T3-BVI-222

$22\overline{)39}$

$2\frac{1}{5} = 3$
$4\frac{1}{5} = 6$
$8\frac{2}{5} = 12$
$17\frac{3}{5} = 24$
$35\frac{1}{5} = 48$
$70\frac{2}{5} = 96$

$6\frac{4}{5}$

$1 \cdot 60$

$11\overline{)15}$

$3 - 2\frac{1}{5}$
$6 - 4\frac{2}{5}$

$2 - 1\frac{1}{5}$
$3 \cdot 2\frac{2}{5}$
$6 \cdot 3\frac{3}{5}$
$6 \cdot \frac{4}{5}$
$9 \cdot 6$

$9\frac{2}{5}$

$2\frac{1}{5}$ 6 2 24
$9\frac{1}{5}$ $18\frac{1}{5}$ 36 $73\frac{1}{5} - 96$

6th Edition

Business Principles and Management

Bernard A. Shilt
Lecturer, State University of
New York at Buffalo
Formerly, Director of Business Education,
Public Schools, Buffalo, New York

Kenneth E. Everard
Professor of Business
Trenton State College
Trenton, New Jersey

John M. Johns
Professor of
General Business Administration
Ball State University
Muncie, Indiana

Published by

G27   **SOUTH-WESTERN PUBLISHING CO.**

CINCINNATI   WEST CHICAGO, ILL.   DALLAS   PELHAM MANOR, N.Y.
BURLINGAME, CALIF.   BRIGHTON, ENGLAND

Copyright © 1973

Philippine Copyright 1973

by

South-Western Publishing Co.
Cincinnati, Ohio

All Rights Reserved

The text of this publication, or any part thereof, may not be reproduced or transmitted in any form or by any means, electronic or mechanical, including photocopying, recording, storage in an information retrieval system, or otherwise, without the prior written permission of the publisher.

ISBN: 0-538-07270-9

Library of Congress Catalog Card Number: 72-88294

5 6 7 8 K 0 9 8 7

Printed in the United States of America

PREFACE

Business Principles and Management, Sixth Edition, is the out-growth of more than 30 years of experience in teaching students in courses which have titles such as business principles, business administration, business management, and advanced business. This edition is the result of the suggestions of many teachers who have used previous editions, together with the helpful evaluations of many businessmen. This edition will provide instructional materials for the following students:

(a) those who will enter business as employees.
(b) those who will enter business as beginning employees and who may eventually have an opportunity to manage a business for others.
(c) those who will eventually own and operate their own business.
(d) those who are not yet sure of their vocational objectives but are exploring the possibility of a career in business.

The materials presented are designed to facilitate the accomplishment of the following basic goals:

(a) aid the students in acquiring a vocabulary of business terms.
(b) give the students an understanding of the many activities involved in the successful operation of a business.
(c) give the students an appreciation of the importance of businesses in our economy.
(d) assist the students in deciding on specific career objectives from among the great number of employment opportunities in the business world.
(e) provide the students with facts, procedures, and concepts that will aid them in becoming more effective employees as they begin their careers in business.

Two new chapters appear in this edition: Chapter 2, Social Environment of American Business; and Chapter 21, Information Systems—Data Processing. Chapter 2 reflects the concerns and responses of businesses to the social problems that have developed in recent years. Chapter 21 presents the growing use by businesses of more effective means for handling information in making management decisions.

In addition to the new chapters, considerable new material has been added to Unit VIII, which deals with the management functions. Pertinent information relating to business has been updated to reflect recent changes.

Those who are familiar with the Fifth Edition will see that some organizational changes have been made in this Sixth Edition. The shifting of some chapters to different units has been done in a belief that the new locations will provide a more logical organization from a teaching and learning standpoint. This shifting to new locations has resulted in most of the units being given new titles.

The material on career information which has proved so helpful in assisting students in deciding on specific career objectives has been retained and expanded in this Sixth Edition and appears at the end of appropriate units.

The wealth of learning aids at the end of each chapter include two major sections titled Review What You Have Learned and Apply What You Have Learned. *Achievement Tests* and *Study Guides and Problems* are additional learning aids which are available as supplementary items to users of this text.

Although changes have been incorporated in this Sixth Edition, the basic purpose which guided the preparation of previous editions remains unchanged—to provide instructional materials which will enable students planning a career in business to gain an understanding of the characteristics, the organization, and the operations of business. The authors believe that these understandings are best achieved when abstract theory is minimized in favor of practical treatment that deals with concrete principles applied through specific procedures and practices of business. For example, purchasing is treated as an important function of business, but the student learns specific purchasing procedures and practices. Realistic examples are taken directly from both large and small businesses, but the emphasis is placed upon small business because the examples are easier for most students to understand and because most businesses are small. The student is, however, shown how the principles involved in operating small businesses also apply to large businesses. Since many types of small businesses are retail establishments, considerable emphasis is placed on those organizations.

We are deeply indebted to the many teachers and businessmen whose helpful suggestions over the years have contributed much to the evolution of this book and regret that space does not permit recognizing them by name.

Bernard A. Shilt

Kenneth E. Everard

John M. Johns

CONTENTS

Chapter		Page

UNIT I
Business and Its Environment

How many businesses are there in the U.S.?

What has made possible the increased output of today's worker?

What is the place of small business?

What is a franchise business?

What is meant by the risks of ownership?

What are the causes of business failures?

BACKGROUND OF CHAPTER

In this country a multitude of industrial and commercial enterprises exist to satisfy the product and service needs of our more than 200 million people. There are a great variety of businesses; and as the population increases and new products are developed, new businesses will be needed.

This chapter is concerned with what characterizes American business. It also discusses certain aspects of business ownership and management and gives some of the advantages and disadvantages of owning a business.

CHAPTER I

CHARACTERISTICS OF AMERICAN BUSINESS

There are nearly 12 million businesses in the United States today. They vary in size from one employee to 800,000 employees and in assets from a few dollars to more than $50 billion.

If one were to make a survey of his home, he would find that it probably contains products from many different producers. The slipcover on the couch may have been made by a self-employed seamstress, the electric light bulbs manufactured by a business with 200,000 employees, a rug manufactured by a business with 500 employees, a loaf of bread from a bakery with 20 employees, and so on.

Supplementing these producers are a great number of other businesses—suppliers of raw materials, transportation companies, finance businesses, and distributors of various kinds. For example, the rug could not have been made without the dyes a chemical firm provided, or the loom that another firm built, the yarn produced by a textile company, transportation companies that transported the various products from one business to another, and banks that loaned money to one or more of the businesses.

NATURE OF AMERICAN BUSINESS

Because the businesses in this country are so varied, it is important that one get an overall understanding of the major characteristics of American business before he begins to study the problems and practices that are found in operating the many different activities of a business.

Types of Businesses

A broad classification of businesses would divide them into two groups—industrial and commercial. *Industrial businesses* are those that produce things. Mining, manufacturing, and construction on a building site are examples of industrial businesses. *Commercial businesses* are those engaged in marketing (wholesalers and retailers), in finance (banks and investment businesses), and in furnishing services (transportation, electric power, gas, hotels, theaters, and the like).

An indication of how important the major types of businesses are is shown in Illustration 1-1. The graph shows the approximate number of persons employed in each of eight classifications. It does not include persons engaged in farming or those in the armed services.

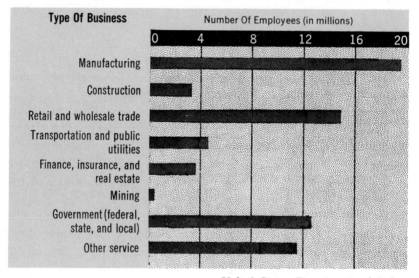

United States Department of Labor

ILLUS. 1-1. Employment in major types of businesses, 1970.

Specialization

Workers have become quite specialized. For example, instead of finding an automobile repair shop in which all workers are general mechanics, one now finds in the larger shops one worker who is a specialist in automobile body repair, another worker who is an expert in repairing automatic transmissions, another worker who is an expert on the motor, and so on. Similarly, in a manufacturing plant one worker may perform just one small operation. A worker in a television manufacturing plant, for example, may do nothing except attach the company's nameplate to the front of television sets.

Just as there has been specialization on the part of workers, there has been specialization in production. For example, a company manufacturing automatic washing machines might buy the electric motors

ILLUS. 1-2. Workers are trained to perform specialized tasks.

from a company which specializes in manufacturing motors rather than produce its own motors. The motor manufacturer, by specializing in making motors which it can sell to other companies needing electric motors in products they are manufacturing, can produce motors at less cost than could the other companies. Since a large percentage of our businesses are specialized, it is easy to understand why businesses are so dependent on each other.

Mass Production

Many of our large businesses manufacture huge quantities of standardized goods by using power-driven machines and assembly-line methods. This process is known as *mass production* (also called *large-scale production*). Mass production makes it possible for the worker to turn out a larger quantity of goods. During the past 20 years the average productivity of a factory worker has increased approximately 60 percent. This increased productivity results in a lower cost for each unit produced. Lower prices for the articles produced enable people with lower incomes to buy more of such articles.

The high production of manufactured products per worker is an important characteristic of American industry. It has come about largely because manufacturing businesses have equipped their plants with the most modern machinery which enables the worker to produce more goods with less physical effort. The figures in Illustration 1-3 indicate the average amount of investment for each production worker in certain industries in the United States in a recent year.

Industry	Investment
Petroleum (includes extraction and pipeline transportation) ..	$205,000
Motor vehicles and equipment	52,000
Tobacco manufacturers	51,000
Chemical and allied products	38,000
Primary metal industries	35,000
Food products	27,000
Paper and allied products	27,000
Transportation equipment	26,000
Stone, clay, and glass products	23,000
Rubber and miscellaneous plastics	19,000
Printing and publishing	19,000
Lumber and wood products	14,000
Textile mill products	14,000
Furniture and fixtures	8,000

Source: The Conference Board, October 1, 1970

ILLUS. 1-3. Capital invested per production worker.

Changing Nature of Business

Today's businesses in our country might be characterized by the terms "constantly changing" or "dynamic." For centuries the principal means of transportation had been by horse. With the coming of the railroads about a century ago (the first transcontinental rail route was completed in 1869), goods and people were transported at a much more rapid rate. For about fifty years rail was the principal means of transportation. Then came the widespread use of the automobile, and a large percentage of the transportation of people and goods began to move by passenger automobile, bus, and truck. Airplane facilities then became so developed that they began to transport rapidly increasing numbers of passengers and quantities of merchandise. The slow 100-mile-per-hour planes were quickly succeeded by faster planes; next followed the jet planes which cross our country carrying people and goods in only a few hours.

There have been similar changes in many other types of business and industry. For many centuries the natural fibers, such as wool, cotton, flax, and silk, were the basic materials for nearly all fabrics used in clothing, bedding, draperies, and similar items. As a result of chemical research there have developed many synthetic fibers, such as rayon, nylon, polyester, and even glass, which are now being used in rapidly increasing quantities in place of natural fibers.

Since World War II, businesses have been spending large amounts of money for research in order to develop new products, processes, and services. Many new products and services have become the bases for new businesses and for increased sales for older businesses.

Not only have many changes occurred in the products manufactured and the services rendered, but many changes have also taken place in the ways businesses are operated. Methods of selling, advertising, buying, and warehousing; credit and collection procedures; and personnel practices have changed and are changing. Many firms have established branches in foreign countries. In some cases this was done to facilitate sales in those countries of products produced in this country. In other cases the purpose was to produce articles for sale in those countries and for importation of other products to sell in this country.

The changing nature of business is also indicated in the comparison of the number of business establishments by types over a period of years. Illustration 1-4 shows the changes that have taken place in selected categories of businesses over a 28-year period. As shown in the illustration, all four types of businesses have increased substantially since 1940; the slight decline in manufacturing and wholesaling firms in recent years has been more than offset by the large increase in retail and service firms. The decline in the number of manufacturing and wholesaling establishments since 1960 has been the result of a decrease in the number of small manufacturing and wholesaling businesses. The rapid increase in the number of service type firms during the last several decades is especially noteworthy.

Type of Business	1940	1950	1960	1968
Manufacturing ...	226,000	321,000	406,000	397,000
Wholesale Trade ..	186,000	266,000	464,000	453,000
Retail Trade	1,567,000	1,816,000	1,907,000	2,113,000
Service	626,000	736,000	2,246,000	2,795,000

Source: U. S. Treasury Department and Department of Commerce

ILLUS. 1-4. Growth in number of selected types of businesses.

Business Growth and Prosperity

Much of America's prosperity has been due to business growth. Around the world people have admired and envied this country's economic strength. A discussion of how a nation can measure its economic wealth and its benefits to citizens is presented next.

Gross National Product. The total market value of all goods produced and services rendered in a year is called the *gross national product* (GNP). Whenever something is purchased, the dollar amount is counted by the federal government. The GNP of the United States may be compared from year to year and it may be compared with the GNP of other countries. In this way, it provides a measure of economic growth.

In 1971 the total GNP for the United States exceeded the staggering figure of $1 trillion. As can be seen from Illustration 1-5, the GNP nearly doubled in size between 1960 and 1970. By 1980 it is expected to approach the $2 trillion mark. In a recent year, the GNP of the United States was equal to the combined GNP of four other leading nations of the world—the Soviet Union, Japan, West Germany, and the United Kingdom. The rate of growth and the current size of the GNP indicate in a very striking way the accomplishment of the United States in its short history.

Year	Gross National Product (In Billions)
1971	$1,047
1970	974
1965	685
1960	504
1950	285
1940	100
1900	20
Source: U. S. Department of Commerce	

ILLUS. 1-5. Growth in GNP since 1900.

Individual Well-Being. General GNP figures are helpful in judging the growth of a nation. By themselves such figures tell little about the economic worth of individuals. However, the United States Department of Commerce has gathered a great deal of information that reveals the economic well-being of Americans.

Year	Average Family Income
1970	$9,867
1965	6,957
1960	5,620
1955	4,421
1950	3,319

Source: U. S. Department of Commerce

ILLUS. 1-6. Rising family income improves the level of living for many Americans.

Average family income between 1950 and 1970 increased steadily, as can be seen from Illustration 1-6. With increased income the average family has been able to improve its level of living over the years. How income is spent for goods can be seen in Illustration 1-7. Three out of four households have one or more cars and over 90 percent of the households possess television sets. The total personal savings of individuals in a recent year totaled $44 billion. Americans have also invested much in education. One out of every three adults under 35 years of age will have had some college training by 1980.

ownership of cars and appliances

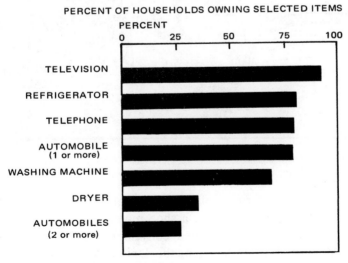

PERCENT OF HOUSEHOLDS OWNING SELECTED ITEMS

Source: U. S. Department of Commerce

ILLUS. 1-7. Families buy cars and appliances with their income.

Place of Small Business

It has been the American tradition to encourage the system of free enterprise in which businesses are permitted to exercise considerable freedom of action and are relatively free from government domination and regulation. Nearly anyone who wishes is permitted to start in business for himself. Consequently, a large number of new businesses are organized each year, and this fact accounts for the high percentage of small businesses.

ILLUS. 1-8. Small businesses dominate the street scenes of American towns and cities.

Small business is a term applied to a single retail store, a dry-cleaning establishment, a restaurant, a shoe repair shop, or some other type of business that can be operated conveniently by one or a few individuals. Most of the businesses in the United States are small, as shown by the statistics for retail businesses which are given in Illustration 1-9 on page 9.

Number of Paid Employees	Number of Retail Businesses
0	609,545
1 to 3	541,198
4 to 7	247,378
8 to 19	182,388
20 to 49	68,700
50 to 99	15,274
100 or more	6,087

Source: U. S. Department of Commerce

ILLUS. 1-9. Most retail businesses are small.

Many of the businesses in America are small, one-man or family estab-lishments with no additional employees. According to the U.S. Depart-ment of Commerce, about 90 percent of all service businesses have an annual income of less than $100,000. About 70 percent have an annual income of less than $25,000. *Annual income* is the total of all income received in one year, out of which all expenses and costs are paid. Illus-tration 1-10, page 10, shows examples of small businesses.

Most of the large businesses of today began as very small businesses. Because they supplied products and services desired by the public and because they were well managed, they became larger and larger. A few of the many such successful businesses are briefly described here.

William Procter and James Gamble formed a partnership in 1837 in Cincinnati, Ohio, with an investment of $3,500 each to start a soap-making business. Today Procter & Gamble has more than 40 manu-facturing plants in the United States and 17 plants in 14 different foreign countries. In addition to being a leading producer of soap products, it manufactures such other items as toilet goods, food products, and paper products. In a recent year its sales totaled nearly $3 billion.

About one hundred years ago, George H. Hartford opened a small tea store in New York City. It has since grown into the Great Atlantic & Pacific Tea Company, the second largest retailing business anywhere with yearly sales amounting to approximately $6 billion. At one time this company had nearly 16,000 stores in operation. In recent years it has reduced the number of stores by combining most of them into super-markets. However, its total yearly sales have continued to increase. It provides employment for some 135,000 employees. In addition, the company owns and operates more than 50 food-processing plants.

Film developing studio	Music store
Bakery	Shoe repair shop
Beauty shop	Book and stationery store
Toy shop	Candy store (including manufactur-
Restaurant	ing)
Gift shop	Tailor shop
Newsstand	Doll hospital
Tobacco shop	Auto repair shop
Barber shop	Gasoline service station
Printing shop	Toy manufacturing
Trucking service	Manufacture of men's ties
Radio repair shop	Machine shop
Dry cleaning and pressing business	Poultry or game bird raising
Manufacturing of window display	Millinery manufacturing
fixtures	Accounting and tax service
Photographic studio	Mimeographing, addressing, and let-
Manufacture of small articles	ter service
Lamp shade manufacturing	Window cleaning
Doughnut shop	Rug cleaning
Bowling alley	Television repair
Motel	Manufacture of store front signs
Self-service laundry	Manufacture of jams, jellies, etc.
Florist shop	

ILLUS. 1-10. Typical small businesses.

Frank W. Woolworth began business in a Pennsylvania town by opening a very small store called the "Great 5¢ Store." Woolworth stores are now found in all 50 states and in six foreign countries. There are over five thousand such stores, the majority of which are located in the United States. Many new outlets are being opened each year. Total international sales in a recent year exceeded $2.5 billion.

Howard Johnson's businesses, numbering approximately 1,300, include restaurants, motor lodges, and food-processing firms which prepare and distribute more than 600 items. The Johnson Company began in 1925 as a small store selling tobacco, candy, and newspapers and having a soda bar. Nearly one third of the restaurants and most of the motor lodges are franchised. The rest belong to the parent company. The franchised restaurants and motor lodges are owned by individuals who use the Johnson name, sell Johnson products, and get suggestions on management from the Johnson Company.

As businesses grow larger, they sometimes restrict certain small businesses; but more often they encourage the growth of other small businesses. For example, in 1900 there were approximately one million persons in this country engaged directly or indirectly in horse and buggy transportation. Now, nearly ten million persons are engaged in making, selling, financing, insuring, and servicing automobiles. Many of the businesses that perform these functions are small. Thousands of roadside stands, restaurants, drive-in theaters, motels, tourist camps, and pleasure resorts also have been established as a result of the growth of the automobile industry. Thus, while many small businesses engaged in horse and buggy transportation, such as blacksmiths, harness shops, and livery stables, were put out of business by the automobile industry, a much larger number of small businesses took their place.

Place of Franchise Business

For the person with limited funds, a popular way of launching a small business today is through a franchise. A *franchise* is a legal agreement between a parent company and a distributor to sell a product or service under specific conditions. Businesses such as Carvel ice cream and McDonald's hamburger stands are operated by small business owners under such agreements. The two parties to a franchise agreement are the *franchiser*, the parent company that provides a popular product or service, and the *franchisee*, the distributor.

In a typical franchise arrangement, the franchisee pays an initial fee and a monthly percentage of sales. The money needed to start a franchise business varies greatly, with many requiring between $5,000 and $25,000. For his payments, the franchisee gets exclusive rights to sell the franchised product or service in a specified geographical area. In addition, he receives expert help in selecting a location and special training and advice in how best to operate the business. Advertising and promotional materials are also provided. The odds of being successful with a franchise business are much greater than with a firm starting totally on its own. This is a primary reason for the popularity of franchise arrangements.

Franchise businesses have grown very rapidly during the last 15 years. Most gasoline service stations and new car dealerships, for example, operate under franchise agreements. The list of enterprises in Illustration 1-11 on page 12 is only a sample of the nationally franchised operations. According to a recent Congressional report, there are more than 1,000 franchisers in the United States with over 600,000 franchisees doing over $90 billion of business each year. Nearly 40,000 new outlets open each year. It is estimated that soon 70 percent of all goods and services will be sold through franchised operations.

A & W Root Beer	House of Fabrics
A to Z Rental	House of Nine
Arnold Palmer Golf Course	House of Pancakes
Avis Rent A Car	Howard Johnson's
Aero Mayflower Transit Company	Kentucky Fried Chicken
Baskin-Robbins Ice Cream	Manpower, Inc.
Beltone Hearing Aids	Mary Carter Paints
Ben Franklin Store	McDonald's Hamburgers
Burger King	Midas Muffler Shop
Budget Rent-a-Car	Mister Donut
Carvel Ice Cream	Mister Steak
Chicken Delight	One Hour Martinizing
Culligan Soft Water Service	Puppy Palace
Dairi-Delite	Putt-Putt Golf Course
Dairy Queen	Robo-Wash
Food Mart	Sawyer Business College
Fred Astaire Dance Studio	Schwinn Bicycles
H & R Block, Inc.	Sheraton Inn
Hertz Rent A Car	Snap-on Tools
Holiday Inn	Stuckeys

ILLUS. 1-11. Many small businesses are franchised operations.

Risks of Ownership

The person who invests his money in a business has confidence that he is smart enough to produce a product or render a service that people will want and that he can sell the product or service at a price and in sufficient quantity to enable him to make a profit.

From the point of view of business operations, profit must include payment for the time, mental effort, physical effort, and worry of the businessman, as well as compensate him for the risk that he takes and the interest on the investment of his money. He runs the chance of losing all his investment if the business fails. If his money were in a savings account, he would earn interest on it; but instead he invests it in his own business where he hopes to earn more.

Not all businesses make a profit; some of them lose money. That is why anyone who invests money in a business takes a certain amount of risk. He may not make any profit and, in fact, he may lose the money he has invested in the business. *Risk*—the possibility of failure—is, therefore, one of the characteristics of American business. Risk involves competition, changes in prices, changes in style, competition with new products, and the dangers that arise from poor economic conditions.

Businesses cease operations for a number of reasons; a large percentage do so because of financial failure. Illustration 1-12 gives an analysis of the reasons why some 15,000 businesses ended operations because of financial failure. Lack of managerial ability and lack of experience were the main reasons for the failures.

Apparent Causes	Percent of Failures	
Inadequate sales	40.7	
Heavy operating expenses	13.3	
Accounts receivable difficulties	9.0	These failures result from
Inventory difficulties	5.1	lack of managerial ability
Excessive fixed assets	4.1	and lack of experience.
Competitive weakness	21.0	
Poor location	3.6	
Neglect due to poor health, bad habits, family difficulties, and the like	3.8	
Fraud: False financial statements, irregular disposal of assets, etc.	1.8	
Disaster: Fire, flood, burglary, employees' fraud, and the like	1.2	Protection against some of these could have been provided by insurance.

Note: Because some failures are attributed to more than one cause, the total of the various percents exceeds 100 percent.

Sources: Based on Dun & Bradstreet, Inc., reports and on opinions of informed creditors.

ILLUS. 1-12. Causes of business failure.

Surveys indicate that failures in small businesses are very high, with from 40 to 45 percent going out of business within the first two years. Of course, not all failures are for financial reasons. Other reasons for going out of business might include retirement, illness, and death.

Illustration 1-13 on page 14 shows the total number of annual failures for financial reasons over a 5-year period. Retail trade firms account for nearly half of all such failures.

In recent years, over 400,000 firms have been formed annually and between 350,000 and 400,000 have been discontinued. Financial failures, though large, represent only a fraction of the total businesses discontinued in a given year.

Year	Number of Failures
1970	10,748
1969	9,154
1968	9,636
1967	12,364
1966	13,061

Source: Dun & Bradstreet, Inc.

ILLUS. 1-13. Yearly financial failures of business firms.

In addition to the large number of new businesses and discontinued businesses, there are yearly more than 350,000 business transfers—firms which continue as businesses but have a change in ownership, such as changing from a partnership to a corporation, or a sole proprietor selling his entire business to another person, or a partner retiring and another person succeeding him as a partner.

OWNERSHIP AND MANAGERIAL OPPORTUNITIES

Anyone who owns a business or a share of a business is called a *capitalist*. He has taken the risk of investing his money in a business in the hope that the business will produce a profit and he will earn an income on his investment.

Much of the money of insurance companies and a great deal of that which is in retirement funds is invested in business. It has been estimated that more than 30 million people in the United States own stock directly in corporations, and more than 120 million own stock directly or indirectly. These are in addition to the many thousands of small business owners.

Most large corporations are owned by many people. For example, there are several large corporations which have more than 500,000 owners each. At the present time General Motors Corporation is owned by more than one million persons. The number of individuals owning shares in business is increasing each year. Therefore, it may be truthfully said that American business is owned by the people and not by just a few wealthy individuals.

Whether one works in a business or owns a share in a business, his success depends on the success of the business. Income from sales and services makes it possible for labor to be paid, interest to be paid on loans, taxes to be paid to government, and profits to be paid to the owners. If a business does not make a profit, it cannot continue.

Advantages of Operating One's Own Business

Many advantages are to be found when one operates a business of his own rather than working for someone else.

Opportunity for Increased Income. When operating one's own business, earnings are not limited to a salary. If the business is successful, the owner earns the equivalent of a salary plus a profit on his investment.

Satisfaction of Being One's Own Boss. There is much satisfaction in being one's own boss. An individual can form his own policies and make his own decisions without consulting the home office as must be done even by a branch manager of a large company. He is free from constant supervisory pressure to produce results, although when one is working for himself there is a strong incentive (increased profits) to produce.

Job Security. An employee of a large company is often worried that he may be discharged. Although many independent businesses are

ILLUS. 1-14. When one operates his own business, he is free of pressure from higher-ups.

short-lived, statistics indicate that when a business is firmly established and efficiently managed the owner enjoys considerable job security.

Opportunity for Constructive Ideas. Because large companies have a research staff to develop products, ideas, and methods, the ordinary employee has little opportunity to put into operation constructive ideas that he may have. As the operator of his own business, however, he can give full play to his ideas. If he has an idea for a new type of display window, a new plan for collection procedures, a new idea for the type of products to be carried or services to be offered, or a new sales promotion idea, he is free to try the new idea. After a reasonable trial, the new idea can be dropped if it does not work as expected. The independent business operator is provided unusual opportunities for giving full play to his constructive ideas.

Social Standing. The owner of a business usually enjoys a higher social standing in his community than does an employee with the same income or even a higher income. He is recognized as one of a group who helps keep the community going. Because of his business ability he is frequently asked to take an active part in community activities.

Disadvantages of Operating One's Own Business

There are disadvantages in operating one's own business that should be kept in mind by one who is thinking of going into business for himself. The principal disadvantages are given here.

Risk of Financial Loss. A business may fail and cause the owner to lose all or part of the money he has invested. In many cases the failure of the business may also cause him to lose property other than that in the business. Some studies have shown that more new businesses fail than succeed, but most of those that are in danger of failure quit before losing all their original investment. Many quit while they still show a profit, and others suffer little or no financial loss.

There are many risks in operating a business. Its delivery truck may injure a person or property, and the business may be sued for damages; a customer or employee may be injured while on the premises; there may be losses from flood, tornado, fire, burglary, explosion, and the like. However, most of such losses may be covered by insurance. Many other risks are not easily covered by insurance. New products, new inventions, new styles, new processes, or new equipment may make one's business obsolete and unable to compete with others; goods purchased may prove unsalable or may drop in price.

Increased Responsibilities. The individual in business for himself has many more responsibilities than the ordinary employee, and he may not forget them when he goes home at night. For example, an employee who drives a truck has only a few tasks, such as picking up loads at different places and delivering them with care. He may have to see that the truck is greased and may sometimes be required to make small repairs. If this man should buy the truck and operate a trucking business of his own, however, he must not only look after the same tasks but also take on others. He may be able to run the business from his home, but he probably must incur some additional expense for an office or a garage. He must assume the responsibility for finding customers who will do business with him, he must persuade those customers to pay a fair price, and he must collect the bills. Furthermore, he must assume responsibility for damage that may occur to the merchandise hauled; he must see that various licenses, taxes, and all bills are paid. Should the business require some additional employees, he must hire, train, and supervise their work and see that the payrolls are met.

Long and Irregular Hours. Usually, the owner of a small or rapidly growing business has to give it constant attention. Many owners work for years without taking a vacation. It is impractical for them to be away from the business because it is too small for them to have qualified assistants to operate the business during their absence. To develop a business the owner must often work long hours; an employee may be sick or quit and the owner must do the work; any one of a hundred things may come up suddenly to demand extra work on the part of the owner.

Difficulty of Retirement. It is usually rather difficult for the owner of a small business to retire without selling the business. Selling one's business may mean receiving less for it than it is worth It also means that one's income from that source is stopped. Frequently, as the business owner becomes older, he does not retain his business ability and fails to keep up with the times. His inclination to take things easy permits his competitors gradually to take over much of his business so that, when his age compels him to retire, he frequently has little financial security.

Possibility of a Low Income. Nearly 50 percent of the businesses in this country are one-man businesses with no employees. Most of these businesses are able just to exist rather than to succeed in making more income for the owner than he could have obtained from some regular job as an employee. However, the great majority of those who fail to earn satisfactory profits do so because of lack of experience, poor managerial ability, or laziness.

Becoming a Business Manager

A thoughtful consideration of the preceding discussion of the principal disadvantages of owning and operating one's own business should cause many to decide that it is more desirable to work for someone else than to start in business for themselves. Unless one is prepared by temperament, talent, experience, and training, he might be more content to work as an employee.

Ability to manage successfully is one of the characteristics of an employee that is most sought by an employer. Knowledge of what to do, how to do it efficiently, and when to do it are so rare that the employee who possesses such ability is rapidly promoted.

On his first job an employee should master the details of the job just as quickly as possible by constantly studying and finding out all that is to be learned. When he has thorough mastery and understanding of the job, he should then begin studying the job above his present one so that, when the opportunity arises, he will be able to step into the new job and handle it efficiently.

While one is gaining experience as an employee and in managing certain phases of a business for his employer, he can decide whether he prefers to continue as an employee, probably rising to positions of greater responsibility, or whether he wishes to start a business of his own. Should his decision be for the first plan, he will find unlimited opportunity among the many large businesses of the country for his managerial ability in such positions as department head, branch manager, district manager, and the like. Should his decision be for starting in business for himself, he will probably have to begin with a small business because his capital will likely be somewhat limited.

OBLIGATIONS OF THE BUSINESSMAN

Anyone who starts an enterprise assumes an important obligation for his welfare is closely related to that of the entire community in which he operates and to the people with whom he deals. Any failure in business is an economic loss that must be borne by society. For example, when a retail merchant fails, he probably owes money to several wholesalers or manufacturers and to other creditors, who must absorb part of the loss. When there are many such losses, business in general is seriously affected. In fact, several such losses may cause additional failures because certain individual creditors may suffer so badly.

One of the executives of the Chamber of Commerce of the United States has pointed out the following obligations of a businessman:

1. To *customers:* That they may have the best at the lowest cost, consistent with fairness to all those engaged in production and distribution.

2. To *workers:* That their welfare will not be sacrificed for the benefit of others, and that in their employment relations their rights will be respected.

3. To *management:* That it may be recognized in proportion to its demonstrated ability, considering always the interest of others.

4. To *competitors:* That there will be avoidance of every form of unfair competition.

5. To *investors:* That their rights will be safeguarded, and that they will be kept so informed that they can exercise their own judgment respecting their interests.

6. To the *public:* That the business will strive in all its operations and relations to promote the general welfare and, without yielding its rights of petition and protest, to observe faithfully the laws of the land.

IMPORTANCE OF A STUDY OF BUSINESS MANAGEMENT

Whether one plans to operate a business of his own or to be an employee who expects to rise to responsible positions, he needs to have a knowledge of numerous things concerning the many complicated activities of a business, such as salesmanship, advertising, store display, merchandising, finance, accounting, credit and collections, shipping and transportation, employee relations and regulations, law and governmental regulations, and public relations. As the owner of a business, he must have a complete understanding of all such phases of a business. Similarly, such an understanding is necessary if he is to be a competent employee in a particular department of a business; and, if he expects to become a department head or an executive of the company, he must thoroughly understand how the various activities of all departments are coordinated in a smoothly operating business.

A study of business management will also give him an excellent picture of the many types of jobs that are to be found in business, the requirements of the jobs, and the possible lines of advancement. In addition, it will give him an appreciation of the many problems and risks of business management.

REVIEW WHAT YOU HAVE LEARNED

Business Terms Checkup:

Each of the following business terms is italicized when first presented in this chapter. Make these terms a permanent part of your business vocabulary by learning their meanings and by using them often.

(1) industrial businesses
(2) commercial businesses
(3) mass production or large-scale production
(4) gross national product
(5) small business
(6) annual income
(7) franchise
(8) franchiser
(9) franchisee
(10) risk
(11) capitalist

Reading Checkup:

1. Approximately how many businesses of all kinds are there in this country?
2. Which major type of business gives employment to the largest number of employees?
3. What is meant by saying that businesses are dependent on other businesses?
4. During the past 20 years, what has been the approximate percentage of increase in the average productivity of a factory worker?
5. Would it be correct to characterize today's businesses as being dynamic? Why or why not?
6. Why is the gross national product important?
7. In a typical franchise agreement, what are the advantages to the franchisee?
8. How much business is done in the country through franchising?
9. Why are businessmen willing to take risks in operating a business?
10. (a) As shown in Illustration 1-12, what percentage of the business failures were due to inadequate sales?
    (b) In the same illustration, what percentage of the failures were caused by competitive weakness?

11. What are the chief advantages of operating one's own business?
12. What are the chief disadvantages of operating one's own business?
13. What characteristic in an employee is usually most desired by an employer?
14. Are there many opportunities among large businesses for persons in managerial positions?
15. State some values to a prospective employee that should result from a study of business management.

APPLY WHAT YOU HAVE LEARNED

Questions for Class Discussion:

1. Explain how specialization of workers increases their productivity.
2. Why are most businesses increasing their spending for machinery and equipment?
3. "As businesses grow larger, they sometimes restrict certain other businesses." Give some examples to illustrate this statement.
4. What proof is there that the average American is well off?
5. Why might a person who wishes to go into business not want to consider a franchise arrangement?
6. Give examples of risks that the owner of a gasoline service station might have.
7. Illustration 1-12 indicates that losses from accounts receivable were responsible for many business failures. How might better management have prevented such losses?
8. In Illustration 1-12 heavy operating expenses were given as a cause of business failures. What is meant by heavy operating expenses?
9. Explain how losses from a disaster might cause the failure of a business.
10. What is meant by indirectly owning stock in a corporation?
11. What is meant by the statement that one has increased responsibilities when one goes into business for himself?
12. How might one prepare himself for the next job above his present one?
13. Not only does the owner of a business have an obligation to his employees, but likewise the employee has an obligation to his employer. Mention some specific obligations that each has.

Problems and Projects:

1. A small retail business, owned and managed by one person, has a total income of $35,000 for a certain year. If the cost of the goods sold was

65 percent of the total income, what amount did the owner have for rent, insurance, light, heat, and other expenses, and for his net profit? (This net profit represents both the salary for his services and the income from his investment in the business.)

2. Make a list of the new businesses that have started in your community during the last year, and see if you can draw any conclusions with regard to new types of businesses.

3. Visit the owner of a small business, preferably some person you know, and find out how many days and hours each week his business is open and approximately how much additional time he finds necessary to devote to his business. Make a report to the class.

4. Make a list of five different kinds of businesses of which you think there are too many in your community; also make a list of any kinds of businesses of which you think there are too few.

5. Make a list of the members of your family and keep a record of the total amount of money each family member spends for a day (or for a week). Add the total spent by all members. If you used a daily total, multiply this figure by 365 days (if you used a weekly figure, multiply by 52 weeks) to find out about how much, on the average, your family contributes yearly to the gross national product figure.

6. Make a list of as many products as possible that you have in your home that were not available when your grandparents were your age. You may want to talk to some older people you know to get ideas for your list. Give a short report to the class on the items included in your list.

7. Look at the list of franchise businesses shown in Illustration 1-11. Make a list of those shown that can be found in the local telephone directory.

Case Problem 1-1:

Fred and Irene Johnson recently inherited $20,000 and wish to start their own business. They feel their prior work experience will be of great value. Johnson has been a supervisor in a large dairy plant for the past 15 years, and his wife has had some work experience as a cashier in a small grocery store. Neither is quite sure, however, what type of business to start although Irene Johnson prefers a small grocery store and her husband has a slight preference for an ice cream stand. Both of the Johnsons have skill in handling people. Their greatest need, it is felt, would be for legal, financial, and technical business advice.

Required:

1. What matters should the Johnsons consider before they reach a decision on the type of business to open?

2. Make a list of the principal responsibilities that the Johnsons will have after they decide which business to start.

3. Should the Johnsons consider a franchise business? Why?

Case Problem 1-2:

Roy Lake has been working for five years as an employee in a television sales and service business where he has had considerable experience in the repair department and some experience in selling. He has decided that he wishes to go into a similar business for himself. Ed Lowrey, who owns and manages a similar business, has indicated that he wishes to retire and that his business is for sale.

Required:

What are the principal points that Lake should consider in deciding whether to buy the business from Lowrey or whether to establish a new business?

Continuing Project:

The fact that you are studying this course is an indication that you expect to be employed in business. There is also a possibility that you will eventually have a managerial position in business or that you may eventually own and operate your own business. With the aid and advice of your teacher, select the kind of small business in which you are interested and in which you think you would like to work and one that you would like to own and operate if you have the opportunity in the future. Obtain a loose-leaf notebook and, under the direction of your teacher, begin assembling materials to construct an operational manual for the business that you have selected. The first part of your continuing project deals with Chapters 1, 2, and 3. Select a business and give your reasons for selecting it.

How do the nation's social problems affect business?

What has caused the need for a large labor force of skilled workers?

What is "recycling" and how does it help solve the pollution problem?

Have the values of people changed in recent years?

What are the social responsibilities of business?

What are the basic rights of consumers?

BACKGROUND OF CHAPTER

Business is an important element of society. The actions of business have an effect on society and the problems of society have an effect on business. To best understand American business, therefore, one should study business principles as well as examine important problems facing the nation.

A growing population, unemployment, poverty, and pollution are some of the significant social problems which the business world must face. The changing values of people also affect the way business owners and managers operate.

This chapter will acquaint you with some of the social problems of the business world and show how American business has changed in response to society's problems.

CHAPTER 2

SOCIAL ENVIRONMENT OF AMERICAN BUSINESS

In its relatively short history, America has attained remarkable achievements. It has moved from an agricultural community to the world's leading industrial society. Horse-drawn wagons have been replaced by diesel-engine trains, jet planes, and missile-powered vehicles for outer space. Technology has provided telephones, television sets, teletypewriters, and Telstar satellites. Problems that once required teams of mathematicians months to compute are now solved in minutes by complex computers. And while our ancestors had few choices among commodities, millions of American consumers now purchase thousands of products in hundreds of varieties.

When one considers the accomplishments of this nation during the 20th century alone, he must marvel regardless of his personal philosophy. The combination of an industrious people, a democratic form of government, and a business system that includes basic rights has produced a prosperous, business-oriented society. Accompanying the rapid economic development of America, however, have come serious problems, such as poverty, pollution, and unemployment. Some of these problems are discussed in this chapter.

The economic growth of the country has been due, in part, to the qualities of the American business system. The business system, however, must be seen in light of the total society in which it operates. As a major element of society, business affects people in material ways. Society, in turn, influences the conduct of business. Political, economic, and social forces help shape the general nature of the country and frequently affect business decisions within individual firms. Thus, one cannot study business organization and management without also having an awareness of the social forces that shape business.

Economic characteristics will be examined in the next chapter. The political system is a separate field of study. Special laws passed by government that affect business are discussed in Chapter 30. In this chapter you will learn about the problems business owners and managers must face in the social environment and about how business in general has responded to those problems.

SOCIAL PROBLEMS AND BUSINESS

Since business does not operate in a vacuum, it cannot isolate itself from society. Often, the dilemmas of business and society are closely interwoven. The social problems presented in this section are those that have a direct bearing on the operations of business and on the well-being of individuals.

Population

The gross national product cannot grow rapidly unless there are sufficient people to provide the necessary labor force and to buy the goods and services produced. Population statistics enable businesses to plan how much and what kinds of goods and services to offer. However, the GNP of a country must grow at a faster rate than its population if the level of living is to be raised. Not only is the size of the population important in business planning, but so is the nature of the population.

Growing Population. The population of the United States has grown steadily over the years, as can be seen in Illustration 2-1. It does not take many years for the population to double in size. For that reason many experts have become concerned about an overly large population for an area the size of this country. Some experts have suggested that the population growth rate be lowered or even reduced to zero. For example, all families would have an average of two children each in order to keep the population at its present size (zero growth). With an existing population of over 200 million and a high birth rate, it would be possible for the United States to exceed 300 million people by the year 2000. While the GNP is likely to grow in proportion to the population, certain problems become more significant. The problem of pollution increases, for example, as more people use more goods.

Changing Population. Not only is the size of the population important to business, but so is the nature of the population. It is younger and getting more mobile and more urbanized.

Over half the population is less than 28 years of age. In fact, nearly 20 percent of the population is between the ages of 14 and 24. This segment of the population represents a youth market to which many

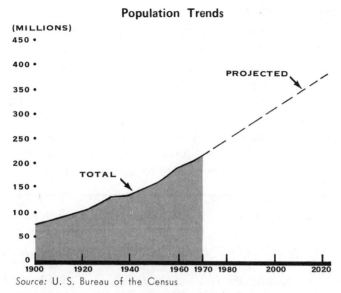

Population Trends

ILLUS. 2-1. Population growth has been steady.

small and large businesses cater. By 1980 these young adults will represent one third of the population.

While the population is getting younger, it is also getting more mobile. About one fifth of the people move from one address to another each year. Young people change addresses twice as frequently as the average American. However, the majority of mobile Americans, on the average, do not move far. In a recent year, 60 percent chose new addresses within the same county in which they had lived.

Moving Americans have tended to go to urbanized areas, according to federal government statistics. Seven out of ten people now live in a city or a suburb. The population has tended to concentrate around metropolitan areas. Nearly half the population is found in the 50 largest metropolitan regions. For example, the 450-mile area between Boston and Washington, D.C., contains over 15 percent of the country's people.

The concentration of the population has caused a variety of problems. Making wise use of limited land for homes and businesses is one. Another problem is that of transportation. How to move people and goods efficiently in heavily populated areas has received much attention by business and government. Arising from densely populated areas are other social problems, such as that of providing adequate medical, recreational, and educational facilities.

Employment and Education

A large labor force is necessary to support a large GNP. As the population expands, the labor force also grows. The *labor force* is composed of all those people who are available for work, whether they are employed or unemployed. Not included in the labor force are those people under 16 years of age, full-time students, housewives, and retired and handicapped people. In a recent year, there were 86 million workers in the total labor force including the armed forces. The growth in the labor force, excluding the armed forces, may be seen in Illustration 2-2. The GNP must increase if people are to be employed.

Year	Employed	Unemployed	Labor Force (Excluding Armed Forces)
1970	78,600,000	4,100,000	82,700,000
1965	71,100,000	3,400,000	74,500,000
1960	65,700,000	3,900,000	69,600,000
1955	62,100,000	2,900,000	65,000,000
1950	58,900,000	3,300,000	62,200,000
Source: U. S. Department of Labor			

ILLUS. 2-2. Employment status of the civilian labor force.

With improved technology has come the need for additional skilled employees. The demand for accountants, secretaries, managers and other business specialists, for example, has never been greater. To become skilled usually means that workers need to be educated. More and more Americans, as a result, are going to school longer than ever before and are becoming trained in specialized jobs.

While the demand for skilled workers has been rising, the need for unskilled workers has been declining. A problem to the businessman is to find adequately trained employees. Education and specialized training, therefore, must be readily available in a highly industrialized society.

Poverty

Closely related to employment and education problems is the puzzle of poverty. Despite this nation's wealth and prosperity, many persons live in poverty. According to the United States Bureau of the Census, over 12 percent of the population was classified as below the poverty level in a recent year. This means that millions of families are receiving little for annual income. The poverty income level, which is not the same for all, is based on family size, age of members, and location. Families within this level are usually poorly housed, poorly clothed, and poorly fed.

The large majority of people living in poverty are unemployed. Many are unskilled workers who lack sufficient education or training to obtain or keep jobs. By training unemployed workers, many corporations have gained badly needed skilled workers while helping to reduce the number unemployed and on welfare. Business firms have also worked with schools and government training programs to help prepare unemployed and unskilled workers for the labor force.

A successful example of business effort to reduce poverty was the establishment of the National Alliance of Businessmen. This voluntary organization of thousands of business executives created a partnership with the federal government to help hire, train, and retrain the disadvantaged urban poor. It has labeled its special program *JOBS* which comes from Job Opportunities in the Business Sector. Since 1968 when it started, the JOBS program has trained many of those previously unemployed.

Pollution

During the last decade, Americans have become conscious of a serious problem regarding their physical environment. This nation cannot continue to produce goods and then carelessly discard waste without upsetting the balance of nature. Pollution affects the land we use, the water we drink, and the air we breathe. The survival of mankind depends on how well society controls its natural environment.

When the country was young, pollution did not show its great effect on the land, water, and air. Few goods were produced and the population was small. Now that there are more than 200 million people and the quantity of goods produced is so great, the environment is seriously affected. One does not have to go far to detect pollution. In many cities the air is filled with harmful fumes from cars and factories. As expressed in Illustration 2-3, many rivers and lakes have been filled with waste to the point of killing fish or making the water hazardous to drink. Even the land has been misused in various ways, such as the wasteful removal of natural resources, the creation of unsightly junk piles, and the use of harmful chemicals to destroy insects.

The condition of the environment has reached a critical stage. Local and state governments have passed control laws, as has the

ILLUS. 2-3. Lakes and streams have become polluted.

federal government. Business firms have become much more conscious of the need to take deliberate—sometimes costly—action to help improve the physical environment. In addition to efforts to clean the air, land, and water, firms have launched recycling programs. *Recycling* means using waste products for making new products. Numerous examples of recycling may be found in business today. Waste paper from schools and offices may be collected and reprocessed to produce new paper products, such as envelopes. Glass containers, such as soft drink bottles, are collected from customers and reprocessed for use. By recycling, businesses use fewer natural resources and thereby conserve the limited supply.

Changing Values

Mankind's values generally remain rather stable for long periods. There are times, however, when values undergo change. Evidence suggests that during the last half of the 20th century values have been shifting. The change is brought about in part by such factors as pollution, poverty, consumer unrest, a high level of technology, economic growth, expanding population, and war.

Society is concerned about the quality of goods and services and the quality of the environment. Americans desire more time to enjoy life and more variety in ways to fulfill themselves. For example, shorter workweeks and longer vacations are requested. Absenteeism on Mondays and Fridays has become a major problem for managers and union officials. However, absenteeism may be a symptom of the changing values of people toward work and life's fulfillment.

The desire to improve the human side of life has been especially evident among youth. Poverty, discrimination, and war are problems attacked by young and old. Freedom for self-expression and participation has been strong, as evidenced by changing dress styles and by establishing the right to vote for 18-year-olds. The desire for a fuller life is also expressed through increased recreation, extensive traveling for leisure, and additional education. As can be seen from Illustration 2-4, personal expenditures for recreation have increased tremendously in recent years.

personal expenditures
for recreation

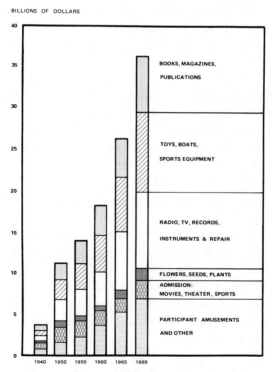

Source: U. S. Department of Commerce

ILLUS. 2-4. Value changes are reflected in increased recreational expenditures.

Individuals are becoming more and more concerned about the quality of their lives. Consumers are now less concerned about obtaining new material goods than about getting better quality in standard items purchased. The majority of Americans possess goods their parents and grandparents could not dream of owning. Society's changing values provide clues to the business owner or manager. Consumers are concerned about the type of product or service offered as well as about the quality.

EFFECT OF SOCIAL PROBLEMS ON BUSINESS

Rapid population growth, unemployment, poverty, and pollution are some of the problems of concern to society in general and to business in particular. Simple solutions to problems such as these are not easily available but are being sought by responsible groups. The business world has responded to social problems in a variety of ways, some of which have already been indicated. To be discussed next are specific areas in which business has demonstrated some change, namely: objectives of business, management of workers, and dealing with consumers.

Objectives of Business

There are two objectives of business: profit and social responsibility. *Profit* (total income less costs) has always been the primary objective of business. Because profit is such an important element in our economic system, it is discussed more fully in Chapter 3. The business owner (or owners) seeks to make a fair profit by offering goods or services to prospective customers. While profit is the central objective of business, in recent years the social responsibility objective has received a great deal of attention.

Social responsibility is the obligation of business to contribute to the good of society in a meaningful way. In a narrow sense a firm is socially responsible when it employs workers and pays taxes. But these actions are either necessary to run a business or are required by law. Under the current meaning, social responsibility extends beyond that which is necessary. It includes voluntary actions that contribute to improving the quality of life.

Forms of social responsibility vary a great deal. The firm that makes a large donation to a charity or builds a recreational facility for a community is socially responsible. So is the firm that provides equal job opportunities or voluntarily installs antipollution equipment.

The profit and social responsibility objectives of business involve ethics. *Ethics* is the concern of people for establishing fair rules of conduct. There is no shortage of rules for fair business play. Numerous state and federal laws exist that help protect the public from unethical businessmen. The business world, however, has developed its own rules for business firms to follow.

The *Chamber of Commerce,* a national association representing the interests of businesses, is one organization that is concerned about ethical practices among its members. *Better Business Bureaus,* located throughout the country, are nonprofit organizations established through the Chamber of Commerce to help protect consumers from dishonest business operators. Qualifications for membership by businesses in a Better Business Bureau include those shown in Illustration 2-5.

THIS IS A BBB MEMBER

- He is a businessman who has been in business for at least six months.
- He believes in the self-control of private business.
- He tries at all times to conduct his business along proper business principles.
- He values the goodwill of his customers and tries to treat them so they will want to do business with him again.
- He expects the Better Business Bureau to give him an impartial opinion when one of his customers complains.
- He supports the Better Business Bureau so that the whole community may have the information and assistance which the Bureau provides.
- He expects to be in business for a long time to come.

Source: Better Business Bureau

ILLUS. 2-5. Qualifications for membership in the Better Business Bureau.

Business organizations, such as the Chamber of Commerce and Better Business Bureau, help to weed out the unethical business operators. Businessmen who follow ethical practices, however, far outnumber dishonest operators. Unethical business practices are harmful to society.

The pressures and problems of society have placed new demands on business organizations, large and small. In addition to the right to make a reasonable and honest profit, business owners must become socially responsible. The effect of business actions should not be harmful to society in the short or long run. There are times, however, when an owner must take action that is socially questionable. For example, when sales drop and profits dwindle, is it proper for the owner to cut expenses by discharging workers? Is it better to cut expenses in this way in order to survive or to keep employees and risk being forced out of business completely? In the latter case, all the employees would ultimately lose their jobs. Such decisions are difficult, but they must be made.

Management of Workers

In addition to affecting the objectives of business, social problems have influenced how owners and managers deal with employees. Attention has been given to making jobs more satisfying. Employees get bored when work they are doing is too specialized. While specialization improves efficiency and is highly desirable from an economic point of view, too much specialization may cause workers to feel more like machines than people. The dullness of overly specialized work may cause the employee to feel unimportant and insignificant.

The human factor in business has taken on added importance. What motivates workers, for example, is being studied with renewed vigor. Psychologists have been hired by some firms to find ways to stimulate employees. Large corporations, especially, have tried to make life on the job more enriching for individual workers. Personal goals and business goals are being brought together as much as possible. This was not always so in the past.

To overcome boredom and frustration, managers have tried to get variety into jobs. Making jobs more interesting through more variety in tasks is called *job enlargement*. An example of job enlargement would be an assembly line involving three separate steps to finish a product, namely, drilling a hole, installing a bolt, and checking the finished product for quality. If the work were highly specialized, each of three workers would perform one task only. Job enlargement might allow each worker to do all three steps or permit the employees to rotate the three jobs periodically.

Another relatively new managerial technique is to get employees personally committed to their work through participation in decision making. For example, managers may request opinions of workers on matters affecting them or may allow employees to get involved in setting job goals. The practice of allowing workers to assume some of the decision making previously done by managers only is called *job enrichment*.

Dealing with Consumers

A third area of change by business firms has been brought about by consumers. The consumer revolt, as labeled by some, has caused firms to become more sensitive to the needs of the buying public. In the past, consumers expressed themselves to business primarily by either buying or not buying goods or services offered. Today the consumer uses other means to communicate as well.

Consumers have relied on government for protection from undesirable business practices and conditions. With the change in values has come the desire for added consumer safeguards. As you will learn in Chapter 30, new laws have been passed in recent years to assist consumers. In 1962 President John F. Kennedy delivered to Congress a special message on consumer protection that included his now famous four rights of consumers as shown in Illustration 2-6. This message was the first of its kind by a president of the United States.

1. *The right to safety*—to be protected against the marketing of goods which are hazardous to health or life.

2. *The right to be informed*—to be protected against fraudulent, deceitful, or grossly misleading information, advertising, labeling, or other practices, and to be given the facts needed to make an informed choice.

3. *The right to choose*—to be assured, wherever possible, access to a variety of products and services at competitive prices, and in those industries in which competition is not workable and government regulation is substituted, to be assured satisfactory quality and service at fair prices.

4. *The right to be heard*—to be assured that consumer interests will receive full and sympathetic consideration in the formulation of government policy, and fair and expeditious treatment in its administrative tribunals.

Source: Consumer Advisory Council
Executive Office of the President

ILLUS. 2-6. President John F. Kennedy's Special Message on Protecting the Consumer Interest

To assure that the "right to be heard" was practiced, President Kennedy created a Consumer Advisory Council to work on behalf of all consumers. The Council influences the passage of consumer laws and has offered advice to businesses regarding products and services.

The consumer movement, launched during the 1960s, continued to gain support during the 1970s. In addition to relying on government to aid their interests, consumers have become an active force through other means. The public has supported individuals who have spoken out for consumer rights. For example, Ralph Nader, a leader among consumer crusaders, formed an organization of young people to represent consumer interests on many matters. Groups of specialists, known as Nader's Raiders, have issued reports on various consumer topics.

Primary consumer concerns deal with such matters as quality products, safe products, unethical business practices, and pollution. The consumer's voice has been heard clearly by business owners and managers. In order for large corporations to become more responsive to consumer interests, firms have recently hired special executives to deal with matters affecting public interest. Leading companies, like General Motors, have allowed individuals representing the public interest to serve on the major ruling body of their organizations. In this way, the public's view—including the consumers'—is heard by leaders before important business decisions affecting firms are made.

THE FUTURE

The growing economy and the rising level of living are measures of success for the American business system. With bigness and wealth, however, have come problems. Many of the problems have been social in nature; for example, unemployment, pollution, and poverty. Such problems have had a direct impact on the way people think and the way business firms operate.

Changing human values have grown out of the problems of life during the second half of the 20th century. People are now more concerned with the quality of life than ever before, and this is not likely to change as time goes on. From businesses of all types, people will expect improved quality in products and services offered and active involvement in improving the physical environment. The responsible business owner or manager will give greater attention to the human aspects of jobs for employees. Large and small companies will be extremely concerned about the social environment in which they operate while at the same time attempting to earn a fair profit. Because business in the past has been responsive to changing conditions, there is every reason to believe business will continue to be flexible and socially responsible in the future.

REVIEW WHAT YOU HAVE LEARNED

Business Terms Checkup:

(1) labor force
(2) JOBS
(3) recycling
(4) profit
(5) social responsibility

(6) ethics
(7) Chamber of Commerce
(8) Better Business Bureau
(9) job enlargement
(10) job enrichment

Reading Checkup:

1. The combination of what three factors helped this country achieve its economic success?
2. For the current population of the nation not to increase or decrease, how many children would each family need to have?
3. What percentage of the population is less than 28 years of age?
4. What are some of the problems caused by people concentrating in metropolitan areas?
5. What effect has improved technology had on the labor force?
6. What percent of the population is classified as living at the poverty level?
7. How does recycling conserve the supply of natural resources?
8. What evidence is there that people have had a desire for fuller, more satisfying lives?
9. What are the two objectives of business?
10. Why has the Chamber of Commerce established Better Business Bureaus?
11. How does too much specialization in work affect employees?
12. Explain two techniques that managers use to make work more interesting for employees?
13. List the four rights of consumers that were identified by President Kennedy.
14. What have businesses done to help overcome some of the complaints of consumers?

APPLY WHAT YOU HAVE LEARNED

Questions for Class Discussion:

1. Why should one who studies American business principles and management also study the social problems of the country?
2. What kinds of businesses would be most affected by the fact that the population is getting younger?

3. Why are the unemployed considered as part of the total labor force?

4. Why has the demand for unskilled workers declined over the years?

5. What is the business world doing for unskilled and unemployed workers?

6. Why does the survival of mankind depend on how well society controls its physical environment?

7. Explain how a large population and GNP can contribute to the problem of pollution.

8. What are some of the ways in which the individual citizen can participate in controlling pollution?

9. Give examples of how values toward work have changed.

10. What does Illustration 2-4 tell us about Americans in general?

11. Give various examples of how business demonstrates social responsibility.

12. Give an example of how the profit objective can conflict with the social responsibility objective of business.

13. How have consumer crusaders, such as Ralph Nader, affected businesses?

Problems and Projects:

1. Visit your school library for assistance in preparing a list of American inventions and scientific discoveries that have occurred since 1950. From the list write a paragraph or two on the effect you think the group of items has had on business and on the individual well-being of people.

2. Contact a large business in your community to find out what it is doing to help control pollution. Prepare a report of your findings.

3. Interview the director of the Better Business Bureau nearest you. Find out how your community has benefited from the work of the Better Business Bureau. Write a report of your interview.

4. Prepare an oral or written report on any one of the following social problems as it applies to your state or area: pollution, unemployment, or poverty. In your report be sure to indicate what business firms have been doing to help solve the problem.

5. In your library find an article on the population problem and report on it to the class.

Case Problem 2-1:

Curtis Miller has been operating a small manufacturing business for about a year. The business makes a special type of heavy-duty paint which is used by many businesses. While Miller made a profit of $5,000 the first year, he felt that it was small based on all the money he had invested and all the time he had put into building the business.

A few of the local citizens have complained to Miller that some of the waste from his plant is getting into the nearby river. An engineer checked this and found that while some waste was seeping into the water it was not enough to be in violation of any laws. The engineer also mentioned that Miller could install a special piece of equipment for about $10,000 that would solve the problem. Miller was not sure, however, whether his new business was going to be successful enough during the next few years to justify such an expenditure.

Required:

1. What is the problem facing the community?
2. What is the problem facing Miller?
3. Should Miller install the equipment?

Case Problem 2-2:

At the annual meeting of stockholders (owners) of a large automobile manufacturing company, it was proposed that the membership of the ruling body of the corporation be changed. The ruling body, which meets about once a month or so, either discusses or makes major policy decisions for running the firm on behalf of the thousands of stockholders. The proposal presented at the annual meeting of stockholders is that one employee and one consumer representative be added to the 12-man ruling body.

The reason for the proposal by one of the small stockholders is that the firm is large and its actions affect many people. Millions of persons either own cars, work for the company, or live in or near communities where the corporation has plants and offices. It is argued that all those affected in a major way by the corporation should be able to influence policies of the firm. Thus, employees and customers should be represented on the ruling body along with owners.

The current members of the ruling body have asked the stockholders to vote against the proposal, stating that (1) employees already have a right to be heard through their supervisors; (2) since we are all consumers, the consumer point of view is already represented; and (3) only the owners of the company should have the right to decide how the company should be run.

Required:

1. If you owned one of the company's cars but did not own any of its stock, would you favor the proposal? Why?
2. If you were a large stockholder in the corporation, would you vote for the proposal? Why?

Continuing Project:

See instructions at the end of Chapter 1, page 23.

What is economics?

How does saving affect an economy?

What is the economic system of the United States?

Why do people own businesses?

How are prices of goods determined?

How does competition benefit society?

What are socialism and communism?

BACKGROUND OF CHAPTER

Every individual is involved in problems related to his efforts to obtain the goods and services he wants. To understand and solve these problems, every individual needs to have some knowledge of economics. For example, a knowledge of economics is helpful to the individual in deciding how he should spend his income. Today's citizen must also have economic knowledge in order to vote intelligently on such things as farm price supports, labor-management relations, and foreign aid.

This chapter explains the basic concepts which citizens, particularly businessmen, need to know to understand the operation of our economic system.

CHAPTER 3

ECONOMIC ENVIRONMENT OF AMERICAN BUSINESS

All societies face the problem of trying to satisfy the wants of their citizens for goods and services. Although all societies have this common problem, many different systems have been developed for producing and using goods and services. The body of knowledge which relates to producing and using goods and services which satisfy human wants is called *economics*.

Business is the term used to identify the efforts of a group of individuals, or a single individual, to produce and distribute useful goods and services. Since business is a central part of economic activity, having economic knowledge is particularly important for those who are engaged in business or who are preparing themselves for a career in business.

Concepts which are essential to the understanding of any economic system are discussed first in this chapter. The economic system which exists in the United States is then described. Finally, brief attention is given to other economic systems.

BASIC ECONOMIC CONCEPTS

A helpful beginning point in understanding the nature and scope of economics is the consideration of the kinds of wants which are the concern of the economic system.

Economic Wants

People have many kinds of wants, but the economic system is only concerned with their economic wants. *Economic wants* are for material goods and services which are scarce. People want material goods, such as food, clothing, automobiles, and TV sets. They also want services, such as haircuts, medical attention, and bus transportation.

Items such as these are scarce because the economic system cannot satisfy all of the wants of all people for these material goods and services.

Other wants of people are not economic wants because there is no scarcity of the thing desired. Such wants include, for example, wants for air and sunshine. Nor are nonmaterial wants for such things as friendship and a happy marriage economic wants.

ILLUS. 3-1. People have many kinds of economic wants.

Production

The goods and services people want have to be produced. For example, clothing must be made, automobiles manufactured, and barbers must cut hair. In economics *production* is defined as the creation of utility.

Utility. *Utility* is the ability of a good or a service to satisfy a want. In other words, a good or a service which has utility is a useful good or service. The most common types of utility are form utility, place utility, time utility, and possession utility.

Form Utility. Changes in the form or shape of a product which make the product more useful create *form utility*. Form utility is added to cotton, for example, when a bathing suit is manufactured from cotton. Form utility can be added only to products, but the other types of utility can be added to services as well as to products.

Place Utility. To be useful a product or a service must be in a place where it is needed or wanted. If an individual is vacationing in Florida and wants to buy a bathing suit, a bathing suit at a manufacturing plant in California is not useful to him. *Place utility* is created by having a good or service at the place where it is needed or wanted.

Time Utility. In addition to being at a place where it is wanted, a product or a service to be useful must be at the place at the time it is needed or wanted. A bathing suit which can be delivered to Florida in one month is not useful to the individual who is on a two-week vacation in Florida. *Time utility* is created when a product or a service is available when it is needed or wanted.

Possession Utility. Possession utility is created when the ownership of a good or service is transferred from one person to another. This transfer of ownership is usually accomplished when an individual buys a product or a service. A bathing suit in the window display of a department store is not useful to the individual vacationing in Florida. The bathing suit is useful when the individual possesses it after buying it from the department store.

Anyone who aids in the creating of utility is a producer and is entitled to a reward for the usefulness which he has added to the good or service. The barber is entitled to a reward for the usefulness of the service he provides. The price paid for the bathing suit includes a reward for the manufacturer who made the bathing suit, the transportation companies and merchants who made it possible to buy the suit in Florida at the time it was wanted, and the salesman who sold the suit to the vacationer.

Factors of Production. Four basic resources must be combined in order that useful goods and services may be produced. These resources, called *factors of production*, are: natural resources or land, labor, capital goods, and management.

Natural Resources or Land. The extent to which a society is able to produce goods and services is, in part, determined by its natural resources or land. The productive ability of the United States, for example, is related to its having fertile soil, minerals in the ground, water and timber resources, and a good climate.

Labor. Labor is the human effort, either physical or mental, which goes into the production of goods and services. Without labor there could not, of course, be much production of goods and services.

Capital Goods. Before goods which people want are produced, it is often necessary or desirable to produce tools and machines which will aid the production process. Goods such as buildings, tools, machines, and other equipment, which do not directly satisfy wants, are called *capital goods.* Capital goods are produced because their use greatly increases the productivity of labor and management. Later you will learn that the term "capital" is also used when referring to the money that is invested in a business.

Management. For the production of goods, more is needed than the mere availability of natural resources, labor, and capital goods. Someone, or some group, must bring these factors together and plan and organize the production of a final product. *Management* is the term used to identify this fourth factor of production which brings together the other three factors.

ILLUS. 3-2. For the production of goods, management utilizes natural resources, labor, and capital goods.

Because government provides many services which are essential to the operation of business, it is often listed as a fifth factor of production by economists. Some of the essential services provided by government are streets and highways, police and fire protection, courts that settle disputes, and a postal system which provides communications.

Consumption

The process of using goods and services is called *consumption,* and the people who use goods and services are called *consumers.* Using a service, such as the service of a barber, is just as much "consumption" as is the eating of food or the wearing of clothes. Goods and services which satisfy people's economic wants directly, such as food and the service of a barber, are called *consumer goods and services*.

Capital Formation

An important concept which relates to both consumer and capital goods is that capital goods are only possible as a result of saving. In economics *saving* means not using productive resources to make consumer goods but using them to produce capital goods. To say this in another way, saving means refraining from consumption for the purpose of capital formation. Capital formation takes place, for example, when steel is used to produce tools (capital goods) for making automobiles rather than using the steel for manufacturing automobiles (consumer goods).

When productive resources are used for capital formation, the capacity for producing more consumer goods is created. For example, when tools are produced for making automobiles, it is then possible to

ILLUS. 3-3. To produce or buy capital goods, business depends in part on the money savings of individuals.

manufacture more automobiles. However, using steel, labor, and management to produce tools (capital goods) means that these resources cannot be used to produce automobiles (consumer goods), and the immediate result is that consumers have fewer automobiles to buy. But because tools were made, consumers will have more automobiles to buy in the future. The scarcity of consumer goods in the Soviet Union is, in part, the result of that country's using a large portion of its productive resources in capital formation.

The term "saving" as used above means the use of productive resources to make capital goods. Much saving is, of course, in the form of money. As you will learn later, business saves money from its profits in order to produce or buy capital goods. In order to produce or buy capital goods, business also depends upon the saving of money by individual citizens. Some individuals who save money instead of spending it for consumer goods invest this money directly in existing businesses. Other individuals invest their savings in buildings and equipment and start new businesses. Still others place their savings in financial institutions, such as banks. These financial institutions lend this money to businessmen who use it to obtain capital goods.

Economic Systems

As has been mentioned, no society has enough productive resources to enable it to satisfy all of the wants of all people for material goods and services. Because productive resources are scarce, difficult decisions must be made as to how to use these limited resources (e.g., deciding which is better—more capital goods and fewer consumer goods or more consumer goods and fewer capital goods).

Each society must have some organized way for making decisions as to how it will use its resources. After goods have been produced, decisions must also be made as to how the goods will be divided among the people in the society. The organized way developed by a society for making these decisions is its *economic system.*

Different societies have developed vastly different economic systems. The sharply contrasting economic systems which exist today are commonly referred to as capitalism, socialism, and communism.

CAPITALISM—THE ECONOMIC SYSTEM OF THE UNITED STATES

The importance of the individual has always been emphasized in America. Because of our belief in the importance of the individual, we have designed political and economic systems which permit the individual much freedom. History tells us that there has been a relationship between political and economic freedom. That is, there has been more political freedom in countries in which individuals have economic freedom.

Our economic system is most commonly referred to as capitalism or the free enterprise system. *Capitalism* is an economic system in which private citizens are free to go into business for themselves, produce whatever they choose to produce, and distribute what they produce as they please.

The above definition of capitalism would have accurately described our economic system during much of the 19th century and the early part of the 20th century. In the past few decades, however, government has come to play a significant economic role in the United States. As our economy developed without intervention by government, certain abuses occurred. For example, some individuals began to interfere with the economic freedom of others, some larger businesses began to exploit smaller businesses, and some employers did not pay fair wages. To correct such abuses, it was necessary to pass laws. Although most of the government intervention is for protecting and promoting the general welfare, many individuals feel that some of the intervention is unnecessary. Further attention to the regulation of business by government is given in Chapter 30.

Because there are now many government controls of business, our economic system is sometimes called *modified capitalism*. In our economy today, private citizens are free to go into business for themselves, produce whatever they choose to produce, and distribute what they produce as they please as long as they conform to the rules and regulations set forth by government.

Private Property

The institution of private property is essential to our capitalistic system. *Private property* means that individuals have the right to own, use, or sell things of value. Thus, individuals can control productive resources. Individuals can own land, they can hire labor, they can own capital goods, and they can use these productive resources to produce goods and services. And, individuals own the products made from their use of land, labor, and capital goods. Thus, the company that produces furniture owns the furniture it makes. The furniture company may sell its furniture to customers, and it owns the money received from selling the furniture.

Profit

In a capitalistic system the incentive and reward for producing goods and services is profit. Briefly defined, *profit* is the difference between costs and receipts. The company making furniture has costs for land, labor, capital goods, materials, etc. Profit is what the furniture company has left over after subtracting these costs from the amount received from selling its furniture to customers.

The profit earned by a business is frequently overestimated. The average profit is about 5 percent of total receipts while the remainder, 95 percent, represents costs. Consider a motel with annual receipts of $100,000. If the profit amounts to 5 percent, then the owner earns $5,000, that is, $100,000 times .05 (change percent to a decimal before multiplying). Costs for the year are .95 times $100,000, or $95,000. Some types of businesses average higher profit percentages but many have lower ones, too. Owners, of course, try to earn a profit percentage that is better than average.

ILLUS. 3-4. Profit is the incentive and reward for producing goods and services.

Merely engaging in business does not, by itself, ensure that a profit will be made. Among other things, to be successful a company must produce goods or services that people want at a price they are willing to pay.

Demand, Supply, and Prices

Demand for a product means how many of the product will be bought at a particular time at a certain price. Thus, "demand" is not the same thing as "want." Wanting a Cadillac without having the money to buy one does not represent demand. Demand for a Cadillac is represented by the individual who wants it, has the money to buy it, and is willing to spend his money for it.

Usually, the more demand there is for a product the higher the price will be for that product. When the Mustang was placed on the market by the Ford Motor Company, there was such a great demand for the car that it was not possible to obtain one for lower than the listed price. At the same time other Ford models for which there was less demand could be obtained for lower than the listed price.

The supply of a particular product also influences its price. *Supply* of a product means how many of the product will be offered for sale at a particular time at a certain price. If there is a current shortage in the supply of a product, the price of the product will usually rise as consumers bid against one another to obtain the product. For example, if bad weather has damaged the apple crop and apples are in short supply, the price of apples will go up. When apples become more abundant in supply, their price will go down. Thus, changes in prices of products are the result of changes in both the demand for and the supply of a product.

In the main, changes in prices determine what is produced and how much is produced in our economy, for price changes indicate to businesses what is profitable or not profitable to produce. If consumers want more shoes than are being produced, they will bid up the price of shoes. The increase in the price of shoes makes it more profitable to make shoes and provides the incentive for businesses to increase the production of shoes. As the supply of shoes increases to satisfy the demand for more shoes, the price of shoes will fall. Since it is now less profitable to make shoes, businesses decrease their production of shoes.

Prices, then, are determined by the forces of demand and supply. That is, prices are the result of the decisions of individual consumers to buy products and of individual producers to make and sell products.

In the final analysis, therefore, it is all of the people in the United States who decide what will be produced and how much will be produced.

Competition

In our free enterprise system, sellers are trying to make a profit, and buyers are trying to buy the maximum amount of quality goods at minimum prices. This conflict of interests between buyers and sellers is resolved to the benefit of society by competition. *Competition* is the rivalry among sellers for the customer's dollars.

Competition in a free enterprise system benefits society in many ways. To attract customers away from other sellers, a business must try to improve the quality of its products, develop new products, and operate efficiently in order to keep its prices down. Thus, competition serves to insure that consumers will get the quality products they want at fair prices.

In addition to benefiting consumers, competition benefits the society in that it tends to make businesses use our scarce productive resources efficiently. If a business does not operate efficiently, the business will fail because customers will buy lower priced or higher quality products from a business which is operating efficiently. The element of competition in our economic system also provides the opportunity for people to enter business for themselves and try to share in the profits being made by those already in business.

One aspect of competition is price competition. Price competition means getting business away from competitors by lowering prices. Today, though, more and more competition takes the form of nonprice competition. For example, customers are attracted away from other sellers by providing products which have superior quality or by adding

ILLUS. 3-5. **Competition is the rivalry among sellers for the customer's dollars.**

something to the product which the competitor does not have, such as an automatic starter on a lawn mower. Or, customers may be attracted by the packaging of a product, such as wrapping vegetables in cellophane. Extensive advertising campaigns aimed at convincing customers that, for example, a particular brand of deodorant is more effective than other brands are also important in nonprice competition.

Competition is the opposite of monopoly. *Monopoly* exists when there is only one seller and the seller is able to avoid most of the elements of effective competition. For example, if a seller does not have to compete with other sellers for the consumer's dollars, he can increase his profit by selling his product for a higher price. As you will learn in Chapter 30, an important area of government intervention in business is for the purpose of maintaining competition and avoiding monopolistic practices.

Distribution of Income

As was discussed earlier in this chapter, all societies must not only decide how scarce productive resources are to be used but must also decide how the goods produced will be divided among the people in the society. In a free enterprise economy, the share of goods produced which an individual receives is determined by the amount of money he has to purchase goods and services.

People receive money for wages and salaries by contributing their labor to the production of goods and services. Money is also received by people as interest on money that they lend to others, as rent for land or buildings which they own, and as profits if they are owners of businesses.

The amount of money which an individual receives in wages or salary is determined by numerous factors, including the personal traits and abilities of the individual. The same factors which determine the prices of goods are also important factors in determining wages and salaries. That is, the amount of wages paid for a particular kind of labor is affected by the supply of and demand for that kind of labor. The demand for unskilled workers is relatively low, and there is a large supply of unskilled workers. Thus, the "price" (income) of unskilled workers is low. On the other hand, the demand for brain surgeons is high in terms of the supply of brain surgeons, and their "price" (income) is high.

By means of taxing and spending, government influences the distribution of income. For example, government takes money away from people who have high incomes by imposing high income tax rates on their incomes. The government then spends the money on such things as public housing, police protection, welfare, and public education which benefit people who pay little or nothing in income taxes because their incomes are low.

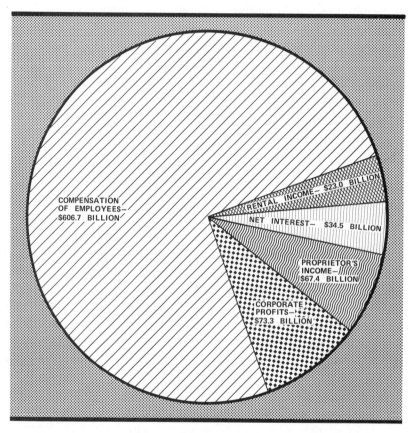

Source: U. S. Department of Commerce

ILLUS. 3-6. How our national income was divided in 1970.

Economic Growth

Economic growth occurs when a country produces goods and services at a faster rate than the population is increasing. When a nation can do this, there are more goods and services for each person. By means of rapid economic growth, the free enterprise system has provided the citizens of the United States with a rapidly increasing quantity of goods and services.

The following are the basic ways in which expansion of the production of goods and services can be achieved:

1. Increase the number of workers in the labor force.
2. Increase the productivity of the labor force by means of education and training.
3. Increase the supply of capital goods so that more tools and machines are available to increase the productivity of labor and management.
4. Improve technology by inventing new and better machines and new and better methods for producing goods and services. (Automation is an example of technological improvement.)

For economic growth, though, more is required than just the expansion of the production of goods and services. There must also be expansion in the consumption of goods and services by consumers, business, government, and foreigners. The incentive for producing goods and services in a free enterprise economy is profit. If the goods and services being produced are in demand and are profitable, business has the incentive to increase production.

Rapid growth of the economy is important for a number of reasons. Rapid growth is important so that we may have more automobiles, TV sets, schools, etc. More importantly, rapid economic growth is needed so that there will be enough jobs as the population increases.

However, in an attempt to expand the economy by increasing the production and consumption of goods and services, problems may arise. A recession may occur when most goods and services available are not consumed. That is, the demand for goods and services for the nation is less than the supply. A *recession* is a slowdown or a decline in the gross national product (GNP) that runs six months or more. It is accompanied by decreased production, unemployment, and other national problems.

Another problem can arise when the amount which consumers, business, and government want to spend is greater than the goods and services currently available for the country. This causes prices to rise. *Inflation* is the rapid rise in prices caused by total demand exceeding supply. Inflation is accompanied by a decline in the purchasing power of money. That is, more dollars are needed to buy the same items bought before inflation occurred. Those with fixed incomes, such as retired people, are financially hurt the most when their dollars buy less.

DOLLARS NEEDED TO BUY AN ITEM COSTING $100
DURING THE PERIOD 1957-1959

If the item were bought in	It would have cost
1950	$ 84
1955	93
1957	100
1960	103
1965	110
1970	116

Source: U. S. Department of Labor

ILLUS. 3-7. Inflation has reduced the purchasing power of the dollar.

Neither a recession nor inflation is desirable for the country, businessmen, or consumers. To help prevent a recession or inflation, the federal government can take steps such as raising or lowering taxes. The businessman needs to be aware of the problems of economic growth and government actions because individual businesses are often affected.

World Trade

Rapid technological advances in such areas as communications and transportation result in our world becoming smaller and smaller. Thus, our relations with other countries become more and more important. Increasingly, we are involved with the rest of the world in economic as well as political problems.

Over $40 billion of goods are exported each year from the United States. If we did not export these goods, many farmers would have less income, many people who have jobs would be unemployed, and the profits of many businesses would be reduced. For example, in a recent year the United States exported over $17 billion of machinery and transportation equipment and over $4 billion in food and live animals.

Imports are also essential for our economy. We need some products which we do not produce at all, such as tin and coffee. Copper and iron ore are illustrations of products which we need to import because we do not produce them in quantities adequate for the needs of our economy.

Many Americans have provided the money or capital goods to start businesses in other countries. These businesses abroad help provide our economy with products which it needs, such as oil from Venezuela. In addition, our helping other countries to develop their productive resources has enabled these countries to make money with which they can buy products we want to export.

OTHER ECONOMIC SYSTEMS

As noted earlier in this chapter, different societies have developed different economic systems. The economic systems which differ radically from capitalism are commonly called socialism and communism.

Socialism

Socialism exists in many different forms, but all socialists believe that the government should own productive resources and should plan production for the entire economy.

Socialists disagree as to the extent to which government should own productive resources. The most extreme socialists want the government to own all natural resources and capital goods. Socialists who are more moderate in their beliefs think that planning production for the entire economy can be achieved if the government owns certain key industries, but they feel that other productive resources should be owned by individuals. For example, when a socialist government was elected in England after World War II, the Bank of England, the coal mines, and the steel, transportation, and communications industries were the only segments of the economy which were nationalized.

Socialists also believe that government ownership of productive resources should be achieved gradually through democratic processes. That is, socialists expect their programs to be carried out when socialist governments are elected.

Socialism is generally opposed in the United States for two basic reasons. First, socialism even in its most moderate form limits the right of the individual to own property for productive purposes, and this is a right which most Americans cherish. Second, most Americans fear that socialism might eventually result in government by one party or by a dictatorship. A socialist party which controlled the important segments of the economy could use its economic power to win elections. For example, a party which controlled the communications industries would be in a strong position to influence public opinion.

Communism

Briefly defined, *communism* is forced socialism. Extreme socialism is the economic system of communism. All, or almost all, of the productive resources of a nation are owned by the government. Decisions regarding what is to be produced, how much is to be produced, and how the results of production are to be divided among the citizens are made by government agencies on the basis of a plan which has been drawn up by the government. Government measures how well producers perform on the basis of the volume of goods and services produced without regard to the quality of or demand for the goods or services. Even though consumer goods are in short supply in the Soviet Union, communism has created situations in that country in which the products made were of such poor quality that they were not purchased by consumers. Because of these situations, some adjustments are being made by the Soviet Union which introduce some capitalistic principles of supply and demand. For example, adjustments are being made to judge the performance of producers by the demand for their products and to permit control of production in terms of consumer demand.

As contrasted to socialism, communism believes in a revolutionary change from capitalism to communism and from democratic processes to dictatorship. The members of a communist society have few of the freedoms which Americans believe are so important.

REVIEW WHAT YOU HAVE LEARNED

Business Terms Checkup:

(1) economics
(2) business
(3) economic wants
(4) production
(5) utility
(6) form utility
(7) place utility
(8) time utility
(9) possession utility
(10) factors of
　　　production
(11) land or natural
　　　resources

(12) labor
(13) capital goods
(14) management
(15) consumption
(16) consumer goods
　　　and services
(17) saving
(18) economic
　　　system
(19) capitalism
(20) modified
　　　capitalism
(21) private property

(22) profit
(23) demand
(24) supply
(25) competition
(26) monopoly
(27) economic growth
(28) recession
(29) inflation
(30) socialism
(31) communism

Reading Checkup:

1. What are the four most common types of utility?
2. What are the four basic factors of production? Why is government often listed as a fifth factor of production?

3. What is the difference between consumer goods and capital goods?

4. Why is our economic system sometimes called modified capitalism?

5. Why is the institution of private property essential to our economic system?

6. What is the significance of profit to the operation of our economic system?

7. How do businessmen know what to produce and how much to produce?

8. What are the four basic ways in which expansion of the production of goods and services can be achieved?

9. Why is socialism generally opposed in the United States?

10. How does communism differ from socialism?

APPLY WHAT YOU HAVE LEARNED

Questions for Class Discussion:

1. What kinds of wants do people have? Which of these wants are the concern of the economic system?

2. Describe the various ways in which producers can add usefulness to goods and services.

3. Distinguish between the two basic meanings of "saving." How are the savings of individuals important to the economy?

4. Explain the effects which the production of capital goods has on consumer goods.

5. Why has some intervention by government in our economic system been necessary?

Problems and Projects:

1. A barber is a producer who performs a service. List as many other jobs as you can in which the person doing the job is performing a service.

2. Identify the most recent action by the federal government that could be labeled an attempt to control either a recession or inflation. Write a paragraph or two indicating how your family was affected directly or indirectly.

3. Select three different types of businesses (dry cleaners, supermarkets, beauty salons, furniture stores, etc.) and from the yellow pages of the telephone directory for your area find out how many firms are in each type of business. Account for why one line of business may have more or fewer competitors than the others.

4. Discuss with a businessman the problems he has in competing with other businessmen. Report what you learned to the class.

Case Problem 3-1:

George Jackson operates the only shoe shop in his neighborhood. For several years he has paid particular attention to the sales volume of a popular but inexpensive sneaker that is imported from the Orient. These sneakers normally sell for $3.00 a pair; demand at this price has been about the same for each month of the year. Jackson is concerned about satisfying his customers pricewise but he is also concerned about making the most profit possible. With this sneaker, he has wondered whether the $3.00 price should be raised or lowered. To aid in his decision, he has been changing the price on an experimental basis for the past five months. Here is his record of sales and profit:

Month	Selling Price	Number Sold	Profit
September	$2.75	130	$ 97.50
October	3.00	100	100.00
November	3.25	90	112.50
December	3.50	70	105.00
January	3.75	40	70.00

Required:

1. What affect did the price have on the demand for the sneaker?
2. From a profit viewpoint, what selling price should Mr. Jackson set?
3. Might there be an advantage to selling the sneaker for $2.75?
4. What would most likely happen to the profit and the number of sneakers sold if Mr. Jackson lowered the price to $2.50?

Case Problem 3-2:

Robert Frakes has had experience in a machine shop, and Harold Thompson has had experience selling small parts which are included in the manufacture of large machinery. They decide to start a business of their own to make certain types of special valves, gears, drills, and compressors because they are most familiar with these. They were able to invest $20,000 of their own money in equipment but needed $20,000 more which they were able to borrow. They received some promises that their parts would be purchased if they could quote satisfactory prices.

Frakes and Thompson had planned to start the business with six employees working in the garage and the basement of Frakes' house; however, they discovered that a city zoning ordinance would prohibit this kind of work in a residential area. Therefore, they had to rent a part of an old factory building. After they started production and were able to figure their costs, they were able to fill some good orders for valves and gears but were not able to obtain any orders for compressors or drills because competitors were always able to offer a lower price.

Required:

1. What kinds of utility in terms of economics is this business performing?
2. What elements or factors of production are involved in this business?
3. What did Frakes and Thompson discover about free enterprise?

Continuing Project:

See instructions at the end of Chapter 1, page 23.

CAREERS IN BUSINESS

Since you have decided to study business principles and management, you probably are considering a career in business. Perhaps you want to go into marketing, accounting, or personnel work. Maybe you are interested in government service, or maybe you want to operate your own business. Perhaps you have not yet made up your mind. This book will help you achieve a better understanding of business and its career possibilities.

Specific career information is given in the various sections of this book listed below. If you are considering a career in marketing, for example, you would be interested in reading now about the many different career possibilities in marketing. If you do not have a specific career interest, you might like to browse through all of the sections below which contain information about careers in business.

UNIT II
Business
Ownership

What is meant by a sole proprietorship?

What businesses are organized as sole proprietorships?

What are the advantages of a partnership?

Why are articles of copartnership needed?

What is unlimited financial liability?

What is meant by a limited partnership?

BACKGROUND OF CHAPTER

Many a small business is started as a sole proprietorship—that is, the business is owned by one person. Barber shops, newsstands, and television repair shops are businesses which are often organized as sole proprietorships. Many businesses are owned by two or more persons as partners. Retail grocery and meat markets, restaurants, and automobile repair and painting shops are businesses well suited to the partnership form of organization.

In this chapter you will learn about the advantages and disadvantages of the sole proprietorship and partnership forms of organization.

CHAPTER 4

SOLE PROPRIETORSHIPS AND PARTNERSHIPS

A dominant characteristic of business in this country is that nearly all businesses are owned by individuals. One person, or a group of persons, invests his savings in a business with the hope of obtaining profits from its activities. There are several legal forms of organization for a business. The most popular forms are the sole proprietorship, the general partnership, and the corporation. The particular form of organization that owners may choose depends on several factors, such as the nature and size of the business, the capital needed, the type of managerial services desired, the tax laws, and the financial liability the owners are willing to assume. Determining which is the best form of organization is one of the first things to be decided in starting a new business.

SOLE PROPRIETORSHIP

An enterprise that is owned and managed by one person is known as an *individual proprietorship,* an *individual enterprise,* or a *sole proprietorship.* Over 9 million businesses in this country are sole proprietorships. Under this form of organization one person usually owns the business, manages it, and is the sole recipient of the profits. The sole proprietor may thus perform the functions of a capitalist, a landowner, and a laborer. He is a capitalist because he owns the business and receives profits from it. He may be a landowner by owning the land on which the place of business is located. He is a laborer because he performs at least part of the labor in operating the business.

It is evident that all the responsibility for the successful operation of the business rests on the shoulders of the sole owner. He must furnish the money, the management, and usually at least part of the labor. For assuming all this responsibility, however, he is the only one who is entitled to the profits that the business earns.

Provided the sole proprietor does not owe any debts, he has full claim to the *assets* (property) of the business. If he has business debts, however, his *creditors* (those to whom he owes money) have prior claims against the assets. The following illustration is a simple financial statement of Mr. B. L. York, who operates a retail grocery as a sole proprietor:

Assets		Claims Against Assets	
Cash	$ 3,700	Accounts Payable (Debts)	$ 3,000
Merchandise	6,600	B. L. York, Proprietorship	42,500
Equipment	5,200		
Land and Building	30,000		
	$45,500		$45,500

This simple financial statement, known as a *balance sheet,* shows that the assets of the business are valued at $45,500. Since York has debts of $3,000, his *proprietorship* (also known as *equity* or *net worth*) is $42,500 ($45,500 — $3,000). If there are any earnings, he gets the total amount. Since he owns the land and the building, he does not have to pay any rent, although he must pay the cost of maintenance and taxes for his property.

ILLUS. 4-1. A sole proprietorship is a business that is owned by one person.

Advantages of Sole Proprietorship

The fact that the majority of businesses today are individual enter-prises indicates that this form of organization has definite advantages. Some of these are discussed below.

Owner Is His Own Boss. When one is the sole owner of a business, he usually has a certain pleasant feeling that he is his own "boss" and is responsible only to himself. He feels that he has more of a chance to be inventive or creative in working out his own ideas. This feeling stimulates him to work hard to make his business a success.

Owner Receives All Profits. Very closely related to this first advantage is the fact that all the profits belong to the sole proprietor. As he is the sole gainer, he is more likely to work overtime and to think continually of how his business can be operated more efficiently.

Owner Personally Knows Employees and Customers. Because most sole proprietorships are small, the proprietor and his employees get to know each other personally. This relationship is conducive to a better understanding and a greater mutual interest between employer and employees. These same benefits should result from the close touch that the sole proprietor has with his customers.

ILLUS. 4-2. The sole proprietor can make decisions quickly, for he does not have to consult anyone else.

Owner Can Act Quickly in Decision Making. The sole proprietor is not hindered in making decisions. As he need not consult business associates, he can act promptly in emergencies. If an unusual opportunity to buy merchandise or equipment arises, or if there is a desire to change the location of the business or to sell on credit terms rather than on a cash basis, there are no dissenting partners to hinder such action. Thus, the management of an individual enterprise is flexible and can adjust itself easily to changing conditions.

Owner Is Free from Red Tape. One can usually commence or cease business activities as a sole proprietor without legal formality. One does not need to consult a lawyer and go through a large amount of "red tape" in order to organize an individual enterprise. In some types of businesses, however, such as a restaurant, it is necessary to obtain a permit or license before operations can be begun.

Owner Usually Pays Less Income Tax Than a Corporation. In most sole proprietorships the income tax is usually less than in the corporation type of business. This is explained in the next chapter.

Disadvantages of Sole Proprietorship

Although there are many advantages, there are some disadvantages that confront the sole proprietor. Some are discussed below.

Owner May Lack Special Skills and Abilities. Each individual usually has a special aptitude or ability. In one, it may be to sell merchandise; in another, it may be to purchase goods; in another, it may be to keep records; in another, it may be to manage employees. All these activities are important to the success of a business, but the sole proprietor is likely to be deficient in judgment or ability in one or more of them. It is therefore easy to understand why many sole proprietorships end in failure within a short time.

Owner May Lack Funds. Often there is need of additional funds (capital) for emergencies. Financial assistance on a large scale may be difficult to obtain when so much depends upon one person. The expansion of the business may be retarded because of the lack of capital of the sole owner.

Owner Bears All Losses. The sole proprietor assumes a great amount of risk. It is true that he receives all the profits of the business; but likewise, he bears all the losses if the business is not successful. Should the business fail and be unable to pay its debts, the creditors have a claim against any of the assets of the proprietor. He may therefore lose not only the money he has invested in the enterprise but also his personal property, such as his automobile or home.

Owner's Illness or Death May Close the Business. The extended illness or the death of the owner may force the business to close.

Kinds of Businesses Suited to the Sole Properietorship Form of Organization

The kind of business that is primarily concerned with rendering personal service is well suited to the sole proprietorship form of organization. Dentists, accountants, auctioneers, landscape gardeners, carpenters, painters, tourist camps, barber shops, beauty shops, shoe repair shops, and radio and television service stores are examples of businesses operating as sole proprietorships.

Another type of business that seems to be well adapted to the single proprietorship is the one that sells merchandise or service, principally of one kind, and does not require a large amount of capital. Newspaper and magazine stands, roadside markets, rental libraries, tearooms and restaurants, flower shops, gasoline service stations, retail grocery stores, retail meat markets, dress shops, automobile parking lots, movers of household goods, and dry-cleaning establishments are examples of this type. In general, the type of business that can be operated suitably as a sole proprietorship is one (a) that can be managed by the proprietor or by persons hired by him and (b) that does not require a great amount of capital. There are, of course, exceptions to this general rule.

PARTNERSHIP

Mr. York, who operates the sole proprietorship mentioned in the preceding discussion, is confronted with the problem of expanding his business. He is now 55 years old and has operated the business successfully for many years. He sees new opportunities in his community for increasing his business, but he does not wish to assume full responsibility for the undertaking. He realizes that the expansion of the business would place on him considerable additional financial and managerial responsibilities. He also realizes that in order to expand the business he needs additional capital, but he does not wish to borrow the money. Because of these reasons he decides it would be desirable to change his business from a sole proprietorship to a *partnership,* a business owned by two or more persons.

ILLUS. 4-3. In a partnership two or more persons own the business.

Mr. R. R. Burton operates an adjoining meat market. He is a younger man than Mr. York and has proved to have both honesty and considerable business ability. It is thought that combining the two businesses should result in more customers for both groceries and meats. Customers who have been coming to the meat market will possibly become grocery customers also, and those who have been buying at the grocery may become meat customers. A discussion between the two men leads to a tentative agreement to form a partnership if a third person can be found who will invest enough cash to remodel the present two stores to form one large store and to purchase additional equipment.

The financial statement of Mr. Burton's business is as follows:

Assets		Claims Against Assets	
Cash	$ 2,200	Accounts Payable (Debts)	$ 1,500
Merchandise	1,500	R. R. Burton, Proprietor-	
Equipment	4,800	ship	32,000
Land and Building	25,000		
	$33,500		$33,500

The net worth of Mr. Burton's business is $32,000. In other words, after deducting the amount of his debts ($1,500) from the total value of his assets ($33,500), he has a net ownership of $32,000. According to the financial statement on page 62, Mr. York's business is worth $42,500. In order to have an equal investment in the partnership, Mr. Burton must therefore invest an additional $10,500 in cash.

They find Mr. King, a person with accounting experience, who has $30,000 and is able to borrow the remaining amount of $12,500 to be an equal partner. The articles of copartnership, shown in Illustration 4-4 on page 68, are then written and signed by the three men.

After the partnership is formed, the financial statement (balance sheet) of the business appears as follows:

Assets		Claims Against Assets	
Cash	$ 58,900	Accounts Payable (Debts)	$ 4,500
Merchandise	8,100	B. L. York, Proprietor-	
Equipment	10,000	ship	42,500
Land and Buildings ...	55,000	R. R. Burton, Proprietor-	
		ship	42,500
		M. O. King, Proprietor-	
		ship	42,500
	$132,000		$132,000

In operating the partnership, York, Burton, and King divide the responsibilities. Mr. York supervises the grocery department; Mr. Burton supervises the meat department; and Mr. King has charge of finances and records.

During the year the three partners remodel the stores and combine them. They also buy some new equipment. At the end of the year the financial statement which follows is prepared to show the status of the partnership.

Assets		Claims Against Assets	
Cash	$ 12,000	Accounts Payable	
Merchandise	24,000	(Debts)	$ 4,000
Equipment	22,500	B. L. York, Proprietorship	47,000
Land and Buildings	86,500	R. R. Burton, Proprietor-	
		ship	47,000
		M. O. King, Proprietor-	
		ship	47,000
	$145,000		$145,000

Has the partnership had a successful year? Each partner has received a salary of $500 a month (according to the terms of the

ARTICLES OF COPARTNERSHIP

This Contract, made and entered into on the first day of June, 19--, by and between Benjamin L. York, of Olean, New York, party of the first part, Raymond R. Burton, of Olean, New York, party of the second part, and Marshall O. King, of Ceres, New York, party of the third part:

WITNESSETH: That the said parties have this day formed a copartnership for the purpose of engaging in and conducting a retail grocery and meat store under the following stipulations, which are made a part of the contract:

FIRST: The said copartnership is to continue for a term of ten years from date hereof.

SECOND: The business shall be conducted under the firm name of York, Burton, and King, at 4467 Goodson Street, Olean, New York.

THIRD: The investments are as follows: Benjamin L. York: Cash, $3,700; Merchandise, $6,600; Equipment, $5,200; Land and Building, $30,000; Total Assets, $45,500, less Accounts Payable, $3,000, equals Net Investment, $42,500. Raymond R. Burton: Cash, $12,700; Merchandise, $1,500; Equipment, $4,800; Land and Building, $25,000; Total Assets, $44,000, less Accounts Payable, $1,500, equals Net Investment, $42,500. Marshall O. King: Cash, $42,500.

FOURTH: All profits or losses arising from said business are to be shared equally.

FIFTH: Each partner is to devote his entire time and attention to the business and to engage in no other business enterprise without the written consent of the others.

SIXTH: Each partner is to have a salary of $500 a month, the same to be withdrawn at such time as he may elect. No partner is to withdraw from the business an amount in excess of his salary without the written consent of the others.

SEVENTH: The duties of each partner are defined as follows: Benjamin L. York is to supervise the grocery department. Raymond R. Burton is to supervise the meat department.
Marshall O. King is to have charge of finances and records.

EIGHTH: No partner is to become surety or bondsman for anyone without the written consent of the others.

NINTH: In case of the death, incapacity, or withdrawal of one partner, the business is to be conducted for the remainder of the fiscal year by the surviving partners, the profits for the year allocated to the withdrawing partner to be determined by the ratio of the time he was a partner during the year to the whole year.

TENTH: In case of dissolution the assets are to be divided in the ratio of the capital invested at the time of dissolution.

IN WITNESS WHEREOF, The parties aforesaid have hereunto set their hands and affixed their seals on the day and year above written.

In the presence of: *Benjamin L. York* (Seal)

Frank E. Dougherty   *Marshall O. King*   (Seal)

John A. Thurman   *Raymond R. Burton*   (Seal)

ILLUS. 4-4. Articles of copartnership.

partnership agreement); and, in addition, the proprietorship of each partner has increased from $42,500 to $47,000 as a result of profits made during the year. This increase of the total proprietorship from $127,500 to $141,000 amounts to $13,500 and is an increase of over 10 percent. Mr. King, who had to borrow some of the money he used for his investment, had to pay 6 percent interest. His investment in the partnership has brought him a return that is considerably more than the interest on his loan.

Advantages of the Partnership

Many businesses are organized as partnerships at their very beginning. There are approximately 900,000 businesses operating as partnerships in this country. Discussed below are some of the advantages of the partnership form of business organization.

Skills and Abilities Are Pooled. The business is likely to be operated more efficiently than a sole proprietorship because two or more persons share in the management. One partner may have special sales ability; another may have an aptitude for buying the right kind, quality, and quantity of merchandise. One partner may propose a change in the business, and another partner may be able to point out disadvantages in or modifications of the plan that were not apparent to the one who made the original proposal. The combined abilities of the partners should result in more efficient operation than there would be if each were conducting a business as a sole proprietor.

Sources of Capital Are Increased. When a business is started, more capital can be supplied through the investments of two or more people than could be obtained ordinarily by one person. Some businesses require a greater amount of capital for equipment and merchandise than one person might be able to supply; but sufficient initial capital can be obtained if several persons enter into a partnership. Generally, the additional capital needed for expansion is obtained more easily if there are several partners.

Credit Position Is Improved. Because it has several owners who are responsible for the ownership and the management, the partnership usually has a better credit reputation than the sole proprietorship.

Each Partner Contributes His Goodwill. Each partner is likely to have a large personal following that he can bring to the business.

Increased Concern in Business Management. Because of their financial responsibilities, the partners will take a greater interest in the business than would be taken if they were only employees.

Less Tax Burden Than Corporations. Partnerships usually have a tax advantage over corporations. Partnership businesses prepare a federal income tax report but do not pay a tax on their profits as do corporations. However, each partner must pay a personal income tax on his share of the profits.

Elimination of Competition. In order to eliminate competition, two or more sole proprietors may combine their businesses by organizing a partnership.

Retirement from Management. A sole proprietor who wishes to retire from active management without retiring from the business may admit a partner to take over the active management.

Operating Economies May Be Realized. By combining two or more businesses, an economy may be effected through the reduction of certain overhead expenses, such as advertising, supplies, equipment, fuel, and rent.

Disadvantages of the Partnership

Discussed below and on the next pages are some of the disadvantages of the partnership form of business organization.

Unlimited Financial Liability. According to law each member of the partnership has an *unlimited financial liability* for all the debts of the business. Each partner is responsible for his share of the business debts; but if one or some of the partners are unable to pay their share, one partner may have to pay all the debts. Suppose that the partnership of York, Burton, and King should fail and that, after all the business assets have been converted into cash, the amount due the creditors of the partnership is $9,000 more than the amount of cash. Each partner should contribute $3,000 to the partnership so that there will be enough money to pay the remaining business debts. The creditors, however, may choose to enforce their claims against York because he owns more property outside the partnership than the other two partners. If York pays the entire $9,000, he would have a claim against each of the other two partners for $3,000.

Disagreement Among Partners. There is always danger of disagreement among partners. The majority of the partners may want to

ILLUS. 4-5. Partnerships cannot operate efficiently if the owners disagree on basic policies.

change the nature of the business but are unable to do so because of the refusal of one partner. For example, a partnership may have been formed for the purpose of conducting a retail piano business. After a while the majority of the partners feel it would be wise to stop selling pianos and handle radios and television sets. As long as one partner disagrees, however, the partnership cannot make the change, although the change may seem very desirable. Furthermore, if there are many partners, certain ones may feel that they are not having their proper share in the management. This situation may cause disagreements and impair the efficiency of the business. Such a condition may be partly prevented if the articles of copartnership specifically state the duties of each partner.

Each Partner Bound By Contracts of Others. Each partner is bound by the partnership contracts made by any partner if such contracts pertain to the ordinary operations of the business. There is always the possibility of friction and ill will between partners if one partner makes a contract that turns out to be unprofitable to the partnership.

Uncertain Life. The life of a partnership is uncertain. Sometimes when the contract for a partnership is drawn up, a definite length of time, such as ten years, is fixed for the existence of the business. If one partner dies, however, there must be a legal dissolution of the partnership. The deceased partner may have been the principal manager, and, as a result of his death, the business may suffer. The heirs of the deceased partner may demand from the surviving partners an unfair price for the share of the deceased partner; or they may insist upon the complete liquidation of the partnership so that they can obtain the share belonging to the deceased partner. In the latter case, the assets that are sold usually do not bring a fair price, and consequently all the partners suffer a loss. (Insurance on the life of a partner might be carried to provide money to purchase the interest of a partner who dies.) Under the laws of most states, the bankruptcy of any partner, the entrance of a new partner, and the incapacity of a partner are other causes that may bring a sudden termination of the partnership just at a time when the business is beginning to prosper.

Limited Sources of Capital. The amount of funds that a partnership may obtain is limited by the contributions of the partners, the earnings of the business, and the amount that can be borrowed. It is difficult for a partnership to obtain enough capital to carry on a large enterprise unless the members of the partnership are individually wealthy or unless they are many in number. Too many partners, however, may cause inefficiency in operation.

Unsatisfactory Division of Profits. Sometimes there is not a satisfactory distribution of the partnership profits according to the ability and the efforts of the individual partners. The profits are shared on the basis of the partnership agreement. If no provision is made in the agreement, the law requires an equal division of the profits. Some of the common methods of distributing profits among partners are: equally; in ratio to the capital of each partner; according to some other agreed ratio, such as 40 percent to one partner and 60 percent to the other partner; paying to each partner a rate of interest, such as 6 percent, on the amount of capital he has invested and then dividing the remaining profits equally or in some other ratio.

Difficulty in Withdrawing from Partnership. If a partner wishes to sell his interest, he may find it difficult to do so. Even if he finds a buyer for his share, this person must be acceptable to the other partners.

Limited Partnership

In an ordinary (general) partnership each partner is personally liable for all of the debts contracted by the partnership. The laws of some states, however, permit the formation of a type of partnership in which all of the partners do not have unlimited financial liability for the partnership debts. This type of partnership is known as a _limited partnership_. However, at least one partner must be a general partner who has unlimited liability. In many states the name of a limited partner may not be included in the firm name.

Usually the law requires that a certificate of limited partnership be filed in a public office of record and that proper notice be given to each creditor with whom the limited partnership does business. If these requirements are not fulfilled, the limited partners have unlimited liability in the same manner as a general partner. Limited partnerships are not commonly found in the usual types of merchandising, manufacturing, and service businesses; they are mainly confined to brokerage firms.

Kinds of Businesses Suited to the Partnership Form of Organization

The partnership form of organization is found in many businesses that furnish more than one kind of product or service. Each partner usually looks after some phase of the business in which he has special ability. Some examples of businesses that are well suited to this form are automobile sales and repair companies; retail grocery and meat markets; restaurants; radio and television stores with both sales and repair departments; barber shops and beauty shops; camera stores with film developing and printing services; men's clothing stores and tailor shops; laundries with dry-cleaning departments; and landscape gardeners rendering tree surgery service. For instance, in the case of an automobile company having separate sales and repair departments, one partner may manage sales and the other partner manage repairs. Some automobile businesses have a new-car sales department, a used-car sales department, and a service department, with a partner in charge of each of the three departments. Similarly, if a business operates in more than one location, there can be a partner in charge of each location. Businesses operating longer than the usual eight hours a day, such as restaurants and gasoline service stations, find the partnership organization desirable. Each partner can be in charge for part of the day.

BUSINESS NAME

A sole proprietorship or a partnership may be conducted under the name or names of the owner or owners. In many states the law prohibits the use of "and Company" or "& Co." unless such indicates partners. For example, if there were only two partners, it would not be permissible to use a firm name such as Jones, Smith & Co., for that name would indicate at least three partners. The name or names comprised in the "company" must be identified by registration at some public recording office, usually the county clerk's office. Usually one can do business under a trade, or artificial, name such as The Superior Hat Store, or W-W Manufacturing Company. Likewise, proper registration is usually required in order that creditors may know the person or persons responsible for the business. Operating under a trade name, therefore, does not reduce the owner's liability to creditors.

REVIEW WHAT YOU HAVE LEARNED

Business Terms Checkup:

(1) sole proprietorship
(2) assets
(3) creditors
(4) balance sheet
(5) proprietorship (equity or net worth)
(6) partnership
(7) unlimited financial liability
(8) limited partnership

Reading Checkup:

1. Name at least four advantages of a sole proprietorship.
2. Name at least three disadvantages of a sole proprietorship.
3. What are some common types of businesses operated as proprietorships?
4. Answer the following questions that are based on the articles of copartnership shown in Illustration 4-4:
   (a) The partnership is to last for what length of time?
   (b) How are the profits to be divided?
   (c) In case of dissolution, how are the assets to be divided?
5. Name three or more advantages of a partnership.
6. Name at least four disadvantages of a partnership.
7. If a partnership that fails and ceases operations is unable to pay all its debts, to what extent is each partner personally liable for the unpaid debts?
8. How is a partnership affected when a partner withdraws from the business?
9. What is a limited partnership?
10. Can an individual proprietorship or a partnership operate a business under a trade, or artificial, name?

APPLY WHAT YOU HAVE LEARNED

Questions for Class Discussion:

1. The sole proprietor is not hindered by associates in making decisions. What disadvantage might result from not having partners to help in making decisions?

2. If a sole proprietorship needs additional capital but the owner cannot furnish it from his personal funds, from what sources might it be secured?

3. Why is it desirable that the partnership agreement be made in writing?

4. Why is it a good plan to include in a partnership agreement some such clause as the eighth one shown in Illustration 4-4?

5. Why is it a good plan to include in a partnership agreement some such clause as the ninth one shown in Illustration 4-4?

6. A partner signed a partnership contract for television advertising while the other two partners were on vacation. Upon returning, the two claimed the partnership was not bound to the contract because both of them disapproved of television advertising. Was the partnership legally bound?

7. Most business partnerships consist of only two or three partners. Why is this size of partnership so popular?

8. Why might a partner who invests a smaller amount of money in a partnership share profits equally with a partner who invests a larger amount?

Problems and Projects:

1. Adams invested $40,000 and Cook invested $30,000 in their partnership business. They share profits and losses in proportion to their investments. What amount should each receive of the $4,200 profit earned during a certain year?

2. Johnson, Huffman, and Markel invested $20,000, $30,000, and $40,000 respectively in a partnership. The partnership profit-sharing agreement states that each partner is to receive 6 percent on his investment and the remainder of the profits are to be divided equally. What is the total amount that each partner should receive of profits of $13,500?

3. Carlton and Baker had invested equal amounts in a partnership business. Later the business failed with $40,000 in liabilities (debts) and only $15,000 in assets (property). In addition to his share of the assets of the business, Baker had $35,000 of other property at the time of the failure; but Carlton only had $5,000 of additional property. What amount of property other than the partnership property might be required of each partner to pay the debts of the partnership?

4. Assume that the balance sheet of the partnership of Davis and Miller at the time of dissolution (going out of business) appeared as follows:

Assets		Claims Against Assets	
Cash	$ 9,000	Accounts Payable (Debts)	$ 5,000
Merchandise	20,000	B. S. Davis, Proprietorship	45,000
Fixtures and Equipment	12,000	T. C. Miller, Proprietor-	
Land and Buildings	54,000	ship	45,000
	$95,000		$95,000

In the liquidation (selling the assets) the merchandise was sold for $16,000, the fixtures for $9,000, and the land and buildings for $55,000. After paying off the debts, what amount of the remaining cash should each partner receive?

Case Problem 4-1:

Al Tyler is the owner of a repair shop for radios, both home and automobile, and electrical appliances (irons, dryers, washing machines, etc.). His business has grown until he now employs two full-time employees. He rents the space in which his small shop is located but owns his own home, which is mortgaged.

Tyler believes that it would be profitable to expand his business to include the sale at retail of radios and television sets.

Required:

1. Does this contemplated expansion seem to be a good idea?
2. Does it appear that Tyler would be financially able to make such an expansion of his business?
3. Suggest a plan by which Tyler might accomplish the expansion.

Case Problem 4-2:

Rutherford (aged 57) is the owner and operator of a small boat rental business at a lake resort. He wishes to expand the business to include the renting of outboard motors, but he has had only a small amount of experience in repairing outboard motors. He will need additional capital for the expansion. He is considering taking a partner into the business.

Required:

What type of person would make a desirable partner?

Case Problem 4-3:

Sherron and Caldwell are forming a partnership to operate a restaurant. They plan to have the restaurant open from 7:30 a.m. until 11:30 p.m.

Required:

1. Suggest how they might share the actual supervision of the restaurant.
2. How might they share the purchasing of food and supplies; the keeping of financial records?

Continuing Project:

This part of your continuing project is not to be completed until you have studied both Chapters 4 and 5. You will find directions for doing this part of the project at the end of Chapter 5.

What are the rights of a stock-holder?

What is a proxy?

What advantages come from the corporation form of organization?

What is meant by a holding company?

What is a cooperative?

In what ways are mutual companies different from cooperatives?

BACKGROUND OF CHAPTER

Most large businesses are organized as corporations, and many small businesses also employ this form of organization. Frequently businesses started as sole proprietorships or partnerships later become corporations.

As compared with the sole proprietorship and partnership forms of organization, it is considerably more complicated to organize and operate a corporation. In this chapter you will learn how a business is operated as a corporation and some advantages and disadvantages of this form of organization.

In addition to corporations this chapter also discusses cooperatives and mutual companies.

CHAPTER 5

CORPORATE FORMS OF BUSINESS OWNERSHIP

In the preceding chapter the sole proprietorship and the partnership forms of business organization were discussed. Since a large percentage of new businesses organized in recent years have been organized as corporations, this chapter will be devoted principally to discussing the main features of the corporation.

CORPORATION

York, Burton, and King, of the partnership mentioned in Chapter 4, believe that there is an opportunity to expand their business by purchasing another store and operating it as a branch. They make a study of the *corporation* as a form of business organization and find that it is an association of individuals organized under a charter granted by the state. It is, in a sense, an artificial person created by the laws of the state.

The essential characteristics of a corporation are as follows:

1. The ownership is divided into equal parts called *shares* of capital stock.
2. The *stockholders* (often called *shareholders*) own the business.
3. The stockholders elect directors.
4. The *directors* formulate general plans and policies and appoint the officers.
5. The *officers* in a small corporation usually consist of a president, a secretary, and a treasurer.
6. The officers have charge of the active management of the business.
7. The officers have the privilege of employing additional persons to operate the business.

The corporation is permitted to make contracts, to borrow money, to own property, and to sue and to be sued in its own name. Any act performed for the corporation by an officer or an authorized employee is not done in the name of the officer or the employee, but in the name of the corporation. For example, the treasurer of a corporation has the power to borrow money for the corporation. Since he acts for the corporation, he signs his name as agent of the corporation.

After consulting a lawyer who is experienced in corporation law, and after studying the disadvantages of the partnership and the advantages and disadvantages of the corporation, York, Burton, and King decide to incorporate. The capital of the corporation will be $200,000, to consist of 2,000 shares of $100 par-value common stock. (Common stock is explained in detail in Chapter 16.) The partners have an investment of $47,000 each, or a total of $141,000, in the business. They effect a tentative organization, and each subscribes for a number of shares of stock equal to his investment in the partnership (470 shares each). They then submit to the secretary of state (in some states to the state securities commission) the certificate of incorporation shown in Illustration 5-1 and apply for permission to operate the business as a corporation.

Usually the new business must pay an organization tax, based on the amount of its capital stock, and a filing fee before the state will issue a *charter* entitling the business to exercise its powers or privileges as a corporation. In many states the term "charter" does not refer to a formal certificate issued by the state government but is a collective term referring to the general powers and rights granted to a corporation. In some states the existence of the corporation begins when the application or certificate of incorporation has been filed in the department of state.

In most states the law requires that the corporation name must clearly indicate by words or abbreviation that it is a corporation. Taylor Co., Incorporated, and Bell Company, Inc., are examples of names that indicate that the businesses are corporations.

A certificate of stock is issued to each of the three men stating that he is the owner of 470 shares. The remaining 590 shares are unissued but may be issued later whenever the stockholders decide to sell them in order to expand the business. The corporation is to assume the liabilities of the partnership. After the corporation has been formed, the financial statement shown on page 82 is prepared.

Certificate of Incorporation

OF

York, Burton, and King, Inc.

Pursuant to Article Two of the Stock Corporation Law.

State of New York } ss.

County of Cattaraugus

We, the undersigned, for the purpose of forming a Corporation pursuant to Article Two of the Stock Corporation Law of the State of New York, do hereby make, subscribe, acknowledge and file this certificate for that purpose as follows:

We, the undersigned, do hereby Certify

First.—That all the undersigned are of full age, and ___all___ of them are citizens of the United States, and ___all___ of them residents of the State of New York.

Second.—That the name of said corporation is York, Burton, and King, Inc.

Third.—That the purpose for which said corporation is formed is To operate a retail food business.

Fourth.—That the amount of the Capital Stock of the said corporation is Two Hundred Thousand Dollars ($ 200,000) to consist of Two Thousand (2,000) shares of the par value of One Hundred dollars ($ 100) each.

Fifth.—That the office of said corporation is to be located in the City of Olean, County of Cattaraugus and State of New York.

Sixth.—That the duration of said corporation is to be perpetual.

Seventh.—That the number of Directors of said corporation is three.

Eighth.—That the names and post office addresses of the Directors until the first annual meeting are as follows:

Benjamin L. York   1868 Buffalo Street, Olean, New York

Raymond R. Burton   1309 Main Street, Olean, New York

Marshall O. King   4565 Erie Avenue, Ceres, New York

Ninth.—That the names and post office addresses of the subscribers and the number of shares of stock which each agrees to take in said corporation are as follows:

NAMES	POST OFFICE ADDRESSES	NO. OF SHARES
Benjamin L. York	1868 Buffalo Street	
	Olean, New York	470
Raymond R. Burton	1309 Main Street	
	Olean, New York	470
Marshall O. King	4565 Erie Avenue	
	Ceres, New York	470

Tenth.—That the meetings of the Board of Directors shall be held only within the State of New York at Olean

In Witness Whereof, we have made, subscribed and executed this certificate in duplicate the tenth day of September in the year One thousand nine hundred and ___--___

Benjamin L. York
Marshall O. King
Raymond R. Burton

ILLUS. 5-1. Certificate of incorporation.

Assets		Claim Against Assets	
Cash	$ 12,000	Accounts Payable (Debts).	$ 4,000
Merchandise	24,000	Capital Stock Outstanding	141,000
Equipment	22,500		
Land and Buildings	86,500		
	$145,000		$145,000

The ownership of the corporation is in the same hands as was the ownership of the partnership. The ownership of the corporation, however, is evidenced by the outstanding stock. Each former partner has in his possession a stock certificate indicating that he owns 470 shares of stock with a face value of $100 each.

The three stockholders own the business and they become the directors. Among themselves they select officers. Mr. York is elected president; Mr. Burton, vice-president; and Mr. King, secretary and treasurer. A simple organization chart of the new corporation is shown in Illustration 5-2.

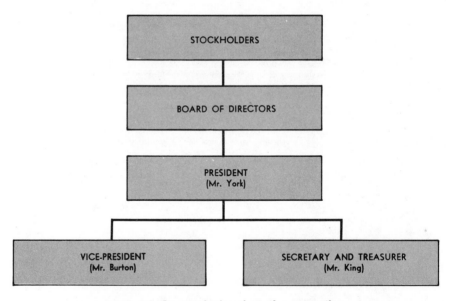

ILLUS. 5-2. An organization chart of a corporation.

Each stockholder will have 470 votes on matters arising in the meetings of the stockholders. Voting stockholders usually have one vote for each share owned. Should Mr. King sell 236 of his shares to Mr. Burton, Mr. Burton would own 706 shares, or more than 50 percent of the total 1,410 shares of stock that have been issued. Then Mr. Burton could control the corporation.

The law usually requires a corporation to send each stockholder, at a specified time in advance, a notice of a meeting to be held by the stockholders. If a stockholder cannot attend the meeting personally, he may be represented by a proxy. A *proxy* is a written authorization for someone to vote in behalf of the person signing the proxy. It is a common practice for a blank proxy to be included in the letter announcing a stockholders' meeting. One form of proxy which a corporation might use is shown in Illustration 5-3.

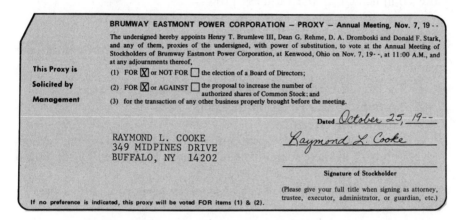

ILLUS. 5-3. Proxy signed by a stockholder.

Close and Open Corporations

A *close corporation* (also called a *closely held corporation*) is one that does not offer its securities for public sale. It is frequently owned by just a few stockholders, some of whom may be actively engaged in operating the business in the same manner as partners would operate a business. York, Burton, and King, Inc., is an example of a close corporation. The three former partners own all the stock and operate the business.

A close corporation, under the laws of most states, does not need to make its financial activities known to the public, for its securities are not offered for general sale. It must, however, submit reports to the state from which it obtained its charter or for tax purposes must submit reports to all states in which it operates.

An *open corporation* (also called a *public corporation*) is one that offers its securities for general public sale. For the benefit of prospective investors, an open corporation must furnish to the public information regarding its earnings, assets, and liabilities. These reports must be furnished in accordance with federal and state laws and the rules of the stock exchanges.

Open corporations often have a very large number of stockholders, some having a million or more. Most of the stockholders in these large corporations own only a few shares; but, because of the great number of stockholders, such a corporation has a very large amount of capital. Naturally, these large corporations are not so simple in organization as York, Burton, and King, Inc. The form of organization becomes more complicated as the business grows.

Rights and Liabilities of Stockholders

The principal rights of one who owns stock in a corporation are as follows:

1. To have a certificate showing the number of shares owned.
2. To transfer his ownership to others.
3. To vote for directors.
4. To receive *dividends* (profits that are distributed to the owners of stock) if there are sufficient earnings, as decided by the board of directors.
5. To subscribe to new issues of stock in proportion to his present share.
6. To share in the net proceeds when the corporation is dissolved.

The ownership of a stock certificate of a corporation is evidence of part ownership in the corporation. A stockholder does not have the same financial responsibility as a partner in a partnership; that is, a stockholder has no liability beyond the extent of his ownership. If the corporation fails, he may lose the money that he has invested in the corporation, but usually the creditors cannot collect any additional amount from him.

Advantages of the Corporation

The corporation has a number of advantages as compared with the sole proprietorship and the partnership. Some of these are given below and on the next page.

Limited Liability of Stockholders. Except in a few situations, the owners (stockholders) are not legally liable for the debts of the corporation beyond their investments in the stock. Thus, persons, whether they have only a few dollars to invest or whether they have thousands of dollars, may invest in a corporation without the possibility of incurring a liability.

Permanency of Existence. The corporation is a more permanent type of organization than the sole proprietorship or the partnership. It may continue to operate indefinitely, or as long as the term stated in the charter, without danger of interruption because of the death of an owner or because of other changes in the ownership.

Available Sources of Capital. The corporation can obtain money from several sources. This advantage makes possible large-scale business operations and the hiring of expert management.

Ease in Transferring Ownership. It is easy to transfer ownership in a corporation. A stockholder may sell his stock to another person and transfer the stock certificate, which represents the ownership, to the latter. When shares are transferred, the transfer of ownership is indicated in the records of the corporation, and a new certificate is issued in the name of the new stockholder.

Stockholders Become Word-of-Mouth Advertisers. A corporation may be able to attract a large number of stockholders, who, in turn, help advertise the business and recommend its products or services.

Disadvantages of the Corporation

Although we have seen that there are several distinct advantages to the corporation, there are also a number of disadvantages. Some of the most significant disadvantages are discussed below.

Charter Restrictions. A corporation is permitted to engage only in those activities that are specified in its charter. Should York, Burton, and King, Inc., wish to add to their business a department selling hardware, they would be unable to do so unless they went through the legal formality of obtaining a new charter or amending the old one. As a partnership they could have added the other department without governmental consent, provided the expansion was agreeable to all the partners.

Lack of Personal Interest. Large corporations with thousands of stockholders are usually managed by salaried employees. Employees usually do not take the same personal interest in the business as that taken by a sole proprietor or a partner.

Taxation. The corporation is usually subjected to more taxes than are imposed on the sole proprietorship and the partnership. Some taxes that are special to the corporation are: a filing fee, which is payable on application for a charter; an organization tax, which is based on the amount of authorized capital stock; an annual state franchise tax, which is usually based upon the profits; and a federal income tax. The first three of these vary in the different states. The minimum rate for federal income tax on the net income in recent years has varied from 22 to 30 percent of the corporation's first $25,000 of net income, and the rate on the net income in excess of $25,000 has been in the 47 to 52 percent range.

Stockholders are frequently said to be doubly taxed. The corporation pays an income tax on its earnings, and the stockholder who receives some of the earnings as dividends must pay an income tax on these earnings. In order to reduce somewhat this disadvantage, legislation has been passed that permits certain small corporations to be taxed as a partnership type of business.

Government Regulations and Reports. The regulation of corporations by states and by the federal government is becoming more strict.

A corporation cannot do business wherever it pleases. York, Burton, and King, Inc., is granted permission to conduct its business only in the state of New York. Should it wish to do business in adjoining states, it would probably be required to obtain in each state a license as a *foreign corporation* and to pay a fee to do business in that state.

A corporation must make special reports to the state from which it obtained its charter, as well as to other states in which it may be doing business. There is consequently an increased need for detailed financial records and reports.

Operating Expenses. Large corporations that have many stockholders have an added expense in the great amount of clerical work required, particularly in keeping the records of stockholders and in paying dividends. For example, the keeping of records of the more than 3 million different stockholders of the American Telephone and Telegraph Company requires a huge amount of clerical work.

Types of Businesses Organized as Corporations

A survey of businesses shows that almost every kind of business exists as a corporation; but the two kinds discussed at the top of page 87 are generally organized as corporations.

1. Those businesses that require large amounts of capital, such as railroads, airlines, companies that supply power and electricity for large cities, automobile manufacturing concerns, iron and steel manufacturing industries, large hotels, and office buildings.
2. Those businesses that may have uncertain futures, such as mining companies, amusement parks, makers of amusement devices, publishers of new magazines, and manufacturers of novelty articles. Persons who organize these types of businesses do not wish to assume the additional risk that falls upon a sole proprietor or a partner in case of failure of the business.

HOLDING COMPANIES

A *holding company,* as its name implies, holds a sufficient amount of the stock of other corporations to control the management of those businesses. In some cases if a holding company can obtain ownership of only 30 to 40 percent of stock of another corporation, known as a *subsidiary,* it can exercise managerial control over that corporation. The ownership of the remainder of the stock may be so scattered that no other group of persons owns enough of the stock to exercise control. A holding company therefore does not necessarily own all the stock of the corporation that it controls. Its success depends upon its ability to own a sufficient amount of stock to control the operations of all its subsidiaries.

The American Telephone and Telegraph Company is an example of a holding company. It does not own the physical assets of its various subsidiary corporations, but it owns enough of the stock of each corporation to control the management.

MERGERS AND CONSOLIDATIONS

Several corporations may actually be combined (a) by discontinuing one or more of the corporations and operating under the name of one of the merged corporations or (b) by forming a new corporation under a new name. For example, in the first case, Williams Company, Inc., and Jackson Company, Inc., merge; and the entire business is operated in the future as Williams Company, Inc. To capitalize on the name and goodwill that Jackson Company, Inc., may have had, Williams Company, Inc., may decide to have what was Jackson Company, Inc., operate as the Jackson Division of Williams Company, Inc. In the second case, Williams Company, Inc., and Jackson Company, Inc., consolidate; and the entire business is operated in the future as Frontier Supply Company, Inc. The transfer of ownership is accomplished (a) by paying cash for the property or (b) by exchanging the stock of the new corporation or of the surviving corporation for the stock of the old corporations.

COOPERATIVES

A *cooperative,* or *co-op,* may be defined as an organization owned and operated by its user-members. It is operated for the purpose of supplying goods or services to its members. If there are any profits, these are distributed among the members. A cooperative is a type of business organization that differs from those previously discussed. In order for a cooperative to operate as a business, it must secure from the state a charter similar to that for a corporation. Federal laws permit the granting of federal charters to cooperative credit unions.

Some of the most common kinds of cooperatives are explained in the following paragraphs.

Consumers' Cooperatives

One of the simplest forms of cooperatives is found where two or more people make purchases jointly. Several housewives may jointly purchase a crate of oranges or a case of soap, each taking a portion of the goods purchased. By making one large purchase, they are usually able to buy the goods at a lower price than if each made a purchase of a smaller quantity. In the farming sections of our country, it is quite common for several farmers to purchase jointly carloads of fertilizer, oil, gasoline, coal, stock feed, fencing, seeds, and farm implements. Many of these are informal cooperative undertakings. More than 7,000 groups, however, are formally organized as supply cooperatives which, according to the United States Department of Agriculture, purchased goods amounting to some $17 billion for approximately 6 million members in a recent year. These supply or purchasing cooperatives also handle such additional items as hardware, paint, electrical appliances, and building materials.

Cooperatives are often criticized by businessmen because it is felt that cooperatives are not subject to many of the same taxes as other businesses with whom they compete.

ILLUS. 5-4. A simple form of cooperative organization exists when two or more people make a joint purchase in order to obtain a lower unit price.

Retail Cooperatives

From the simple type of consumers' cooperative, it is relatively easy to form a large organization and begin to operate stores to serve its members better. Statistics indicate that the number of retail cooperatives declined between 1951 and 1971, but the number of members and the volume of sales increased greatly. The largest number of retail cooperatives are grocery stores (some of which are supermarkets); but there are many other types, such as general stores, gasoline service stations, drugstores, and gift shops.

Wholesale Cooperatives

The next natural step, when a number of retail cooperative societies are functioning in a region, is the formation of a cooperative organization for wholesale buying. About one half of the 3,300 local retail cooperatives have joined to form some 25 wholesale buying associations. Most of these are regional wholesale associations, each of which includes all or parts of several states in its trading area. Some of them overlap because their member societies are sponsored by competing farm organizations—Farm Bureau, Grange, Farmers' Union. In most European countries one national wholesale cooperative serves all the local retail cooperatives of the country.

Local retail member cooperatives do not buy all their goods from the wholesale cooperatives. One reason for not doing so is that the local retail cooperative usually likes to shop around to get the best possible price on the goods it buys. Another reason is that the wholesale cooperatives are not in a position to supply all goods. Some commodities, like fresh fruits and vegetables, milk, and meats, must be purchased locally.

Twenty-five regional wholesale cooperatives pool their purchasing power in National Cooperatives, Inc. This organization, founded in 1933, acts as a broker. It negotiates master contracts under which goods —so far, chiefly oil, automobile accessories, electrical appliances, tractors, farm machinery—are put under the cooperative label and delivered directly by the manufacturers to the member regional wholesale organizations.

Wholesale cooperatives frequently engage in the production of goods and services. For example, The Farm Bureau Cooperative Association, Inc. (Ohio), operates feed mills, fertilizer plants, and an oil refinery. Others operate such businesses as chicken hatcheries, canning plants, paint manufacturing businesses, and bakeries. Because certain production facilities, such as in the oil industry, require large amounts of capital, regional cooperatives sometimes form a national association. National Cooperative Refinery Association, for example, is made up of five regional associations; in a recent year, it owned nearly 500 oil wells and operated pipelines and oil refineries.

Cooperative Marketing

Cooperative marketing has been more successful than most of the other types of cooperative enterprises. Approximately 25 percent of all farm crops in the United States are marketed cooperatively and at least 60 percent of the farmers belong to one or more such cooperative. Growers of fruit, vegetables, grain, cotton, and many other crops cooperate in the harvesting, storing, and marketing of their products. In recent years marketing cooperatives, like retail cooperatives, have shown a decline in number of organizations but have had an increase in number of members and in volume of sales.

Some of the fruit-growers' associations present interesting examples of cooperative marketing. After the fruit is grown, it becomes the property of the cooperative association. It is harvested, packed, and marketed by the association, which may also operate a plant for making boxes and crates in which the fruit will be packed. If there is a surplus of production, the fruit of one grower may not be harvested, but the grower is paid in the same proportion as the other members of the association. Many of these associations have brand names for their products, such as Sunkist oranges and lemons, Sun-Maid raisins, Blue Diamond walnuts, Welch grape juice, and Ocean Spray cranberries. Some of these associations are very large. For example, Sunkist Growers, Inc., has more than 10,000 member growers.

Service Cooperatives

In recent years there has been a large growth in the number of cooperatives providing services. Some of the more common types and the approximate number of members served by each type are shown in Illustration 5-5.

In addition there are several hundred miscellaneous service cooperatives, such as trucking, storage, feed grinding, cotton ginning, funeral groups, nurseries, recreation halls, house insulation businesses, shoe repair shops, laundries, dry-cleaning plants, and water supply associations.

Type of Cooperative	Number of Organizations	Number of Members
Credit unions	23,700	21,600,000
Rural electric groups	1,000	6,700,000
Telephone	235	650,000
Housing	700	250,000
Insurance	1,500	17,000,000
College student organizations (room, board, stores, etc.)	300	510,000
Nursery schools	1,400	45,000

Source: The Cooperative League of the U. S. A.

ILLUS. 5-5. Service cooperatives—number and membership in a recent year.

Management of Cooperatives

There are many variations in the ownership and management of cooperatives, but most of these organizations are patterned along the following plan. The local retail cooperative is composed of members who buy shares in the organization. These shares are usually of a small value, such as $1, $5, $10, or $50. On the shares they hold, members receive a small interest rate. The policies of the cooperatives are controlled by votes cast at membership meetings. One vote is allowed per member regardless of the number of shares owned, and the direct management of the cooperative is by a board of directors elected by the members. Any profits the organization makes are divided periodically in proportion to the purchases made by the members from the retail cooperative. The profits are returned to the members in the form of *patronage dividends (refunds)*. Owners of shares in a cooperative have limited liability similar to that of owners of stock in a corporation.

MUTUAL COMPANIES

Another type of business organization is the *mutual company*. This organization is similar to the cooperative in that its customers are the members that comprise the company. However, no stock is issued even though a charter is obtained from the state. The members elect a board of directors, or trustees, to manage the company.

Many insurance companies are organized as mutual companies. The policyholders are the members or owners. Profits are returned to the policyholders in the form of dividends. Savings banks are usually organized as mutual companies, and the depositors are the members who own the business.

REVIEW WHAT YOU HAVE LEARNED

Business Terms Checkup:

(1) corporation
(2) shares
(3) stockholders (shareholders)
(4) directors
(5) officers
(6) charter
(7) proxy
(8) close (or closely held) corporation

(9) open (or public) corporation
(10) dividends
(11) foreign corporation
(12) holding company
(13) subsidiary
(14) cooperative
(15) patronage dividends (refunds)
(16) mutual company

Reading Checkup:

1. Who elects the directors of a corporation?
2. Who appoints the officers of a corporation?

3. Is a corporation permitted to sue and be sued in its own name?

4. To whom is an application for permission to operate a business as a corporation usually submitted?

5. The certificate of incorporation shown in Illustration 5-1 indicates that the corporation wishes permission to issue how many shares of stock at what value per share?

6. What taxes must a corporation pay before it can begin business operations?

7. What is the stockholder's evidence that he is a part owner of a corporation?

8. State the principal rights of a stockholder.

9. List at least three advantages of a corporation from the point of view of the owners.

10. Name at least three disadvantages of a corporation from the point of view of the owners.

11. What items are handled by farmers' marketing cooperatives?

12. According to Illustration 5-5, how many members were there in rural electric groups?

13. Are cooperative credit unions classed as retail or service cooperatives?

14. Do retail cooperatives usually buy all their goods from wholesale cooperatives?

15. How are the profits of a cooperative divided among its members?

16. What is meant by a mutual life insurance company?

APPLY WHAT YOU HAVE LEARNED

Questions for Class Discussion:

1. Must the directors of a corporation manage the business, or may they hire others to operate it?

2. What authority is granted by the proxy in Illustration 5-3?

3. Discuss the possible advantages of a close corporation over those of an open corporation.

4. Explain what might be an advantage of an open corporation over a close corporation.

5. What is meant by a stockholder sharing in the net proceeds when the corporation is dissolved?

6. What liability does a stockholder have for the debts of his corporation?

7. Stockholders (shareholders) are said to be doubly taxed—the corporation taxed on its earnings and the stockholder also taxed on the dividends he receives. Does this seem fair? Explain.

8. What are some reasons for the large number of mergers and consolidations among corporations that have taken place in recent years?

9. Compare the voting power of members of a cooperative with that of stockholders of a corporation.

10. Do you think the plan of dividing profits among members of a retail cooperative on the basis of the purchases they have made is a good method even though one member may own more shares than another?

Problems and Projects:

1. Assume that you and four other classmates decide to form a corporation. Write the articles of incorporation.

2. Investigate the requirements in your state for: (a) organizing a corporation; (b) obtaining a charter; (c) selling and issuing stock, and (d) making reports to the proper state authority. Write a report of your findings.

3. If the organization tax is 50 cents on each $1,000 of capital stock authorized, what would be the total organization tax for a corporation authorized to issue 15,000 shares of $50 stock?

4. In a certain state the organization tax for corporations is as follows: each share of authorized capital stock of the first 50,000 shares without any face value, ½ cent; each share in excess of 50,000 shares and up to and including 1,000,000 shares, ¼ cent; each share in excess of 1,000,000 shares, ⅕ cent. What is the organization tax for the Mattison Company which is authorized to issue 1,500,000 shares?

5. A corporation's net income before the federal income tax amounted to $130,000 in a certain year. The tax that year was 30 percent of the first $25,000 of net income and 52 percent of the net income in excess of $25,000. (a) What was the total federal income tax for that year? (b) What was the amount available for dividends?

6. The board of directors of Melby Company, Inc., decides to distribute $40,950 as dividends to its shareholders. There are 27,300 shares of stock outstanding. (a) What will be the amount of the dividend to be distributed on each share? (b) John Taylor owns 240 shares. What amount of dividends should he receive?

7. George Thompson purchased stock in the Erie Manufacturing Co., Incorporated, for $76 a share. During a year he received quarterly dividends of $1, $1, $1, and $.80 on each share. His total dividends for the year amounted to what percent of the price he paid for each share?

8. On the books of the Fenwick Company, the assets have a value of $117,000; the liabilities are listed as $37,000; the capital stock, $80,000. The company decides to go out of business. The assets are converted into $97,000 cash. What amount of cash will the stockholders receive?

9. The net profit of a retail cooperative is $2,000, and the purchases made by members amount to $50,000. If the profit is divided in proportion to the purchases, how much should be given to a member who made purchases of $500?

Case Problem 5-1:

Bob Williams, who has had considerable experience in newspaper and magazine work, believes that there is an opportunity for publishing a weekly magazine for businessmen that will give a digest of recent laws and regulations affecting business, current statistical information on business conditions, and business forecasts.

Required:

1. Under which form of business organization should the new enterprise be started? Why?
2. Do you recommend that the new business purchase a printing plant (building and equipment)? Explain.

Case Problem 5-2:

Carl Jackson plans to establish a farm to raise minks (fur-bearing animals).

Required:

Explain whether it would be better to organize the business as a sole proprietorship or as a corporation.

Continuing Project:

This part of your continuing project will deal with both Chapters 4 and 5. After you have studied Chapters 4 and 5, select the type of legal organization (sole proprietorship, partnership, or corporation) that you consider best suited to the type of business you plan to enter or to operate. Give your reasons for selecting this type of organization. Draw up a partnership agreement if you have selected a partnership, or draw up an application for incorporation if you have selected a corporation form of organization.

UNIT III
Marketing

What is meant by direct marketing?

What trade channels may a business use?

Why do some producers use several methods of distribution?

What is a broker?

How should a method of distribution be chosen?

What are the marketing functions of middlemen?

BACKGROUND OF CHAPTER

Customers buy goods, and money from the sales enables the business producing the goods to stay in operation. But there will be no sales or profits unless goods are moved from the producer to the customer. The producer or manufacturer of products must be acquainted with the different channels of distribution in order to decide on the most effective way of getting his products to customers. The retailer and other middlemen must also understand the channels of distribution in order to know how they can serve and be served most effectively.

This chapter will discuss the distribution of various types of products and will explain the different economic functions of middlemen.

CHAPTER 6

MARKETING CHANNELS

Many thousands of different products are produced to meet the demands of the millions of customers. In order that the consumers may be able to purchase these products at the time, at the place, and in the quantity they wish, many businesses perform services in getting the products from the producers to the consumers. Each producer must decide just what method he should use in getting his product to the consumers.

DISTRIBUTING GOODS FROM PRODUCERS TO CONSUMERS

The activities involved in moving goods from the producer to the consumer are known as *marketing*. Sometimes the producer markets goods directly to the consumer without the use of middlemen. This is known as *direct marketing*. Some producers sell their products to retailers; others distribute their goods to wholesalers (sometimes called jobbers) or to other middlemen. Distribution through middlemen is known as *indirect marketing*.

Trade Channels

The various routes taken by goods in getting from the producer to the consumer are known as *trade channels*.

Producer Directly to Consumer. The shortest trade channel is that in which the goods move directly from the producer to the consumer. The manufacturer of airplanes sells his products directly to airlines. The farmer may sell his produce directly to consumers through his roadside market, by house-to-house canvassing, or by taking his produce to a farmers' market in a city, where he may sell it from his

ILLUS. 6-1. Each producer must decide how to get his products to consumers.

truck. A bakery may have trucks which make direct house-to-house deliveries of its baked goods or may operate a retail store in the front part of the building in which the baking is done.

There are three methods by which the producer may sell directly to the consumer: by mail, by having salesmen go to the customers, or by having the customers come to the producer.

Selling by Mail. Selling by mail requires a large amount of advertising and correspondence. Letters with inserts and catalogs are generally used. In the past this method has been used most successfully in selling to people in rural areas where the consumer found it difficult to get to city retail stores. With the extensive building of good roads and the wide popularity of the automobile, people in rural areas find it convenient to shop in nearby cities. However, a large number of products of almost every variety and description are still being sold by mail.

There is more success in selling some products by mail than others. A mail-order business is likely to be most successful if:

1. The shipping expenses are not high in comparison with the value of the articles. For instance, if a 50-cent article would require

a shipping expense of 20 cents when marketed directly by mail in shipments of one item each, it would probably not be marketed in that manner but would be shipped to middlemen in large quantities by freight.

2. The goods sold stand up well in being handled and transported. For example, although eggs have been sold directly by mail, the handling of fragile products by such a method has not proved successful generally.

3. The selling prices of the articles are low. People are afraid to take the risk of investing a large amount of money in articles they cannot see before buying. The largest percentage of buying directly by mail is done by people in the low-income class.

4. There is a warranty permitting return of the goods and refund of the purchase price in case the purchaser is not satisfied. This warranty must be fulfilled in the strictest sense.

5. The goods have mass appeal.

6. It requires only a short time for the mail-order goods to reach the customer.

What success can be expected from direct-mail solicitation? The following figures indicate what is considered to be a good return for articles selling at different prices:

Selling Price of Article	Percent of Prospects Solicited Who Are Likely to Buy
$ 1.00 to $ 5.00	2 to 3%
5.00 to 10.00	1 to 2%
10.00 to 25.00	½ to 1%
Over $25.00	Less than ½%

The more selective the mailing list and the more attractive the mailing piece, the greater the sales results should be.

Selling Through Salesmen. Products that people can do without, but that mean convenience and comfort, are often purchased only when the consumer is urged to buy them. In such cases the producer often sends his salesmen to call directly on consumers in an attempt to intensify the want that is present but inactive. For example, the Fuller Brush Company has approximately 3,000 full-time salesmen calling on housewives, and annual sales amount to some $100 million. Encyclopedias, household goods (including cosmetics), magazines, books, and some items of clothing are often marketed in this manner. Usually the products are those that do not require servicing.

ILLUS. 6-2. For products which consumers must be urged to buy, door-to-door salesmen are often used.

Consumers Come to Producer. In some cases the producer has the consumer come to him to get the product. This plan is sometimes followed because the producer does not wish to devote the additional time to marketing or in order that the customer will feel he is getting a fresher product. In some cases it would be impractical to carry to the consumer a wide variety of products from which the consumer could make his selection. Trees and shrubbery and the produce of farmers are examples of such products.

Producer to Consumer Through One Middleman. Using only one middleman is next to the shortest trade channel. This middleman is usually spoken of as a *retailer* (the one who sells to the consumer). Automobiles ordinarily are distributed by this method; the local dealer, or agent, buys from the manufacturer and sells to the consumer. Milk often follows this trade channel in reaching consumers in cities; the dairy purchases the milk from the dairy farmer and then pasteurizes, bottles, and sells it to the housewife. Some farmers choose to haul certain products to town and market them directly to the consumer. Others find that, if they let someone else handle the marketing, they can spend their time more profitably at home in producing. This specialization tends to create more efficiency.

The manufacturer who expects to market his product to retailers must be able to maintain a sales organization large enough to contact the retailers. If a producer makes a large group of related products, he will probably find it desirable to sell to retailers. Producers of the following types of goods may also find it desirable to use this trade channel: bulky goods, such as brick, cement, lumber, and coal; style goods, such as women's coats and dresses; perishable goods that need to be made available to the customer as quickly as possible; goods of such a high value that they justify a large selling expense; or products that have to be pushed a great deal in order to make sales. For certain items, such as shoes, tires, and gasoline, manufacturers may operate their own retail outlets. However, the majority of retailers handle the products of many manufacturers.

Sears, Roebuck & Company, founded in 1866 and now one of the country's largest retailers with over 800 stores, was a mail-order business selling the goods of several manufacturers for the first 40 years. It continues to conduct mail-order business which currently amounts to about 25 percent of the total sales of the company.

There are several kinds of retail stores. *Specialty stores* handle principally one type of goods such as shoes, jewelry, hardware, women's dresses, or furniture. *Department stores* handle many different types of merchandise. *Supermarkets* carry principally food products, often stocking as many as 10,000 different items. The so-called *discount stores* handle a variety of items that usually sell for less than the price at which they are being sold in other types of stores. Some of these retailers purchase goods from the producer; others make purchases through other middlemen as explained later in this chapter.

Producer to Consumer Through Two Middlemen. The use of two middlemen is frequently thought to be the most typical of the trade channels used in distributing merchandise in this country. Illustration 6-3 on page 102 shows three trade channels with different combinations of two middlemen.

Goods having a steady demand, such as groceries, drugs, and hardware, are frequently marketed through a wholesaler and a retailer. *Wholesaler* is a term given to the merchant who usually supplies the retailers and others who buy in large quantities, such as industrial users and institutions (schools, hospitals, etc.). Many department and chain stores eliminate wholesalers by purchasing from the manufacturers.

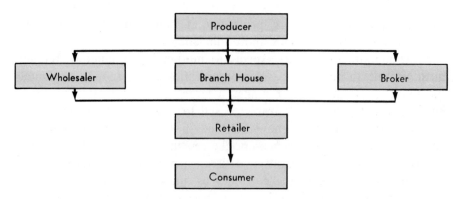

ILLUS. 6-3. Trade channels with two middlemen.

Manufacturers of farm machinery and large meat packers are examples of producers who often have their own *branch houses* that sell to the retailer. In some cases the branch house is owned entirely by the producer; in other cases it is controlled by the producer, who owns a controlling interest in the capital stock of the branch house. This method is likely to be used when other distribution facilities, in the form of suitable wholesalers and brokers, are inadequate; or a manufacturer may feel that if his goods were distributed through wholesalers and brokers, who handle a large variety of goods, his goods might not be promoted as much as they are by his own branch house. Branch houses are usually found only in metropolitan areas.

The output of small coal mines is frequently marketed through a broker, who represents several mines. A *broker* is an agent who specializes in selling, or buying, for his principal without actually having possession of or title to the goods. He is paid a commission which is usually a percent of the amount of the sale or purchase. The coal-mining companies find this method less expensive than that of maintaining their own sales force.

Producer to Consumer Through Three or More Middlemen. Sometimes when the producer has a small business, such as a small canning factory or a textile mill producing only a few kinds of cloth, he may turn the marketing of the goods over to brokers or agents in order to eliminate the need for maintaining sales and related departments. The brokers or agents sell the goods to the wholesaler who sells them to the retailer. Likewise, wholesalers who handle a very large variety of articles, such as wholesale hardware dealers who carry a great number of products made by many manufacturers, find it desirable to get their goods through buying agents, who can keep in close touch with the different manufacturers and the daily price changes. Illustration 6-4 shows several trade channels having three middlemen. In this illustration the *buying agents* receive their compensation from the wholesaler who employs them. *Sales agents,* on the other hand, are em⋅ployed by the producer. In recent years there seems to be little difference between a jobber and a wholesaler. Formerly the jobber bought "job" or odd lots of merchandise and sold them wherever he could sell them advantageously.

Other middlemen, such as local shippers, importers, and auctioneers, may come between the producer and the wholesaler in such a way that there are four middlemen. For example, fruit growers may market their fruit through a local shipper, who sends it to an auction where the wholesaler buys it. It then reaches the consumer through the retailer. The name sometimes given to all these middlemen (retailers, wholesalers, etc.) is *intermediaries.*

Using Several Channels at the Same Time

Usually a manufacturer finds it best to use only one channel of distribution. Sometimes it is necessary, however, for a manufacturer to use more than one if he is to get the greatest distribution of his product. Such goods as razor blades, fountain and ball-point pens, stationery, cigarettes, and soap are stocked by so many different kinds of retail stores that the manufacturers of such items must use different trade channels to get the widest distribution.

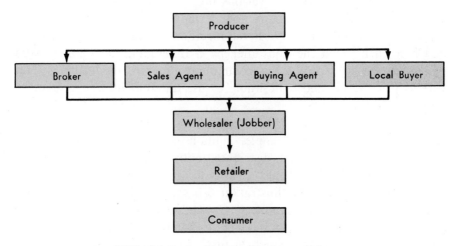

ILLUS. 6-4. Trade channels with three middlemen.

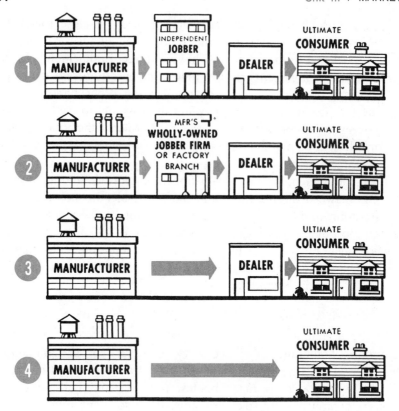

ILLUS. 6-5. Trade channels for radios.

A business that produces various products may find it desirable to use different trade channels. A good example of such a business is a large meat-packing company. Fresh meat, soaps, fertilizers, glue, hides, and hair each reach the consumer by a different route. Some radio manufacturers who produce a great many different models to sell at various price levels find it desirable to use different trade channels, as shown in Illustration 6-5.

For the convenience of customers, some businesses use more than one trade channel. For example, a publishing company might desire to have its weekly magazine distributed entirely through news agencies and newsstands; but it will also distribute copies directly by mail.

The four diagrams in Illustration 6-6 show trade channels used in distributing four different products. Notice how different trade channels may be used for the same product. For example, the dairy farmer sells his milk to the city dairy, which in turn sells directly to the consumer.

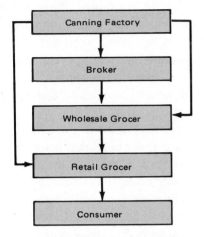

TRADE CHANNELS FOR CANNED
FRUITS AND VEGETABLES

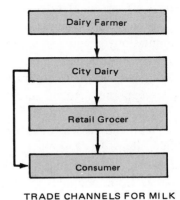

TRADE CHANNELS FOR MILK

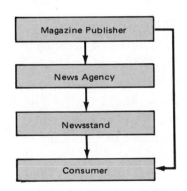

TRADE CHANNELS FOR MAGAZINES

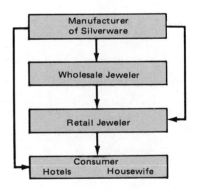

TRADE CHANNELS FOR SILVERWARE

ILLUS. 6-6. Various trade channels.

This same city dairy also sells milk to the retail grocer or delicatessen, which sells it to the consumer.

Changing Trade Channels

There is a growing tendency for some products to be marketed through trade channels different from those used 10, 20, or 30 years ago. For instance, the cooperative marketing organizations of farmers often eliminate one or even two middlemen by selling directly to city wholesalers. In the past the usual trade channel for eggs, for example, was: poultry farmer to country buyer (country store), to shipper (packer), to wholesaler (jobber), to retailer, to consumer. Now the egg-producers' cooperatives sell directly to wholesalers, eliminating the country buyer and the shipper. Several years ago most toilet articles, such as toothpastes, hand lotions, face powders, and soaps, were sold through drugstores that purchased the items from wholesalers. Now a large percentage of such items are sold to the consumers through supermarkets that buy directly from the manufacturer.

With the growth of chain stores and supermarkets of a great many kinds, there has been a tendency to eliminate the wholesaler in many lines of goods. Increased efficiency in transportation also has tended to change trade channels. Good roads and automobiles have resulted in many products being marketed through retailers instead of directly by mail or by peddlers canvassing from farmhouse to farmhouse. Likewise, the retailer need not depend upon some neighboring wholesaler for goods but can get them directly from the manufacturer in almost the same time that it formerly took him to buy from the wholesaler.

Factors Involved in Choosing a Trade Channel

Many factors must be considered by a business in deciding which trade channel or channels will be used in marketing its product. Some of the principal factors are mentioned here.

1. *Perishability of the product.* Highly perishable articles, such as baked goods, ice cream, and certain fruits and vegetables, are usually marketed directly to the consumer or by means of few middlemen.

2. *Distance between the producer and the consumer.* Ordinarily, the greater the distance from the producer to the consumer, the more middlemen will be involved in handling the product.

3. *Financial condition of the producer.* The better the financial position of a producer, the more likely he is to sell to retailers or directly to consumers. Should he be restricted in finances, he will want less money tied up in inventories and can less afford to have a large number of accounts receivable with comparable losses due to bad debts.

4. *Need for special facilities for handling the product.* If the product requires costly fixtures or equipment for handling, it is likely to pass through as few middlemen as possible. For that reason gasoline, which needs special tanks and tank trucks for handling, is marketed directly from the refiner to the retailer. Often the retail outlet is owned by the refiner.

5. *Number of users.* The greater the number of users of a product, the more middlemen there probably will be. For instance, the manufacturer of steel is likely to sell directly to users, whereas the manufacturer of shoes usually sells to retailers.

6. *Number of various products produced.* A manufacturer who has only one product, such as an electric iron, will probably sell his product to a wholesaler as he would find it too expensive to maintain a sales force large enough to contact all the retailers. But if a manufacturer has a large number of electrical products, such as clocks, toasters, waffle irons, heaters, and heating pads, he will probably have salesmen call on retailers because the expense of this plan will be distributed over many products.

Economic Services and Functions of Middlemen

A number of services and functions are performed in moving the product from the manufacturer to the consumer. These are known as *marketing functions* and may be summarized under the following general headings:

1. Transporting—moving the goods to the place where there is a demand for them.

2. Storing—holding of goods until needed.

ILLUS. 6-7. An important function of middlemen is the storage of goods.

3. Grading and standardizing—grouping goods of like quality together.
4. Selling—assisting and persuading customers to buy the product.
5. Financing—obtaining the necessary capital for the operations of the business.
6. Risk-bearing—assuming the risk of losses that may occur from fire, theft, tornado, flood, obsolescence, decline in value, etc.

Regardless of which channel of distribution the goods follow, these services and functions are to be found. If a certain middleman is eliminated, his services and functions must be taken over by someone else. The services may be consolidated, but nevertheless they are still performed. This fact is well illustrated by the experiences of the Emerson Company, which are described below.

CASE EXAMPLE—THE EMERSON COMPANY

Let us suppose that we are starting a company, known as the Emerson Company, that will manufacture vacuum cleaners. We know that already there are many businesses in this field; but we believe that, because of the superior quality of our cleaners, we shall find a ready market, once the cleaners have been introduced sufficiently. We shall start our manufacturing on a small scale until we can determine to what extent the public will desire our product.

We find it difficult to interest retail stores in our goods because they already carry one or more other brands and are doing a satisfactory business with them. They tell us that adding our brand would mean more of their capital tied up in inventories. Furthermore, if they should induce some of their customers to buy our new, untried brand instead of the others and if the cleaners should be unsatisfactory, they would lose their reputation and customers. Therefore, we decide to market our goods directly to consumers.

Advantages of Direct Marketing

In marketing our cleaners directly in this manner, we have to hire salespeople who will solicit business from house to house. We set our prices below those asked by retail stores for cleaners of similar quality because we think that by this direct-marketing method we may be able to eliminate some of the expenses of the middlemen. We find that under this plan:

1. We can promote our product in territories where the retailers might be unwilling to handle it or, if they did, might have a tendency to "push" some other brand that they also handle.

2. We can make more effective demonstrations of our vacuum cleaners in the homes than could be done in retail stores. The various attachments for cleaning rugs, draperies, furniture, walls, and the like can be demonstrated.

Disadvantages of Direct Marketing

After this plan has been in operation for a while, we find there are a number of disadvantages. The principal ones are:

1. Our representatives find it difficult to obtain interviews because of the distrust many people have of house-to-house salespeople and because the housewife may be in the midst of other activities when our representative calls.

2. When adjustments have to be made, the customer resents the delay caused by her having to contact our local representative, who may have to contact headquarters. She says that she can get an adjustment quickly at any local store.

3. We find that our delivery expense is very high.

4. To get a wide distribution of our product, we must employ hundreds of sales representatives. Such a large number increases problems of hiring, training, and supervising.

5. Two trips of our representative are required: one to make the sale and one to deliver the goods at a later date. Often the customer is not at home when delivery is attempted and still another trip must be made.

Selling to Retailers

Now that we have acquainted the public in several localities with our product and the quality of our product has been proved, we are able to interest retailers in handling our cleaners. Retailers, especially in the localities where our product is well known, become middlemen for our product. As the retailer must have a margin for his operating expenses and his net profit, we have to sell the cleaners to him at a price considerably less than that at which we sold it under the former plan. The lower price that we now receive has, however, some offsetting advantages. We do not have the former salespeople's commissions to pay (we still have a few representatives to call on dealers); we have less delivery expense because we can ship in large quantities to the retailer; we need less storage space for the inventory of cleaners since the retailer now will carry stock necessary for supplying the wants of customers; we have less record keeping; and we should be able to increase our volume of sales because many of the reasons why customers did not buy from us when we had house-to-house representatives have been eliminated.

Planning for Future Expansion

Once our product is well established in a section of the country, we may wish to expand our business further by marketing our goods in other sections. Either of two general plans may be followed. We might greatly increase our staff of salesmen who call on retailers and thus attempt to contact retailers in other parts of the country. Since this plan would result in additional personnel problems, as well as delivery and record-keeping problems, we might use another plan, that of selling to wholesale merchants, or jobbers. Under this plan our selling price to the wholesalers or the jobbers would be lower than that at which we would sell to retailers, but there would be offsetting features. We would need fewer representatives to contact all the wholesalers than we would to contact the retailers; we would have only a few accounts receivable; we would need to keep less goods in storage for filling orders; we would ship in larger quantities. Under the latter plan the problem of marketing our goods would require little of our time and attention; hence we could concentrate on improving our processes of manufacturing. If we choose this plan, however, we must establish a definite program of advertising to create consumer demand in the new territories and must have a sufficient number of representatives to create wholesale demand by calling on the retailers.

REVIEW WHAT YOU HAVE LEARNED

Business Terms Checkup:

(1) marketing
(2) direct marketing
(3) indirect marketing
(4) trade channels
(5) retailer
(6) specialty store
(7) department store
(8) supermarket
(9) discount store
(10) wholesaler
(11) branch house
(12) broker
(13) buying agents
(14) sales agents
(15) intermediaries
(16) marketing functions

Reading Checkup:

1. Which is the shortest trade channel?
2. What are three methods by which the producer may sell directly to the consumer?
3. Under what conditions is mail-order selling likely to be most successful?
4. According to the diagram on page 102, what are the three channels by which goods move from the producer to the consumer?
5. Where are branch warehouses of manufacturers usually located?
6. Why is it sometimes necessary for a producer to use more than one channel in the distribution of his products?
7. Refer to the diagram on page 105 showing the trade channels for magazines. State from what two sources the consumer can secure magazines.
8. What are some of the reasons why trade channels are changing?
9. What are the principal factors to be considered in choosing the trade channel to be used?
10. Name the services and functions of middlemen.
11. State two reasons why the Emerson Company decided to sell directly to consumers.

APPLY WHAT YOU HAVE LEARNED

Questions for Class Discussion:

1. What is the reason that the percentage of prospects solicited by direct mail who buy is smaller when selling a $25 item than when selling a $2 item?
2. Why do the producers of such items as household goods and encyclopedias usually employ salesmen to call on the consumer?
3. Why are such items as women's dresses and coats usually not marketed through wholesalers to retailers?
4. Surveys indicate that a large percentage of children's clothing is purchased at discount stores, but the purchase of furniture is usually done in the specialty store. What is the probable reason for this?
5. What is the chief difference between a broker and a wholesaler in acting as a middleman between producer and retailer?
6. Does the elimination of some of the middlemen eliminate any of the marketing functions? Explain.
7. Explain the principal disadvantages that were experienced by the Emerson Company in selling directly to consumers.
8. If the Emerson Company markets its products through wholesalers, what are the principal advantages it will have?

Problems and Projects:

1. A farmer has produced 100 bushels of potatoes for sale. He could sell them in their ungraded condition to a city wholesale produce business at $1.50 a bushel. Instead, he decides to market them directly to housewives by a house-to-house canvass. He finds that it requires 12 hours to clean, grade, and put the potatoes into containers. He is compelled to make a two-hour trip to the city to purchase the containers (bushel baskets). The cost of the containers is 15 cents each. The total time spent in traveling to the city and making a house-to-house canvass to dispose of the 100 bushels is 15 hours on two different days. He sells 80 bushels, which are the large size, at $2 and the remainder, which are the small size, at $1.50. Assume that the expense of operating the truck for three trips to the city is $8 and that the farmer's time is worth $2 an hour. Did the farmer receive more or less by marketing the potatoes directly than he would have by selling them to the produce business? How much?

2. You decide to sell by mail for $5.97 a product that costs $2. You have a selected mailing list of 2,000 names to which you send materials advertising your product. The cost of the advertising materials is 12 cents each (printing, order card, envelope, addressing, folding, inserting, stapling, postage, etc.). Compute your gross profit or loss (a) if you receive 60 orders and (b) if you receive 100 orders.

3. The consumer paid the retailer 30 cents for a can of tomatoes. An analysis of what each of the following persons received for his services in the marketing process is as follows:

Grower	5.61¢
Canner	14.94¢
Wholesaler	3.45¢
Retailer	6.00¢
	30.00¢

Determine the cost price to the retailer, the wholesaler, and the canner.

Case Problem 6-1:

Jackson & Perkins Co., grower of flower bulbs and rose bushes, is doing a nationwide business of selling its products by mail.

Required:

1. What are some of the reasons for its success in marketing these products by mail?

2. The company also sells by mail products closely related to flower bulbs and rose bushes. Suggest what these products might be.

Case Problem 6-2:

The Better Biscuit Company manufactures a line of cookies, crackers, and other bakery products that it has been distributing directly to retail grocers within a radius of approximately 60 miles by its own truck. It is contemplating doubling the size of its baking facilities and marketing its products over a wider area.

Required:

1. If the distribution is to cover a much wider territory, what change in trade channels may be desirable?
2. Are there other possible outlets for the products?

Case Problem 6-3:

There are three furniture stores, all handling bedroom furniture, in a certain city. The Wayne Mattress Company is undecided as to whether it would be desirable to give one of the stores the exclusive agency for its mattresses or have the mattresses sold by all three of the stores.

Required:

Which method of distribution would probably be the better for the Wayne Mattress Company? Give reasons for your decision.

Case Problem 6-4:

A paint manufacturer began to manufacture a new household floor wax and to distribute it through paint and hardware stores which sold its line of paints. Sales did not develop as expected although the wax was superior in many respects to other floor waxes. Upon investigation the manufacturer learned that other brands of floor wax were being sold in supermarkets.

Required:

1. What was the probable reason that floor waxes being sold through supermarkets sold better than floor waxes being sold through paint and hardware stores?
2. If the manufacturer plans to increase the sales of his floor wax, what change should be made in the channels of distribution used?

Continuing Project:

Make a study of the channels of distribution through which you will receive your goods from the time of raw materials until the goods reach you in their final form. Next, prepare a distribution plan for the products that you intend to sell. Drawings will be helpful in this part of your project.

How does competition affect prices?

How is the merchandise turnover rate figured?

Why are psychological prices often used?

What are the operating expenses of a business?

What is net profit?

How are markups and markdowns used in establishing prices?

BACKGROUND OF CHAPTER

A difficult task for the businessman is the determination of prices to place on the goods and services he sells. The prices established will greatly affect the volume of business done and the profits earned. If prices are too high, customers may shop elsewhere. Prices which are too low will not provide a large enough margin of profit to make the business successful.

Fortunately, there are certain guidelines which businessmen may follow in establishing their prices. In this chapter you will learn about these guidelines and about the procedures involved in pricing merchandise.

CHAPTER 7

PRICING POLICIES AND PROCEDURES

Since the price that a business places on its products or services will have a definite effect on its success or lack of success, it is extremely important that a careful study be made of the many factors that should be considered by the business before making a decision as to the price it will place on its goods or services.

PRICING POLICIES

Since a business is operated for profit, it is obvious that the owner will obtain for each item that he sells a price that is as high as is practicable. A businessman may establish high prices and sell very few articles; as a result of that policy, he may make very little profit or may actually lose money. On the other hand, some businessmen establish very low prices in the hope of selling merchandise in quantities large enough to result in a desirable profit, even though the percentage of profit is low. Let us consider the following two examples:

Example A: An article that costs a businessman $50 is offered for sale at $100. The businessman sells three of these in a month, making a gross profit of $150.

Example B: Another businessman, having the same or a similar item costing $50, decides to attempt to sell a greater quantity at a lower price. He therefore offers his item for sale at $60. During a month he sells ten of these at a gross profit of $100.

If we assume that all other factors are equal, the businessman in Example A makes a greater gross profit than the one in Example B, although each may fail to make a net profit. In many cases more expense will be involved in selling ten items than in selling three. The cost of doing business will therefore be greater when the larger volume of business is handled. It is probable, however, that in each of the preceding cases the price is wrong. In one case it is so high that a sufficient quantity will not be sold to yield a fair net profit; in the other it is so low that a sufficient gross profit will not be made. Between these two extremes there is probably a reasonable price; but there are many factors influencing the establishment of that price. Some of these factors are discussed in the following paragraphs.

Competition Affects Prices

The amount of competition among businesses handling similar goods or giving similar services is an important factor in establishing prices. If one business asks a higher price than a competitor, some of its customers are likely to do business with the competitor. Even businesses in neighboring localities are influenced by competition. If prices are too high in one locality, many people will travel to nearby communities to purchase goods or services. For example, if a service station in one neighborhood is selling a certain brand of gasoline for 37 cents a gallon and a station in another locality two miles away is selling the same brand for 35 cents, the customer is likely to buy where he can get it for 35 cents.

Often a business must offer some of its merchandise at a price below that which will yield a fair profit because some competitor has established a similar low price. It is not always necessary to have a lower selling price than competitors. If your product has some distinct

ILLUS. 7-1. **Competition affects prices.**

advantage or if you provide some service, such as delivery, desired by customers, a higher retail price may be obtained without sacrificing your volume of sales.

In businesses in which competition is keen, there is a tendency to set prices to cover only the actual costs of the average business. Net profits are made, therefore, only by the most efficient businesses. Even if there is little or no competition, a business that fixes its prices too high finds that people will do without its products or services, or find substitutes, rather than pay the prices that seem to give that business an unduly large profit. For example, a laundry that asks too high a price for its services will find that many of its customers will go to another laundry or will do their own laundry at home.

When introducing a new product, the manufacturer should acquaint himself with competitive products on the market and check the prices at which they sell. He may find gaps in the price brackets that he can fill by pricing his product accordingly. For example, if a competing manufacturer is selling shoes in the $20 to $25 price range and another competing manufacturer is selling shoes in the $10 to $12 range, he may decide to manufacture shoes to sell in the $15 to $18 price range and thus hit a price bracket that is not being filled.

Fixed Prices During Long Periods of Time

Many businesses, especially in the retail trade, have a tendency to fix a price for a certain item and to keep the item at that price for a considerable period. For example, a store has been selling women's hosiery at $1.19 a pair for several years, even though the cost of the hosiery to the store has varied from time to time. Since the customers have become accustomed to paying $1.19, they naturally expect to continue to buy their hosiery at that price. Should the store raise the price to $1.29, the customers are likely to resent the increase, thinking that the store is attempting to make an unfair profit. On the other hand, should the price be lowered to $1.09, they are likely to become suspicious of the quality. The same situation applies to the dentist, the barber, the shoe repairman, and other businessmen who have had fixed prices for their services over a considerable period of time. Even though operating costs vary, customers may resent price changes. Therefore, many businesses find it desirable to change either the quantity or quality, or both, of their product in order not to change the price. For example, in response to changes in economic conditions over a period of years the manufacturer of a candy bar may keep the price the same but change its size.

Prices Based on Getting a Specified Rate of Return

When introducing a new product, many businesses, especially manufacturers, base their selling price on what will result in a specified rate of return (such as 8 percent after taxes) on the capital invested. This policy could be followed as the basis for determining the price, but the actual rate of return would be influenced by how well the product is received and to what extent the prices of competing products have an effect.

Consumer Demand

The owner of a business that carries fashion goods knows that at certain times the goods will be in great demand, and at other times the demand will be greatly diminished. As an illustration, a retailer will find that swimsuits sell readily early in the season but that later in the season it is almost impossible to sell them unless the prices are much lower. Since the exact number of suits that will be sold cannot be estimated accurately, the retailer will, at the beginning of the season, fix a selling price that should ensure a net profit on the entire lot of swimsuits, even though prices may have to be reduced drastically late in the season in order that no suits need to be carried over to the next spring season.

Sometimes a businessman may buy a group of similar items at the same price; but, because there are variations in the designs, the colors, and the styles, he may charge different prices for the various items. As certain colors or designs will be more attractive than others, customers will be willing to pay higher prices for them.

A manufacturer of a novelty article that suddenly becomes popular finds it necessary to sell at a high price while the demand is great. When new competitors come into the field and the demand begins to subside, the original manufacturer either sells the product at a much lower price or ceases production. For instance, a game that has become suddenly popular is sold at a high price by the manufacturer. Before long, many other manufacturers come into the field. Then the demand soon begins to subside. The original high price cannot be maintained. In such cases the manufacturer should be careful not to overproduce, and the retail store not to overbuy.

The introduction of new products on the market (for example, a new type of electric shaver) presents an interesting study in price policies. During the process of introducing a product of this type, large amounts of money are needed for advertising and promotion. In the early stages there are few, if any, competitors. The price that is established may therefore be the highest price at which the manufacturer feels he can sell a reasonable quantity. Often the manufacturer suggests to the retailer the price at which to sell the product to the consumer. Sometimes he has the suggested retail price printed on the package label. Sometimes when production facilities are limited, a high price is established because, even at that price, buyers will consume all that is produced. As the manufacturer increases his production facilities and develops more economical methods, he can reduce the price and, in many cases, make a greater gross profit. As new competitors come into the field, there is usually a tendency to lower prices. The additional sales promotion of several competitors will help to create a greater total demand. With this greater demand, a larger volume of sales will often result. But, in spite of the greater volume, a severe reduction in price may decrease profits.

Perishability of the Product

In determining his selling price, the owner of a small store who purchases a crate of strawberries must consider, in addition to his usual operating expenses, the probable loss due to spoilage. For example, he pays $6 a crate (25 cents a pint) and establishes a selling price of 35 cents a pint. If he sells all the strawberries, his net profit is:

```
$8.40  = sales (24 pints at 35 cents)
 6.00  = cost
$2.40  = margin, or gross profit
 1.68  = operating expenses (20% of sales)
$ .72  = net profit
```

But if 4 pints should spoil, the result would be:

```
$7.00  = sales (20 pints at 35 cents)
 6.00  = cost
$1.00  = margin, or gross profit
 1.40  = operating expenses (20% of sales)
$(.40) = net loss
```

In the second case, the operating expenses might be as high as in the first case ($1.68). This would result in a still larger loss (68 cents).

The merchant should have figured the approximate loss due to spoilage and made the selling price slightly higher (probably 40 cents a pint) so as to have made a satisfactory net profit in spite of the spoilage of part of the strawberries.

ILLUS. 7-2. The price established for perishable products must include an estimate of losses resulting from spoilage.

Likewise, the baker must consider the loss that will result from unsold baked goods that soon become stale. All other businessmen handling perishable products should be careful in determining their selling prices.

Fragile articles that are easily broken by handling, such as glassware, chinaware, and toys, should be considered in much the same manner as the perishable products just mentioned. The manufacturer of, or dealer in, ice and liquids that evaporate easily has a similar problem.

Sometimes the problem to be considered in establishing a price is not to obtain the greatest net profit but to avoid as much loss as possible. In other words, the problem is to establish a selling price that will permit a minimum loss. A merchant, a distributor, or a manufacturer may discover that he has on hand perishable merchandise that, if not sold soon, will become a total loss. Sometimes if style merchandise is not sold quickly, it will become so out of style that it can be sold only at a great loss. After a price has been established, it may become necessary to reduce it in order to sell the goods. Good judgment and experience are, therefore, important in establishing prices.

Effect of Merchandise Turnover

Articles that sell slowly usually are marked at higher prices than articles that cost the same but sell more rapidly. For example, one article that cost $4 remains in stock for approximately six months and then is sold at a price of $6. Another article that cost $4 and remains in stock for approximately two months is sold for $5.50. Because of the greater rate of turnover, the latter article may yield a larger net profit to the business at the end of the year. Stores often attempt to increase their rate of merchandise turnover by setting lower prices.

As was disclosed previously, it is often dangerous for a businessman to attempt to sell too great a volume at reduced prices because the gross profit may not be sufficient to yield a net profit.

The following methods are used in computing the rate of merchandise turnover:

1. Divide the cost of goods sold by the average inventory valued at the cost price.
2. Divide the net sales by the average inventory valued at the retail price.
3. Divide the total number of units sold by the average number of units in stock.

ILLUS. 7-3. A smaller percentage of profit is usually planned for products which are sold quickly.

The theory of obtaining a higher profit from goods with a low turnover than from goods with a high turnover is based upon two facts: (a) if money is invested for a long period of time in merchandise with a low turnover, a high rate of profit should be obtained; (b) if merchandise moves slowly, it is necessary to obtain a high percentage of profit in order to take care of operating expenses for the longer period of time. For instance, the merchandise in a jewelry store usually is not sold and replenished at the rate of more than once a year. This rate may even run as low as once in two years. The jeweler therefore finds it necessary to obtain a very high gross profit of 50 percent or more.

Retail Prices Fixed by Contract

In some states manufacturers can fix the resale price on their branded, nationally advertised goods. In certain cases, federal legislation also has legalized price-fixing in goods sold across state lines. These so-called "fair trade" laws are discussed in Chapter 30. The important point to consider in this chapter is that the resale prices of some branded items are definitely fixed by the manufacturers, while those of other branded items are controlled through agency agreements. If a businessman accepts the agency for a certain product, he must sell that product at the price prescribed by the manufacturer.

As will be seen in a later discussion, the agreements fixing the prices of certain nationally advertised brands also prevent price-cutting. Some retailers prefer to sell brands on which the prices are not fixed, especially if they are in a "fair trade" state and located near the border of a state that does not have the law.

Prices Affected by Store Services

A business that has a policy of extending credit to its customers and of delivering goods may have larger operating expenses than one that sells on a cash-and-carry basis. Larger operating expenses mean that a higher selling price must be received to yield the same net profit as that earned by a store doing a cash-and-carry business. The attitude of a merchant toward goods returned by customers also has its influence. If a store is liberal in making adjustments, it usually has high original selling prices. Other services, such as free parking space and checkrooms, also have an effect on the prices at which goods are marked for sale. Many retail stores are being established as or changed to self-service stores in order to reduce the number of employees needed and thus reduce expenses.

In establishing a price, a manufacturer or a wholesale distributor should consider all the services that must be performed. The price should not be far out of line with the prices of competing items, but it should be sufficiently high to provide a gross profit that will cover all costs. For instance, a certain amount must be allowed for advertising. Sometimes an amount must be allowed for the expense of installing the product sold. In the case of some kinds of equipment it is necessary to provide for service either free of charge or upon a fee basis. If such service is to be provided free, the cost must be considered in establishing the selling price.

Unit Pricing

Some stores that sell a product in different size packages have introduced what is called *unit pricing*. In addition to indicating the selling price of the package, a price per unit of measurement is given. For example, a package having a net weight of 15 ounces has a selling price of 30 cents and also has a price of 32 cents a pound. This aids the customer in deciding whether the 15-ounce package or a package containing some other amount will cost more or less per pound.

Pricing in Service Businesses

Service businesses generally base their prices on the cost of furnishing the service. Such businesses as automobile repair shops and television repair shops use a fixed-price approach. There is a charge of so much per hour for labor. In addition there is a charge for parts used.

Psychological Prices

When pricing consumer goods, the retailer may find it desirable to use *psychological prices*. A retail price of 97 cents rather than $1, or $4.93 rather than $5, are examples of this type of pricing. Another example is found when a special price is given on multiple-unit selling, such as when a single item normally selling for 10 cents is priced at three for 27 cents.

PRICING PROCEDURES

Knowing the general factors that affect prices is helpful, but this knowledge alone is not enough to enable the businessman to set fair and wise prices. The businessman must also be familiar with many specific pricing terms and procedures.

The diagram shown in Illustration 7-4 explains the component parts of the selling price of an article.

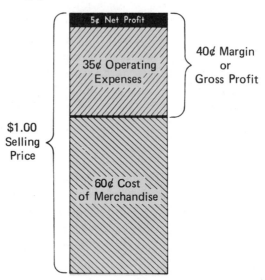

ILLUS. 7-4. Component parts of the selling price or the customer's sales dollar.

Cost of Merchandise. The basic factor in determining the selling price of goods is the *cost of the merchandise* (delivered price). To determine the total cost of merchandise, it is customary to add the transportation charges to the purchase price of the merchandise. For example, if the cost price of an article is 55 cents and the transportation charge is 5 cents, the total cost of that article is 60 cents.

Operating Expenses. *Operating expenses* are the costs incurred in operating a business. The following items are those that make up the operating expenses in most businesses:

Rent

Taxes

Interest paid on money borrowed

Repairs and painting

Salaries

Stationery, bags, paper, twine, and other wrapping materials

Telephone and telegraph service

Allowance for shrinkage due to theft, spoilage, or breakage

Depreciation of furniture, fixtures, and delivery equipment

Bad accounts and collection expenses

Delivery costs

Advertising

Heat, light, power, and water

Donations

Insurance

Miscellaneous and unclassified expenses

Net Profit. *Net profit* is the difference between the selling price and all the costs and expenses of the business. Net profit can be expressed in the following formula:

Net profit = selling price — cost of merchandise sold — operating expenses

Margin. *Margin* is a term used to indicate the difference between the selling price and the cost of the merchandise. Sometimes it is called the gross profit. In Illustration 7-4 the margin is 40 cents. In the terms of a formula it is:

Margin = operating expenses + net profit
or
Margin = selling price — cost of merchandise sold

In business papers and magazines the margin is often referred to as a percentage of the selling price. In the preceding case it would be 40 percent (40¢ ÷ 100¢).

Markup. *Markup* is similar to margin. When both are spoken of in dollars and cents, they are identical. For example, in Illustration 7-4 the markup is also 40 cents. The markup may be expressed as a percentage of the selling price or as a percentage of the cost. Thus, the markup in Illustration 7-4 would be 66⅔ percent (40¢ ÷ 60¢) if expressed as a percentage of the cost. If the markup is expressed as a percentage of the selling price, it is 40 percent (40¢ ÷ 100¢). In department stores, markup usually is expressed as a percentage of the selling price. It is therefore exceedingly important that a businessman, in reading articles about pricing and in discussing margin and markup, be certain of the exact meaning intended when these terms are used.

Markdown. *Markdown* is any amount by which the original selling price is reduced.

Selling Price as the Base

In order to compare figures that are related to sales, it is necessary to have a common base for the computations. If the salaries were figured as a percentage of the cost of the merchandise sold and the net profit as a percentage of the sales, it is quite obvious that an accurate comparison could not be made. Since selling price includes everything (the cost of the merchandise, the operating expenses, and the net profit), it is the whole amount and should be used as the base, or 100 percent. Then the cost of the merchandise, the various operating expenses, the net profit, the margin, and practically all financial items can be stated as percentages of the sales of the business.

The modern businessman thinks in terms of sales. He figures what percentage of his sales are such items as salaries, advertising expense, delivery expense, loss on bad debts, taxes, net profit, cost of goods sold, margin, sales returns, sales discount, interest, and many others. He plans his budget and adjusts expenditures upon the basis of these percentages.

Another important reason why a businessman should use his selling price as the base, or 100 percent, is that most discussions and statistical reports in business magazines and government bulletins use the selling price as a base. Let us assume that a writer in a magazine suggests the following margins of profit: (a) 25 percent on cheese, (b) 30 percent on tea, (c) 12½ percent on cereals, and (d) 20 percent on canned tomatoes. These percentages are based on selling prices. Let us take the example of tomatoes, on which a margin of 20 percent is proposed. Here is the way the profit is computed:

```
                          100%  is the selling price
                           20%  is the margin (20% of 100%)
Therefore                  80%  of the selling price = the cost of the goods
Let us assume that                                $400 = the cost of the goods
Then                       80%  of the selling price = $400
                            1%  of the selling price = $5 ($400 ÷ 80)
                          100%  of the selling price = $500
```

The margin (20 percent) is composed of two elements, the net profit and the operating expenses. Assuming that 2 percent is a reasonable average net profit, the operating expenses will be 18 percent. The final result will therefore be:

```
        $500 = sales
18% of $500 = $90, operating expenses
 2% of $500 = $10, NET PROFIT
80% of $500 = $400, cost of goods
```

But if the reader of the magazine article assumes that the margin of 20 percent is figured on the cost of the goods, the following will then be the result:

```
                              $400  = the cost of the goods
            20% of $400 =       80  = the margin
                              $480  = the selling price
Assume that operating expenses will be  90,  or the same amount as in the
                                             preceding situation
                            $(10) = NET LOSS ($80 − $90)
```

It is evident from these calculations that, when one attempts to utilize published figures on costs and profits, one should know how these percentages are computed. For instance, if a man starts a new business with the assumption that he should have a 20 percent margin of gross profit, and if he figures that margin on the cost price, he probably will lose money.

The cost of selling different kinds of merchandise varies. Competition and other factors, which were mentioned in the first part of this chapter, affect the prices of many kinds of merchandise. These factors make it impracticable to have the same margin on all items. It is necessary, therefore, that the businessman keep records of sales and operating expenses by departments or by kinds of merchandise. Only when such information is available is it possible to price each kind of goods so that it will be sold profitably.

Markup Table

We have already seen how to compute the selling price when the cost price and the margin are known. Because it would be a laborious task to compute the selling price for many different items at various rates of margin, most businesses have *margin,* or *markup, tables* prepared to simplify the process. Illustration 7-5 shows a markup table for a number of margins. Some businesses have more elaborate tables.

Find the desired margin in the left-hand column. Multiply the cost of the article by the corresponding percentage in the right-hand column. Add this amount to the cost in order to determine the correct selling price.

Desired Margin (Percent of Selling Price)	Equivalent (Percent of Cost)
10%	11.1%
12½	14.3
15	17.6
20	25.0
25	33⅓
30	42.9
*33⅓	*50.0
35	53.8
40	66⅔
50	100.0

ILLUS. 7-5. Markup table.

Suppose an article costs $1.50 and the desired margin is 33⅓ percent (of the selling price). The table (see starred items) shows us that we should multiply the $1.50 by 50 percent. This computation gives

us 75 cents, which is the margin. We then add this amount to the
$1.50 (the cost) and get a selling price of $2.25. Let us now check
our work. If the selling price is $2.25, the desired margin of 33⅓
percent of the selling price is 75 cents. The selling price of $2.25 minus
the margin of 75 cents gives a cost of $1.50.

The following formula can be used for changing any desired markup
(margin) as a percent of the selling price into a percent of the cost:

$$\frac{\text{Markup (Margin) as a percent of selling price}}{100\% - \text{Markup as a percent of selling price}} = \text{Markup as a percent of the cost}$$

Applying the formula to the fourth item in the markup table above,
we have

$$\frac{20}{100 - 20} = \frac{20}{80} = .25 \text{ or } 25\%$$

Markdowns

In many cases a merchant is compelled to mark and sell part of
his goods at a lower price than that at which he had been selling them
previously. Some of the principal reasons for markdowns are:

Shopworn, soiled, or damaged   Competitors' lower prices
  goods   Unseasonable weather
Style changes   Overproduction or overpurchases
Remnants   Sudden changes in costs

Naturally the amount of markdown varies greatly with different
items. Some of the variations are indicated in Illustration 7-6.

Although some markdowns can be reduced by a more careful control of buying, there are some that cannot. By an accurate record of
his own past experiences with markdowns, as well as knowing the

Women's dresses	15.6%
Women's suits and coats	12.6
Blouses and skirts	9.3
Women's shoes	8.3
Silks and velvets	7.2
Men's clothing	7.1
Leather goods	6.4
Jewelry	5.4
Drugs and toilet goods	4.0

ILLUS. 7-6. Markdown averages.

experiences of others, the businessman should be able to estimate the probable allowance he should make for markdowns in determining his original selling price. Just as soon as it is learned that an item is not selling as rapidly as expected, it should be marked down.

Sometimes a businessman believes that, by reducing the selling price, he will increase the volume of sales and thus earn more profit. His belief may or may not prove true. Let us see how, in the case of a markdown, the unit sales must be increased in order that the gross profit, or margin, will be the same in dollars and cents as the gross profit that was earned on the original selling price.

Suppose $10 is the selling price
               6 is the cost
            $ 4 is the margin or 40% of the sales
Assume   12 articles are sold daily
          $48 is the daily gross profit ($4 × 12)

If the goods are marked down 10 percent—

$ 9 is the new selling price
  6 is the cost
$ 3 is the margin, or gross profit, on one article

$48 is the daily gross profit desired
  16 articles must be sold daily in order to yield the same amount of gross profit in dollars ($48 ÷ $3)

Thus, if goods carrying a 40 percent margin are reduced 10 percent, it is necessary to increase the volume of unit sales 33⅓ percent (16 — 12 = 4 ÷ 12 = 33⅓ percent) in order to obtain the same amount of gross profit. The smaller the percentage of original margin, the greater must be the increase in sales to bring about the same gross profit. In the preceding example a 10 percent reduction on goods carrying a 40 percent margin necessitated an increase of 33⅓ percent. A 10 percent reduction on goods carrying a 30 percent margin would necessitate a unit sales increase of 50 percent, while the same reduction on goods carrying a 20 percent margin would necessitate an increase of 100 percent. Another factor to be considered is the probable increase in operating expenses that will result from the increase in sales volume.

It is obvious from the previous discussion that a reduction in the unit price requires a considerable increase in the volume of sale of individual units in order to maintain the same amount of net profit. So-called cut-rate businesses are therefore not always profitable. To be successful, a cut-rate business must be in a location where, through the proper sales promotion methods, a sufficient amount of additional

business can be obtained to compensate for the lower unit profit. Supermarkets operate on this plan.

A merchant should consider the likely effect on competitors that
may result from lowering prices in the hope of increasing the volume
of sales. As a result of his lowering prices, he may find his competitors
do the same. In such a case, the merchant has not accomplished his
purpose.

REVIEW WHAT YOU HAVE LEARNED

Business Terms Checkup:

(1) unit pricing   (6) margin
(2) psychological prices   (7) markup
(3) cost of the merchandise   (8) markdown
(4) operating expenses   (9) margin (or markup) tables
(5) net profit

Reading Checkup:

1. In businesses in which competition is keen, the prices are usually at what
   level?
2. Why do some businesses have a tendency to keep the same price on a
   certain item over a long period of time?
3. Why do prices on novelty goods usually become much lower after a time?
4. In pricing articles that are very fragile, should the pricing policy consider
   the possible loss from breakage?
5. How is the merchandise turnover rate computed?
6. Are retail prices sometimes fixed by the manufacturer?
7. How do store services affect prices?
8. What is meant by unit pricing?
9. What are psychological prices?
10. Examine the diagram on page 124 showing the component parts of the
    selling price and state the amount of net profit shown.
11. Does the *cost of the merchandise* include the transportation cost on mer-
    chandise purchased?
12. Name the common operating expenses of a business.
13. Of what two items does margin consist?
14. When do the terms *margin* and *markup* mean the same?
15. Refer to the markup table on page 127. If a margin of 25 percent of
    selling price is desired, what is the equivalent percentage of the cost?
16. State some principal reasons for markdowns.

APPLY WHAT YOU HAVE LEARNED

Questions for Class Discussion:

1. How does competition affect prices?

2. How might a small grocery store successfully compete with a super-market whose prices are lower?

3. A business has very little competition. It therefore fixes the prices of its goods so that it will make a large profit. What will be the probable effect of this policy?

4. Why is it often necessary in the initial stages of introducing a new product to charge a considerably higher price than is later charged? Why is it possible?

5. The perishability of a product should be considered in determining the selling price. Explain this statement.

6. Is it desirable for the retail florist to apply the same rate of markup to cut flowers as to potted plants? Explain.

7. Why does merchandise turnover affect profits?

8. What expenses does a business have in connection with selling to customers on credit terms?

9. Why is the selling price ordinarily used as the base in comparing items relating to sales?

10. Can larger net profits be made if the selling price is reduced but there is a greater rate of merchandise turnover?

11. A printing shop that does job printing prices the usual printing job on a full-cost basis plus a 20 percent markup on the full cost. However, on jobs for envelopes and letterheads it adds only a 10 percent markup. What is a possible reason for the smaller percent of markup on envelopes and letterheads?

Problems and Projects:

1. Suppose a merchant estimates his sales in a year will be $100,000 and that his operating expenses will be $20,000.

   (a) What will be the amount of the margin if he expects to have a net profit of 5 percent of sales?

   (b) What is his percentage of margin?

   (c) What percentage of the total sales is the cost of merchandise?

   (d) If he buys an article for $1.50, what should be its selling price?

   (e) What is his rate of markup on the cost?

2. During a year a merchant sold 180 electric lanterns. The number of lanterns on hand during the year was as follows: January 1, 22; February 1, 28; March 1, 36; April 1, 30; May 1, 42; June 1, 55;

July 1, 50; August 1, 50; September 1, 48; October 1, 43; November 1, 66; December 1, 70. What was the rate of turnover?

3. A business owned by you shows the following figures for a year's operations: sales, $60,000; average inventory (at selling price), $40,000; cost of goods sold, $42,000; operating expenses, $14,400. The figures for the next year showed the following: sales, $100,000; average inventory (at selling price), $40,000; cost of goods sold, $70,000; operating expenses, $24,000.

   (a) Find the annual rate of merchandise turnover for each year.

   (b) What percentage of the average inventory was the net profit each year?

4. A hobby shop has been selling each month an average of 10 model airplane motors that cost $20 each. The regular selling price has been $28. By reducing the selling price to $24, the number of sales was increased to 15 each month. If the average monthly operating expenses were increased $10 by the change, how much was the monthly net profit increased or decreased by the change in price?

5. Find the percentage of markup on the cost price; also find the selling price in the following cases:

COST PRICE	DESIRED MARGIN (PERCENTAGE OF SELLING PRICE)
(a) $6.00	40%
(b) $ .75	25%
(c) $8.40	20%
(d) $4.50	50%

6. A ladies' dress shop buys 100 dresses at $18.00 each. The dresses are marked to be sold at a margin of 50 percent on the selling price. Eighty dresses are sold at that price. The remaining are sold after a markdown of 25 percent.

   (a) What was the original marked selling price of each dress?

   (b) What was the selling price of each dress after the markdown?

   (c) What was the total amount received from the sale of all dresses?

   (d) What was the margin (gross profit) on the sale of all dresses?

Case Problem 7-1:

The Sexton Shoe Store is now selling for $24 a pair a certain style of shoe that costs $14.40. The owner thinks that if the selling price were reduced slightly more sales and more profits might be made since the operating expenses would not increase. The store has sold an average of 30 pairs daily.

Required:

1. If the selling price is reduced 10 percent, it will be necessary to increase the number of pairs sold by what percentage in order that the same amount of gross profit will be made?

2. Comment on the owner's belief that the operating expenses would not increase.

Case Problem 7-2:

The Central Dress Shop plans to add a department that will sell formal evening dresses.

Required:

Should the store plan to have the same percentage of markup on the dresses in the new department as they have been having on the other types of dresses? Explain fully your reasons.

Case Problem 7-3:

The Sheridan Nursery sells plants and shrubbery at wholesale prices to retail nurseries, garden stores, garden departments of variety and department stores, etc. The firm grows most of its plants on its 60 acres of land. It sends price lists to its customers twice a year—March 1 and June 15.

Required:

Would it be desirable for the firm to send price lists more frequently (possibly monthly from March 1 to August 1) in order to adjust prices?

Continuing Project:

From the information in this chapter and from any other supplementary reading, establish a pricing policy, including margins, markups, and markdowns, for the merchandise you plan to sell.

Why must a business continually add new customers?

What are some methods used by business to obtain customers?

What are some kinds of special sales?

What are loss leaders?

What types of delivery service may be offered?

What are the effects of merchandise returns?

BACKGROUND OF CHAPTER

Consumers "run" business; their dollars can determine the success or failure of a business. Their wants influence the choice of goods which are offered for sale, the prices which are placed on the goods, and the customer services which are given. If the business does not provide customers with the merchandise and services they desire, they will soon cease to be customers.

All businesses face the same problem—how to attract customers and persuade them to buy. This unit's remaining chapters—on obtaining and serving customers, salesmanship, and advertising and sales promotion—deal with solutions to this problem.

CHAPTER 8

OBTAINING AND SERVING CUSTOMERS

Customers are the lifeblood of a business. One who wishes to operate a successful business must, therefore, know the methods used to obtain customers and be prepared to provide the services which customers expect.

OBTAINING CUSTOMERS

Whether a business is engaged in manufacturing, in wholesaling, in retailing, or in supplying service, an important problem that confronts the management is the obtaining of customers. This problem must be met not only when a business enterprise is started, but also throughout the life of the business. New customers must be obtained to take the place of old customers who cease to deal with the business because of change in residence, death, change in financial status, or the like.

Securing Prospective Customers

In its continuing efforts to obtain new customers, a business employs many different methods to provide information about its goods and services to those who are most likely to purchase its goods and services.

Advertising. Advertising in its various forms, as discussed in Chapter 10, is one of the main methods that manufacturers, wholesalers, and retailers use in obtaining prospective customers. Manufacturers use various forms of advertising, and much of this advertising is designed to develop demand on the part of consumers. This demand then makes it easier for the manufacturer and the wholesaler to sell to the retailer.

One of the most important means of getting prospective customers for retail stores is newspaper advertisements. To attract his first customers, a businessman opening a new store may insert an announcement

ILLUS. 8-1. Advertising is one of the main methods of attracting customers.

in a newspaper. From time to time the advertisements of a business are designed to attract additional customers. The display windows are one of the best means of drawing prospective customers into the store. The windows should be so attractive that passersby will observe the goods and be stimulated to buy. *Business-promotion letters* are often used to convert prospects into customers. For example, a department store may make a practice of sending a letter, such as shown in Illustration 8-2, to all new residents of the city, welcoming them to the city and inviting them to open charge accounts.

In obtaining possible customers, the small retailer has problems which are simpler than those of the manufacturer and wholesaler; but they require a thorough understanding of the various means of obtaining customers at a minimum of expense. In every kind of business the problem of obtaining prospects is different. Often radio or television programs, magazine advertising, house-to-house canvassing, and demonstrations by manufacturers will help the small businessman to obtain prospects. For instance, if a businessman handles a certain

THE **PLAZA**

Everything from to

881 PATTON STREET   GREEN BAY, WI 54301   DEPARTMENT STORE

August 22, 19--

Mrs. Gerald R. Coleman
2000 Barberry Lane
Green Bay, WI 54304

Dear Mrs. Coleman

May I be among the first to welcome you to Green Bay.

All of us at THE PLAZA hope that you will enjoy living
here and that we shall soon have the privilege of
knowing and serving you. We believe that you will find
THE PLAZA a convenient and pleasant place to shop.

A charge account will make your shopping easier, and
we are therefore enclosing a credit application. If
you will return it to us, we will notify you when you
can pick up your "Charga-Plate" at our store. If you
have any questions, we shall be pleased to hear from
you.

We know that you will make many new friends, and we
hope that THE PLAZA will be among the first.

Cordially yours

Arthur Lawrence

Arthur Lawrence
Credit Manager

AL:cb

Enclosure

ILLUS. 8-2. A business-promotion letter welcoming a new resident to the city and inviting her to open a charge account.

product, the manufacturer may refer to him prospects who have been secured through replies to radio and television commercials, sending in coupons as a result of advertisements, and various other means.

Securing Names of Prospects. Lists of doctors, lawyers, accountants, and other special types of individuals can be obtained. In fact, mailing lists are available for almost every imaginable type of person or business. There are persons who make a business of preparing and selling mailing lists and prospect lists. For instance, lists of various kinds of dealers can be obtained through such agencies as Dun and Bradstreet, Incorporated, and Rand McNally. Such lists include retail grocers, druggists, and others. It is also possible to buy catalogs in which are given various kinds of mailing lists that can be bought from various sources. Additional ways of obtaining mailing lists are discussed in Chapter 10.

Telephone and City Directories. Telephone and city directories contain classified sections from which many businesses may select prospects. A stationery merchant could find in the telephone book a list of local accountants who might be prospects for accounting supplies; a laundry or a linen supply company could obtain a list of all the restaurants and the barber shops in the city; a flour-milling company would be interested in the names of bakers; a list of the beauty shops would furnish prospects for businesses handling beauty-shop equipment and supplies; and automobile and trucking companies should make good prospects for truck salesmen and insurance salesmen.

From city directories that have the residents listed by streets, such neighborhood businesses as public garages, delicatessens, beauty shops, gasoline service stations, and dry-cleaning shops can obtain a list of prospects who live in the immediate neighborhood. Some city directories indicate whether the person living at a certain address is the owner of the property. The owners listed might, for instance, be prospects for fire insurance and building repairs.

Newspapers. The daily newspapers will aid many businesses in finding prospective customers. The lists of building permits granted and contracts let for buildings, roads, and streets should be valuable information to businesses that furnish contractors with raw materials and supplies. News items telling of the promotions of people to higher salaried positions may provide prospects for real-estate companies or life-insurance salesmen. Likewise, the announcements of engagements, marriages, births, newcomers to the community, and political appointments should provide prospects for many businesses.

Other Ways of Securing Names of Prospects. The proprietor of a restaurant located in that section of the city occupied mainly by office buildings could make a list of the people who have offices nearby and use that list for his sales-promotion letters. The landscape gardener, the tree surgeon, the painting contractor, and other persons who render similar personal services can find a large number of prospects by observing closely the condition of shrubbery, trees, and buildings. The names of new prospects can often be obtained from old customers and from friends. Tupperware Products, a firm that sells principally plastic dishes and containers, obtains the names of women attending a "Tupperware Party" held in the home of a person who acts as a hostess. Usually such prospects become customers.

Special Sales

Some businesses conduct many special sales, but others seldom have them. The management must therefore decide the advantages and the disadvantages of special sales and determine which types of sales are most effective for that particular type of retail business.

Many merchants feel that continuous markdown sales have a strong tendency to turn regular customers into bargain hunters. Such sales build up a sales resistance to the merchandise when it is offered at regular prices. More money is generally made on business done at regular prices than on a greater volume produced by a policy of continual special sales. A business may find that winning customers from competing stores by holding continual sales at low prices may actually make profits less instead of greater because the customers may buy only the low-priced goods instead of the items that produce a reasonable profit. A large volume of sales alone does not mean profits.

For every special sale that a business conducts, there should be a good reason. It is better to have a few special sales and to see that the customers are given extraordinary values than it is to have a large number of special sales. The customers of today are better informed than those of a generation ago and so are naturally curious as to the reason for a special sale. If they are given the real reason for the sale, they are more likely to believe in the worthwhileness of the sale.

Types of Special Sales. There are two general types of special sales— clearance sales and stimulative sales.

ILLUS. 8-3. Having a few special sales in which customers may obtain real
bargains is better than having a large number of special sales.

Clearance Sales. Most stores accumulate certain pieces of merchandise that did not sell at the regular prices. In order to make room
for new stock and to dispose of the old items before they become unsalable, stores often have *clearance sales.* These are usually held at the
close of a season. For example, a women's clothing store may have a
clearance sale of summer clothing in August. If a business is careful
in its buying, however, there should be little need for clearance sales.
In order to avoid general clearance sales, many stores use bargain tables
as a means of disposing of excess goods. In some stores the bargain
basement serves the same purpose. The bargain basement, however,
usually handles lower priced merchandise than that carried in the other
parts of the store and does not serve as a place for the disposal of slow-
moving stock.

Stimulative Sales. The other type of special sale is known as the
stimulative sale. Its primary objective is to stimulate business. The
following are some of the purposes of stimulative sales:

1. Introducing new kinds of goods.

2. Offering the customer especially good bargains in new goods purchased at bargain prices.

3. Calling attention to a special department or special kinds of goods that customers have seemingly neglected.

4. Stimulating sales in traditionally slack periods.

Forms of Special Sales. Special sales take many different forms, some of which are listed below:

Anniversary sales	Back-to-school sales
Pre-inventory sales	Half-price sales
Post-inventory sales	One-cent sales
Warehouse sales	After-Christmas sales

If the offerings at these sales are not as they have been represented, customers become rather skeptical of sales in general and doubt the genuineness of a real special sale when one is carried on.

Manufacturers sometimes have various forms of sales, or "deals." As part of such a sale the manufacturer furnishes display materials and sometimes cooperates with the retailer in advertising the merchandise in other ways. In most cases free goods, such as dishes, spoons, and cake pans, that are given with merchandise in retail stores have been obtained by the retailers as special inducements from the manufacturers. For example, the manufacturer may offer ten cases of his product at a special discount and give a certain number of dishes free. The retailer then conducts a special sale and gives away the dishes as an inducement for his customers to buy.

Planning Special Sales. If special sales are to be successful, both in immediate financial returns and in building customer goodwill, they must be planned carefully. In large retail stores there is usually a *sales promotion manager,* who is a specialist in this type of activity. In small businesses the owner is his own sales promotion manager.

Before any sale is started, many factors must be considered. For instance, a special sale may fail if it is promoted at the time that a neighboring competitor is having a similar sale. A merchant must be familiar with the prices of competing merchandise so that when he sponsors a sale his prices will be reasonable in comparison with competitive prices. Business conditions may be so bad that a sale may prove to be a failure. On the other hand, a special sale may be just the thing that is needed to stimulate business.

The advertising should be prepared well in advance of the actual time of the sale. It should be truthful, telling the facts about the merchandise. If the merchandise is slightly soiled from handling or is of second quality, or if the sizes are broken, the advertisement should indicate the fact. Such words as *stupendous, mammoth,* and *colossal* should be avoided. These words long ago lost their power to attract the majority of people. In cities the advertising should appear in the newspapers on the day before the sale. If it should appear too long before the sale, its effect would be lost before the time of the sale. Furthermore, if the sale is announced too far in advance, it may prevent customers from coming into the store for normal purchases because they will wait until the time of the sale.

Regular customers should be mailed notices of the sales event. Illustration 8-4 is an example of such a notice. Special window displays that are dignified, rather than gaudy and cheap, should be arranged for the goods on sale. The merchandise being featured should be indicated clearly by cards that tell the price and something about the quality and the value of the goods. It may be a good plan to place other attractive goods where customers are likely to see them as they walk through the store looking for the goods on special sale.

Leaders and Loss Leaders

Some businesses, such as groceries and drugstores, make use of leaders and loss leaders. *Leaders* are items sold at markups much below the usual ones. *Loss leaders* are items sold below the cost plus the estimated expense of handling the items.

Some state laws prohibit sales below invoice cost; in certain other states sales cannot be made below invoice cost plus 6 percent. Those businesses which follow a policy of offering loss leaders believe that it will create an atmosphere of low prices for a store and will attract attention and draw customers who will buy other articles in addition to the loss leaders. There is danger that some customers will buy only these specially priced items.

For these leader items, businesses usually choose items that customers buy frequently and whose customary prices are well known. Items of standard quality are usually chosen so that customers will not think the lower price means lower quality.

Improving Off-Season Sales

Many businesses have certain periods in the year when the volume of sales declines considerably. For example, the sale of fur coats and

r
r   **RUGGLES & ROBERTSON**
        4565 CHOUTEAU AVENUE   ST. LOUIS, MO 63110

April 17, 19--

Mr. Charles Daniels
1006 Ellington Drive
St. Louis, MO 63121

Dear Mr. Daniels

Since you are one of our faithful customers, we invite
you to a private clearance sale of our spring suits
and slacks on April 24 and 25.

Beginning on April 26 there will be a general sale of
these suits and slacks to the public, but in the meantime, we want to give you a special opportunity to make
your selection before the merchandise is put on general
sale.

We have available for your inspection a fine selection
of colors and weaves with suit sizes ranging from 38
to 46, and slacks, sizes 26 to 38.

If you will come in on either April 24 or 25, I shall
give you my personal attention.

        Sincerely

        RUGGLES & ROBERTSON

        George Robertson

        George Robertson
        Manager

jf

ILLUS. 8-4. Letter sent to customers announcing a sale.

winter clothing is usually very small during July and August; fishing and boating equipment sales are low during the winter months.

To increase sales in traditionally slack periods, special merchandising efforts must be made. Some things that might be done are as follows:

1. Advance the selling season of new merchandise, such as featuring fur coat sales in August.
2. Feature special items in connection with holidays or local historical days, such as July 4, the anniversary of the founding of the city, and the like.
3. Use bargain tables regularly to feature unadvertised special items.
4. Award a prize to each hundredth customer, with the names of the winners posted in the store. The prizes would be from the merchandise being featured.
5. Make value and price the basic appeals of the items being promoted.

SERVING CUSTOMERS

The problem of providing extra services was discussed previously as a factor in determining the selling price. The providing of various services does not necessarily require an increase in selling prices. For instance, a full-service department store does not always have higher prices, but it often does. If a business that offers many services is operated economically, it may make a greater profit than one not offering any. In many types of stores it is necessary to offer certain services in order to obtain business. For instance, credit may have to be extended in order to obtain certain kinds of customers. Because of competition, many department stores have established delivery service, gift-wrapping counters, free parcel checkrooms, restaurants, rest rooms, and beauty parlors. The retailer may find it necessary, especially in cities, to make some provision for parking automobiles if he wishes to attract customers. He may operate his own parking lot, or he may arrange to pay the charges for his customer at a parking lot nearby. Manufacturers quite often have to furnish engineering service, laboratory testing facilities, and technical advice. From the point of view of retail stores, delivery service is one of the most important merchandising services.

Delivery Service

The nature of many businesses requires delivery service for customers. For example, in cases in which the customer purchases heavy or bulky articles, delivery is imperative. In some types of businesses the competition is so keen that delivery service is furnished to build up goodwill in an effort to win and keep customers. Some businesses probably could increase their sales volume by furnishing delivery service.

If delivery service is provided, many customers use the service when they do not need it, thereby adding to the operating expenses of the business. If the item purchased is small and light in weight, the salesperson may ask, "Will you take it?" rather than, "Shall I send it?" The customer's answer to the latter question is almost always "Yes," whereas the former question often results in the customer carrying home his purchase.

Rapidly increasing congestion in city streets makes driving and walking more hazardous and makes parking facilities less convenient. This situation, together with extensive buying by telephone, has a tendency to increase the demand for delivery service.

If a business has decided that it will furnish delivery service, its next problem is to decide on the type of service. The two most common types are (a) individually owned delivery equipment and (b) consolidated delivery service.

Individually Owned Equipment. *Individually owned equipment* for delivery service is widely used in almost all kinds of businesses. Under this type of service the delivery equipment is owned by the business that has goods to be delivered. The business hires the necessary drivers and pays all the costs of equipment repairs, storage, delivery supplies, and insurance. Some of the advantages claimed for this type are:

1. The delivery personnel, being employees of the business, make a better contact between the business and the customer than would employees of a delivery company.
2. The delivery equipment can be used for advertising purposes.
3. The style and the quality of the equipment can be in keeping with the character of the business.
4. This type of service permits more flexibility in delivery routes and schedules.

If this plan of delivery service is used, the personnel should be chosen carefully. The deliveryman is legally a representative of his company, and the company is therefore responsible for his acts. He should have a good personality, since he comes into direct contact with the customer almost as much as does the salesperson. If he is capable, he can do much to facilitate adjustments and to smooth out the complaints of customers.

Consolidated Delivery Service. *Consolidated delivery service* is used when several stores make a contract with some other privately owned business to take care of deliveries for them. Some of the advantages of using such service are:

1. The store need not invest large amounts of capital in equipment.
2. This method usually reduces delivery costs, since the contract commonly provides for a charge of so much per unit. Thus, when sales are slack, the delivery costs are low; but if the business owned its own equipment, the depreciation and other overhead expenses would occur just the same. Stores in a large city found that their delivery expenses were reduced from 15 to 25 percent after they had adopted a consolidated delivery system.
3. Small businesses can have their deliveries made as promptly as larger ones. It may also be possible for the small businessman to give delivery service to his customers, even though his business is too small to warrant purchasing delivery equipment.
4. Consolidated service eliminates the problems of management of the employees needed to operate and service the equipment.
5. Consolidated service shifts to the owners of the delivery trucks the responsibility for damage suits growing out of accidents caused by the delivery equipment.

Other Types of Delivery Service. Other types of delivery service used by businesses include parcel post, express, and freight. It is important to know the costs of each type of delivery service so that the most economical method may be used for various items and for shipments being made over varying distances.

Convenient Hours of Operation

If a business is to serve customers, it must be open at hours that are convenient for the customers. Of course, the hours of operation vary greatly with different businesses. A laundry and dry-cleaning business needs to be open early enough in the morning for customers to leave the laundry and garments on their way to work. Similarly, it is desirable for it to be open so that people on their way home from work may pick up the finished laundry and dry cleaning.

Many businesses stay open in the evenings to encourage family shopping. For large items such as automobiles, stoves, refrigerators, furniture, and clothes, husband and wife frequently shop together. Therefore, they usually do such shopping during the evening or on Saturday. A survey showed that a couple shopping together in a supermarket buys 60 percent more than the husband shopping alone and 30 percent more than the wife shopping alone.

Returned Goods

A survey of eleven department stores in Boston disclosed that in one year's time approximately $20 million worth of merchandise purchased by customers was returned. This amount represented nearly 12½ percent of the total sales. In a survey of the large stores in Pittsburgh, Chicago, and New York City, a similar condition was found. In some stores the percentage of returns was a little smaller than that found in the Boston stores; in others it was a little larger.

Studies made of the kinds of goods returned showed that dresses were returned most frequently (see Illustration 8-5). These surveys indicate that the return of merchandise purchased by customers is an important problem to most stores and particularly to those handling clothing.

Manufacturers and distributors have similar problems pertaining to returned goods. For instance, a manufacturer may sell to a wholesaler or a retailer more goods than the retailer can sell. In order to maintain the goodwill of the retailer, the manufacturer may accept the return of some of the merchandise. Sometimes manufacturers will take back perishable merchandise to protect the reputation of the goods.

Kind of Goods	Percentage of Return
Dresses	25.4%
Women's and misses' wear	10.9
Shoes	10.5
Men's furnishings	6.7
Gloves	5.9
Hosiery	5.7
Furniture	3.3
Notions	3.0
Millinery	2.6
Groceries	2.4

ILLUS. 8-5. Frequency with which different kinds of goods are returned.

Occasionally a new product is put on the market that sells well for a while and then ceases to sell. The manufacturers and the distributors sometimes have to take back from the retailers the unsold goods. These difficulties often arise from the fact that manufacturers and wholesalers sell to retailers larger quantities than they should.

Effect of Returned Merchandise on Profits and Selling Prices. The handling of sales returns is an expensive activity for a business. Some of the usual activities in connection with a sale and a return are: making the original sale, wrapping the merchandise, recording the sale, delivering the merchandise, handling the complaint (either by telephone, by letter, or in person), having the article picked up by the delivery truck, recording and inspecting it upon arrival back at the store or the warehouse, making the proper accounting record of the return, and placing the merchandise back in stock for resale. Some returns may cost several dollars, but some may cost only a few cents, with an average expense of approximately 90 cents for each return.

In addition, there is often depreciation (loss of value) due to handling of the merchandise or delaying the return of it. For example, if a woman purchases a new spring dress and keeps it for two weeks

ILLUS. 8-6. Handling returned merchandise is an expensive activity for a business.

before returning it, the delay in making the return may prevent the store from selling the dress to someone else. If a store has a large number of returns, it must carry a large inventory of merchandise. Some of the merchandise will always be in the hands of customers; and, although it will be returned eventually, it will not be available to show to other customers until it is returned. This loss greatly affects the prices at which goods must be marked originally in order that the business may make a net profit. If stores that have many returns fail to consider this expense, they are likely to operate at a loss.

Reasons for Merchandise Returns. It is good management for a store to attempt to reduce as much as possible the amount of merchandise returned by customers. Before taking action to bring about a reduction in returned merchandise, the management of a business must study the reasons for merchandise returns. The results of one study on customer reasons for returning goods are shown in Illustration 8-7.

Reasons for Returns	Percentage of All the Returns
Wrong size	37.2%
Unsatisfactory merchandise	16.5
Goods that did not match	15.6
Change of mind	15.0
Faulty merchandise	13.0
Misrepresentation of the store	1.2
Disapproval of the person for whom the merchandise was purchased	1.2
Unsatisfactory delivery service	.3
	100.0%

ILLUS. 8-7. Frequency of reasons given for returning goods.

In the study summarized in Illustration 8-7, "wrong size" was the most frequently given reason for returning merchandise. This reason is most prominent largely because of the faulty memory of customers who ask for wrong sizes or because of guesswork when an item is being purchased for someone else. Sometimes the salespersons are to blame because they do not know the correct size to suggest. For example, the customer gives the shoe size of the one for whom hosiery is being purchased, but the salesperson suggests the wrong hosiery size.

REVIEW WHAT YOU HAVE LEARNED

Business Terms Checkup:

(1) business-promotion letter
(2) clearance sale
(3) stimulative sale
(4) sales promotion manager
(5) leaders
(6) loss leaders
(7) individually owned equipment
(8) consolidated delivery service

Reading Checkup:

1. Why must a business be continually looking for new customers?
2. State some methods used by manufacturers to find prospects.
3. Mention some methods used by retail stores in obtaining customers.
4. What are some common types of special sales?
5. Does a bargain basement usually handle lower priced merchandise than that carried in other parts of the store?
6. Is it desirable to make frequent use of such words as *stupendous, mammoth,* and *colossal* in a store's advertising?
7. Do the laws in some states prohibit the use of loss leaders?
8. What is meant by off-season sales?
9. Give three advantages of each general type of delivery service.
10. Merchandise returned by customers was approximately what percentage of the total sales of large department stores in Boston?
11. Examine the statistics on page 147 concerning the kinds of goods returned and state which type had the largest percentage and which the smallest.
12. Examine the report on page 149 showing the reasons given by customers for returning goods purchased and state the principal reason given.

APPLY WHAT YOU HAVE LEARNED

Questions for Class Discussion:

1. How would it be possible for a manufacturer of commercial laundry soaps to prepare a list of prospects for a large city?
2. Why are many people rather skeptical of special sales in general?
3. What policies might a store adopt to avoid having general clearance sales?
4. What are some purposes of stimulative sales?
5. Discuss the characteristics of leader items.
6. Explain why one needs to consider carefully the time for holding a special sale.

Problems and Projects:

1. Compare the total annual delivery costs under the following plans:

    (a) Individually owned equipment. Cost, $10,000; depreciation, 20 percent; truck repairs, $310; gasoline, oil, and grease, $600; insurance, $305; storage, $240; driver's salary, $6,000.

    (b) Contract plan. 4,400 packages at 25¢; 5,650 packages at 40¢; 2,400 packages at 50¢; 1,000 packages at 80¢; 440 packages at $2.50; 200 packages at $6. (Rates vary with package sizes.)

2. Many department stores in large cities recognize that transportation is a problem for customers.

    (a) Name two helps that might be offered to customers who come to the store in their own automobiles.

    (b) Suggest a help that might be offered to those who come on buses.

3. Make a survey of several types of businesses in your community and find out what hours they are open. Give a report on your findings.

Case Problem 8-1:

The Taylor Marine Sales located in Buffalo, New York, sells pleasure boats, outboard motors, and small boating equipment and supplies. Most of their sales are made in April, May, June, and July.

Required:

Explain the special promotion activities that they might use to encourage sales in the so-called off-season.

Case Problem 8-2:

The Barker Appliance Store, located in a neighborhood shopping area in a large city, will stock such household items as refrigerators, automatic washing machines and dryers, electric and gas kitchen stoves, portable electric heaters, and room air-conditioners. The retail store plans to be open daily, Mondays through Saturdays, from 10 a.m. until 5 p.m.

Required:

Do you think it desirable for the store to be open one or more evenings for the convenience of customers?

Continuing Project:

Determine your merchandising policies and procedures, including sales promotion, getting the business started, services that you will offer, specific policies concerning merchandise returns, and your policy relating to hours of operation.

What abilities and traits should a salesperson have?

How does a salesperson greet a customer?

What motives cause people to buy?

What information about a product do customers usually desire?

How should a salesperson close the sale?

What is meant by suggestion selling?

BACKGROUND OF CHAPTER

A good salesperson is always in demand. Since nearly all of a business' income results from the sale of products or services, it is important that the firm have a competent sales staff. A personable, helpful salesman builds a clientele for the business. A disagreeable, uninformed salesperson can drive customers away.

The business manager must select his sales representatives with care to make certain that his staff will properly represent the firm and serve its customers. A sales training program usually helps assure that the individual will make a maximum contribution to the business.

This chapter deals with a number of the problems often faced in selling situations.

CHAPTER 9

SALESMANSHIP

In any sale there are four elements: the customer, the business, the merchandise or the service, and the salesperson. The salesperson bridges the gap between the customer and the business. The success of the business depends, to a great extent, upon the quality and the price of the goods or services; but its success is also very dependent upon good salesmanship.

TRAITS AND ABILITIES NEEDED BY SALESPEOPLE

The salesperson is the employee who probably makes the most contacts with customers and therefore has a good opportunity to build goodwill for his organization; but the other employees also may have a great deal to do with keeping customers satisfied or causing a loss of customers. The delivery boy can easily lose goodwill by poor delivery service. Errors made by employees in the bookkeeping department or in the delivery department also have an undesirable effect upon customers. Even the manner in which telephone calls are handled has its effect.

In a survey of several hundred stores, the customers who had stopped patronizing the stores gave these reasons:

Indifference of salespeople	9%
Lack of knowledge of goods and misrepresentation of goods	8
Haughtiness of salespeople	7
High-pressure salesmanship	6
Mistakes and poor service	17
Unwillingness to make adjustments	10
Attempted substitution of goods	6
Prices too high	14
Merchandise of inferior quality	10
Slipshod store methods	13
	100%

Let us look at the matter from another angle. What do customers like? An investigation as to what customers liked about the businesses with which they were dealing showed the following items, which are arranged according to their importance as stated by the customers:

1. A sufficient variety of stock from which to choose.
2. Prices comparable to the quality of the merchandise.
3. Pleasant and helpful employees.
4. Willingness to make adjustments in case of errors and returns.
5. Truthful statements about the goods and the services.
6. An attractive store (including lighting, ventilation, equipment, and arrangement).
7. Service features, such as delivery, charge accounts, and free parking for automobiles.

Since items 3 and 5 are principally dependent upon the personality of employees, it is evident that the employee plays a very important part in the success of a business.

If a business is so small that one person can take care of all the phases of operation, it is extremely important that this one individual possess or develop a personality that will build goodwill for the business. *Personality* is a term given to a person's attitudes, habits, and traits. Should the business be so large that many employees, in addition to the owner, are needed, it is important that the owner know what qualities are desirable in his employees, especially his salespeople.

Courtesy

Courtesy is not only expected but also demanded by customers. One who is courteous will be patient, sympathetic, and always considerate of the feelings of both the customer and the co-workers in the business. He will devote his attention to the customer, will listen attentively without interruption, will become interested in the problems of his customer, and will give respectful consideration to the opinions of others.

Enthusiasm

Enthusiasm makes work a pleasure instead of a drudgery; it makes one an optimist instead of a pessimist. People like to associate with persons who are cheerful. One can hardly expect customers to be enthusiastic about goods or services unless the salesperson explaining

ILLUS. 9-1. The salesperson should continually check to make sure he is exhibiting desirable personality characteristics.

them is enthusiastic. Likewise, the owner or manager of a business cannot expect his employees to be enthusiastic about methods and procedures used in the operation of the business unless he himself is enthusiastic about them. Enthusiasm is contagious. The attractive personality has a plentiful supply of enthusiasm that can be spread to others. Enthusiasm is based upon knowledge. So to develop enthusiasm, one should find out in what way or ways his goods, services, or ideas are better than those of others. He should then emphasize these points.

Memory

A good memory is a distinct asset to one in business. Remembering the names of customers so as to greet them by name the next time they call makes an appeal to their vanity. Remembering the likes and dislikes of a customer will aid in better serving that customer.

Tact

Many persons in business who have some splendid qualities have lost goodwill and customers for their business because they lacked tact. They did not have the ability to do or say the proper thing so as not to offend others. The shoe salesperson who comments to a customer, "You have a foot that is unusually hard to fit," displays a lack of tact.

Imagination

The ability of a salesperson to form mental images of things and activities enables him to visualize products in use. Most customers are interested more in the use of a product than in the product itself.

Industriousness

Industriousness is essential to business success. The proprietor who is willing to work many extra hours after regular business hours in planning and taking care of the many details of his business will find that his industriousness pays dividends. The industrious salesperson will never have difficulty in finding things to do between sales. He will rearrange and care for his goods. He will call customers to tell them of merchandise in which he knows they will be interested. He will study his merchandise in order to learn more about it and its possible uses. The industrious traveling salesman will plan his schedule of calls so as to make the best use of his time, and he will learn as much as possible about a prospect or customer before he calls on him.

Resourcefulness

Resourcefulness is the ability to deal effectively with different and unexpected situations. It is needed by the salesperson as he deals with different types of customers, answers objections raised by customers, suggests desirable substitute articles, and handles unexpected problems.

Personal Appearance

One's personal appearance makes a definite impression on anyone whom one meets for the first time. One may have many desirable personality traits and still not make a favorable impression because of an unfavorable personal appearance. A good personal appearance helps to command the respect of others and also helps to give one self-confidence in meeting people.

One's personal care has a great deal to do with one's appearance. Care should be taken to have clean teeth, clean hands, clean fingernails, and a scalp that is free from dandruff and greasy hair dressings. Using cosmetics to excess and extreme styles in hair should be avoided by women in saleswork. One should also guard against body odors that may offend others.

The clothing of the owner of a business or that of his employees should be in keeping with the position. For example, the clothing worn by a salesman in an exclusive men's apparel store should be of high quality. The salesperson's clothes should be clean, well pressed, and in good repair. Many kinds of businesses, such as restaurants, service stations, laundries, dairies, and beauty parlors, find it desirable to have their employees wear uniforms. Good taste in clothing avoids extremes of style.

Other physical factors, such as health, physique, posture, and even manner of walking, have an influence on others. The tone and the inflection of one's voice, as well as one's enunciation, have their effect. Some large organizations consider good speech so important that a course in speech training is given to salespersons.

Mannerisms

Successful salespeople must avoid mannerisms that are distracting to the customer. There are mannerisms of speech, posture, voice, gesture, and the like. Continually clearing one's throat, constantly repeating such phrases as "You know what I mean?", winking an eye, and sitting in a slouched position are examples of mannerisms.

KNOWLEDGE AND SKILLS NEEDED IN DEALING WITH CUSTOMERS

There are many types of customers, and the salesman must be able to adjust himself to each type. There are customers who come into the store knowing exactly what they want. They do not want to listen to long explanations about the goods. Some customers constantly change their minds when being shown goods. When handling them, the salesman usually should show only one article at a time. Some people who come into retail stores are not interested in any particular article but are just looking around. These people require detailed information about the goods and a demonstration, if possible. Some customers are talkative, some are the silent type, some are irritable, some are ill-mannered, some are suspicious, and some always want a concession. The successful salesperson must be able to handle all types.

Greeting the Customer

There is no one best way of greeting a customer. Circumstances will vary the greeting to be used. When calling on a stranger who is the manager or owner of a business, it is desirable that the traveling salesman greet the customer by name and introduce himself. Successful salesmen often make some introductory remark about the customer's business that will let him know that the salesman is interested in his business and his problems.

In retail stores there are many suitable greetings. "Good afternoon" or "How do you do?" are rather formal but are suitable in greeting strangers who have not indicated an interest in any specific article. "May I help you?" is commonly used and may be suitable when one does not know whether the customer wishes to be waited on or prefers to look around.

Frequently the best greeting to use when a customer is already look-ing at some article on display in the store is to make some comment about the article. The salesperson, noticing a customer looking at a dress, may say, "That is an unusually attractive pattern, isn't it?" or "That is the dress which is advertised in this month's *Vogue*." Such a greeting stimulates the customer's interest and makes it easy for the salesperson to explain the fine features of the dress. An approach of this kind is known as the *merchandise approach*. It is a commonly used method in retail stores.

Should the name of the customer be known, it is usually effective to include the customer's name in the greeting. The attitude of the salesperson as shown by his manner, by his tone of voice, and by his facial expression should reflect a genuine interest in the customer and is much more important than the actual words used in greeting the customer. Many retail salespeople approach customers in a bored fashion and do not have the proper attitude of helpfulness.

Promptness in greeting a customer is important. A customer in a restaurant appreciates having a glass of water and the menu handed him promptly even though he may be in no hurry. Even if a customer seems to be browsing, the retail salesperson can acknowledge the pres-ence of the customer by a brief greeting.

Studying the Wants of Customers

The salesperson who attempts to sell candy to a child by emphasiz-ing the quality probably will not succeed. On the other hand, the salesperson who emphasizes the quantity of a certain kind of candy that can be purchased for a dime probably will make a sale because he understands the important reason that usually causes a child to prefer one kind of candy to another. If one wishes to be successful in satisfy-ing customers, he must study and understand human nature. Why do people buy? What wants do they have, and how can those wants be satisfied?

Many motives cause people to buy. Some of the most important of these so-called *buying motives* are listed below:

Imitation	Amusement
Desire for ease and comfort	Desire for bargains (thrift)
Affection	Desire for good health
Appetite	Pride of possession
Love of beauty	Desire for recognition
Desire for money	Envy
Fear	

To be successful, the salesperson must know what is likely to be the buying motive of a particular customer and then make his sales talk and demonstration appeal to that motive. In many cases appeals can be made to more than one buying motive. For instance, a laundry representative, in attempting to sell the services of his company to a housewife who has a family of three persons and financial means that are a little above average, may talk about the comfort and convenience of having her laundry done by his company rather than doing it herself. He may also explain that it is less expensive to send the laundry to his company because of all the expenses that are involved in doing it at home.

Suppose that this same laundry representative were calling upon the proprietor of a barber shop or a beauty parlor. In such a case he

ILLUS. 9-2. To be successful the salesperson needs to know the customer's buying motive.

could emphasize the special sterilizing treatment given to linens and the high degree of whiteness in the laundered linens, factors which would aid in keeping customers of the barber or the beauty-parlor operator satisfied and also help in attracting other customers.

When several buying motives may be appealed to, the salesperson can often make brief appeals to different ones and carefully observe the reaction of the customer. He can usually discover which is the most important appeal and then emphasize that particular one.

In other words, it is a sound policy in selling to attempt to determine human wants and buying motives and then attempt to satisfy those wants and motives. Providing satisfaction through a sale is the ultimate goal of a salesperson. This method of selling does not mean high-pressure selling; it means intelligent selling.

Giving Information About the Product

If a salesperson is to be of the most service to his customer, he must understand the wants or needs of his customer. In addition, he must have a thorough knowledge of his goods or services in order that he may be able to suggest that which best fits the needs of the customer. In many cases the customer looks to the salesperson for expert advice. The landscape gardener who suggests the wrong kinds of plants and shrubs for a particular kind of soil in which they are to be planted; the salesperson who suggests the wrong kind of furniture polish for a particular kind of furniture; the oil salesman who suggests the wrong kind of oil for a certain machine; and the hairdresser who uses a coiffure that is not becoming to her customer will quickly lose the goodwill of their customers.

Uses of the Product or Service. Customers are usually interested in what the articles or the services will do for them and how they can be used. Hence it is important that the salesperson should have a thorough knowledge of the various uses of his product, as well as its limitations. Even in the simple case of apples, the successful salesman will know which apples are best suited for baking, which are to be preferred for making sauce, and which are desirable as eating apples. Likewise, in selling dry-cleaning preparations, the salesperson must know upon what type or types of materials each preparation should be used. He can render a very valuable service to his customers in this way.

The primary uses of an article are usually known to the customer, but the salesman should be able to convince the customer that the article is suited for the customer's particular purpose. The salesman should also point out the versatility of the article by explaining its secondary uses. For example, the primary use of a vacuum cleaner is to clean rugs and carpets; but a particular cleaner may also be used to clean drapes or upholstery and even to mothproof articles.

Knowledge of the Merchandise. A thorough knowledge of the merchandise is necessary so that the salesperson may answer questions that are asked about the merchandise. The following questions are examples of those that customers might ask: "How much paint will I need for a bathroom six feet by eight feet?" "Which paint is best for a concrete basement floor?" "Can this dress be laundered?" "Why is this pair of shoes $18 and that pair $15?"

One of the best ways for a salesperson to prepare himself to render service to the customer is to obtain information concerning the kind, quality, cost, and source of materials used in the manufacture of his product. These factors affect the price, wearing quality, appearance, uses, and the care of an article. For example, the fact that a certain piece of clothing is made of cotton, wool, rayon, nylon, orlon, dacron, silk, or a combination of two or more of these has a decided effect upon the care that should be given the article in cleaning. It also has a definite influence upon the wearing quality, appearance, and price.

A knowledge of the processes used in manufacturing an article should be valuable to a salesperson. The dyeing of a piece of cloth or clothing may have been done by the process known as *stock dyeing*. Under this method the raw material is dyed before it is spun into yarn and woven into cloth. Thus, the cloth will be colorfast because the dyes have thoroughly penetrated the fibers. Another piece of cloth may have been dyed by the process called *piece dyeing*. Under this method the dyeing is done after the cloth has been woven. The piece of cloth is dipped into the dye bath. This method is less expensive, but such color is less durable than that which was stock dyed. Knowing that certain products are "handmade" and still others are "not touched by human hands" is important information.

Different items of information about the same product may appeal to different persons. For instance, a safety feature on a washing machine will appeal to both the wife and the husband. Simplicity of operation or some novelty feature may appeal to the wife. Sturdiness of construction will appeal to the husband. In order to find out the various features of a product, a successful salesman should study his product as well as competing products and should always be prepared to show why his product is worth the price that is being asked for it.

Proper Care of Article. In order that the customer will receive a full measure of service, he should be given definite information as to the proper care of the article he is purchasing. The purchaser of a dry-cleaning preparation should be given complete directions for using it. The customer who has purchased a pair of gloves should be told whether they should be laundered or dry-cleaned. If they should be laundered, she should be told the best means of laundering, including the kind of soap to be used, the correct temperature of the water, and the best method of drying. A company selling plants and shrubs will want to give the customer suggestions as to the best methods of caring for them. Failure to give the customer proper instructions on the use and care of the product he has purchased is likely to result in the customer's failing to get the best service from the product. He may, therefore, become dissatisfied with both the product and the business that sold it, even though the product is of the proper quality.

Sources of Information. The salesperson may obtain specific selling points about merchandise from many sources such as the following:

1. Examination of the merchandise. The salesperson should carefully examine the goods and also use them, if possible. Labels put on products by the manufacturer often contain helpful information.
2. The manufacturer. Booklets and circulars explaining the principal characteristics of the product are usually published by the manufacturer. Additional information may be secured by writing to the manufacturer.
3. Magazine and newspaper advertisements.
4. Representatives of the manufacturer. They possess valuable information about their products and are willing to pass it along to interested persons.
5. Technical books and magazines found in public libraries.
6. Customers, if they have already had experience with the product.
7. Fellow salespeople who are acquainted with the merchandise.

Showing the Goods

In addition to giving the customer information about the goods, the salesperson should effectively show the goods in order that the customer may be convinced that they will best fit his needs. This is sometimes referred to as creating desire on the part of the customer.

ILLUS. 9-3. The salesperson should show the product as he is giving information about it.

It is usually a good plan to show the article as information about the article is being given. The attention of the customer is then centered on the article as its merits and advantages are convincingly explained.

Goods should be shown to the best advantage. By handling the article carefully and showing respect for it, the salesperson enhances its value in the customer's mind. For example, the value of a piece of sterling silver is enhanced when the salesperson handles it very carefully and admiringly places it on a piece of velvet.

An effective way of convincing the customer is to show the article in action as it would be used by the customer. A sewing machine may be demonstrated by sewing some samples for the customer; a furniture polish, by actually polishing a piece of furniture; a radio or television, by tuning in different stations.

Whenever possible, the customer should be encouraged to participate in the demonstration—to operate the vacuum cleaner, to type on the typewriter, to try on a hat, or to drive the automobile. Such activity on the part of the customer has much influence in changing his interest to a desire to own the article.

Handling Objections

Even though the sales talk and demonstration are carefully given and seem to have proved the worth of the goods, some customers will raise objections. Some objections are only excuses and are not the real reason why the customer has not bought the goods. He may object to the particular style of the goods when the real reason is the fact that the price is too high. Often, because the salesperson has not been convincing in his sales talk, the customer states that he wishes to "think it over before deciding." It is necessary that the salesman use his keenest powers of observation to decide whether the objection raised is the real reason why the customer does not buy. Many sales have not been made because customers have not expressed their objections and the salesmen have not been clever enough to discover them.

The successful salesperson learns as much as possible about products of his competitors. This enables him to better answer questions about competing products raised by his prospective customers. Such knowledge also will enable him to stress the qualities of his product that are superior to the competing products.

A commonly used method of meeting an objection is to turn the objection skillfully into a selling point. For example, a businessman states, "Business is so poor I cannot afford to buy calendars." The salesperson meets the objection by saying, "That is just why you need calendars. They will stimulate your business." Some salesmen insist that practically every objection can be met in such a manner.

Another method of meeting an objection is to admit the truth of the objection but show that such is only a slight disadvantage when compared with the advantages. Thus, the salesman of advertising space in a newspaper in answering the objection that there was waste in such advertising stated, "It is true that some few readers of the newspaper are not potential customers for you; but your message will reach those who are potential customers for less than one fourth the cost of direct-mail advertising."

When a prospective buyer raises a price objection, it probably indicates that the sales talk has not convinced him of the value of the product. It is necessary that he then be presented with more reasons why the price is reasonable. Although the salesman should be ready to answer objections effectively, a careful presentation of his sales talk and demonstration will prevent many objections from being raised. It is, therefore, a good plan to give considerable time and study to the preparation of the presentation.

Closing the Sale

The successful closing of a sale comes as a result of a sales talk and demonstration so convincing that the customer is thoroughly sold on the product. When the salesperson believes that the customer is ready to give his approval, a skillful closing will make it easy to complete the sale. Most customers resent a salesperson who uses high-pressure methods in closing the sale, but tactful suggestions may secure favorable action on the part of the customer.

A simple method of closing is to ask the customer a question that requires him to make a buying decision. The following are frequently used:

"Do you prefer the Empire Brand or the Carter Brand?"
"Will three shirts be enough?"
"Do you wish to take it with you or shall I send it?"
"Shall I wrap this one for you?"
"Shall I charge it to your account?"

The salesperson should not attempt to close the sale until the customer seems ready to make a decision. To do otherwise would cause the prospective customer to regard the act as pressure salesmanship.

The customer can be made to feel satisfied with his purchase by the salesperson who makes such comments as the following: "I am sure you will be pleased with your dress" or "You have made a wise choice in selecting this machine." The customer should be thanked sincerely for having made the purchase. Should no sale have been made, the salesperson should thank the customer for the opportunity of showing the goods and extend a cordial invitation to come again.

Suggestion Selling

Have you had the experience of buying a fountain pen and having the salesman suggest that you buy a mechanical pencil to match the pen? Or have you observed a man when he purchased a shirt and the salesperson suggested a necktie to match? Such activity on the part of salespeople is known as *suggestion selling*. Suggestion selling takes place when the salesperson calls the attention of the customer to goods not definitely asked for.

One kind of suggestion selling takes place when the salesperson recommends the purchase of an item related to what the customer has just bought. A customer has just purchased a can of paint. The salesman says, "We have just the kind of brush to use with this paint," and hastens to show it to the customer. A women has just purchased some yard goods for a dress, and the salesperson suggests thread and trimmings to match. Gift cards are suggested to a customer who has purchased gifts. These are examples of the suggestion of related articles.

ILLUS. 9-4. Through suggestion selling a salesman can often sell a customer additional items.

Another kind of suggestion selling is recommending to the customer that a larger quantity be purchased. You ask the grocery clerk for a small-sized package of cocoa. He brings you a package that sells for 25 cents and one that sells for 50 cents and tells you that the larger one contains three times as much as the smaller one and yet it sells for only twice as much. Or you ask for a 20-cent can of a certain brand of corn, and the clerk tells you that you can purchase two cans for 35 cents. In self-service supermarkets there is an effort to induce customers to buy in larger quantities by the use of multi-unit packs. Several individual items are fastened together and priced at a reduction from the per unit cost.

You may have asked a salesman to show you medium-priced shirts, but he shows you also a higher priced shirt that has really more quality for its price. This type of selling is called suggestion of higher priced goods.

You may often have gone into a store for a particular brand of goods, but the salesman told you that that brand was not carried. He did, however, show you a similar brand stocked by the store. Or you may have told the salesman the purpose for which you intended to use the particular brand, and he may have suggested that another brand was more suitable for your needs. This type of selling is known as the suggestion of a substitute.

In addition to the four kinds of suggestion selling explained in the preceding paragraphs, there is another kind in which the customer's attention is called to merchandise that at that time has been specially priced or that is being featured in the advertising of the store or the manufacturer.

Is Suggestion Selling Desirable? If the salesperson really uses suggestion and does not attempt to force unwanted goods upon the customer, then suggestion selling is desirable from the viewpoint of both the customer and of the store. Calling attention to related goods may save the customer from making an extra trip to the store later to buy the related article. It may also furnish him with related goods that more closely suit his original purchase than would related goods that were purchased elsewhere. Likewise, suggesting to the customer that by purchasing a larger quantity he can get the goods at a lower price, suggesting a higher priced article when it means more quality for its price, and suggesting substitute brands should be of value to customers and should be considered part of the service a salesman can give.

To a business suggestion selling has great possibilities for increasing sales by getting customers to purchase related items instead of buying them from competitors. The increased sales should result not only in larger net profits but also in a greater percentage of net profit because the additional sales cause only a little increase in overhead expenses.

Guides in Suggestion Selling. All suggestions should be based on a thorough knowledge of the merchandise and on a sincere desire to be of service to the customer. To be effective, the suggestions should be positive, not negative. "Will that be all for this time?" "You wouldn't like some nice strawberries today, would you?" and similar questions are likely to be futile in increasing sales. It would be more effective to say, for instance, "These Tennessee strawberries have an exceptionally fine flavor." The suggestion should be made in an enthusiastic manner, and the salesman should attempt to show or demonstrate the suggested article. In suggesting substitutes, one should avoid such indefinite statements as, "This is just as good as the X brand." If the X brand is a shirt that gained its reputation because of its fast colors, the salesperson might say, "This shirt carries a money-back guarantee that its color will not fade. It also has a collar that needs no starching when being laundered."

Selling by Telephone

There is a growing use of the telephone in selling. It provides a quicker and less expensive method of calling on customers than making personal calls. The telephone is also a convenient method for the customer to use in placing an order. Large stores usually have a person or persons (often known as *shopping service*) who devote all their time to telephone selling. Such persons must have a thorough knowledge of the goods or services of the business and possess an excellent telephone voice and manner.

The telephone can be used by a business as a follow-up to its advertising, as a method of reviving inactive accounts, and to call to the attention of customers special items that may be of interest to them.

How Salesmanship Can Be Improved

An investigation made by the University of Oregon concerning the relative efficiency of 501 retail salespeople in representative lines of business showed the following percentage of salespeople that satisfactorily met the four basic selling requirements:

Making favorable approaches 75%

Having adequate knowledge of goods 54%

Effectively answering objections 36%

Effectively closing sales 30%

This investigation showed that the majority of the salespeople were able to greet customers satisfactorily. Handling them afterward was more troublesome. Approximately one fourth of the salespeople needed to improve their selling approaches; one half needed to increase their knowledge of the goods being sold; about two thirds should improve in their ability to answer objections effectively; and more than two thirds needed to become more proficient in closing deals.

Most businesses find it desirable to provide special training for their salespeople so that they may become more effective. Discussion of different methods of training is given in Chapter 25.

SELF-SERVICE MERCHANDISING

Some types and forms of merchandise can be sold without the aid of a salesperson. Variety stores, supermarkets, greeting card stores, and record shops are examples of stores that have been changing to *self-service* in recent years. Customers are permitted to select the goods they

ILLUS. 9-5. Self-service merchandising is being used today by many types of stores.

wish, take them to a cashier or checkout counter, and pay for them. In some such stores it is desirable to have a few clerks to aid the customers in making selections. Surveys have indicated that customers in self-service stores frequently buy additional items that were not on their original shopping list.

Experts generally agree that successful self-service merchandising requires products which do not require demonstrations or explanations, which have well-known brand names, and which are packaged so that they can be easily handled.

The arrangement (display) of merchandise in self-service stores should be such that it attracts attention and makes it convenient for the shopper to examine the merchandise. It is desirable that the labels on the merchandise provide adequate information about the merchandise for the shopper.

Another type of selling without the aid of a salesperson is that done by vending machines. There has been a large increase in the sale of products by vending machines in recent years.

REVIEW WHAT YOU HAVE LEARNED

Business Terms Checkup:

(1) personality
(2) merchandise approach
(3) buying motives
(4) suggestion selling
(5) shopping service
(6) self-service

Reading Checkup:

1. What four elements are involved in a sale?
2. Give several reasons why customers stop patronizing certain stores.
3. State several reasons why customers like certain stores.
4. Is the merchandise approach considered a good approach?
5. What are some of the most common so-called buying motives?
6. Where can a salesperson obtain information about the products he sells?
7. Why is it desirable to have the customer participate in the demonstration of an article?
8. What is a commonly used method of meeting an objection?
9. Why does a prospective customer usually raise a price objection?
10. Name three kinds of suggestion selling.
11. State two ways in which a store can use the telephone in selling.
12. According to the figures shown by the University of Oregon survey, what percentage of the salespeople seemed to be effective in closing sales?
13. Has self-service merchandising been increasing in recent years?

APPLY WHAT YOU HAVE LEARNED

Questions for Class Discussion:

1. "Every employee is an ambassador of goodwill for his organization." Explain this statement.
2. State six personal traits that are desirable in salespeople and give a specific example of the importance of each.
3. Explain the importance of a good personal appearance to a salesperson.
4. Explain how lack of knowledge about merchandise on the part of the salesperson might build ill will for a business.
5. Is suggestion selling desirable? Discuss.
6. Should the training of salespeople include effective speaking? Explain.
7. What might be desirable information to include on the plastic package containing a man's shirt that is displayed in a self-service store?

Problems and Projects:

1. Give a report on some salesperson you have observed, pointing out good characteristics and also traits that you think are not desirable.

2. List the selling points that you should emphasize in selling each of the following articles: (a) a bicycle, (b) an electric clock, (c) glue.

3. How might the salesperson meet the following objections:
   - **(a)** "I cannot afford the article."
   - **(b)** "A less expensive article will serve my purpose."
   - **(c)** "I shall wait until they are marked down."
   - **(d)** "I want to think it over."
   - **(e)** "I want to see what the other stores have before I decide."

4. Make a report on the different products that are being sold through vending machines. Include those you have observed and those you have learned about from friends, advertisements, and other sources.

Case Problem 9-1:

The Greeting Card and Gift Shop plans to feature in October a box of fifteen assorted Christmas cards for $1.98.

Required:

Make a list of objections that might be encountered and suggest how each might be answered effectively.

Case Problem 9-2:

Ken Harper purchased a television set from your store five years ago. You have just received a shipment of new models.

Required:

Prepare the exact statements you would use in telephoning Harper to tell him about the new models.

Case Problem 9-3:

Assume that you are a salesperson in a furniture store. Explain how you can make appeals to more than one buying motive in attempting to sell to a housewife an upholstered chair for a living room.

Continuing Project:

Set up a plan for selecting, hiring, and training salespeople and policies in regard to selling.

What are the purposes of advertising?

What advertising media may a business use?

How can a businessman obtain mailing lists?

What characterizes a good window display?

How much should a firm spend for advertising?

What is meant by false advertising?

BACKGROUND OF CHAPTER

In a large city there are hundreds of grocery stores, and there are thousands of persons who buy food supplies. How can each store manager reach these persons and try to convince them to shop at his store? He can advertise.

Advertising allows a business to tell customers what makes it unique, what makes it different from all similar businesses. Perhaps it offers low prices, a convenient location, credit, or special customer services. By advertising in newspapers, magazines, over radio or television, the business can tell customers these things. If the advertising is convincing, the business will have the shoppers it needs.

CHAPTER 10

ADVERTISING AND SALES PROMOTION

Before a business can be successful, it must interest persons in buying its goods or services. The principal method used to tell prospective customers about a business and its goods or services is advertising.

Many different kinds of advertising are available. Some kinds are useful for a large business operating on a nationwide scale but are of no value to the person operating a small local business. This chapter will explain the advantages and disadvantages of the principal kinds of advertising and will explain some of the things a businessman should know when planning and conducting an advertising campaign.

PURPOSES OF ADVERTISING

Simply stated, the purpose of advertising is to influence people to buy the merchandise or the service of a business. Thus, advertising is one form of selling. There are many types of advertising, but their main purposes may be summarized as follows:

1. To make a direct sale of goods.
2. To create demand.
3. To create a favorable impression of the firm.
4. To familiarize the consumer with the use of the product.
5. To introduce new styles or customs.
6. To induce people to enter a store.
7. To get a list of prospects.
8. To prepare the way for a salesman.
9. To establish the popularity and familiarity of a trade name, trademark, or slogan.
10. To create goodwill.

ILLUS. 10-1. Many types of advertising or advertising media are available to the businessman.

KINDS OF ADVERTISING AND SALES PROMOTION

The following *advertising media* (means or kinds of advertising) are available:

1. Publication advertising: newspaper display advertising (advertising scattered throughout the newspaper) and classified advertising; general magazines; trade, technical, and professional magazines; directories; and programs.
2. Mass advertising: outdoor, bus and car cards, station posters, point-of-sale advertising, window displays, loud speakers, radio, television, and theater signs.
3. Direct advertising: circular letters, catalogs, booklets, folders, package inserts, handbills, calendars and novelties, premiums, and house organs.
4. Store advertising: window displays and counter displays.

The importance of these forms of advertising to the modern business is evidenced by the fact that advertising expenditures increase every year. Illustration 10-2 gives a comparison of expenditures for various media in three different years.

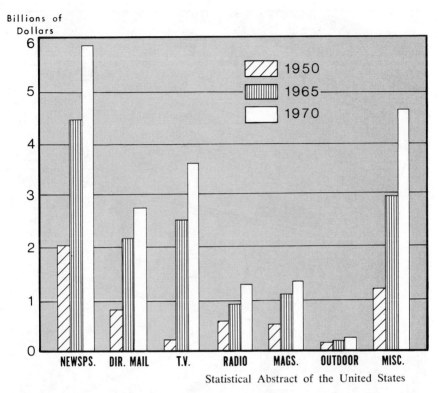

ILLUS. 10-2. Advertising expenditures by media—1950, 1965, and 1970.

Some large companies use practically all these forms of advertising, but many small businessmen must be content to use a few. For instance, a merchant in a small town would not utilize national magazine advertising, but he could use the local newspaper. The classified advertising section in the newspaper would probably not be as good as newspaper display advertising with an attractive layout.

Billboards, bus and car cards, and local radio and television programs are considered good advertising for many localized businesses. Such advertising is effective in attracting the general public within a particular area. It is doubtful, however, if a grocer in a section of a large city would find radio or television advertising profitable. The cost would probably be so great that the results would not justify the expense. Radio or television advertising in this case would not be effective because such a small percentage of the listeners or viewers would be potential customers. However, a supermarket chain in a metropolitan area might find it desirable.

ILLUS. 10-3. Direct-advertising literature.

Almost any businessman, particularly the small retailer, can use most forms of direct advertising. Examples of direct-advertising literature are given in Illustration 10-3, page 176.

Because of their low cost, handbills are a popular means of advertising used by neighborhood stores and by centrally located stores in large cities. In many cities there are agencies that make a business of distributing handbills at a contract price. One of the bad effects of distributing handbills is the littering of porches and lawns. In some cities there are ordinances against this practice. It is illegal to place handbills in a mailbox because the mailbox is considered the property of the U.S. Postal Service. Of course, they may be mailed. A substitute for distributing handbills is to wrap the bills in customers' packages or enclose them in the envelope containing the monthly statements mailed to charge account customers. Items of this type are often referred to as *package inserts*. In these instances, however, the handbills do not reach noncustomers.

Television Advertising

During the last 20 years the number of households having one or more television sets has increased from approximately 10 percent to approximately 95 percent. Because of this increase many large businesses are finding television a desirable medium for advertising. The cost of television advertising varies depending on the time of the telecast, the number of television stations carrying the telecast, and the nature of the program in which the advertising will appear. The most expensive time is between 6 p.m. and 11 p.m. and is called *prime time*. Short advertising messages (generally 30 or 60 seconds in length) are called *commercials*. When used in a network program of from 200 to 300 different television stations, commercials are much more expensive than commercials prepared by and used only on a local station since commercials run on a network program reach more people.

Mailing Lists

Mailing lists can be bought from many commercial agencies. The names on these lists are often classified according to professions and occupations, sex, or age. The best mailing lists for a local businessman are, however, those that he compiles carefully from selected lists. Some means of obtaining satisfactory mailing lists for an advertising campaign are given at the top of page 178.

Records of former customers and prospects	Records of permits issued
Names of prospects supplied by customers	Records of marriage licenses issued
News and society items in papers	Records of charters of incorporation issued
Telephone directory	Records of births and deaths
City directory	School annuals
Classified business directory	Lists of faculty members and students of universities and colleges
Financial and trade directories	
Mercantile directories	Lists of municipal and state employees
Voting lists	
Lists of real-estate transfers	Social register
Records of automobile licenses issued	Club membership lists
	Convention rosters

Display Advertising Versus Direct-Mail Advertising

In some businesses display advertising in newspapers or magazines is the most economical form of advertising. In other businesses *direct-mail advertising* (literature mailed directly to prospects) has been found to be most effective and economical. In many businesses it is necessary to use a combination of these types of advertising.

Almost every business has an opportunity to use direct-mail advertising as well as other forms of advertising. Small businesses cannot afford expensive advertisements in large city newspapers, magazines, or over radio and television; therefore, they find it necessary to use small advertisements in local newspapers, neighborhood newspapers, and various types of direct-mail advertising. Many types of items and services can be advertised effectively in the classified section of a newspaper at a low cost. Some businesses find the postal card, such as that shown in Illustration 10-4, a very economical and effective means of direct-mail advertising.

Direct-mail advertising makes it possible for the businessman to direct his advertising message to individually selected recipients. In newspapers the effect of his advertising is influenced by its position in the paper and its particular location on the page, by its size in relation to other items on the page, by the reader's interest in adjacent material on the page, and by the attention-getting quality of the advertisement. A piece of direct-mail advertising can be easily saved for future reference by an interested recipient. A newspaper, however, is ordinarily discarded within a day after publication.

SPRING HAS ARRIVED AT LAST!

BRING YOUR CAR IN FOR

• Clean crankcase breather cap • Check fluid in battery, radiator, brake master cylinder, power steering pump and transmission - fill to correct level as necessary • Lubricate throttle, transmission and parking brake linkage • Inspect front suspension, steering linkage and ball joint seals • Check operation of manifold heat valve • Check rear axle lubricant level • Lubricate hood mechanism, door hinges and latches and other body hardware where applicable • Use special lubricant on rubber parts • Check and adjust all belts for proper tension • Inspect and open body and door drain holes.

IMPORTANT: Change oil every 6000 miles or 60 days (whichever comes first). Change oil filter with oil change nearest 6000 miles.

REHME *Pontiac, Inc.*

3553 KENNEDY ROAD   CINCINNATI, OHIO 45275   PHONE: 661-7677

ILLUS. 10-4. Postal card used for direct-mail advertising.

Cooperative Advertising

In *cooperative advertising* two or more persons or groups share the costs of advertising a common product. The cooperative advertising arrangement most often found in business is called *manufacturer's cooperative advertising*. According to an agreement between manufacturer and retailer, the local retailer advertises the manufacturer's product in a local medium and then is reimbursed by the manufacturer for part of the advertising costs. A 50-50 division of costs is common.

Another type of cooperative advertising arrangement is one in which competitors selling a common product sponsor jointly an advertisement featuring that product. Sometimes all the businesses in a city selling a particular make of television cooperate in sponsoring a large newspaper advertisement featuring that product. Still another kind of cooperative advertising arrangement is one in which Chambers of Commerce and organizations of retailers share the advertising costs of promoting special community sale days.

Trading Stamps

It is estimated that more than 200,000 retailers are now using trading stamps as an aid in promoting business. Supermarkets and gasoline service stations are the largest users. A trading stamp is usually a small piece of gummed paper on which is printed the trade name of the company which sells the stamps to the retailer. The retailer gives the stamps to customers in a ratio to their purchases, such as one stamp for each ten cents of purchases. The customers exchange their accumulated stamps (usually pasted in a stamp-saver book) for merchandise. In some cases the customer has the choice of redeeming the stamps for either cash or merchandise. The cost of stamps represents a promotional expense for the retailer and should be considered in determining the selling price of goods.

Coupons

There has been a large increase in the use of coupons for promoting the sale of goods. Coupons have proved to be an effective psychological spur to buying. They are used principally to introduce a new product or to maintain and increase a company's share of the market for established product brands. Coupons usually appear in newspaper and magazine advertisements, but they are also distributed by direct mail.

There are several types of coupons. One requires the purchaser of an article to send to the manufacturer a label or coupon from the package; the manufacturer then makes a small cash refund to the purchaser. Frequently coupons may be used by the consumer to purchase a certain product at a reduced price in a local retail store; and the retail store, in some cases, will have the coupons redeemed by the manufacturer. Retailers who use trading stamps sometimes issue coupons which can be exchanged for extra stamps when purchasing certain items. Illustration 10-5 shows two types of coupons.

ILLUS. 10-5. Coupons used in promoting the sale of goods.

Manufacturer and Dealer Aids

You have already learned that the manufacturers and distributors of many products cooperate with merchants in advertising those products. In addition to sharing advertising costs, manufacturers also cooperate with merchants by providing certain materials—called manufacturer and dealer aids—to be used in advertising the products. Some of these materials commonly furnished without cost or at a low price are:

Window displays	Mailing enclosures
Counter displays	House-to-house canvassing
Handbills	and sampling
Layouts and illustrations for	Store demonstrations
newspaper advertisements	

It is advisable for manufacturers and wholesalers to aid all retailers with their promotional campaigns. If the local dealer expects to tie in his advertising and promotion with a national campaign, he should keep himself posted on the advertising program and obtain all of the free materials and suggestions that are available. For example, when a dealer who distributes phonograph records or cassettes learns that a particular artist is appearing on a national radio program or is performing locally, it is advisable to feature the records and tapes of this particular artist and obtain all of the displays that are available.

The obtaining of such cooperation in advertising is sometimes dependent upon the buying of a certain quantity of merchandise. Overloading one's stock in order to participate in such a plan is undesirable, but buying a certain quantity may often be advantageous. When merchants buy a certain quantity of goods, some manufacturers or distributors agree to provide special window displays that will be set up by a specialist.

When producers are introducing new merchandise or a new product into a new territory, they commonly distribute samples. The purpose of this practice is to familiarize people with the product so that there will be a demand for it in local stores.

Producers and distributors also cooperate with merchants by arranging special displays and demonstrations within stores. Samples are given to customers as they enter. This practice usually helps the merchant to sell the new product. He, of course, gives this merchandise a preference over other competing products. Sometimes distributors pay merchants for the privilege of giving demonstrations or offer special inducements for such a privilege. If conducted properly, the demonstration and sampling process is of common advantage to the merchant and to the producer or the distributor. Before granting the privilege, the merchant should be sure, however, that the product is of a quality that he is willing to recommend.

Window Displays

Windows of a building in which a business displays some of its goods are known as *display windows*. Since prospective customers get the first impression of a retail store chiefly by its display windows, such windows are a very valuable part of a retail store. Windows are considered so valuable by large department stores that the various departments are charged for the window display space used by them. The plan of displaying merchandise to the people who pass the store should serve the purpose of telling them that the store handles the items displayed and should result in increased calls for the items. Stores have estimated increases of from 30 to 50 percent in the sale of items when they are effectively displayed in windows. To the small store located in a large city, the window display is the chief means of advertising. Small stores can provide for additional window display space by recessing the doorway and by using *island display cases* (display cases separated from the display windows). In addition to providing added window display space, the recessed doorway enables the passerby to stop and look at the window display without being in the way of pedestrian traffic.

Window displays should be changed frequently. To a great extent the same people pass the windows daily; and, if the displays are not changed frequently, the passersby become tired of looking at the same exhibits. Furthermore, the merchandise eventually becomes soiled.

A merchant should bear in mind that the windows and the front of his store greatly influence the first impression of the customer. They should therefore be kept attractive and in harmony with the rest of the store and with the merchandise that is being sold.

The Merchants Service Bureau of the National Cash Register Company has made a study of the points for measuring the quality of window displays. These criteria are listed in Illustration 10-6.

Interior Displays

In planning *interior display* (display within the store) it is necessary to take into consideration a whole interior and not just an individual

- Make the windows advertise the merchandise to be sold as well as the character of the store.
- Put human interest into displays.
- Suggest the use of the articles displayed.
- Mark prices plainly.
- Display related articles together.
- Display seasonal goods; tie in displays with local events and needs.
- Group merchandise; don't scatter it.
- Tie in displays with advertising.
- Don't crowd the windows.
- Make displays simple.
- Plan displays ahead.
- Get together everything needed before starting to work in the window.
- Improve the window lighting.
- Study and use harmonious color combinations.
- Don't expose to sunlight merchandise that will be harmed by it.
- Change displays frequently.
- Keep the windows and displays spotlessly clean inside and outside.
- Make the displays sell merchandise.

Source: National Cash Register Company

ILLUS. 10-6. Criteria of good window displays.

display. In order to obtain a harmonizing effect from displays, the interior planning should include decorations, layout, and merchandise displays. Decorations include the lights, fixtures, walls, ceiling, and floors. The layout involves the placement of the tables, showcases, racks, and other equipment. The displays involve the actual placing of merchandise on the counters, the floor, the shelves, or in showcases.

The special displays within a store should be in harmony with the window displays. If something is featured in a window, it should also be featured in the interior of the store. Above all considerations, the displays within a store must be neat and clean. They should be changed frequently.

Large department stores, chain stores, and associations such as the International Grocers Alliance have made studies that disclose the most useful display space for certain products. For instance, products in a grocery store have certain preferred locations. Fresh fruits and vegetables must be displayed prominently, whereas soap, unless it is on special sale, may be placed in a less prominent place. Spices and various luxuries should be displayed prominently because people do not ask for them as they do for the usual necessities. It is a common practice in restaurants to display chewing gum and candy near the cash register. After eating a meal, customers are usually in a receptive mood for such items and may use some of their change in buying them. Unless such items are within sight, however, they will not be requested.

- Tie in this display with the window display.
- Harmonize with the store decorations.
- Place displays at eye level.
- Make displays accessible if they are to sell merchandise.
- Keep displays filled with merchandise.
- Make the displays self-explanatory.
- Mark the prices plainly.
- Display related items.
- Display seasonal items.

ILLUS. 10-7. Interior display checklist.

To assure good interior displays, many businessmen use a checklist, such as the one shown in Illustration 10-7, to evaluate their displays.

PLANNING AND MANAGING THE ADVERTISING PROGRAM

The preceding discussion points out the various types of advertising and helps to evaluate their usefulness. Every businessman, however, has an individual problem in determining what kind of advertising program to follow. In many cases the businessman will imitate his competitors or at least follow a similar plan, but he should always be looking for a new and more effective means of advertising.

The small businessman often has to rely on his own ability in making all the advertising plans and in writing the advertisements. The printer may help him in writing the copy and designing the advertisement. Paper supply houses often help to select the proper kind of paper. Newspaper publishers will offer suggestions in preparing newspaper advertisements. Radio and television broadcasting companies will also help to plan advertising.

Other sources of help in planning and carrying out an advertising program are as shown at the top of page 185:

1. Newspaper advertising representatives.
2. Salesmen.
3. Manufacturers.
4. Advertisements of competitors.
5. Trade associations.
6. Exchange of ideas with other businessmen.
7. Free-lance artists and writers.
8. Advertising agencies.

As the business grows larger, the owner has the option of hiring someone to handle the advertising or of placing all his advertising problems in the hands of an advertising agency, which will take care of everything. For their services, advertising agencies usually charge a percent of the total amount spent for the advertising.

Cost of Advertising

The amount that one can spend for advertising should be determined by budgeting, which is discussed in Chapter 22. When this amount is known, it should be distributed over the various forms of advertising that one chooses to use. The next step is to plan the advertising program for one year. Of course, emergencies will arise that require a decision at that particular moment; but, unless some planning is done, the program cannot be executed economically and most effectively.

A person engaged in business should know what constitutes a reasonable expenditure for his advertising. Illustration 10-8 on page 186 shows the average percent of net sales spent for advertising by various types of retail businesses; or, in other words, the number of cents of each dollar of sales spent in promoting sales.

Firms that advertise nationally or in large areas have a wider variation in the amount that they spend for advertising. Manufacturers of patent medicines, drugs, soaps, and toilet articles often spend more than 25 percent of the sales dollar for advertising purposes. This great amount of advertising creates a demand for the products and sometimes permits large enough and economical enough production to permit products to be sold at a relatively low price. Examples for other products of the amounts spent nationally for advertising in relation to sales are: paints and varnishes, 7 percent; automobile accessories, 6 percent; heating equipment, 5.7 percent; petroleum products, 5.7 percent; sporting goods, 5.7 percent; footwear, 4 percent; textiles, 1.8 percent; and office equipment, 2.6 percent.

Kind of Business	Percent of Net Sales
Automobile dealers	0.74
Used-car dealers	0.84
Bakeries	0.65
Beauty shops	1.58
Camera stores	2.06
Department stores	3.80
Drug stores	1.23
Electrical appliance stores	2.45
Furniture stores	5.32
Grocery stores	0.65
Hardware stores	1.45
Jewelry stores	3.5
Laundries	1.70
Men's wear stores	2.9
Paint stores	1.52
Shoe stores	2.78
Sporting goods stores	2.0
Tourist courts	3.53
Toy stores	2.3
Women's wearing apparel stores	3.2

Source: *Better Retailing*, The National Cash Register Company

ILLUS. 10-8. Percent of net sales spent for advertising.

From these figures it is possible to get at least a general idea of how much one should anticipate spending to advertise a business. However, a particular business may find it desirable to spend more or less than the average percents indicated, depending on the competition it has and the nature of the product or service it sells.

Timeliness of Advertising

In nearly every type of business there are certain times when advertising can be done more effectively than at others. For instance, manufacturers and sellers of toys advertise widely before the Christmas holidays. Outdoor furniture is advertised in the spring and early summer. Blankets are advertised in the late summer and early fall. Laundries and dry-cleaning establishments feature special advertisements for curtains and draperies in the spring and the fall. Rug-cleaning companies make a special advertising drive at housecleaning time in the spring. At other times of the year advertising may be wasted to a great extent. One should therefore study his business to determine the most opportune times to advertise—times potential customers would be willing and able to purchase goods or services advertised.

For a local merchant, payday for his customers is an important date. The alert advertisers in every city study payroll records very carefully to determine the most effective day of the week to spend most of their money for advertising. These dates determine when they should feature their sales. Figures on payroll payments are available in almost every city through the local newspaper or the Chamber of Commerce. In the smaller city they can be determined by investigation among employers and the banks. For instance, in most cities wages are usually paid on Friday. Employees who are paid twice monthly usually receive their pay about the middle of the month and at the end of the month; and those who are paid monthly, at the end of the month. If one is going to advertise at a time when a consumer has the most cash available, it should correlate with these paydays.

Frequency of Advertising

A single advertisement may produce temporary results, but the cumulative effect of advertising is important in building a steady stream of customers. If advertising does not appear often enough, customers will tend to forget about a business. Continuous advertising, regardless of its nature, helps to hold old customers and to get new ones. It builds confidence and familiarity. Not all customers will read a business' advertisement at any particular time; but if advertising is repeated often enough, most of the prospective customers will be reached. Therefore, it is desirable for most businesses to spread their advertising appropriations over the entire year by using smaller and less expensive advertisements frequently rather than to spend all advertising funds on a few expensive advertisements.

Effectiveness of Printed Advertising

A printed advertisement in the newspaper has characteristics different from a radio advertisement. A billboard or poster certainly has characteristics different from a window display. However, certain general characteristics are often listed for effective printed advertising. Illustration 10-9 on page 188 shows a checklist that may be used in evaluating printed retail advertising. Any advertisement that has a rating of seventy points or better on this scale will ordinarily prove to be satisfactory for a retailing firm.

		Rating	Your Score
1.	Does the headline contain news value?	15	.....
2.	Is there a promise to the reader's self-interest?	15	.....
3.	Is there an appeal for direct action?	10	.....
4.	Is the advertisement of proper size for the importance of the offer and for its most favorable presentation?	10	.....
5.	Is the advertiser's name clearly displayed?	5	.....
6.	Is the merchandise or service mentioned in the headline?	3	.....
7.	Does the headline include the name of the firm?	2	.....
8.	Does the illustration show the merchandise or service in use?	5	.....
9.	Does the illustration invite the reader to project himself into it pleasantly, profitably, or favorably?	3	.....
10.	Does the layout locate elements logically and eye-invitingly?	5	.....
11.	Is the layout exciting or attention-compelling?	3	.....
12.	Does the copy tell what is new, different, or better about the merchandise or service, especially from the style angle?	3	.....
13.	Does the copy inspire enthusiasm for the merchandise or service?	3	.....
14.	Does the copy have a definite ring of truth and sincerity?	5	.....
15.	Does the copy tell that the merchandise or service is priced to save money?	2	.....
16.	Does the copy tell that the product is guaranteed, lasting, and gives good service?	3	.....
17.	Does the copy develop an appeal to price?	2	.....
18.	Does the copy or illustration imply the merchandise increases sex appeal?	3	.....
19.	Does the copy tell why the merchandise is so priced?	1	.....
20.	Does the copy tell of the seasonal appeal of the merchandise?	1	.....
21.	Does the copy describe the merchandise or service with reasonable completeness?	2	.....
22.	Does the copy indicate a personal loss for not buying or using the product?	1	.....
23.	Are all negative thoughts connected with the product eliminated from the copy?	2	.....
24.	Does the copy indicate enthusiasm of users, such as testimonials?	2	.....
25.	Does the copy bring out superiorities of the merchandise or service over competitive products?	1	.....
26.	Is the urge to action repeated three times—in the heading, in the first paragraph, and in the closing?	5	.....
27.	Is the price displayed so it will command sufficient attention?	3	.....
28.	Is there a free deal, free offer, free trial, or something free included?	3	.....
29.	Have all details to facilitate action been included? (Phone number, order blank, store hours, mention of air conditioning, parking, etc.)	2	.....

Source: *Small Business Aids*, No. 216, United States Department of Commerce

ILLUS. 10-9. Checklist for evaluating printed retail advertising.

Correlating All Forms of Sales Promotion

To be effective, space advertising should be correlated with direct-mail advertising and all other forms of promotion. The ideal purposes of such correlated advertising are as follows:

1. To have a possible customer pick up a magazine or a newspaper, read the manufacturer's advertisement, and be impressed with a need for the product.
2. To have the prospect receive at about the same moment a folder from his retailer telling the advantages of this product.
3. To have the prospect go down to the dealer's store and be reminded again of this product by a window display.
4. To have the dealer's sales clerk suggest to the prospect the purchase of this product, pointing out its advantages and merits.
5. To have the prospect buy the product and, on opening the package at home, find an insert reviewing product uses.

An important point in correlating sales promotion is to take advantage simultaneously of all means of promotion so that the greatest impact or impression can be made upon the prospective customer. From the list given above, it is evident that if a local merchant, for example, wishes to get the best advertising from his advertising dollars he should correlate his efforts with those of the manufacturer and the wholesaler. When something is being featured or given special emphasis in a national magazine, on the radio or television, and in local newspapers, it is a good time for the local merchant to have window and store displays as well as to use handbills and feature special sales.

Relation of Other Policies to Sales Promotion

In addition to advertising and displays, other activities of a business have a direct relation to advertising, selling, and sales promotion. These additional factors are covered in Chapters 8, 19, and 20. Some of the policies of a business that directly affect the success of an advertising and promotion program are as follows:

Credit and collections	Lighting
Pricing	Store arrangement
Return privileges	Parking facilities
Special sales	Appropriateness of merchandise
Delivery and other services	

The study of these additional factors emphasizes the necessity of correlating all the activities of a business so that they have a combined effect that is desirable.

Truth in Advertising and Selling

There is a federal law against *false advertising* in interstate business. False advertising is defined by the federal law as being "misleading in a material respect," including the failure to reveal facts as to the consequences that may result from the use of the advertised commodities.

Permanent business success must be built upon honesty, understanding, and fair practices. A businessman may be tempted occasionally to exaggerate or to imitate some other competitor who seems to be stretching the truth. In the long run it does not pay, however, to break the confidence of customers.

The Council of Better Business Bureaus has established standards to be followed in selling and advertising. Particular attention is given to misleading statements. The following paragraphs give some examples of misleading terms and statements that should not be used in selling and advertising.

Terms of Purchase. Statements such as "Pay as You Please" and "Your Own Terms" are usually inaccurate, as the customer is seldom permitted to name his own terms. Credit terms should be explicit.

Sales. The public construes or understands the term "sale" to mean an offering of merchandise at a price concession.

Special Sales. Special sales or offerings should fulfill the accepted meaning of the word "special," namely, "out-of-the-ordinary practices."

Time Limits on Sales. Time-limited sales should be rigidly observed. All offers to purchase under the terms of a time-limited sale, received after the expiration of the period, should be refused. "One-Day Sale" means that merchandise either is no longer sold or reverts to a higher price on the day following the sale.

Going Out of Business. Such terms as "Going Out of Business," "Selling Out," and "Closing-Out Sale" should not be used unless the concern so advertising is actually going out of business.

Reliability of Guarantee. A *guarantee* is a promise of the seller or manufacturer to protect the buyer in some specific way if the merchandise is unsatisfactory. A guarantee is only as good as the concern that

1. Serve the public with honest values.
2. Tell the truth about what is offered.
3. Tell the truth in a forthright manner so that its significance may be understood by the trusting as well as the analytical.
4. Tell customers what they want to know—what they have a right to know about what is offered—so that they may buy wisely and obtain the maximum satisfaction from their purchases.
5. Be prepared and willing to make good as promised and without quibble on any guarantee offered.
6. Be sure that the normal use of merchandise or services will not be hazardous to public health or life.
7. Reveal material facts, the deceptive concealment of which might cause consumers to be misled.
8. Advertise and sell merchandise or service on its merits and refrain from attacking your competitors or reflecting unfairly upon their products, services, or methods of doing business.
9. If testimonials are used, use only those of competent witnesses who are sincere and honest in what they say about what you sell.
10. Avoid all tricky devices and schemes such as deceitful trade-in allowances, fictitious list prices, false and exaggerated comparative prices, bait advertising, misleading free offers, fake sales, and similar practices that prey upon human ignorance and gullibility.

ILLUS. 10-10. Fair Trade Code for Advertising and Selling adopted by the Council of Better Business Bureaus.

makes it. When merchandise or service is "guaranteed," the consumer has a right to expect that the terms of the guarantee will be fulfilled by the guarantor. Accordingly, a guarantee should not be made on merchandise or services unless the guarantor is in a position to fulfill the guarantee in case he is called upon to do so. In their advertising, retailers should not use statements regarding a manufacturer's guarantee unless the manufacturer is known to be in a position to carry out his guarantee; nor should retailers refer to their merchandise merely as "guaranteed" unless they are willing to make good if they are called upon to do so.

Free Offers. The common meaning of the word "free" is "without cost or obligation," or "gratuitous"; that is, given without recompense or payment. The word "free" may therefore have the capacity to mislead when used in any other sense.

Derogatory Statements. Statements derogatory (unfavorable or damaging) to the price, the merchandise, or the service of competitors should not be made. Such statements not only are unethical and unfair but also destroy public confidence in advertising.

Satisfaction Guaranteed. When such claims as "satisfaction or your money back" are made, the customer should be the judge of whether or not he is satisfied, and such guarantees should be honored at once. If a guarantee covers a certain length of time, the amount of time should be specified definitely.

REVIEW WHAT YOU HAVE LEARNED

Business Terms Checkup:

(1) advertising media
(2) package inserts
(3) prime time
(4) commercial
(5) direct-mail advertising
(6) cooperative advertising
(7) manufacturer's cooperative advertising
(8) display windows
(9) island display cases
(10) interior display
(11) false advertising
(12) guarantee

Reading Checkup:

1. What are the principal purposes of advertising?
2. Name the four kinds of advertising.
3. Approximately how much was spent for newspaper advertising in 1970?
4. From what sources can a new store in a community obtain a satisfactory list of prospects?
5. Compare the advantages and the disadvantages of display advertising in newspapers and magazines as contrasted with direct-mail advertising.
6. Give two examples of cooperative advertising.
7. Is the cost of trading stamps a promotional expense for the retailer?
8. What are the principal uses of coupons?
9. What are some of the advertising aids that manufacturers often provide for retail merchants?
10. Explain the chief purpose of window displays.
11. Mention several things that must be done in order to have good interior displays.
12. From what sources can a small business that does not have an advertising department obtain help in preparing advertisements?
13. Do different types of businesses spend different percents of their sales for advertising?

14. What aspects of timeliness in advertising should be considered in planning a program?

15. Explain the importance of frequency of advertising.

16. Name the four most important items in the checklist for evaluating printed advertising given in this chapter.

17. Why is it desirable to correlate all forms of sales promotion?

18. What organization is the sponsor of the Fair Trade Code for Advertising and Selling?

19. From the viewpoint of truth in advertising, what should a "sale" mean?

APPLY WHAT YOU HAVE LEARNED

Questions for Class Discussion:

1. In your opinion, why is television advertising not a desirable advertising medium for a meat store in a large city?

2. Illustration 10-2 shows that the largest percentage of increase from 1950 to 1970 in money spent for advertising was that spent for television advertising. Discuss the possible reasons for this.

3. Why is the cost for television advertising between 6 p.m. and 11 p.m. the most expensive?

4. What time is probably the best for television commercials for household products such as soaps and cleaning materials?

5. Name some businesses that might advertise in a school newspaper.

6. Announcements in newspapers of engagements and coming weddings could be the source of a mailing list for what businesses?

7. The five Chevrolet automobile dealers in a city jointly pay for a full-page ad in the city newspaper. The names and addresses of all five dealers appear at the bottom of the ad. How is it possible for any one dealer to benefit from such an ad?

8. Why are coupons an effective booster of sales?

9. What items might be arranged in a display window of a sporting goods store if the display is to feature golf?

10. Give an example of timeliness in advertising.

11. State briefly how various forms of advertising and sales promotion can be correlated.

12. Mention some examples of advertising practices that you feel are unfair.

13. Do you think a company that is continuing in business is justified in featuring a "closing-out sale" to clear out some old stock? Why or why not?

Problems and Projects:

1. A suburban store that has average annual sales of approximately $100,000 spends 3 percent of its sales for advertising. Its advertising budget is divided as follows: handbills, 30 percent; calendars, book matches, etc., 7 percent; window displays, 15 percent; newspaper advertising, 15 percent; direct mail, 20 percent; and miscellaneous, 13 percent.

   (a) How much is the annual advertising budget?

   (b) What is the amount spent for each type of advertising?

2. Obtain a sample of a handbill, a package insert, or a piece of direct-mail advertising literature, and criticize it from the following points of view: (a) attractiveness, (b) specific information, (c) effectiveness, and (d) any other points that seem important.

3. Plan an advertising campaign for a small shoe store in your community, being sure that the total expenditures for a year will not exceed $3,000.

4. Two young men are launching a new radio and TV repair and sales business with a moderate investment. They have decided to use about half of their advertising budget for direct-mail advertising.

   (a) Using this chapter as a guide, select six suitable sources of customer prospects for their mailing list.

   (b) How often should this list be revised?

   (c) What steps should be taken to keep the lists up to date?

Case Problem 10-1:

In an outlying district of a large city, an attractive new residential community was developed. The contractor built a small business community with eight store buildings in it which were offered for rent. Within close walking distance or short driving distance there were 3,000 families whose incomes were estimated to be twice the normal average of the city. A successful grocer in another part of the city rented one of these buildings with the idea of developing a high-grade grocery store catering to the people in the new community.

Required:

Suggest ways in which the owner of this new grocery store could appeal to the customers in this community to get them to buy from him.

Case Problem 10-2:

You are opening a new retail shoe store in a community that already has two shoe stores. One of these established stores has been advertising about four times a year in the local newspaper, using about one eighth of a page each time. The other store usually has advertised in the local newspaper only once a year, advertising a special clearance sale of ladies' summer shoes.

Required:

Suggest what might be a desirable plan for advertising your new store.

Case Problem 10-3:

The china and glassware department of a large city department store decides that it would be desirable to write personal letters to newly engaged women inviting them to visit the department to select dishes and glassware for their new homes.

Required:

1. From what source might the names and addresses of the newly engaged women be obtained?
2. What might be the general contents of the letter?

Case Problem 10-4:

The Main Muffler Company, located in a city of 350,000 persons, is one of two businesses that specialize in the replacement of mufflers on all makes of automobiles. It wishes to stimulate business by using advertising to announce a special reduced rate for installing mufflers during a two-week period. It considers using the daily newspaper, radio, and television. There are three radio and two television stations in the city.

Required:

Explain which method or methods of advertising might prove effective and give reasons for your choice.

Continuing Project:

Make a complete advertising plan for the business that you have selected, indicating the types of advertising you plan to use, the frequency, the schedule, and the cost.

How is a town or city evaluated as a possible business location?

What is meant by zoning restrictions?

What are common errors in locating a store?

How can a study of customer traffic help in planning a layout?

What are the advantages of leasing, rather than buying, equipment?

BACKGROUND OF CHAPTER

Before a person can begin operation of a business, he must decide upon a desirable location. All too often an individual who is just starting in business pays too little attention to the selection of a location. He simply chooses a vacant building or one which is convenient to his home. The man who chooses his business location in this haphazard way usually discovers that few people are passing or entering his establishment.

When one is selecting a location for a retail business, there are many important factors that should be considered. This chapter discusses those factors and factors to be considered in planning the arrangement of equipment and merchandise.

CHAPTER 11

LOCATION AND LAYOUT

Two of the major problems of a business are determining where it is to be located and the arrangement of its physical facilities. The selection of a location for a business has much to do with its success. A convenient location for customers, the cost of the land or rent, transportation and labor costs, and similar factors influence greatly the ability of a business to compete successfully.

LOCATION OF RETAIL STORES

Because retail businesses are so numerous and deal directly with the consumers, considerable study needs to be done to determine for a particular business a location that will help it to be profitable.

Selecting the Community

Is it desirable to locate the business in a city or in a village? Does one community seem to offer better opportunities than some other community? These are only two of the questions a businessman must seek to answer when selecting the community for his business. In the discussion that follows, you will learn more about how the best community for a business is chosen.

In any city, shopping area, or trade center, there is only a certain amount of purchasing power. That amount is determined by the number of people in the area and how much money they have to spend. If there are too many businesses of a certain kind, they cannot all prosper.

Some kinds of businesses are more numerous than others. For example, in any given city you will usually find that there are many more eating places than there are furniture stores.

Before selecting a community in which to locate a retail business, a careful survey should be made. If the area is overpopulated by the kind of business one wants to start, one may have some difficulty becoming established; but if the number of competing establishments is relatively low, there is an indication of possible success. Many other factors, however, must be taken into consideration.

The United States Department of Commerce made a study of 23 large companies to find out what factors are examined in evaluating a town for a store location. The factors most commonly mentioned as being important for a community were the following: total population, nature of the population, population trends, per capita income, industries (trend, permanence, and prospects), amount of competition, area growth, labor conditions, banking and credit facilities, rent range of business buildings, insurance rates, local taxes, standard of living, and transportation costs.

Selecting the Store Site

After the community in which to locate a particular business has been chosen, the site for the store must be selected. This site may be in the downtown area or in a suburban location. Such factors as traffic, parking facilities, zoning, and rent play an important role in the choice of a particular site.

Downtown Locations. Downtown locations in large cities are good for such businesses as department stores, jewelry stores, variety stores, theaters, restaurants, parking lots, and hotels.

Shopping Centers. In large cities, stores congregate in groups forming what are commonly called *neighborhood shopping centers*. Such a center that includes a drugstore, a grocery store, a meat market, an electric supplies shop, a beauty shop, a restaurant, a dry cleaners, and a barber shop is reasonably well balanced. If it included three drugstores, however, instead of one, it would not be a particularly attractive business location for a new drugstore.

Since World War II suburban shopping centers (often called *shopping plazas*) have developed in rapidly growing suburban areas near large cities. Approximately 12,000 such shopping centers have been established. Usually they are located on heavily traveled streets or highways. They are generally built around a department store branch, several large supermarkets, two or more variety stores, and a drugstore. Thirty to fifty stores are often found in such a center. The shopping center is usually owned as a total real estate venture by a developer.

Some of the newer centers are called *shopping malls*. In this type of arrangement, all or most of the stores face a central pedestrian shopping area. All of the stores may be under one roof, forming an enclosed mall.

Influence of Traffic on Store Location. The traffic problem is a serious one for stores. Merchants have found that a scarcity of parking facilities discourages shopping, for people usually buy at stores that can be reached easily. Some merchants have found it profitable to provide free parking space for customers or to make arrangements with the managers of garages and parking lots to reduce rates for the customers of the stores. Some stores that are not located in the shopping district provide special transportation facilities, such as buses. The added cost for free parking or free bus service must be included in the selling price of the merchant's goods.

Another important aspect of traffic has to do with what is called the *traffic count*. This term refers to the number of vehicles or the number of people who pass a specific location. Real estate firms, large stores, and chain-store organizations conduct traffic counts to determine the relative values of different locations. For example, if a person is considering two locations for a women's shoe store, he may have a traffic count made of each location. If the traffic count shows that 300 women pass one location in an average day, whereas 500 pass the other location during the same time, the latter is to be considered the better location. If a count of automobile traffic were made, it might show that 100 women pass the first location in automobiles during an average day, whereas only 50 pass the second location. The latter would still be the better location because the number of people who walk by a store is more important than the number who ride by.

A high automobile traffic count is more important if there are parking facilities in the immediate vicinity than it is if there are no parking facilities. Many people may pass a location in automobiles; but if they cannot stop and park their cars, the location has no particular advantage from the point of view of shopping, although it does have an advantage from the point of view of publicity. The traffic count of automobiles is, of course, more important than the pedestrian count in the case of determining a location for a garage or a service station.

To the drive-in retail establishment, such as a gasoline service station, a food and refreshment stand, and a dry-cleaning business, location on a traffic artery with ease of entry and adequate parking space is necessary. A location at a street intersection is preferred because traffic can enter the drive-in from more than one direction.

Since a stop sign slows traffic, a drive-in location before or after a stop sign is usually desirable.

Traffic and Parking Problems. Transportation and traffic have had some interesting influences on business in the past 50 years. As roads have been improved and automobiles have become widely owned, many people have quit trading in the small rural areas. They have gone to the cities to do their purchasing where there is a greater selection of merchandise. Cities and towns have grown in size.

Since this trend has continued and more automobiles are now owned and driven into cities for shopping purposes, the traffic problem has become very serious. Because of the narrow streets and the congestion brought about by heavy traffic, some locations are undesirable.

As a result of this congestion, there has been a steady trend in recent years in most cities for some businesses to move out of the center of the city into suburban shopping centers or to establish branches in the suburbs. In other words, the automobile, which caused the original concentration of city shopping areas, is now causing a movement away from the center of the city.

As highway traffic becomes more congested, roads are often re-located, with the result that motels, service stations, roadside restaurants, and similar businesses suddenly find that what were once good locations are now very poor locations. Before starting a business, it is desirable to check with government authorities to see if changes in locations of highways are planned.

Zoning Restrictions. Most cities have *zoning restrictions,* which specify that in certain zones or districts, only certain types of businesses may be established. It is important to check on such conditions in a search for a suitable location for a particular business.

Rent as a Factor in Location. The rent to be paid for a location should have a satisfactory ratio to the anticipated sales volume. Since good locations usually have high rents, rent should be considered only as a percentage of the anticipated sales volume. In other words, a location that is poor requires only a low rent because the anticipated sales volume in such a location will be lower than it would be in a better location.

Sometimes it is better to pay a high rent than a low rent. For example, it would be better to pay $300 a month for a location that would produce $60,000 in annual sales than it would be to pay $200 a month for a location that would produce annual sales of only $20,000.

Some Common Errors in Store Location. When people go into a retail business or when retail merchants change their location, they frequently make mistakes in choosing the site for the business. Some of the most serious mistakes are:

1. The retailer is influenced too much by vacant space and low rent and the expectation that customers will come to him. He bases the selection of his location on cost rather than on suitability for customers.

2. The fact that several stores are already located in a section encourages the retailer to select the same location. The volume of business available in this section may not be sufficient, however, to support all the merchants there.

3. The retailer may choose a location that is suitable for some types of business but unsuitable for his particular business.

ILLUS. 11-1. Selecting a location because the rent is low is an error commonly made by businessmen.

EQUIPMENT AND LAYOUT

After a businessman has found a desirable location and building, he must obtain the equipment the business needs and plan the *layout*. Layout means the arrangement of fixtures, equipment, and merchandise in the building.

Retail Store Layout

The layout that is planned and the equipment and fixtures that are installed should be such that customers will be served efficiently and effectively.

Types of Merchandise. A store handling groceries would need different fixtures and a layout different from that of a furniture store or a dress shop. It is important that the equipment and fixtures be suitable for the merchandise to be sold. A visit to similar stores and consultations with the salesmen of the manufacturers of store fixtures and equipment should be helpful to the business being planned.

Types of Service. The recent trend of permitting customers to select the items wanted and to take them to a cashier in such businesses as food, drug, and variety stores requires different fixtures and a different layout than the stores having salespersons who wait on the customers. For self-service operations *open display fixtures* are needed. These include such fixtures as tables, racks, and bins that make it

ILLUS. 11-2. Open display fixtures allow the customer to see and examine the merchandise.

possible for the customer to see, handle, and examine the goods. In such businesses as jewelry stores and camera shops, the goods are usually displayed in closed glass display cases for greater protection and are demonstrated and sold by salespersons.

Effect of Customer Traffic. Customers tend to turn to the right when entering a store, especially if there is no large center aisle. Thus, the space at the right of the entrance is the place where the owner should display merchandise that yields large profits or that might otherwise be overlooked by the shopper. For example, in a grocery store the fresh fruits and vegetables or fancy groceries might be placed at the right of the entrance in the front part of the store.

If there is a large center aisle leading from the entrance, most of the traffic will be confined to this one aisle, and customers may not see other parts of the store. A large center aisle is therefore undesirable unless the store is very narrow. Even a store that has a width of only 25 feet may be arranged without a center aisle. Illustration 11-3 shows a possible arrangement of a small grocery.

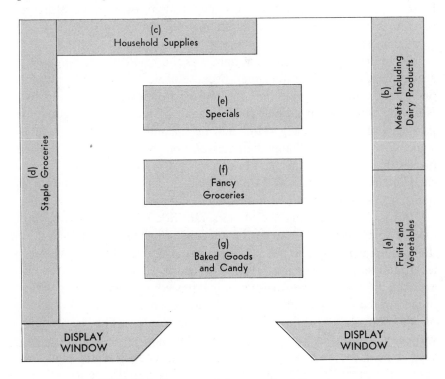

ILLUS. 11-3. Arrangement for a small retail grocery.

Because people usually follow the widest space offered them upon entering a store, it is possible to get them to turn to the left if the aisle on that side is wider than the one at the right. Some studies show that customers tend to turn to the right if the aisles are equal in width.

In large stores having elevators and escalators, there are also rather definite traffic routes taken by customers. Such routes are usually the most direct aisles between the entrance and the elevator or escalator. On these routes the merchant often places aisle tables containing merchandise that he wishes to move quickly.

Effect of Customer Attitudes. The attitudes of customers toward various types of merchandise and services should be given much attention in planning the layout of a business. When buying items classed as necessities, the customer usually enters the store with a definite plan to buy. For that reason such items may be placed in less desirable and less accessible parts than other items. For example, household cleaning supplies, such as laundry soaps, may be placed in the rear part of a grocery store; the prescription counter of a drugstore may be located similarly; the furniture department of a large store may occupy an upper floor; the repair shop of an automobile dealer may be located in space at the rear of the display room.

Some articles are purchased mainly as the result of an impulse upon seeing them displayed, rather than because of definite plans to buy them. Such goods are known as *impulse goods*. For instance, as a customer is paying a restaurant cashier for his meal, he sees chewing gum, small packages of candy, or cigarettes and cigars and immediately purchases some with part of the change being given him by the cashier. Experience proves that people at that particular moment are more inclined to make such an additional purchase than at other times. Furthermore, such items are usually consumed immediately after a meal.

Bottles of meat sauces and horseradish are placed on the top of meat display cases so that customers may buy them on impulse. For the same reason some items are displayed at eye level; some, below eye level; and some, above eye level. For instance, on the lowest shelf of an open display fixture, there may be placed the best selling kind of bread; on the next shelf, the special breads; on the next, the cookies; and on the top shelf (about eye level), the cakes. The best location vertically is about eye level and the best location horizontally on a long shelf is near the end of the shelf. Wrapping counters and places near cash registers are valuable places for arranging impulse goods. Displays near the entrance of a store are usually effective last-minute reminders.

When customers are shopping for goods that represent a large expenditure of money, they usually do not want to hurry in making their decisions. Such goods should not be placed on congested aisles. For example, when buying dresses, women do not want to be hurried in making their decisions. Department stores therefore find it undesirable to have their dress departments on the street floor. Such a department is frequently made into a sort of store with a main entrance of its own. It then has more seclusion and quiet than it would have if it were just open space on a floor with other departments.

Arrangement of Related Items. Whenever possible, it is a good plan to arrange *related,* or *complementary, goods* near each other. When men's ties are placed near men's shirts, the purchaser of a shirt is likely to see the ties and to purchase a new tie to wear with the new shirt. Such arrangement also makes it easy for the salesperson to suggest related goods.

Illustration 11-4 shows an effective arrangement of related items. By displaying flowers in various glass and pottery holders, the florist

Armstrong Cork Company

ILLUS. 11-4. An effective arrangement in a florist's shop.

increases the sale of both flowers and holders. The arrangement of this merchandise suggests to the shopper ideas on using flowers in the home. No doubt many shoppers who had never thought of using certain flowers in such ways were stimulated to buy them when they saw how attractively they could be arranged.

Convenience of Customers. The aisles in a store should be wide enough to allow plenty of room for customers to pass around the displays without crowding. Upon finding the main aisles crowded, many people will walk out of a store and buy elsewhere. If the aisles are narrow, some items may be damaged as a result of being knocked off their display fixtures by passing customers. Many supermarkets have very wide aisles so that it is easy for customers pushing shopping carts to move along the aisles and select purchases from shelves and display tables.

Checkrooms, public telephones, and branch post offices maintained for the convenience of customers are usually located toward the rear of stores in order to get customers to walk past several displays of

ILLUS. 11-5. Check-out stations provide customers with speedy service.

merchandise. In large stores there is usually a rest room and lounge for women. This is situated on an upper floor so that persons using it may see as much of the store as possible. As the elevator stops at the different floors, the customer may get a view of each floor which may suggest certain purchases to her. If the store has an escalator, the customers using it get a longer and a wider view of each floor than they do from an elevator. Some stores have a mezzanine floor which makes a desirable place for chairs to be placed for customers who wish to rest.

While resting, they get a view of the entire street floor and, seeing certain items on display, might make purchases.

Reserve Stock Location. To provide for a minimum amount of travel time in moving goods from the reserve stock location to the selling area, the storage area should be located as near as possible to the selling area it will serve. An example of this principle is shown in Illustration 11-6. This illustration gives the location of storage areas and selling, or display, areas for produce departments in two different retail stores. Note that Store B has used an arrangement which requires much less travel time of the stock clerk when replenishing produce in the selling area.

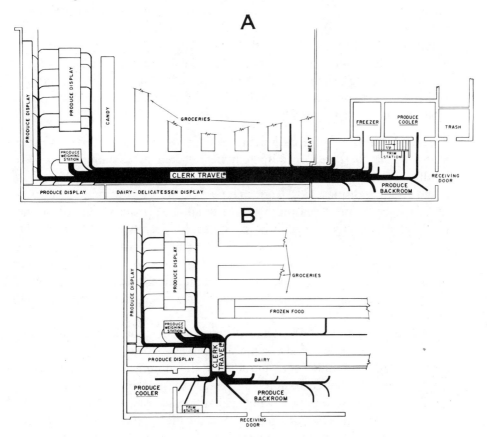

* The black areas indicate the amount and location of stock clerk travel.

ILLUS. 11-6. Stock clerk travel between storage area and sales area in two retail produce departments.

Obtaining Equipment

Most businesses require equipment of various kinds for efficient operation. In planning the layout of a business, the equipment that will be needed must be considered.

Determining the Kind of Equipment Needed. By consulting trade papers, directories, and businesses using similar equipment, one can obtain the names of equipment manufacturers. From these manufacturers one should obtain literature descriptive of the equipment that will probably best fit the needs of the business. The next step should be to interview representatives of the equipment manufacturers and let them offer suggestions with regard to the most suitable kind of equipment. Most manufacturers will give demonstrations and furnish technical data on the operation of machines. Some of them will leave equipment on trial so that a thorough test may be made. Often it is possible to observe the equipment in use in other businesses. Comparisons as to the original cost, the probable life, the rate of depreciation, and the repairs or services required should be made of similar equipment manufactured by competing businesses.

Standardization of Equipment. As far as possible, it is desirable that a particular type of equipment be selected as a standard for use in all similar work. If display cases are of the same size and make, it is easy to shift a display case from one part of the store to another during special sales or busy seasons without breaking up the harmony of the entire store display. Furthermore, a neat appearance is given to the store if all the equipment is alike. If all the cash registers in a store are manufactured by the same company, it is easy to obtain service on them and for employees to shift from one machine to another. Likewise, if all the typewriters in an office are of one make, the typists can use any machine.

Another advantage of standardization is that one can usually purchase a large number of the same articles at a lower price per article than if a small number were purchased. If equipment is purchased in large quantities, better maintenance service is ordinarily available.

Less variety in supplies, which means less cost per unit, is needed when equipment is standardized. When all the typewriters in an office, for instance, are of the same make, only one kind of typewriter ribbon need be carried in stock. If various kinds of display cases are used in a store, it may be necessary to stock a variety of electric light bulbs for the proper illumination of each kind.

Buying and Leasing Equipment. There are many forms of contracts under which equipment may be purchased. In some cases the contract may be a conditional sales contract, but in others it may be a chattel mortgage contract. (In some states these two contracts are known as a security interest.) In the case of the conditional sales contract, the purchaser does not receive title to the equipment until it has been fully paid for. In the case of the chattel mortgage contract, the equipment becomes the property of the purchaser at the time it is delivered, but the seller holds a mortgage claim against it until the amount specified in the contract is paid. These types of contracts are explained in Chapter 19. Occasionally, for a small unpaid balance, the seller does not require any special contract. The buyer is merely billed on open account.

During the last few years businesses have been turning more and more to leasing equipment rather than purchasing it. Making a contract to use a piece of equipment without buying the item is known as *leasing*. Nearly any kind of equipment that a business needs—from adding machines to plant equipment—can be leased.

Most lease contracts range from three to ten years. Usually provision can be made for the lease payments to be applied against the purchase price if the lessee should decide to buy the equipment after having used it for a time.

Advantages of Leasing Equipment. The principal advantages of leasing are as follows:

1. It conserves cash, for less immediate cash expenditure is required.
2. It eliminates the necessity for borrowing money and possibly paying high rates of interest.
3. It provides the business with the latest and most efficient types of equipment.
4. No maintenance expense is required because maintenance service is included in the lease payments.

Disadvantages of Leasing Equipment. It should be pointed out that there are some disadvantages to leasing equipment. The principal disadvantage is that the total cost of leasing over a number of years is likely to be more than if the equipment had been purchased.

Renting Equipment. Frequently a business may need a particular piece of equipment for only a short time. For example, a business may need a long-carriage typewriter for the preparation of annual reports, a truck to transport some goods, or additional typewriters and calculating machines during peak seasons. In such cases it is possible to rent the equipment for a short period of time.

Preparing a Scaled Layout

It is often difficult to visualize accurately and in advance a good arrangement of equipment. A simple way to plan for such arrangement is to draw a floor plan to scale and then cut small pieces of cardboard, also to scale, to represent the various items of equipment. By shifting these about, the best arrangement should be found. Some equipment manufacturers have miniature *three-dimensional models* (representations made to scale which show the length, width, and thickness of an article) which are available as an aid to prospective customers for determining the best arrangement.

Trade association journals frequently contain articles and pictures of layouts of successful businesses that may be helpful. Manufacturers of equipment and display fixtures, as a result of their many experiences in equipping stores, can make suggestions as to effective layouts. One can also make visits to businesses similar to the one being planned and observe the arrangement and layout.

Store Modernization

Most stores find it desirable to modernize at intervals of 15 to 20 years. Such modernization usually results in increased sales and profits. It provides a more inviting climate for customers to shop, enhances the image of the store in the eyes of the community, and increases the efficiency of store operation. Modernization includes such improvements as changing the lighting, repainting the walls and ceiling, installing new types of display fixtures, rearranging merchandise, air-conditioning the building, and installing a new type of flooring.

REVIEW WHAT YOU HAVE LEARNED

Business Terms Checkup:

(1) neighborhood shopping center
(2) shopping plaza
(3) shopping mall
(4) traffic count
(5) zoning restrictions
(6) layout
(7) open display fixtures
(8) impulse goods
(9) related (or complementary) goods
(10) leasing (equipment)
(11) three-dimensional models

Reading Checkup:

1. In evaluating any town for the purposes of a store location, what are at least three of the factors that are investigated by large companies?

2. Why is a traffic count of automobiles not always an indication of a good location for a retail business?

3. Name at least three major factors used as guides in selecting a specific site for a retail store.

4. Name several common errors made in selecting locations for retail stores.

5. Why is that part of a retail store near the entrance the most valuable selling space?

6. Why is a large center aisle usually undesirable in a large store?

7. In the illustration on page 203, the baked goods, fancy groceries, and specials were arranged at right angles to the other items. What is a reason for such an arrangement?

8. Where might it be desirable to place items classed as (a) necessities, (b) impulse goods?

9. Name some ways in which businesses have planned their layouts for the convenience of customers.

10. What is meant by a scaled layout?

APPLY WHAT YOU HAVE LEARNED

Questions for Class Discussion:

1. If you are making a traffic count to determine the suitability of a particular location for a beauty salon, to which of the following factors would you give most consideration: (a) the number of women who pass the location, (b) the number of men who pass the location, (c) the number of automobiles that pass the location, or (d) the number of men and women who pass the location in couples?

2. Competitors in retail businesses often try to obtain store locations near one another. Can you explain the reason for this practice?

3. What factors do you think would help to determine a good location for a gasoline service station?

4. Discuss the advantages and the disadvantages of a business' leasing delivery trucks rather than purchasing them.

5. Why might it be desirable for a dealer who sells equipment to suggest to the businessman just starting a new business that he buy used instead of new equipment?

6. A drugstore plans to sell cigars and cigarettes. What might be a good location for the display of the items?

Problems and Projects:

1. Assume that you wish to start one of the following business activities in your city: a gift shop, a hobby shop, children and teens' shop, or a restaurant.

    (a) Secure an outline map of your community, or draw an outline map (partially real and partially imaginary). Indicate on this map the principal features, streets, types of zoning (industrial, business, and residential). Indicate the location you have chosen for the business.

    (b) Why is this particular business location to be preferred over other places?

2. (a) Make a pedestrian count for a certain location within the center of a block. Make this count during a particular time—the longer the time, the better.

    (b) On the same day a week later, and at the same hour, make a pedestrian count for an adjacent corner location. In each case tabulate the number of women, children, and men who pass the location.

    (c) Draw some conclusions with regard to the value of each location.

3. A store in the downtown (central shopping) district has a rental expense of $10,000 for the year and has sales for the year of $125,000. A similar store in a neighborhood shopping center has a rental expense of $8,000 for the year and has sales for the year of $80,000. Considering only the rental expense as a percentage of sales, which location would be considered better?

4. Visit at least two stores, such as a jewelry store and a drugstore, and make a list of items found in closed display cases (not windows). Give reasons for such goods being displayed. Observe whether there are other goods that might have been displayed to advantage in cases.

Case Problem 11-1:

On a main highway just outside a large city are three motels with a total of 64 units (apartments). The nearest restaurant is approximately two miles from the motels and is located in a shopping center on the same highway as the motels. J. D. Howe is considering opening a restaurant near the motels.

Required:

Explain some of the important factors he should consider in making a decision.

Case Problem 11-2:

Fred Case, after working for several years as a salesman of used cars, decided to establish himself in the used-car business. In the community he found two lots that were of sufficient size. One lot was located near three other used-car lots operated by agencies selling both new and used cars. The other lot was located at the edge of a shopping center nearly two miles away from the other three used-car lots.

Required:

Which is likely to be the better location for Case's used-car business? Explain your answer.

Continuing Project:

(a) Make a study of possible locations for your business, then choose the best location. Draw a map of the location, including nearby businesses, and give your specific reasons for selecting the location.

(b) Make a detailed list of the equipment that will be needed in your business and make a drawing of the building, placing the equipment where you think it should belong. The outline of each piece of equipment should be drawn to the same scale as the layout of the building. With your list of equipment include the cost of each item.

 **CAREERS IN MARKETING**

In the chapters in this unit, you have learned that there are many different activities involved in marketing or getting goods from the producer to the consumer. In large businesses many of these activities are handled by persons who have become specialists in a particular type of work. To give you an idea of some of the areas of marketing in which one may find a career, information about the principal ones is given here.

Very large businesses usually employ a marketing specialist, known as the marketing research director, and marketing research technicians. Such specialists are employed also by management consultant firms, who offer their services to a business for a fee.

Specialists in marketing need a superior background in economics, marketing, transportation, warehousing, finance, statistics, business management, accounting, and research techniques.

Careers in Distribution. In recent years specialists have been developed to aid the manufacturer in determining what are likely to be the best markets for his products and what are the most efficient distribution channels for these products. If a business plans to increase or decrease its sales territory, to add or drop products or lines, it is important that a study be made of the possible effects of such changes on the costs of distribution and the possible effects on the sales volume and profits. As business conditions change, a business may find it desirable to use a different method of distribution.

Careers in Merchandising. Most large retail stores have positions filled by persons who are experts in merchandising. These persons have control of the buying and the selling of goods. They see that the store has the goods that will satisfy the customer demand—the proper goods, at the proper prices, at the proper time, and in the proper quantities.

The person who has the full responsibility for merchandising in a particular store usually is called the merchandise manager. He may have as his assistants persons known as divisional managers, each of whom is a specialist in a particular line of merchandise.

To gain the proper experience for such a responsible position as merchandise manager, one needs to have had experience as a salesperson, then as a buyer, and then as divisional merchandise manager.

Careers in Selling. There are such a variety of career opportunities in the field of selling that only a few of the principal types of selling will be explained here.

One type of selling is the *consumer route,* in which the salesman, such as the dairy products salesman or the laundryman, calls on homes on a regular schedule. A similar type is the salesman who has a regular business route—selling merchandise on a repeat basis to business establishments.

Retail selling is that which is done when the consumer comes into the place of business of the seller. *Consumer specialty selling* is that type which involves calling on prospective buyers in their homes to sell specialty products, such as vacuum cleaners and storm windows. *Business specialty selling* refers to calling on business establishments to sell products, such as air-conditioners, accounting machines, and cash registers, that will facilitate the operation of the business.

Another type of selling is that which is involved in selling *services* rather than goods. Persons selling insurance, advertising space, consulting services, repair and maintenance services, and transportation are examples of the selling of services.

A successful salesman enjoys being with and studying people. He needs a great deal of imagination and ability to deal with unexpected situations. Initiative, enterprise, and determination to get ahead are important qualities. It is desirable that a salesman have a broad background; excellent ability in communication (both oral and written); and a knowledge of salesmanship, advertising, and business management.

Careers in Advertising and Sales Promotion. Advertising is big business. About 160,000 persons are now working in the advertising field, and it is estimated that a minimum of 15,000 jobs in this field are being filled each year.

There are advertising jobs in different areas. One area is in advertising agencies (there are more than 5,000 of them). These agencies prepare the majority of the advertisements that we see and hear. Agencies are engaged by firms to decide what is the best type of advertising medium and to prepare the actual advertising material. A second area is that of working directly for the advertiser—a manufacturer, a retailer, a utility company, and the like. In such companies the advertising department prepares the company's advertising. A third area is working for businesses that carry advertising, such as magazines, newspapers, outdoor poster and sign companies, and television and radio stations.

A great variety of specialists are found in advertising. They include those who write copy, artists, those who decide which medium (TV, magazine, newspaper, radio) best meets the advertiser's needs, those who invent product names and slogans, those who help design packages for products, TV producers, and researchers who interview users of the products advertised.

It is desirable that one study courses in advertising, marketing, economics, and salesmanship. Liberal arts courses with emphasis on English, literature, history, and sociology are also good basic preparation for advertising careers.

Large stores have employees who are specialists in preparing window displays and in arranging for special interior displays. Generally, such specialists also have the responsibility for the overall decorations for the store on special occasions, such as the Christmas season and the Easter season.

Manufacturers frequently employ similar specialists who visit retail stores, usually smaller stores, and arrange special window displays of their products. These specialists also suggest how to (or actually do so) arrange attractive interior store displays. Some businesses that sell display materials and equipment have specialists to aid the merchant in arranging displays.

Since the size and shape of display spaces vary so greatly and the merchandise to be displayed is in all sizes, shapes, and colors, a great deal of creative ability and imagination is needed for this special type of advertising and publicity work. A background in art work, advertising, and display materials and methods is important for a person in this work.

UNIT IV
Purchasing and Production

Where may a business obtain information about prices?

What is the job of a comparison shopper?

Through what sources can goods be bought?

When is it desirable to buy merchandise in small quantities?

What are the types of merchandise discounts?

BACKGROUND OF CHAPTER

Buying is not always easy. Consider, for instance, what an individual must think of before he can make a simple purchase of some shirts: Do I need one shirt, three, or a half dozen? Will the department store or the neighborhood men's shop give me the selection and values I want? When is the best time to buy—now or during the spring sales? Should I take the budget shirt or the more expensive, higher quality one?

The answers to those questions help in making the purchasing decision. A businessman asks similar questions before he buys supplies and merchandise for resale. This chapter tells how he answers his questions and makes some of his purchasing decisions.

CHAPTER 12

MERCHANDISE PURCHASE AND CONTROL

Whether a business is purchasing merchandise for resale, raw materials for manufacturing, equipment for use in operating the business, or supplies to be consumed in its operation, it must solve certain purchasing problems and determine purchasing procedures. No business can conduct its purchasing activities efficiently unless certain policies are established. This chapter discusses the problems and procedures of purchasing and controlling merchandise, especially as applied to retail stores.

PURCHASING PROBLEMS

Anyone who enters business should remember that his existence can be justified only on the basis of the service that he renders to the community. He should therefore consider himself as serving in the capacity of purchasing agent for his community. If he has that attitude, he will study the people he is to serve; he will find out their wants, their tastes, and their methods of living.

If a store is located in the section of a city where people with average incomes live, the store should not be stocked with only highest priced goods. Stocking medium-priced goods would probably be better. Should the goods of the store be bought only by women, the management should study feminine likes and dislikes before deciding what to buy. A business' purchasing policy decisions should always be determined by what is known about its customers.

What to Purchase

Keeping the right kinds of goods in stock is extremely important to the success of a business. Discussed on the next pages are those factors which businessmen must consider in making decisions about the type of goods to purchase.

Quality. Many merchants have injured their businesses by thinking more about quantity than quality. They have been anxious to give greater quantity than their competitors without regard to quality. In other words, the price factor has been uppermost in their minds. Winning the confidence of the public and holding it is the principal factor in the success of any business. A customer may be fooled for a short time; but when he finds that he has been fooled, he will look for another place to buy.

ILLUS. 12-1. The store that purchases goods without regard to quality in order to price below competitors may lose customers.

Brand Names. The businessman who is just beginning an enterprise is confronted with the problem of deciding what brand or brands of goods to handle. Well-known or nationally advertised brands are probably the best for a new business. After the business is well established and has earned a good reputation, the customers might be induced to try private brands, which usually yield a larger profit.

A decision must be made as to how many different brands of similar products are to be carried in stock. For instance, the grocer must decide just how many different brands of canned corn he should handle. A study of the customers and the community should be of aid to him in making this decision. He must serve his community by attempting to give customers what they wish; but if he carries five or six brands instead of two, he will have a larger amount of his capital tied up. Most stores do not find it necessary to carry more than three brands in different price ranges.

Related Items. Just how many different items should be handled cannot be answered definitely, for the number will vary with each business. Should the person who is opening a men's clothing store handle suits only, or should he also stock shoes, shirts, underwear, socks, neckties, and hats? There are two factors that should influence him in reaching a decision. The amount of competition is one. If there are already a number of nearby stores that carry the same quality of merchandise, the proprietor of the men's clothing store would probably find it unwise to handle all the related items. If, in a survey, he found that there was seemingly a lack of such stores selling hats, then he might find it desirable to handle hats in addition to suits. The other factor is the financial ability of the business to handle many items in addition to suits. Keeping in mind these two factors, the merchant should handle as many related items as possible.

Size. Because many items come in different sizes, the merchant has to decide what sizes of various items should be stocked. For example, should the merchant stock sugar in 2-pound, 5-pound, or 10-pound packages? The shoe store will have to determine what sizes and what quantities of each size, style, and color should be purchased.

Guides in Determining What to Purchase

There are several guides the businessman can use in determining what to purchase. Catalogs and salesmen are valuable guides. Trade associations and their publications can also help. Two aids readily available to every merchant are records of past purchases and sales and comparison shoppers.

Records of Past Purchases and Sales. An important guide to buying is found in the records of past purchases and sales. These records, which also show factors that affected sales of past seasons, can be interpreted in connection with new circumstances that may have an important effect in the future season. For instance, the records may show that during the last three seasons the average number of men's tropical worsted suits sold was 400. But the fashion news for the coming season indicates that men's summer suits of double-knit fabric will be in vogue. So it probably would be unwise for the store to plan to purchase 400 tropical worsted suits for the coming season. There are many publications that will aid the buyer in forecasting the demands of a season.

Comparison Shoppers. Making a study of what other stores are doing may help the businessman with his purchasing problems. He may study the advertising and examine the merchandise displayed in the windows of competing stores. Many of the larger stores in cities send someone to competitors' stores to find out what merchandise, prices, and services are offered by those stores. This person is usually known as a *comparison shopper*. He may actually buy goods in a competitor's store and take them back to his establishment for comparison with his own goods.

When to Purchase

The determination of when to purchase is influenced by the type of merchandise, the type and location of the supplier, and style and price trends. Orders have to be placed in advance of the selling season so that the merchandise will be in the store at the right time. For example, orders for women's shoes for summer wear are usually placed in January. If a new item comes on the market, the businessman might find it desirable to delay placing his order for a short time until he feels certain that the item will be in style for a sufficient time for him to sell the item. Should the businessman believe that prices for certain items are likely to be much higher in the near future, he may wish to place his order for such items before the price rises.

How to Purchase

Through trade papers and other magazines, businessmen should be able to obtain information as to important sources of supply. The leading methods of buying are: (1) ordering through traveling salesmen; (2) making personal trips to the market; (3) ordering through buying offices; and (4) ordering by mail by means of a catalog.

Traveling Salesmen. The operators of small stores often cannot afford to take the time and incur the expense of making personal trips to large markets to buy their goods, so they usually order their goods from traveling salesmen.

Trips to the Market. The buyers for large stores usually go to the chief markets, such as New York City. One advantage of such a method is that it gives the buyer a chance to visit a large number of businesses and to compare their merchandise.

Making personal trips to the market is the usual procedure followed in buying clothing for women, most of which is sold on a style basis. Wholesalers do not like to handle such goods because of the great risk of loss due to style changes. Direct contact between the buyers for retail stores and the manufacturers of women's clothing is also advisable so that a style that is proving popular can be manufactured quickly and placed on sale in the stores. Unless the clothing is produced quickly, there may be no demand for it when it is placed on sale.

ILLUS. 12-2. Many small businesses buy their goods from traveling salesmen.

Buying Offices. In the chief markets the buyer may visit a *buying office* that will give him information about the products of many manufacturers and help him with making purchases.

Ordering by Catalog. This method is used mainly for placing repeat orders of staple goods when the merchant finds his stock getting low and the representative of the manufacturer or the wholesaler will not call again for some time. Directories of different kinds such as those published by trade associations, manufacturers, wholesalers, and telephone companies may also provide information as to possible sources from which to buy.

Choice of Suppliers

Another purchasing problem the businessman must solve is whether to buy goods from several suppliers or to concentrate his purchases among a few. In addition, he must decide whether to buy from local suppliers or those in a distant city.

Concentrating Purchases Among a Few Suppliers. Whether to buy most of his goods from a few suppliers or whether to scatter his orders among many business concerns is a problem that the businessman must resolve. Most successful businessmen believe that to concentrate buying among a few suppliers is the best plan. The businessman who follows this plan usually develops friendly and personal relations with the manufacturer or wholesaler, and the supplier consequently gets to know the store, methods, and needs of the businessman. Better prices and better credit terms, as well as better service, are likely to result.

Buying from Nearby Suppliers. Since the transportation cost, whether prepaid by the seller or paid by the buyer, affects the total cost of the purchase, the merchant should buy his goods from concerns located as near as possible to his place of business, other factors being equal. Buying from nearby suppliers also results in orders being filled more quickly.

The sources of supply do not remain the same. Some business may develop a better article or one that costs less. The successful buyer will be constantly alert for better sources from which to buy.

How Much to Purchase

After the businessman has decided what to buy, when to buy, and how to buy, there is still the problem of how much to buy. The increasing amount of attention paid in recent years to stock turnover has greatly changed buying policies. Formerly a six months' supply of goods was bought at a time. Such a policy would result in the money of the business being tied up in merchandise for a long time. For example, a clothing merchant might estimate that he could sell 3,000 suits of clothes during the spring and summer season. If all the suits were purchased at one time at a cost of $50 a suit, the merchant would have $150,000 of his capital tied up in suits for a considerable time. It would be better for him to purchase approximately 1,500 suits at one time, 1,000 suits at a later date, and the other 500 at a still later date. By that method he would require only about $75,000 (1,500 suits at $50) to finance the purchase.

With modern transportation and communication facilities so excellent, it is a good practice to buy in small quantities, for this permits a minimum investment in merchandise. If only small quantities of merchandise are kept in stock, the danger of loss from obsolescence, spoilage, shrinkage, or changes in demand will be small. When the stock of merchandise is large, there is a greater chance of loss.

When buying small quantities, however, the transportation costs should be considered. By buying in larger quantities one may be able to realize a savings in transportation costs. For example, if the freight

ILLUS. 12-3. To minimize the investment in merchandise, it is usually best to buy in small quantities.

rate is based on a minimum weight of 100 pounds, the cost of a shipment of 100 pounds would be no more than for 60 pounds.

Many merchants cannot resist the temptation to buy large quantities of merchandise when they are offered a discount for buying such a quantity. A clothing store may be quoted a price of $40 for 100 pairs of men's socks or a price of $38 for 100 pairs on a purchase of 1,000 pairs. If the store should buy 1,000 pairs at one time, the cost would be $380 instead of $400 for 1,000 pairs purchased at the rate of 100 pairs each time. But suppose the store were able to sell only 800 pairs during the season. The remaining 200 pairs would have to be stored until the next season. In that case capital would be tied up; there would be danger of deterioration and damage; and styles might change during the next season. The store would probably suffer a larger loss on the 200 pairs than would have been saved in buying the larger quantity.

PURCHASING PROCEDURES

A business must have merchandise and materials on hand at the time they are needed. To accomplish this requires many persons and a great deal of clerical work. In large businesses several departments and many people will have something to do with the purchase of goods and materials. It is necessary, therefore, that the different procedures involved in purchasing be carefully organized.

A well-organized purchasing procedure depends on obtaining and keeping detailed information on supply, consumption, quality, and prices as shown in Illustration 12-4. For each product that is purchased and consumed, there should be information on sources, specifications

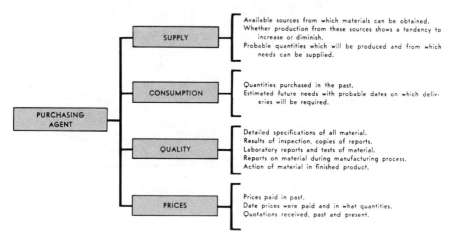

ILLUS. 12-4. Information needed by a purchasing department.

(detailed description), quantity consumed, quantity purchased in the past, time required for delivery, the satisfaction obtained from previous purchases, prices, and price trends.

Much of this information can be obtained from the catalogs of the various manufacturers and distributors. There should be a systematic method of filing and indexing such catalogs or the information obtained from them. For instance, each catalog should be analyzed according to the different kinds of goods listed in it. A separate card showing all pertinent facts for each class of goods can then be prepared and placed in a convenient file.

The Purchasing Department

Many businesses have a large staff of skilled employees who do nothing but handle the purchases. Each person has specialized duties to perform. The person in charge of the purchasing department is known as the *purchasing agent*. In large businesses the procedures involved in the purchasing and receiving of goods also involve departments other than the purchasing department. The departmental interrelationships which result from the purchase and receipt of goods in one large company are shown in Illustration 12-5.

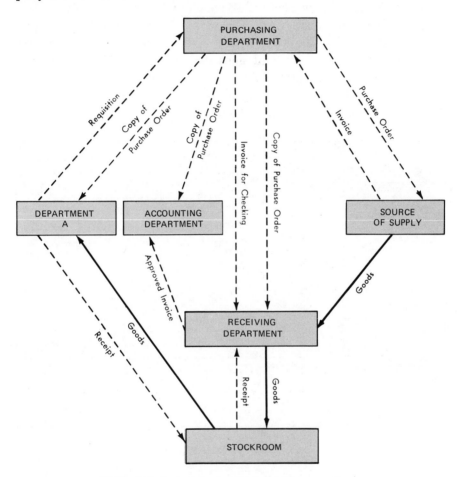

ILLUS. 12-5. A chart tracing the purchasing procedures.

Ordering and Receiving Goods

Two important parts of the purchasing process are the ordering of goods and the receiving of goods. The following discussion explains how these operations are handled in the large and in the small business.

Placing the Order. The proprietor of a small business can easily discover that the stock of certain items is getting so low that additional orders should be placed. As a check or reminder he should list his purchase needs in a memorandum book of some kind as he discovers them. As he places the order, he can check off the items ordered.

It is impossible for the owner or even the purchasing department of a large business to know when goods should be ordered. For that reason *purchase requisitions* are used. These are forms requesting the purchasing agent to buy the items listed. A department head or the chief stock clerk usually fills out and signs the requisition. Illustration 12-6 shows a purchase requisition. At least one carbon copy is made. The original is sent to the purchasing agent, and one copy is kept by the person requesting the purchase of the goods.

PURCHASE REQUISITION			**27994**
ORDER FROM Fordson Office Supplies Co.		DATE March 6, 19--	
ADDRESS 906 Berry Avenue, Waynesboro, VA 22980			
SHIP TO The George D. Barbey Co., Inc.			
ADDRESS Charlotte Avenue and Third Street			
VIA Fordson delivery truck	F.O.B.		

QUANTITY	NO.	DESCRIPTION	PRICE
2 boxes	324	3½" Loose leaf fasteners	4.75/box
50	754-21	Pressboard folders, half cut tab	.58/ea.
5	12R	8½ x 11 Ring binder, steerhide line	3.10/ea.
20	45-150	8½ x 11 Analysis pads	.70/ea.
5	45-110	8½ x 14 Analysis pads	.75/ea.

INDICATE USE BELOW:

DEBIT MEMO	CHG. ACCT.	EXPENSE ORDER	PROD. ORDER	OTHER
	Office Supplies #5102			

PURCHASE ORDER NO. *F14518*   REQUESTED BY *J. Harris*   APPROVED BY *M. Fuller*

ILLUS. 12-6. A purchase requisition.

The proprietor of a small business places his order for goods by writing a letter, while a large business makes use of a business form, known as a *purchase order,* to accomplish the same result. Such a form is shown in Illustration 12-7 on page 227.

Several copies of a purchase order are made by the purchasing department. The original is sent to the company from which the goods are being ordered. Usually a second is sent to the vendor, who returns it as an acknowledgment of the order. One copy is kept in the purchasing department files; another is sent to the person who prepared

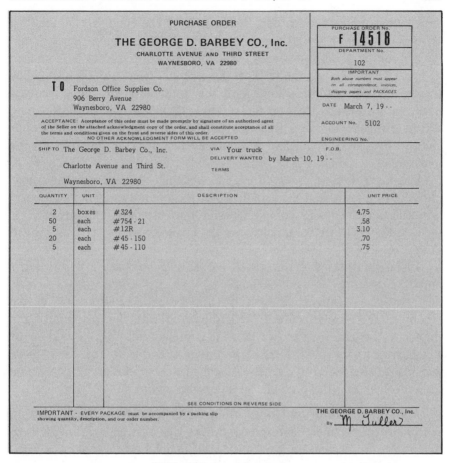

ILLUS. 12-7. A purchase order.

the purchase requisition so that he will know the goods have been ordered; one copy may be sent to the receiving department; and another may be sent to the accounting department. These copies are usually made on paper of different colors so that the proper copy will be sent to the proper department or person.

Handling Incoming Goods. After goods have been ordered for a business, other fundamental operations must be carried out in preparation for the resale or use of the goods. All incoming shipments should be received at a specified point, and a complete and correct record should be made there. Before signing the receipt of the transportation company, the receiving clerk should examine each shipment to see if the case or the wrappings are damaged, wet, or broken. If the shipment is not in good order, a statement of the condition in which it is received should be written on the receipt. This precaution will aid in establishing a claim if some of the contents are found to be damaged or lost. Before signing the receipt, the receiving clerk should also check to see that the shipper's name and the number of packages received agree with the statements on the receipt. It is desirable that a detailed record be made of the shipment received. Should some of the goods shipped by the seller be lost or damaged in transit, a claim should be made against the carrier.

The next step is unpacking and checking. When merchandise is unpacked and checked in a small store, the quantity of goods received is usually counted and compared with that listed on the invoice. If the count agrees with the quantity on the invoice, the invoice is approved in that respect.

In larger businesses the goods are checked against a copy of the purchase order. Another system used by some businesses is known as the *blind-check system*. In such a case the checker does not receive a copy of the purchase order for comparison with the contents of the shipment. Instead the checker lists the contents on a form, one copy of which goes to the purchasing department and one to the department that placed the order. This list is checked against the invoice by some person other than the one who counted the contents.

Marking the Price on Goods. In a merchandising business marking the prices on the merchandise is the next step. In a department store this procedure becomes a great task. All major items are marked individually. Whenever it is feasible, a price ticket should be placed on every article. Items such as handkerchiefs can be grouped together with one price notation applying to each item in the group. These items are, however, often marked individually. Sometimes the price is placed upon the carton or the display compartment. In many grocery stores the price is indicated by movable numbers placed on the display shelf under the items. However, some grocery stores do indicate the price on each individual item of merchandise whose price is not subject to frequent changes. In such cases the price is usually marked by means of a crayon pencil or a rubber stamp. This marking is an aid to the cashier in the self-service type of store.

The practice of marking prices on merchandise in retail stores advertises the merchandise to those who are hesitant about asking the price. It avoids the misquoting of prices to customers. The price ticket may also aid in taking a physical inventory. The retail price should be marked in large, plain figures. Price tickets may be stitched, pinned, tied, or pasted on merchandise.

The efficient merchant wants to know which stock is old and which sells slowly, so that he can better decide about his future purchases and also make plans to dispose of the older merchandise. Information of this and other types can be indicated on the price tag. An example of a tag containing various items of information is shown in Illustration 12-8. Tags of this general type are made so that when an item is sold

The Williams Bros. Company		Explanation of the information on the tag:
45	828	45 department
117	W 1118	828 style number
	2.89	117 business from which the article was purchased
45	828	W 1118 date of purchase
117	W 1118	W 1973
	2.89	11 November (11th month)
		18 18th day
		2.89 selling price

ILLUS. 12-8. A duplicate price ticket, sometimes called a two-part ticket or a stub-type ticket.

a stub can be torn off and turned in by the salesperson to the department head or the stock room. Such stubs not only indicate how well particular articles are selling but also serve as a check on the supply of each item. In other words, as each item is sold, management gets a stub and can watch the inventory of that item. Many businesses, however, do not use a price ticket with a stub.

Many kinds of tags, tickets, or labels are used. They may be printed by ticket machines or marked by hand. The most common types of tags, tickets, and labels are:

1. Gummed labels for towels, handkerchiefs, books, and appliances.
2. String tags for jewelry, dresses, and large articles.
3. Pin tickets for socks, underwear, and other articles that pins do not damage.
4. Tickets that are fastened to cloth goods by looping part of the goods into a slot on the ticket.

When new merchandise has been marked and is ready to be placed on sale with other goods of its kind, it should be so placed that the merchandise already in stock and still in good condition will be disposed of first. Should the new merchandise be placed on top of or in front of the old merchandise, the latter becomes shopworn before it is sold. Many food items such as eggs, dairy products, cookies, and bread are marked with a code to indicate when they should be removed from sale.

Dating and Terms

Since the dating and the terms of purchase offered by sellers vary a great deal, the businessman should be familiar with the more common ones in order to know which are most advantageous to him.

FOB. When purchases are made, a free delivery point is indicated. Ordinarily merchandise is bought *FOB* (free on board) *shipping point.* The seller then pays only the expense of delivering the goods to the carrier, such as a railroad, in the city in which he is located. *FOB destination* means that the seller will pay the transportation charges to the destination. These transportation charges do not include charges for trucking the goods from the railroad to the purchaser's place of business. As will be seen, however, in Chapter 14, store-door delivery can be obtained at no extra cost under some conditions. Most trucking lines provide store-door delivery.

As an example of shipping practices, consider the following case: Mr. Jones, who operates a store in Buffalo, orders a washing machine from a Chicago business, the price being $200, FOB Chicago (the shipping point). The transportation charges from Chicago to Buffalo are $15. Mr. Jones therefore pays the transportation company $15 and the seller in Chicago $200. Suppose that Mr. Jones wanted the machine shipped FOB destination. In that case the Chicago business would probably ask a price of $215 because it would have to pay the $15 to the transportation company.

There is a legal point in connection with these two situations that the buyer should keep in mind. In the first situation, when goods are purchased FOB shipping point, the title to the goods passes to the buyer as soon as the seller delivers the goods to the carrier. Thus, if the goods sold to Mr. Jones should be damaged en route to Buffalo, the loss would fall upon Mr. Jones, the buyer. In some cases Mr. Jones might be able to collect damages from the transportation company. In the second situation, however, when goods are sold FOB destination, the title to the goods and the risk of damage remain with the seller until the goods reach their destination.

Regardless of the responsibility for damage to goods, it is usually good practice for the seller to make whatever adjustment is necessary and to handle the claim with the transportation company. If there is a justifiable claim against the transportation company, the seller can usually collect damages readily.

Net 30 Days. A common way for the terms of a purchase or sale to be stated is "net 30 days," which means that payment is to be made within 30 days from the date of the invoice. The date of the invoice is usually the date of shipment of the goods. Some businesses offer longer terms, such as net 60 days. The longer the terms, the better for the buyer since he will have a chance to sell some or all of the goods by the time he is to make payment for them.

Open Account. Open-account terms usually imply payment within one week or ten days or a period agreed upon by the buyer and seller.

Advance Datings. In order to encourage buyers to purchase in advance, that is, to place their order for goods several months before they will actually sell them, some businesses offer *advance datings*. Under such a dating the date for payment is computed from a certain day in advance (after) of the date of shipment. For example, goods may be shipped in February but have a dating of April 4. If the terms are net 30 days, payment need not be made until May 4.

EOM. Another form of dating is *EOM* (end of month). The time of payment is then computed from the end of the month in which the merchandise is shipped. If goods are shipped on May 14 with EOM terms of net 30 days, payment need not be made until June 30.

ROG or AOG. When the buyer is located a great distance from the seller, *ROG* (receipt of goods) or *AOG* (arrival of goods) terms may be given. For example, the seller in New York gives terms of ROG net 30 days to the buyer in San Francisco. If the buyer receives the goods on May 1, he is to make payment by May 31.

COD. Under COD (collect on delivery) terms, payment is made in cash by the buyer when the goods are delivered to him.

Discounts

The businessman is often offered discounts on goods that he purchases. The common types of discounts are: trade discount, quantity discount, seasonal discount, cash discount, and anticipation discount.

Trade Discount. A *trade discount* is a special deduction from the *list price* (price quoted in price lists and catalogs) that is made to buyers in certain classes, such as wholesalers, retailers, or jobbers. For example, a manufacturer may give retailers a 30 percent discount but may give wholesalers a 45 percent discount. Sometimes a series of trade discounts may be offered. For instance, in the catalog of a manufacturer a particular article may be quoted as $40, less 25 percent, less 10 percent. The net cost would be figured as follows: $40 less $10 (25 percent of $40), or $30; less $3 (10 percent of $30), or $27.

The trade discount serves as a simple method of adjusting prices. On a rising market, the manufacturer can drop one or more discounts from a series or replace a larger one with a smaller one without publishing an entirely new price schedule or catalog. Likewise, on a falling market, prices can be adjusted by increasing the rate of discount.

Quantity Discount. A *quantity discount* is used by sellers to encourage customers to buy in larger quantities. One kind of quantity discount applies to the total purchases by a business over a period of time. Another kind applies to individual shipments or sales. Quantity discounts may be based on the number of units purchased or on the value of the entire order.

Seasonal Discount. A *seasonal discount* is one given to the buyer for ordering or taking delivery of goods in advance of the normal buying period. It is an inducement to buy earlier than is really necessary from the purchaser's standpoint. An example is a discount offered on fuel oil bought in the summer.

Cash Discount. If payment is made within a given time, most manufacturers and wholesalers offer a discount known as *cash discount* or *time discount*. It may be offered with various advance datings and credit terms. The terms of a purchase may be net 30 days with a 1 percent discount for payment within 10 days. If the invoice is dated May 1, the buyer will be permitted to deduct 1 percent provided he pays for the merchandise on or before May 11; otherwise he must pay the full amount by May 31. It is customary in business to express such terms as "1/10, n/30."

If a discount is to be granted for payment within a 10-day period, the remittance should be in the hands of the seller before the close of the tenth day of the credit period, or the envelope should bear a postmark indicating that it was mailed within that period.

If a cash, or time, discount is offered, the buyer should attempt to make payment in time to get the discount because (a) discounting purchase invoices gives the merchant a good credit rating and (b) such a practice effects a saving. For example, under the terms 1/10, n/30, the saving amounts to approximately 18 percent on an annual basis. In other words, if 1 percent is saved by making payment 20 days before the due date, there is an equivalent saving of approximately 18 percent in 360 days. Illustration 12-9 gives the amounts which a businessman can save by taking advantage of cash discounts.

Terms	Approximate Saving
1/2% in 10 days, net 30 days	9% a year
1% " 10 " " 30 "	18% " "
2% " 10 " " 30 "	36% " "
2% " 10 " " 60 "	14% " "
2% " 30 " " 120 "	8% " "
3% " 10 " " 120 "	10% " "
3% " 10 " " 60 "	21% " "

ILLUS. 12-9. Approximate annual savings on discounts.

The figures in Illustration 12-9 show that a businessman will actually profit by borrowing money at 6 percent annual interest in order to take advantage of cash discounts. It is quite apparent that he should keep his finances in such a condition that he can discount invoices.

Anticipation Discount. A business that has sufficient working capital may sometimes be granted an *anticipation discount*. As an example, suppose that the terms on a $400 invoice are net 90 days. The buyer has sufficient funds to make payment at the end of 30 days. Since he will be paying 60 days before the due date, he may deduct interest for the 60 days anticipated. Sixty days' interest at 6 percent on $400 is $4, the anticipation discount. The buyer accordingly makes a payment of $396 to settle his account. An anticipation discount should not be taken, however, unless the privilege is granted by the seller or unless the granting and taking of such discounts is an established practice within the particular industry. Taking an anticipation discount without having the privilege is certainly unethical.

Some sellers state on their invoices, "Interest at 6 percent a year will be charged on all past-due accounts." This is the reverse of allowing anticipation discounts and is intended to encourage buyers to pay their bills before they become overdue.

STOCK CONTROL

From the time of receipt of the goods until their final sale or use, goods are said to be "in stock." Since the period during which they must be "in stock" may vary from a few hours to several months, orderly methods of storing them and of keeping track of how many items are on hand must be planned.

Storing Goods

Some merchandise may be placed immediately upon display for sale or be used immediately in the operation of the business, while other goods must be stored temporarily. The amount of space needed for storage will vary with different types of businesses, and the location of such space will vary. It is desirable to have the storage space so located that needed goods may be obtained quickly and easily. In retail businesses the storage space is frequently in the rear part or in the basement of the building, utilizing space which is undesirable for selling space. In some retail businesses a considerable amount of reserve stock is stored near the selling space in order to provide prompt service to customers who may wish to take their purchases with them.

The type of storeroom and equipment needed varies a great deal. Certain goods should be stored in a cool place, or even in a refrigerator; others in a warm place. Some goods require a very dry atmosphere; others a damp one. Shelving is needed in most storage rooms, and the type varies greatly for different products. In many instances it may be desirable to stack full cases and boxes of unopened goods on the shelves. In such a situation they should be stacked so that the labels may be read easily. Those items that are most frequently needed should be stacked on lower shelves and near the door of the storeroom for easy accessibility. Whenever a new shipment is received, the older supply in storage should be placed on top or in front of the new so that the older supply will be taken out first.

Methods of Controlling Stock

Every businessman should have some definite means of controlling his stock so that he knows which items are selling best, how rapidly the various items of stock turn over, when goods should be reordered, and in what quantities repeat orders should be placed. **Too many business-men** depend on their memories and, because of the lack of records, are compelled to guess about the most important facts of their business.

A practical policy is to fix high and low limits for every item carried in stock. In a retail store the low limit, or the point below which management does not wish the supply to fall at any time, is a safeguard against being unable to supply items called for by customers; in a manufacturing business, the low limit is a safeguard against a lack of supplies needed in the process of manufacturing. In a manufacturing business, a shortage of supplies will hold up production and cause a serious loss. The low limit is determined largely by the time required to have more goods delivered and made ready for resale or use. The high point is established to serve as a check against buying too large a quantity and thus overstocking with probable bad results.

A simple plan for calling attention to the low limit is to place a strip of ordinary gummed tape, such as that used for packing and wrapping, around the group of items that is considered the low-limit quantity. For example, the low limit for a certain brand of toothpaste may be four dozen tubes. The gummed tape is placed around a group of four dozen tubes, together with a gummed label, or "sticker," that contains information about the article. When, days or weeks later, a clerk sells the last loose tube of that particular brand of toothpaste and is confronted with the taped group of four dozen, he tears off the tape and gives the "sticker" to the one who does the buying.

When items have individual tickets attached, these tickets can be removed from the goods when they are sold and can then be given to the buyer as a guide in making future purchases.

Many businesses use *stock cards* as an aid in deciding what to buy, when to buy, and how much to buy. Stock cards are also used as the basis of the inventory record. Individual stock cards are kept for all items. Illustration 12-10 on page 236 shows a stock card. This type of card is quite useful in a manufacturing enterprise, in a department store, and in some specialized stores, such as a shoe store. In a small grocery store or a hardware store, however, too much detailed work would be involved in keeping a record of this kind for each individual product. In such stores two methods of controlling stock are generally used: (1) observation or inspection and (2) physical inventory. Most small-store managers rely on constant observations as a guide to know what is happening to their stock. A *physical inventory*, which is made by a personal count of every item in stock, is made only once or twice a year.

| Manufacturer | Ordered | | Received | | Unit Cost | Selling Price | Sold | | Balance | | Remarks |
	Date	Quantity	Date	Quantity			Date	Quantity	Quantity	Value*	
M. M. Co.	19 - - Feb. 15	48	19 - - Feb. 17	48	.26	.39	19 - - Feb. 18 19 20 21 22 24	3 2 4 1 5 2	48 45 43 39 38 33 31		

Article __Plastic tape__ Stock No. __871__ High __72__ Low __24__

* This column may be used for either cost value or retail value. Usually the value column is used only at the end of a fiscal period, as at the end of a month.

ILLUS. 12-10. A stock record card.

Taking an Inventory

At the close of each fiscal period an inventory of the merchandise is taken primarily to determine the amount for the financial records and also to discover what merchandise is moving slowly. Either of two general methods—the cost method or the retail method—may be used in taking an inventory.

Cost Method. Under the *cost method,* the values of the items on hand are computed at the prices paid for the articles. It is therefore necessary that the cost price of each item be known. The price can be determined by locating the invoice for each item, but this plan is laborious and therefore little used. The cost price is sometimes marked in code on each item at the time of purchase. Ten different letters or symbols may be used to represent the ten different figures 1, 2, 3, 4, etc. "Black horse" and "come and buy" are examples.

```
1  2  3  4  5  6  7  8  9  0
B  L  A  C  K  H  O  R  S  E
C  O  M  E  A  N  D  B  U  Y
```

As each item is counted, the cost value is determined by the code mark. For example if "black horse" were used as the code, the letters A R K on an item would indicate a cost of $3.85. If the market value of the goods being inventoried is less than the cost price, the former is used. The cost method is used in manufacturing businesses and in some retail stores.

↗**Retail Method.** The *retail method* of taking an inventory is the listing of all the items on hand and determining their value on the basis of the retail prices marked on them. Thus, it is easier to inventory goods by the retail method than by the cost method. The total value of the goods secured by this method cannot, however, be used on the balance sheet because on this statement the assets are to be listed at their cost, not their sale, value. To adjust this retail value to cost value requires that detailed records be kept, especially when a large number of items are handled. The costs of the merchandise purchased are accumulated along with the retail values. Then, at the end of a fiscal period, the ratio of the cost value to the retail value is applied to the retail value of the stock in order to adjust the inventory to cost value. The basic method is given in Illustration 12-11.

	Cost	Value at Retail Price
Inventory at beginning of period	$ 20,000	$ 40,000
Purchases during the period	100,000	160,000
Totals	$120,000	$200,000

The ratio of cost to retail is 60% ($120,000 ÷ $200,000). If the physical inventory at the end of the period had a total value of $75,000 at the marked selling prices, then 60% of $75,000 would give a cost value of $45,000 for use in the financial statements.

ILLUS. 12-11. Method of adjusting inventory retail value to cost value.

If there are such items as purchase returns, freight charges, markups and markdowns, they must be included in the calculations.

↘**Perpetual Inventory.** Manufacturing and large wholesale and retail businesses frequently use a *perpetual-inventory system*. Such a system provides records showing the amount of merchandise or raw materials on hand at any time without the necessity of making a physical count. Illustration 12-12 on page 238 shows a perpetual-inventory card used in a manufacturing business. A card record is kept for each item. Whenever a purchase of any item is made and the material is received,

| \
 PERPETUAL-INVENTORY CARD | | | | |
Item:			#12 bolts	
Date	Pur. Req. or Stock Req. No.	Put in Stock	Withdrawn	Balance
2/3/--	2192	1,200		1,200
2/10/--	126		100	1,100
2/12/--	128		500	600
2/26/--	2198	1,000		1,600
3/1/--	140		300	1,300

ILLUS. 12-12. Perpetual-inventory card.

an entry is recorded on the card. Whenever a quantity of an item is withdrawn from stock, it is recorded on the card. The balance on hand at any time is always shown in the last column. If the business has a computer, perpetual-inventory records are generally kept on it.

Even when perpetual-inventory records are kept, it is desirable occasionally, usually once a year, to make an actual count of all goods available to see whether the physical inventory agrees with the records.

REVIEW WHAT YOU HAVE LEARNED

Business Terms Checkup:

(1) comparison shopper
(2) buying office
(3) purchasing agent
(4) purchase requisition
(5) purchase order
(6) blind-check system
(7) FOB shipping point
(8) FOB destination
(9) advance dating
(10) EOM
(11) ROG (or AOG)
(12) COD

(13) trade discount
(14) list price
(15) quantity discount
(16) seasonal discount
(17) cash (or time) discount
(18) anticipation discount
(19) stock card
(20) physical inventory
(21) cost method
(22) retail method
(23) perpetual-inventory system

Reading Checkup:

1. What thought should be kept uppermost in mind by the businessman in deciding what goods to purchase?

2. What brand or brands of goods should be carried by a new business?

3. What are the principal methods of buying?

4. Under what circumstances do retailers order goods by mail?

5. Are women's dresses usually handled by wholesalers?

6. Is it usually a better plan to buy from many business houses or from only a few?

7. Why is it usually a good practice to buy in small quantities?

8. What is a purchasing department?

9. Examine the purchase order on page 227 and state from whom the goods are being ordered.

10. Does the checker of incoming goods receive a copy of the purchase order when the blind-check system is used by the business?

11. Mention some commonly used methods of marking prices on merchandise.

12. What is meant by terms of 2/10, n/30?

13. According to the table on page 233, what would be the approximate annual saving if the buyer took advantage of terms of 2/10, n/30?

14. What is meant by goods "in stock"?

15. What is meant by low and high stock limits?

16. If the code for indicating cost prices were "black horse," how should a cost of $4.18 be indicated?

17. Why is the retail value of goods not used when reporting the value of the inventory on the balance sheet?

APPLY WHAT YOU HAVE LEARNED

Questions for Class Discussion:

1. Should the goods handled by a bookstore and gift shop in a small college town be the same as that handled by a similar store in a noncollege town? Explain.

2. (a) Name three articles that quickly deteriorate.

   (b) Name two articles that are subject to sudden style changes.

3. Why is it usually a good policy for a new business to carry nationally advertised products?

4. What related items might be handled profitably by a ladies' shoe store?

5. Which of these three buying methods—from catalogs, from traveling salesmen, by making trips to the market—is usually used by the following retail stores:

   (a) Small grocery.

   (b) Women's exclusive dress shop.

(c) Radio and television store.

(d) Men's shoe store.

6. What are the possible advantages to the retailer of buying from nearby suppliers?

7. Why is it desirable for a business to use a purchase-order form?

8. Why should the receiving clerk examine incoming goods before signing the receipt for the transportation company?

9. Give examples of goods that require cool or cold storage space; give examples of those requiring a dry storage place.

10. Discuss the desirability of having the price of each article plainly marked for the customer to see.

11. Why do buyers insist on advance datings when they purchase goods a considerable time before they will actually sell them?

12. When goods are bought at different times on EOM terms of net 30 days, does the buyer always have the same length of time between the date of purchase and the date of payment?

13. What are the principal reasons for taking an inventory of the merchandise at the close of each fiscal period?

Problems and Projects:

1. Visit a small clothing store and observe how many different kinds of wearing apparel are stocked. Also observe if there are neighboring stores that stock similar items.

2. A dress shop purchased 200 dresses at $25 each. The dresses were marked to sell at $35 each, and 100 dresses were sold at that price. Because the dresses did not sell as well as expected, the selling price was reduced to $28; 60 dresses were sold at that price. To dispose of the remaining dresses, a half-price sale was held; and the remaining 40 dresses were sold for $17.50 each. What was the total gross profit (ignoring the operating expenses) on the dresses?

3. If the dress shop in the preceding problem had purchased only 160 dresses at $25 each and was able to sell 100 dresses at $35 each and the remaining dresses at $28 each, what would have been the total gross profit on the dresses?

4. An appliance store can purchase a certain make of electric heater for $25 from either a firm in City A or a firm in City B. Transportation cost from City A is $2.88 per heater; transportation cost from City B is $2.17. What would be saved if 50 heaters were purchased from the firm in City B?

5. A business uses approximately 850 packing cases daily. It requires approximately two weeks to place an order for and to receive a new shipment. What might be a desirable low stock limit to set for this item?

6. Refer to the illustration on page 229 showing how information concerning the date of purchase was listed on the duplicate price ticket. If the letter "Y" were used to indicate the year 1973, how should a purchase made on March 23, 1973, be indicated?

7. What is the percent of approximate annual savings effected by taking advantage of each of the following discounts: 1/10, n/60; 2/10, n/90; 3/10, n/90?

8. On March 1 you make a purchase of $400 on terms of 2/10, n/30. Suppose you do not have the money to take advantage of the discount, so you borrow at 6 percent for 20 days the amount needed to pay the invoice on March 11. What is the net saving you make by borrowing to take advantage of the discount?

Case Problem 12-1:

Ann Williams is opening a retail apparel store in an exclusive apartment-house district of a city of 400,000. She is considering what type of apparel should be carried.

Required:

1. Do you think it advisable for the store to specialize in infants' and children's wearing apparel?

2. What price clothing should be stocked?

Case Probem 12-2:

Today Tom Henderson, owner of the All Star Sporting Goods Store, received shipments of merchandise containing thermos bottles, baseballs in a cardboard box, binoculars, and men's socks.

Required:

Make a recommendation for Henderson as to the kinds of price tickets (string tag, gummed label, pin ticket, etc.) that should be placed on the merchandise he received today.

Continuing Project:

(a) For one of the items that you plan to sell in your business firm, establish a purchase plan. Indicate when to purchase the item, how much to purchase, where to purchase, and the credit terms.

(b) Set up for your business a plan for determining goods that are needed, a plan for purchasing, a plan for receiving, and a plan for handling stock.

What location problems does a manufacturer face?

How should a production department be organized?

What is involved in scheduling?

What is the most efficient method of production?

What is meant by quality control?

How does layout affect manufacturing operations?

BACKGROUND OF CHAPTER

A service business sell services; retail and wholesale businesses purchase merchandise from someone else and resell it; a manufacturing business makes useful products from raw materials and sells the finished products to wholesalers or retailers.

A manufacturing business faces the usual problems in accounting, finance, sales, and other functions. In addition to the problems which are common to all businesses, a manufacturing business has many problems connected with the production of goods. This chapter discusses the operations of a manufacturing business.

CHAPTER 13

MANUFACTURING PROBLEMS AND PROCEDURES

The management of a manufacturing business faces the usual problems in accounting, finance, sales, credit, collections, and the other activities that are common to retailing, wholesaling, and service businesses. A manufacturing business, however, has some additional problems.

Determining a location for the plant is one situation in which a manufacturer faces problems and considerations different from those encountered by the retailer or wholesaler. Location and extent of the market; transportation; access to raw materials; power, labor, and water supplies; climate; and political considerations are examples of factors which the manufacturer must study before making a plant location decision.

Also, a manufacturing business has an *engineering problem*, which usually involves research and study in regard to new products and the improvement of old products, designing and planning new products, designing and planning new equipment, and other related work.

Production problems which involve such factors as labor, equipment, plant layout, and work scheduling will be encountered. The purchasing problems related to production are often complicated because purchases must be scheduled carefully to fit in with the production program. Purchasing and related problems include receiving, inspecting, testing, storing, and issuing the materials as needed.

A manufacturing business has important problems of keeping the building and equipment in repair, and these problems may require a separate maintenance department. There are also problems of personnel and wages. These often require a separate personnel department for the selection, training, placement, and payment of employees.

The main emphasis of this chapter will be on the location and the production problems of the manufacturer.

LOCATION PROBLEMS OF A MANUFACTURER

The manufacturer has location problems that are distinct from those of the retail merchant, and selecting a location for a manufacturing enterprise is quite a complicated procedure if it is done scientifically. The manufacturer must consider carefully such factors as:

1. Location and extent of the market he expects.
2. Transportation facilities, including costs and services.
3. Access to markets.
4. Source of supply of raw materials needed.
5. Focal points for raw materials.
6. Power supply and cost.
7. Water supply.
8. Labor supply.
9. Climate.
10. Kindred industries.
11. Political considerations, such as taxes.

Location and Extent of the Market

In the following paragraphs we shall see how the selection of a location is influenced by such considerations as the extent and concentration of the marketing area.

Regional Markets. Many businesses that operate in local markets eventually extend into *regional markets* (markets that take in more than one state). For instance, some ice-cream manufacturers expand from one city to another until they cover a regional market, such as New England, the Ohio Valley, or the West Coast. Seldom, however, does an ice-cream manufacturer extend marketing into a particularly large area. Some candy manufacturers who start as small enterprises eventually expand into regional markets, and a few of these expand into national markets. Numerous food and other products are sold in regional markets, but often no attempt is made to market them nationally.

Producers and distributors often find that they cannot reach into national markets without establishing branches. They hesitate to establish branches because the problem of management then becomes more complicated and expenses increase. Many manufacturers have found that the most profitable plan is to confine activities to a reasonably restricted area. When they attempt to expand into larger markets, competition and the costs of service make increased sales unprofitable.

National Markets. Many businesses, such as book publishing companies and manufacturers of automobiles, steel, and breakfast foods, have developed what are called *national markets*. In other words, they sell products in all states. In catering to a national market, a business enterprise must take into consideration the location from which it can produce and distribute its products most economically. Some of the factors that influence the location are discussed later in this chapter. It is obvious, however, that the producer who expects to sell in a national market must give very careful attention to his location in relation to the market. For example, a company that manufactures a breakfast food largely from wheat with a national market for its products would not find it economical to be located in the northern part of Maine or in New Mexico. In many cases, however, accessibility to raw materials, power, and labor may be more important factors than the location in relation to the market.

Transportation

A manufacturer's market is not always close to him. He frequently serves a wide area, whereas the retailer serves a relatively small area. Thus, in a manufacturing business, special attention must be paid to transportation facilities such as trucking routes, railroads, waterways, airlines, and pipelines.

Transportation Facilities. Before locating their factories, manufacturers who must ship large quantities of material by freight investigate carefully the freight service in and out of all cities. They may find that freight moves more quickly from one city than it does from another. This small difference in time is frequently important in selecting a location.

A business that is located where it has access to all types of transportation facilities is in a desirable situation provided other conditions are satisfactory.

Cost and Service in Transportation. The cost and the reliability of transportation service must be considered together. Some businesses could operate more profitably by maintaining a single large plant, with a central office in one city, and shipping to all customers from this point. The cost could then be kept at a minimum. Service is, however, extremely important. For example, a textbook publisher with a central office in Chicago may find it necessary to establish branches in San Francisco, Atlanta, and New York in order to serve the entire United

States. Books must be sent to each branch from the central point in Chicago. From each branch books are shipped in smaller lots to customers. This type of organization often adds to the cost of distribution, but it accelerates service. A customer in San Francisco would not have to wait until his order is shipped from Chicago.

Access to Markets. Manufacturers that have a large export business usually find it more economical to have their plant, or at least a branch, at a seaport or at a point where they can obtain good transportation to a seaport. Some businesses located in the Middle West send shipments down the Ohio and the Mississippi Rivers for transfer to ocean-going vessels. Others located within the interior of the United States ship by rail to the East or the West Coast for *transhipment* (transfer to another means of shipping) by water. With the completion of the St. Lawrence seaway, ocean-going vessels can deliver their cargo, as well as accept cargo, at the many ports on the Great Lakes. Use of this seaway will avoid the necessity for transhipment of certain cargo and will result in lower transportation costs.

Raw Materials

For many manufacturers the availability of raw materials must be considered in choosing a location. Specific factors which must be evaluated are discussed on the following pages.

Source of Supply of Raw Materials. The source of supply of raw materials is extremely important in some industries, whereas it is not important in others. If the raw material is used in small quantities and has a very high unit value, the source of supply is not so important as in the case of raw material that is used in large quantities at a low unit cost. For instance, the jewelry business is not so much interested in the source of its supply of gold as it is in other factors. It would be foolish for a manufacturer of fine jewelry to locate his plant near a gold mine. If he did, his plant would be situated somewhere in the mountainous sections of the West, in Alaska, or in some other place away from large centers of population that provide markets for the jewelry.

If the goods to be processed are perishable, the plants that process them are usually located near the perishable raw materials. For example, plants processing fruits, fruit juices, and vegetables are located in the agricultural sections where the fruit and vegetables are grown.

Focal Points for Raw Materials. The location of iron and steel mills is a good example of the importance of care in the selection of producing points. Coal, from which coke is made, iron ore, and certain amounts of limestone are the principal raw materials used in the production of iron and steel. Some mills are located near iron deposits, while many others are located near coal deposits. The ideal location is one near a good grade of iron ore and a good grade of coal.

Some iron and steel mills are located at points that are not near the source of supply of coal, iron ore, or limestone (the basic raw materials). They are located at what might be called *focal points* (places where raw materials can be assembled economically) for all these materials. From these focal points the mills have easy access to their markets for the finished products of iron and steel. The steel mills of Ohio, Pennsylvania, West Virginia, Illinois, and Indiana are not located at original sources of all the raw materials. None is at the source of iron ore. Some are located at the source of coal, and others at the source of limestone; but a few of them are not located near any of the raw materials. They operate successfully, however, because they are situated at focal points in areas where they are able to serve large markets economically.

Power Supply and Cost

Power is an extremely important factor in modern industry. It may be derived from waterfalls or from some fuel, such as coal, oil, gas, or wood. Power that is generated by a waterfall is usually converted into electricity, whereas that derived from fuels is used to generate steam. The steam may operate engines directly and thus furnish the power for manufacturing, or it may operate engines that convert the mechanical power into electric energy.

Many manufacturers buy electricity from a public utility company. Others have their own power plants in which they generate steam to be used in steam engines or to be converted into electrical energy. Still other plants generate electric power through the use of diesel engines, which burn crude oil. The generation of steam power depends upon good supplies of coal and water. The generation of electric power through the use of diesel engines depends upon obtaining a supply of crude oil at a reasonable price.

Sometimes there are other large plants that have surplus power nearby that is sold cheaply. Plants that need much electric power usually locate in areas where there is plenty of power at a low price, such as near the TVA or other large power developments. In some small communities other manufacturing conditions might be desirable, but the power supply might not be dependable.

Water Supply

Many of the modern industries require very large quantities of water. For example, approximately 50,000 gallons of water are required for the manufacture of one ton of steel. Such industries would probably find it more desirable to locate on a large body of water rather than to depend on wells dug in inland areas.

Labor Supply

Some industries require highly skilled labor, whereas others can use unskilled labor. Still others require a combination of the two. Producers of machine tools, jewelry, musical instruments, and watches require a large number of highly skilled workers and only a few unskilled workers. In selecting a location, such a manufacturer finds that the supply of labor has an important bearing unless workers can be "imported" easily.

Most industries have no difficulty in obtaining large supplies of un-skilled labor. Some of the textile plants moved to the South so that they could obtain large supplies of unskilled labor at low prices and, at the same time, be near the raw material and cheap power. When new plants are organized in small communities, however, labor is frequently imported. Unskilled workers are sometimes encouraged to move to a new location in order to increase the supply of labor and thus to keep the price of labor low.

Some manufacturers need seasonal labor, whereas others need permanent labor. For instance, canneries that pack fruits, vegetables, and fish need labor only during their canning seasons. They therefore find it necessary to use a small percentage of skilled labor and a large percentage of unskilled labor.

Climate

The favorable and unfavorable aspects of an area's climate should also be considered in locating an industrial plant. Heating and air-conditioning facilities add much to the cost of a building and increase operating costs. Severe storms such as hurricanes, tornadoes, and snow storms can affect power lines and interfere with transportation. Excessive rainfall leading to floods also can be harmful to poorly located plants.

Kindred Industries

Industries tend to group themselves into "families" or kindred industries. *Kindred industries* (sometimes called *related industries*) are those industries that are similar in nature. Woodworking industries of various types frequently congregate. Machine industries also group themselves together. Cincinnati, Ohio, for instance, is one of the most important machine-tool centers. This fact has led to the manufacture of a great many other types of machinery in Cincinnati. In Detroit and surrounding cities a large percentage of our automobiles are made. Because of the automobile industry in this area, there are many factories that make automobile accessories, tools, and equipment.

The supply of labor in kindred industries can be transferred from one enterprise to another without serious difficulty. Another advantage of the grouping of such industries is the fact that the necessary service agencies are developed in the same community. For instance, if a factory needs some kind of repair, the service can be obtained without difficulty provided the factory is located in a community in which there are many kindred industries and also service agencies that aid these industries.

Political Considerations

Sometimes political considerations influence the location of a manufacturer. Certain units of government (state, county, city, etc.) may offer more favorable rates on such taxes as business profits taxes, workmen's compensation taxes, real estate taxes, franchise taxes, and special license taxes than do other political units. Some communities even postpone the levying of taxes for a period of time in order to entice new businesses to locate in the community.

PRODUCTION PROBLEMS

As was discussed in Chapter 3, economists define production as the creation of utility (the ability of a good or a service to satisfy a want). Of the types of utility (form, place, time, and possession), this discussion involves business operations which create form utility—making a product useful by changing its form or shape. As commonly used in business, the term "production" means the creation of form utility; or, in other words, "production" means the manufacturing of products.

Production (or *manufacturing*) *problems* involve obtaining the proper labor, selecting and obtaining the proper materials, selecting and using the proper equipment, arranging the plant and its equipment in the proper manner, planning and scheduling the work, and inspecting and testing products.

Organizing for Production

In a small plant employing only ten men, the manager may be able to remember all of the necessary production data. He may issue verbal orders and instructions and supplement these instructions as work progresses. In a plant of this size he knows all the workers well, what they can do best, when any part of the work is finished, and what work is still to be done. He can use his best judgment to change plans and schedules quickly in order to meet changing conditions. If a breakdown of a machine occurs, he will know about it immediately and can take steps to remedy the situation. If an employee is absent because of illness, he can change the work schedule. If an employee quits, he can replace him and train the new employee.

If a product is changed, the manager will know immediately what materials and tools are needed and can show his men how to incorporate the changes in the production methods. He will know what to do if production is increased or decreased. If an order is cancelled, he can adjust the work and quickly shift to another product.

In this small plant the manager can keep a daily watch on inventories and supplies. His management control can be effective, economical, and flexible. Only a minimum amount of paper work is required.

Even in small plants, however, it is advisable to put things down on paper and to think out plans carefully because one's memory is not always dependable. If the manager is ill or absent, production must go on under the guidance of someone else. A one-man organization is, therefore, inadequate even in a small business.

Now let us see what happens if a plant increases in size with more workers, more products, more materials, and more orders to be filled. The production management of one man who carries all the information in his head begins to break down. Supervision and paper work are needed. Orders must be written to avoid mistakes, reports must be made by various individuals, and these must be cleared through someone who is in a position to make decisions and to make sure that all factors of production are working together smoothly. These factors are orders, labor, materials, supplies, tools, and equipment. They must be checked constantly with production schedules to be sure that no part of the production system drops behind in the schedule.

There are many types of production organizations. Illustration 13-1 is an example of how one production department is organized. Illustration 13-2, page 252, shows the functions performed in a production department of a manufacturing business.

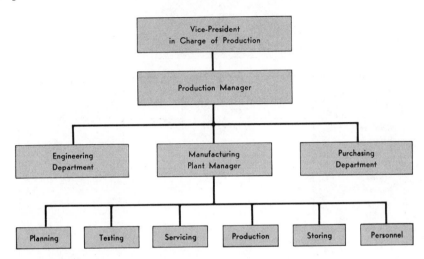

ILLUS. 13-1. Organization of a production department.

Controlling Production

Production control means controlling factors of labor, materials, layout, and equipment that are used in the production process. These factors must be used efficiently in order to satisfy customers, to keep employees busy and happy, and to make a profit. To achieve effective production control, management must obtain proper timing and a smooth and uninterrupted flow of work.

Planning Production

Illustration 13-3, page 253, is an example of how the operations of a manufacturing plant are scheduled. These operations are based upon plans. Plans are based upon actual orders and forecasts of orders. The manager must be able to answer questions such as the following:

1. What and how much are we going to make?
2. When are we going to make it?
3. How will we make it?
4. How much and what kinds of materials will be needed?
5. When shall we order the materials and supplies to be sure that they are available when needed?

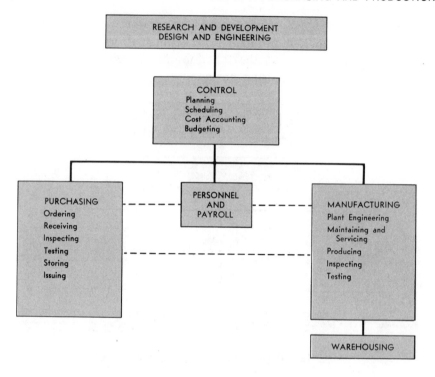

ILLUS. 13-2. Production department functions.

6. What parts and how many parts must be manufactured on contract by someone else?
7. From what sources can we get these parts, and when shall we order them to have them when we need them?
8. What tools and equipment are needed, and is it necessary to obtain additional or special tools and equipment?
9. How much and what kinds of labor and special skills are needed?
10. How shall we schedule the production of the orders?

In Illustration 13-3 the product being manufactured is a piece of machinery that will necessitate the making of metal castings, the manufacture of several parts, and the obtaining of special parts from *subcontractors* (other manufacturers).

The needs of labor, materials, and equipment are estimated. These estimates are known as *budgets*. From these budgets, the money needed is estimated. Illustration 13-4 shows a sample of a materials budget.

The purchasing agent should know or find out how long it takes to obtain all of these materials and parts so that they will be available

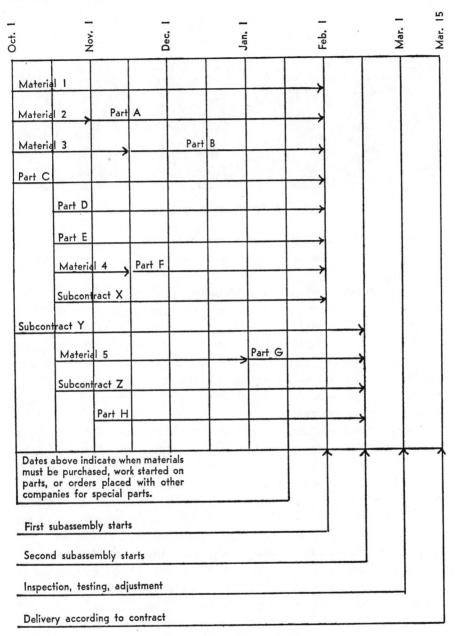

ILLUS. 13-3. Production schedule.

when the various stages of assembly take place. This kind of planning is very similar to the planning of a meal in a home. The housewife must start the cooking of various foods so that they will all be ready

Materials Budget
for Six-Month Period, January I to July I, 19—

| Material or Parts | January | | February, etc. |
	Quantity Required	Estimated Cost	
# 6064 casting	200	$1,986.00	etc.
# 125 shield	200	894.00	
# 306 casters	800	193.50	

ILLUS. 13-4. Example of materials budget.

for serving at the same time. Some foods require longer to cook than others. Therefore, the cooking of all foods will not be started at the same time.

In Illustration 13-3, if the calculations have been made correctly, the materials and parts needed in the first subassembly will be ready at the same time (Feb. 1). Those needed in the second subassembly will be ready when needed. Adequate time for delivery and production must be allowed, and in most cases some spare time must be allowed so that there will be no costly delay in assembling the final product simply because one part was not ordered early enough or was not started in production early enough.

The problems outlined above are particularly true of certain types of products made on special orders for special purposes. Standard parts can be made in quantity at any time and kept in stock. The manufacture of these can be scheduled in production to fill in idle time. Other standard parts can be purchased from other manufacturers and kept in stock until they are needed. However, no manufacturer likes to keep more parts in stock than are necessary for efficient production. To do so would mean an investment in idle parts and materials.

When production is ready to start, all factors of production must be set in motion. This is the *scheduling process*. Illustration 13-5 shows how production is scheduled and cost figures collected.

The scheduling department, which is a part of the whole manufacturing or production department, issues the orders for jobs or processes to be started in production. The requisition for materials goes to the stores (stored materials) department. The instructions for the work orders go to the manufacturing department. The personnel department receives instructions as to the work and men required. The stores

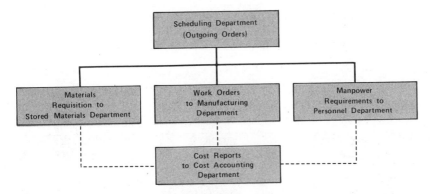

ILLUS. 13-5. **Scheduling department functions.**

department, manufacturing department, and the personnel department refer all costs figures to the cost accounting department.

Organizing Production Routine

There are two steps in efficiently organizing production routine. The first step is illustrated by the chart in Illustration 13-6 on page 256. It is necessary to list the various steps in any production process to determine the various jobs that must be performed. The second step is arranging the plant and equipment so that this production process can be carried out smoothly.

In order to get smooth production routine, it is necessary to move from one process to another without interruption or delay and with a minimum of labor and machinery to do each job. This efficient method of production is often referred to as *straight-line production*. This method is usually the most economical because the goods do not back-track but move steadily forward from operation to operation with a minimum of handling. The term straight-line method applies even though the goods do not move forward exactly in a straight line.

Straight-line production is important because it will usually save space as well as bring about economy in production. Space is often saved by eliminating unnecessary steps and by joining together the various related functions. Efficiency in production is automatically obtained by eliminating wasted motion. For example, in some factories materials are moved from one bench to another or from one department to another on trucks. Using trucks requires wider aisles, causes confusion, and requires more time. By joining the tables or the departments together so that the production flows smoothly from one step to another, there is more efficiency.

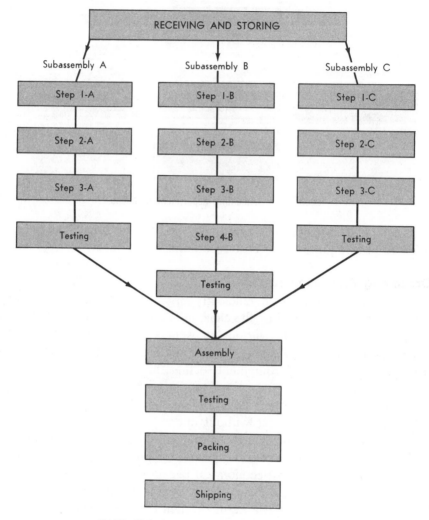

ILLUS. 13-6. Organizing straight-line production.

Handling Materials

If one were to define manufacturing in its simplest terms, it could be said that manufacturing is the productive movement of materials through the factory. Materials are brought in and are moved from one point to another. They are stopped at various stages at machines, benches, bins, or shelves. They are sometimes stored on the floor. They may be put onto a cart and taken off a cart.

The first step in handling materials is storing. Illustration 13-7 is a simple record of stores. This is typical of the kind of record used in

Balance of Stores Record

Item Casters # 306   File number   B12.4
Maximum   1000   Minimum   100
Time required for delivery   10 days

Location
A-1-3

Date	Units Ordered	Received			Issued		Balance		Remarks
		Units	Price	Amount	Units	Amount	Units	Amount	
1/1/—	Balance	820	$2.00	$1,640.00			820	$1,640.00	
1/10/—					350	$700.00	470	$ 940.00	
1/12/—	500								
1/18/—					200	$400.00	270	$ 540.00	
3/1/—		505	$2.10	$1,060.50			775	$1,600.50	
3/2/—					100	$200.00	675	$1,400.50	

ILLUS. 13-7. Record of materials and parts.

a manufacturing business. There is a card or sheet used for each item. Every bolt, nut, and screw must be recorded and accounted for carefully. Each item must be marked on the records when it is received and checked out when it is placed in production. The person in charge of stores is responsible for seeing to it that there is always sufficient material on hand when needed. Before the quantity on hand gets too low, the purchasing department must buy an additional quantity.

Besides a written record of materials that are stored for use in manufacturing, there are other ways to be sure that the supply of any item does not fall below the minimum requirement before reordering. One method of handling small parts that are placed in bins is to have two sections in the bin for each item. One section will hold the minimum quantity needed before reordering. When all other parts are used and only the minimum quantity is remaining, the person in charge of the stores is required to notify the purchasing department immediately. The same principle can be used with items that may be stacked. A marker can be placed at one place in the stack, and when the supply is reduced to this level, the clerk immediately notifies the purchasing department.

The handling of the materials throughout the entire production process is time-consuming and costly. It has been estimated by some experts that the handling of materials represents 75 percent of manufacturing activity. In some businesses 50 percent of all the labor cost is in the handling of materials and parts. The handling of materials does not contribute anything directly to the value of a product, but it adds greatly to the cost. Therefore, a manager of a manufacturing plant must ask himself the questions listed in Illustration 13-8 and attempt to find solutions to these problems.

1. Could the supplier of materials and parts package or deliver them in a manner that would save time and labor?
2. Can special trucks, platforms, conveyors, or containers be used?
3. Can materials and parts be moved by gravity rather than by mechanical power or manpower?
4. Are there idle periods during which materials and parts can be handled?
5. Does the movement of materials proceed smoothly without interruption and with a minimum of handling?
6. Can production processes be combined to avoid rehandling of material?

ILLUS. 13-8. Questions regarding the efficient handling of materials.

Improving Production Methods

The manager of a small plant may determine his own production methods, or he may hire a specialist to advise improved methods.

Methods of production must be carefully studied at all times. New materials and new machinery may make it possible to develop better methods of production. Even with old materials and old equipment it may be possible to improve the methods of production. For example, four metal stamping machines each had an operation rate of 60 units per minute. At this rate the output per machine should be 27,000 units for each working day of 7½ hours. The actual production was 22,800 per day. The difference between the rated, or maximum, output and the actual output was due to the fact that the operators had to obtain their own materials, transport them to the machines, and arrange them for their use. This work took approximately ten minutes out of each hour. There are two solutions to this problem. One is to put an inexperienced person in charge of supplying the materials to each operator as needed. The other solution is to take one operator off his machine for half of each hour and give him the job of supplying the other operators with the materials they need.

"I'm beginning to think we need a better system around here."

ILLUS. 13-9. Production methods must be continually evaluated.

Use of Time and Motion Studies. In order to improve the methods used by employees at different jobs, a business should have studies made of the jobs. These are called *motion study* (a study of movements) and *time study* (a study of the time required on each process). Such studies should result in an economy of time and motion on the part of the employee and possibly a simplification of the work. For example, a study was made of a person doing assembly work while seated at a bench with the various parts to be assembled placed in small boxes on the bench. This study showed that the parts to be picked up by the left hand and the right hand should be placed within the semicircles shown in Illustration 13-10. If the various parts were not placed in those positions, the employee would have to get up from his seat to reach the necessary parts.

In making studies it is usually desirable to determine the actual time required for the different operations performed by the worker. By that means one can determine how much each operation costs. Those

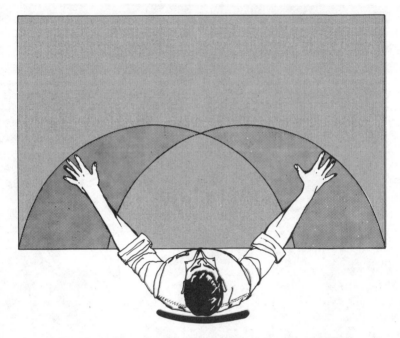

ILLUS. 13-10. Areas showing results of one form of motion study.

operations that cost the most are studied with special care to see if they can be made less costly.

Study of Equipment. When trying to improve production methods, it is always necessary to take into consideration the tools and equipment that are used in the plant. In many plants there is considerable time lost because small tools are not available when needed. There is time lost in making adjustments on machines and in setting them up for operation. Tools and equipment are lost, and very often there is considerable inefficiency because of the lack of knowledge as to how to use tools and equipment. In well-organized plants there are special maintenance men, and there is a centralized toolroom where all equipment is available quickly when needed.

In some plants the equipment is inadequate to do the job that is being performed. Machines are sometimes overloaded or the machine is too small to do the job properly. In other cases the wrong type of machine is being used. A different type of machine would be better and faster. Every plant manager must make decisions as to whether machines are running at the proper speed, whether machines are being fed properly, and whether there is a smooth flow of production from one process to another. In planning production it is necessary to know what each machine can do. The table in Illustration 13-11 shows how the capacities of machines are scheduled.

Many manufacturing processes that formerly were done by machine with the guidance and assistance of a worker are now done through automation. Both large and small businesses can benefit from automation. Some people assume that automation in a manufacturing plant

Schedule of Machine Requirements
for Six-Month Period, January 1 to July 1, 19—

Machine Number	January				February, etc.
	Machine-Hours Required	Capacity	Excess Capacity Available	Additional Capacity Needed	Etc.
1	180	160		20	
2	240	200		40	etc.
3	120	160	40		
etc.					

ILLUS. 13-11. Planning and scheduling production in terms of machine capacity and work load.

means that the whole plant operates automatically. Such is usually not the case. Automation is most often achieved through a step-by-step improvement of the manufacturing operations. The first step usually is to make machines automatic and then tie them together with automatic handling of materials with electrical control.

Quality Control

Quality control is involved in engineering, manufacturing, and purchasing. Essentially, *quality control* is the checking of products to make sure they measure up to certain prescribed standards. It involves research, improvement in design, testing of materials, inspection, and testing of finished products. To obtain the facts that are needed, it is often necessary to check on the product when it is in use by customers. Salesmen often can get information as to how well the product stands up in use and how satisfied the customers are. It is always desirable to watch competitive products and examine them to see what improvements have been made. Another part of quality

1. Can the job be done better at a previous or subsequent point in the production process?
2. Can this operation be combined with another operation?
3. Does the operation add any usefulness or salability to the product?
4. Can the part be purchased at a lower cost than it can be made?
5. Does the operator stand in the right position and sit at the right height?
6. Are both hands being used efficiently?
7. Will a foot control or an automatic control save time?
8. Is the best operator using any particular method that other operators can use?
9. Will specially designed tables, tools, or machines improve production?
10. Are parts and tools within easy reach?
11. Can more than one machine be operated efficiently by one operator?
12. What are the most frequent causes for rejection during inspection?
13. What can be done to correct mistakes or low quality in production?
14. Are standards higher or finer than is necessary for quality needed in the product?
15. Can a standard and cheaper part be substituted for a special and more expensive part?
16. Can holes, bolts, and screws be standardized as to size?
17. Can the design be improved to simplify the manufacture and assembly but still meet the requirements of salability?
18. Can different material be used?

ILLUS. 13-12. Questions to be asked when attempting to improve production methods.

control involves the consideration of new and better materials, the use of improved methods of manufacture, the use of newer and better machinery in manufacturing, and the training of workers so they can produce a better product.

It has already been mentioned that inspection is one means of controlling quality. Poor quality may be due to the machine or to the workman or both. Usually each workman is held responsible for checking his work to be sure that it meets requirements. However, additional inspections by experts are necessary. Good inspection practices will include the following:

1. Inspection and testing of materials and purchased parts.
2. Inspection at various stages in the manufacturing process as indicated in Illustration 13-6.
3. Final inspection and testing.

Failure to have good quality control can cause great losses. Some of these losses arise from:

1. The cost of materials that are scrapped.
2. The cost of labor and other manufacturing expenses wasted on a defective product.
3. The cost of correcting a defect.
4. Special discount on a defective product that is sold below the usual price.
5. The cost arising from the return of defective merchandise from a customer.
6. The loss of goodwill of a customer.

Factory Layout and Expansion

The purpose of factory layout is to provide the arrangement of building facilities, machinery, and equipment that will produce quality products at the lowest cost per unit.

There are hundreds of thousands of different kinds of products being manufactured. Different kinds of machinery and lengths of time are required for their manufacture. Consequently, there are different layouts for the different types of manufacturing. For example, an automobile manufacturing plant layout would be considerably different from that of a small candy manufacturing plant.

Illustration 13-13 shows the layout of a bakery and illustrates how the incoming materials move through the manufacturing processes.

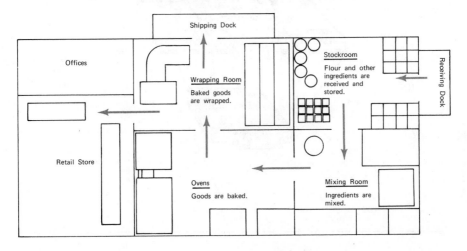

ILLUS. 13-13. Layout of a bakery.

As new technical inventions in equipment and machinery are made, a factory usually needs to revise its layout to accommodate the new machinery and to expand operations. Frequently a study of the building, the location of the areas for receiving and for shipping, and the location of the different machines and equipment used in the manufacturing process will result in finding changes that can be made to reduce the cost of manufacturing. A visit to plants manufacturing a similar product may be an aid in revising one's plant. Revised layouts are usually necessary when the plant is enlarged as the volume of business increases.

Many small manufacturing plants of today will become the medium-sized plants of tomorrow. This means that the building must be enlarged. It is desirable in planning the original building to design it so that additions can be made from time to time as the business grows. Illustration 13-14 shows a plan for making additions to a manufacturing plant.

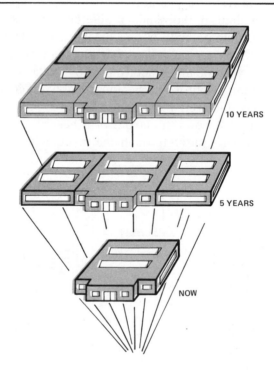

ILLUS. 13-14. Plans for future expansion.

REVIEW WHAT YOU HAVE LEARNED

Business Terms Checkup:

(1) engineering problem

(2) regional markets

(3) national markets

(4) transhipment

(5) focal points

(6) kindred industries

(7) production problems

(8) production control

(9) subcontractors

(10) budgets

(11) scheduling process

(12) straight-line production

(13) motion study

(14) time study

(15) quality control

Reading Checkup:

1. What are some of the factors that should be considered by a manufacturer in selecting a location?

2. How does the adequacy or the inadequacy of the supply of raw material affect the location and the successful operation of a business?

3. What bearing do kindred industries have upon the location and the operation of a business?

4. Name some of the problems that a manufacturing business has that are not found in retailing and wholesaling businesses.

5. Why is a one-man management system, even in a small plant, unsatisfactory?

6. Indicate at least three things that the manager must know in planning and scheduling work.

7. Why must there be a budget of materials in manufacturing?

8. In a manufacturing business, what department gets the reports from which costs of manufacturing are determined?

9. In organizing an efficient straight-line production system, what are the two necessary steps?

10. Why is proper handling of materials so important in manufacturing?

11. Since the handling of materials is costly, what are at least two of the questions that a manufacturing plant manager should ask himself to improve the handling of materials?

12. How can time and motion studies be helpful in improving production methods?

13. Give some examples of how tools and equipment affect manufacturing efficiency.

14. In scheduling the use of machinery in production, what information is needed on each machine?

15. Indicate at least two questions that should be asked when one is attempting to improve production methods.

16. In controlling the quality of manufacturing, what functions are involved?

17. What are some of the losses that will occur as a result of poor inspection and quality control?

APPLY WHAT YOU HAVE LEARNED

Questions for Class Discussion:

1. In what ways must electric power be dependable for some types of industry?

2. Why do some companies have branch offices and warehouses when they could operate more economically from one central point?

3. Name some of the natural resources that give certain sections of the country an economic advantage over other sections that do not have these resources.

4. What utilities are usually very important to manufacturing plants?

5. Explain why management is so important in a manufacturing process.

6. Explain how the failure to purchase or to acquire a single item when it is needed might completely stop production and add to the cost of manufacturing.

7. Why is a manufacturing process such as the production of wheat flour simpler than the production of special jobs such as a machine to stamp automobile tops?

8. Some manufacturers feel that they should make all the parts that go into the final product that they are manufacturing and selling. Why may this not be the cheapest way in which to make the product?

9. Examine the production schedule shown in Illustration 13-3, page 253. Explain why the purchasing function plays a very important part in production.

10. Why is accurate cost accounting important to a manufacturer?

11. Straight-line production is emphasized in all kinds of manufacturing. Why is it considered so important?

12. Why is it so important in production to have a written record of incoming and outgoing materials?

13. Explain what you think are the essentials of quality control.

14. What are some factors a manufacturer must consider in deciding whether to sell a defective product for junk, correct the defect and sell it as a standard product, or sell the defective product at a discount?

15. Why do growing manufacturing plants need to revise their layouts?

Problems and Projects:

1. In factory production, costs are referred to as: (a) raw materials, (b) direct labor, and (c) factory expense or factory overhead. The Huron Electric Manufacturing Company, a manufacturer of small motors, produced during a certain month a total of 12,340 units. The costs were as follows:

Raw materials	$ 3,220
Direct labor	11,250
Factory expense:	
Depreciation of machinery and building	170
Heat, power, and lighting	175
Supplies	64
Insurance	75
Management and supervision	700

Give the total cost of production and the cost per unit.

2. In manufacturing, one of the important costs is depreciation. Depreciation means loss of value due to use and age. Therefore, as equipment and tools wear out in the manufacturing process, part of the original cost of these tools and equipment is charged as manufacturing cost.

The simplest method of computing depreciation of equipment is to assume a certain life and to estimate the scrap value or trade-in value at the end of that period; the difference between the cost and the trade-in or scrap value is charged off as an expense during the estimated life of the machine. If depreciation is computed on a monthly basis, the yearly charge is divided by twelve. To complete the table below, figure the yearly and monthly depreciation on the four different kinds of equipment.

Property	Original Cost	Scrap or Trade-In Value	Estimated Life	Yearly Depreciation	Monthly Depreciation
Conveyors	$3,000	$100	15 years		
Lathe #2	4,600	150	12 years		
Press #5	1,500	100	10 years		
Drill press #1	250	50	10 years		

3. In a manufacturing business there are three classifications of costs: (a) raw materials, (b) direct labor, and (c) factory expense or factory overhead. Factory overhead expense includes rent, depreciation, repairs, power, heat, light, supplies, supervision, and general salaries and wages not charged directly to any specific product.

In the Tredwell Shoe Company the following were the costs of manufacturing shoes during a three-month period ending December 31 of last year:

Raw materials, $55,872.80.
Direct labor, $73,309.20.

Factory overhead consisted of: salaries and wages, $7,200; rent, $3,260; depreciation and repairs, $4,150; power, heat, and light, $1,141.65; factory supplies, $2,638.25; miscellaneous factory expense, $818.75.

(a) What was the total factory overhead for the quarter?
(b) What was the total factory cost?
(c) Taking into consideration the following factors, what is the cost per pair of shoes manufactured during this period?

Shoes are grouped into classifications based upon a study determining how much it costs to produce one pair of shoes in relation to the cost of producing shoes in another classification. The shoes manufactured are in the following groups, each with an index of cost or a cost factor:

Group 1, index 1.0, 20,000 pairs
Group 2, index 1.3, 35,000 pairs
Group 3, index 1.5, 15,000 pairs
Total .... 70,000 pairs

In other words, shoes in Group 2 cost 1.3 times as much to manufacture as those in Group 1. (Suggestion: Multiply the index numbers times the quantity produced and find the total for each group; divide the grand total into factory cost; multiply this basic unit cost times the index number for each group in order to find the factory cost of manufacturing each pair of shoes in each of the three groups.)

Case Problem 13-1:

The American Radio Company produces small radio sets that are sold under its own brand name and under various brand names of other companies for which sets are manufactured. The sets are tested once, just before packing. The purpose of the test is to see whether the radio works satisfactorily. About 5 percent are defective. About 10 percent more are returned under a guarantee. The checking of each of these defective sets and putting it in working condition costs almost as much as making a new set. Management is concerned because of the cost due to defective sets. Profits are low.

Required:

1. What do you think is the cause of this problem?
2. What do you recommend be done to reduce the number of defective sets that are produced?
3. How may the supervision within the plant be at fault?

Continuing Project:

If your business is a manufacturing business, prepare detailed plans for scheduling, testing, production, handling material, and managerial controls.

What is meant by a common carrier?

How are railroad rates determined?

What materials are shipped by water?

What functions are performed by the traffic manager?

What forms are used in freight shipments?

What should be considered in choosing a method of shipment?

BACKGROUND OF CHAPTER

The need to transport goods from place to place is a problem for all businessmen. Sales can depend on the choice of a method of shipping. If transportation costs are too high, if products arrive in damaged condition, or if shipments are delivered too slowly, customers may become dissatisfied and stop their dealings with the business.

Anyone who is receiving or shipping merchandise is concerned with the speed, cost, care, and packaging necessary for the safe handling of the goods. In this chapter you will learn about the various types of transportation available to businessmen and will find out how costs and services may be compared.

CHAPTER 14

SHIPPING AND TRANSPORTATION OPERATIONS

Most businesses—retail, wholesale, or manufacturing, large or small —have some contact with problems of shipping and transportation. They must receive goods, ship goods, or both. The goods may be cotton for a textile mill, an order of dresses for a retail store, or supplies for a barber shop. Businessmen, of course, want the most convenient method of transportation at the lowest possible cost.

TYPES OF CARRIERS

Transportation is provided by common, contract, and private carriers. The term *common carrier* is generally applied to carriers engaged in the carrying of personal property or goods for the public. They include railroads, trucking companies, express agencies, steamships, and air transport companies. A common carrier must perform the same service for all persons without discrimination. His rates are fixed by the government.

A *contract carrier* undertakes for hire in special cases and under special arrangements to carry the goods of another to a particular place. He does not offer his services to anyone who desires them, and he reserves the right to select his customers. Moving vans, ordinary truckmen, delivery agencies, and some short railroads are examples of contract carriers. When a business owns trucks and other transportation units which it uses for transporting its goods, the business is usually referred to as a *private carrier*.

Duties and Rights of Common Carriers

The common carrier must furnish adequate service and must make uniform charges in accordance with the nature of the goods hauled and

ILLUS. 14-1. Most companies have transportation problems, for they must receive goods, ship goods, or both.

the distance moved. A common carrier is bound to provide ample facilities for receiving and caring for a freight shipment and for protecting it after it has arrived at its destination and until it is delivered to the business or person who is to receive the goods. A carrier must furnish equipment that is suitable for the safe and efficient transportation of the goods. The carrier is under a duty to protect the goods from the weather. The carrier must also protect the goods from loss or injury while they are in transit; in the case of perishable goods, he must provide refrigerator cars. If the contract calls for delivery at a specified time, the carrier will be held accountable for failure to comply with that provision.

A common carrier is liable for any loss or damage occurring to the goods while they are in his possession, whether the loss or damage is due to his negligence or not (except in situations indicated on page 273). The liability of the carrier begins when the goods are delivered by the shipper and received by the carrier.

Common carriers may make reasonable rules and regulations for the operation of their business, provided such rules apply alike to all persons. They may require goods to be crated for protection. They cannot be compelled to carry goods that are in violation of the law or that do not come within the class of goods that they usually carry. Thus, an express agency is not obliged to carry heavy freight shipments because its business is confined to small and valuable articles. Carriers have a right to demand the payment of their charges in advance; and if they do not exercise this right, they have a lien (claim) on the goods for the charges. Such a lien may include charges necessarily incurred for storage or charges advanced to connecting carriers.

Factors Limiting the Liability of Common Carriers

In the absence of laws or custom limiting the liability of the common carrier, he will be regarded as an insurer of the goods while they are in transit. He is not liable, however, for any loss or damage that is caused by: (a) an act of God, (b) an act of a public enemy, (c) the fault of the shipper, (d) government seizure, and (e) the inherent nature of the goods.

An Act of God. A cause of injury that human power cannot prevent nor human prudence avert is considered an act of God. Acts of God include floods, earthquakes, tornadoes, lightning, and the like.

An Act of a Public Enemy. By the phrase "public enemy" is meant an organized force with which the nation is at open war.

A carrier may also exempt himself from liability for loss caused by rioters and strikers through an expressed agreement with the shipper.

The Fault of the Shipper. If a loss is due either to the improper packing, marking, or addressing of the goods, or to the failure of the shipper to inform the carrier of the nature of the goods, the carrier is excused from liability.

Government Seizure. Seizure might arise because of illegality or dangerous nature of the goods, or need of them for emergency use.

The Inherent Nature of the Goods. A loss is due to the inherent nature of the goods when it arises from the natural decay of fresh fruits, vegetables, or other perishable commodities; the evaporation or the fermentation of liquids; and the death or the injury of animals through their own fault or the fault of other animals. In the case of such a loss, the carrier is released from liability. Although the loss does arise from one of these excepted causes, the carrier may be held liable if he or his agent is guilty of negligence.

Duties and Rights of Contract Carriers

A contract carrier is liable only for failure to use the skill and care that an ordinarily prudent person would exercise in the conduct of his business. Since the contract carrier has the right to make special arrangements and contracts with his clients, he may restrict his liability to any degree, even to the extent of not being liable for his own negligence. A businessman dealing with a contract carrier must therefore recognize such arrangements with the contract carrier.

METHODS OF SHIPPING

There are methods of shipping to fit the needs and budgets of every business. The businessman can study each method and decide whether he will use railroad, water, pipeline, motor freight, air express, or parcel post as a means of shipping his goods. He may use one method for certain shipments and different methods for other shipments depending on cost, time, and convenience factors.

Railway Freight Shipments

Railway transportation is one of the most common forms of shipping in the United States. It includes carload freight (*CL*), less-than-carload freight (*LCL* or *package car*), and express.

The rates for a less-than-carload shipment, or package-car shipment, are lower than those for express but are higher than carload freight rates. Under the LCL plan the shipments of several companies are placed in the same car for the same destination. Carload freight is self-explanatory; one shipper uses a complete car at a fixed rate for the car or at a fixed rate per 100 pounds, the rate depending upon the destination. Express shipments are discussed on page 277.

As carload shipments are routed through from the point of origin to the destination, they are handled speedily. It is a common practice in large cities to pack less-than-carload shipments in one car for through shipment to another city. For instance, a car of miscellaneous merchandise may be packed in Chicago for shipment directly to Cincinnati. This car will be routed through without interruption. Not all less-than-carload shipments, however, can be handled in this manner. For instance, a train leaving New York may have a car of merchandise for distribution to Buffalo, Pittsburgh, Chicago, Cincinnati, and Indianapolis. In such a case the train stops at transfer points where the less-than-carload shipments are unloaded from the original car and reloaded into other cars according to their final destination. Carload shipments comprise the majority of railroad freight shipments. In a typical week there are approximately 350,000 carload shipments.

Freight Forwarding Companies. In most large cities there are companies that gather together small shipments and pack them in railroad freight cars, each car going to a specific destination. These companies are called *freight forwarding companies.*

A freight forwarding company obtains cars from the railroads at the carload rate. It collects small shipments and provides the services of a full car between two points but charges LCL rates. For example, a freight forwarding company in Pittsburgh may collect thousands of small shipments for various destinations such as New York, Chicago, and St. Louis. These small shipments are sorted, and full cars are packed and sent straight through to these destinations. On arrival in these cities, the cars are unpacked and prompt delivery is made.

Special Railroad Freight Services. Besides the regular services of carload and less-than-carload shipping, railroads offer several types of special services to all shippers. Some of these are available at special rates that are higher than the standard rates.

Store-Door Delivery. Most railroads in most cities will pick up goods at the office or the plant of a shipper, deliver these goods to the railroad, load them in cars, ship them to their destination, unload them, and deliver them by truck to the person for whom they were intended. This service is called *store-door delivery.*

ILLUS. 14-2. Most railroads provide store-door delivery.

Terminal Service. In many cities the railroad will deliver a car to a private railroad track owned by the business to which the car has been shipped. If a company does not have a private railroad track or siding, the railroad will leave the car for unloading purposes along a track (called a team track) that can be reached by truck. This service is called *terminal service.*

Pool Car Service. If a shipper has enough goods going to several customers in the same direction, he can pack the goods in one car at the carload rate, which will be charged between the point of origin and the point at which the first goods from the car are unloaded. The rest of the merchandise can be unloaded at various points farther on the route, and the less-than-carload rates will be applied. This service is called *pool car service.*

Changes in Transit. There are several kinds of services available to shippers who may decide to have a shipment returned after it has been sent, stop it and put it in storage, hold it in transit for further instructions, or change instructions for delivery. This kind of service is often used in shipping fresh fruits and vegetables. Cars from California, Arizona, Texas, or Florida may be started toward certain cities, but the shipper may give instructions to the railroad to change the delivery of any car. These services are sometimes called *in transit privilege* or *diversion in transit.*

Railroad Rates. Railroad freight rates are determined on (a) a classification basis and (b) a commodity basis. More than 25,000 articles and commodities are divided into groups referred to as classes. All items within each class are shipped at the same rate. The classification books contain information describing articles in each class and giving special rules pertaining to packing, marking, quantity, billing, and rights and obligations of the carrier, the shipper, and the one who receives the goods.

A *class rate* is one that applies to a related group of goods. A *commodity rate* is a special rate for a specific commodity. Commodity rates commonly apply to such products as coal, sand, steel, and other heavy or bulky products. So many special rates have been established in relation to class rates that there has almost become a new classification of railroad rates, sometimes referred to as *exception rates.*

If a class rate, as well as a commodity rate, is established for a certain product to be shipped between two points, the commodity rate is used because it is always cheaper. From the point of view of tonnage, most freight is shipped under commodity rates. These rates are established by setting for a particular commodity, such as coal, a flat rate per ton between the point of origin and the destination. The exact mileage is not considered. In this way a railroad having a long haul can compete with a railroad having a short haul between the same two points. However, one route may provide faster service than another.

The United States is divided into railway freight territories. The classification of products for rate purposes is not always the same in all territories; therefore, the rates vary. It is necessary to know the classification before determining the rate. While there formerly were wide variations in classification rates of the different territories, the Interstate Commerce Commission has started a program of developing uniform classifications and a narrower difference between rates.

Ordinarily the charge for a freight shipment is determined by multiplying the rate by the weight. For example, if the rate is $1.20 a 100 pounds and if the shipment weighs 245 pounds, the freight charge is $2.94 ($1.20 $\times$ 2.45). Regardless of the weight of the shipment, however, there is a minimum freight charge. The minimum charge is usually a specified amount or the rate per 100 pounds, whichever is the larger. There is a minimum weight set for a carload.

The rates are not the same, however, for all products shipped the same distance. For instance, commodities of a high unit value, such as silk, have higher rates than commodities of a low unit value, such as coal.

The preceding discussion indicates that a shipper should be acquainted not only with the proper class rate or commodity rate under which he may ship his product but also with any other conditions that affect the rate. For instance, furniture and some large toys are usually shipped unassembled because they can then be sent at a lower rate than they could be if they were assembled. In shipping terms, unassembled is *knocked down* or *KD*. If the product is assembled, it is *set up* or *SU*.

Railway Express Shipments

There formerly were several express companies in operation in the United States, but there now is only one express company—the REA Express, previously known as the Railway Express Agency.

Express shipments are carried in special cars on passenger trains or on special fast trains. Recently the express company has been transporting some shipments by trucks as the number of passenger trains has decreased. Express shipments are faster than other railway shipments, but they are also more expensive. Ordinarily large, bulky material is not shipped by express because the express rate is higher than the freight rate; but when speed is a factor more important than cost, express is preferable to freight.

Shipment by Water

Canal, lake, river, or coastwise shipping by boat is cheaper than railway freight, but it is much slower. This type of shipping is usually considered economical for heavy, bulky merchandise that does not need to be delivered promptly. For instance, some shippers on the East Coast send merchandise by boat through the Panama Canal to the West Coast and thus save money in comparison with railway freight rates. Bad weather may, however, delay a shipment and cause serious difficulties.

In considering the water shipments that travel at least partially by ocean, one must take into account the increased cost of packing that is usually required in order to protect the shipment from damage. There are also extra charges incidental to loading and unloading. This extra cost must be considered as a part of the freight rate in making comparisons with other forms of transportation.

Pipeline Transportation

Many years ago most liquids were shipped by tanks on railroad cars or on trucks and in tanker boats. Pipelines were first used to transport water and gas. Now pipelines are used extensively for transporting liquids such as oil and gasoline.

Motor Freight

Motortrucks are considered most advantageous for shipments to be sent two or three hundred miles. Within this radius the truck competes favorably with railway freight because it can pick up the merchandise at the door of the shipper and deliver it at the door of the receiver of the goods in the destination city. Trucks also often compete favorably with railroads on long trips. Trucks, in many cases, can give more prompt service than that obtained by railway freight; but sometimes traffic congestion, bad weather, and breakdowns cause this form of transportation to be undependable. Trucks are used for both packaged goods and bulk shipments. In handling bulk shipments the truck has the disadvantage of having less capacity than the freight car. For most of the bulky freight with low unit value, the railroad can compete more effectively than the truck on long trips. Trucks are very important in serving communities that have no railroad service.

Truck-Rail Service. Trucklines sometimes have difficulty competing with railroads on long trips just as the railroads have difficulty competing with trucklines on short trips. However, a truck is always involved in part of the transportation unless goods can be loaded directly into a railroad car from a plant and unloaded directly from a railroad car into another plant.

Some trucking companies load trucks or trailers and place them on railroad cars to be shipped to the destination. The truck or trailer is rolled off the railroad car and delivered. The trucking line pays the railroad for hauling the trucks or trailers. Some railroads own their trucking lines and trailers and provide this service themselves. This service is called *piggyback* service. Similar to the piggyback freight of railroads, there is *fishyback* freight in which trucks are driven onto ships.

ILLUS. 14-3. Some railroads offer piggyback service.

Motor Freight Rates. Motor freight rates are regulated by the states and the federal government. The rates charged are based upon classifications and the distance traveled.

Bus Service. Some passenger bus lines are permitted to transport small shipments in very much the same way as any other motor express or railway express. The shipment has to be delivered to the bus terminal and must be picked up by the addressee at the destination bus terminal.

Air Express and Freight

Commercial airlines and private planes are carrying an increasing volume of express and freight shipments. This means of transportation is costly for many types of shipments. Items most commonly shipped by air express are perishable or high in value. Examples are jewelry, furs, flowers, and fashion dresses. Emergency repair parts and other emergency shipments are also shipped this way. Air transportation does provide the greatest possible speed, although in bad weather the delivery service may be delayed.

The Air Express Division of the REA Express makes shipments over the main transport airlines throughout the United States and

REA Express

ILLUS. 14-4. Emergency shipments, perishable goods, and goods of high value are often shipped by air.

into Canada, South America, and other countries as well. Through arrangements made with the Western Union Telegraph Company, a messenger will pick up at one's home or office a package to be sent by air express. Any Western Union office will accept a shipment. Illustration 14-5 provides examples of air express rates.

The REA Express has also made arrangements with several airlines to provide a combination of air and rail service to and from points that are not directly linked by air service.

Regular airlines traveling on schedule and chartered airlines traveling on special trips are now offering special lower rates on air freight.

Destination (from Cincinnati)	2 lbs.	5 lbs.	25 lbs.	40 lbs.	50 lbs
Memphis	$9.50	$9.50	$ 9.65	$11.00	$12.10
Dallas	9.50	9.50	13.15	16.70	18.76
Albuquerque	9.50	9.50	15.16	18.73	21.11
Salt Lake City	9.50	9.50	15.65	19.62	22.26
Los Angeles	9.50	9.50	17.37	22.18	25.12

ILLUS. 14-5. Examples of air express rates (minimum charge, $9.50).

These rates are based upon large shipments. The rates vary according to the commodity, the distance, and the weight.

Parcel Post

Parcel post shipments (fourth-class mail) get essentially the same handling as express shipments, except that they are handled by the U.S. Postal Service. They are often hauled on the same train with express shipments. Two important disadvantages of parcel post, however, are the small limit in the size and the small limit of the weight as compared with other forms of shipping. These limits are subject to frequent change by federal laws or regulations. The maximum limit on weight is 70 pounds (lower if sent to large cities classed as first-class post offices). Consequently, if merchandise in a large quantity is to be sent by parcel post, it must be shipped in packages of the appropriate size and weight. Another disadvantage of parcel post shipping is the fact that the shipper cannot get a signed receipt that will prove delivery of the package.

The rates on parcel post shipments are based upon the weight and the distance. The distance is determined by zone. For instance, items of the same weight may be sent for the same cost to any destination in the same zone. One of the great advantages of parcel post, however, is the fact that one may send a shipment by parcel post to any destination in the United States and to almost any destination in the world. This is not true of other forms of shipping.

There is a special fourth-class rate for educational materials. This is essentially a parcel post rate, but it is special for books and other materials used for educational purposes. The charge is based upon weight regardless of the distance the shipment is to travel.

Parcel post packages can also be sent by airmail. This service is called *air parcel post*. The rates are higher than for regular parcel post.

ILLUS. 14-6. **A shipment by parcel post may be sent to any destination in the United States and to almost any destination in the world.**

PROBLEMS OF TRAFFIC MANAGEMENT

Traffic management is the management of all aspects of obtaining transportation for the products of a business. The person who is in charge of this function is often called the *traffic manager*. The traffic manager selects the best method for shipping goods, supervises the preparation of merchandise for shipment and the preparation of the various forms required, traces missing shipments, and negotiates claims for damaged or lost merchandise. A good traffic manager who can ship merchandise quickly, carefully, and at the lowest possible cost can save money and earn customer goodwill for the business.

Choosing the Method of Shipping

When one is deciding upon a method of shipment, he must consider: (a) speed, (b) carefulness in handling, (c) convenience in pickup and delivery, (d) packing requirements, (e) insurance, and (f) cost.

A person can usually decide readily whether he prefers to send a shipment by freight, express, parcel post, or some other method; but, without having available some definite figures, he cannot easily make a decision based upon cost. The costs of the various methods must be compared to determine the most economical method. The table in Illustration 14-7 shows a comparison of the costs of shipping one commodity, ruled paper, to five different destinations by four different methods of transportation.

Item	Value	Weight	Destination from Cincinnati	REA [1]	Air [2]	Motor Truck [1]	Parcel Post (Fourth Class) [2]
Ruled Paper	$25	25 lbs.	San Francisco, California	$13.85	$20.08	$12.72	$6.50
Ruled Paper	$25	25 lbs.	Traverse City, Michigan	9.25	12.73	9.85	3.05
Ruled Paper	$25	25 lbs.	Lakeland, Florida	8.65	14.22	9.45	3.75
Ruled Paper	$25	25 lbs.	Dayton, Ohio	8.75	12.20	8.00	2.35
Ruled Paper	$25	25 lbs.	Omaha, Nebraska	10.95	12.73	11.13	3.75

[1] Includes pickup and delivery.
[2] Includes delivery, but not pickup.
Truck rates are minimum load charges.
Insurance: Insurance is included in all of these amounts for comparison.

ILLUS. 14-7. Comparison of shipping costs.

In addition to the consideration of the rate, the size of a shipment will often have an influence on how it is sent. For example, a shipment of 150 pounds cannot go by parcel post unless it can be divided into at least three smaller packages.

Insurance is included in freight and express rates. In the case of express, however, the amount of insurance is only $50. When an express shipment exceeds $50 in valuation, there is an extra charge for each additional $100 in valuation or fraction thereof. The U.S. Postal Service makes a separate charge for the insurance of parcel post shipments. If the shipper wishes, he may assume his own risk or may insure his shipment through a private agency.

Packing Goods for Shipping

The cost of packaging and packing goods for shipping is often very great. However, some kind of wrapping, boxing, or crating is necessary for most goods for most types of transportation. The kind of packaging and packing that is necessary may help determine the method of shipping. For example, it might be very expensive to build a crate around a piece of machinery that has to be shipped by railroad freight. The machinery possibly could be shipped by truck, however, without any kind of boxing or crating.

In shipping an entire carload or truckload of merchandise, the shipper can make sure that the goods are packed tightly and will be shipped without damage. However, if the small shipments of one shipper are mixed with those of many others, there may be damage unless the goods are packed very carefully. For example, a truckload of books packed in cartons can be shipped for a thousand miles without damage. However, if these same cartons were shipped by parcel post, they would be handled roughly several times and would very likely be damaged to some extent upon arrival at their destination.

Forms Used in Freight Shipments

Three parties are involved in the process of shipping: the person or business who is shipping the merchandise, the carrier, and the person or business to whom the merchandise is being shipped. When shipping goods by freight, several forms must circulate among these three parties. The most commonly used forms are the bill of lading, freight bill, waybill, and notice of arrival.

Bill of Lading. The *bill of lading,* one of the most commonly used forms in shipping, represents a contract between the shipper and the carrier company. There are two forms, the straight bill of lading and the order bill of lading, or negotiable bill of lading. Examples of these are shown in Illustrations 14-8 (page 285) and 14-9 (page 286). Three copies of a bill of lading are made. These copies are distributed as shown below.

Bill of Lading { three copies }
{ 1. Original ⟶ to buyer (consignee)
{ 2. Shipping order ⟶ to transporting agency (carrier)
{ 3. Memorandum ⟶ kept by shipper (consignor)

The original copy of the *straight bill of lading* should be sent by the *consignor* (shipper) to the *consignee* (the one who receives the merchandise). Upon presenting the bill of lading and signing for the merchandise, the consignee can obtain his shipment. The *order,* or *negotiable, bill of lading* requires the railroad to withhold the shipment until the original bill of lading has been endorsed to show that payment has been received for the merchandise. A draft may accompany an order bill of lading. If it is a *sight draft* (one payable upon presentation), the merchandise is released when the draft is paid. If it is a *time draft,* the merchandise is released when the draft is accepted (or signed), for the acceptance (or signing) converts the draft essentially into a note that will become payable on an agreed date.

STRAIGHT BILL OF LADING—SHORT FORM—ORIGINAL—NOT NEGOTIABLE

RECEIVED, subject to the classifications and tariffs in effect on the date of the issue of this Bill of Lading,

FROM **FRANK'S ELECTRIC COMPANY**

AT CINCINNATI, OHIO.

CONSIGNED TO

John Kelley & Son
604 Regent Blvd.
Detroit, Michigan 48205

CUST. ORDER NO.   L409-3

DELIVERING CARRIER   ASSOCIATED TRUCK

CAR INITIAL AND NO.

the property described below, in apparent good order, except as noted (contents and condition of contents of package unknown), marked, consigned, and destined as indicated below, which said carrier (the word carrier being understood throughout this contract as meaning any person or corporation in possession of the property under the contract) agree to carry to its usual place of delivery at said destination, if on its route, otherwise to deliver to another carrier on the route to said destination. It is mutually agreed as to each carrier of all or any of said property over all or any portion of said route to destination, and as to each party at any time interested in all or any of said property, that every service to be performed hereunder shall be subject to all the terms and conditions of the Uniform Domestic Straight Bill of Lading set forth (1) in Official, Southern, Western and Illinois Freight Classifications in effect on the date hereof, if this is a rail or a rail-water shipment, or (2) in the applicable motor carrier classification or tariff if this is a motor carrier shipment.

Shipper hereby certifies that he is familiar with all the terms and conditions of the said bill of lading, including those on the back thereof, set forth in the classification or tariff which governs the transportation of this shipment, and the said terms and conditions are hereby agreed to by the shipper and accepted for himself and his assigns.

NO. PACKAGES	DESCRIPTION OF ARTICLES	WEIGHT	RATE	CHK.
3	cartons electrical appliances	350 lbs.		

*If the shipment moves between two ports by a carrier by water, the law requires that the bill of lading shall state whether it is "carrier's or shipper's weight." Note—Where the rate is dependent on value, shippers are required to state specifically in writing the agreed or declared value of the property. The agreed or declared value of the property
is hereby specifically stated by the shipper to be not exceeding _____ per _____

FRANK'S ELECTRIC COMPANY

Per *B. L. K.*   Agent, Per _____

PERMANENT POST-OFFICE ADDRESS OF SHIPPER; 10 Mesa Street, CINCINNATI, OHIO 45227

YOUR INVOICE MUST SHOW OUR BILL OF LADING NUMBER

AGENT'S NO. __

February 6   19 __

Subject to Section 7 of conditions of applicable bill of lading, if this shipment is to be delivered to the consignee without recourse on the consignor, the consignor shall sign the following statement:
The carrier shall not make delivery of this shipment without payment of freight and all other lawful charges.

FRANK'S ELECTRIC COMPANY

(Signature of Consignor)

If charges are to be prepaid, write or stamp here, "To be Prepaid."

TO BE PREPAID

Received $ _____
to apply in prepayment of the charges on the property described hereon.

Agent or Cashier

Per _____
(The signature here acknowledges only the amount prepaid.)

Charges Advanced: $ _____

†Shipper's imprint in lieu of stamp; not a part of bill of lading approved by the Interstate Commerce Commission.

† The fibre boxes used for this shipment conform to the specifications set forth in the box maker's certificate thereon, and all other requirements of Uniform Freight Classification.

SHIPPER'S NO.

1 36644

ILLUS. 14-8. A straight bill of lading.

(Uniform Domestic Order Bill of Lading, National Motor Freight Classification No. 5, Effective Dec. 31, 1940.)

UNIFORM ORDER BILL OF LADING
ORIGINAL—DOMESTIC

ABC TRUCKING COMPANY, INC.

RECEIVED, subject to the classifications and tariffs in effect on the date of the issue of this Bill of Lading,

Shipper's No. 126

Agent's No. _____

From Frank's Electric Company _____, Date February 6 , 19 —

At 10 Mesa Street Street, Cincinnati City, Hamilton County, Ohio 45227 State

the property described below, in apparently good order, except as noted (contents and condition of contents of packages unknown), marked, consigned, and destined as shown below, which said company the word company being understood throughout this contract as meaning any person or corporation in possession of the property under the contract) agrees to carry to its usual place of delivery at said destination, if on its own railroad, water line, highway route or routes, or within the territory of its highway operations, otherwise to deliver to another carrier on the route to said destination. It is mutually agreed, as to each carrier of all or any said property over all or any portion of said route to destination, and as to each party at any time interested in all or any of said property, that every service to be performed hereunder shall be subject to all the conditions not prohibited by law whether printed or written, herein contained, including the conditions on back hereof, which are hereby agreed to by the shipper and accepted for himself and his assigns.

The surrender of this Original ORDER Bill of Lading properly indorsed shall be required before the delivery of the property. Inspection of property covered by this bill of lading will not be permitted unless provided by law or unless permission is indorsed on this original bill of lading or given in writing by the shipper.

Consigned to ORDER OF Frank's Electric Company

Destination 1201 Main Street, Marietta City, Washington County, Ohio State

Notify American Hardware Company

At 880 Rosemont Street, Marietta City, Washington County, Ohio State

Routing _____

Delivering Carrier ABC Trucking Co

Vehicle or Car Initial _____ No. _____

No. Packages	DESCRIPTION OF ARTICLES, SPECIAL MARKS, AND EXCEPTIONS	*Weight (Subject to Correction)	Class or Rate	Check Column	
10	cartons electrical wiring	380			Subject to Section 7 of conditions, if this shipment is to be delivered to the consignee without recourse on the consignor, the consignor shall sign the following statement: The carrier shall not make delivery of this shipment without payment of freight and all other lawful charges.
					_____ (Signature of Consignor.)
					If charges are to be prepaid write or stamp here "To be Prepaid." TO BE PREPAID
					Received $_____ to apply in prepayment of the charges on the property described hereon.
					Agent or Cashier
					Per _____ (The signature here acknowledges only the amount prepaid.)
					Charges Advanced: $_____

*If the shipment moves between two ports by a carrier by water, the law requires that the bill of lading shall state whether it is "carrier's or shipper's weight."

NOTE—Where the rate is dependent on value, shippers are required to state specifically in writing the agreed or declared value of the property.

The agreed or declared value of the property is hereby specifically stated by the shipper to be not exceeding _____ per _____

Frank's Electric Company Shipper Per _____ Agent.

© 1 Per Roger Haney, Clerk

Permanent Address of Shipper: 10 Mesa Street Street, Cincinnati City, Ohio 45227 State

ILLUS. 14-9. An order bill of lading.

Freight Bill. Freight charges may be prepaid by the shipper or collected from the consignee. If they are prepaid, the receipted freight bill is often attached to the bill of lading. The *freight bill* is merely an itemized statement from the railroad covering the charges for handling the shipment.

Waybill. A *waybill* is a sheet of instructions prepared by the shipper or by the transportation company showing the point of origin, the destination, the route, the consignor, the consignee, the description, and the transportation charge. It accompanies the shipment to its destination.

Notice of Arrival. The *notice of arrival* is sent to the consignee by the railroad when the shipment has reached its destination.

When a carload shipment arrives at its destination, the consignee is given a certain amount of time to unload the shipment and to release the car. After the lapse of this specified time, a charge known as *demurrage* is assessed against the shipment. The consignee cannot obtain the shipment until he has paid the demurrage charge in addition to all other charges due the transportation company.

COD Shipments

COD shipments may be sent by any form of transportation, but some trucklines refuse to handle them. When a shipment is sent COD, the consignee must pay the cost of the merchandise upon delivery to him. In the case of express and parcel post shipments, an extra fee is charged for this service. The express agent or the postman collects the amount due the shipper, transportation charges, and the COD fee.

If a freight shipment is sent COD, a sight draft may be attached to a copy of the order bill of lading. This draft, with the bill of lading, is then sent to a bank. The bank presents the sight draft to the consignee for payment. Upon paying the draft, the consignee receives from the bank the bill of lading which he then presents to the railroad company when claiming his shipment. A comparison of the order bill of lading on page 286 with the straight bill of lading on page 285 will indicate a fundamental difference in the way the shipment is consigned. In the case of the order bill of lading, the shipment is actually being sent to the American Hardware Company but on the *order* of Frank's Electric Company. The shipment cannot be released to the American Hardware Company except on the order of Frank's Electric Company.

The order bill of lading has space on the reverse side that permits the consignee to transfer title of the property to another person by endorsement (signing).

Under another method of sending freight shipments, the railroad company charges a COD fee for collecting the amount of the shipment. Collection is made in cash unless some other form of payment is specified on the bill of lading. The letters *COD* must be marked on each package. The shipment must be sent on a uniform straight bill of lading accompanied by the invoice. All documents must be stamped in a manner similar to the following:

COD Shipment (Sent Freight Collect)

COD Amount	$250.00
Collection Fee	1.00
Total Charges	$251.00

A shipment by truck may be merely billed as COD and a copy of the invoice given to the driver. The driver collects for the COD shipment and makes payment to his company, which in turn gives it to the consignor.

Collect and Prepaid Transportation Charges

All forms of freight and express shipments may be sent with the transportation charges collect or prepaid. If a shipment is sent *collect,* the transportation company collects the transportation charges from the consignee on delivery to him. The transportation charges on a *prepaid shipment* are paid by the consignor. On a parcel post shipment transportation charges must be paid by the consignor and are added to the total charge when a package is sent COD.

As you learned in Chapter 12, the term *FOB* means free on board. If a shipment is sent from Cincinnati to Chicago under the terms FOB Cincinnati, it means that the shipper will pay for loading the goods or turning them over to a transportation company in Cincinnati; but the transportation costs from Cincinnati to Chicago must be paid by the purchaser.

If a shipment is sent from Cincinnati to Chicago with the terms FOB Chicago, the seller of the goods must deliver the goods to the transportation company and pay the transportation charges.

Tracing Shipments

If a shipment sent by insured parcel post is lost, the U.S. Postal Service is responsible. The department will conduct an investigation and, if the shipment is not found, will make payment for the loss. Even if the shipment was not insured, the U.S. Postal Service will do its best to find the shipment.

Under all other forms of shipping, it is possible to ask the transportation company to start a tracing procedure. Even though the transportation company is responsible for the loss of the shipment, the consignee is going to be very unhappy if the shipment is not delivered. It is therefore important to notify the customer what action is being taken to trace the shipment, and it may even be necessary to send a new shipment to replace the one lost.

Auditing Freight Bills

Any company handling many shipments should know enough about freight classifications and freight services to be able to check freight bills carefully. Since items are quite often sent under the wrong classification, shippers may be paying higher rates than are necessary. For instance, there may be two freight rates on beds. One rate may be for a bed set up; the other, for a bed knocked down. Assume that a manufacturer has been shipping beds knocked down and has been paying the higher rate that is charged for shipping beds set up. If such an error is detected, the shipper can claim reimbursement upon furnishing satisfactory proof. Furthermore, there are chances of errors in figuring the amounts of freight bills. For that reason such bills should be checked carefully. There are some companies that specialize in auditing, or checking, the freight bills of various shippers. A flat service charge is made or a fee is collected by the auditing company on the basis of the adjustments that are made.

Claims

Claims other than those based upon rates arise from the fact that shipments may not be delivered or may be totally or partially destroyed. Such a *freight claim* should be presented by the party who possesses the title of ownership. When a claim is presented, the freight bill, the bill of lading, and the invoice should be presented. A photostatic copy may be used if the original bill of lading cannot be presented. A sworn statement of nondelivery should be attached to these papers. The affidavit should be made by the consignee, regardless of whether the consignee or the consignor is filing the claim. When a claim for partial loss is submitted, the affidavit should specifically state the extent of the loss.

When any loss is claimed because of damage, it is important that a representative of the transportation company examine the merchandise to help prove the claim.

REVIEW WHAT YOU HAVE LEARNED

Business Terms Checkup:

(1) common carrier	(18) air parcel post
(2) contract carrier	(19) traffic manager
(3) private carrier	(20) bill of lading
(4) CL	(21) straight bill of lading
(5) LCL or package car	(22) consignor
(6) freight forwarding company	(23) consignee
(7) store-door delivery	(24) order, or negotiable, bill of
(8) terminal service	lading
(9) pool car service	(25) sight draft
(10) in transit privilege or diversion	(26) time draft
in transit	(27) freight bill
(11) class rate	(28) waybill
(12) commodity rate	(29) notice of arrival
(13) exception rates	(30) demurrage
(14) knocked down (KD)	(31) collect
(15) set up (SU)	(32) prepaid shipment
(16) piggyback	(33) FOB
(17) fishyback	(34) freight claim

Reading Checkup:

1. What is the primary distinction between a private carrier and a common carrier?

2. What are some of the obligations of common carriers?

3. When is a common carrier relieved of responsibility for damage?

4. For what reason may a railroad shipment of less than a carload require a longer time for delivery than a carload shipment?

5. If you send a carload shipment to a destination, is there any way that you can change the destination after the car is en route?

6. What determines railroad rates and classifications?

7. In the case of a commodity such as coal or wheat, is the cost of shipping determined by the mileage and the commodity rate?

8. Why is it sometimes advisable to send furniture or other similar items unassembled?

9. If the railroad delivers a loaded car to the door of a manufacturer, what will happen if the manufacturer fails to unload the car promptly?

10. What is the justification for railroad express rates being higher than railroad freight rates?

11. For what kind of goods is water transportation usually suitable?

12. Explain how railroads and trucklines combine their services in providing freight transportation.

13. What are some of the items that are commonly shipped by air express?

14. What is the difference between air express and air freight?

15. (a) What are some of the disadvantages of parcel post shipping?
    (b) What are some of the advantages?

16. What are some of the duties of a traffic manager?

17. (a) On a shipment of 25 pounds of ruled paper from Cincinnati to San Francisco, which is the cheapest method of transportation?
    (b) On a shipment of 25 pounds of ruled paper from Cincinnati, Ohio, to Traverse City, Michigan, which is the cheapest method?

18. How will crating or packing requirements influence the decision as to the method of shipment?

19. What are the essential points of difference between a straight bill of lading and an order bill of lading?

20. What are two ways of sending railroad freight shipments COD?

21. When a claim is made for a lost freight shipment, what information should be presented?

APPLY WHAT YOU HAVE LEARNED

Questions for Class Discussion:

1. From the viewpoint of a railroad shipper, what are some of the advantages of using a pool car?

2. Suppose that you are a shipper of fresh vegetables grown in Florida. After watching the market conditions in Chicago and New York, you start a carload shipment to Chicago because the market is most favorable there. However, you discover after starting the car that the market has changed and is more favorable in New York. What can you do to take advantage of the favorable New York market?

3. If you had a carload of sand to ship for the making of glass, under what type of freight rate do you think it could be shipped at the lowest price?

4. Under certain circumstances some retailers and wholesalers of women's fashion clothing use air express and air freight quite extensively. Can you give any explanations of why and when this rather expensive method of transportation would be used?

5. Give some reasons why a shipper who ordinarily would prefer to use parcel post may be forced to use express or some form of freight.

6. If a freight shipment is sent to a consignee through the use of an order bill of lading and a sight draft, what must the consignee do before receiving the goods?

7. Explain what you would consider to be some of the advantages of the piggyback method of shipment.

8. Assume that you have a factory from which you wish to ship a full carload of goods to be delivered along a route to three of your branches. What kind of railroad service could you obtain that would be most satisfactory?

9. What are some of the factors that will determine whether a large piece of machinery will be shipped by truck or by railroad freight?

10. If a common carrier, such as a railroad, accepts a shipment from you, can it refuse a similar shipment from someone else?

11. Give an example of how a railroad might be relieved of responsibility for damage because of the inherent nature of the goods.

Problems and Projects:

1. T. R. Jeffreys, a citrus grower in Florida, received an order for a carload of citrus fruit from the Eastside Fruit Market in Chicago. Jeffreys loaded the railroad car and shipped it "sight draft to bill of lading." Answer the following questions:
   (a) What type of bill of lading is used?
   (b) What is done with the papers (sight draft and bill of lading)?
   (c) What must be done by the Eastside Fruit Market to claim possession of the fruit?
   (d) How does Jeffreys get his money?
   (e) What can Jeffreys do if, after the fruit has been shipped, he gets a telegram from the Eastside Fruit Market cancelling the order?

2. Select a specific product to be shipped to a destination at least 50 miles from your community and determine (a) the railroad freight rate, (b) the truck rate, (c) the express rate, and (d) the mail rate.

3. The following table shows the information in a section of the parcel post and rate book:

Pounds	Local	Zones 1 and 2	Zone 3	Zone 4	Zone 5	Zone 6	Zone 7	Zone 8
49	$1.80	$3.20	$3.65	$4.50	$5.95	$7.30	$9.20	$11.00
50	1.80	3.25	3.70	4.60	6.05	7.40	9.35	11.15

Compute the cost of sending an insured shipment to a destination in Zone 5. Assume that the shipment comes within the size limit and that it weighs 50 pounds. The value is $50. Insurance on parcel post shipments is computed from the following information:

Value of Contents	Fee
$ 0.01 to $ 15	$0.20
15.01 to 50	.30
50.01 to 100	.40
100.01 to 150	.50
150.01 to 200	.60

4. At 5:00 a.m. on January 10 the weather bureau at Pittsburgh sent out a warning that there would be a flood. On January 12 the railroad company still had negligently allowed a car to remain on the tracks in Pittsburgh until the water had reached the car and damaged the goods in it. The owner of the goods brought suit against the railroad for damages. The railroad company claimed that the damage was due to an act of God.

(a) Who do you think is liable for the loss and why?

(b) What would be your answer if the flood had reached the car at 10:00 a.m. on January 10?

Case Problem 14-1:

The Cincinnati Milacron Company makes large machinery for other manufacturers. It built a machine, costing $200,000, for the Ford Motor Company of Detroit. An important part of that machine has broken. The cost of a replacement is $100. It weighs 75 pounds. Production on the machine is shut down and 20 men are out of work. It is important to get the machine back into production. A new part has been ordered from the Cincinnati Milacron Company with instructions to rush it.

Required:

1. What choices does the Cincinnati Milacron Company have in sending this part from Cincinnati to Detroit, a distance of approximately 300 miles?

2. What should the Cincinnati Milacron Company do? Why?

3. Suppose the replacement part weighed 1,800 pounds. What do you think the decision should be in regard to shipping it?

Continuing Project:

In the business selected, you may have either incoming or outgoing shipments and possibly both. Select the types of transportation that will be used and give your reasons for selecting these types of transportation.

CAREERS IN PURCHASING, PRODUCTION, AND TRANSPORTATION

Careers in Purchasing. The purchasing of materials, supplies, and equipment for businesses is such a large and widespread activity that there are approximately 80,000 persons employed as specialists in purchasing.

The largest number of trained purchasing specialists are in manufacturing plants. Other businesses which have large-scale purchasing departments are transportation companies (railroads, airlines, bus and truck companies, and steamship lines); large commercial enterprises (hotels, insurance companies, banks, motion picture producers, and radio and television companies); governments (national, state, and local); and large universities and colleges.

The person in charge of all purchasing activities is known by some such title as director of purchases or purchasing agent. Other specialized personnel include the following: assistant purchasing agents, buyers (each a specialist for certain products), specifications engineers, testing engineers, inspectors, warehousemen, and stock clerks.

Usually, one begins his career in purchasing by starting in lower level jobs and is promoted to higher level jobs as he grows in purchasing knowledge and ability. Entrance to most positions in purchasing departments in the government is by competitive examination (civil service).

A knowledge of such subjects as business law, marketing, economics, manufacturing processes, and accounting is essential for a successful career in purchasing.

In large department stores there are special positions for people who spend the major part of their time in buying merchandise. Usually, each department has a buyer, and in the larger departments there may be an assistant buyer. A large percentage of department store buyers and assistant buyers are women. The buyer has the responsibility for determining what to buy, when to buy, where to buy, how much to buy, and what price to pay. The success or failure of the department mainly depends on the capability of the buyer. In addition to buying the merchandise, the buyer supervises the display of the goods, aids in preparing advertising material for the goods, and provides salespeople with information about the goods.

It is essential that a buyer have a thorough knowledge of merchandise and be aware of consumer preferences and style trends. He must have an excellent knowledge of advertising, salesmanship, business law, budgeting, and accounting.

Careers in Production. Many people do not like office work as we normally think of it in an office. These people can find many interesting and challenging jobs in manufacturing. Some of these jobs are those of stores clerk, time study clerk, product designer, efficiency engineer, production engineer, and testing engineer. Each worker in a plant has his special responsibility in creating a good product at a low cost. There is a good future for the right person in manufacturing.

An individual with some vocational training may start as a machine operator in the factory. Some on-the-job training will probably also be necessary. Competent men who demonstrate managerial ability may be promoted to foreman and eventually may become involved in the planning, scheduling, routing, dispatching, and recording of production.

Most people who seek careers in manufacturing have training in engineering. They supervise the actual production. Business administration graduates are found, however, in such positions as that of efficiency engineer who makes studies of the workers to be sure that their time is being most efficiently utilized.

The person who wants a career in manufacturing should study cost accounting, business and factory organization, production, statistics, labor problems, and management.

Careers in Transportation. The two major sources of jobs for young people who are considering a career in shipping and transportation are carriers, such as railroads, airlines, and motor freight lines, and the traffic departments of businesses. A limited number of jobs are also available in government agencies such as the Federal Aviation Agency and the Bureau of Public Roads, in transportation trade associations, and the Chambers of Commerce.

A person with a high school education or less might start with a carrier as a driver or loader and later advance to the position of guard, inspector, or dispatcher. Managerial jobs with carriers are found in the departments of sales, claims, and accounting. Some carriers sponsor training programs for their new managers.

A new employee in a business' shipping or traffic department would probably be placed first in the shipping room to gain experience. His duties would be the packing and unpacking of shipments and the preparation of shipping forms. He might also prepare freight rate schedules and compute freight charges. More experienced clerks analyze rates and transportation statistics and may assist the traffic manager by tracing missing shipments and by handling claims.

The highest position in a business' shipping and transportation operations is that of traffic manager. His duties were outlined earlier in the unit. It is still possible to become traffic manager by starting as a clerk and working upward. However, most companies now recruit their traffic manager trainees from colleges. They want people with training in management, marketing, statistics, economics, transportation, and accounting.

UNIT V
Finance

What types of capital do businesses need?

How can one determine the price to pay for a business that is up for sale?

What is meant by merchandise turn-over?

What is cash flow?

How are capital needs estimated?

How can internal and external standards be used to determine capital needs?

BACKGROUND OF CHAPTER

All businesses need capital. Capital is invested in land, buildings, and equipment. Capital is also needed to buy goods for sale and to meet day-to-day expenses. An individual wanting to own a business needs enough money to start a new business or buy an established business, and he must have enough money to keep it running until profits can pay the operating costs.

This chapter discusses the different types of capital which a businessman may need, how capital requirements are determined, and how capital is used.

CHAPTER 15

FINANCIAL REQUIREMENTS OF A BUSINESS

Whether one is starting a new business, buying a going business, or operating a going business, there is the problem of having enough capital to operate the business. Even a profitable business can get into trouble if it does not have enough cash. In this chapter the problems of capital needs are studied, and in the following chapters the sources of capital will be studied.

CAPITAL

In economics, as explained in Chapter 3, the term "capital" is used to refer to money invested in equipment and merchandise as well as actual cash available for operating the business. In this chapter we shall use "capital" to mean the money and credit used to run a business. *Fixed capital* is the term applied to money invested in fixtures, equipment, and real estate. *Working capital* represents the excess of current assets over current debt. The term *current* refers to those assets and debts which have a life of one year or less.

In a study made by the United States Department of Commerce, lack of sufficient capital is given as one of the important causes of business failures. The lack of sufficient capital may be caused (a) by failure of the businessman to have enough money to start a business or (b) by the failure to borrow wisely. Sometimes a business with sufficient capital will fail because the owner invests too much money in equipment and buildings and does not keep enough for working capital.

In starting a business, a person should not be too eager to own his own building or to buy expensive equipment. This caution applies equally well to the person who has already established a business, for there have been many businessmen who, considering themselves successfully established, bought a building or expensive equipment. Then they found that they could not operate their businesses profitably because of a lack of working capital.

Funds that are put into assets that cannot be sold readily will not be available to pay current bills. Until the business produces enough earnings to ensure plenty of money for operating purposes, it is unwise to put more than a minimum amount into a building or equipment. A building can be rented, and frequently equipment can be obtained on some plan of payment that does not require the immediate outlay of the total amount in cash.

ESTIMATING CAPITAL NEEDS

There is always uncertainty about the amount of capital needed to start and to operate a business. How can the buyer of a going concern, for example, be certain that the price asked is correct and within his ability to pay? Starting a new business requires as much capital, if not more, than the outright purchase of a going concern.

The two basic measures commonly used in estimating capital needs are (1) external standards and (2) internal standards.

External Sources of Information

Clues to capital needs are available from several external sources. One source, the Department of Commerce, makes a report available to businessmen which gives the average amount of money it takes to invest in a particular type of business. This report makes reference to the size of the business, its community description, and anticipated annual sales volume. The amount needed to purchase equipment and inventory is also suggested by these national averages.

Probably the second most important external source of information about capital needs is local commercial banks. Banks have constant contact with businesses and in the process of lending money develop a knowledge of capital requirements for various types of businesses. Of further value is the contact made with the bank as a potential source of capital.

Some prospective businessmen have had success in contacts with others in the same line of business. Although it would appear natural that the competition would withhold some information, many will give basic information freely. The buyer of a going business should compare the data of several external sources before making the final decision on his capital needs.

It might be well worth the expense of employing a person from another city who is in the same type of business to help in the planning for capital needs.

Other external sources include the local Chamber of Commerce, Small Business Administration, accountants, and lawyers.

Internal Sources of Information

When an individual takes a close look at the business itself, he can get an estimation of capital needs. This is known as the internal source of information. For example, when buying an existing business there is an advantage of visual observation of the location, assets, and many times the financial records. When starting a new business the observation is done from a statistical or mathematical base. In the statistical base certain assumptions have to be made concerning sales, profits, equipment, and other asset requirements. Statistical observation includes (1) asset cost, (2) equity capital, (3) return on investment, and (4) sales projection.

Asset Cost. Capital needs can be estimated by determining what assets are required. Illustration 15-1 shows the basic types of assets

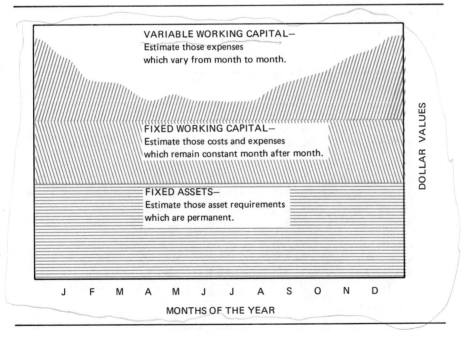

ILLUS. 15-1. Estimating annual assets required.

needed—fixed assets and working capital assets. By listing the types of fixed assets which will be needed, a cost value of acquiring those assets can be established. An estimate of business costs and expenses such as inventory, payroll, utilities, rent, supplies, and the many other day-to-day expenses of doing business can establish an amount for working capital.

If $20,000 is the amount an individual has to invest, the amount for investment in fixed assets, working capital, and other operating expenses is limited to that amount unless more money is borrowed.

Another method of determining asset cost is by the application of average ratios such as those suggested by Dun and Bradstreet as shown in Illustration 15-2. For example, to determine the amount for fixed assets, net worth (owner's investment) is multiplied by the average percentage of fixed assets to net worth for the kind of business being considered. If the owner's capital in a jewelry store is $20,000, the amount he would need for fixed assets would be approximately $1,800 ($20,000 × 9%).

Following the above example, $18,200 remains for working capital ($20,000-$1,800). The inventory for the jewelry store can be valued at approximately $14,200 ($18,200 times 77.8% = $14,159.60). The remaining amount, $4,000 is needed for variable working capital. A summary of the capital investment for the jewelry store is given in Illustration 15-3. A rule of thumb suggests that the relationship

Line of Business	Inventory to Working Capital	Current Debt to Inventory	Current Debt to Net Worth	Fixed Assets to Net Worth	Net Profit on Net Worth
Retailing					
Department Stores	76.9%	72.1%	41.9%	24.7%	6.46%
Gasoline Service	63.2%	159.7%	38.1%	47.4%	7.50%
Jewelry Stores	77.8%	67.3%	45.6%	9.0%	8.13%
Family Clothing	82.5%	51.4%	36.9%	11.4%	8.38%
Wholesaling					
Automotive	94.8%	64.3%	46.3%	12.5%	8.11%
Hardware	93.4%	59.8%	45.1%	13.8%	4.85%
Furniture	83.0%	107.3%	84.4%	10.5%	7.93%

Source: Dun and Bradstreet

ILLUS. 15-2. Asset values from selected ratios.

Owner's Equity	$20,000
For Fixed Assets	1,800
For Inventory	14,200
For Variable Working Capital	4,000

ILLUS. 15-3. Asset value of a jewelry store.

between inventory and working capital should not exceed 80 percent.

In using a statistical observation for asset cost, the nature and kinds of assets must be determined and a value placed upon them.

Equity Capital. Those who have loaned capital to the business have an equity (claim against assets) in the business. Thus, *equity capital* includes owned capital as well as borrowed capital. Because the business owns things of value, it can borrow other funds. When a business borrows money based upon its owned capital, the process is called *trading on its equity*. The extent to which it can borrow is called *leverage*. Obviously, the amount which can be borrowed is limited by the amount owned. If the creditor's share of the equity is greater than the owner's, lenders would hesitate to loan money to the firm. If a business owned $20,000 in assets, it would be difficult to borrow an additional $20,000. The question would arise as to who owned the business, the owners or the creditors?

How much current debt can a business sustain? In Illustration 15-2 various relationships were given. The extent of the current debt can be determined by the line of business and the amount of inventory. For the jewelry store in the previous example, 67.3 percent is average for the relationship of current debt to inventory. With an inventory of $14,200 the current debt can approximate $9,550 (67.3% × $14,200 = $9,556.60). By a comparison of debt to net worth, the jewelry store current debt can approximate $9,120 (45.6% × $20,000).

The amount to invest in the assets of a business is limited to the combination of owned capital and an amount that could be borrowed safely.

Return on Investment. One method of determining profitability is the return on invested capital. The average return of 8.13 percent for jewelry stores is shown in Illustration 15-2. This return provides the income for the owner as well as for the future development of the business. If the net profit is equal to 8.13 percent return on the invested capital, a payback of 12.3 years (100 ÷ 8.13) results. *Payback* is the period of time it takes for net profits to equal the original investment of the owner.

One method of determining the capital needs of a business is to *capitalize the profits.* This means to place a value on the assets based upon the net profit. For example, if it is assumed that the net profits for a year are anticipated to be $5,000 and a return on investment of 8.13 percent is desired, an investment of $61,500 ($5,000 ÷ .0813) would be required. To prove the result, an investment of $61,500 times 8.13 percent return equals $5,000.

In using the return on investment for an estimation of capital requirements, the owner must estimate accurately the net profit and the percentage of return needed to make the investment worthwhile.

Sales Projection. Money invested in merchandise is a part of working capital because the funds will be used over and over again as sales are made, money is received, and new merchandise is purchased. An additional amount of cash is also needed to pay wages and all other operating expenses. Of course, it is assumed that sales will provide cash that can be used again and that sales will provide a profit, but it may take a new business a long time before any profit is made. Thus, it is important to estimate sales carefully. The cost of the building and the equipment can be computed accurately, but the amount of sales must be estimated.

If one is going to sell on credit, his money will be tied up until he can make collections. It is therefore important to have a sufficient amount of capital available to finance the business until collections can be made. If sales are to be made on a cash basis, the cash to pay creditors will be available earlier.

Illustration 15-4 shows the working capital cycle. Note the various steps in the process where merchandise is sold and converted into cash. Each time the cycle is completed, merchandise is replaced. A *merchandise turnover* rate indicates the number of times the merchant will buy and sell all the merchandise in his store during the year. A business with a high turnover needs less working capital than one with a low turnover because the former has less money invested in merchandise.

A turnover of three times a year means that the merchandise is on the shelves an average of four months from the time it is bought until it

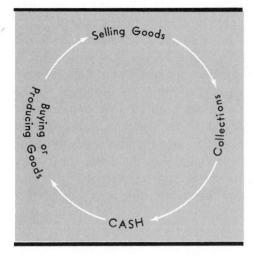

ILLUS. 15-4. The working capital cycle.

is sold. If the turnover is twelve times a year, the merchandise is on the shelves an average of thirty days. Figures like those in Illustration 15-5 will help a businessman to estimate the financial requirements for his merchandise inventory. For instance, if one is contemplating starting a business in which the turnover is four times a year, with most of the goods sold on thirty days' credit (the average collection period being thirty days), the estimated time from the purchase of merchandise until the collection of cash from sales will be about four months (3+1).

Type of Business	National Average Turnover of Merchandise
Retail:	
Grocery stores	16.8
Furniture stores	4.6
Gasoline service stations	9.9
Jewelry stores	2.9
Motor vehicle dealers	7.6
Wholesale:	
Grocery	12.6
Manufacturing:	
Communication equipment	4.7
Household appliances	4.6
Source: Dun and Bradstreet	

ILLUS. 15-5. Examples of merchandise turnover rates.

If the businessman buys merchandise on thirty days' credit, he therefore must have enough cash available to operate for three months.

It will be seen from this analysis that the rate of turnover has a definite relation to the amount of working capital that is needed. If businesses have the same amount of sales, the one with a high turnover can operate with less capital than the one with a low turnover.

Turnover also is related to the gross profit on merchandise that is sold. That is true because one must obtain a greater profit on merchandise that is held on the shelves a long time than he needs to obtain from merchandise held only a short time. For example, the typical retail grocery store with a high turnover can operate successfully with a smaller gross profit on each item sold than a typical jewelry store, which has a low turnover.

ESTIMATING CASH FLOW

Sales, collections, and profits will determine how much cash is available for working capital. Even if sales and profits are good, there may be a shortage of cash if collections are bad or if too much is invested in merchandise and equipment.

It is possible to estimate sales and to estimate profit. From this information it is then possible to estimate how much cash will be available and whether it will be necessary to borrow money. The table in Illustration 15-6 shows the estimated cash flow or working capital

Estimate of Cash Flow, Month of March

Beginning cash balance	$ 3,375.00
Collections from customers	17,500.00
Total cash available	$20,875.00
Payments:	
Accounts to be paid	$11,250.00
Labor	2,375.00
Other operating expenses	3,250.00
Sales expense	3,750.00
Salary of executives	1,750.00
Purchase of fixed assets	....
Repayment of bank loan	....
Total payments	$22,375.00
Expected cash shortage	$ 1,500.00
Bank loan needed	$ 2,500.00
Ending cash balance	$ 1,000.00

ILLUS. 15-6. Estimate of working capital.

available for a company which has sales of $17,500 in February and expected sales of $20,000 in March. Notice, for example, that this company has cash of $3,375 at the beginning of the month. It was estimated that collections from customers would amount to the same as the sales for the previous month. Of course, some of these collections will be from customers who purchased merchandise in previous months.

The company did not expect to purchase any new fixed assets, and there are no bank loans that must be repaid in March. However, it will be observed that there is an expected cash shortage of $1,500. Therefore, it will probably be necessary to borrow $2,500 so that there will be some cash left over with which to operate. Money will continue to come in from collections from customers.

SECURING ADEQUATE FINANCIAL ADVICE

Although there is much the individual can do in the estimation of capital needed for starting and operating a business, it is still a good idea to secure the opinion of several competent individuals. Using the services of a commercial bank in the planning of financial requirements is of primary importance. Among the many advantages of the banker's opinion are two which stand out. First, he works daily with businesses and knows their problems and needs. Second, the banker who knows the businessman's needs from the outset is in a better position to make positive judgments concerning potential loans to him.

Accountants work with ratios and financial statements. They are another valuable source of information and advice. Chamber of Commerce and Better Business Bureau officials are involved with the economics of the community and can offer advice. Other businessmen normally stand ready to help the beginning business.

These sources of information should be considered before the potential businessman invests his time and money in operation.

REVIEW WHAT YOU HAVE LEARNED

Business Terms Checkup:

(1) capital

(2) fixed capital

(3) working capital

(4) current assets

(5) current debt

(6) equity capital

(7) trading on the equity

(8) leverage

(9) payback

(10) capitalize profits

(11) merchandise turnover

Reading Checkup:

1. According to a study of the United States Department of Commerce, what is one of the most important causes of business failure?
2. What do the terms internal and external sources of information mean?
3. Distinguish between visual observation and statistical observation.
4. What is meant by equity capital? Name the two types of equity capital.
5. What is meant by variable working capital? Fixed working capital?
6. Are leverage and trading on the equity the same?
7. How is payback calculated?
8. Capitalizing of profits means to place a value on assets. How is this done?
9. What is merchandise turnover? How does it affect the profitableness and the working capital of a business?
10. Name the various individuals and institutions which might be consulted about financial requirements?

APPLY WHAT YOU HAVE LEARNED

Questions for Class Discussion:

1. Why does one usually avoid investing money in a building when a new business is being organized?
2. How do credit terms on sales affect working capital?
3. Why will a business find it difficult to borrow money unless the owners have a substantial amount invested in the business?
4. Which type of business is likely to have the greater turnover of merchandise—a jewelry store or a grocery store? Why?
5. How does merchandise turnover affect profits?
6. Would you consider it good judgment on the part of the manager of a retail business to use the same percentage of gross profit on all items?
7. Why would a stone and clay products company have a greater percentage of its total assets invested in fixed assets than would a wholesale paper products company?
8. Why is it likely to take less time for a retailer to become successfully established than a manufacturer who is seeking a nationwide distribution?
9. Using information given in Illustration 15-2, page 300, assume the jewelry store owner had $50,000 to invest. Construct a summary of capital investment for the store like Illustration 15-3.

10. Examine Illustration 15-6 showing the cash flow for March and explain what action is going to be necessary in some future month in regard to the bank loan of $2,500 in March.

Problems and Projects:

1. In this chapter you have studied fixed capital and working capital. Select a small business, such as a flower shop, a gift shop, or a hobby store, and make an estimate of the fixed capital and working capital required for starting and operating this business in your community. The fixed capital requirements will be for equipment; working capital requirements will be for merchandise, rent, wages, and other regular expenses. Remember that you must have enough working capital to provide capital needed until you obtain money from sales. You must also take into consideration whether sales will be for cash or on account.

2. The motel business has expanded very rapidly in all parts of the nation. Using your own area for analysis:

(a) Give two reasons why this business is likely to continue its rapid growth.

(b) Give two reasons why such expansion is not likely to continue.

(c) City hotels are feeling the competition of motels. Suggest two ways in which hotels can meet this competition.

3. You are planning to open a hardware store. A study discloses that you can sell in your community each month an average of approximately $2,500 worth of hardware, which will cost $1,250. Figures compiled by the United States Department of Commerce show the average expenses (not including wages and salaries) of hardware stores to be the following percentages of net sales:

	Percent
Rent	4.0
Heat, light, and power	.4
Taxes and licenses	1.4
Insurance	.8
Interest	1.2
Telephone and telegraph	.4
Boxes, wrapping, and other packing material	.1
Postage, including parcel post	.3
Maintenance and depreciation of delivery equipment, etc.	1.1
Depreciation other than that on delivery equipment; repairs	.8
Collection costs, including credit association dues	.03
Advertising	1.4

(a) Prepare a list showing the amount of each expense and the total for the month. For this purpose, do not include the cost of the hardware in your figures.

(b) Complete the following form to find the estimated profit.

```
Sales ............................... xxxx.xx
        Less cost of goods sold ............ xxxx.xx
Gross profit from sales ................ xxxx.xx
        Less total estimated expenses ...... xxx.xx
Estimated profit ..................... xxx.xx
```

4. (a) In starting a new business, assume the following cash expenditures are necessary: rent, $200; insurance, $142; customer convenience, wrapping paper and other supplies, $75; wages, $430; telephone service, $17; heat, light, and water, $180; advertising, $125; license, $30; purchase of merchandise, $3050; down payment on equipment, $300; office and related accounting supplies, $60.

Determine the amount of money that will be needed to start a business if you ignore the possibility of any cash income during the first month of operation.

(b) Assume that during the first month of operation the cash sales will total $1675 and that $2000 can be borrowed for sixty days from a bank at the beginning of the month, interest at 8 percent deducted in advance. What is the minimum amount of additional cash that will be needed for the month?

Case Problem 15-1:

Philip Crone started a lumber and building materials business. He invested $20,000 of his own money and borrowed $5,000 from a bank. He bought $1,000 of equipment and purchased $23,000 of merchandise which he maintained at this level. His sales for each of the first two years amounted to about $45,000, but he was always short of cash and had difficulty paying his bills.

Required:

1. What do you think are some of the causes of his difficulty?
2. What can he do to remedy his difficulties?

Case Problem 15-2:

Felix Cune owned and operated a small fabric store in a neighborhood shopping center. He had, however, been considering ways of expanding his interests. The opportunity arose when a building adjacent to his fabric store became vacant. He was interested in starting a self-service laundry since (1) he could operate such a business in conjunction with the fabric store, (2) the area had many apartment buildings, (3) competition was thin and poorly managed. The owner of the building agreed to permit Cune to use the building as a self-service laundry on the basis of a two-year lease at $375 a month with an additional three-year option.

Total initial cost of the necessary equipment amounted to $27,800, of which Cune paid $5,560 down and borrowed the balance of $22,240 from a banker for two years at 8 percent interest. Initial equipment consisted of washers, dryers, and supplemental equipment, such as tables, chairs, and soft-drink machines.

After two years of operation, Cune reported the following:

1. Sales averaged $2,827 a month.

2. Monthly operational costs and other expenses amounted to:

Electricity	$ 160.00
Water	65.00
Gas	80.00
Rent	375.00
Insurance	42.00
Interest and principal (first two years)	1,074.00
Part-time help	525.00
Repair bills (first 18 months)	200.00
Total	$2,521.00

3. During the last 6 months, as the equipment became older, repair bills averaged around $250 per month.

4. Sales remained steady and showed no tendency to decline.

After two years Cune became interested in selling the business because of increasing costs and the steady drain on his time from performing most of his own repair work.

Arthur Meyer spent some time inspecting the business and asked Cune what his selling price was. Cune stated that he wanted $22,500. Meyer offered to purchase the business for $20,000, a price which would include all of the equipment, tools, and supplies. Cune accepted the offer.

Required:

Did Cune receive a fair price?

Continuing Project:

For your business make an estimate of your capital needs for equipment and fixtures, an opening inventory of merchandise (if applicable), and a cash reserve for working capital.

What are the sources of capital?

How can proprietary capital be obtained?

What kinds of stocks are issued by corporations?

What are the sources of borrowed capital?

What kinds of bonds are issued by corporations?

How may securities be marketed?

BACKGROUND OF CHAPTER

When the capital needs for buying or starting and for operating a business have been determined, the businessman then must obtain the necessary capital.

Money may be obtained from various sources. It may be furnished by the owners as an investment in the business. It may be borrowed from banks, loan companies, and other lenders. Often a corporation is formed and stock in the corporation is sold.

This chapter explains where and how a businessman may obtain the capital he needs.

CHAPTER 16

FINANCING A BUSINESS

In Chapter 3 you learned that in economics the term "capital" means tools, machinery, buildings, and equipment used in production. In Chapter 15 you learned that, in financing a business, capital means the money and credit needed to run the business; and this is the sense in which the term "capital" is used in this chapter. Capital to run a business is furnished by the owners, by those who lend money to the business, by commercial credit extended to the business, and by earnings left in the business.

Much of the capital is made available to business through money invested by individuals. One individual may invest money and start a business; he may form a business with partners; or many individuals may put their money together in the form of a corporation to acquire assets and start a business. Illustration 16-1 gives the results of a study of 80 small businesses. The study was made for the Small Business Administration, an agency of the federal government. The study shows that the owners of these businesses provided 60.6 percent of the needed capital from their own funds in starting the businesses.

The sources of money for the capital needs of business depend upon the accumulated savings of individuals or the profits of business. The profits of business, if they are kept in the business, can be used to invest in new capital equipment and buildings that will create new production or to buy materials and pay expenses. Savings of individuals are not only invested directly in business to provide new capital, but savings of many individuals are also deposited in banks and other financial institutions (such as insurance companies) and are then loaned to businesses to provide new capital. In addition, those who sell on credit to a business are providing some of the capital in the same way that lending to a business provides capital.

Sources	Percentage of Total
Cash and savings of operator	52.5%
Previous investment in the business	8.1
Loans from banks and other institutions	15.7
Loans from family	6.9
Loans from friends	4.7
Credit from suppliers	6.0
Loans from previous owners	2.7
From surrendered insurance	0.1
Other unspecified sources	3.3
	100.0%

Source: Small Business Administration

ILLUS. 16-1. Sources of initial capital investment.

SOURCES OF CAPITAL

At this point it is necessary to determine where the money will come from to start and to operate a business. The sole owner of a business is known as the proprietor. Any money an owner invests in the business is called _owned_ (or _proprietary_) _capital._ This capital may be personal funds or money obtained by borrowing on a home or on some personal property. Others may invest in the business as part owners. This investment is also owned capital. Profits that are kept in the business are another source of capital and are called _retained earnings._ Any capital that is loaned to the business by others is called _borrowed capital._ Banks and other lenders will usually not lend money to a business unless the owned capital exceeds the borrowed capital. Illustration 16-2 indicates the relationship of the two kinds of capital to the assets of the business.

Owned Capital

To finance his business by acquiring proprietary capital, the individual proprietor can tap several sources. He can sell some of his personal assets, borrow from an individual, mortgage the business property, or mortgage his personal property.

The sole owner of a business may also obtain additional money by (a) forming a partnership and requiring the new partner to invest money in the business or (b) forming a corporation and selling stock. A business that is expanded in one of these ways may make greater sales

Balance Sheet

Assets $10,000	Liabilities (Borrowed capital obtained from bank) . . . . $ 4,000
	Proprietorship (Proprietary capital invested by owner) 6,000
$10,000	$10,000

ILLUS. 16-2. Borrowed and proprietary capital.

and greater profits, but the percentage of profits based on the invested money may decrease. The owner of the business must therefore make an estimate that will help him decide whether he can make more profit by himself or more profit by bringing additional money and owners into the business.

Let us say that the proprietor decides to secure additional proprietary capital by incorporating and selling stock. The two kinds of stock most frequently issued by a corporation are known as common stock and preferred stock. A copy of a stock certificate is shown in Illustration 16-3.

Common Stock. So far as profits are concerned, the owners of *common stock* are in much the same position as the partners in a partnership. They participate in the management of the business and share in the profits (called *dividends*) if there are any. They do not obtain earnings, however, until all other investors have been paid. Furthermore, there is no fixed rate of earnings on common stock.

Preferred Stock. As its name indicates, *preferred stock* has some kind of preference over the ordinary, or common, stock. One preference may be in the distribution of profits. Whenever profits are distributed, the preferred stockholders must receive their dividend first. A corporation must, of course, pay its regular debts and interest on borrowed money before any dividend can be paid. Holders of preferred stock usually receive a fixed dividend, ranging from 4 to 7 percent of the face value of the stock.

Let us see just how this plan works out. Suppose that a certain corporation has issued $50,000 of 7 percent preferred stock and also $50,000 of common stock, and that the profits for a certain year are $4,000. The preferred stockholders will receive their 7 percent of $50,000, which is $3,500. Then there is only $500 remaining, which

ILLUS. 16-3. A corporation obtains capital by selling stock.

is available for the common stockholders. But suppose that the same corporation should earn $12,000 in profits during a certain other year. In this case the preferred stockholders would be paid their fixed rate of dividend (7 percent), or $3,500; and there would be $8,500 left for distribution to the common stockholders. If this whole amount were distributed, the common stockholders would receive a dividend of 17 percent. It is, however, usually not a good policy to distribute all the profits. It is better to keep some of the profits as a reserve (or surplus). If all the profits are paid out in the form of cash, a company may later need to borrow money in order to carry on its operations. As shown in Illustration 16-4, some corporations prefer to leave a surplus in the business so that, if no profit is earned during a particular period, they may still pay a dividend out of the surplus that was previously earned. If a corporation pays out all its earnings and profits, it may have serious difficulty if a loss is suffered during any particular year.

Ordinarily the preferred stockholders do not have any voting privilege in the management of the business, although the ownership of certain types of preferred stock does permit such activity in case dividends are not declared and paid regularly. Some kinds of preferred stock carry a special privilege with regard to claims against the assets.

ILLUS. 16-4. A corporation distributes part of its profits as dividends to stockholders and retains the rest as a reserve or surplus.

For instance, if the corporation ceases operations, the preferred stockholders must be paid before the common stockholders.

To illustrate, suppose that a corporation has outstanding $50,000 of common stock and also $50,000 of stock that is preferred as to assets. During the liquidation process all the assets are converted into cash and all the creditors are paid. There then remains $80,000 in cash. The sum of $50,000 must be paid to the stockholders whose stock is preferred as to assets. Consequently the holders of common stock receive only $30,000. Thus, the common stockholders receive only 60 percent of the full face value of their stock. Had there been no preference as to assets, all the stockholders, both common and preferred, would have shared equally, each group receiving $40,000.

When a corporation goes out of business, however, both the preferred and the common stockholders seldom get much from the assets because the assets often do not sell for enough to pay the creditors.

Par Value and No-Par Value Stock. In many states corporations have the privilege of issuing par value stock or no-par value stock.

Par Value Stock. Each stock certificate must show the number of shares it represents. In addition, it may show a *par value* or *stated value*. A par value or stated value shown on the certificate has nothing to do with the worth of the stock. For example, a stock with a par value of $10 may be worth $50, or it may be worth nothing. The par value of a stock is simply an amount used for bookkeeping purposes on the balance sheet of the issuing company.

A par value on shares of stock may be required by the corporate laws of the state. A corporation can choose almost any amount for the par value of its stock. It could be 10¢, $1, $50, or $100.

The value indicated on a stock certificate should not be confused with the *market value,* which is the value at which the stock is bought and sold. A share of a certain stock may have a par value of $50; but, because the company that issued it has been prosperous and has been paying large dividends, certain people may be willing to pay $60 for it. If a corporation has not been successful financially, the market value of its stock is likely to be less than the par value.

Another term, book value, is often used in connection with the value of a share of stock. The *book value* of a share is found by dividing the net worth (assets minus debts) of the corporation by the total number of shares outstanding. Thus, if the net worth of a corporation is $75,000 and the number of shares of stock outstanding is 1,000, the book value of each share is $75, regardless of whether the stock has a par value of $50 or $100, or whether it has no par value.

No-Par Value Stock. No-par value stock is essentially the same as par value stock except that it has no value stated on it. This is done to avoid the inference that the stock is worth a certain amount. Dividends on no-par value stock are always stated as a certain amount per share.

Which Kind of Stock to Issue? One of the problems that must be decided in organizing a corporation is the amount of capital stock to be issued and the kind or kinds. The certificate of incorporation states whether all the stock of the corporation is to be common or whether part is to be common and part preferred. The corporation can issue no other kinds unless authorization is received from the government.

In starting a business, it is usually a good plan to issue only common stock. Even though profits may be made from the very beginning, it is often desirable to use those profits in the expansion of the business. When preferred stock is issued, the corporation is under an obligation to pay the specified dividend if profits are made. If the company begins business with common stock and later finds it desirable to expand the business, it may then issue preferred stock in order to induce others to invest in the company.

Sometimes the preferred stock is issued to the original owners of the business. The original owners may desire to have the first dividends available and to have their investment returned in case of failure of the business.

Retained Earnings

Unforeseen happenings make it necessary for the manager of a business to build a reserve to take care of them. This is called "plowing back" earnings. If the business makes a profit, the owner should not take out all the profits in the form of cash or other assets, but he should attempt to leave sufficient cash for some or all of the following:

1. Replacement of buildings and equipment needed as the result of depreciation (wearing out).
2. Replacements needed as the result of obsolescence (out of date).
3. Additions that are necessary for expansion.
4. Financial protection during periods of low sales and low profits.
5. Purchases of goods at times when bargains can be obtained.

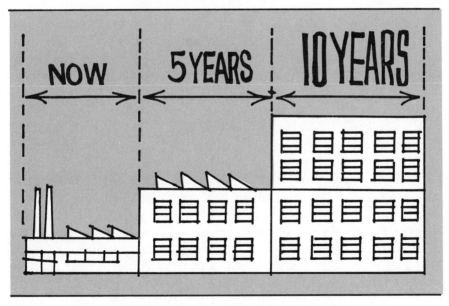

ILLUS. 16-5. Some of the earnings of a business should be retained to provide for future expansion of the business.

Even if the business is not making a profit but is just breaking even, it should make provision for replacing the assets that decrease in value because of depreciation or obsolescence. For instance, a bus company may start operations with new buses. The business may not make a profit, but there may be considerable cash available each month. If the owners of the business take out all the available cash, there will not be any funds with which to buy new buses when the present ones are worn out.

It should be realized that retained earnings are not kept in the form of cash only. Cash may be reinvested in many assets, particularly inventories and other short-lived assets, which are in turn converted to additional cash. Since retained earnings are a part of owned capital, the owners and their management can use these earnings for investment purposes and for future expansion.

Borrowed Capital

From the point of view of the business, borrowed capital is of three types: (1) short term, based on short-term credit; (2) intermediate term; and (3) long term, based on long-term credit.

Sources for these three kinds of borrowed capital are listed in Illustration 16-6 on page 319.

Short-Term Capital. *Short-term capital* is borrowed capital that must be paid back in a relatively short time of 30, 60, or 90 days and usually in less than a year. It is also referred to as *short-term credit* when it is obtained from a bank or from a creditor from whom merchandise or equipment is purchased.

In borrowing from a bank or other lending agency, the lender will want to be certain that the loan will be repaid. Some of the questions that may be asked about the borrower are indicated in Illustration 16-7 on page 320. If satisfactory answers are given to these questions, the bank may grant an *open line of credit* which will permit regular borrowing and repaying. If there is some doubt about the ability of the business to repay the loan, the bank may ask that the accounts receivable of the business or the merchandise inventory be pledged to the bank as security for the loan. If the loan is not repaid, the bank would have a right to the money collected from the accounts of customers or could claim the merchandise and sell it.

Borrowing on Insurance Policies. A life insurance policy can be used as security for obtaining a loan from an insurance company, and

1. Commercial banks.
2. Industrial banks.
3. Small loan companies.
4. Factoring companies (which will purchase the accounts receivable and notes receivable of a business at less than face value).
5. Commercial credit companies (that will lend money on securities, such as accounts receivable and notes receivable or warehouse receipts).
6. Sales finance companies (which are used primarily when installment sales are involved and will purchase the installment sales contracts).
7. Insurance companies.
8. Individual investors.
9. Corporations that are seeking branches or outlets (and will therefore lend to a small businessman to set him up or help finance him to serve as a branch or outlet).
10. Investment bankers.
11. Community industry-development groups (which are formed in some communities to encourage new business and which will lend to a new business getting started or help an old one to expand).
12. Equipment manufacturers (which will not actually lend money but will sell needed equipment on an extended-time payment plan).
13. Loans from the federal government.

ILLUS. 16-6. Sources of borrowed capital.

the loan can be repaid when it is convenient. If death occurs before the loan is repaid, the amount of the loan is deducted from the payment due the beneficiary.

The amount that can be borrowed on an insurance policy depends entirely on the face of the policy and the length of time the policy has been in force. A bank will occasionally lend on an insurance policy in the same way as an insurance company.

Other Sales Financing. Besides borrowing from banks, there are other financial institutions from which money can be borrowed to finance sales. One type of company is called a *factoring company*, or *factor*. Factors specialize in making loans to businesses based upon their accounts receivable. The usual practice is that the factor will purchase the accounts receivable and then collect them.

A *sales finance company* is one that is engaged in purchasing installment sales contracts from businessmen. The contracts are purchased at a discount, and the finance company makes the collections. However,

1. Is he of good character?
2. Is the borrower putting up enough cash?
3. What experience has the borrower had in this business?
4. Will loan be secured properly? Will payments on debt be made from profits only?
5. Will financing be sound? (Net worth to debt and cash to cash needs ratios. Also debt payments to net income ratio.)
6. Is enough cash being raised to supply needs—
    for repairs on buildings and equipment?
    for modernization, new equipment?
    to build up accounts receivable?
    for build-up of inventory expansion?
7. How good is the estimate of expenses, salaries, wages, utilities, advertising, supplies, taxes, insurance, etc.?
8. What are the terms of lease? What amount must be paid in taxes?
9. Does borrower have good accounting knowledge and does he keep proper accounting records?

ILLUS. 16-7. Questions that may be asked about the borrower.

in some cases finance companies loan the money to the businessman with the installment contracts as security, and the businessman continues to collect the installments.

Notes are purchased by the finance company at a discount. For example, a customer may buy a refrigerator on the installment plan and sign a mortgage contract. This contract may then be sold to a finance company for less than the amount that is owed on the contract when it becomes due. The finance company collects the full amount of the contract and thereby makes its profit for handling the transaction. In many cases the contract is endorsed *without recourse*; that is, it is endorsed in such a way that the finance company will have no claim against the merchant if the debtor refuses or is unable to pay. In a few cases, however, contracts are sold to finance companies with the understanding that the merchant is responsible for handling the collections.

Loans from the Federal Government. Because small businesses sometimes have difficulty obtaining loans or obtaining them under favorable conditions, the federal government has established the Small Business Administration. This agency is authorized to make short-term or long-term loans to small businesses. This agency also makes funds available to regular lending agencies so that these agencies can lend to small businesses.

Special Sources of Loans. Some states, cities, counties, and other special organizations have money to lend to businesses to encourage them to locate in a particular place or to encourage a business not to move away. Money is loaned at favorable rates, and often buildings are constructed and leased to a business at a favorable rate.

Intermediate-Term Capital. When the term of financing falls somewhere between one and ten years, the financing is referred to as intermediate financing. There are needs of business to acquire property which has a short productive life. Although retained earnings are utilized for the most part in this period of time, intermediate-term credit is also available from banks, insurance companies, and other lending institutions.

Long-Term Capital. *Long-term capital* is usually obtained by issuing bonds, long-term notes, or mortgages. When bonds are issued by a corporation, the corporation usually pledges some security to the bondholders. This security is either some specific property or a right to certain earnings. In other words, the corporation tells the bondholders that, if the interest on the bonds or the principal is not paid according to the agreement, the owners of the bond can take over the property or collect certain earnings that have been pledged.

A long-term note has some of the aspects of a mortgage, but it does not extend for such a long time.

It can be seen from the preceding discussion that a sole proprietorship or partnership cannot issue bonds and obtain the usual long-term credit that is thus available to corporations. The sole proprietor or members of a partnership can obtain ordinary short-term credit from a bank; but in order to obtain long-term credit, they must usually mortgage their personal property or the property of the business, or pledge some other security for the loan.

Bonds. The *corporation bond* is a long-term written promise to pay a definite sum of money at a specified time. It contains an agreement to pay interest at a specified rate at certain intervals. Bonds do not represent a share in the ownership of the corporation; they are evidence of a debt owed by the corporation. All bondholders have a preferred claim against the earnings of the corporation, for they must be paid before stockholders share in the earnings.

There are two general types of bonds: (a) mortgage bonds and (b) income, or debenture, bonds.

The issuer of *mortgage bonds* pledges some specific assets as a guarantee that the interest and the principal will be paid according to the terms specified in the bonds. Land, buildings, and machinery are commonly used as security for such bonds.

Debenture bonds have no specific assets pledged as security. They are secured by the faith and the credit of the corporation that issues them. Public corporations, such as city, state, and federal governments, usually issue debenture (revenue) bonds when they need to borrow money. Private corporations usually find it difficult to sell debenture bonds, although they probably prefer to issue debenture bonds instead of mortgage bonds. If the latter type is issued and the corporation is unable to meet some of the interest payments as they fall due, the bondholders may start foreclosure proceedings against the corporation. Such legal proceedings are usually begun by the trustee of the bondholders—the one who holds the mortgage for the bondholders.

The bonds above may also be further classified as: (a) coupon bonds, (b) registered bonds, and (c) convertible bonds.

Coupon bonds are generally payable to the bearers (holders). Thus, the corporation that issues them has no way of knowing who are the owners at the time interest payments are due. Because of this fact, coupons, one for each interest-due date, are attached to such a bond (see Illustration 16-8). The owner of the bond may collect the interest by clipping a coupon and cashing it at the office of the corporation or at a bank on or after the date specified on the coupon.

If *registered bonds* are issued, the corporation keeps a record of each owner and pays the interest and the principal by check to the registered owner. This type of bond means more clerical work for the corporation, but it is preferred by many people who buy bonds.

Sometimes *convertible bonds* are issued. The holder of such bonds has the privilege of exchanging them for a definite number of shares of stock. This feature is attractive to the holder. He receives a fixed rate of interest as long as he holds the bonds; and later, if the corporation should begin to earn large profits and to pay large dividends, he may exchange the bonds for stock and begin receiving dividends instead of interest.

Long-Term Notes. As a method of financing, long-term notes are a significant source of capital in modern business. Term loans are

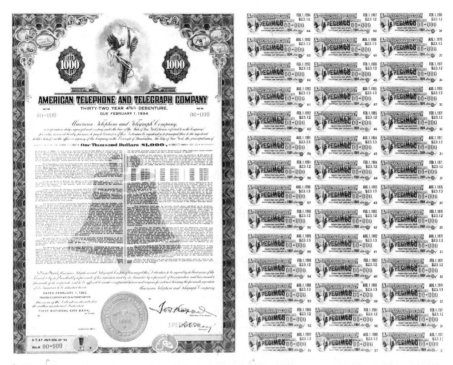

ILLUS. 16-8. A coupon bond from which some of the coupons have been clipped. There were originally 70 coupons.

obtained from commercial banks, insurance companies, and various government agencies. Notes are written for periods of time which provide for a reduction of the principal and interest in anticipation of immediate earnings.

Term loans are more readily available when banks have a surplus to loan. Interest on such loans has normally been slightly higher than for short-term loans for the same firm.

Mortgages. Mortgage loans are given to firms that have some type of property to use as security for the loan. Property often used as security includes real estate, equipment, stock and bond certificates, and life insurance policies. Lending institutions which make most of the mortgage loans are insurance companies and commercial banks.

If the loan and interest are not paid when due, the lender may take legal action against the firm to collect the value of the debt. Sometimes the lender may cause the property to be sold in order to recover the amount of the loan.

Like most loans, recovery of the principal and interest is dependent on the earning ability of the firm and not necessarily on the value of the security pledged. Most property cannot be sold for the amount of the loan. The lender may choose to attach (or claim) other assets of the firm.

DETERMINING WHICH SOURCE OF CAPITAL TO USE

Three important factors should be considered in deciding the source from which capital should be obtained: (a) the original cost of procuring the capital, (b) the interest rate, and (c) the authority exercised by the various contributors of capital.

Original Cost of Procuring the Capital

The original cost of obtaining capital from bondholders, holders of long-term notes, and stockholders is usually larger than the original cost of obtaining it from mortgage holders or short-term creditors. Considerable preliminary investigation usually has to be carried on before bonds and stocks can be sold, and considerable expense is usually incurred in doing this. Further and larger expenses are usually necessary in reaching prospective buyers. Investment banking firms that specialize in the sale of bonds and stocks will usually not sell an issue of securities of less than $500,000 in amount. They contend that the minimum expense that must be incurred on any issue is so large that a profit cannot be made on a small issue. A business that desires to obtain capital of less than $500,000 in amount will usually resort to borrowing on a mortgage or on a short-term note, unless it is prepared to market its own securities. This procedure, however, is usually costly. A business may, of course, have a market that it can reach with little expense. For example, the present stockholders of a corporation may be willing to purchase additional stock. They may also be willing to purchase bonds issued by the corporation. Employees may be ready purchasers of the securities of the company for which they work. Customers may be potential purchasers. Most businesses, however, have to follow the costly procedure of appealing to the public.

Interest Rates

Interest rates vary from month to month and from year to year. A business needing money when interest rates are high may issue short-term obligations with the expectation that interest rates will be lower at the time these obligations mature. If this expectation is realized, long-term obligations may then be issued at a lower interest rate to obtain funds with which to pay the short-term obligations. By this means the high interest rate is paid for only a short period of time; whereas, if the long-term obligations had been issued originally, the high interest rate would have been paid during the whole period of their life. In following this plan, however, a business exposes itself to possible difficulty in procuring funds when the short-term obligations fall due and to the possibility that interest rates may rise even higher.

Authority Exercised by Contributors of Capital

If short-term creditors contribute capital, they usually have no control over the affairs of the business. If the obligations are not paid, the creditors may bring a legal action to recover the amount due them; but otherwise the owners of the business are in no way restricted in their conduct of the business.

If capital is obtained by the use of bonds or mortgages, the holders of these usually have a lien on at least part of the assets of the company. This lien may impose restrictions on the use of these assets, and the agreement under which the bonds or the mortgages were issued may impose restrictions on the use of the income of the company.

If new stockholders or new partners contribute proprietary capital, they thereby gain a voice in the management of the business. The original owners may not desire to relinquish any of their authority to outsiders. It is possible in most states to issue stock that does not have voting rights, but such stock may be hard to sell. Of course, if the old stockholders or partners provide the additional funds, the control of the company is not affected, provided they contribute in the proportion of their past holdings. New stockholders or partners also share in the earnings. For example, if the number of shares is doubled by selling new shares, there are twice as many shares among which earnings must be divided.

MARKETING SECURITIES

When bonds, stocks, or long-term notes are offered to the public, the procedure becomes complex. There are two methods by which these securities may be sold: (a) directly to investors or (b) through investment banking channels.

Direct Sales to Investors

The corporation may wish to give existing stockholders the first opportunity to buy available securities. This may be accomplished by issuing *stock rights* which allow the stockholder to buy additional stock at a price lower than the current market price and in relation to the number of shares he now owns. The lower price may attract more funds to the corporation without the additional expense of selling the securities through other investment channels.

Seldom will the corporation attempt to sell its own securities to an unknown public since there is no assurance that the public will buy them, while the current stockholders can easily be asked if they desire to buy additional stock.

It may be desirable to appeal directly to investors in the following cases:

1. When small issues are made. In such cases bankers will either refuse the issue or charge a proportionately large amount for its sale.
2. When a company desires to obtain the influence as well as the investments of certain classes. For example, a business may sell its securities directly to employees with the hope of enlisting their goodwill. Again, it may sell to its customers with the hope of increasing their goodwill and patronage.
3. When the concern has a national reputation for financial success and the fair treatment of investors and, consequently, has a market for the securities that already exist.
4. When the concern desires and can afford to create an investment clientele (persons who will look to the company for investment opportunity) for future financing. This situation may exist if a company issues large quantities of securities periodically and has a national reputation for financial strength. The American Telephone and Telegraph Company follows this plan.

Investment Banking Channels

The process of selling securities through investment banking channels requires the corporation to contract with an investment company group to buy the securities and remarket them through their own channels. The advantage to the corporation is that the entire amount of cash becomes available immediately. The cost of such marketing is generally higher than the sale of securities directly to shareholders.

REVIEW WHAT YOU HAVE LEARNED

Business Terms Checkup:

(1) owned (or proprietary) capital
(2) retained earnings
(3) borrowed capital
(4) common stock
(5) dividends
(6) preferred stock
(7) par value
(8) market value
(9) book value
(10) no-par value stock
(11) short-term capital
(12) short-term credit
(13) open line of credit
(14) factoring company (or factor)
(15) sales finance company
(16) endorsement without recourse
(17) long-term capital
(18) corporation bond
(19) mortgage bonds
(20) debenture bonds
(21) coupon bonds
(22) registered bonds
(23) convertible bonds
(24) stock rights

Reading Checkup:

1. In this chapter how is the term *capital* used as distinguished from its use in the economics sense?

2. Explain the differences between the two main types of capital.

3. In a corporation, which of the owners participate in the management and share in the profits?

4. Are preferred stockholders guaranteed a fixed dividend?

5. What is the relationship between the par value of stock and the market value?

6. Name at least three sources from which a business may borrow needed capital.

7. What are the types of questions that a businessman must be prepared to answer when he attempts to borrow money?

8. What is the principal difference between mortgage bonds and debenture bonds?

9. In the case of a corporation, what are the principal means of obtaining additional working capital?

10. What type of claim does a bondholder have against a corporation?

11. From the point of view of control and income, what are some of the disadvantages of selling additional stock to acquire new capital?

12. Give some reasons why a business should not pay out all the profits to owners but instead should retain some of the earnings.

13. In the case of a small corporation, why is it often necessary to sell securities directly to investors?

APPLY WHAT YOU HAVE LEARNED

Questions for Class Discussion:

1. If you have real estate valued at $5,000, from what source might you be able to obtain a loan of $3,000 with your property pledged as security?
2. If more capital is needed, is it usually more desirable to issue additional stock than to issue bonds? Explain.
3. What advantage does a corporation have in selling common stock as compared with selling preferred stock?
4. What is the advantage to a corporation of selling preferred stock as compared with selling common stock?
5. What is the advantage to a corporation of selling preferred stock instead of bonds?
6. Explain why a small business could probably not get an investment banker to handle an issue of stock but would probably have to sell the stock itself.
7. Why do you think that preferred stock of a corporation would probably sell at a higher price than common stock?
8. Between the owners of bonds and the owners of stock, which have the greater protection?
9. What is the disadvantage to present stockholders if new shares of common stock are issued and sold?
10. Why would common stock tend to sell on the market at an increasing price if the value of retained earnings is steadily increasing?

Problems and Projects:

1. The assets of the Rosemont Corporation are $750,000; the accounts payable, $45,000; bonds payable, $100,000; common stock, $350,000; preferred stock, $150,000. Does the corporation have a surplus or a deficit? What amount?
2. The Orville Corporation has sales of $75,246.50. The net profit is 3 percent, or $2,257.40. There are outstanding 400 shares of stock with a par value of $100.
   (a) Compute the earnings per share of stock.
   (b) Assume that, if 200 additional shares are sold, the sales can be increased to $90,000 and the percentage of net profit will remain the same. What will be the earnings per share?
   (c) What must the sales be in order for the expanded business to earn a sufficient net profit at the rate of 3 percent in order to pay the same rate of dividends on the increased number of shares as was paid on the original shares?

3. The Ohio Casting Company, a small corporation, decides to sell 200 shares of common stock for $100 a share. A bank has agreed to take the stock at a 7 percent discount and market it. The miscellaneous costs, including printing and registering the stock, will amount to $1,365. What will be the net proceeds from the sale?

4. Refer to the following balance sheet and answer these questions:

   (a) If the par value of both common and preferred stock is $100 a share, how many shares of each kind are outstanding?

   (b) If the preferred and common stock have equal claims, what is the book value of each share?

   (c) If the directors decide to distribute $4,800 as dividends, how much will be paid to preferred stockholders and how much to common stockholders?

   (d) If a person owns 10 shares of preferred stock and 10 shares of common stock, how much of the dividends in part (c) should he receive?

The Barker-Trowe Corporation

Balance Sheet

Assets		Liabilities and Capital		
Cash	$ 18,500	Notes Payable		$ 1,000
Notes Receivable	500	Accounts Payable		3,500
Accounts Receivable	7,500	4% Bonds Payable		25,000
Merchandise	35,000	Common Stock:		
Equipment	8,000	Authorized	$50,000	
Real Estate	48,000	Unissued	10,000	
		Outstanding		40,000
		7% Preferred Stock:		
		Authorized	$50,000	
		Unissued	10,000	
		Outstanding		40,000
		Surplus		
		Retained Earnings		8,000
Total Assets	$117,500	Total Liab. and Capital		$117,500

5. B. C. Apple and H. O. Mason each owns 1,000 shares of stock, representing all the common stock outstanding in a rural bottled gas company. They need $10,000 and have three choices of securing the funds: (a) borrowing $10,000 for a period of three months—April, May, and June—and again for a period of three months—October, November, and December—at a yearly interest rate of 6 percent; (b) selling 1,000 additional shares of common stock at $10 each to raise a total of $10,000 for permanent working capital; and (c) selling 1,000 shares of preferred stock at $10 a share with a dividend rate of 7 percent. In other words, these owners are faced with a need for cash to finance their

operations; and they must decide whether to borrow money, to sell common stock, or to sell preferred stock.

Assume that the profit of the company is $18,000 a year without anticipating any interest charges.

(a) How will the interest on the borrowed money affect the profits to Apple and Mason if $10,000 is borrowed as indicated above?

(b) How will the profits to Apple and Mason be affected if 1,000 shares of common stock are sold?

(c) How will the profits to Apple and Mason be affected if 1,000 shares of preferred stock are sold?

6. The net profit of the Ajax Corporation has averaged $10,000 a year. There are 2,000 shares of common stock authorized, but only 1,000 are issued and outstanding. The owners feel that more capital is needed and are considering selling the additional 1,000 shares at $100 a share. It is estimated that the new capital will make it possible to increase the net profit to $15,000.

(a) What is the net profit per share now?

(b) What would be the expected net profit per share if 1,000 new shares are sold?

(c) Does it appear to be a good action to take?

Case Problem 16-1:

Paul Wescott decides to buy a successful business. He has consulted bankers, accountants, and friends who are familiar with the business. They all agree that the price of $75,000 is a fair price for the business. Wescott has had successful experience as an employee in this type of business, and he has $5,000 to invest. He expects to borrow the rest.

Required:

1. Will a bank lend the $70,000 that Wescott needs?

2. From what other sources do you think he might borrow enough money?

3. Is there any other way of financing the purchase of this business besides borrowing as he has planned to do?

Case Problem 16-2:

A business in which you are interested is offered for sale. The price is $5,000 for which you get the equipment and merchandise. You feel that the record of profits is such that this is a fair price. Before you can buy it, you must have enough cash or credit to buy $2,000 worth of new merchandise and be able to pay rent and other expenses of $1,000 the first month. You have $2,000 of your own money to invest.

Required:

1. What is the total cash and credit needed?
2. How much must you raise besides your investment?
3. What do you consider good possible sources of capital and credit to help you finance the business?

Continuing Project:

On the basis of the information you compiled in the Continuing Project in Chapter 15, prepare a financial plan for your business. Make certain assumptions as to how much proprietary capital will be available and how you are going to finance the rest through borrowing and commercial credit.

How should a bank be selected?

What services can the businessman receive from his bank?

What information does a lender request from a borrower?

What is meant by a collateral loan?

What is bank discount?

In what ways may a check be endorsed?

BACKGROUND OF CHAPTER

As explained in Chapter 16, a businessman can obtain some of the capital he needs by borrowing from a bank. Since businesses, large and small, must have dealings with banks, one of the first steps a new businessman should take is to establish a banking connection.

This chapter discusses the factors to consider in choosing a bank, the types of banks and their services, and how to deal with banks. In addition, attention is given to requirements for loans, interest rates, and repayment of loans. Since negotiable instruments relate to banking, their use is also presented.

CHAPTER 17

BANKING SERVICES

If you are going into business, the first step you should take, even before buying a business or starting a new business, is to consult a banker. You should consult the banker in regard to your plans because he has a background of experience in dealing with other business concerns. The banker should be in a position to give helpful advice both in starting a business and in operating it. He knows the inside story of many businesses. If he knows the history of a business from the beginning, he can help in making decisions as to when to borrow, how much to borrow, and when to expand or to restrict operations.

Under our economic system, dealing with a bank is absolutely essential. There are usually two important relations with a bank. One is opening a checking account, and the other is borrowing money. Practically every businessman uses both of these services.

SELECTING A BANK

Integrity is the first important factor in considering the choice of a bank. The size and the type of the bank are considerations also. In some communities there is an advantage for a small business to place an account in a small bank because the officers and the personnel of such a bank learn to know each customer and appreciate his business. The advantages of a small bank, however, are sometimes offset by those of a larger bank. Dealings with a large bank may be impersonal, but such a bank can offer facilities that are not otherwise available. Small banks may not be able to make a loan at a favorable interest rate or may not be able to make as large a loan as is desired. The businessman who has many dealings in other cities may find the larger bank more helpful because it may have better connections in

ILLUS. 17-1. A banker can give helpful advice about starting and
operating a business.

those cities and can therefore handle his financial transactions more
conveniently.

As a summary, therefore, the following six guides are suggested.

1. Choose a bank whose officers possess character, leadership, and
   the willingness to assume a risk provided there is a reasonable
   chance of repayment.

2. Choose a progressive bank—one whose officers are alert to current industrial trends and are willing to make loans for new
   products and more efficient processes.

3. Choose a bank that stresses an attitude of friendliness to a small
   business.

4. Choose a bank that has confidence in the future of your community and thus is willing to invest in it.

5. Choose a bank that quotes reasonable interest rates.

6. Choose a bank that gives good service.

These facts and other information can be learned from the reputation of a bank and of its officers. Other businessmen may be consulted
as to their experience with banks.

BANKS AND THEIR FUNCTIONS

Large banks provide many specialized services in regard to taxes, real estate, and other matters. However, the four main services that are performed by all banks are as follows: (1) providing a safe place to deposit money; (2) providing an efficient service in collecting checks, drafts, and notes; (3) giving financial advice; and (4) lending money needed in the operation of business.

Banks classified according to their function are: (1) commercial banks, (2) savings banks, and (3) trust companies.

Commercial Bank

A *commercial bank* may be a private bank, a state bank, or a national bank. This well-known type of financial institution accepts checking and savings accounts and makes loans to individuals and businesses. Among the many other services extended to their customers are availability of safe deposit boxes, operation of trust departments, and offering of financial advice.

When a commercial bank offers all of the services permitted by the state, it is sometimes referred to as a *full-service bank*. Many of the activities a bank may carry on for its customers, in addition to those mentioned above, include: tax information and preparation, bill-paying services, legal services, insurance planning, estate planning, and vault service.

Savings Bank

A *savings bank* specializes in accepting savings accounts. A *mutual savings bank* is one that is owned by the depositors and is operated primarily for their benefit. A mutual savings bank has no stockholders, and income earned by the bank goes to the depositors in the form of interest on their accounts. While the commercial bank will make short-term loans, the mutual savings bank will make mortgage loans which extend one year or longer. The following customs are relatively uniform among mutual savings banks and the savings departments of commercial banks:

1. Deposits are usually accepted for amounts as small as one dollar.
2. Checks cannot be drawn against deposits.
3. The bank reserves the right to demand several days' notice before the withdrawal of funds.

Trust Company

A *trust company* may be a separate company or a department of a commercial or a savings bank. The trust company will receive property from individuals and manage the property for the benefit of the person. Property may be real estate, marketable securities, or cash. The trust company may also manage property for the benefit of a third person. For example, an individual may place property in trust for a minor. Trust companies also manage estates and pension funds.

LOANS

Bankers are usually eager to lend money, but they must lend it cautiously, even though at times they take reasonable risks. You should not hesitate to borrow money if it will help you to make more money. That is the way that most businesses are able to grow. However, the banker will expect complete facts to be given beforehand so that the decision can be made as to whether or not the business will be able to repay the loan under the terms of the agreement.

Regulations of Loans

State and federal laws limit banks, according to their classification, in the types of loans that can be made. State banks are governed by the laws of their respective states. Member banks of the Federal Reserve System are governed by the following restrictions:

1. The Federal Reserve Board has power to fix the percentage of loans that the banks in any federal reserve district can make with bonds and stocks as collateral.
2. Member banks may make loans secured by staple agricultural products, goods, wares, or merchandise.
3. Loans secured by direct obligations of the United States, such as government notes or bonds, may be made to individuals, partnerships, or corporations.
4. No member bank is permitted to lend money to an affiliated organization or to individuals in an affiliated organization. For instance, a bank may hold the controlling interest in an investment company, but the bank is not permitted to lend money to this affiliated organization or to individuals in that organization. It may not accept securities of an affiliated organization as collateral for a loan if the loan exceeds 10 percent of the lender's capital and surplus.

5. Loans can be made on improved real estate, including improved farm land. These loans are limited as to the percentage of the value that can be loaned and the length of the loan. Only a limited amount of the funds of a member bank may be used for loans on real estate.

Requirements for Obtaining a Loan

Besides the questions of character and security, most banks and other lending agencies want additional information when making a loan. This information involves the business ability of the borrower, his past business experience, his chances of success in the future, his own investment in the business, the need and purpose of the loan, and the probability of its repayment on time and in full. More complete lists of the information that most lenders will require of a borrower are shown in Illustrations 17-2 and 17-3.

1. Proper identification.
2. Nature of business.
3. How the business is organized, its ownership, and any special agreements.
4. Personal data on all principal owners as to age, connection with the business, connection with other businesses, life insurance, banking connections, and civic activities.
5. Other financial relations of the business, such as other bank connections and indebtedness.
6. The amount, the purpose, the need, and the plan for repaying the loan that is requested.
7. A detailed balance sheet showing the assets, liabilities, and ownership of the business.
8. A detailed income and expense statement showing the income and expenses of the business.
9. Detailed information in regard to liabilities and claims, such as unpaid taxes and other business debts that are due or will become due.
10. Proof as to the future prospects and the plans of operation of the business.

ILLUS. 17-2. Information usually requested from borrowers.

Kinds of Loans

Most regular bank loans are called *short-term loans* because they extend for 30, 60, or 90 days. These loans are often renewed.

Unsecured Loans. Under normal conditions, bank credit is widely extended on *unsecured loans* (nothing of value pledged to the bank) merely by the signing of a note. However, bank practice varies in this respect, and the type of business will often determine whether a bank will give an unsecured loan.

FINANCIAL STATEMENT **PARTNERSHIP**

NAME OF FIRM Foster & Smith Shoes

BUSINESS Retail--shoes and accessories ADDRESS 90 Bryant Square, Tulsa, OK 74101

STATEMENT FOR

LEAVE NO BLANKS. INSERT "O" OR WORD "NONE" WHERE NECESSARY TO COMPLETE INFORMATION

CONDITION AT CLOSE OF BUSINESS May 31 19-- FILL IN DATE

ASSETS	DOLLARS	CTS.	LIABILITIES	DOLLARS	CTS.
CURRENT			CURRENT		
CASH ON HAND	2 350	70	NOTES PAYABLE—TO BANKS (SCHEDULE 1)	500	00
CASH IN BANKS—(SCHEDULE 1)	2 177	05	BANKERS ACCEPTANCES—MADE FOR OUR ACCOUNT	0	
U. S. GOVERNMENT OBLIGATIONS	5 000	00	NOTES PAYABLE—COMMERCIAL PAPER BROKERS	0	
TRADE ACCEPTANCES—CUSTOMERS	0		NOTES PAYABLE—PARTNERS AND EMPLOYES	0	
NOTES RECEIVABLE—CUSTOMERS—(SCHEDULE 2)	0		NOTES PAYABLE—OTHERS	0	
ACCOUNTS RECEIVABLE—CUSTOMERS—(SCHED. 2)	0		NOTES PAYABLE—FOR MERCHANDISE	1 880	00
MERCHANDISE—FINISHED (GIVE FULL	990	00	TRADE ACCEPTANCES PAYABLE	0	
MERCHANDISE—IN PROCESS DATA ON	0		ACCOUNTS PAYABLE—NOT DUE	957	60
MERCHANDISE—RAW PAGE 3)	0		ACCOUNTS PAYABLE—PAST DUE	0	
			ACCOUNTS PAYABLE—PARTNERS AND EMPLOYES	400	00
TOTAL CURRENT ASSETS	10 517	75	ACCOUNTS PAYABLE—OTHER	0	
CONTROLLED AND AFFILIATED CONCERNS—			PROVISION FOR FEDERAL TAXES	0	
INVESTMENTS IN (SCHEDULE 3)	0		ACCRUED INTEREST, OTHER TAXES, ETC.	170	15
DUE FROM — FOR ADVANCES (SCHEDULE 3)	0		DEPOSITS OF MONEY WITH THIS FIRM	0	
DUE FROM — FOR MERCHANDISE (SCHEDULE 3)	0		MORTGAGE OR LONG TERM DEBT—PAYMENTS DUE WITHIN ONE YEAR	0	
TOTAL	0		DUE TO CONTROLLED AND AFFILIATED CONCERNS— (SCHEDULE 3)	0	
INVESTMENTS					
STOCKS, BONDS & INVESTMENTS (SCHEDULE 4)	1 750	00			
REAL ESTATE NOT USED IN BUSINESS	0		TOTAL CURRENT LIABILITIES	3 907	75
MORTGAGES RECEIVABLE (SCHEDULE 7)	0		DEFERRED—(DUE AFTER ONE YEAR)		
CASH SURRENDER VALUE LIFE INSURANCE	662	00	MORTGAGES OR LIENS ON REAL ESTATE (SCHED. 5)	0	
			CHATTEL MORTGAGES—(DETAILS ON PAGE 3)	0	
TOTAL INVESTMENTS	2 412	00	LOANS ON LIFE INSURANCE	0	
FIXED ASSETS					
LAND (SCHEDULE 5)	0				
BUILDINGS (SCHEDULE 5)	0		TOTAL DEFERRED	0	
MACHINERY, FIXTURES AND EQUIPMENT	875	00	RESERVES		
			RESERVE—FOR DOUBTFUL RECEIVABLES	0	
TOTAL FIXED ASSETS	875	00	RESERVE—DEPRECIATION—BUILDINGS	0	
MISCELLANEOUS ASSETS			RESERVE—DEPRECIATION—MACH., FIXT., EQUIP.	260	00
PREPAID INTEREST, INSURANCE, ETC.	295	00	RESERVE—OTHER—(ITEMIZE)	0	
MISCELLANEOUS MATERIALS AND SUPPLIES	120	00			
MISCELLANEOUS DEPOSITS—(WATER, POWER, ETC.)	0				
DUE FROM—PARTNERS AND EMPLOYES (SCHED. 6)	0		TOTAL RESERVES	260	00
DEFERRED EXPENSE, ETC.	0				
GOODWILL, PATENTS AND TRADE-MARKS	0				
TOTAL MISCELLANEOUS	415	00	NET WORTH (SEE PAGE 2)	10 052	00
TOTAL ASSETS	14 219	75	TOTAL	14 219	75

CONTINGENT LIABILITIES	DOLLARS	CTS.
LIABILITY UPON TRADE ACCEPTANCES AND/OR NOTES RECEIVABLE DISCOUNTED OR SOLD	0	
LIABILITY UPON TRADE ACCEPTANCES AND/OR NOTES RECEIVABLE ASSIGNED OR PLEDGED	0	
LIABILITY UPON CUSTOMER'S ACCOUNTS SOLD, ASSIGNED OR PLEDGED	0	
LIABILITY UPON ACCOMMODATION PAPER OR ENDORSEMENTS OR UPON NOTES EXCHANGED WITH OTHERS	0	
LIABILITY AS GUARANTOR FOR OTHERS FOR NOTES, ACCOUNTS OR CONTRACTS—BONDS, ETC.	0	
ANY OTHER CONTINGENT LIABILITIES	0	
TOTAL CONTINGENT LIABILITIES	0	

—1—

ILLUS. 17-3. The first page of an application for a loan.

Character, capacity, and capital are the principal factors that a banker will consider in granting an unsecured loan. Unsecured loans are generally made for a shorter period than secured loans. Unsecured loans are ordinarily granted only to an established, successful business or to individuals in business who are well known by the lender.

A *demand loan* is one kind of unsecured loan. It is a loan at a low rate of interest for no specific length of time. It simply must be repaid when the bank demands it. Obviously, it is the type of loan on which a business cannot reliably depend because it must be repaid on demand.

Many businesses open a *line of credit* with a bank. This arrangement is made when a business has good credit ratings and is a customer of the bank. Basically, the business arranges ahead of time for an amount of money which it may borrow if the need arises. The business can show the line of credit to secure credit from a dealer. The credit letter has limits as to the amount the bank will guarantee. For example, Mr. Gilbert secures a line of credit from his bank for an amount not to exceed $1,000. Mr. Gilbert may travel some distance to purchase merchandise or supplies. The credit letter is shown to the Cargo Supplies Company. The company ships the merchandise to Mr. Gilbert knowing that Mr. Gilbert's bank will lend him up to $1,000.

Secured Loans. A *secured loan* is also called a *collateral loan*. For this type of loan the borrower pledges something of value to the bank as security. Collateral loans are usually the easiest to obtain because they give the banker more protection. Therefore, a collateral loan is usually made at a lower return of interest than an unsecured loan. The following types of security or collateral are those most commonly used:

1. Warehouse receipts (negotiable types).
2. Machinery and equipment.
3. Cash value of life insurance.
4. Bonds, stocks, and other marketable securities.
5. Buildings and real estate.
6. Accounts receivable or notes receivable.
7. Merchandise.

For instance, a person who wishes to borrow from a bank may have placed one thousand bushels of wheat in a grain elevator. If he has receipts for this wheat, he may turn these receipts over to the bank, thus transferring to the bank the right of ownership to the wheat in case he does not pay his loan when it becomes due.

A person may borrow money on real estate and grant a mortgage that gives the lender the right to take possession of the real estate if the loan is not paid. An example of a real estate mortgage is shown in Illustration 17-4.

Any stock or bond that has a value can usually be used as collateral. Some banks prefer stocks and bonds that are listed on recognized exchanges because such bonds and stocks can be marketed easily if they must be sold to pay the loan. A bank will ordinarily lend about 50 percent of the value of a good stock or a good bond.

Sometimes a businessman cannot obtain a loan without getting a friend to guarantee that the loan will be repaid. When the borrower signs the note and gets a friend to sign the note also, this process is called *endorsement*. It is a form of security or collateral. The friend who signs the note is a *cosigner*.

In the case of a short-term loan, usually one note which must be paid at a specified time or on demand is signed. In the case of a long-term loan, the borrower ordinarily signs a series of notes, each coming due on a specific date so that the loan is paid off gradually. There are also loans, classified as intermediate-term loans, which may extend over a period of a few years. Usually the borrower signs a series of notes, each coming due at a specified time.

Interest Rates

Although interest rates are governed to some extent by law, bank rates are largely based upon the supply of and the demand for money. The lowest rate of interest is called the *prime rate*. This is the rate at which large banks will make large loans to the best qualified borrowers. Smaller loans and loans to less desirable customers will be made at higher rates. All rates vary from day to day and from month to month.

On short-term commercial loans it is common for a bank to deduct the interest in advance. Interest deducted from a loan in advance is called *discount*. Suppose, for example, that a loan of $200 is needed for three months and that the bank charges 6 percent interest. As shown below, the borrower would receive $197. Goods, bonds, or stocks with a market value of approximately $400 may be required as security by the bank.

```
Amount to be paid to bank in three months ...... $200
Six percent interest deducted in advance ........    3
Amount of cash given to borrower ............. $197
```

Know All Men by These Presents:

That   James D. Graham   of   Montgomery   County, Ohio, *in consideration of the sum of* Three Thousand ($3,000) Dollars *to*   him   *in hand paid by*   Raymond E. Kelly

         does hereby **Grant, Bargain, Sell and Convey**

to the said   Raymond E. Kelly   *his heirs and assigns forever, the following described* **Real Estate**, *situate in the*   City *of*   Miamisburg   *in the County of*   Montgomery   *and State of Ohio.*

    Lot No. 103 on Blanchard Road of the Far Hills subdivision.

and all the **Estate, Right, Title and Interest** *of the said grantor in and to said premises;* **To have and to hold** *the same, with all the privileges and appurtenances thereunto belonging, to said grantee,*   his   *heirs and assigns forever. And the said*   James D. Graham   *does hereby* **Covenant and Warrant** *that the title so conveyed is* **Clear, Free and Unincumbered,** *and that*   he   *will* **Defend** *the same against all lawful claims of all persons whomsoever.*

    Provided Nevertheless, *That* if the said James D. Graham shall well and truly pay or cause to be paid, his certain promissory note of even date herewith, for Three Thousand ($3,000) Dollars drawn to the order of Raymond E. Kelly and payable in three years from date, with interest at six (6) per cent per annum

then these presents shall be void.

In Witness Whereof, *the said*   James D. Graham   *who*   *hereby releases*   *his*   *right and expectancy of dower in said premises, has*   *hereunto set*   his   *hand , this*   seventh *day of*   November *in the year of our Lord one thousand nine hundred and* -------

Signed and acknowledged in presence of us:

Dennis Gray

Howard Wright

James D. Graham

The State of   Ohio   **County of**   Montgomery   **ss.**

   Be It Remembered, *That on the*   seventh   *day of*   November   *in the year of our Lord one thousand nine* hundred and ------   *before me, the subscriber, a*   Notary Public   *in and for said county, personally came*   James D. Graham *the grantor*   *in the foregoing Mortgage, and acknowledged the signing thereof to be*   his   *voluntary act, for the uses and purposes therein mentioned.*

       In Testimony Whereof, *I have hereunto subscribed my name, and affixed my* official   *seal, on the day and year last aforesaid.*

Warren J. Lascure

ILLUS. 17-4. A real estate mortgage.

In this example the interest charge is slightly more than 6 percent, for $3 is being charged for the use of $197 for three months. If the loan is not repaid in three months, the bank has the privilege of selling the securities to obtain the $200. Suppose that, at the end of three months, this loan has not been repaid. It may be possible for the borrower to have the loan renewed by paying $3 interest in advance and by signing a new note. Or he may pay $100 and sign a new note for $100 after paying $1.50 interest in advance on the new loan.

If the securities are sold to protect the bank, more or less than the amount of the loan may be obtained, depending upon the fluctuation of the market prices of the securities. Suppose that, in the preceding example, nothing is paid on the loan and the bank sells the securities at the end of the three months for $300. The additional $100 will go to the person who obtained the loan. If the securities are sold for only $175, however, the person who obtained the loan still owes the bank $25.

Repayment of a Loan

Bankers have found that borrowers will pay long-term obligations with less difficulty if some provision is made for repaying the loan at intervals instead of in one amount at the expiration of the loan period. If the average borrower is given the privilege of waiting until a specified date to pay the entire amount, he may carelessly or intentionally utilize his income for other purposes and not have available the proper amount of money when the loan becomes due. The property that was given as security may by this time have depreciated so much that the bank will not have adequate protection on its loan.

Some borrowers have a tendency to borrow money without giving specific thought as to when and how it can be repaid. They assume that, if they cannot repay a loan when it becomes due, they may renew it and continue to pay the interest without making payments on the principal. Borrowing without a definite intention and specific plan of repaying the principal is a dangerous practice for both the borrower and the lender. It will eventually result in trouble for those involved. The borrower will be forced into bankruptcy; the banker will be unable to collect all of the debt, and he may then be unable to pay his depositors all that he owes them.

A loan may be payable on demand, or it may have a term up to ten years or occasionally longer. The *maturity date* of a loan refers to the date on which it must be repaid. In borrowing, it is important to set up a schedule of loan maturities based upon a budget of cash as explained in Chapter 22. In estimating one's flow of cash, a reasonable margin of safety should be allowed so that funds will be available to pay a maturing loan.

NEGOTIABLE INSTRUMENTS

The relation of borrowing and lending centers largely around a negotiable instrument. A *negotiable instrument* is a written evidence of some contractual obligation and is ordinarily transferable from one person to another by endorsement. It is frequently referred to as *negotiable paper* or *commercial paper*.

The person who endorses a negotiable instrument and transfers it to someone else is known as the *endorser*. The person to whom he transfers the negotiable instrument is referred to as the *endorsee*.

The most common forms of negotiable instruments are (a) promissory notes and (b) checks. Other forms of negotiable instruments commonly used include certified checks, bank drafts, cashier's checks, and bank money orders.

Promissory Note

A *promissory note* (see Illustration 17-5) is an unconditional written promise to pay a certain sum of money, at a particular time or on demand, to the bearer or to the order of one who has obtained the note through legal means. The one who promises to pay the amount specified in the note under the terms indicated is the *maker*. The person to whom the note is payable is known as the *payee*.

DUE _August 10, 19—_	NO _528_

$ _500.00_   MUNCIE, IND., ____May 10____, 19__

____Three months_____AFTER DATE, WE, OR EITHER OF US, PROMISE TO PAY

TO THE ORDER OF ____J. J. McKissick____

Five hundred and 00/100_____**DOLLARS**

WITH ATTORNEY'S FEES. NEGOTIABLE AND PAYABLE AT **INDUSTRIAL TRUST & SAVINGS BANK OF MUNCIE, IND.,** FOR VALUE RECEIVED, WITHOUT RELIEF FROM VALUATION OR APPRAISEMENT LAWS. THE DRAWERS AND ENDORSERS SEVERALLY WAIVE PRESENTMENT FOR PAYMENT, PROTEST, NOTICE OF PROTEST AND NOTICE OF NON-PAYMENT OF THIS NOTE, WITH _7_ PER CENT INTEREST AFTER DATE, AND EIGHT PER CENT INTEREST AFTER MATURITY UNTIL PAID.

T Oliver Reese
J. B. Burton

1145 South High

Industrial Trust & Savings Bank of Muncie, Indiana

ILLUS. 17-5. A promissory note.

Checks

A *check* is a written order on a bank to pay previously deposited money to a third party on demand. The person who writes the check is the *drawer*. The person to whom the check is payable is the *payee*. The bank that is ordered to pay the check is the *drawee*.

The drawer of a check or the maker of a note is unconditionally required to pay the amount specified. This obligation assumes, of course, that the transaction represented by the instrument has been proper and legal. The drawer of a check is required to pay the amount of the check if the drawee (the bank) does not pay it. There are, however, certain limitations on this rule in many states.

Bad Checks. A *bad check* is one that is not honored (paid) when it is presented to a bank for payment. It may not be paid because there are insufficient funds in the account on which it is drawn, or because it was written by a dishonest person who did not have an account in the bank on which it was drawn. In either case it is possible in every state to prosecute the person who has written the check.

Ordinarily banks and business people are courteous and considerate whenever a person unknowingly writes a check on an account in which there are insufficient funds. Both the person who drew the check and the person to whom the check was issued are notified. Ordinarily no legal action is taken if the matter is cleared up satisfactorily. On the other hand, if there is an apparent intention of fraud, the person to whom the check was issued is usually responsible for starting any legal action.

When a check or any other negotiable instrument is presented to a bank for payment but is not paid, it is returned, along with a *protest form*, to the one who submitted it. The bank makes a charge for protesting the nonpayment of a negotiable instrument. Thus, it is advisable to avoid submitting to a bank any item that probably cannot be collected. It should be borne in mind that, when a bank accepts a check for deposit, it is acting only as the collecting agent until the check has been collected. If the bank cannot collect the check, it deducts the amount from the account of the depositor.

Stopping Payment on Checks. After you have drawn or issued a check to someone, you may direct your bank to refuse to pay it when it is presented. This procedure is called *stopping payment* on a check. In most states when a bank has been properly ordered to stop payment on a check, it is the bank's responsibility to do so, and the bank is liable if it fails to stop payment. This procedure should be used only as a protection and should not be abused. For instance, a businessman may discover after issuing a check that fraud or deception has been involved and may want to stop payment on the check before it is cashed. Illustration 17-6 gives an example of a stop-payment order.

(97-19) THE FIFTH THIRD UNION TRUST CO.

STOP PAYMENT ORDER—PHONE ORDER Cincinnati, O.

Check Number 242 Date March 10, 19-- Payee Stephen O'Hara Amount $57.95

Checks not filed and in process of being paid have been examined by ________ Bookkeeper.
Checks in the **CURRENT** file have been examined by ________
Checks of same amount shown on Ledger and on Bulk Lists in file checked by ________

Stop Payment order taken by M S
Phone call by Edwin Lansbury Time 1:05 P.M.
Branch
Informed by M S
Time 1:10 P.M. to ________

ACCOUNT OF Edwin Lansbury
1006 Hill Crest Road
Cincinnati, OH 45224

ILLUS. 17-6. A stop-payment order.

Deposit Checks Promptly. Checks accepted by a businessman in payment for merchandise or services should be deposited promptly. A person should not be negligent or cause unreasonable delay in presenting a check for collection.

For instance, Mr. Kyle issues to Mr. Yates a check drawn on the Union City Bank. Mr. Yates delays 30 days before presenting the check for payment. In the meantime the Union City Bank has been closed because of some financial difficulty. There is some legal question in this case as to whether Mr. Yates can force Mr. Kyle to make a new payment because, as a result of Mr. Yates' negligence, the check was not presented for payment within a reasonable time. On the other hand, if Mr. Yates had not been negligent, Mr. Kyle would probably be legally bound to make a new payment.

Reconciliation of the Bank Statement. Illustration 17-7 shows a bank statement. The accuracy of this bank statement can be proved by following the steps listed below:

1. Verify the checks recorded on the bank statement by comparing them with the canceled checks accompanying the statement.
2. Verify all deposits by checking those listed on the bank statement with those recorded on the check stubs.

STATEMENT OF
YOUR ACCOUNT

PACIFIC
NATIONAL BANK

Ronald B. Gordon
1813 Baxter Street
Fresno, CA   93725

CHECKS	CHECKS	DEPOSITS	NO. OF CHECKS	DATE	BALANCE
				May 1	350.72
78.00	9.21		2	May 3	263.51
22.80			3	May 8	240.71
		125.00		May 10	365.71
52.93	16.20		5	May 15	296.58
65.45			6	May 20	231.13
32.75	12.25		8	May 23	186.13
		95.00		May 25	281.13
23.19			9	May 29	257.94
1.35 SC				May 31	256.59

CC—Certified Check   EC—Error Corrected   OD—Overdrawn
CM—Credit Memo   LS—List of Checks   RT—Returned Item
DM—Debit Memo   NC—Check Not Counted   SC—Service Charge

ILLUS. 17-7. A bank statement.

Cash balance on statement	$256.59	Checkbook balance	$309.20
Deposit not shown on statement	100.00		
	$356.59		
Less checks outstanding:			
No. 152 .... $15.50			
No. 153 .... 33.24			
Total checks outstanding	48.74	Less service charge	1.35
Correct bank balance	$307.85	Correct checkbook balance	$307.85

ILLUS. 17-8. Reconciliation of the bank statement.

3. Determine from the checkbook stubs which checks were outstanding on the date of the bank statement.

4. Subtract from the cash balance shown on the bank statement the total of the checks outstanding, and add the amount of any deposits made but not shown on the bank statement. This should give the adjusted, or correct, bank balance.

5. Subtract from the checkbook balance (on the date of reconciliation) any charges, such as a service charge, made by the bank and not recorded on the check stubs. Add the amount of any deposits made but not recorded on the check stubs. The balance is the adjusted checkbook balance, and it should be equal to the adjusted, or correct, bank balance.

The bank statement was reconciled as follows:

1. The checks and deposits were verified. The outstanding checks were found to be for $15.50 and $33.24, a total of $48.74. A deposit of $100 was made May 31 but does not appear on the bank statement.

2. The checkbook balance was found to be $309.20, but a bank service charge of $1.35 had not been recorded on the check stubs.

3. The reconciliation was then recorded in the manner shown in Illustration 17-8.

Certified Check

It is sometimes desirable to transfer money by using a certified check. A *certified check* is one upon which the bank certifies that there is money being held specifically to pay the check when presented. An example of a certified check is shown in Illustration 17-9. A certified check is useful when the person receiving it must be assured that the drawer of the check has sufficient money in his bank for the payment of the check. Such a check certifies that it will be paid upon presentation. As soon as the cashier of the bank certifies the check, he charges the amount to the depositor's account.

For instance, Mr. Pippin must make a payment of $345.67 on a purchase. He writes his check and presents it to the cashier of his bank for certification. Immediately the bank reserves this amount for payment of the check.

Industrial Trust & Savings Bank of Muncie, Indiana

ILLUS. 17-9. A certified check.

Bank Draft

A *bank draft* (see Illustration 17-10) is a check that a bank draws on funds deposited to its credit in some other bank. A bank draft is a convenient means of transferring money when the individual who is making payment is not known by the person or firm to which the remittance is to be sent.

For example, Mr. Adams, who lives in Winchester, Indiana, wishes to make a payment of $500 to Hartford & Sons in Chicago, Illinois. Since Mr. Adams is not known in Chicago, his personal check may not be accepted. Mr. Adams therefore buys a draft that the Industrial Trust and Savings Bank in Muncie, Indiana, draws on its funds in the First National Bank of Chicago. When the draft is presented to the latter bank, it is paid as any other check would be paid.

Industrial Trust & Savings Bank of Muncie, Indiana

ILLUS. 17-10. A bank draft.

Cashier's Check

One may buy a cashier's check in somewhat the same way that a person buys a bank draft. The *cashier's check* (see Illustration 17-11) is a check on the bank that issues it, payable to the person designated by the purchaser of the check.

For example, Mr. Grant's personal check for $1,000 may not be an acceptable means of payment to his creditor, Mr. Carr. Mr. Grant therefore purchases from the Industrial Trust Bank a cashier's check made out to Mr. Carr. Mr. Grant pays the Industrial Trust Bank $1,000 plus a fee. Mr. Grant presents the check to Mr. Carr, who in turn presents it to the Industrial Trust Bank for payment. Banks also use cashier's checks to pay their own debts and expenses.

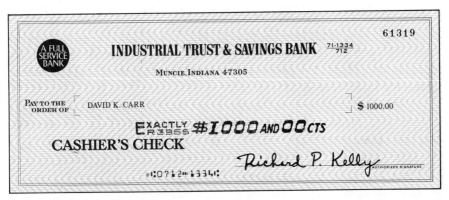

Industrial Trust & Savings Bank of Muncie, Indiana

ILLUS. 17-11. A cashier's check.

Bank Money Order

A *bank money order* (see Illustration 17-12) serves essentially the same purpose as a cashier's check. The main difference is that the name of the remitter (the sender) of the bank money order is written on the money order but usually is not written on a cashier's check.

Endorsements

The proper endorsement of checks, notes, and other negotiable instruments is quite important. There are various kinds of endorsements that can be used for different purposes. Examples of these endorsements are shown in Illustration 17-13. The most common is the *blank endorsement* which permits the negotiable instrument to be transferred to someone else without any restriction.

Industrial Trust & Savings Bank of Muncie, Indiana

ILLUS. 17-12. A bank money order.

A *restrictive endorsement* means that the negotiable instrument is payable to and the funds are for the use of only one purpose as specified.

The *special* or *full endorsement* gives the name of the person to whom the instrument is to be transferred.

A *qualified endorsement* is used when the endorser does not want to assume any further responsibility for the negotiable instrument. For example, when a note arising out of an installment contract is sold to a bank or a finance company, the customer's note is often endorsed "without recourse" by the seller.

T. S. Mason	*Pay to the order of Thomas Keene T. S. Mason*
Blank endorsement	Endorsement in full
For deposit only T. S. Mason	*Without recourse T. S. Mason*
Restrictive endorsement	Qualified endorsement

ILLUS. 17-13. Examples of typical endorsements.

COLLECTION SERVICE

Banks provide a collection service for such items as notes, drafts, trade acceptances, checks, and interest and principal on bonds. For instance, when a note that he owns becomes due, a businessman may turn it over to his bank for collection. The bank charges a fee for this service.

Attached to many bonds are coupons that are to be torn off and submitted for collection when interest on the bonds is due. A bank will perform this collection service. Likewise, when the principal of a bond becomes due, the bank will act as the collecting agent. Sometimes there is no charge when such collections are made locally, but in most cases there is a charge. Banks will also take care of the collecting and the exchanging of securities, such as stocks and bonds. A service charge and a shipping charge are included in the fee for handling securities. Charges such as these can be deducted from the balance in the depositor's account.

REVIEW WHAT YOU HAVE LEARNED

Business Terms Checkup:

(1) commercial bank
(2) full-service bank
(3) savings bank
(4) mutual savings bank
(5) trust company
(6) short-term loan
(7) unsecured loan
(8) demand loan
(9) line of credit
(10) secured loan or collateral loan
(11) endorsement
(12) cosigner
(13) prime rate
(14) discount
(15) maturity date
(16) negotiable instrument
(17) negotiable paper or commercial paper
(18) endorser
(19) endorsee
(20) promissory note
(21) maker
(22) payee
(23) check
(24) drawer
(25) drawee
(26) bad check
(27) protest form
(28) stopping payment
(29) certified check
(30) bank draft
(31) cashier's check
(32) bank money order
(33) blank endorsement
(34) restrictive endorsement
(35) special or full endorsement
(36) qualified endorsement
(37) without recourse

Reading Checkup:

1. Why should a person see a banker before he starts a business?
2. (a) What may be the advantage of dealing with a small bank?
   (b) What may be the advantages of dealing with a large bank?
3. What are some of the guides that one can follow in selecting a bank?
4. What are the four main services that are usually performed by all banks?
5. How are banks classified according to their functions?
6. Give at least three kinds of information or facts that a borrower will be expected to furnish when requesting a loan.
7. Distinguish between a secured loan and an unsecured loan.
8. What are the most common types of security or collateral used in obtaining loans?
9. How can the signature of a friend be used as security?
10. In order to obtain more money to operate a business, what can a company do if it has made sales on the installment plan?
11. How is the interest on a short-term loan usually handled by a bank?
12. If you have written a check and want to prevent it from being cashed at your bank, what should you do?
13. Explain what is meant by the reconciliation of the bank statement.
14. Why would you use and how would you obtain a cashier's check?

APPLY WHAT YOU HAVE LEARNED

Questions for Class Discussion:

1. How would a businessman go about obtaining a line of credit?
2. If a businessman accepts an unsecured note from one of his customers, can this note be sold to a bank or used to obtain a loan?
3. Why are interest rates often lower on secured loans than on unsecured loans?
4. What happens to your collateral if you fail to repay a loan to a bank as agreed?
5. From the point of view of a businessman, what do you think might be one of the disadvantages of using accounts receivable to secure a loan?
6. Why do you believe that the prime rate of interest is lower than other regular interest rates?
7. Is there any difference between the method by which a note and a check can be transferred from one person to another? How can you transfer it in each case?

8. Assume that you have issued a check to someone and, after he has left your office, you discover that what he has sold you is not in accordance with his statements. What action can you take to protect yourself and to prevent his cashing your check?

9. If you wish to transfer money to a person in another city who will probably not accept your regular personal check, what kind of instrument mentioned in this chapter could be used to transfer the money?

10. If you are willing to accept a personal check from someone for a large, important payment and want to be sure there are adequate funds available and that it will be paid when you present it, what can you ask the drawer of the check to do to protect you?

Problems and Projects:

1. Assume that you are in business and have an invoice for $1,153 on which the terms are 2 percent ten days, net thirty days. You wish to take the discount but find it necessary to borrow money at 6 percent until the end of thirty days in order to pay the invoice. You will need to borrow $1,000. How much money will be saved by borrowing the money for twenty days in order to obtain the discount?

2. On March 25, W. E. Scott discounted at the bank at 6 percent his 60-day noninterest-bearing note for $325, dated March 25.
   (a) What are the proceeds of the note?
   (b) What is the date of maturity of the note?
   (c) What amount must Scott pay the bank at maturity?

3. The following figures (except check numbers) appeared on the bank statement of R. E. Matthews on December 1:

Checks

No. 31	$24.50	Balance, November 1	$321.42
No. 32	2.36		
No. 33	26.00	Deposits	$ 49.30
No. 35	18.00		18.05
No. 36	11.25		26.50
No. 38	32.81		10.00
No. 39	14.30		19.55
Service Charge	$ 1.65	Balance, November 30	$313.95

Reconcile the bank statement, taking the following into consideration:

Checks outstanding .... No. 34 .... $ 12.60
                                           No. 37 .... 47.35
Checkbook balance, November 30 .... $355.65
Deposit of December 1 not shown on bank statement $100.00

4. Assume that you borrow $100 from a bank for sixty days at 6 percent interest, deductible in advance. At the end of thirty days you are able to pay off the debt. The bank is willing to accept payment and to allow you credit for the remaining thirty days of interest. How much will you repay the bank?

5. The Corner Appliance Store sells mostly on the installment plan and has most of its working capital tied up in merchandise sold on the installment plan. Added to the sale price is a service charge plus interest amounting to about 12 percent. Losses over a period of years amount to about 7½ percent of installment sales. The store can sell the accounts at their face value (value of merchandise) to a sales finance company or borrow money at 6 percent from a bank. Which is the more economical choice?

Case Problem 17-1:

The Home Furnishings Company has borrowed all it can borrow on unsecured credit from its bank. It owns its own building. Many of its sales are on the installment plan, and it has $10,000 outstanding on accounts receivable. Orders have been placed for a substantial amount of furniture for a special sale, but it is not expected that sufficient money will be available to pay the bills promptly and to take advantage of special discounts. The company wishes to protect its credit standing but needs additional cash.

Required:

1. Can the Home Furnishings Company borrow on an unsecured loan from another bank?
2. What are the ways in which the Home Furnishings Company can probably obtain the cash needed?

Case Problem 17-2:

The Platz Manufacturing Co. has been considering the desirability of trading in all of its lathes for new models of the same type of machines. The total cost to make the trade will be approximately $400,000, but only $100,000 of the cash on hand can be spared from current operating needs.

It is estimated that the new machines will save an amount equal to their cost in about three years, and perhaps even sooner. The maker of the machines is willing to extend 90-day credit terms but would expect to be paid in full at the end of that time. As an alternative, the manufacturer is willing to accept a series of 6 percent $10,000 notes, one due each month for 30 successive months, which Platz should be able to pay. These notes would be payable starting at the end of 30 days.

The local bank has indicated a willingness to loan $300,000 for six months at 5½ percent; and it has given every assurance that, if a part payment is made at the end of six months, the balance can be extended for six months, and so on until the note is retired.

Required:

Assuming that the Platz Manufacturing Co. decides to purchase the new machines, what source of financing seems most appropriate? Justify your decision by indicating the factors that influenced your conclusion.

Continuing Project:

Select a bank and obtain the forms necessary for opening an account, making a deposit, and applying for a loan. Fill out one of the bank's deposit tickets, and complete a form requesting a loan from the bank.

What business risks are insurable?

What is meant by a mutual insurance company?

What causes insurance rates to change?

What is coinsurance?

For what purpose is a surety bond used?

What business risks are noninsurable?

BACKGROUND OF CHAPTER

Every business must carry some form of insurance and usually many forms of insurance. Insurance takes some of the gamble out of business operations. A business must have insurance before anyone will lend money or extend credit to the business. Without adequate insurance a great loss could cause the business to fail, and it would not be able to pay its debts.

In this chapter you will learn the fundamentals of the common types of business insurance and how to buy insurance for the protection of the business, the customers, and the employees.

CHAPTER 18

BUSINESS RISKS AND INSURANCE

Every sensible businessman carries proper insurance, for a loss without insurance could cause a business to fail and to be unable to pay its debts. In particular, a small business cannot afford to take serious risks when it is possible to obtain protection through some kind of insurance at a reasonable cost. A large business may sometimes take risks that would be too great for a small business. For instance, a large corporation operating a fleet of 500 automobiles finds from its experience that not more than an average of one car is stolen in a year. Not only is it cheaper for the business to stand such loss of stolen cars than to pay the cost of insuring them, but also the unusual loss of two or three cars in a year would not be serious. However, if a small business owns one automobile and that one car is stolen, the loss would be serious.

Businesses must also carry adequate insurance in order that they may secure the needed credit. In other words, unless the business is properly insured, a bank will not lend it money and goods often cannot be purchased on credit.

There are many types of *risks* (possibilities of loss) for which a businessman can obtain protection through insurance. Some of the most common insurable risks are:

Fire	Embezzlement by employees
Theft	Injury to employees
Forgery	Injury to customers
Windstorm	Loss of shipments
Auto damage	Disruption of business due to fire
Death	Credit loss
Health	

INSURANCE OPERATIONS

To understand a discussion of insurance operations, one must first become acquainted with certain insurance terms. The insurance company is called the *insurer*. The person or business purchasing insurance is the *policyholder*. The written agreement, or contract, between the insurer and the policyholder is called the *policy*. The policyholder is also called the *insured* and is sometimes known as *the risk*. The term "risk" is a little confusing because any possibility of a loss is also called a risk.

Insurance companies collect from policyholders amounts that are called premiums. A *premium* is a payment for protection against some risk, such as fire, sickness, accident, or death. Premiums are paid weekly, monthly, quarterly, semiannually, yearly or less frequently—the time of payment depending upon the nature of the insurance, the type of policy, and the kind of insurance company. The funds collected from policyholders are used by the company in somewhat the same manner as cash deposits are used by banks. In other words, with the funds paid by policyholders, insurance companies make investments that earn an income. An insurance company must, of course, keep a reasonable amount of cash available to pay the claims of policyholders. The manner in which an insurance company handles its affairs is governed by law.

Types of Insurance Companies

There are two general types of insurance companies. One is known as a stock company and the other as a mutual company. The *stock company* is a corporation that is formed according to the laws of the particular state. The stockholders own the company and operate it although they are not necessarily policyholders. An insurance company of this type obtains money from the sale of stock to stockholders, as well as from the collection of premiums from policyholders. The profits of the company are paid to the stockholders, who are the owners of the business. In some companies the policyholders also share in the earnings after the stockholders have been paid a specific amount.

A *mutual company* must also be organized under the laws of the particular state. The policyholders in such a company are, however, the owners. Each person or business that is insured in a mutual company becomes a member of the company and is entitled to a share in the ownership, the control, and the earnings. The ownership of the members is not evidenced by shares of stock as it is in a stock company.

Although the policyholders in a mutual company do not own shares of stock, they are in a sense partners or members of a cooperative organization. The only way in which they can exercise their power or control of management is for a sufficient number of them to register a protest or to act as a group in demanding changes in the management or the operation of the business. Of course, the insurance departments of the various states look after the interests of policyholders and scrutinize the management of these companies.

Policyholders in mutual companies usually pay premiums at a predetermined fixed rate, comparable to the rate established by stock companies. The policyholders in mutual companies, however, may receive from the company *dividends* (part of the profits) or have to pay *assessments* (extra charges) to the insurance company. If the company makes a profit, each policyholder shares in proportion to the amount of his policy. If the company fails to make a profit, each policyholder is assessed a certain amount so that the income of the company will be equal to its expenditures. Usually the maximum amount of an assessment cannot exceed the original premium.

Insurance Rates

Insurance rates vary according to the risk that is involved. For instance, if there are a large number of robberies in a particular community, theft insurance rates are high in that community. If fire protection is bad, buildings are not fireproof, and fires are frequent in a certain community, the fire insurance rates are high in that community. Rates charged for insurance are based upon the past experience of the insurance company in distributing losses over all the property that is insured. The rates established for any particular year are therefore in anticipation that the losses for that year will be essentially the same as those of the previous year.

Rates for various kinds of insurance in each state are determined by the experiences of insurance companies, and the basic rates must be charged by all companies for the same kind of risk in the same location within the state. However, some of the cost of insurance may be returned to policyholders through dividends.

Regardless of the basic rates, the charge made to any policyholder may be lower than or higher than the basic rate depending on certain circumstances. For example, a modern fireproof building with an automatic sprinkler, located where there is good fire protection, can be insured at a lower rate than a frame building without a sprinkler, located where there is poor fire protection. In many states automobile rates vary from the basic rate depending upon whether the driver has a good or bad accident record and also depending upon the age of the person who drives the car.

Cancellation

Most property or liability insurance contracts may be canceled by the insurer or not renewed when they expire. If they are canceled, notice must be given to the policyholder. Generally, life insurance contracts may not be canceled except for nonpayment of premiums.

Insurable Interest in Property

The policyholder must have an insurable interest in the property. An *insurable interest* is generally defined as any interest in property that will suffer a possible financial loss if there is a loss of or damage to the property. A person who has purchased a piece of property but has not paid for it also has an insurable interest. A person who uses a building as a warehouse has an insurable interest in the building, even though he does not own the building. A person who has a mortgage on a piece of property has an insurable interest in the property. The interest in property to be insured must be specifically indicated in the policy.

How to Buy Insurance

In every community there are reputable agents and brokers of all types of insurance. In buying insurance for the first time, one should consult other businessmen and a banker and then depend upon a reputable insurance man to make recommendations for the types and amounts of insurance. Points to consider when choosing an insurance agent are given in Illustration 18-1.

In buying insurance the primary objectives are (a) to get the proper coverage of risks and (b) to make certain that the claim will be paid in the event of loss. For example, if one has fire insurance,

1. Can the company he represents furnish the right kind of insurance?
2. Does he have the proper knowledge of insurance?
3. Are his rates reasonable?
4. What kind of extra service can he furnish?
5. What kind of reputation does he have for helping when losses occur?
6. What reputation does his company have for settling claims?

ILLUS. 18-1. Points to consider in selecting an insurance agent.

he wants to be sure that the company from which he buys the insurance will make a fair adjustment promptly and without legal action. If one is buying liability insurance, he wants to be sure that the insurance company will settle promptly and fairly the claim of the injured person.

TYPES OF INSURANCE

A businessman may obtain various types of insurance to fit his needs in protecting his property and employees. The major types of insurance which a business might possess are: (1) fire insurance, (2) transportation and cargo insurance, (3) automobile insurance, (4) burglary and robbery insurance, (5) fidelity bonds, (6) performance or surety bonds, (7) liability insurance, (8) life insurance on owners or executives, and (9) insurance for employees.

Fire Insurance

Fire insurance usually provides funds to replace such items as buildings, furniture, machinery, raw materials, and finished goods destroyed

ILLUS. 18-2. A business should be insured against losses caused by fire.

by fire. Insurance on a building usually does not cover equipment, machinery, and stock. Ordinarily separate policies are required to give full protection from fire loss. The owner of a building should be interested in insurance to protect his investment. The occupant of a rented building should be interested in insurance to protect his business. In buying insurance one should know just what is covered by the policy.

The actual loss in property destroyed by fire is not the only loss to a business. The interruption to business until a new place can be obtained and operations can be resumed will result in a loss of profits and considerable incidental expense. Special types of insurance can be obtained to cover such losses caused by the inconvenience of a fire.

Features of Fire Insurance Policies. When a businessman is buying fire insurance, he should know what he is buying and how he will be protected. He should give careful consideration to the amount of his protection, the kind of protection, and special clauses in the policy. Illustration 18-3 shows a typical fire insurance policy.

No businessman has any advantage in being overinsured. As a matter of fact, he will save money by keeping his insurance down to an amount that actually equals the value of the property. Policies when renewed should be revised in amount so that they cover the real value of whatever is being insured. It is therefore important to check the policies carefully before they are renewed.

In most states the actual amount of the loss (usually replacement cost less depreciation on the property destroyed) is paid, rather than the insured value. In some states there are so-called *valued policy laws*. These laws require the face value of the contract to be paid in the event of a total loss, regardless of the value of the property at the time of the loss.

Instead of paying only for the damage to a replaceable article, the insurance company may exercise the right given in the policy to take all or part of the insured article at an appraised value. In such a case the company may repair, rebuild, or replace the damaged property with other property of like kind and quality within a reasonable time. In the case of a building that is insured, the insurance company may likewise repair, rebuild, or replace the damaged property. Insurance companies ordinarily do not exercise this option but usually follow the practice of compensating for the damage and letting the policyholder take care of the property.

The policyholder is required, according to the contract, to be responsible for the property that has been damaged. In other words, he may not abandon it to the insurance company, for it still remains his property. The policyholder cannot assume that, immediately after the fire, the company is responsible for the damaged property.

In every fire insurance policy the property that is covered should be clearly identified as to description and location. The property

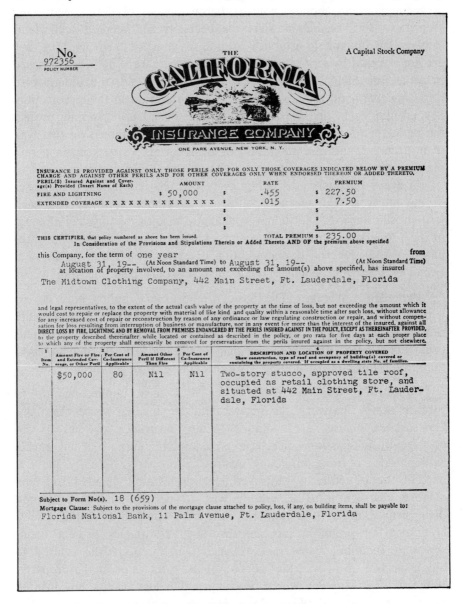

ILLUS. 18-3. A fire insurance policy.

included in the policy and the property excluded should be definitely understood. In the event of a fire, property may be moved to another location for protection. In this location it is covered by the insurance for a certain amount of time, usually about five days.

The standard insurance policy usually excepts or omits such items as accounts, bills, money, notes, other evidences of debt, deeds, and securities. This fact emphasizes the necessity for keeping such items safely. It is difficult to establish a value for most of them; and, as they are not covered by an ordinary policy, extreme care should be exercised in protecting them. Even if such items are insured, the difficulty of replacing them still remains the prime consideration in their protection. Special clauses in an insurance policy or special policies may protect the items mentioned above. A lower rate can be obtained on this type of insurance if the insured person or business agrees to keep in a safe place duplicates of such items as plans, maps, and invoices.

In every fire insurance policy there are restrictions as to increases in the hazards. For instance, after an insurance contract has been written, the hazards may undergo changes because of physical changes in the property, alterations or repairs, changes in the use or the occupancy of the property, or the addition of explosives, gases, or the like. Fraud or the concealment of facts may void any insurance policy.

Extended Coverage. The basic fire insurance policy may be extended to cover such additional risks as windstorm, hail, explosion, riot, civil disorder, aircraft or auto damage, and smoke damage. This protection, called *extended coverage,* is obtained by paying an additional premium and by adding a special clause to the contract.

Coinsurance Clauses. *Coinsurance* is a term applied to an insurance policy in which the insurer and the insured share the risks. Coinsurance clauses are included in fire insurance policies to encourage businessmen to purchase an adequate amount of insurance. Seldom does a fire completely destroy a property. Usually, only a part of the structure is destroyed. If businessmen decided that the average destruction to a building was 40 percent and they insured their properties for that amount, insurance companies would lose a great deal of premium income. Insurance companies protect themselves by including coinsurance clauses which require the insured to buy insurance up to a certain portion of the total value of the property. If the individual underinsures property and a loss occurs, the insured must bear a portion of the loss. Thus, coinsurance means that the insured must take some of the risk of loss from fire if he has failed to insure for the required amount.

Coinsurance clauses are normally written for 80 percent of the coverage. For example, if the insured and the insurance company place a value of $50,000 on a building, under an 80 percent coinsurance clause the insured is required to carry at least $40,000 of insurance (80 percent of $50,000). If a loss occurs, the insured can recover any amount of the loss up to $40,000. However, if the insured carries only $30,000, he can collect only 75 percent of any loss (since he is carrying only 75 percent -of the required $40,000 of insurance). Illustration 18-4 contains examples of how 80 percent coinsurance clauses operate.

Value of Property	Percentage Required by Policy	Amount Required by Policy	Actual Percentage Carried	Amount Carried	Loss	Amount Paid by Insurance Company	Loss Borne by Insured
$10,000	80%	$8,000	90%	$9,000	$9,000	$9,000	$ 0
10,000	80%	8,000	80%	8,000	8,000	8,000	0
10,000	80%	8,000	80%	8,000	5,000	5,000	0
10,000	80%	8,000	80%	8,000	9,000	8,000	1,000
10,000	80%	8,000	60%	6,000	6,000	4,500	1,500
10,000	80%	8,000	60%	6,000	9,000	6,000	3,000

ILLUS. 18-4. How 80 percent coinsurance clauses operate.

All examples of coinsurance can be summarized in one formula:

$$\frac{\text{Amount carried (face)}}{\text{Amount required}} \times \text{Loss} = \begin{array}{l} \text{Amount recoverable from the} \\ \text{insurance company, which, how-} \\ \text{ever, must never exceed the face} \\ \text{of the policy.} \end{array}$$

It is important to the individual to reappraise the value of his property from time to time to make certain the value carried on the insurance policy is adequate.

Coverage for Large Fire Risks. In many communities it is impossible for any particular business to obtain all the insurance it desires through one insurance company. Insurance companies follow a plan, particularly in certain high-risk districts, of insuring only a certain percentage of the value of property. There are two ways, however, in which a businessman may obtain complete coverage. One is by obtaining two or more policies that together cover the entire value of the property. The other is by purchasing complete coverage from one insurance company, which in turn will reinsure part of the value of the property with one or more other insurance companies. When any particular insurance company issues a large insurance policy, it usually sells or reinsures part of the risk with other companies. This practice is considered good management on the part of the insurance company because it distributes the risk among a number of companies. Any particularly large loss might cause serious financial harm to a single company; but when it is distributed over several companies, it is not so significant. In other words, several insurance companies bear the loss instead of one company.

Use and Occupancy Insurance. *Use and occupancy insurance* is sometimes referred to as *business interruption insurance*. For instance, after a fire in an office, a factory, or a store, the business suffers an additional loss because it cannot carry on its operations in the normal manner. Some of its expenses continue in spite of the fire. These are such expenses as interest on notes, taxes, rent, royalties, certain insurance, advertising, telephone service, and certain salaries. The business may lose not only the normal income from sales but also its customers, who may go to other sources and never come back. On the other hand, during the period when the business may be shut down because of the fire, it may save the salaries of certain employees and a few other miscellaneous expenses.

In determining the amount of such insurance to carry, the businessman should consult an insurance representative. He will find it advisable to prepare a list of items that are customarily considered as fixed charges and to make an estimate of his normal profit, taking into consideration past experience and future expectations. When such an estimate has been made, a record should be kept of the method of computing the estimate so that these figures can be submitted in justifying a claim.

Transportation and Cargo Insurance

Protection against damage, theft, or complete loss of goods shipped by water is obtained by purchasing *marine insurance*. The person who owns the goods may obtain this insurance, or the company that transports them may provide it as a part of the cost of transportation. The transportation company may insure all its shipments through an insurance company, or it may assume its own risks and pay its own losses.

The insurance cost on freight shipments is included in the rate charged for transportation.

Parcel post packages may be insured by the U.S. Postal Service upon the payment of an extra fee, or they may be sent uninsured.

Common carrier trucking companies must carry cargo insurance, and a special form must be submitted by the insurance company to the Interstate Commerce Commission whenever a policy is issued on a cargo.

Automobile Insurance

An individual may purchase several different kinds of automobile insurance to protect himself against such losses as theft, property damage, or personal injury.

Comprehensive Coverage. Most basic automobile insurance policies include a coverage called the *comprehensive clause*. Insurance paid for under this clause usually includes loss caused by glass breakage by a flying object (but not collision), fire, theft, explosion, windstorm, hail, water, vandalism, or riot; coverage may also extend to wearing apparel in the automobile.

In the case of insurance covering fire and theft, the most common practice is to issue policies which state that the market value of the automobile at the time of the loss will be paid. For instance, a new car may be insured on January 1 for its actual value, or cost, of $3,200. If it is stolen six months later, the amount that the insurance company is obligated to pay is only the market value of a secondhand car of that particular age and model. Most policies are worded in such a manner that the insurance company may replace the car with a similar one or pay the market value at the time of the loss, regardless of the amount of insurance carried on the car. When there is only a partial loss, the insurance company repairs the damage or pays an amount of cash equivalent to the cost of repairs. Most policies include protection against fire and theft while an automobile is being transported on a boat or a railroad.

Collision Insurance. *Collision insurance* is usually meant to be protection against damage to one's own car. This type of insurance is becoming somewhat unpopular because it is costly and because some unscrupulous people damage their own cars to collect insurance.

A way to get collision insurance protection at a lower cost is to buy it with a *deductible clause*. For example, a policy with a "$50 deductible clause" means that the owner of the insured car must pay his

ILLUS. 18-5. Collision insurance provides protection against damage to
one's own car.

own losses up to $50; the insurance company will pay all losses
above $50. By increasing the deductible portion to $100 or more,
the premium can be decreased even further.

Property Damage Insurance. *Property damage insurance* provides
protection against damage caused by the insured's automobile to the
automobile or to some other property of another person.

Ordinarily it is considered wise to carry not less than $10,000 worth
of property damage insurance. If an automobile driver who carries
$10,000 worth of property damage insurance damages the automobile
of another person or the front of a store, for instance, the person whose
property has been damaged may collect damages from the insurance
company to the extent of $10,000.

Bodily Injury Insurance. *Bodily injury insurance* is also called *personal injury insurance*. It provides protection against an injury to a
person.

Property damage insurance and bodily injury insurance are usually
sold together in the same policy. They are both important because the
risks are unknown and the claims for damages may be very great.

The so-called *ten-and-twenty-clause* in an automobile insurance policy refers to $10,000 of bodily injury insurance for injury to one person and $20,000 for injury to two or more persons in the same accident. Damage claims above the amount of insurance must be paid by the insured. These amounts are usually the minimum amounts for which bodily injury insurance should be carried, but it is common practice to carry more protection. Amounts of $50,000 and $100,000 are quite common.

Nonownership Clause. For an extra charge a special clause can be included in the automobile insurance policy that will provide protection to the policyholder in case he drives a car belonging to some other person. This kind of protection is usually referred to as the *nonowner-ship clause.* It is similar to another type of clause, the *hired-car clause,* which can be included in the policy to protect the driver if he hires a car.

Medical Payments Insurance. For an extra fee a clause can be inserted in an automobile insurance policy which will cover the medical, surgical, hospital, and nursing expenses caused by accidental injuries to any occupant of the insured automobile, including the policyholder himself. These payments will be made regardless of the legal liability of the policyholder. This type of insurance is called *medical payments insurance.*

No-Fault Insurance. Some states have passed *no-fault insurance* laws. Under the provisions of the various laws, the insurance company does not attempt to fix the responsibility of an accident to a driver. Each insurance company is required to pay losses incurred by their insured regardless of who might have been responsible for the loss.

Arguments for the approach are varied. It is reasoned that there can be quicker financial settlements and lower administrative costs as a result of reducing the number of court cases resulting from accidents.

Opponents to the various plans claim that while the damage to an automobile can be immediately assessed, that is not the case with physical injury. There are many instances in which the extent of personal injury is not known for several months. The company will be required to pay only to the extent of the policy coverage. The question arises as to who might have to pay amounts above the policy amount if the injured person were not legally at fault in the accident. The injured person may have no further claim against his own insurance company and may not be in a financial position to secure legal action against the other person.

Burglary and Robbery Insurance

Various policies provide protection from loss due to personal holdup, robbery of merchandise, robbery of a safe, robbery of paymaster, messenger robbery, and interior office or store robbery. Because of the differences in the types of businesses and the methods of operating businesses, the risks vary considerably. Consequently, the rates also vary considerably. Individual policies may be obtained to cover different risks, or one policy may be obtained to cover several risks. The rate on the latter type of policy will depend upon the number of risks covered.

A risk of loss which it is very difficult for the businessman to protect himself against is the loss resulting from *shoplifting* (customer stealing of merchandise). Although it is possible to include protection against shoplifting losses in theft insurance policies, such protection is very expensive. In addition, the guilt of the customer accused is difficult to prove, and the possibility of falsely accusing a customer can greatly harm the business. To reduce losses from shoplifting, some stores employ detective agencies to apprehend shoplifters.

Coinsurance may be obtained with various forms of burglary and robbery insurance. For instance, a coinsurance clause is often used in burglary insurance policies on merchandise which is in stock or openly displayed. In burglary insurance, as in the case of fire insurance,

ILLUS. 18-6. **To reduce losses from shoplifting, some stores employ detective agencies.**

usually only a limited loss is sustained at any particular time, for seldom is all the merchandise stolen. The greater number of coinsurance clauses are therefore confined to smaller percentages. If the policyholder is willing, however, to insure for 90 or 100 percent, he will obtain more complete protection at a lower rate.

Fidelity Bonds

Fidelity bonds, which are used in business, are really a form of insurance against dishonesty of employees or agents. For instance, when a person employed by a bank will be required to handle money, he must be bonded by a surety and bonding company. Then, in case the employee later embezzles or steals money from the bank, the bonding company is required to make good the loss provided the employee is not able to return the money. Some employers pay the cost of the bond, but others require the employee to pay it. Bonds on individuals are issued only on the basis of reputable character. The rate is dependent upon the risk involved. For instance, a person handling a small amount of money will not require a large bond, and the rates will probably be reasonably low. On the other hand, if the person handles a large amount of money, the bond will probably be rather large and the rate will be higher.

There are many kinds of fidelity bonds. Some bonds, known as *blanket bonds,* cover all employees. Other bonds cover only the individuals who are named. This type is called a *name schedule bond.* Another type of bond, the *position schedule* or *blanket schedule bond,* covers persons occupying certain positions, but these persons are not specified by name. For example, the treasurer, the bookkeeper, and the secretary might be bonded regardless of who occupies those positions.

Performance or Surety Bonds

Performance bonds or *surety bonds* are also commonly used in business. For instance, if one obtains a contract to construct a building or to furnish merchandise at a specified price and under specified conditions, it may be necessary for him to give a bond. If the contract is not carried out according to its terms, the bond is forfeited; and the company that issued it must pay damages to the person for whom the building was being constructed or the merchandise was being produced. Such bonds are used quite generally in business. For instance, if a company establishes an agency, the agent may be required to give a performance bond.

Liability Insurance

Businessmen operating retail stores or dealing directly with the public in other ways usually find it necessary to carry various forms of special insurance, such as *liability insurance,* to provide protection from loss due to the personal injury of customers. A claim may result from an injury sustained by slipping on a floor, falling down steps, being hurt on an escalator, or from being harmed by an employee or by some other customer. Damage claims may also result from the use of merchandise that was sold by a store. For instance, the dye in some clothing may cause a skin infection. A cosmetic may result in injury to a user. A piece of machinery may be defective and cause personal injury. Claims can result from all these cases, but there is liability insurance available to provide protection against them.

Even though insurance is carried as protection against such claims, the owner or the management has an important responsibility to prevent accidents. When an accident occurs, it creates ill will. The prevention of accidents is therefore really as important as insurance providing protection against them.

ILLUS. 18-7. Businessmen should carry insurance which protects them against claims because of injuries to customers.

Life Insurance on Owners or Executives

Life insurance plays an important function in business. In the case of a sole proprietorship, the owner will usually find it easier to borrow money if he carries adequate life insurance. He may specifically carry life insurance so that if he should die the proceeds from the insurance will pay any indebtedness of the business, permitting the business to be turned over free of debt to his son or some other successor. Some sole proprietorships are so dependent on the owner and originator of the business that, when he dies, it is difficult for the business to continue successfully. If proper insurance is provided, there will be funds available to carry on the business until it can be sold or until someone can be obtained to manage it.

Life insurance has an especially important place in partnerships. Generally a partnership is dissolved upon the death of one partner. One partner may attempt to carry sufficient insurance so that when he dies his heirs will be able to use the proceeds of the insurance to purchase the shares of other partners. Another plan is one in which a partner carries life insurance on the other partner so that when his partner dies he will obtain, as beneficiary of the insurance policy, sufficient money to buy the share of the partnership owned by the deceased partner.

Important executives of corporations are usually insured. The theory behind this plan is that, if a key executive dies, the progress of the corporation will be impaired, but the proceeds from the insurance will help the corporation to make any adjustments that are necessary until a new executive can be obtained.

In a small corporation owned by just a few stockholders, it is also a practice for stockholders to carry insurance on each other so that if one stockholder dies it is possible for the remaining stockholders to purchase the stock of the deceased stockholder and continue the operation of the business within the small group.

Insurance for Employees

The so-called *group insurance* plan has a prominent place in business. The business and the employees usually share in the payment of the premiums. Under this plan life insurance is provided for many employees who could not individually obtain insurance because of their health. Usually no medical examination is required. From the viewpoint of employees, the insurance is available usually at a relatively low rate.

Most employers are required by law to carry workmen's compensation insurance to cover accidents or illness caused by the work. Most employers and employees are also taxed by the federal government to provide social security in the forms of pensions, unemployment compensation, and medical care. These kinds of protection are discussed in Chapter 26.

Special Types of Insurance

In addition to the types of insurance already discussed in this section, a businessman may sometimes need certain special types of insurance, such as credit insurance, credit life insurance, and forgery insurance.

Credit Insurance. A businessman may purchase *credit insurance* to protect himself against losses on credit that he extends to his customers. If he cannot collect an amount due him, the insurance company will pay the loss. However, the insurance company still has the right to try to collect from the customer.

Credit Life Insurance. Credit insurance should not be confused with *credit life insurance*. This type of insurance is used commonly by small loan companies, banks, and dealers who sell on the installment plan. The borrower or the installment purchaser must buy sufficient life insurance to pay the balance of his debt if he dies.

Forgery Insurance. *Forgery insurance* may be obtained by businessmen, individuals, banks, and other institutions to provide protection against loss caused by forged or altered checks and securities. Losses may occur as a result of the wrong person cashing a check, altering a signature, or altering an amount on a check. Businessmen are constantly exposed to these risks. Any businessman who cashes any great number of checks should carry this kind of insurance for protection.

Other types of insurance that a businessman may wish to consider are those covering glass breakage, water damage, and boiler explosion. In fact, it is possible to obtain insurance on almost every type of risk, except those involving business judgment.

Noninsurable Risks

The businessman is also concerned with certain special types of risks for which there is no insurance. For instance, anyone who has operated a business has discovered that people change in their needs, desires, and wants. These changes cause serious business risks. Most products are produced in anticipation of sale. If the needs, desires, and wants of consumers change, however, those who have produced goods are likely to suffer a loss.

Fashions, particularly in women's clothing, change frequently. Manufacturers and merchants of such clothing are sometimes stocked heavily at a time when styles change or when buyers fail to accept new styles. Whoever is stocked with the merchandise therefore suffers a loss and probably has to sell the goods at a special sale. A wise merchant watches his purchases carefully so that he does not overstock.

Methods of heating, transportation, and lighting cause serious business risks. For instance, the owner of a store that was thoroughly modern a few years ago may find all his customers going to another store that has recently installed air-conditioning equipment. New decorations and new lighting equipment may attract customers away from an old, established store. Improved methods of transportation may give one type of business an advantage over another. For instance, private passenger automobiles may injure the business of bus companies. Television affected the sales of radio manufacturers, motion-picture producers, and theater owners. Drive-in theaters reduced the receipts of regular theaters. There are numerous such changes going on constantly.

Changes in the weather are sometimes serious business risks. For instance, a delayed summer season may prevent manufacturers and stores from selling their stock of summer clothing. A cool summer may injure the business of pleasure resorts because people may stay comfortably at home.

The fluctuation or change in business conditions is another serious risk. It can be overcome to some extent by studying business conditions and by planning carefully in anticipation of changes in business. Therefore, a knowledge of economics is valuable to a businessman.

Within any business community there are numerous local risks, such as the relocation of highways, which may cause customers to change their sources of supply to more convenient ones or destroy the value of a location for a motel; the development of new highways, which may take customers to larger communities to do their shopping; the improvement of streets, which may make one location better than another and therefore draw customers away from an old location; parking restrictions and the establishment of no-parking zones, which may have a bad effect upon certain types of businesses; the shift in population and the types of population in a community, which may make it necessary to move businesses. These and similar risks must be considered by every businessman. Unless he recognizes them, he may wait too long and find that his business has been totally or partially destroyed.

REVIEW WHAT YOU HAVE LEARNED

Business Terms Checkup:

(1) risk
(2) insurer
(3) policyholder
(4) policy
(5) insured or the risk
(6) premium
(7) stock company
(8) mutual company
(9) dividends
(10) assessments
(11) insurable interest
(12) fire insurance
(13) valued policy laws
(14) extended coverage
(15) coinsurance
(16) use and occupancy insurance or business interruption insurance
(17) marine insurance
(18) comprehensive clause
(19) collision insurance
(20) deductible clause
(21) property damage insurance
(22) bodily injury insurance or personal injury insurance
(23) ten-and-twenty-clause
(24) nonownership clause
(25) hired-car clause
(26) medical payments insurance
(27) no-fault insurance
(28) shoplifting
(29) fidelity bond
(30) blanket bond
(31) name schedule bond
(32) position schedule bond or blanket schedule bond
(33) performance bond or surety bond
(34) liability insurance
(35) group insurance
(36) credit insurance
(37) credit life insurance
(38) forgery insurance

Reading Checkup:

1. Why is proper insurance coverage considered essential if a business is requesting credit?
2. What are some of the risks that can be covered by insurance?
3. Explain the differences in ownership between a mutual insurance company and a stock insurance company.
4. How are insurance rates established?
5. Describe what may be considered an insurable interest in property.
6. Does a fire insurance policy on a building usually cover the equipment and the materials in the building?
7. Is there any advantage in carrying fire insurance for a greater amount than the actual value of the property?
8. Under a fire insurance policy with a coinsurance clause, why are the rates per thousand dollars of insurance lower than they are under an ordinary fire insurance policy?

9. Under an automobile theft insurance policy, on what basis is the value of the car determined when the insurance company pays for loss due to theft?

10. If you carry collision insurance on an automobile, what kind of protection is provided?

11. Why is bodily injury insurance important?

12. In what way can a business obtain protection against possible loss due to theft by an employee?

13. What is a performance or surety bond? .

14. How does a performance bond provide protection on a contract?

15. What is the main reason that group insurance is so important to many people?

16. Name some of the business risks for which it is impossible to buy insurance protection.

17. What types of insurance protection can be obtained for a person who may drive a car not owned by him?

APPLY WHAT YOU HAVE LEARNED

Questions for Class Discussion:

1. Does a person who rents a building have an insurable interest in the building?

2. A manufacturing plant is located in a very modern, fireproof building, but there is poor local fire protection. How will the fire insurance rates be affected?

3. How does the nature of the product being manufactured in a factory determine fire insurance rates?

4. If you operate a store, what are some of the possible claims for damages that might be incurred on the part of your customers?

5. What would be your opinion of a mutual fire insurance company that would insist that you correct certain defects in your building before insuring the building for you?

6. Why is business interruption insurance so important to some companies?

7. Many large corporations operating large fleets of cars driven by salesmen carry a nonownership clause in the automobile insurance contract. Why do these corporations feel that the addition of this clause is important?

8. Is it possible to carry too much insurance? Explain.

9. Assume that you are able to make what appears to be a very favorable contract with a new construction company. The contractor does not have

much money with which to operate, and he asks that you pay part of the cost of the construction in advance. Mention how you might protect yourself in case the contractor does not perform his work.

10. In recent years many companies that have made just one product have begun to manufacture more than one product. This practice is called diversification. Why do you think that these firms have diversified their lines?

11. Discuss the advantages and disadvantages of no-fault insurance.

Problems and Projects:

1. From the information in the following table indicate for each of the examples a, b, c, and d how much of the loss will be paid by the insurance company.

Example	Value of Property	Coinsurance Clause	Face of Policy	Amount of Loss
a	$10,000	80%	$ 8,000	$ 8,000
b	40,000	80%	25,000	30,000
c	60,000	80%	48,000	50,000
d	20,000	80%	16,000	5,000

2. Obtain a sample of a fire insurance policy used by a business on a building, merchandise, or equipment. Study it and write a report on the nature of losses covered, the losses that are excluded from coverage, and any other special features that you discover.

3. Obtain an automobile insurance policy and make a report on the different kinds of losses covered by the policy, the obligations of the policyholder, and the kinds of liabilities or losses that are not covered.

Case Problem 18-1:

The Henderson Electric Company owns two trucks that are covered by insurance, including a nonownership policy as a part of its automobile insurance. One day a truck needed extensive repair, and the Madison Garage loaned one of its trucks to the Henderson Electric Company. The driver, John Nelson, in the performance of his duties, was at fault in an accident causing $1,000 damage to a car owned by Walter Meeks.

Required:

1. Can Meeks collect from Nelson or Nelson's insurance company?

2. Can Meeks collect from the Madison Garage or its insurance company?

3. Can Meeks collect from the Henderson Electric Company or its insurance company?

Case Problem 18-2:

The Western Publishing Company makes about 5,000 shipments by mail a year. It has been insuring these shipments through U.S. Postal Insurance at the rates shown below.

Value of Contents	Fee
$ 0.01 to $ 15.00	$0.20
15.01 to 50.00	0.30
50.01 to 100.00	0.40
100.01 to 150.00	0.50

There are seldom any shipments over $50. The insurance fees paid and the losses over a period of ten years are listed below.

Year	Insurance	Losses
1963	$700.00	$400.15
1964	685.20	515.10
1965	810.15	450.15
1966	640.40	350.60
1967	750.00	470.60
1968	688.20	270.50
1969	710.15	500.50
1970	850.00	600.40
1971	600.50	300.45
1972	675.50	420.15

The company wants to consider the policy of self-insuring—setting up a fund by making a charge on each shipment from which losses can be paid.

Required:

1. What is the average amount of insurance paid during the past ten years?
2. What is the average yearly loss during the past ten years?
3. If 5,000 shipments are sent each year, what is the average loss per shipment?
4. The company is considering putting into an insurance fund an allowance of 10 cents for each shipment. Would this be a wise decision?
5. What action would you recommend?

Continuing Project:

For the business that you have selected, make a list of your insurance needs, the kinds of insurance that you will carry, and the insurance cost.

What are the types of retail credit?

What are advantages and disadvantages of extending credit?

What policies should be followed when extending credit?

What are the types of installment contracts?

What are sources of retail credit information?

BACKGROUND OF CHAPTER

Much of the world's business is conducted on credit. Buying on credit can be a convenience, a privilege, and a service. Credit has many advantages to the seller and the buyer, but it adds to the cost of doing business and often adds to the price of the goods and services that are being sold.

To avoid losses, a businessman must extend credit carefully and observe good credit policies and procedures. This chapter explains the terms used in credit dealings, discusses the advantages and disadvantages of extending credit, tells how credit information can be obtained, and recommends credit policies and procedures which the businessman should follow.

CHAPTER 19

CREDIT POLICIES AND PROCEDURES

Some businesses sell for cash only; others extend credit to their customers. If a business extends credit, much of its success will depend upon its policies and the care with which credit is extended and collections are made.

RETAIL CREDIT

Retail credit is ordinarily credit that is extended by the retailer to the consumer. The average person is, of course, more interested in retail credit than in wholesale credit.

Types of Retail Credit

A retail store owner may extend short-term, long-term, or revolving credit to his customers. The factors which most commonly influence the terms of a sale are the credit customs in the community and the credit practices of competitors.

Short-Term Credit. *Short-term credit* is credit extended on account. When a customer buys merchandise, the sale is charged to his account. At the end of each month he is expected to pay for the purchases made during the month. A retailer usually submits a monthly statement to each customer. Retail stores with a large number of accounts use a plan of sending the monthly statement to certain customers at one date of the month and to certain other customers at other times in the month. This plan is known as *cycle billing*. In most communities the practice is to require the customer to pay his account within ten days after the date of the statement. A discount is seldom allowed on retail purchases.

ILLUS. 19-1. Credit cards are now commonly used to facilitate
charging goods and ser-
vices to one's account.

National Car Rental

Large local stores and national chain businesses issue credit cards
to their charge customers. For example, most oil companies issue
credit cards to automobile owners who request them for making credit
purchases at service stations. The cardholders are billed monthly for
their purchases and are expected to pay when the bills are received.
BankAmericard, Master Charge, American Express, Diners' Club, and
Carte Blanche are examples of businesses which offer credit card
service for those businesses that do not wish to establish their own
credit card system. Usually the business which permits a customer to
charge a purchase by the use of such cards pays a fee of from 5 to
7 percent to the credit card company for doing the clerical work and
collecting from the customer.

Long-Term Credit. *Long-term credit* may be extended on account
or through an installment plan. In the latter case the customer is required to enter into a formal contract.

An *installment contract,* which will be discussed later in this chapter,
is the agreement under which the buyer of goods promises to make
regular payments until the goods are paid for. The principal difference
between short-term credit and long-term credit is that in the latter case
the customer is given a longer time to pay. He is sometimes required
to pay an extra amount for this privilege, and he is often required to
make regular small payments on the amount he owes.

In department stores, furniture stores, and similar stores, regular customers who have charge accounts may be allowed to purchase

some of the major items on 60 or 90 days' credit without having to pay any additional charge. For instance, a store may permit a customer who has a good credit record to buy furniture amounting to $200 and allow him 60 to 90 days to pay for it without having to pay any extra charge or to sign any installment contract.

Revolving Credit. In some cities retail stores have established what is called a *revolving credit* plan, also referred to as a program of *planned credit*. It combines the features of an ordinary charge account and an installment contract. Under the revolving credit plan the customer is required to make a regular monthly payment depending upon the amount of the unpaid balance of his account. The amount of the regular monthly payment required in each case is determined by the store. Often the customer pays an extra charge of some stipulated amount, such as 1.5 percent, on the unpaid balance.

Advantages of Extending Retail Credit

As has been stated before, business could not be transacted without some form of credit. Merchants recognize the advantages of credit in dealing with their customers. Some of these advantages are:

1. Credit develops permanent customers. It makes regular customers and creates a more personal relationship between the seller and the purchaser.
2. As a rule, credit sales are larger than cash sales, although they are not so frequent as the latter. Customers usually buy in larger quantities when they do not have to pay immediately. The larger quantities last a longer time.
3. Good credit relations develop the customers' confidence in a merchant and build goodwill for the merchant.
4. Customers who have good credit and are not concerned with price may prefer to buy where they can get credit rather than pay cash, even though the prices may be lower in a cash-only store.
5. Credit may create a larger volume of business. If the cost of credit is not too great, the company may make more profit.

Disadvantages of Extending Retail Credit

Extending credit also has its disadvantages. A major disadvantage of extending credit is that it increases the cost of doing business. Since a credit business has more money tied up in accounts owed by customers, it takes more money to run a credit business than to run a cash business. A credit business also will lose some money on accounts that cannot be collected, and it has additional costs for keeping records and collecting accounts.

Other disadvantages of extending credit are the result of unwise credit practices. The businessman who allows his customers to buy recklessly is not only abusing his credit relations but also is encouraging his customers to abuse their credit relations. Any merchant who encourages extravagance through urging customers to make thoughtless purchases soon finds that he cannot collect the accounts that are owed to him.

Determining Credit Standing

A commonly recognized formula for determining the credit of a person or a business is the *"three C's"*—character, capacity, and capital.

Character is the first consideration. Many businessmen feel that an individual's character is more important than his wealth. Wealth alone cannot determine one's credit, nor, of course, can one get unlimited credit on his character alone.

Capacity is merely another term for earning power. An individual may have an honorable character and perfectly good intentions of paying an obligation; but unless he has the ability or capacity to pay, he cannot pay satisfactorily.

The third measuring standard, *capital,* applies only to people who have property. A person with a temporary lack of earning power may be entitled to receive credit, provided he has good capital resources (wealth) and a good character.

Capacity and capital without character will, however, usually disqualify any credit applicant.

Illustration 19-2 on page 385 shows the results of a survey to determine how credit managers rate in importance various kinds of credit information. *Mercantile* refers to extending credit to merchants; *retail* refers to extending credit to individuals. It will be observed that character ranks first. The payment record, which shows both the ability and the willingnes to pay, ranks second. The financial statement, which ranks third, is important in determining credit extended to a merchant; but it is not so important when a merchant extends credit to a retail customer. The financial statement shows what is owned and what is owed by the business.

When a credit manager examines financial statements that are submitted by a business, he will investigate carefully to determine the

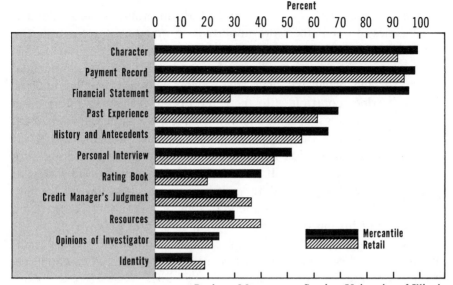

Business Management Service, University of Illinois

ILLUS. 19-2. Types of credit information considered most valuable by credit managers.

amount of insurance carried by the business. If the business is not carrying sufficient insurance, it may be considered a poor risk.

Sources of Retail Credit Information. The following sources of retail credit information are available to the merchant who is dealing with individuals:

1. Information may be obtained from the applicant by asking questions (personal interview) and by requiring the applicant to fill out a credit application blank.
2. Information may be obtained from a local retail credit agency which obtains information from all businesses that cooperate in supplying such information. The functions of a credit agency will be explained later.
3. Information may be obtained from other businesses or stores.
4. Information may be obtained from the applicant's bank or employer.

Credit Agencies. In general there are two types of credit agencies: (a) agencies that provide credit information on individual purchasers and (b) agencies that provide credit information on businesses.

Banks sometimes give confidential credit information on individuals and businesses. It is therefore important to maintain satisfactory relations with a bank if a good credit rating is desired.

Private credit agencies collect information and publish confidential reports for the benefit of their subscribers, who are usually retailers. Each subscriber contributes to these reports by furnishing information and periodic ratings. Additional information is gathered from local newspapers, notices of change in address, death notices, and court records. Such information is valuable to the retailer in protecting himself from loss on accounts. If one of his customers moves, he will want to know of the change in address. If a customer dies, he will want to be sure that his claim is presented. If someone is taking court action against one of his customers, he will want to protect his own claim.

The National Retail Credit Association is composed of local associations in various cities. These associations are organized to cooperate in furnishing credit information.

Approximately 4,000 credit bureau and collection offices of the Associated Credit Bureaus of America maintain credit records of millions of persons and write more than 50 million credit reports each year. These records are kept up to date constantly through the cooperation of local bureaus. The information is at the fingertips of any merchant who is a member of a local bureau. When a person establishes a credit rating, the information is available to merchants even though the person may move from one city to another.

This huge network of credit-reporting agencies is beneficial not only to the merchant but also to the individual who seeks credit. Anyone who is honest and desires to maintain proper credit should be willing to have a report submitted on him. Under this system of credit reporting, it is difficult for anyone to establish a bad credit reputation without the information being made available to other merchants who extend credit.

In many communities there are associations of credit men that are a part of a nationwide organization known as the National Association of Credit Management. This national organization operates a credit interchange service. Through the credit interchange service members report their credit relations with their various customers. This information is assembled and is furnished in the form of a confidential report to members who pay a fee for this service. Illustration 19-3 is an example of the kind of information furnished in these reports.

REPORT ON:

X Y Z Company   Cleveland, Ohio   December 11, 1972

BUSINESS CLASSIFICATION	HOW LONG SOLD	DATE OF LAST SALE	HIGHEST RECENT CREDIT	AMOUNT OWING INCLUDING NOTES	AMOUNT PAST DUE	UNFILLED OR FIRST ORDERS	TERMS OF SALE	MANNER OF PAYMENT DISCOUNTS	PAYS WHEN DUE	DAYS SLOW	COMMENTS
GRAND RAPIDS 326-240 165 MTL	10-70	10-70					COD				
CLEVELAND 324-309 D 66 PNT	*Yrs	3-71	$ 83	$ 58	$ 33		2-10-60			30-90	
CD 170 PNT	Yrs	3-71	816	733	399					3-5 Mos	
C 1 HDWE	Yrs	3-71	1403	687	449		2-10-30			120	
C 258 MISC						12					
C 46 ELEC							COD				
C 218 ELEC		12-70	85	35	35					60-90	
A MISC	Yrs	3-72	50							30	
GRAND RAPIDS CONT'D 86 MTL	Yrs	2-71	240	18						30-60	
NEW ENGLAND 326-342 260 HDWE	Yrs	8-72	40				2-10			30-90	

* Several years

ILLUS. 19-3. Report of National Association of Credit Management.

Cost of Credit to the Seller

Merchants who sell on open account may be classified .as follows: (a) those whose prices for credit and for cash sales are the same and (b) those who charge more for credit than for cash sales.

The extending of credit adds extra costs to every sale. The principal extra costs result from (a) the clerical work necessary for recording credit sales and collecting accounts and (b) interest on the money that is invested or has been borrowed in order to extend credit. Additional costs result from occasional losses due to bad debts and the tendency of credit customers to return goods for exchange.

The extra cost for clerical help is obvious. It is also a known fact that merchants find it impossible to collect all their accounts. Furthermore, a merchant who does a large credit business must have available enough money to provide a stock of goods, to pay his expenses, and to operate his business until collections can be made. In other words, he always has some debts outstanding. If he had all the money that is due him, he could invest it and earn an income from it. He is therefore entitled to some extra income because he is deprived of the use of some of his own money for business or for investment purposes. Most merchants find it necessary to borrow money. They extend credit and at the same time borrow money to finance their own businesses. The interest they must pay on the loans is an added operating cost.

Surveys made by Dun and Bradstreet indicate clearly that in most businesses it costs more to sell on credit than it does to sell for cash. This finding is shown in Illustration 19-4.

Trade	Percentage of Sales
Grocery stores	+1.9
Grocery and meat stores	+1.5
Meat and fish stores	—0.3
Drugstores	+1.3
Country general stores	+0.7
Dry goods and general merchandise	+2.5
Men's furnishings	—2.6
Men's and boys' clothing	+4.3
Women's ready-to-wear	+4.9
Family clothing and children's wear	+3.3
Shoe stores	+0.5
Hardware stores	+0.7
Service stations	+2.3
Automotive accessories and parts	+5.9
Average	+2.13

This table shows that, with but two exceptions, the percentage of expense of operating credit stores is higher than that of cash stores.

ILLUS. 19-4. Excess expense of operating credit stores over cash stores.

These comments should not be construed to mean that a merchant who sells on credit must necessarily sell at higher prices than a merchant who sells for cash. If selling on credit results in greater sales than selling for cash, the increased sales may produce a greater profit in spite of the additional costs.

Recommended Retail Credit Policies and Procedures

Credit policies and procedures must be related to collection policies. The following are the four main types of credit and collection policies:

1. Liberal credit is granted with a liberal treatment in collections.
2. Liberal credit is granted but with strict collection policies.

3. Strict credit is granted, but collection policies are liberal.

4. The granting of credit is strict and collection policies are strict.

It is desirable to have uniform credit policies and procedures in each community so that all merchants will treat their customers alike and so that customers will become accustomed to the policies. The following credit policies are those followed by merchants in one typical city:

1. Standardize all terms, classifying accounts as follows:

   (a) Monthly charge accounts (open accounts).

   (b) Budget, or deferred-payment, accounts (time-payment accounts of short duration, not exceeding ten weeks, on which no carrying charge is made).

   (c) Installment accounts (time-payment accounts of long duration on which a carrying charge is made).

2. State the terms, including all costs of financing and the interest rate charged, to the applicant for credit, stressing a definite due date.

3. Consider all accounts to be past due on the day following the definite due date.

4. Make no deviation from the terms of credit.

5. When an account has not been paid in full within 60 days following the end of the month of purchase, use at this point a uniform "term" letter.

6. Charge interest at the rate of not less than one-half percent a month on all balances of monthly charge accounts that have been due for 60 days.

7. Use a credit application blank requiring the signature of the applicant and carrying a notice of the interest charge.

8. Check all applicants for credit through the credit bureau before opening any new accounts, and do not open an account when the credit report is unfavorable.

9. Require a down payment of not less than 10 percent on all installment, layaway, or will-call sales.

10. Record all installment accounts with the credit agency if they are not recorded with the county clerk and recorder.

11. Furnish to the credit agency each month a complete list of all accounts that have been delinquent 90 days. (Example: January purchases would be reported on May 1st.)

12. Report promptly to the agency all accounts that have been closed with cause; report, at the time of repossession, any merchandise that has been repossessed; report all unfair claims and any other special information that might affect the credit standing of the customer in the community.

These credit policies and procedures, which have been suggested for a uniform community policy, are also recommended for individual stores. In addition, it is suggested that when a new account is opened a letter of confirmation should be written to the new customer. It should be a friendly letter and a letter of welcome, but it should also explain the policies in regard to credit and the amount of credit that is being extended the customer.

Secured Transactions

When selling a high-priced item, such as a refrigerator or an automobile, the business usually will not sell it on open credit, but will insist on an agreement which enables the business to retain a security interest in the property until the obligation has been completely paid. Under the Uniform Commercial Code which has been adopted as the law in all states but one (Louisiana), this contract is called a *security agreement,* of which there are different types. Two common types are (a) a chattel-mortgage contract and (b) a conditional sales contract. Illustration 19-5 (page 391) shows a chattel-mortgage contract; Illustration 19-6 (page 392), a conditional sales contract. In most states the laws specify the particular form that must be used, whereas in a few states either form may be used.

When merchandise is sold on any kind of installment contract, the terms of the sale, as well as the plan of payment, should be clearly explained to the purchaser. The seller should insist that the purchaser read the contract carefully before signing to be sure he understands all of his obligations.

Chattel-Mortgage Contract. When goods are sold under a *chattel-mortgage contract,* the seller has a lien (a claim) against the goods until the amount of the contract is paid even though the title of the goods has been transferred to the buyer. If merchandise is sold under a chattel-mortgage contract, it may be *repossessed* (taken back) by the seller if the payments are not made as agreed. However, under this kind of contract, it is usually necessary to get a court order in order to regain possession of the goods.

TAYLOR APPLIANCES
LOUISVILLE, KENTUCKY

County_____Jefferson_____ State____Kentucky_____ City____Louisville____ Date___June 14, 19--

CONSIDERATION ACKNOWLEDGED. — I do hereby grant, bargain, sell, convey and confirm unto TAYLOR APPLIANCES (mortgagee) or assigns, the following described merchandise, to have and to hold said merchandise forever, provided, however, that I shall pay to the mortgagee or its assigns the full purchase price in installments on the day of each month that the installment becomes due, then this mortgage to be void.

DESCRIPTION AND TERMS

Item____Major Washer____ Serial No.__4974206KM____ Cash Purchase Price $____179.95____

_____Ajax Dryer_____ ____M01-A263____ $____129.00____

_____ $_____

Less Down Payment Received by ___Wm. L. Keel___ $____50.00____
                                        (Signature)

Balance to be paid as follows: Principal $___21.47___   BALANCE $____258.95____

                                Carrying Charges $____1.73____

                                Total $ ___23.20___ each and every month.

If I fail to make any monthly payment then all remaining installments may be declared due and payable, and upon failure to make any monthly payment, or all, if all declared due, I agree to deliver said Merchandise as described, upon demand to the Company, or its assigns, and all payments made and the used Merchandise applied on purchase as described shall be retained by said Company, or its assigns, as stipulated damages. I Further Agree to take good care of said Merchandise and to be responsible for its loss by theft, fire or other casualty, and not to remove it from

___4876 Austin Drive_____ ____Louisville_____ ____Kentucky_____ ____JA 1-9021___
      Name of Street   City   State   Tel. No.

unless I first obtain the written consent of said Company, or its assigns.

It is Understood and Agreed that no other agreement or guaranty, verbal or written, expressed or implied, shall limit or qualify the terms of this contract.

Not valid unless accepted by Dealer.

Accepted_Michael Jonas, Treasurer_ Signed _Gil E. Murray_____
                                                              Customer

Date_____June 14_____ 19--   Salesman __Wm. L. Keel___
                                                       Salesman sign here

ILLUS. 19-5. A chattel-mortgage contract.

Conditional Sales Contract. If merchandise is sold on a *conditional sales contract*, the title of the merchandise does not pass to the customer until full payment of the price has been made. This should be explained to the customer. The merchandise can be repossessed by the seller if the purchaser does not pay as agreed.

Terms of Payment. The percentage of down payment and the length of the credit term vary according to the product, the amount of the down payment, and custom. Illustration 19-7 on page 393 provides a summary of the usual percentages of down payment and the usual maximum periods for making payment for particular types of merchandise.

Installment Sales Policy. It is obvious that some kinds of merchandise, because of the amount of the sale, can be sold on installments more easily than for cash or on ordinary credit terms. However, installment selling should be confined to merchandise that does not deteriorate rapidly from age or wear. It certainly is a bad policy to sell anything on an installment contract that will be worn out before full payment is made. The following are suggested as good policies in selling any goods on an installment plan:

1. Sell the merchandise instead of the terms. If the salesman places more emphasis on the ease of buying merchandise rather than

CONDITIONAL SALES CONTRACT

<u>4580</u>
Account No.

The undersigned seller hereby sells, and the undersigned purchaser hereby purchases, subject to the terms and conditions hereinafter set forth, the following property, delivery and acceptance of which in good order is hereby acknowledged by purchaser, viz.:

DESCRIPTION	SERIAL NO.	PURCHASE PRICE
1 Norstad Radio	T-10006-31	$ 95.00
Salesman Raymond Ellis	Tax	2.85
	Total	$ 97.85

Purchaser's Down Payment .... $ 20.00

Unpaid Balance of Purchase Price .... $ 77.85

Time Price Differential .... $ 6.40

Deferred Balance of .... $ 84.25

Payable at the office of The Philip Stern Company in ___11___ installments of $ ___7.02___

each and in one final installment of $ ___7.03___, on the ___15th___ day of each month,

commencing _____June 15_____ 19___, making a total time sale price of $ __84.25__

Interest is due on installments after maturity at the highest lawful contract rate, and if this contract be placed with any attorney for collection, 15% of the amount due hereunder shall be paid by purchaser as attorney's fees, or if prohibited, the amount permitted by law.

The title in the property above described shall remain in the seller until the terms of this contract have been fully complied with. In case of any default in the performance of the terms and conditions hereof, the seller shall have the right to declare the full unpaid amount immediately due and payable and/or retake all the property. Buyer agrees not to move, sell, mortgage, encumber, pledge, or otherwise dispose of the property until paid for in full. Upon the performance by the buyer of all the conditions of this contract, title to the property is to vest in the buyer. It is mutually agreed that this instrument sets forth the entire contract.

Executed this_____23rd_____day of_____May_____19___

William Sayler	466 Elm	Canton	Michigan
(Purchaser's Signature)	(Street)	(Town)	(State)
Raymond Ellis	105 East First	Canton	Michigan
(Seller's Signature)	(Street)	(Town)	(State)
Edward Burnet		*Lawrence Davis*	
(Witness)		(Witness)	

ILLUS. 19-6. A conditional sales contract.

Product	Usual Percentage of Down Payment	Usual Time Allowed the Buyer to Pay (Months)
New automobiles	10 up	12-36
Used automobiles	10 up	12-33
Used automobiles— not late models	20 up	12-24
Mobile homes, new	10-25	12-120
Furniture	10-25	12-36
Refrigerators	5-10	18-36
Television sets	10-25	12-36
Jewelry	10-25	6-18
Men's clothing	10-25	3- 9

ILLUS. 19-7. Down payments and time allowed on installment sales.

on the need for the merchandise and its quality, he may be making a sale that will result in a dissatisfied customer.

2. Because of the extra cost of selling on an installment plan, it is necessary to price the merchandise high enough to cover all costs, including carrying charges, collection cost, interest on money invested in the merchandise, bad debt losses, cost of repossessing merchandise, and cost of reconditioning merchandise that is returned.

3. Get the highest percentage of down payment that is possible. Ten percent of the selling price is a minimum; 20 percent is very desirable; but 30 percent is better. When a customer feels that he has a relatively large amount invested in the merchandise, he is more likely to want to finish paying for it.

4. Regular payment dates, such as weekly, biweekly, or monthly, should be set; and the payments should not be spread out over any longer length of time than is absolutely necessary for the customer.

5. On installment sales of substantial amounts, such as for the sale of an automobile, it is a good practice to require the customer to buy credit life insurance, as described in Chapter 18.

6. For the protection of the dealer and the customer, the customer's ability to pay should be studied. The businessman should either adjust the payments to fit the customer's ability to pay or not sell to him.

WHOLESALE CREDIT

The credit granted by wholesalers and manufacturers is called *wholesale credit*. The very nature of the sales of manufacturers and wholesalers to retailers makes the need for some kind of credit necessary. Requiring retailers to make their purchases in cash would be very inconvenient. Wholesalers therefore usually sell *on account* (ordinary credit of 30 to 60 days) to retailers who have proved worthy of the extension of credit. The granting of credit by the wholesaler permits the retailer to purchase goods and to sell at least part of them before he is required to make payment to the wholesaler.

Manufacturers also sell equipment on long-term credit which may extend from 90 days to a year or even more. Such equipment is usually sold under some kind of installment contract.

When a businessman deals with other businesses, he has problems different from those encountered by the retail merchant who deals with individuals. An important source of information on the credit of commercial houses and manufacturers is Dun and Bradstreet, Incorporated. A book of credit ratings is published regularly by this agency and sold as a service to subscribers. The service covers the entire United States. In addition, a subscriber can obtain a special report on any businessman or professional man in any part of the country. The reliability of this agency has been established through many years of effective service to all types of businessmen and professional people.

Illustration 19-8 on page 395 shows how business firms are rated by Dun and Bradstreet. They are classified as to financial strength and credit rating. In addition, business firms are classified by a numerical system as to the type of business, such as lumber dealer, men's furnishings, and plumber.

In the Dun and Bradstreet credit rating table, *financial strength* means the amount that the business would be worth if it paid all its debts. The *composite credit appraisal* represents the general opinion of the agents of Dun and Bradstreet from all the information they have available. In checking a name in the Dun and Bradstreet reference book, if the name of the business has the marking "BB3" after it, the "BB" means that the financial strength is between $200,000 and $300,000 and the "3" means that the credit rating is fair. These two items of information are given on the same line across the page of the key. If the name of the business has just a single numeral "2" after it, the financial strength is estimated to be $20,000 to $125,000, and on this basis one must determine how much credit to extend.

KEY TO RATINGS U.S. AND CANADA

Estimated Financial Strength			Composite Credit Appraisal			
			HIGH	GOOD	FAIR	LIMITED
5A	Over	$50,000,000	1	2	3	4
4A	$10,000,000 to	50,000,000	1	2	3	4
3A	1,000,000 to	10,000,000	1	2	3	4
2A	750,000 to	1,000,000	1	2	3	4
1A	500,000 to	750,000	1	2	3	4
BA	300,000 to	500,000	1	2	3	4
BB	200,000 to	300,000	1	2	3	4
CB	125,000 to	200,000	1	2	3	4
CC	75,000 to	125,000	1	2	3	4
DC	50,000 to	75,000	1	2	3	4
DD	35,000 to	50,000	1	2	3	4
EE	20,000 to	35,000	1	2	3	4
FF	10,000 to	20,000	1	2	3	4
GG	5,000 to	10,000	1	2	3	4
HH	Up to	5,000	1	2	3	4

CLASSIFICATION FOR BOTH ESTIMATED
FINANCIAL STRENGTH AND CREDIT APPRAISAL

Financial Strength Bracket		Explanation
1-	$125,000 and Over	When only the numeral (1 or 2) appears, it is an indication that the estimated financial strength, while not definitely classified, is presumed to be within the range of the ($) figures in the corresponding bracket and that a condition is believed to exist which warrants credit in keeping with that assumption.
2-	20,000 to 125,000	

NOT CLASSIFIED OR ABSENCE OF RATING

The absence of a rating, expressed by two hyphens (–), is not to be construed as unfavorable but signifies circumstances difficult to classify within condensed rating symbols. It suggests the advisability of obtaining a report for additional information.

ILLUS. 19-8. Dun and Bradstreet credit ratings.

Some of the main sources of credit information used by a business when it checks the credit of other businesses are as follows:

1. Dun and Bradstreet.
2. National Association of Credit Management (Credit Interchange).
3. Special credit agencies operated by trade associations of which the business is a member.
4. Information collected by the firm's own salesmen.
5. Information secured from banks.
6. Financial statements and other information obtained directly from the customer.
7. Confidential information obtained from other businessmen dealing with the same customers.

In evaluating a business for the purpose of granting credit, information must be taken into consideration besides the ordinary facts that may show up in credit reports. Some of this information is available in certain types of credit reports or special investigations. For instance, one of the services of certain credit agencies is to furnish special reports based on special investigations and covering such topics as those summarized in Illustration 19-9.

1. Willingness and general attitude of customer in submitting complete credit and financial information.

2. Reputation in the business, living standards, habits, and competency of the owner and manager.

3. Fire risks and other hazards of the business and the proper insurance coverage.

4. The history of any previous bankruptcy or receivership.

5. The nature of present or previous lawsuits against the business, the history of any previous fire losses, and settlements with insurance companies.

6. The nature of the business, as to its stability and competition.

ILLUS. 19-9. Factors to investigate in evaluating a business for the purpose of granting credit.

REVIEW WHAT YOU HAVE LEARNED

Business Terms Checkup:

(1) retail credit
(2) short-term credit
(3) cycle billing
(4) long-term credit
(5) installment contract
(6) revolving credit or planned credit
(7) three C's
(8) character
(9) capacity
(10) capital

(11) mercantile
(12) retail
(13) security agreement
(14) chattel-mortgage contract
(15) repossessed
(16) conditional sales contract
(17) wholesale credit
(18) on account
(19) financial strength
(20) composite credit appraisal

Reading Checkup:

1. Is an installment contract considered to be short-term credit or long-term credit?

2. What are the generally accepted terms of credit on open accounts in retail stores?

3. What are some of the advantages that a merchant derives from extending credit?

4. Name some disadvantages to the merchant of extending retail credit.

5. Explain the meaning of capacity in relation to credit.

6. In extending mercantile and retail credit, what kind of credit information is ranked first in importance by credit managers?

7. Name the sources of credit information that a retail merchant may use.

8. Explain the credit interchange service of the National Association of Credit Management.

9. Refer to the report of the National Association of Credit Management, page 387. Indicate how many firms are selling to this customer on COD terms; indicate how many firms report this customer as being 30 to 60 days slow in paying.

10. What are the four main types of credit and collection policies?

11. Examine the list of recommended credit policies on pages 388-390. How much is recommended as a minimum down payment on installment sales?

12. If you look in a Dun and Bradstreet credit rating book and find the name of a business marked with the symbols CC2, what does this information indicate?

APPLY WHAT YOU HAVE LEARNED

Questions for Class Discussion:

1. What advantage is there for a business to adopt cycle billing?

2. What advantages are there for a small business to sell on credit by using a national credit system such as BankAmericard or Master Charge?

3. In the case of a new business, explain why character might be more important than capital in extending credit.

4. What is the importance of having a uniform community credit policy?

5. What is meant by the statement, "Credit develops permanent customers"?

6. Why do you think a seller is justified in charging interest on a past-due account?

7. Suggest what may be some of the dangers of extending installment credit payments over too long a period.

8. What are some of the dangers of requiring no down payment, or a very small down payment, on installment sales?

9. In this chapter there are four fundamental sources of credit information that are listed for retail stores. Which of these sources do you think will provide the best credit information?

10. If you as an individual move from one city to another, how is it possible for a retail store in the second city to obtain information on your credit record?

11. In extending credit to a business firm, of what importance would you consider the willingness or lack of willingness of the customer to submit complete credit and financial information?

12. What would you do as a businessman if your customer pays you very slowly and you find that his credit rating and credit reputation rank very high?

Problems and Projects:

1. The Washington Department Store has sold a refrigerator for $298. The customer has made a down payment of 10 percent and is to pay the balance in 12 monthly installments.

   (a) Compute the unpaid balance after the down payment.
   (b) Compute the equal monthly installments.
   (c) If the department store sells the contract to the Universal Finance Company at a discount of 5 percent, what will the store receive for the contract?

2. The Ace Appliance Store sold an electric range on the installment plan. The price of the range is $300. An old range was traded in for an allowance of $30. A down payment of 10 percent of the amount of the sale (the selling price less the trade-in allowance) is required.

   (a) Compute the unpaid balance, taking into account the trade-in allowance and the down payment.
   (b) Add 5 percent to the amount of the unpaid balance to take care of the extra costs of selling the range on the installment plan. Compute the amount of each installment payment, assuming there will be 12 equal installments.

3. Make an investigation in your community to find out the procedures that retailers must follow to obtain credit from wholesalers and manufacturers from whom they buy. Write a report of your findings.

4. In most communities the credit policies of retail stores are reasonably uniform. They often are established by the Retail Credit Bureau, if there is one. Investigate the policies in your community in regard to extending retail credit. Write a report on these policies as to amount of credit

allowed, kinds of investigations made, credit information that must be furnished, payment period, and other policies.

5. Tom Howard is starting a retail carpet and rug store and decides to give credit to his customers. He estimates the following costs of selling on credit during the first year: salary of bookkeeper, $5,200; losses on bad debts, $1,600; stationery, business forms, postage, etc., $3,000; depreciation of office equipment needed, $120. He estimated the total sales for the year will be $100,000.

(a) What is the total of estimated expenses for selling on credit?

(b) What percent of the estimated sales are the estimated expenses related to credit sales?

(c) The selling price of the merchandise sold on credit should be what percent larger than if it were sold for cash?

Case Problem 19-1:

The Star Department Store is located in a city where all the other merchants have followed a policy of granting credit on a very careful and strict basis and using strict collection procedures. The owners of the Star Department Store decide to follow a new policy which is advertised as "no down payment; liberal credit extended; 12 months to pay."

Required:

1. What kind of customers are most likely to be attracted?
2. What will happen to sales?
3. Explain any dangers that may be involved.

Case Problem 19-2:

The Hyde Park Store is experiencing increased competition because other stores are selling on the installment plan without any down payment and are extending longer terms of credit. The manager feels he must do something to meet competition by (a) doing the same as his competitors or (b) reducing Hyde Park's finance charges.

Required:

1. What would you do?
2. Why?

Continuing Project:

Establish credit plans, procedures, and policies for your business and indicate why you have selected these particular plans, procedures, and policies.

What steps should be taken to collect an unpaid account?

Can a business take back goods if the bill for them is not paid?

What is garnishment?

What is a statute of limitations?

What are the types of bankruptcy?

Is a man responsible for his wife's debts?

BACKGROUND OF CHAPTER

The study of credit in Chapter 19 is closely related to the study of collections. Good collection policies and procedures may make the difference between the success or failure of a business. If collections are not made properly and promptly, the business will not have the money with which to operate, and customers may get into the habit of not paying their bills. Proper handling of collections is also extremely important to a business in building and holding the goodwill of customers. Collections must be managed as carefully as any other function of the business.

This chapter will explain policies, procedures, and practices in collection.

CHAPTER 20

COLLECTION POLICIES AND PROCEDURES

Any business which extends credit to its customers is concerned with losses from debts that are not collected. Surveys show that the losses from uncollected debts usually range from 0.5 to 1.5 percent of net sales. In some businesses there are practically no bad-debt losses; in others the losses run rather high. Most of the open-credit losses do not exceed 1 percent of the net sales, whereas many of the installment credit losses often exceed 4 percent of the net sales.

The extent to which a business has losses from uncollected debts is related to its basic credit and collection policies. As is discussed in Chapter 19, the basic types of credit and collection policies followed by businesses are:

1. Liberal credit is granted with a liberal treatment in collections.
2. Liberal credit is granted but with strict collection policies.
3. Strict credit is granted, but collection policies are liberal.
4. The granting of credit is strict and the collection policies are strict.

In order to minimize losses from uncollected debts, the basic credit and collection policies of a business must be supported by effective collection procedures.

COLLECTION PROCEDURES

The person who has charge of making collections should bear in mind the two major objectives of the collection procedure: first, to get the money and, second, to retain the goodwill and patronage of the customer. When one considers the second objective, it is evident that much tact is necessary in making collections.

The usual collection procedures include the sending of a statement each month followed by impersonal reminders, first reminding the customer that the amount is past due and then asking why payment has not been made. Eventually, a letter must be written indicating that no further credit can be extended until the account has been paid or other arrangements have been made. At this stage it is important to talk with the customer to find out what the problem is.

All honest persons who cannot pay debts when due are embarrassed and worried. As long as there is a desire and a willingness to pay, there should be a frank discussion to work out a payment plan. Part of the fault may come from the fact that too much credit was extended too easily. This is as much the fault of the seller as it is of the buyer.

If the customer wants to pay but cannot pay, it is necessary to work out some kind of deferred-payment plan that will enable him to pay. If the customer cannot pay and there does not appear to be

ILLUS. 20-1. Extravagant and thoughtless purchases on account may prove to be uncollectible.

any chance in the future that he will be able to pay, there may be little practical choice except to cancel the charge and to write it off as a loss.

Collections on installment accounts are usually handled in the same manner as the collection of other accounts. If it is found that the customer is willing to pay but cannot pay the monthly installments as originally agreed, it is wise to arrange for a new agreement with smaller payments. The last recourse is to repossess the merchandise, as described later in this chapter.

A fundamental fact that affects the procedures followed in collecting past-due accounts is that the longer the account is overdue, the less are the chances for collecting the money owed. Illustration 20-2 indicates, for accounts which are unpaid for varying lengths of time, the degree to which it is likely that the accounts will be paid. The data given in Illustration 20-2 are based on the experiences of retail stores.

Age of Account	Possibility of Collecting
60 days or more	90%
6 months or more	50%
12 months or more	30%
24 months or more	25%
36 months or more	15%
5 years	almost none

ILLUS. 20-2. Possibility of collecting past-due accounts.

Example of a Collection Sequence

The preceding discussion has pointed out some general procedures in collection. Each businessman must develop a specific procedure of his own. Ordinarily, the type of procedure used must be varied according to whether the person is "slow pay" or "good pay." Special cases require individual handling. The following is an example of a collection sequence used in a business:

1. An invoice is issued at the time the order is filled.

2. A statement is mailed at the end of the month during which the sale was made.

3. A statement is mailed at the end of the second month. Some companies follow a practice of attaching to the statement or

typing on it some comment, such as "Now due" or "Just a friendly reminder that your account is now due."

4. A statement with a typewritten comment such as the following is mailed on the 15th day of the third month: "Did you overlook paying this amount, which is 45 days overdue?" or "Past due. No doubt payment has been overlooked."

5. A statement with a sticker pasted on it containing a comment such as the following is mailed at the end of the third month: "You must have overlooked this amount because it is 60 days overdue." (Illustration 20-3 shows some collection stickers which might be used.)

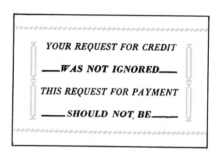

ILLUS. 20-3. Collection stickers.

6. If there is no response, a telephone call may be effective to find out the trouble and to suggest that the customer come in for a friendly discussion of the problem.

7. On the 15th day of the fourth month, a brief friendly letter is written calling attention to the amount due and the length of the overdue period. The letter should point out the advantages

of making prompt payment and remind the customer of his obligations.

The following is an example of an appropriate letter:

> Dear Mrs. Kraft
>
> You have overlooked paying your account of $98.50. Our credit terms are 30 days, and your account is now four months overdue. We are sure that you appreciate your credit privileges, and we appreciate your business.
>
> Please make payment promptly so that we can continue to extend credit to you.
>
> Sincerely yours

8. At the end of each 15 days thereafter, another letter is written, each letter becoming stronger in its demand for payment. The first letter of the series, however, is personally dictated and discusses the whole matter.

The following is a typical example of one of the collection letters in this series:

> Dear Mrs. Kraft
>
> We should like to keep your credit account open so that you can make purchases. However, we have instructed our credit department that no more credit purchases can be made on your account until you settle your balance of $98.50, which is now six months overdue.
>
> We urge you to call or come in so that we can discuss this matter with you. If there is any misunderstanding or any question about your account, please let us know.
>
> Sincerely yours

9. If no collection has been obtained after a reasonable length of time, a letter is written stating that the account will be placed in the hands of a collection agency. If such a threat is made, it should be carried out.

The following is a typical letter for this purpose:

Dear Mrs. Kraft

We have always valued you as a customer, and we want you to continue to be a customer. However, we have sent you a total of ten notices of a past-due account of $98.50, which is now eight months overdue. To protect your own credit standing in the community, you should pay this amount promptly and reestablish your credit.

It is still not too late; but unless we hear from you within ten days, we shall place your account in the hands of a collection agency.

Sincerely yours

A certified letter may be sent with a request for a receipt for the delivery of the letter to be returned by the U.S. Postal Service. This will prevent the customer from having the excuse that he did not receive a notice. This method can also be used to secure the address of a customer who has moved and has failed to give his new address.

Of course, if a partial payment is made or some agreement is reached, the collection procedure is stopped. A new similar series is started, however, if payment is not made according to the agreement. The collection procedure that has been explained is a relatively mild procedure. In most businesses the procedure is more forceful.

Final Drastic Steps

Credit and collection policies must be enforced. However, before any drastic steps are taken, the collection manager must determine whether the customer cannot pay or will not pay. If he cannot pay, it is a waste of time and expense to try to force payment. If a customer can pay but simply will not pay, it is then necessary to take whatever steps are necessary to collect the amount due.

Collectors are frequently engaged in collecting installment or contract accounts, but they sometimes create ill will. Past-due accounts may be turned over to a collection agency or sold to the agency. Such a procedure may result, however, in ill will because the businessman is at the mercy of the collection agency in handling the matter.

A lawyer may be employed to write letters as a last appeal, threatening to begin legal proceedings for collection. In some cases he may actually begin such proceedings. If a suit is brought against a debtor,

1. The older an account becomes, the harder it is to collect it.
2. If a business fails to collect accounts promptly, some customers will buy elsewhere because they will be ashamed to return until their accounts are paid.
3. Carrying unpaid accounts for a long time increases the cost of operating the business.
4. Customers tend to have respect for the businessman who has a courteous but systematic method of handling the collections according to agreements.
5. If all customers are treated essentially alike, good customers realize that they are not being penalized because of other customers who are slow in paying.
6. Failure to have a prompt and effective system will encourage customers to become slow in paying.
7. Continuous bad practice as a result of not having a system will increase bad-debt losses.

ILLUS. 20-4. Reasons for a systematic follow-up of unpaid accounts.

it may be possible to have the court attach some of his personal property and hold it until the debt is paid or to sell the property to satisfy the debt. If the debtor does not have enough money or property to be attached, the businessman may bring a lawsuit to obtain a *judgment* whereby the debtor is ordered to pay the debt whenever he gets sufficient money.

Special agencies, such as Dun and Bradstreet, Incorporated, the National Association of Credit Management, and credit bureaus, have services through which accounts can be collected.

Some businessmen follow the procedure of drawing a sight draft on a delinquent customer for the amount of the account. (A *delinquent customer* is one whose payments are overdue.) The draft is given to a bank, and the customer is requested to pay the draft to the bank that presents it for collection. Should he fail to pay the draft, his credit standing with the bank will be lessened.

Many firms follow a practice of trying to get the customer to sign a promissory note (or a series of notes payable at regular intervals) when an account has become past due. It is legitimate to expect a person to pay interest on this note. A promissory note is legally a little easier to collect than an account, and sometimes a note may be discounted at the bank.

Some customers who owe accounts may not have the money but expect to have it in the future. In such cases it is sometimes desirable to ask for a *postdated check*. This is simply a check dated ahead to a time when a customer knows he will have some money in the bank. If a postdated check is obtained, it is a good policy to deposit it promptly on the date indicated on the check before the funds are withdrawn. Accepting a postdated check is not a very desirable practice, but sometimes it is the only way to get money from a customer.

One who receives a check that he believes is a bad check or drawn on insufficient funds will save a lot of trouble by sending it directly to the customer's bank for payment rather than depositing it in his own bank.

Repossession of Property

When merchandise is sold on open account but is not paid for, the only way that a merchant can protect himself is to sue for the amount of the debt. If merchandise is sold under a conditional sales contract, the title to the merchandise does not pass to the customer until full payment of the price has been made. The merchandise therefore still remains the property of the seller and can be repossessed by him. If merchandise has been sold under a chattel-mortgage contract, the seller has to go through definite legal proceedings to regain its possession.

In many states a customer may not lose all if he has paid a substantial part of the purchase price at the time the goods are repossessed. For example, if the unpaid balance is $50 and the goods are repossessed and sold for $150, the customer is entitled to some return of his payments if money remains after deductions have been made for service charges, interest, and other expenses.

On the other hand, the customer may owe additional payments. For example, assume that the amount owed is $250 and the goods are sold for only $150 after being repossessed. In this case the seller may get a court order, called a *deficiency judgment*, requiring the customer to pay $100 plus any other expenses involved.

Garnishment

If a debtor refuses to pay, the creditor may in most states bring a legal action to force the payment of the debt. By an order of a court, the employer of the debtor may be required to pay to the creditor a certain percentage of the debtor's wages until the amount of the debt or the amount specified by the court has been paid. This procedure is called the *garnishment,* or *garnisheeing,* of wages. The laws on garnisheeing wages vary in the different states. In some states only a certain percentage of a person's wages can be collected in this way. In other states a worker cannot be forced to pay small debts through the garnishment process.

Guaranteed Accounts

When it is difficult for a person to establish credit, some merchants require the customer to get some responsible person to guarantee that the account will be paid. If the account is not paid by the customer, the guarantor can be held legally responsible for paying it. The form in Illustration 20-5 shows the kind of contract used for such a purpose.

GUARANTY OF ACCOUNT

In consideration of The Merriman Builders' Supply Company, Augusta, Maine, granting credit for merchandise purchased or to be purchased by or on the account of ...... James Esterbrook ....

.... at present residing at ...... 161 Belle Avenue ....

.... Augusta, Maine ...., to an amount not exceeding

.... Twenty-Five .... Dollars per month, I hereby agree to become responsible as surety for the payment of and will pay on demand said monthly accounts. Notice of separate transactions is waived. This surety is to continue from month to month until revoked by me in writing and the account due thereon is settled in full to date of receipt of said notice of revocation.

Augusta, Maine ...... December 8, ...19 ..... _William Stiles_
Signature of Guarantor

Witness: _Henry Dodson_ .... 980 Terrace Park, Augusta, Maine
Address of Guarantor

Property Owned by Guarantor ...... House and lot at 980 Terrace Park, Augusta, Maine

---

ILLUS. 20-5. A guaranty of account.

Recording Credit History of Customers

Every businessman should be very cautious in extending credit. A convenient record of the credit history of every customer should be kept. This record should show the credit experience of the business in dealings with the customer, as well as information obtained from outside sources. A card is often used for this purpose. It may contain space for indicating the dates on which statements and collection letters are sent.

After there has been enough experience with customers, they should be classified as (a) prompt pay, (b) slow pay but good, (c) slow pay but doubtful, and (d) bad pay. Those in the first two groups should be treated with more consideration than those in the last two. For the former, the collection process should be drawn out longer. Those at the lower end of the scale should be handled with more firmness and promptness so that they will not become too far in arrears (payment overdue). Every account should be studied carefully from time to time to be sure it is classified properly.

Analyzing Accounts Receivable

In every business it is important to watch *accounts receivable* (the debts or money owed to the business) in order that their total does not get out of proportion to the amount of credit sales. For example, if credit sales are not increasing but accounts receivable are gradually growing larger each month, an effort should be made to collect the accounts more efficiently.

The total of accounts receivable may not show the true picture of conditions. For instance, an analysis of the accounts receivable may show that most of them are only 30 or 60 days old, while only a few are 90 days old or older. The situation may therefore not be particularly alarming. On the other hand, if an analysis of the accounts receivable shows that most of them are 90 days old or older, it may prove necessary to have some of the customers sign notes, to place some accounts with a collection agency, to start lawsuits for collection of some accounts, and to strengthen and speed up the collection procedure generally so that accounts in the future will not become so old.

The most common method of studying accounts receivable is often referred to as *aging the accounts*. The form in Illustration 20-6 is an example of the type of analysis that can be used to show the true situation. The following is an explanation of the analysis of accounts receivable: The amounts owed by the Adams-Jones Company and the Artwell Company have not been due 30 days. However, in the case of Brown and Brown, $27.41 has been due for a period of more than 60 days but less than 90 days; an amount of $40 has been due for a period of more than 30 days but less than 60 days; an amount of $52.50 has been due less than 30 days. The amount due from

ANALYSIS OF ACCOUNTS RECEIVABLE						
Date January 2, 19—						
Name and Address	1 to 30 Days	30 to 60 Days	60 to 90 Days	Over 90 Days	Total	Explanation
Adams—Jones Company, Cincinnati, Ohio...	$235.00				$235.00	
Artwell Company, Chicago, Illinois..	$426.51				$426.51	
Brown and Brown, Gary, Indiana......	$ 52.50	$40.00	$27.41		$119.91	They wrote "will clear up account this month."
A. Davis, Inc. Detroit, Michigan..				$175.00	$175.00	Account in hands of attorney.
Custer Stores, Granville, Ohio....			$76.06		$ 76.06	Now on C.O.D. basis.

ILLUS. 20-6. An analysis of accounts receivable.

A. Davis, Inc., has been due more than 90 days. The amount owed by Custer Stores has been due more than 60 days but less than 90 days.

A second method of analyzing accounts receivable is to determine what percentage of the accounts outstanding is collected each month. For example, if the total amount outstanding is $10,000 and collections are $8,000, 80 percent of the accounts receivable have been collected.

A third method of measuring the efficiency of collections is to compute the percentage of delinquent accounts in relation to the total outstanding accounts. For example, if 10 percent of the accounts in January are delinquent, 15 percent are delinquent in February, and 20 percent are delinquent in March, this is an unfavorable trend.

A fourth method of determining the efficiency of collecting accounts is to compute the bad-debt losses. Remember that bad-debt losses run from less than 1 percent of the net sales to a high of usually not more than 5 percent of the net sales.

COLLECTION LIMITATIONS

A business trying to collect a past-due account may find its collection procedures legally restricted. For example, a state's statute of limitations can prevent a business from collecting the money due it.

Statute of Limitations

Nearly every state has a law commonly known as the *statute of limitations*. Under this law the debtor cannot be forced to pay after the expiration of a certain period of time unless the debt has been partially paid or otherwise *reinstated* (put back in effect) during that period. For instance, the law in most states makes it impossible to bring a court action to collect a debt after four years from the date of the sale. The seller can, if possible, collect the debt after that time; but he cannot resort to court action in doing so. Perhaps during the period allowed by the statute of limitations, the seller has obtained an additional *acknowledgment* of the debt—an admission that the debt is owed or that it will be paid. If so, the time allowed by the statute begins again from the date on which the debt was reinstated by the acknowledgment.

There are various ways of reinstating an account by acknowledgment. For instance, a partial payment reinstates an account in most states. A written acknowledgment, or a new promise to pay, reinstates accounts in most states; and an oral acknowledgment or promise is sufficient in a few states.

Bankruptcy

Bankruptcy proceedings, either voluntary or involuntary, are at times the last resort for a debtor unable to pay his bills or for a creditor unable to collect from the debtor.

Voluntary Bankruptcy. A debtor, except a municipal, railroad, insurance, or banking corporation, or a savings and loan association, may voluntarily apply to the proper court for release from debts on a plea of bankruptcy. This is called *voluntary bankruptcy.* If the court finds that the debtor is incapable of paying his debts, it may discharge him from any claims as a result of his old debts. The assets owned by the debtor (with the exception of certain exempt assets) must, however, be used to pay as large a part of the outstanding debts as possible. For instance, a person may voluntarily petition the court to declare himself bankrupt, but the court may discover that he has assets of $525 and debts of $3,000. The court will allow him to retain certain assets of a minimum amount, possibly $150; but the remaining assets, equal to $375, must be distributed among his creditors, who hold the claims totaling $3,000. If there are several creditors, they may not all get a part of the assets because some of the creditors may have a higher *priority* (a claim ranking ahead of others). This may leave little or nothing for some of the unsecured creditors.

ILLUS. 20-7. Newspaper item announcing the filing of a bankruptcy petition.

Partners File in Bankruptcy

A bankruptcy petition was filed yesterday in U.S. District Court for Jeffrey A. Brinkley, 4456 Savannah Ave., and Donald Stevenson, 887 Georgetown Rd., partners in the Apex Mobile Home Co., from June, 1969, to August, 1973. Debts were listed at $175,496, with $1,044 being in taxes, and assets at $1,823. Two addresses, 9233 Springdale Rd., and 4624 Beckett Rd., were given for the firm which was in the mobile home sales and trailer park development and operation business. A total of 80 creditors were listed.

A debtor may file with the court a petition requesting the court to arrange for the settlement or the satisfaction of an unsecured debt, or the extension of the time for payment of such a debt. A debtor may also petition a court for an arrangement affecting debts secured by real estate or chattels (such as equipment and livestock). The filing of a petition with a court does not make the debtor a bankrupt. In other words, the court has the power to decide upon a proper settlement or extension of the terms. Under the same law the court is given broad authority to halt or delay actions for the collection of debts and the foreclosure of mortgages.

Involuntary Bankruptcy. Creditors sometimes force a debtor into bankruptcy in order to collect their claims. This is called *involuntary bankruptcy*. They believe that, if they allow the debtor to continue his business, he will go more deeply into debt and will dissipate or waste whatever assets are available; but if they force him into bankruptcy, they may collect at least part of their claims before it is too late. This process is therefore a means of protection to the creditors. When involuntary bankruptcy proceedings are started, the creditors assume that they will lose less by forcing the debtor into bankruptcy than they would if they allowed him to continue to operate his business. It is impossible for creditors to file an involuntary bankruptcy petition against a wage earner, a farmer, a municipality, a railroad, an insurance company, a bank, or a savings and loan association.

Responsibility for Debts

Every individual or businessman should have a sufficient knowledge of law to be familiar with his own responsibilities and the responsibilities of those with whom he deals. For instance, it is important to know to what extent a husband is responsible for his wife's debts. Let us assume, by way of illustration, that a young married woman opened charge accounts in two stores. Her purchases of household necessities amounted to $150. The husband refused to pay the debts. The stores could sue for the collection of these debts because in most states the wife has an implied authority to pledge her husband's credit for necessities of the household.

On the other hand, the husband may give a legal written notice that he will not be responsible for his wife's debts. He may publish the announcement in a newspaper or may write a notice to the various retail stores with which his wife has charge accounts.

Parents are not responsible for debts incurred by minor children in purchasing luxuries or other unnecessary articles. The laws of most states do place responsibility upon parents for the payment of debts incurred by children in purchasing the necessities of life. In most states, however, a parent cannot be held responsible if a minor child, without the parent's permission, purchases goods or services not necessary for preserving the life or the health of the child. A businessman should therefore always be cautious in dealing with minors.

REVIEW WHAT YOU HAVE LEARNED

Business Terms Checkup:

(1) judgment

(2) delinquent customer

(3) postdated check

(4) deficiency judgment

(5) garnishment or garnisheeing

(6) accounts receivable

(7) aging the accounts

(8) statute of limitations

(9) reinstated

(10) acknowledgment

(11) voluntary bankruptcy

(12) priority

(13) involuntary bankruptcy

Reading Checkup:

1. What is the average amount of loss from bad debts?

2. In granting liberal credit, what two choices of collection policies may be applied?

3. What is the first step usually followed in collection procedures?

4. If the customer is willing to pay but cannot pay, what collection procedures should be followed?

5. Name at least the first four steps in a typical collection sequence.

6. Give at least three reasons for using a systematic follow-up system for collecting accounts.

7. If a customer has owed an amount for some time, what is the advantage of having the customer sign a note promising to pay this amount?

8. What procedure must a seller follow to obtain repossession of property sold under a chattel-mortgage contract which has not been paid for according to the agreement?

9. Explain the process of collecting money by garnisheeing wages.

10. If a person guarantees an account of a friend, what obligation does that person assume?

11. What are the common ways of classifying customers as to their bill payment habits?

12. What should be done if the aging of accounts receivable indicates that many accounts have been past due for a long period of time?

13. Explain how a statute of limitations operates.

14. Name and explain briefly the two types of bankruptcy.

15. What types of individuals or organizations may apply to a court for voluntary bankruptcy?

16. Does a wife have legal authority to buy merchandise on account and obligate her husband for the debt?

APPLY WHAT YOU HAVE LEARNED

Questions for Class Discussion:

1. What collection procedure would you recommend be followed for a customer who has a reputation in the community of not paying until there is a threat of a lawsuit or action by a collection agency?

2. What collection policy would you follow in regard to a customer who has good character, adequate capital, and adequate earning capacity but is very slow in paying?

3. How would your collection procedure for a customer be affected if a customer makes a part payment of the account?

4. What are some of the disadvantages of repossessing property when an installment account is not paid?

5. Why is it recommended that before drastic action is taken in collecting an account, there should be a discussion with the customer?

6. Why do states have a law limiting the time in which one must start a lawsuit to collect a debt?

7. Assume that in your state the statute of limitations outlaws the collection of a debt after four years from the date the debt was incurred. What should you, as a businessman, do to be sure that your debt does not become uncollectible?

8. You are one of three creditors of a person in bankruptcy who owes you $400. What are your chances of being paid, and to what extent, if the total assets of this individual amount to $600 and the total claims of the creditors amount to $3,200?

9. If a youth 15 years of age arranged with you to open an account to charge his purchases at your record shop, could you collect these debts from his parents?

Problems and Projects:

1. Assume that you are the owner of a retail clothing store and that you have five customers who have ordinarily paid regularly at the end of 30

days when the statements of their accounts have been mailed. At the end of 60 days these accounts have not been paid. You decide that some kind of special message should be sent with next month's statements. Indicate what you would attach to each statement, write on it, or include in a separate letter.

2. Frank Stein is the credit manager of the Sayre Department Store. He has tried over a period of a year to collect a long overdue account of $225 from Dan Worthington. The best he has been able to do is get a few small payments on account, but the account balance is still $190. In exasperation at the long delay, he wrote a letter containing the following closing statement: "We regret that our business relationship must be terminated and that we can no longer permit you to make any purchases in our store."

(a) Was this decision by the credit manager a wise one to make?

(b) What other steps could have been taken first?

(c) If all other steps had been taken and a decision had then been reached to deny further credit, what door should have been left open for future purchasing by the customer?

3. Assume that you have been hired as the credit and collection manager of the Midwest Wholesale Hardware Company. You have been hired because the former credit manager has just retired and the owners of the business have discovered that there are many overdue accounts because of a poor collection system.

(a) Prepare a detailed plan and schedule for the mailing of invoices, notices, and collection letters. Indicate at what stage the collections will be turned over to a collection agency or a lawyer.

(b) Write the notices that will be sent out and the models of collection letters.

4. The average annual sales of the Whitman Appliance Store on the installment plan amount to $20,000. In selling on the installment plan, the store includes in the financing charges an amount of 10 percent above the cash sale price. Some of the appliances must be repossessed and then sold secondhand. The average annual losses and costs of repossession and selling the appliances secondhand are $1,300. As compared with selling on a cash basis, are the installment sales as profitable or less profitable and to what extent?

Case Problem 20-1:

Ludington purchased from Williamson an appliance store, including all accounts receivable and all other debts due the store. Ludington immediately made a study of the debts due the business and discovered that many payments were long overdue because of the poor collection methods of Williamson.

Required:

1. What do you think should be the first steps taken by Ludington?

2. What should Ludington do in regard to the customers who fail to respond to normal collection procedures?

3. What should Ludington do with those customers who can pay but will not pay?

4. What should Ludington do with the customers who are not able to pay?

Case Problem 20-2:

Richards, who had had eight years of experience as a mechanic, planned his business venture quite carefully. He and his wife had saved $9,000, and he waited until he found what he considered an almost ideal location for a service station. Richards bought all new equipment for which he paid $7,000 in cash. With $2,000 left for working capital, he was very confident that he would succeed.

Richards has now been in business for 13 months, and sales have increased every month. Although all of his bills are paid, the financial condition of the business is not as good as the sales record indicates; for much of the capital is tied up in accounts receivable which Richards cannot collect. Despite his intentions of selling only for cash, Richards is soft-hearted and has been extending credit.

Required:

On the basis of the experience which Richards has had in operating his business for 13 months, what actions should he take?

Continuing Project:

Establish plans for the collection procedure and policies of your business firm. Give the reasons for your policies.

CAREERS IN FINANCE

Anyone seeking a career in finance will find numerous opportunities in the various types of financial institutions, such as banks and insurance companies. Many other opportunities in finance exist within departments of business organizations which are not financial institutions.

Banking positions. Bank jobs range from that of the lowest paid clerk to that of bank president. Duties of bank employees include clearing checks, transferring currency, lending money to individuals and businesses, keeping securities and other valuables in safe-deposit boxes, making investments, and administering estates. Clerks of various types, interviewers and investigators of loan applicants, tellers, stenographers, secretaries, bookkeepers, cashiers, and accountants are needed to perform these duties.

Insurance Positions. The greatest career opportunities in insurance may be found in jobs with insurance companies. There are many types of jobs available, such as the actuary who determines insurance rates, the salesman who renders a service by selling the proper kind of insurance needed by business, the adjuster who settles claims, the operator who runs a computer, the manager who runs an office, and a great variety of clerks and supervisors.

The insurance problems of a small business are usually handled by the owner. In a large business insurance is handled by one of the officers, frequently the treasurer or some person responsible to the treasurer.

The insurance program of a business is extremely important. Insurance must be adequate, but it is wasteful to carry too much insurance or the wrong kind of insurance. The insurance program should be studied frequently and investigations should be made to see if the right kind of coverage is being purchased and whether it is being obtained at the most reasonable cost. A duplication of coverage should be avoided. In large businesses there are employees who have the responsibility for studying the insurance and being sure that payments are made and policies are renewed.

There are some specialists in insurance who make a business of studying the insurance programs of businesses and making recommendations.

Credit and Collection Positions. There are many opportunities in credit work. In a credit department of a business, one can specialize in checking credit applications to determine if people can and will pay their debts. In a business firm there are also jobs of credit interviewer, credit investigator, and credit clerk who records and makes information available quickly when needed. Credit manager is the top job in this field.

Except in large businesses, credit and collections are handled by the same staff. However, when the work is divided, there are specialists who age the accounts, call accounts to the attention of the credit and collection manager, send notices and letters as instructed, and handle the incoming payments. In some offices there are investigators and collectors.

Insurance companies, banks, and loan companies also have credit departments. In a credit agency one will have an opportunity to collect and record credit information about many buyers and borrowers and will make this information available to members of the agency.

Educational and Personal Qualifications. The individual who hopes to advance to a responsible position in the field of finance must secure a good understanding of economics, business management, finance, accounting, and law, plus special subjects related to a particular field of finance.

On-the-job training is available in almost all aspects of finance. A beginner must start in a job and then begin to learn all about the business. Special training courses are also available to employees in finance. These include special programs in banking, insurance, credit and collections, and almost all other phases of finance.

All jobs in finance require absolute honesty, accuracy, and dependability. Those engaged in credit and collection procedures must be especially courteous, tactful, and patient in their dealings with customers.

UNIT VI
Managing
Information

What is an information system?

How is data processing a part of an information system?

What are the functions of electronic data processing equipment?

How is a flow chart used?

Are speed and accuracy the only reasons for automating an activity?

Are management decisions a result or cause of the information system?

BACKGROUND OF CHAPTER

As business and industry move into the mid- and late-70's, there will be greater need for information relating to business activity. Data will be processed faster and more accurately for those firms that understand the workings of an information system.

Manual and mechanical tools used in processing data join with more advanced equipment in achieving an operative information system.

This chapter will discuss methods of designing an information system and the tools used in data processing activities.

CHAPTER 21

INFORMATION SYSTEMS — DATA PROCESSING

A business relies on information to make significant decisions in its operations. Regardless of the size of the business, the flow of information to owners and managers is a constant need if the management is to operate the business in its most efficient manner.

Data is raw information which, when combined with other information, becomes a useful tool of management. Processing of data is not a new concept. Only the methods used to process data are undergoing change. Compared with some of the techniques of today, the methods used in the past seem very slow and time-consuming. Business entries and transactions were recorded by a person using a pen or some mechanical means. Today, those transactions are recorded and processed quickly with the help of new types of electronic equipment.

NEED FOR AN INFORMATION SYSTEM

In the business world of today, transactions must be made and summarized faster because of the increasing population and the greater number of transactions. In modern banks, for example, the millions of checks and other instruments handled require speed in the transferring of funds from one account to another. In the modern supermarket or retail store, the speed with which inventory is changed has created a demand for a better and more rapid method of ordering, producing, and pricing of goods. As the requirements become more complex in processing data, a system or method of handling the vast amount of information produced becomes more important.

A *system* is a way of accomplishing an activity. For example, a highway system is designed to move traffic in an organized manner from one place to another with the minimum amount of interruption. Other familiar systems are the communications systems of telephone, radio, television, and newspapers. A manufacturing concern must have a system in the production of a product. That system must begin with the raw material and logically follow a pattern to end with a finished product.

An *information system* is a method of collecting, processing, and reporting data which is desired for a particular activity. An information system is most effective when all parties know the system and how it works. For example, most business firms have a procedures book which informs the employee about his duties, to whom he reports when questions arise, and his position within the framework of the organization. An information system includes not only verbal or written communications, but it may also include manual, mechanical, and electronic devices which help collect and report data for further processing.

Data processing is an organized way of handling facts in the information system. This chapter will discuss the development of an information system utilizing concepts of data processing.

TOOLS FOR PROCESSING DATA

Processing data for an effective information system includes the basic operations of classifying, sorting, calculating, summarizing, recording, and reporting. Tools have been developed to assist in these operations. This section discusses two kinds of tools (1) manual and mechanical and (2) automated.

Manual and Mechanical Tools

The processing of data may be accomplished by a manual system or by a system in which the major activities are accomplished by automated equipment. A *manual system* is one identified as a specific job or routine which is performed by an individual. The job is accomplished by an individual who may be using a machine, such as a typewriter, adding machine, or calculator, or some other tool. The tool may be the simple pencil used to make notes in books, on sales slips, or on other types of business forms. As another example, a mail clerk opens mail with a letter opener and sorts the mail into stacks for another person. He may put the correspondence into mailboxes or incoming files. The tools required or used in such a system included the letter opener, a table or desk, the mail sorting boxes or desk files, and a wastebasket for discarded paper. He may have used a stamping machine to indicate the time and the date the correspondence was received.

When an adding machine or calculator is utilized for problem solving, a *mechanical tool* is substituted for the calculations done by the person's mind. The introduction of a mechanical tool to assist the individual does not alter the system. It is still a manual system. The mechanical tool is substituted to improve the elements of speed and accuracy. Of course, the person's ability to use the mechanical tool also affects the speed and accuracy of the process.

Because of the cost factor in moving to a method using mechanical tools, some thought has to be given to the savings in time and payroll and the money needed to purchase the mechanical tools to replace a simple manual system. It is only when the savings of time and money are greater than the cost of the mechanical tool that such a purchase should be considered.

Automated Tools

When equipment plays the major role and the work is done with a minimum of human effort and regulation, the process is automated. The equipment is designed to complete a process or a portion of an entire process. For example, the operator will furnish the data and "instruct" the equipment to complete an activity. Although the operator controls the machine, the machine completes the various calculations and reports the results. The operator is thus relieved of the activities formerly done manually. *Automated data processing* is the term used to describe information handling which uses both mechanical and electronic equipment. *Electronic data processing* refers to the use of equipment which processes data in the form of electronic impulses. Abbreviations for these terms are ADP and EDP.

In the use of this equipment in data processing, raw data is converted into usable information. Useful information is the result of data processing.

When the computer system consolidates and coordinates operations in order to avoid duplication and overlapping of information, it is called *integrated data processing*. The system normally involves a number of machines. The purpose of such a program is to save time and to cut down the flow of duplicated information. Thus, rather than having several types of the same information, the computer will consolidate the information.

Hardware. Equipment used in an automated system is specialized. It completes a particular activity. *Hardware* is the name given to the equipment. Basic in the equipment hardware is the computer.

The computer is a type of equipment which will receive data, process the data, and produce an informational response. Illustrations 21-1 and 21-2 show examples of computer installations with accompanying hardware. A *console* is the operator's "switchboard." It is at the console that the operator can turn the system on or off and monitor the system as it works. The operator can enter data into the system or alter the data when necessary. The *card reader* can read data which has been punched into cards by the *card punch* machine.

Honeywell Information Systems

ILLUS. 21-1. Computer hardware system.

After the computer has received the data and made its calculations, the *printer* will record the information on paper. *Magnetic tape units* utilize a tape (similar to film) on which data or information can be stored for further use. Thus, the tape can be used in two ways (1) to put information into the computer and (2) to receive information from the computer. Storage of information can be done internally

Honeywell Information Systems

ILLUS. 21-2. Computer, tape, and printout equipment.

with a *disk storage unit* or externally in equipment which is independent of the system. Illustration 21-3 shows disk storage and magnetic tape units.

Honeywell Information Systems

ILLUS. 21-3. Disk storage and magnetic tape units.

Computer Activity. The computer acts and reacts only when a complete set of instructions is given. Needless to say, the data given to the computer must be correct. Incorrect or inadequate information and human error will produce incorrect results in the system. To describe this fact systems workers use the expression "GIGO," which means "garbage in—garbage out."

Data input refers to information which has been gathered and communicated to the computer by the use of codes. The data may be on punched cards or magnetic tapes. In a unit-record system, which utilizes the punched card, data is recorded into the card by punching holes in numbered spaces on the card. Illustration 21-4 shows an 80-column punched card and the interpretation of the punched holes at the top of the card. This card has digits 0 through 9 in 80 columns on the card.

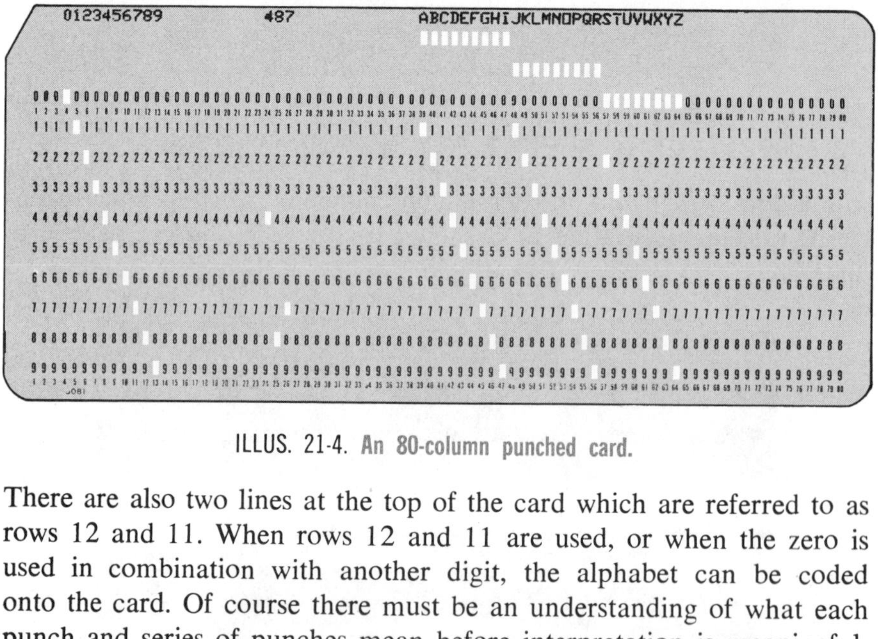

ILLUS. 21-4. An 80-column punched card.

There are also two lines at the top of the card which are referred to as rows 12 and 11. When rows 12 and 11 are used, or when the zero is used in combination with another digit, the alphabet can be coded onto the card. Of course there must be an understanding of what each punch and series of punches mean before interpretation is meaningful. For example, 487 may refer to an amount, date, or customer number.

There is also a 96-column punched card which can hold 20 percent more information than the 80-column card but is only one third the size. An example is shown in Illustration 21-5 on page 427.

The computer must be told what to do with the data after it is punched into the card. The set of instructions is known as the *program* or *software*. The computer has the ability to store data in a *memory unit*. With the data in the memory unit, further instructions will tell the computer what to do with the data. The central activity of a computer is

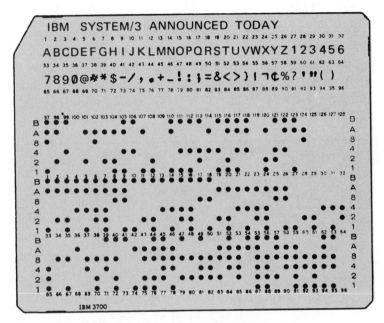

ILLUS. 21-5. A 96-column punched card.

the processing of the data. A *control unit* within the computer acts as a double check to determine if the instructions are being carried out. When the process has been completed as the instructions were given, an *output unit* functions to translate the results into information on printed pages, punched cards, or magnetic tape. Illustration 21-6 shows the steps in a unit record system where data is recorded manually and put into a computer system which processes the data according to a program and prints a report.

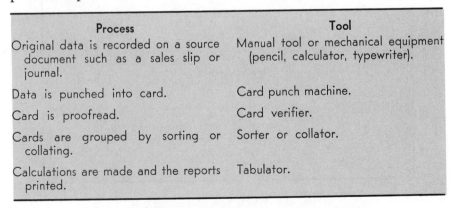

Process	Tool
Original data is recorded on a source document such as a sales slip or journal.	Manual tool or mechanical equipment (pencil, calculator, typewriter).
Data is punched into card.	Card punch machine.
Card is proofread.	Card verifier.
Cards are grouped by sorting or collating.	Sorter or collator.
Calculations are made and the reports printed.	Tabulator.

ILLUS. 21-6. Information processing for a unit-record system.

FLOW CHARTS

Flow charts are graphic presentations that show a sequence of steps needed to complete a data processing procedure. They aid in understanding the steps that must be followed to accomplish some business activity. Although programming symbols vary, there are national and international standards. Illustration 21-7 shows some of the typical symbols.

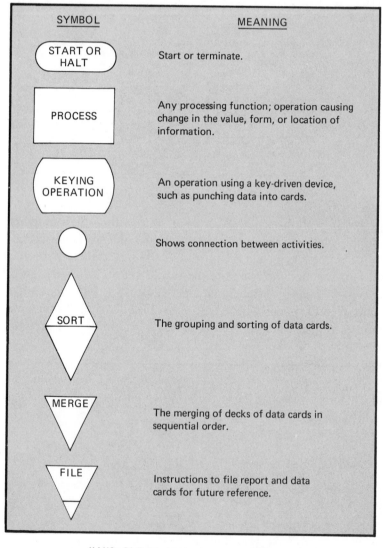

SYMBOL	MEANING
START OR HALT	Start or terminate.
PROCESS	Any processing function; operation causing change in the value, form, or location of information.
KEYING OPERATION	An operation using a key-driven device, such as punching data into cards.
◯	Shows connection between activities.
SORT	The grouping and sorting of data cards.
MERGE	The merging of decks of data cards in sequential order.
FILE	Instructions to file report and data cards for future reference.

ILLUS. 21-7. Typical programming symbols.

DESIGNING AN INFORMATION SYSTEM

Before any information system can be put into operation, it is imperative that care be taken to check all aspects of the system. In order for the system to produce results which can be used, it must have available correct information, in the correct order, at a particular time. It must also have built-in check points to test the accuracy of the system. The following discussion concerns the process of establishing a system.

Establishing Goals

Information systems are not set up without purposes or identifiable goals. In an information system these goals are referred to as *output*. Some examples of output for an information system include:

1. Summaries of certain business transactions for a particular period of time, such as amounts of sales made on account. Balances of specific inventory items could be summarized at the end of fiscal periods.
2. Information for the preparation of desired financial reports such as the balance sheet and income statement.
3. Comparisons of certain data for corresponding periods of time. Sales amounts for specific months could be compared with other specific months.
4. Indications of trends of particular operations which allow management to make decisions concerning future activities. Patterns of sales growth by geographical areas could signal expansion or termination in that area.

Identifying Source Material

Now that the information system has a definite set of goals or output, attention should turn to the source input data. *Input* is the basic data used in the data processing system. Where will the basic data be obtained?

This data is gathered at the operational level where it is created and recorded. The operational level is where the transaction occurs. The transaction may occur at the point of sale or delivery, in the warehouse where inventory is controlled, or in the accounting department. It is necessary to go directly to the areas where the data is known and available.

It should also be recognized that the source data must be of a quantitative nature. That is, it must be expressed in numbers if the material is to be processed through electronic data processing equipment. Even if electronic equipment is not used in the information system, management can better utilize data in numeric form since it allows for comparisons, ratios, and accumulation.

The source data required to produce an output of net sales is shown in Illustration 21-8. Figures for sales, sales returns and allowances, and other amounts that reduced or increased the sales account are needed. By putting the data into a program, the data processing equipment will be able to place the amounts in such a manner that the result is known.

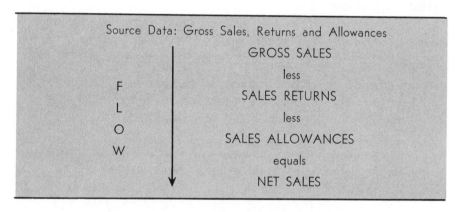

ILLUS. 21-8. Source data used to obtain net sales.

The processing equipment could make other significant calculations, such as the percent of sales returned and why the goods were returned. When the goods were returned, for example, a numeric code system could be used to indicate why the return was necessary. Reasons might include damaged goods, incorrect size or style, not needed, or any other reason.

If net sales is the desired output, it is necessary to know what the total sales were for the period of time and deduct from those sales the items which reduced the total. With this information it is possible to determine other data and to make management decisions. If returns and allowances reduced total sales by 6 percent and management feels that the acceptable limit is 3 percent, a decision can be made to determine why such a percentage exists and how to correct the situation.

Securing the Desired Output

After it is determined just what the information system is designed to accomplish and what data is necessary and what form is desirable, it becomes the task of a programmer to put this data into a logical sequence for an output. A *programmer* creates a flow chart or program by which the data is to be put together with other information to arrive at a solution to the problem. The previous illustration shows the flow of information. The bookkeeping cycle is another familiar type of flow of information designed to summarize special activities of a business.

Illustrations 21-9 and 21-10 on pages 432 and 433 show a program form giving the various steps required to solve a specific problem. In the illustrations, the firm has received a roll of film to be developed for a customer. Notice the use of symbols used to program the activity that is being carried on. The data is in numeric form and the company utilizes unit-record data processing. That is, a punched card will be processed by a key punch operator from the information a clerk has written on an envelope containing a roll of film. The customer desires color prints from the 8 exposures. The company wants an output which will produce a bill including the customer's name and the amount charged for the film processing. The company also wants to know the total sales for filing and for income tax records.

Evaluating the System

Just because the output of the system has been determined, there is no assurance that the system will work. The immediate task is to test the system through a double check to determine if it does provide adequate information. During the evaluation period of the system, overlapping and duplicating of materials may be evident and the system can be modified.

In the evaluation of the output from Illustration 21-10 immediate information is given. The question should be raised of whether additional information is needed. Will there be a need for data relating to sales specifically for prints, color, or black and white? Is there a need to build in a control for the ordering of supplies and other inventory items? Is the customer's address needed? If so, this particular program would need modification.

From the problem (Illustration 21-8) relating to the sales of an organization, assume that one output desired is information concerning the geographical location of the sales market. From what areas are customers attracted? How large are the orders from this market? What geographical areas are not active? If the objective was to determine these factors, can a source of data be provided? Suppose that the company had provided for all of the above questions except the one concerning the inactive market. An evaluation of the system would point up this omission.

THE CAMERA SHOP

The Camera Shop processes film in one of two ways; either as slides (Code A) or as prints (Code B). Prints may be either black and white (Classification C) or color (Classification D). Slides are processed at the price of 8¢ per exposure. Black and white prints are 5¢ and color prints are 12¢ per exposure.

The customer leaves film with a clerk. The clerk fills out an envelope which shows the customer's name and the details concerning slides, prints, color, and number. A number is preprinted on the envelope and the customer receives a duplicate tab which will become his claim check.

From the information given on the envelope, a punched card is processed by a key punch operator and placed in the computer.

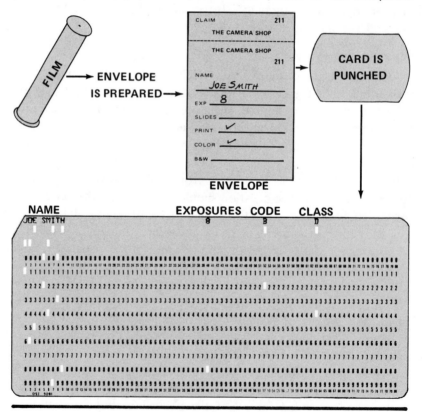

ILLUS. 21-9. Source data for programming.

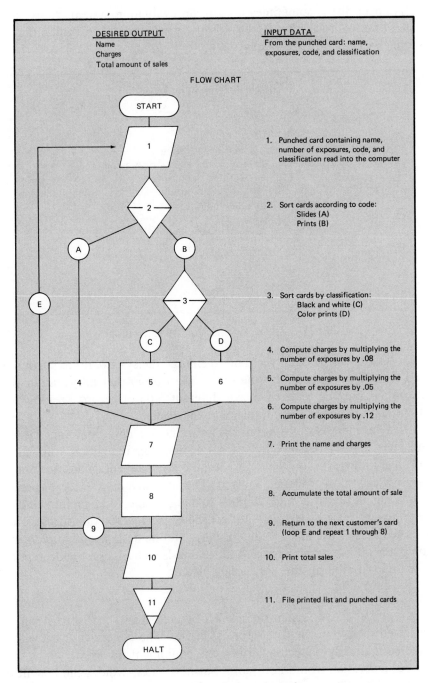

DESIRED OUTPUT
Name
Charges
Total amount of sales

INPUT DATA
From the punched card: name,
exposures, code, and classification

FLOW CHART

START

1

2

A   B

3

C   D

E

4   5   6

7

8

9

10

11

HALT

1. Punched card containing name,
   number of exposures, code, and
   classification read into the computer

2. Sort cards according to code:
   Slides (A)
   Prints (B)

3. Sort cards by classification:
   Black and white (C)
   Color prints (D)

4. Compute charges by multiplying the
   number of exposures by .08

5. Compute charges by multiplying the
   number of exposures by .05

6. Compute charges by multiplying the
   number of exposures by .12

7. Print the name and charges

8. Accumulate the total amount of sale

9. Return to the next customer's card
   (loop E and repeat 1 through 8)

10. Print total sales

11. File printed list and punched cards

ILLUS. 21-10. Flow chart programming.

A check list is sometimes used in an evaluation system. A list such as the one in Illustration 21-11 might be appropriate in evaluating the output on sales.

Output Evaluation—Sales

Check
Yes   No

                    Does the system
(✓)   (   )   1. locate customers geographically?
(✓)   (   )   2. allocate the sales dollar geographically?
(   )   (✓)   3. determine the sales distribution on a percentage base?
(   )   (✓)   4. give the average dollar value of the order?
(✓)   (   )   5. provide the volume of sales in a territory?
(   )   (✓)   6. determine why sales are not made in a particular area?
(   )   (✓)   7. measure competition in the area?

(   )   (   )   8. _____

(   )   (   )   9. _____

(   )   (   )   10. _____

ILLUS. 21-11. Checklist for evaluating an information system.

It is much easier to correct and to enlarge the system at the beginning than to find out later that some of the most important information was left out. It may be realized that a different type of record keeping and source data is needed to complement the system.

If a business is considering the introduction of a computer system and feels that its personnel does not include an individual who has a working knowledge of the area, it might be advantageous to obtain the services of a systems analyst. The *systems analyst* is a person possessing those skills and abilities to look at the total picture and to determine the needs. He does not set the objectives for the business nor does he in any sense manage the business. But he designs and implements computer information systems to fit the needs of businesses and prepares flow charts outlining the processing of data.

Systems Controls

In any effective system there must be controls so that errors can be corrected before a final output is made. These controls are either handled manually or technically by the equipment involved.

An individual would not mail a business letter without the benefit of proofreading. The proofreading is a control which is done manually. In the checking of extensions on an invoice, very often the accounting department will have an individual verify the computations by using a calculator. This would be a combination of manual and technical control for accuracy. Information systems use the expression *"debug."* What is implied by the expression is that errors are found and corrected before final action takes place.

Often news stories report on individuals who receive tax refunds amounting to several thousands or millions of dollars more than they should have been. Obviously, the system did not have adequate controls to "toss out" the information and stop the processing. In one instance, a payroll which was printed by a computer awarded a principal of a high school a paycheck for $2.70 while one of the teachers received a check for $22,500. If a control had been in effect, the payroll checks would not have been processed.

Generally, a computer system will have controls built into the program. For example, after the source data has been processed into a punched card, the card will be sent through a machine called a verifier. This machine is similar to the card punch but, rather than punching cards, it checks or verifies that the holes were punched correctly.

Another control technique where the electronic equipment can find its own errors is a check system on specific data. For example, the programmer could include a control of net pay. Each employee would have an average net pay and the computer could determine if the current paycheck was within "limits" which were predetermined. The limits might be 10 percent more or less than the average. If the printout noted an amount greater than the 10 percent, the computer would stop and the error could be traced before the check was issued to the employee. Perhaps it would be found that the computation was correct because of a change in pay rate or hours worked. This type of control would also help to solve the problem of extreme refunds in income tax or the overpayment (underpayment) of invoices.

If inventory is kept by computer records, control can be written in to alert the stock room that inventory of a particular item is low and needs to be reordered. Airlines and motels use a system which gives a degree of certainty that space is available when a customer makes advance reservations. The control system matches reservation requests with availability and completes the transaction.

Controls used by the trucking industry provide for the loading and directing of trucks so that maximum space and the minimum of time are utilized in transporting goods from place to place.

UTILIZING INFORMATION

The immediate use of information is of great importance to the business operation. Information may have value for various departments in the organization and the information must be available to these departments when they need it. To make this information available requires storage and the ability to recall the information. *Terminals* are often used to record data and to recall information from storage. Illustration 21-12 shows a terminal being used to record a sale. The

National Cash Register Company

ILLUS. 21-12. Terminal used to collect data at point of sale.

instrument held in one hand can read credit cards and price tags. The data can later be used in billing and inventory control.

Which information should be stored and for what period of time? Some information has value at one step along the process and may never be required again. Such information could be discarded. Other information which has been accumulated is still very necessary for the purpose of updating other information. The sales for January are important to use if added to the sales for the months of February and March. At the end of March, the first quarter of operations, it may be of value to compare the separate months and later to compare the second quarter sales to the first. At the year end, it would be of interest to note the quarter of greatest activity and the quarter of least activity so that management could concentrate on correcting any deficiency.

From information obtained through the use of an information system, management can arrive at basic decisions at a more rapid pace and also have some assurance that the information is correct within the limits of the system.

REVIEW WHAT YOU HAVE LEARNED

Business Terms Checkup:

(1) data
(2) system
(3) information system
(4) data processing
(5) manual system
(6) mechanical tool
(7) automated data processing
(8) electronic data processing
(9) integrated data processing
(10) hardware
(11) console
(12) card reader
(13) card punch
(14) printer

(15) magnetic tape units
(16) disk storage unit
(17) data input
(18) program or software
(19) memory unit
(20) control unit
(21) output unit
(22) flow charts
(23) output
(24) input
(25) programmer
(26) systems analyst
(27) debug
(28) terminal

Reading Checkup:

1. What can an effective information system do for a business manager?
2. Can an information system be effective for a small business? Why?
3. How does electronic data processing affect the information system?
4. What is meant by the expression, "garbage in—garbage out"?

5. What is the purpose of a program? Of a flow chart?

6. Why must there be goals established for an information system?

7. Name various sources where business data might be obtained for use in the information system.

8. Why must an information system be tested before it is put into operation?

9. Why is it important to consider which information should be stored for future use?

10. How is a terminal used? What is its advantage?

APPLY WHAT YOU HAVE LEARNED

Questions for Class Discussion:

1. What is the major activity of the computer?

2. Discuss: The accuracy of the source data determines the accuracy of the report.

3. Discuss: It is necessary for a business to determine the goals or output before introduction of the information system.

4. What is meant by flow charting of a project?

5. How does the manager go about evaluating the output of the system?

6. When is it of benefit to a business to secure the help of a systems analyst?

7. Why is a control needed in the electronic data processing system?

8. Why is some information stored and other information discarded? How do you determine which information to discard?

Problems and Projects:

1. Select some city or point of interest within your state which is at least 100 miles from where you are. Write a line by line set of instructions to direct another person to that city. Use a recent road map for your source material. Without telling another the location you have selected, see if he can find the city.

2. From the problem given in Illustrations 21-9 and 21-10, assume that Joe Smith brought in 2 rolls of film, one had 8 exposures for color prints and the other had 20 exposures for color slides. Also, Mary Hawkins left one roll of 8 exposures for black and white prints.

   Instructions: Find the following information by tracing each of the punched cards through the various steps.

   (a) Joe Smith's charges.

   (b) Mary Hawkins' charges.

   (c) The company's total sales.

3. Assume that you are going to find the net pay for an employee in order to process his paycheck. List all of the information which is needed as source data and put it in the order in which it will be processed.

4. Most electric household appliances have some form of automation. Describe the steps of the program involved in arriving at the output of the appliance. Select one appliance such as a coffee maker, automatic dishwasher, electric dryer or washer, stereo, electric range, or any other appliance. Write a list of activities necessary to describe the system using the following:

(a) Establish the goal or output

(b) Identify the source materials or input

(c) Secure the desired output

(d) Evaluate the system

(e) Control the system

(f) Conclusion

An example is given to help guide your solution:

An electric toaster: (a) a light brown slice of toast, (b) a slice of bread, (c) turn toaster on, heat, and produce toasted bread, (d) the toast is too light, just right, too dark, (e) turn the dial which controls the heat and time if correction is necessary, and (f) test again.

Case Problem 21-1:

The Robinwood Country Club has three types of memberships: (a) family, (b) husband and wife, and (c) single. The dues are (a) $100, (b) $75, and (c) $50 for adult and $30 for school age. The yearly membership gives full privileges to members to use the golf course, driving range, and putting greens. Other facilities are available on an admission basis. The management of the Robinwood Country Club wants its data processing system to give the annual membership charge for each applicant.

Required:

Using Illustration 21-10 as a guide, prepare a flow chart to show the steps needed to give the information desired.

Continuing Project:

Select one department or activity center from your business and show how information collected within that department could be used by other departments and management. You might select personnel, inventory control, purchasing, accounting, or any area you consider vital to the business.

What information is obtained from accounting records?

What are the types of record systems?

What methods should be used in handling cash?

What is depreciation?

What information must a business have for income tax purposes?

What is a budget?

BACKGROUND OF CHAPTER

A business cannot operate successfully without proper bookkeeping and accounting records. One of the main reasons for failures of businesses is the lack of adequate financial records.

This chapter does not attempt to teach the methods of maintaining bookkeeping and accounting records. It does, however, indicate the types of records that are needed, the importance of these records, and how they are used.

Part of the chapter is also devoted to a discussion of the use of budgets and methods of control applied to business activities.

CHAPTER 22

FINANCIAL RECORDS IN BUSINESS

Bookkeeping and *accounting records* are financial records of the transactions of the business. If a person is going to own or operate a business, he must maintain records in one of the following ways: (1) know enough about bookkeeping and accounting to keep his own records; (2) hire a full-time bookkeeper or a part-time bookkeeper; (3) obtain a standard set of records that he can follow from a set of rules; (4) use a bookkeeping service organization (local or national); or (5) use a data processing service center if the service will justify the cost.

It is important for financial records to be kept accurately, because the businessman must use the many different kinds of information which can only be provided by these records. Some of the types of information that a businessman should expect to secure from his accounting records are listed below and on the next page:

1. Kinds and values of assets.
2. Amount of debts that are owed by the business, including withholding and payroll deductions.
3. Amount owed to the business (daily or monthly).
4. Cash balance in the bank and cash on hand (daily).
5. Amount of cash deposited in the bank (daily).
6. Amount of cash withdrawn from the bank (daily).
7. Amount of cash received (daily).
8. Amount of cash sales (daily).
9. Amount of credit sales (daily).
10. Kinds and amounts of expenses.
11. Total expenses, including depreciation and bad debts.
12. Amount of merchandise bought.
13. Transportation charges paid.
14. Amount sold by each salesperson.

15. Profit or loss.
16. Percentage of profit or loss.
17. Trends in sales, expenses, profits, and net worth.
18. Comparison with other similar businesses.

RECORD SYSTEMS

Modern accounting records are not difficult to maintain. Model sets of records can be obtained from the manufacturers of some cash registers. Some standardized systems can be purchased at stationery stores. Some associations, such as those of oil dealers and hardware stores have standard records they recommend for their members.

Types of Record Systems

There are two general types of record-keeping systems that can be used in business. One is called the double-entry system, and the other is called the single-entry system.

Double Entry. The *double-entry system* involves recording each item in two different ways by means of a debit and a credit. For example, when a customer pays a bill for $10, his charge account on the books of the business is credited (reduced) by $10 while the cash account on the records of the business is debited (increased) by $10. Thus, this single payment of $10 shows up on the books of the business in two places. All other transactions are recorded in terms of debit and credit. In this manner two sets of figures are developed. The total of one set should equal the total of the other. If the totals do not balance, a mistake has been made. Because of this safety factor, the double-entry system is more commonly used than the single-entry system.

Single Entry. The *single-entry system* involves just one recording of each item. Therefore, only a single set of figures is available. This system is easier to operate than the double-entry system, but if a mistake is made, it is extremely difficult to locate it.

Automated System

In many offices automated data processing equipment performs much of the bookkeeping work formerly done by hand or machine. This kind of equipment is widely used in large businesses. Businesses of medium size are also installing automated equipment. Small businesses are making use of automated equipment by sending certain information to data processing service centers which, for a monthly fee, prepare the bookkeeping records and return complete financial reports to the business. These service centers may keep accounts of customers and prepare monthly statements.

There are many types of automated equipment available. The kinds of equipment that might be used for automating the accounting department in a business are (1) tabulating or punched-card equipment and (2) the electronic computer. Various types of automated equipment were discussed in Chapter 21.

Systems in Small Businesses

Small businesses, especially retail stores, do not need elaborate records; and many such businesses use a cash register as a basis for obtaining most of the information for their financial records. An example of a financial record which might be kept by a gasoline service station is shown in Illustration 22-1.

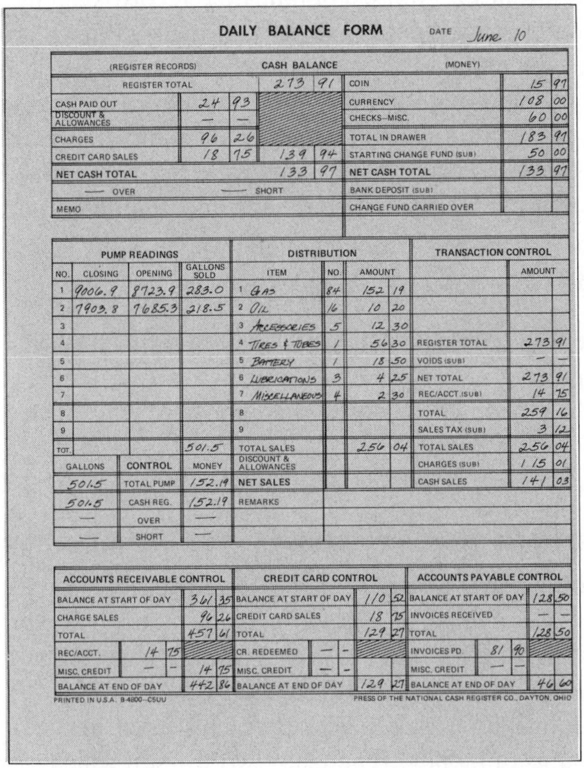

DAILY BALANCE FORM DATE June 10

CASH BALANCE

(REGISTER RECORDS)				
REGISTER TOTAL			273	91
CASH PAID OUT	24	93		
DISCOUNT & ALLOWANCES	—	—		
CHARGES	96	26		
CREDIT CARD SALES	18	75	139	94
NET CASH TOTAL			133	97
— OVER	— SHORT			
MEMO				

(MONEY)		
COIN	15	97
CURRENCY	108	00
CHECKS–MISC.	60	00
TOTAL IN DRAWER	183	97
STARTING CHANGE FUND (SUB)	50	00
NET CASH TOTAL	133	97
BANK DEPOSIT (SUB)		
CHANGE FUND CARRIED OVER		

PUMP READINGS

NO.	CLOSING	OPENING	GALLONS SOLD
1	9006.9	8723.9	283.0
2	7903.8	7685.3	218.5
3			
4			
5			
6			
7			
8			
9			
TOT.			501.5

GALLONS	CONTROL	MONEY
501.5	TOTAL PUMP	152.19
501.5	CASH REG.	152.19
—	OVER	—
—	SHORT	—

DISTRIBUTION

ITEM	NO.	AMOUNT	
1 Gas	84	152	19
2 Oil	16	10	20
3 Accessories	5	12	30
4 Tires & Tubes	1	56	30
5 Battery	1	18	50
6 Lubrications	3	4	25
7 Miscellaneous	4	2	30
8			
9			
TOTAL SALES		256	04
DISCOUNT & ALLOWANCES			
NET SALES			
REMARKS			

TRANSACTION CONTROL

	AMOUNT	
REGISTER TOTAL	273	91
VOIDS (SUB)	—	—
NET TOTAL	273	91
REC/ACCT. (SUB)	14	75
TOTAL	259	16
SALES TAX (SUB)	3	12
TOTAL SALES	256	04
CHARGES (SUB)	115	01
CASH SALES	141	03

ACCOUNTS RECEIVABLE CONTROL

BALANCE AT START OF DAY			361	35
CHARGE SALES			96	26
TOTAL			457	61
REC/ACCT.	14	75		
MISC. CREDIT	—	—	14	75
BALANCE AT END OF DAY			442	86

CREDIT CARD CONTROL

BALANCE AT START OF DAY			110	52
CREDIT CARD SALES			18	75
TOTAL			129	27
CR. REDEEMED	—	—		
MISC. CREDIT	—	—		
BALANCE AT END OF DAY			129	27

ACCOUNTS PAYABLE CONTROL

BALANCE AT START OF DAY			128	50
INVOICES RECEIVED			—	—
TOTAL			128	50
INVOICES PD.	81	90		
MISC. CREDIT	—	—		
BALANCE AT END OF DAY			46	60

PRINTED IN U.S.A. B-4800–C5UU PRESS OF THE NATIONAL CASH REGISTER CO., DAYTON, OHIO

National Cash Register Company

ILLUS. 22-1. Daily balance form.

If a cash register, showing detailed kinds of transactions, is used in the business, this information can be taken from the cash register tape (or audit strip) and copied in the daily balance form.

A special form listing the daily cash payments should be maintained. Some cash registers provide for these amounts to be shown on the daily audit slip. In the absence of an adequate cash register, a written record should be made of all types of sales, other receipts, and payments, and these should be recorded at the end of the day.

If there are sales made on credit, a charge ticket should be issued to each customer and a copy kept for accounting records. A detailed account must be kept for every charge customer showing what he purchased, when he purchased it, amounts paid, and the balance. A receipt should be issued for each payment received from a customer.

Systems in Large Businesses

In large businesses more complicated record-keeping systems are necessary; and many people, usually organized into an accounting department, are required to maintain the records. An accounting department is commonly divided into the following sections: (1) general ledger, (2) cost accounting, (3) accounts receivable, and (4) accounts payable. There may sometimes be additional sections for branch accounting, payroll, disbursing, and tabulating.

TYPES OF RECORDS NEEDED

Bookkeeping records in all types of businesses have many points of similarity, but they differ in some respects because of the nature of the businesses. The kinds of records that are kept will also depend upon the size of the business.

Accounting for Cash

A cash register is used in most retail businesses for handling cash. Regardless of whether a bookkeeper is employed or whether the records are kept by the owner of the business, similar procedures must be followed in accounting for cash. Several suggestions for the safe handling of cash are listed in Illustration 22-2.

In accounting for cash, special problems arise in making payments of small amounts of money. There are two ways in which small payments are usually made by businesses. When a cash register is used and there is no special petty cash fund, the usual practice is to pay the amount and

1. A petty cash fund adequate for small emergency payments should be kept in a safe place with somebody responsible for it. A written record of all money put into the fund and all money paid out must be kept. Receipts for payments should be obtained where possible, and the fund should be replenished by check to provide a further record.
2. If a cash register is used, small emergency payments can be made out of cash register funds instead of through a petty cash fund; but adequate records of payments must be made and receipts obtained.
3. If a cash register is used, there should be a daily change fund of a fixed amount, which is never deposited in the bank but is kept available to start each day's operations. This fund should be counted and verified daily.
4. Deposit all receipts in a bank account.
5. Make payments by check for all items except small emergency payments.
6. Verify by a double check any cash overages or cash shortages in the daily transactions.
7. Do not keep any more cash around the office than is necessary and, if convenient, make more than one deposit in the bank daily.
8. Pay salaries by check instead of by cash.
9. Audit regularly the amounts received on account.
10. Audit regularly the receipts by comparing them with the bank deposits you have made.
11. Audit regularly the actual cash paid out by comparing the check stubs with bills paid.
12. Endorse all checks for deposit with a company rubber stamp or, when signing checks for endorsement, write "For deposit."
13. Reconcile the monthly bank statement promptly and regularly as explained in Chapter 17.

ILLUS. 22-2. Suggestions for the safe handling of cash.

put a slip, such as that shown in Illustration 22-3 on page 446, in the cash register drawer. When money is put aside (often in a special box or drawer) for a petty cash fund, a petty cash record is kept which shows why the cash was paid and to whom it was given.

Keeping a careful watch on one's bank account is of particular importance in accounting for cash. A bank always provides a monthly statement that should be reconciled with the checkbook. In other words, the balance on the bank statement should be verified with the balance in the checkbook. The process of reconciling the bank statement was discussed in Chapter 17.

PETTY CASH VOUCHER

NO. _6_   DATE _February 9, 19--_

PAID TO _Sims Typewriter Service_   AMOUNT

FOR _Repairing typewriter_   3 | 50

CHARGE TO _Miscellaneous Expense_

PAYMENT RECEIVED: REED AND MALLOCH

Helen Jones   APPROVED BY _George Ajax_

ILLUS. 22-3. Petty cash voucher.

Debt Records

Nearly every business owes money on account or owes money on notes. It is important to keep in a systematic way an accurate record of these amounts due so that they will be paid at the proper times. A file can be used for this purpose. The unpaid invoices are placed behind tabs indicating the date on which they must be paid in order to get the cash discounts. When the invoices are paid, they are removed and placed in the file under the creditor's name.

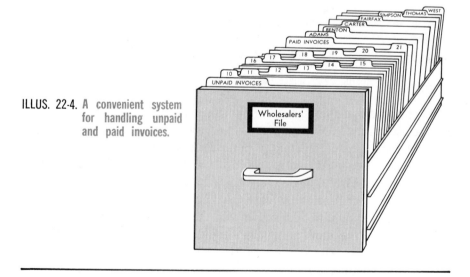

ILLUS. 22-4. A convenient system for handling unpaid and paid invoices.

Depreciation Records

Every businessman should recognize the problems that result from the decrease in the value of property through use. For example, a service station operator buys a pump that costs $300. He knows from experience that at the end of five years the pump will not be worth any more than its value as junk, about $25. He estimates therefore that it will wear out at the average rate of $55 a year.

Assets are recorded on the books of a business when they are purchased. They become part of the property owned by the business. As they wear out or become of less value, the business is allowed by law to charge the loss in value each year as an operating expense.

The general term that is applied to such a decrease in the value of an asset is *depreciation*. Property may also decrease in value because of *obsolescence;* that is, the asset may become out of date, or it may become inadequate for a particular purpose. For all practical purposes, however, any decrease in the value of an asset can be considered depreciation. A cash register, for instance, may wear out gradually, or it may become inadequate because the business has expanded.

The loss due to depreciation is very real, although it usually cannot be computed definitely. Any businessman who fails to recognize depreciation is failing to observe good business principles. The depreciation of assets is part of the cost of doing business. When equipment is worn out, it must be replaced. If money is not available to replace the equipment, the business enterprise may be handicapped seriously.

Register Records

Financial statements provide information on such items as insurance, fixed assets, and real property but do not provide the detailed information that is needed with regard to these assets. Special forms that are referred to as *registers* are used for keeping the detailed information on these items. For instance, a businessman may have insurance policies on equipment, merchandise, trucks, buildings, plate glass, and various other items. He therefore needs to know such information as the face of each policy, the amount of the insurance expense to be charged off each month, the date of expiration of each policy, and the like. This information may be kept in an insurance register and a fixed assets register. These registers provide additional information that is helpful to the bookkeeping and to the management of the business.

An *insurance register* is one that identifies type of policy, company from which it is purchased, amount, date of expiration, and premium.

A *fixed assets register* is a permanent record that includes such information as description of the asset, date of purchase, cost, accumulated depreciation, and book value.

Tax Records

The federal income tax law requires every business to keep satisfactory records so that its income and expenses can be reported. Preparation of an income tax return for a small business is relatively simple. The information needed for an income tax return of a business can be obtained from any good set of business records kept under the double-entry method. The income tax form and the sheet of instructions with the form will explain most of the information needed.

Employers are required to withhold a certain percentage of the wages of each employee for federal income tax purposes. Each employee is required to fill out a card in regard to his family status. From a table furnished by the Internal Revenue Service, the employer can determine the amount to withhold from each salary payment. Periodically these withholdings must be paid by the employer to the Internal Revenue Service.

Most employers are subject to social security taxes for old-age benefits and unemployment compensation payments. The employer is also required to withhold taxes from each employee's wages for social security purposes. The employer is required to pay to the federal government his own taxes and those withheld from employees. Further discussion concerning federal taxes will be found in Chapter 26.

Payroll Records

In order to keep satisfactory payroll records to provide the information needed by the business operator and to satisfy federal and state authorities, there must be a comprehensive record kept for all employees and for each employee showing the hours worked, regular wages paid, overtime wages, and all types of deductions from wages. It is from these records that an employer can make his regular reports. A simple set of payroll records is shown in Illustration 22-5, page 449.

Records for Self-Employed

All self-employed persons must pay the federal income tax. Self-employed persons, except those specifically excluded or exempted by the law, must also pay taxes for federal old-age benefits insurance. Self-employed persons include independent contractors, independent

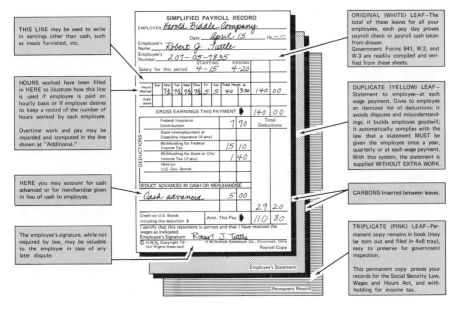

ILLUS. 22-5. Simplified payroll record.

businessmen, partners in business, independent commercial salesmen or agents, life insurance agents, commissioned truck drivers, newspaper and magazine distributors over 18 years of age, and similar workers. Self-employed persons must keep careful records of their incomes and expenses for income tax purposes.

KEEPING RECORDS SAFE

The financial records, including the accounts of customers and all other vital information, should be kept safe. They should be protected from such hazards as fire and theft. Many records, such as the accounts of customers, would not be stolen; but they could easily be destroyed by fire. In every office, therefore, there should be a fireproof safe or vault for such records. So-called fireproof filing cabinets made of sheet metal with insulated walls will withstand heat; but if the building burns and something heavy falls upon such a cabinet, the cabinet will be crushed.

Many business firms are making use of a photographic technique called *microfilming*. By this process a great amount of data is stored on small frames of film and can be recalled for showing through projection on a screen. Not only does this process save valuable storage space but also, through effective filing and information retrieval, it is generally a fast reference.

Unusually valuable documents, such as notes, deeds, leases, mortgages, and contracts, should be placed where they are secure from theft or fire. Many of these are often placed in bank safe deposit boxes if there is no adequate protection in the office.

BUDGET SYSTEMS

Because of the intricate business relations in modern civilization, budgeting has become extremely important. A study conducted by the United States Department of Commerce reveals the fact that stores that budget their financial operations are more successful than stores that do not budget. The stores that are most successful are those that (a) keep double-entry bookkeeping records, (b) have their accounts audited or checked by an experienced accountant, (c) take an inventory of merchandise more than once a year, and (d) operate under a financial budget.

In its simplest form a *budget* is an estimated plan for the future that helps keep expenses in line with income. Use of a budget should prevent overbuying and help to anticipate when borrowing is necessary.

The actual procedures in budgeting will depend on the type of business. For a retail store the process is principally one of budgeting sales, expenses, purchases, and cash. For larger types of businesses, budgeting is more complicated, as is indicated in Illustration 22-6.

TYPES OF BUDGETS

The final overall budget for a business is made up of several different types of budgets, such as the sales budget, the merchandising and purchasing budgets, the advertising budget, the cash budget, and the budgeted income statement. Most individual budgets are based upon sales. At some times, however, in some types of businesses, either the production capacity or the financial capacity must be determined first. The sales and all other estimates are then based upon the ability to produce.

The traffic manager, the office manager, the employment manager, and the engineer in a large production plant must be acquainted with all the individual budgets because their departments are affected by the budget requirements. The small businessman, obviously, will not have

1. The estimate of sales is based upon past experience and future expectations. As will be explained later, there is more than one method of making this estimate.
2. The advertising budget is based upon the expected sales and the amount that can be afforded in promoting new products and in opening new territories.
3. The production plans should be based upon the expected sales of the individual products. It is therefore necessary to take into consideration the production capacity and the equipment needed.
4. The purchasing requirements are based upon expected sales and production. Purchases must be made far enough in advance to allow time for production. It is therefore necessary to be familiar with the times of the year when the sales are greatest.
5. In a large manufacturing business it is necessary to anticipate the labor requirements. The budget of labor must therefore be based upon the production requirements.
6. The budget of administrative costs, office costs, and the cost of supplies must be based upon all the previously mentioned factors.
7. The mass or complete budget is made up after all the preceding budgets have been made.
8. The cash budget, which is explained later in this chapter, is a budget that shows the manager of the business or the treasurer what cash balance he can expect at any particular time. Such a budget is necessary to anticipate borrowing.

ILLUS. 22-6. Budgeting procedure for a manufacturing business.

such a detailed budget as that described previously. He will in all cases, however, be concerned with budgeting sales, purchases, expenses, and cash.

Sales Budget

The *sales budget* is strictly a forecast of the sales for a month, a few months, or a year. Estimated sales may be computed on the basis of sales territories, salesmen, branch offices, departments, or particular commodities. Sometimes independent estimates are made on all these bases and, after some compromises, a final sales budget is compiled. Sometimes sales estimates are prepared with the idea of developing sales quotas or goals for salesmen and territories. These estimates provide a goal for the sales department, as well as a basis for preparing the merchandising, purchasing, and other operating budgets.

Illustration 22-7 shows sales estimates determined in two different ways for the same company. Since the two sets of estimated figures are

Budget Based on Analysis of Salesmen

Salesman	Sales 1973	Estimate 1974
T. A. Nader	$ 71,344	$ 76,000
H. E. Loch	69,676	72,000
C. D. Heidel	94,248	88,000
J. H. Sharmon	88,588	88,000
C. F. Powell	85,396	88,000
J. G. Dunbar	81,672	80,000
Total	$490,924	$492,000

Budget Based on Analysis of Products

Product	Sales 1973	Estimate 1974
Washers	$128,568	$136,000
Dryers	40,464	40,000
Ranges	37,852	36,000
Lamps	41,872	40,000
Refrigerators	242,168	260,000
Total	$490,924	$512,000

ILLUS. 22-7. Two ways of budgeting sales.

not the same, someone must be responsible for combining them into one satisfactory estimate that can be followed.

Numerous factors influence the making of the sales estimate. General business conditions have an important bearing, although one concern may enjoy good business while another, at the same time and under the same conditions, may suffer a decline in business. If a good harvest and favorable prices for the crops are anticipated in a certain section, there should be good prospects for selling farm machinery in that section. A retail store located in such an area should expect good business. A flood or drought may affect certain businesses adversely but others favorably. These are examples of some of the influences that should guide one in making a sales estimate.

The following is suggested as a checklist of factors to be used as a guide in a budget of sales:

1. Previous sales.
2. The economic trend.
3. Factors such as weather conditions.
4. Shifting population.
5. Sales force.
6. Availability of merchandise.

7. Buying habits.

8. Season of the year.

When a person is starting a new business, it is advisable to investigate the experiences of other operators in the same line of business and secure what information can be obtained from wholesalers and manufacturers.

Merchandising and Purchasing Budgets

The *merchandising and purchasing budgets,* which are prepared after the sales budget, must be closely correlated. The kinds of stock to have on hand and the time when they should be available are determined. Maximum and minimum supplies are established. Purchases are planned, and information is passed on to the financial department so that the cash needs can be estimated. Sources of supply are checked, and delivery dates are scheduled. The production department and the receiving department are notified. Requisitions and orders are tentatively planned. Orders are sometimes placed in advance, subject to cancellation later; or minimum orders are placed, subject to increase later.

Advertising Budget

The *advertising budget* is a plan of spending for advertising based on estimated sales. Advertising should be kept within some reasonable bounds, for it is not true that sales will always be in direct proportion to advertising. In other words, if the estimated sales are pretty well known, it would be unwise to spend an unusual amount for advertising. Such a plan might result in a loss. On the other hand, a special advertising campaign, properly planned, might increase the sales of a certain product; and the advertising budget would consequently have an influence on the sales budget. These two budgets should therefore be planned together. Likewise, the person in charge of finances should be aware of the plans for advertising in order to control those expenses and to have the necessary cash at the proper time.

Cash Budget

The *cash budget* is an estimate of cash income from all sources and of cash payments. Budgeting cash is sometimes referred to as providing working capital. Working capital comes from either or both of two sources: (a) from the income of the business or (b) from borrowing. When money is borrowed, it must eventually be paid back. In the cash budget, therefore, borrowed money should be included as a special item under receipts. When it is to be repaid, it should be included in the cash budget under disbursements.

The form in Illustration 22-8, may be used for the cash budget of a small business. This type of budget, however, should be prepared by every business, regardless of size. It should show the anticipated necessity of borrowing and the possibilities of repaying borrowed money. For instance, it is possible for a business to make a sizable profit; but at some particular time during the year it may not have enough cash for its operations and may therefore have to borrow.

Cash Budget
For Three Months Ending March 31, 19—

	January	February	March
Net Sales ⟶	$20,000	$20,000	$22,500
Beginning cash balance	8,375	1,000	1,750
Collections from customers	17,500	17,500	20,000
Total cash available	25,875	18,500	21,750
Payments (disbursements)			
Accounts to be paid	11,250	11,250	15,000
Labor	2,375	3,000	4,000
Salaries and administrative expense	1,750	1,750	1,750
Sales expense	3,750	3,750	3,750
Other operating expense	3,250	4,500	6,000
Purchase of fixed assets		2,500	2,500
Repayment of bank loan	2,500		
Total cash payments	24,875	26,750	33,000
Expected cash shortage		8,250	11,250
Bank loans needed		10,000	12,500
Ending cash balance	1,000	1,750	1,250
End-of-month situation:			
Materials purchased	11,250	15,000	20,000
Accounts receivable	37,500	40,000	42,500
Accounts payable	11,250	15,000	20,000
Bank loans		10,000	22,500

ILLUS. 22-8. A cash budget.

Income Statement Budget

Illustration 22-9 is an *income statement budget* that Mr. Anderson prepared for his grocery and meat store on June 30. His budgeting process consisted of (a) tabulating the items from his income statement, (b) computing percentages on the basis of the total sales, (c) comparing his experience with the experiences of others by using the standard percentages of a large group of other similar stores, (d) estimating for the next six months each item on the income statement

J. A. Anderson
Budgeted Income Statement
For Six Months Ending December 31, 19—

Income, Expense, and Profit	Amounts for Past Six Months (a)	Percent of Sales (b)	Standards for Comparison (c)	Amounts Budgeted Next Six Months (d)	Estimated Percent (e)
Sales	$63,400.00	100.00%	100.00%	$65,000.00	100.00%
Cost of merchandise sold	52,495.20	82.80	82.60	53,755.00	82.70
Gross profit	10,904.80	17.20	17.40	11,245.00	17.30
Selling expenses:					
Supplies	266.28	.42	.43	286.00	.44
Wages	2,371.16	3.74	3.77	2,457.00	3.78
Advertising	1,020.74	1.61	1.60	1,046.50	1.61
Miscellaneous expense	190.20	.30	.31	208.00	.32
Total selling expenses	3,848.38	6.07	6.11	3,997.50	6.15
Administrative expenses:					
Repairs and maintenance	329.68	.52	.53	325.00	.50
Bad debts	12.68	.02	.02	13.00	.02
Administrative and legal	247.26	.39	.40	260.00	.40
Rent	890.00	1.40	1.40	890.00	1.37
Utilities	576.94	.91	.93	585.00	.90
Insurance	215.56	.34	.35	227.50	.35
Taxes and licenses	583.28	.92	.91	598.00	.92
Interest on loans	107.78	.17	.16	110.50	.17
Depreciation of assets	538.90	.85	.85	559.00	.86
Total administrative expenses	3,502.08	5.52	5.55	3,568.00	5.49
Total expenses	7,350.46	11.59	11.66	7,565.50	11.64
Net income	3,554.34	5.61	5.74	3,679.50	5.66

ILLUS. 22-9. An income statement budget.

on the basis of his past experience and his plans for the future, and
(e) calculating the percentages of his estimates to see how his budget
compares with experiences of others. After computing his estimated
percentages, he might have found one of his figures to be considerably
out of line with his previous experience or with the standard percentage.
He might then revise the budget and try to operate within the new
limit.

ADMINISTERING THE BUDGET

No budget can be followed exactly in a business. One must remember that a budget is an estimate and that it therefore cannot be exact.
It is merely a guess of what may happen. If the sales increase more
than was anticipated, all elements of the budget can be adjusted,
particularly purchasing. If the sales decrease more than was anticipated,
economies must be put into effect as soon as possible.

The operations of the business should be checked periodically,
preferably monthly but in some cases weekly, to determine whether
the business is making a profit and whether the budget is being followed.
If the budget is not being followed closely enough to insure a profit,
it may be necessary to reduce some items of expense or to find new
ways of promoting business.

An important analysis is to check the budget periodically to see how
the actual operating performance compares with the budgeted estimates.
(Illustration 22-10 shows a comparison of actual sales and advertising
expenditures for the first quarter of a year with estimated sales and
advertising for the same quarter.) If a comparison of actual operating performance with the budget estimates reveals that the business

Items	Estimated Sales First Quarter	Actual Sales First Quarter	Estimated Advertising First Quarter	Actual Advertising First Quarter
Radios	$ 3,000	$ 2,770	$ 55	$ 49
Televisions	4,200	3,605	100	87
Ranges	1,500	1,620	40	42
Refrigerators	4,250	4,335	75	67
Gas stoves	750	695	30	25
Lamps	3,900	4,223	105	118
Furniture	4,150	4,100	135	142
Household furnishings .	2,725	2,897	75	77
Household equipment .	3,050	2,816	60	46
Total	$27,525	$27,061	$675	$653

ILLUS. 22-10. A comparison of estimated figures with actual figures.

will not make the anticipated profit or will have a loss, the manager must review the expenses to determine what can be done to reduce them. Economies can be effected by budgeting the inventories carefully to avoid buying unnecessary new merchandise and to reduce the quantity of old items in inventory. If sales are considerably below the anticipated level, it may be necessary to make drastic adjustments, such as the reduction of delivery service, the elimination of part of the personnel, or the cancellation of certain purchases.

CONTROLLING BUSINESS OPERATIONS

In addition to budgeting, many other accounting and financial techniques are available to the businessman for controlling the operations of his business.

Interpreting Financial Statements

The study of the financial statements is the main means of control in the management of a business. Businessmen use the *income statement* (also called the *profit and loss statement*) and the *balance sheet* as part of the means of controlling their operations. Every business should have these two statements prepared at least once a year, but preferably every six months. In many cases they are prepared every month.

Let us consider a grocery business that is operated by Mr. J. A. Anderson. His income statement is shown in Illustration 22-11, page 458. It provides Mr. Anderson with an analysis of the results of his operations during a period of six months ending on December 31. The information reported on this statement was obtained from the accounting records. The statement discloses the fact that a net profit of $3,742.20 was made during the six-month period.

Illustration 22-12 on page 459 is a balance sheet that was prepared at the same time as the income statement. The purpose of the balance sheet is to show the condition (assets, liabilities, and ownership) of the business on a specific date. According to this statement, on December 31 the net worth, or capital, of Mr. Anderson is $11,724.50. On July 1 his net worth amounted to $10,382.30. During the six months between July 1 and December 31, Mr. Anderson withdrew $2,400 for his own purposes. If he had not made these withdrawals, the net worth would be $2,400 more.

Quite often it is important to compare the results of one year with those of the previous year or years. For instance, the income and

J. A. Anderson
Income Statement
For Six Months Ended December 31, 19—

Income from sales		
Sales		$64,500.00
Cost of merchandise sold		
Merchandise inventory, July 1	$ 5,687.50	
Purchases	54,405.50	
Total cost of merchandise available for sale	$60,093.00	
Less merchandise inventory, December 31	6,816.00	
Cost of merchandise sold		53,277.00
Gross profit on sales		$11,223.00
Operating expenses:		
Selling expenses:		
Supplies	$ 273.00	
Wages	2,430.50	
Advertising	1,025.00	
Miscellaneous expense	197.25	
Total selling expenses		$ 3,925.75
Administrative expenses:		
Repairs and maintenance	$ 327.00	
Bad debts	11.50	
Administrative and legal	255.00	
Rent	890.00	
Utilities	582.00	
Insurance	232.50	
Taxes and licenses	593.00	
Interest on loans	109.25	
Depreciation of assets	554.80	
Total administrative expenses		3,555.05
Total operating expenses		$ 7,480.80
Net income		$ 3,742.20

ILLUS. 22-11. An income statement.

expenses of one year may be tabulated alongside the income and expenses of the preceding year or the statements of several years. Such tabulations are known as *comparative reports*. At a glance, one is then able to make a comparison of various items for two or more years. Similar comparisons may be made of balance sheet items for two or more years.

J. A. Anderson
Balance Sheet
December 31, 19—

Assets		
Current assets:		
Cash	$ 2,026.50	
Accounts receivable	714.50	
Merchandise inventory	6,816.00	
Supplies	72.13	
Insurance	77.00	
Total current assets		$ 9,706.13
Fixed assets:		
Equipment	$13,500.00	
Less depreciation	2,475.30	
Total fixed assets		11,024.70
Total assets		$20,730.83
Liabilities		
Current liabilities:		
Accounts payable	$ 5,259.63	
Accrued wages payable	160.10	
Taxes payable	86.60	
Total current liabilities		$ 5,506.33
Long-term liabilities:		
Bank loan, 5-year		3,500.00
Total liabilities		$ 9,006.33
Proprietorship		
J. A. Anderson, Capital, July 1	$10,382.30	
Net income for period $3,742.20		
Less withdrawals 2,400.00		
Net increase in capital	1,342.20	
J. A. Anderson, Capital, December 31		11,724.50
Total liabilities and proprietorship		$20,730.83

ILLUS. 22-12. A balance sheet.

As you examine the balance sheets in Illustration 22-13, page 460, you will notice that there are some changes in most of the figures. The most important change is in the merchandise inventory, which has increased. Possibly the business is carrying too much inventory in December. Notice also that the proprietorship has increased.

There are many items on a balance sheet that may need examining. We have already mentioned the matter of merchandise. Accounts

J. A. Anderson
Comparative Balance Sheet
June 30, 19—, and December 31, 19—

Assets	June 30		December 31	
Current assets:				
Cash	$ 1,875.75		$ 2,026.50	
Accounts receivable	682.30		714.50	
Merchandise				
inventory	5,687.50		6,816.00	
Supplies	68.42		72.13	
Insurance	65.00		77.00	
Total current assets		$ 8,378.97		$ 9,706.13
Fixed assets:				
Equipment	$13,500.00		$13,500.00	
Less depreciation	1,920.50		2,475.30	
Total fixed assets		11,579.50		11,024.70
Total assets		$19,958.47		$20,730.83
Liabilities				
Current liabilities: ...				
Accounts payable	$ 5,825.42		$ 5,259.63	
Accrued wages payable	153.00		160.10	
Taxes payable	97.75		86.60	
Total current liabilities		$ 6,076.17		$ 5,506.33
Long-term liabilities:				
Bank loan, 5-year ..		3,500.00		3,500.00
Total liabilities		$ 9,576.17		$ 9,006.33
Proprietorship				
J. A. Anderson, beginning capital	$ 9,132.30		$10,382.30	
Net increase in capital	1,250.00		1,342.20	
J. A. Anderson, ending capital		10,382.30		11,724.50
Total liabilities and proprietorship		$19,958.47		$20,730.83

ILLUS. 22-13. A comparative balance sheet.

receivable is another item which must be studied frequently. In Chapter 20 there was a discussion of aging accounts receivable. The aging of accounts receivable refers to the examination of each account to determine if it is past due. Accounts payable must also be examined regularly to be sure that the creditors are paid when their accounts are due and to be sure that the creditors are paid promptly in order to obtain the cash discount.

Trends in business may be determined by monthly or yearly comparisons of the items in the balance sheet statement and items in the income statement. When figures are available, it is desirable to make comparisons for three or four years, or even more years, in order to show the trends of the business.

Ratio Analysis

The simple financial statements that have just been presented are not always sufficient to enable the manager to interpret the condition of the business. An accountant can prepare numerous ratios that will help to analyze the business. For instance, he may compute a ratio to show the relationship between current assets and current liabilities. Such a ratio helps to determine the ability of the business to pay its current debts. For example, if a business has $3 of current assets for every $1 of current liabilities, the business is better able to pay its liabilities when they become due than it would be if the ratio were two to one or one to one. No ratio can be set as a standard because some types of businesses do not require as large a ratio as others.

Another important ratio is the relationship between sales and cost of merchandise sold, an analysis of which is usually handled by an accountant. The manager of the business must understand something about accounting in order to understand these figures. For instance, even though the businessman may not be sufficiently familiar with accounting procedure to prepare the financial statements, he should be able to look at them and understand the figures. As an example, assume that during one year the cost of merchandise sold amounted to 80 percent of the gross sales and that during the next year the cost of merchandise sold amounted to 85 percent of the gross sales. Obviously, therefore, the manager should be concerned with figuring a way of reducing the cost of merchandise sold or of increasing the selling price. Otherwise the trend indicates that eventually gross profit, and therefore net income, will be eliminated.

Illustration 22-14 shows a ratio analysis for various types of wholesalers and retailers that was prepared by Dun and Bradstreet, Incorporated. Such ratios are of interest to the businessman because he can compare his business with others. For instance, the ratio of current assets to current debts is computed by dividing the total amount of such assets as cash, accounts receivable, and merchandise by the total amount of such liabilities as accounts payable and notes payable. If a

	Current Assets to Current Debt (Ratio)	Net Profits on Net Sales (Percentage)	Average Collection Period (Days)	Net Sales to Inventory (Times)
Wholesalers:				
Automobile parts, accessories	2.75	2.13	35	4.9
Dairy products	1.73	1.03	29	30.5
Drugs, drug sundries	2.11	1.34	36	6.3
Groceries	2.07	.58	13	11.2
Hardware	2.89	1.48	44	4.5
Retailers:				
Clothing, men's and boys'	2.71	2.40	..	4.0
Farm, garden supplies	2.48	2.46	..	9.1
Lumber	3.21	1.98	51	5.8
Women's specialty shops	2.50	2.18	..	6.1

Source: Dun and Bradstreet, Inc.

ILLUS. 22-14. A ratio analysis.

businessman has such comparative ratios prepared for his own business each month or each year, he is kept aware of his financial condition.

Reports and Exhibits

In large organizations numerous reports and exhibits are prepared for the benefit of executives. These types of reports are also useful in smaller organizations. Such reports may be classified as follows:

1. Reports showing the anticipated results of future operations. These reports include estimates of sales, purchases, production, financial condition, income, and similar reports.
2. Reports showing a comparison between the actual results and the estimated results. These reports make possible the enforcement of budgets and provide data for use in revising the budgets when revision is necessary.
3. Reports showing the present financial condition. The balance sheet, with various subsidiary schedules, is the most commonly used report.

4. Reports showing the results of past operations in terms of income and expense. The various forms of income and expense analysis and the standard form of income statement with subsidiary schedules are used for this purpose.

5. Reports showing information necessary for the daily actions of executives and employees. These reports may include a statement for the treasurer showing a summary of cash transactions; a report for the collection manager showing accounts 30, 60, and 90 days past due; a report for the sales manager showing the slow-moving items of stock; and other reports of a similar nature.

6. Reports providing data on conditions external to the business but affecting the plans and policies of the business. These reports are usually of a statistical nature and present data helpful in making the departmental budgets, as well as in deciding policies for the business as a whole. Many of the reports are prepared from data collected and analyzed by agencies outside the business itself.

REVIEW WHAT YOU HAVE LEARNED

Business Terms Checkup:

(1) bookkeeping and accounting records
(2) double-entry system
(3) single-entry system
(4) depreciation
(5) obsolescence
(6) insurance register
(7) fixed assets register
(8) microfilming
(9) budget
(10) sales budget
(11) merchandising and purchasing budget
(12) advertising budget
(13) cash budget
(14) income statement budget
(15) income statement
(16) balance sheet
(17) comparative reports

Reading Checkup:

1. If a businessman cannot keep accounting records or have a bookkeeper, what can he do to keep the records?

2. Name at least five kinds of information that a manager or an owner of a business should expect to obtain from his accounting records.

3. Why is a double-entry system of bookkeeping better than a single-entry bookkeeping system?

4. From the daily balance form of a service station shown on page 443:
   (a) What is the amount of cash sales?
   (b) What is the amount of the charge sales?
   (c) What is the cash register total?
   (d) How much was received on account during the day?
   (e) How much was outstanding as accounts receivable at the end of the day?
5. In a large business how are some of the functions in an accounting department divided?
6. Give at least two suggestions for the safe handling of cash.
7. Explain a system of handling unpaid invoices.
8. Why is depreciation a part of the cost of doing business?
9. What kind of information is shown in an insurance register? In a fixed assets register?
10. What are the principal types of information that must be reported for federal income tax purposes?
11. Is an employer required by law to make income tax deductions from the wages of employees?
12. What information with regard to wages must the employer give to each employee?
13. Name the types of information that must be recorded for social security and payroll tax purposes for each employee and for all employees as a group.
14. If a business cannot afford to purchase automated data processing equipment, how may such equipment be used by the business?
15. What is an advantage of microfilming of records? A disadvantage?
16. What is a budget?
17. Name some classifications or bases on which it is possible to estimate the sales of a business.
18. Is a budget ever changed after it has been prepared?
19. What is the purpose of a balance sheet?
20. What is meant by comparative financial statements?
21. How is a ratio analysis of benefit to the businessman?

APPLY WHAT YOU HAVE LEARNED

Questions for Class Discussion:

1. Explain what types of bookkeeping information should be recorded daily in a business and give your reasons why.

2. Since depreciation does not involve a cash expenditure, why is it an expense?

3. If you had a machine that normally would last 10 years and then could probably be sold for a certain amount of money, how would you proceed to set up a depreciation rate on the machine?

4. Why do you believe that a fixed assets register is necessary?

5. What are some of the advantages of an insurance policy register?

6. How important do you think it is to include accurate information in the federal income tax return?

7. Why must the production manager know the estimated sales budget?

8. Why is the cash budget so important from the viewpoint of the owner of a small business or the director of a large business?

9. Give examples of some situations in which there would be a favorable condition if the percentages in a budgeted income statement were different from those which are standards or averages of other businesses.

10. What value is there in basing a budget of income and expenses on past experiences?

11. In this chapter there is a list of certain factors that may influence sales estimates. How will the economic trend affect a sales budget?

12. What would be considered the better ratio: (a) $2 in current assets for every $1 of current liabilities or (b) $1 in current assets for every $2 of current liabilities? Give your reasons.

13. If a businessman hires boys during school vacation, do you think it is necessary to deduct the usual amount for federal income taxes from their wages?

14. Why may it be an advantage to have monthly statements of customers prepared on a computer, even though the cost may be greater than doing this work by hand?

Problems and Projects:

1. L. A. Hendricks has assets as follows: (a) a store building that he bought two years ago at a cost of $20,000, not including the value of the land; (b) store equipment that cost $3,000 and was installed when the building was bought; (c) a used delivery truck that was bought two years ago for $2,000. Assume the following with regard to depreciation: (a) the building decreases in value at the estimated rate of 5 percent a year; (b) the store equipment decreases at the estimated rate of 10 percent a year; and (c) the truck will last one more year and can be traded in then for $300. What is the depreciated value of the assets now?

2. J. P. Caswell, who operates an appliance store, asks you in your capacity as a bookkeeper to prepare a budgeted income statement for

the year ending December 31, 19——. The estimated sales are $248,000 and the percentages which Caswell wishes to allow for the various items are as follows: Cost of merchandise sold, 65% of the sales; salaries and wages, 15.8%; advertising, .8%; donations, .1%; supplies used, .4%; miscellaneous office expense, .15%; telephone expense, .12%; delivery expense, 1.2%; taxes and insurance, .8%; rent, 2.5%; heat, light, water, .52%; loss from bad debts, 1%; interest paid, .3%; repairs and depreciation, .6%; other expenses, .5%.

3. George Maddox operates a shoe store. His income and expenses for a calendar year are as follows:

Sales	$114,609.04	Delivery expense	$ 460.00
Cost of		Taxes	1,104.00
merchandise sold	87,586.00	Insurance	345.00
Salaries and wages	12,800.00	Rent	2,880.00
Advertising	833.20	Heat, light, and water	607.00
Donations	180.00	Interest paid	268.00
Supplies	369.20	Depreciation	
Office expense	164.60	and repairs	988.00
Telephone	192.00	Miscellaneous expense	392.40

Compute the gross profit on sales, total operating expenses, the net income, and the percentage of each item in relation to sales, which represent 100 percent.

4. On page 455 there is a budgeted income statement for J. A. Anderson for six months ending December 31, 19——. Instead of the estimated sales of $65,000 in the budget, assume sales of $90,000 for the next six months and prepare an estimated budget based upon the estimated percentages in the last column of Anderson's illustrated budget.

Case Problem 22-1:

The Jetworth Manufacturing Company had the following income statement for the past year:

Sales (10,000 units)	$200,000
Cost of Merchandise Sold	120,000
Gross Profit	$ 80,000
Selling Expense	$40,000
General Expense	36,000
Total Expense	76,000
Net Income	$ 4,000

The management was not happy with this low profit and asked the sales manager to make a study. His recommendation was to reduce costs through a 50 percent increase in production. He promised to sell the increased number of units if the price were reduced 10 percent.

Estimates were then made; and it was determined that the cost of each unit would decrease 15 percent, the total selling expense would increase 20 percent, and general expenses would increase 5 percent.

Required:

Prepare a budget for the next year based on these estimates.

Case Problem 22-2:

The following assets are owned by S. A. Smith:

Item	Original Cost	Date of Purchase	
Building	$25,000	July	1
Truck #1	6,000	March	2
Truck #2	3,000	October	3
Equipment			
Group #1	4,000	July	22
Group #2	1,000	September	1
Group #3	6,000	November	18

Smith is interested in setting up a fixed asset register which will show the depreciation expense per year and the book value at the end of this year and for the next four years. The building will depreciate 5% per year while the equipment depreciates 10% per year, and the trucks will last an anticipated five years.

Required:

Rule a sheet of plain paper and list headings for the item, original cost, yearly depreciation, and the book value for the next five years starting with the current year.

Continuing Project:

(a) Under the guidance of your teacher, prepare a list of accounts that will be used in the bookkeeping system of your firm. Select the different kinds of records that will be used and draw up a plan for your bookkeeping system. Indicate what policies will be followed in regard to your bookkeeping practices.

(b) Based upon the knowledge that you have gained in your previous study and the information you have collected, prepare a detailed budget for the operations of your business for one year.

What functions are performed in an office?

What is contained in an office manual?

What machines are used in handling mail?

What filing systems do offices use?

Why do offices want standardized supplies?

Why are office flow charts prepared?

BACKGROUND OF CHAPTER

Every business, no matter what its size, must perform office work, such as handling mail, filing, and communications. The office of a small business may consist of one desk and a file cabinet. Contrasted with this is the office of a large business in which many trained employees and the most modern equipment are required to handle office work. Whether small or large, though, the office provides services needed by all segments of the business.

This chapter describes the specific services performed in an office and the essential problems of organizing and operating an office.

CHAPTER 23

OFFICE SERVICES

The office provides services such as the handling of incoming and outgoing mail, correspondence, filing, telegrams, supplies, equipment, and many types of records. Some of the functions performed in a large office are shown in the organization chart in Illustration 23-1.

There are several departments of a business that must obtain service through the office. These departments that require office service are accounting, credit, sales, advertising, purchasing, finance, and production. Of course, each of these departments may have its own staff but will depend upon the general office for some of its work and service. Several of these specialized functions that are performed in the general office are described in Chapters 12, 19, and 20.

MANAGEMENT OF THE OFFICE

Business establishments differ widely in their methods of fixing responsibility for the management of an office, because different types and sizes of business organizations have widely differing needs for office services.

Organization of Large Offices

In a large business the office manager often ranks with the managers of such departments as credit, accounting, and purchasing. If the head of the accounting department or of some other department is responsible also for managing the office, the management of the office is likely to be neglected.

When the office work is organized as a department of the business, the office manager will work in close cooperation with other departmental executives. Under this type of organization much can be done to promote harmony and efficiency. Furthermore, the duplication of work.

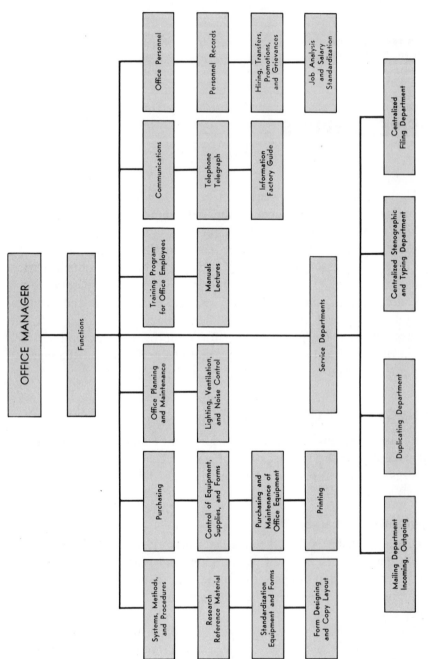

ILLUS. 23-1. Organization of an office.

can be eliminated. For example, there can be a centralized filing unit and a centralized stenographic force. If, on the other hand, the stenographic force is divided among the various departments, there is a likelihood that at certain times one department will be extremely busy while another will be idle; but the busy department may not be able to call upon the idle department for assistance. Under a centralized system the office help can do whatever work is necessary at the time.

Organization of Small Offices

In a small office most of the functions of a large office are performed, but they are performed by fewer individuals. In some respects the managing of a small office is more difficult than that of a large office because each individual must perform more duties.

When the first office worker is hired, the work may then be divided. The manager may continue to take care of the bookkeeping, purchasing, and general management of the business; the new clerk or stenographer may take care of the stenographic, billing, and other general clerical duties. On the other hand, the first employee may be a bookkeeper who will also perform duties such as filing and mailing.

Even though a small office may have employees who ordinarily take care of the stenographic, filing, bookkeeping, and general clerical work, it is often advisable to send out work to other agencies. This particularly applies to reproduction and duplicating services, such as mimeographing, production and mailing of large quantities of letters, mailing of large quantities of advertising literature, and other similar functions. These cannot be performed economically with a small staff.

Importance of Office Manuals

There are some who believe that in a small office an office manual is not necessary because there are so few workers and because they work so closely together. However, in a small office a manual may be needed more than it is in a large office. Whoever is running a small office usually has many duties, and he may not always be available for consultation about company policies and procedures. A manual that presents all information clearly will therefore be very helpful.

Certainly in a large organization there is need for at least one general office manual. For example, if there are hundreds of employees in an office, it is quite likely that they will be following many different policies and procedures unless these have been developed in written form for the employees.

There are two main types of office manuals. One is the *general company manual* which covers matters of (1) organization, (2) policies, and (3) procedures and practices. In other words, in the general manual there is complete coverage of the matters that are important to everyone in the entire organization.

A second type of office manual is the *departmental manual* which deals with specific policies relating to a particular department and covers the procedures and practices in that department. It may include specific job instructions, or they may be included in a separate manual.

Various types of manuals are commonly prepared for stenographers and secretaries. A manual of this type will cover in detail the procedures, standards, styles, and policies in regard to correspondence. In a similar manner, a manual for the filing department will explain the filing system, procedures, practices, and will describe in detail how every job in the filing department is to be performed.

Functions of Office Management

Regardless of who performs the functions of office management and regardless of whether the office is large or small, there are certain functions that must be performed. Some of the most important functions are:

1. Providing proper working space and satisfactory arrangement of workers and equipment.
2. Obtaining proper equipment.
3. Preparing and obtaining supplies of office forms and stationery.
4. Providing for the handling of dictation and transcription of correspondence.
5. Providing and maintaining a filing system.
6. Directing the system of handling incoming and outgoing mail.
7. Setting up and supervising a system of internal communications.
8. Selecting, training, and supervising office workers.
9. Studying office procedures to find ways to improve them.
10. Preparing an office manual that will provide information and instructions for employees.

PERFORMING OFFICE SERVICES EFFICIENTLY

The performance of office work is not a profit-making function in a business organization. However, inefficiency in the performance of office work will reduce profits, and this section is devoted to a discussion of the effective performance of certain of the office services.

ILLUS. 23-2. Inefficiency in the performance of office work will reduce profits.

Handling Mail

The system a business uses to sort and distribute incoming mail and to address and send outgoing mail will depend on the size of the business. In a small business one person may be able to take care of both incoming and outgoing mail. Larger businesses will require one or more persons to handle incoming mail and others to handle outgoing mail.

Handling Incoming Mail. In every office, large and small, some particular person or persons should be responsible for sorting and distributing the incoming mail. In some offices it is desirable to hand to the proper persons the unopened mail. In many large offices, however, a special mailing department will open the mail, stamp it with the time of arrival, and distribute it to the proper persons or departments. Mail within the office is usually delivered by means of an organized messenger system.

Particular care should be taken in scanning mail to discover its general contents, to check enclosures (particularly such items as cash or checks), and to verify any mistakes that might be evident before the mail is distributed. If there is a difference between the statements in a letter and the actual enclosures, this discrepancy should be marked on the mail. Checks and other enclosures should be attached to letters before the mail is distributed.

The incoming letter should always be checked with the envelope before destroying the envelope. If the letter does not contain a complete name and address, the envelope should be attached to the letter or the necessary information should be recorded on the letter.

Handling Outgoing Mail. Even in a small business some system should be followed in handling outgoing mail. Some one person should be in charge of it if the quantity of outgoing mail is large. The internal messenger system should provide not only for distributing mail but also for collecting outgoing mail. Under an organized mailing system the mailing department collects all outgoing mail, checks enclosures, and further prepares the letters for mailing. In some offices the mailing department is responsible for folding, weighing, stamping, sealing, and tying the mail in bundles according to ZIP codes.

It is ordinarily not advisable to allow everyone in the office to handle stamps. If a postage meter machine, as described in the following paragraphs, is not used, some one person should be responsible for handling the stamps and usually for stamping the mail.

Special Mailing Equipment. Businesses having a large amount of outgoing mail usually make use of some types of special mailing equipment.

Postage Meter Machines. Postage meter machines, which in one operation seal, stamp, and stack the mail, are commonly used as time-saving devices. These meters print the postage on mail instead of affixing adhesive stamps. Such a meter is taken to the local post office where it is set for the amount of postage for which the business pays. When the meter has printed the full amount for which it was set, it automatically locks and prevents further operation. Most models, such as the one shown in Illustration 23-3, can be adjusted to print postage in various denominations. Use of a postage meter is especially desirable in the shipping department of a business that sends out small packages requiring various amounts of postage. The postage and the postmark are printed on a gummed tape that can be affixed easily to a package.

Some advantages of using a postage meter machine are:

1. It speeds mail delivery by eliminating time-consuming operations at the post office. Stamps printed on this machine do not have to be canceled at the post office.
2. It safeguards the postage account by eliminating the mutilation, waste, theft, and misuse of postage.

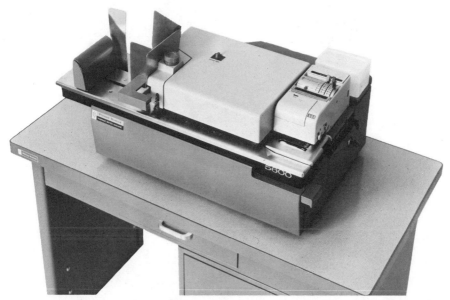

Pitney-Bowes, Inc.

ILLUS. 23-3. Postage meter machines can seal, stamp, and stack mail in one operation.

3. Daily or departmental costs for postage are available by reading the meter registers, which show the number of pieces mailed, the amount of postage used, and the balance still on hand.
4. Such a machine saves time in the preparation of mail because it affixes the postage, seals the envelope, and stacks the mail.
5. It gives the mail a uniform and neat appearance.
6. Special advertising can be printed on the mail at the same time that the postage is printed.

Parcel Post Scales. Businesses that need to mail many parcels usually make use of a special parcel post scale. By means of a precision indicator which acts fast, stops instantly, and is easy to read, the proper amount of postage may be automatically determined.

Addressing Equipment. Any office that has large amounts of material to be mailed to the same people regularly needs some kind of addressing equipment. For example, if a business has a mailing list of 5,000 names to which advertising pieces are sent regularly, it would be much cheaper and quicker to address the material by machine than by hand. The usual method is to make an address plate or a stencil for

Cheshire Incorporated

ILLUS. 23-4. Equipment such as the Cheshire 514 can save many hours in addressing correspondence.

each name and address. These can be fed through a machine which automatically addresses envelopes and other kinds of matter to be mailed. Such a machine is shown in Illustration 23-4.

Many utility companies, insurance companies, and others punch the names and addresses of customers on cards. When it is time for bills to be sent, the name and address card with one or more additional punched cards showing the amount of charges are inserted into electronic equipment which will print the name and address as well as the amount of charges due.

Handling Calls and Visitors

In most offices the switchboard operator acts as the receptionist for those who visit the office. In some offices, however, a special reception clerk is used in order to avoid interference with the duties of the tele-phone operator.

Regardless of who handles this function, the person should have exceptional qualities. She should be calm, pleasant, and courteous. Her diction should be clear and precise. She should have a good working knowledge of the organization so that, if she is questioned about it, she can answer satisfactorily. She should be acquainted with the policies of the organization so that she will know what to do in giving informa-tion and in handling callers. Since this person represents the company to the public, her position is very important.

Internal Communications

In most offices the messenger who distributes the incoming mail and collects the outgoing mail is also responsible for distributing *interde-partmental* or *interoffice communications*. In some small offices the stenographer or the secretary who types an interdepartmental com-munication may pass it from one person to another; but in large offices where there are many such communications, such a plan will cause con-siderable confusion, delay, and inefficiency. It is common for each department to have baskets or trays for incoming and outgoing com-munications. Communications coming to the department are placed in

anderson importers   interoffice memo

```
        TO:  Thomas Duffy
      FROM:  Donald Romero
      DATE:  September 5, 19--

   SUBJECT:  Centralized Stenographic Unit

   For some time I have been thinking that we should centralize
   the stenographic services in the office.  I have worked out a
   plan that I think will be satisfactory to everyone.  Before
   putting the plan in operation, however, I want to discuss it
   with all department heads.

   I wish you would meet with the other department heads in my
   office on Friday, September 9, at 2:00 p.m. to discuss this
   matter.  If you will be unable to attend, please send one of
   your assistants.

   av
```

ILLUS. 23-5. A good form of interoffice communication.

one tray; those that are to be distributed to other departments are placed in the other.

The messenger who handles the interoffice communications should pass through the office at regularly established intervals to collect and to distribute communications. He should also be on call at any other time to handle any necessary messages.

The internal telephone system, handled through the switchboard or through another type of speaking system, may be used for oral communications within the office.

Stenographic Services

As a business grows beyond the one-man stage, it is usually necessary to have some kind of stenographic service. This service can be obtained by hiring at least one stenographer or by using a public stenographer or stenographic agency.

In many small offices the first stenographer who is hired serves in many capacities. She may, for instance, keep the books, do the filing, and perform other office duties. She may or may not write shorthand. Many small businesses find the use of voice-writing machines quite advantageous. While the stenographer is busy with other duties, the manager of the business may dictate letters and other communications that are recorded on plastic discs, belts, tapes, or wire. When the stenographer has time, she transcribes the correspondence and presents it to her employer for his signature.

Businesses differ widely in the extent to which they centralize the responsibility for the preparation of outgoing and interdepartmental communications. In some cases each executive or employee regularly responsible for the preparation of such communications has his personal stenographer. The employees who are only occasionally responsible for the preparation of communications use stenographers available for such service or dictate to a machine.

On the other hand, it may be that none of the executives or employees have personal stenographers. A central stenographic "pool" provides a stenographer on request. A further development of this plan is the use of dictating machines and a centralized transcription department. The executives and employees dictate to the machines whenever they desire. The discs, belts, or tapes are collected at regular intervals and taken to the transcription department where the transcripts are made. The transcribed material is then returned to the dictators who inspect and sign it. It is then collected by the mail messengers.

ILLUS. 23-6. Most businesses require some kind of stenographic service.

In some offices recording machines are located in a centralized transcription department with wires running to each dictator's desk. The dictator, by means of a sort of telephone connection, dictates directly to the machine located in the transcription department. This plan saves considerable equipment and expense.

In some businesses there are some *correspondents* (specialists in writing letters) who handle the routine correspondence. It is unnecessarily expensive to have high-salaried executives devoting their time to answering routine inquiries and complaints that can be handled just as well by medium-salaried employees. In some cases, too, the use of correspondents leads to the preparation of better letters.

Filing Services

In most businesses the correspondence and other material for filing soon reach such proportions that it is not feasible to have separate files for each office, executive, or employee. Both efficiency and economy are promoted by the use of a centralized filing service.

As soon as the one who receives any correspondence or other material has completed his present use of it, it is sent to the files. If it is

ILLUS. 23-7. In most businesses it is more efficient and more economical to have a centralized filing service.

desired later, a memorandum requesting it is sent to the filing department. When the material is removed from the file, an "out card" containing a memorandum of the material that has been removed from the file (see Illustration 23-8) is inserted in its place. If anyone goes to the files for this particular correspondence, the out card shows who has the correspondence. In some offices a duplicate of the out card, prepared on a different colored form, is used as a *follow-up card*. It is placed in a tickler file with other follow-up cards so that the proper follow-up will be made if the borrowed material is not returned. A *tickler file* (file of reminders listed in chronological order) may also be used for other types of follow-up cards.

The filing department should be located near those departments that make most frequent use of it, or some mechanical means should be employed to transfer material as quickly as possible. If an executive has frequent need for specific material, he may keep this material in a private file.

When a central filing system is used, only the filing clerks should be permitted to file correspondence or to take correspondence from the files. If others are permitted to go to the files, there are too many chances of errors, and no one can be held responsible.

OUT			
SUBSTITUTION CARD			FILE AT EXTREME RIGHT OF FOLDER
NUMBER, NAME OR SUBJECT	DATES OF LETTERS	ISSUED TO	DATE ISSUED
Shaw Equipment Supply	June 14, 19—	G. Breem	August 13, 19—
Keystone Savings and Loan	May 9, 19—	P. Cox	August 21, 19—
Vulcan Brick Company	July 1, 19—	C. Guzi	Sept. 9, 19—

ILLUS. 23-8. Out card: a memorandum of material removed from the files.

If there are individual departmental files in addition to the files of the central filing department, there should be close correlation between them. If something is filed in a departmental file that has a relation to the general files, a duplicate should be placed in the general files or there should be some other method of cross-referencing.

Indexing and Filing Systems. There are fundamentally four systems of indexing and filing correspondence: alphabetic name, subject, geographic, and numeric. However, there are variations of these.

Under the *alphabetic name filing system* general alphabetic divisions are indicated on the tabs of the guide cards, and material is filed by names between these alphabetic divisions.

Under the *subject filing system* the subjects are indicated on the tabs and are generally arranged alphabetically.

Under the *geographic filing system* the guide cards are arranged alphabetically according to the states, the cities, or the counties indicated on the tabs; and within these geographic divisions material is filed alphabetically according to the names of the correspondents.

Numeric filing requires the classification of correspondence into groups that are numbered. Such a plan necessitates the keeping of a separate card index to indicate in what section of the numeric files particular correspondence can be found.

Visible Files and Indexes. Besides filing cards in boxes, there are several different kinds of systems used for filing cards with information on them so that the information can be quickly found. These are called *visible files* (see Illustration 23-9). A portion of the card, usually showing the name or subject, remains visible even when the card is filed. The cards may be filed under any one of the indexing systems. The two most common types of visible files are the flat drawer type and those arranged on a wheel, which can be turned quickly to the proper position.

Handling Supplies

The modern tendency is to standardize office supplies as much as possible. *Standardization* is the elimination of numerous unusual sizes and kinds of supplies used in the office. For instance, one company found that it was using twelve different kinds of paper and finally standardized on three. Eight different types of pencils were used. One kind of mechanical pencil was selected as the standard, and leads of different colors were purchased for this pencil.

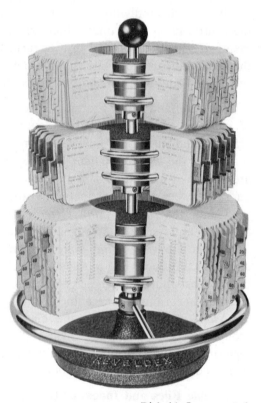

ILLUS. 23-9. Visible files make it possible to find information quickly.

Diebold, Incorporated

Standardization leads to economy in the purchase and the use of supplies. In order that standardization may be established, control should be centralized in the hands of the office manager. Naturally, he must cooperate with employees and department heads.

After the supplies have been selected and requisitioned, they are ordered by the purchasing agent. To facilitate the purchasing process, a card containing all information pertinent to the particular item being ordered is kept on file in the purchasing department and is referred to each time the item is ordered. Such a card, called a *supply specification card,* is shown in Illustration 23-10.

The quantities to be purchased should be determined by the office manager in consultation with the department heads. It is advisable to

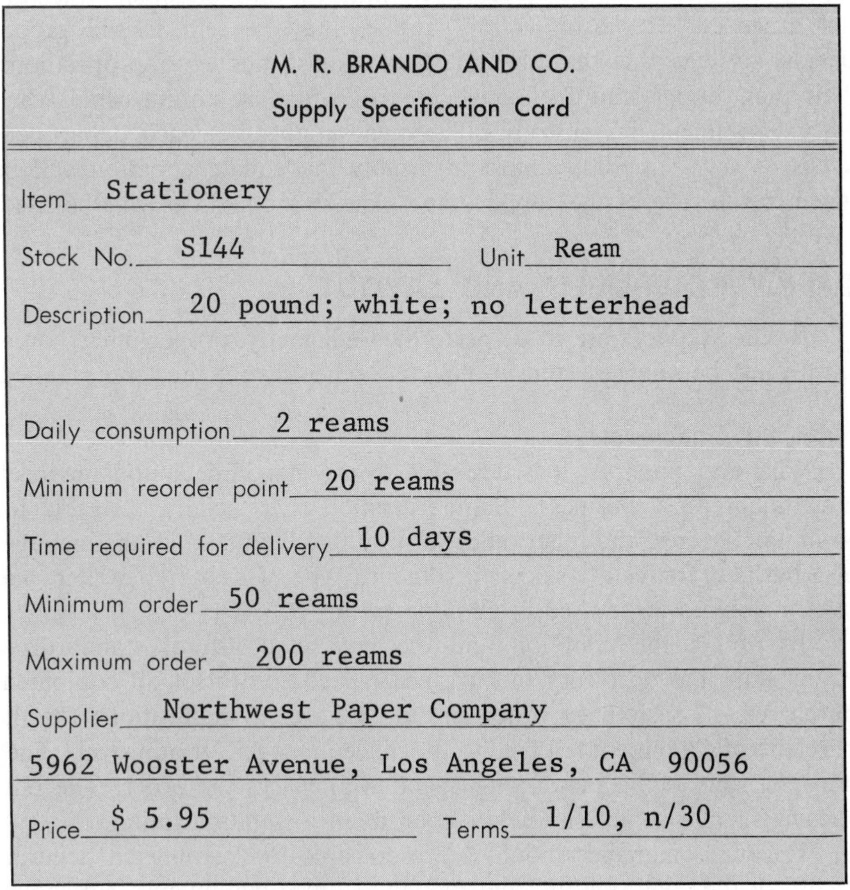

M. R. BRANDO AND CO.
Supply Specification Card

Item___Stationery_____

Stock No.___S144_____ Unit___Ream_____

Description___20 pound; white; no letterhead_____

Daily consumption___2 reams_____

Minimum reorder point___20 reams_____

Time required for delivery___10 days_____

Minimum order___50 reams_____

Maximum order___200 reams_____

Supplier___Northwest Paper Company_____

5962 Wooster Avenue, Los Angeles, CA 90056

Price___$ 5.95_____ Terms___1/10, n/30_____

ILLUS. 23-10. A supply specification card.

establish minimum quantities for stock so that the supplies will not
be exhausted at any time. The maximum quantities to be purchased
will be determined by the savings that can be made in purchasing and
the amount consumed. The purchasing procedure for supplies is
the same as that for merchandise. This procedure is discussed in
Chapter 12.

If supplies are to be used economically, they should be placed in a
central storeroom and issued only upon the request of department heads.
As supplies are checked in or out of stock, the amounts received or
removed should be recorded on a stock-control card similar to that
shown on page 236. The quantity that each department is permitted
to requisition at one time, or within a definite period of time, can
be established; and the storekeeper can see that these amounts are
not exceeded. Requisitions for supplies may be sent to the proper
person so that they can be checked against budget appropriations.
This plan brings about effective control which is not possible when
each department has custody of its own supplies. If each department
keeps its own supplies, almost invariably inadequate attention will be
given to the care of the supplies and excessive quantities will be used.

OFFICE EQUIPMENT AND LAYOUT

If office services are to be performed efficiently, proper office equipment must be selected, and an effective office layout must be planned.

Selecting Equipment

Whenever possible, it is desirable to use standard equipment in all
departments of a business. Standardization is especially desirable for
furniture, fixtures, and other office furnishings. To that end, the manager
of a business frequently selects a standard type of desk, typewriter, and
other machines to be used in all departments.

To obtain the adoption and the continued use of standardized
equipment, it is necessary to have centralized control of all equipment
purchases. A customary procedure is to have all requisitions for the
purchase of equipment referred to the office manager for approval. They
are then sent to the purchasing agent, who places the order. The purchasing agent is sometimes held responsible for standardization.

The office manager should be responsible for keeping an accurate
record of the condition and the repairs of office equipment. He should
make arrangements for servicing, reconditioning, and replacement, and

should also keep himself well informed on new developments in equipment that can be purchased as time-saving devices. Large offices use many types of time-saving equipment. In some small offices such equipment is used only to a limited extent because not many types are needed. Examples of time-saving equipment are listed in Illustration 23-11.

Adding machines	Envelope openers
Addressing machines	Envelope sealers
Billing machines	Letter-folding machines
Bookkeeping machines	Metered mailing machines
Calculating machines	Numbering devices
Card-and-tape punching equipment	Package taping machines
Cash registers	Pencil sharpeners
Check-writing devices	Stamp affixers
Coin changers	Stapling machines
Coin counters and sorters	Tabulating machines
Dating devices	Telegraph receivers and senders
Dictating and transcribing machines	Teletypes
Duplicating machines	Time stamps

ILLUS. 23-11. Time-saving equipment.

A common fault of a man starting a new business is that he invests too much of his money in expensive equipment. It is better to start with

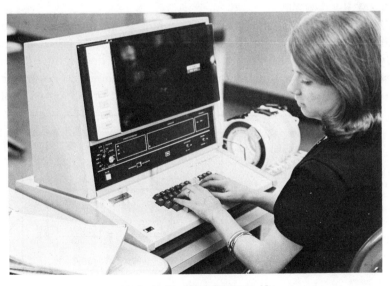

ILLUS. 23-12. Key-to-tape machine.

a minimum of essential equipment and then add new items as they are needed and as money is available.

Of course, every piece of equipment must be selected carefully in terms of the use for which it is intended. For example, there are many kinds of dictating machines, duplicating machines, and bookkeeping machines. Take the problem of selecting an adding or calculating machine, of which there are many varieties. The less expensive ones are hand operated, but most machines are electrically operated. Some are fast and some are slow. Some are very expensive and some are cheaper. Some will perform all types of mathematical calculations, but some will not. Some provide a printed tape record, but others do not. However, there is a machine available that will satisfy the needs for any purpose and often for a variety of purposes.

Great progress is being made in the development of equipment for handling office operations. The types of equipment that we have already mentioned make office work more economical, faster, and more accurate. In Chapter 21 you learned that there are many types of electronic equipment now available for various uses in the office. Although it is not necessary to understand the technical aspects of how this equipment functions, you should understand some of the operations that this equipment will perform. Perhaps you will want to review the discussion of electronic equipment contained in Chapter 21.

Planning the Layout

The layout of an office, large or small, is an important factor in adding to the efficiency of the office. There are two ways of making a study to determine the proper layout. One is to devise an *office flow chart,* such as that in Illustration 23-13, showing how the normal transactions of the office proceed from one department or person to another.

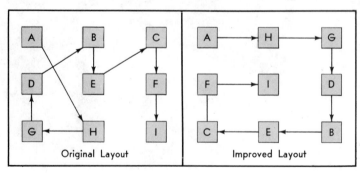

Original Layout   Improved Layout

ILLUS. 23-13. Office flow charts.

The charts in Illustration 23-13 show the original layout of an office and the improved layout. Notice how the rearrangement in the improved layout has eliminated the overlapping and confusion.

Another means of checking the layout of an office is through the use of an *office relationship chart*. For instance, each department will have certain relationships with other departments each day. The department that has the most relationships with another department during an average day should be located nearest the latter department. Of course, certain compromises must be made. Illustration 23-14 shown below shows a chart that was made to determine these relationships and one that was constructed to show an improved layout. Each line indicates that a relationship or a communication is established between the departments or individuals a certain number of times each day.

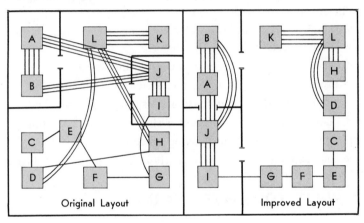

Original Layout · Improved Layout

ILLUS. 23-14. Office relationship charts.

REVIEW WHAT YOU HAVE LEARNED

Business Terms Checkup:

(1) general company manual
(2) departmental manual
(3) postage meter machine
(4) interdepartmental or interoffice communications
(5) correspondents
(6) follow-up card
(7) tickler file
(8) alphabetic name filing system

(9) subject filing system
(10) geographic filing system
(11) numeric filing
(12) visible files
(13) standardization
(14) supply specification card
(15) office flow chart
(16) office relationship chart

Reading Checkup:

1. What are the office functions?
2. In a large office what is likely to happen if a department head, such as the head of the accounting department, is also the general office manager?
3. Why is an office manual sometimes more essential in a small office than in a large office?
4. Name at least three functions of office management.
5. Give some reasons why it is desirable for one person in an office to sort and distribute the incoming mail.
6. If an office has a mailing department that takes care of outgoing mail, what are the responsibilities of that department?
7. State at least two advantages of using a postage meter machine if there is sufficient mail to justify the cost.
8. In large offices what provision can be made for handling written inter-office communications?
9. What are the main advantages of a central filing system?
10. What are the advantages of standardizing the supplies for an office?
11. Who should handle the purchasing of supplies in an office?
12. What plan can be used to prevent a shortage of office supplies?
13. Name some examples of time-saving office machines.
14. Name and explain two types of charts used to plan office layouts.

APPLY WHAT YOU HAVE LEARNED

Questions for Class Discussion:

1. Explain why the office manager in a large office usually does not supervise such persons as the advertising manager, the accountant, the credit manager, or the sales manager.
2. What are some of the things that are likely to happen in an office if there are no office manuals?
3. Suggest as many items as you can that you believe should be covered in a departmental office manual for the stenographic department.
4. What is a disadvantage of an interoffice communication that is addressed to several individuals, each of whom is to check off his name as he passes the communication on to the next person?
5. What is an important disadvantage of an office organization in which there is a secretary for each executive but no stenographic department for all the executives?

6. If a central filing system is used, why is it desirable to have a ruling that no one but the filing clerks be permitted to remove correspondence from the file?

7. The company with a small office of ten employees has no receptionist, but there are instructions that each employee should be alert to receive and take care of any guest. What do you think of this policy? Can you suggest any improvements?

8. Suggest the kind of indexing and filing system that you believe a whole-sale electrical supply company might need. The filing system should take care of customers and the firms from which the company makes purchases.

Problems and Projects:

1. Make a list of the equipment, both large and small, that will be needed in a small office in which there are approximately five employees; two are stenographers, one is a billing clerk, one is the manager, and one is a file clerk. For each piece of equipment indicate the estimated cost, and then determine the total cost.

2. The writing of business letters is expensive. The Apex Company writes 200 letters a week with direct costs as follows: stationery, $8; enve-lopes, $6; postage, $16; wages of stenographers, $160; that part of the dictator's salary devoted to letter writing, $135; depreciation on two typewriters, $1. Ignoring the cost of rent, desks, and other supplies and costs and using only the cost figures as given in this problem, compute the direct cost of each letter.

3. Assume the following facts with regard to the hand stamping of mail and to the use of a postage meter machine:

```
Rate of hand stamping ................1,000 pieces an hour
Cost of labor for hand stamping ........$2 an hour
Rate of stamping with a postage-meter
    machine ..........................2,000 pieces an hour
Cost of labor for machine stamping .....$2 an hour
Cost of machine .....................$295
Length of life of machine ...........10 years (trade-in value, $30)
Rental of postage meter .............$7 a month (average, 21 days a month)
```

(a) If the company has an average daily mailing of 5,000 pieces, which method would be the more economical?

(b) If the company has an average daily mailing of 25,000 pieces, which method would be the more economical? Assume that in either case the person who handles the stamping will be kept busy at other work when no mail is to be prepared.

4. A manufacturing company, the Morley-Black Equipment Company, has customers in all states. There are approximately 1,000 customers. For each customer there must be a file folder in which correspondence and copies of all orders and invoices are placed. Select a filing system suitable for this business and indicate by which method the customer records should be indexed and filed. Give your reasons for your recommendations. If possible, obtain and include in your report some illustrations of the filing system that you select.

Case Problem 23-1:

The Suburban Advertising Company uses machine and manual methods of addressing envelopes and writing letters, using two typists at $420 each a month and four clerks at $400 each a month to handle a certain monthly job. The owner and manager of Suburban Advertising Company is considering automation. To do the same work by automated equipment, the requirements will be one typist at $420 a month; two clerks at $400 each a month; an auto-coder at a monthly rental of $92.04; a key punch at a monthly rental of $90; an electric typewriter at a monthly rental of $15.37; special cabinets that will be depreciated at an expense of $16.67 a month; and an increase in the cost of special envelopes needed for the special equipment amounting to $71.67 a month above the cost of present envelopes. All other equipment presently being used will still be used and should not be included in any calculations.

Required:

1. What are some of the problems that the manager of Suburban Advertising Company must solve when the system is changed?
2. Under which system is there the greatest economy of operation?

Case Problem 23-2:

You are the operator of the Hilltop Dry Cleaners. You have one full-time helper, one part-time helper, and one girl who handles the cash register, keeps the books, and does whatever stenographic or clerical work is necessary. You extend credit to your customers. You operate the delivery truck personally.

Required:

1. List the office equipment that you are most likely to need.
2. What kind of records of customers will show the sales for each customer and will permit you to send out advertising literature to these customers regularly?
3. Recommend the most efficient method of sending out monthly circulars to 500 customers and prospects.
4. What standard procedure would you set up for answering the telephone?

Continuing Project:

Every business, even a retail store, has office problems. Draw a layout of the office for the type of business you have selected. Make a list of the work that should be performed, indicate who is to be responsible for the work, and make a list of the equipment and supplies needed, including their cost. Indicate in what part of the building the office is located and the reasons for locating it there.

What are the changing conditions which affect business?

How should business decisions be made?

What is the scientific method?

Why is economic research important to business?

Who conducts business research?

Where can business and economic data be obtained?

BACKGROUND OF CHAPTER

Yesterday's businessman could operate his business on the basis of the experience he had accumulated in running the business. Business operations today, however, are complex and ever-changing; and much more is involved than the making of "educated guesses" in operating a successful business. Effective plans and wise decisions must be made by management if the business is to survive. Adequate and accurate information must be available to management if it is to make effective plans and decisions. This information is provided by business research, the central topic of this chapter.

CHAPTER 24

RESEARCH FOR PLANNING AND DECISION MAKING

In a free enterprise system the business owner's incentive and reward for producing goods and services is profit. Engaging in business, though, carries with it risks which can result in the businessman's incurring a loss rather than making a profit. Many important risks faced by businessmen result from the fact that business operates in a constantly changing economic world. The following are some of the most important changes in conditions that may affect any business:

1. Economic conditions, such as declining payroll payments that cause a decrease in purchasing power.
2. Competition.
3. Changes in the markets, such as shifting of the population.
4. Changes in marketing methods.
5. Changes in the products that are made or sold.
6. Laws and other governmental regulations.
7. Changes in social values.

A prime function of management is to minimize the element of risk through careful planning and effective decision making. *Planning* is the preparation of a guide for future action. Business plans for future action include determining what should be done, how it should be done, when it should be done, where it should be done, who should do it, and how the results will be evaluated. These plans must take into consideration such things as the demand for the company's product, pricing of the product, supply of raw materials, actions of competitors, relations with the union, and general level of business activity. Although forecasting the future is difficult in areas such as those listed above, it is an indispensable part of planning for business operations.

ILLUS. 24-1. Planning can minimize the risks of doing business.

In the process of implementing business plans in the operations of the business, management must make many decisions. That is, many questions will come up in business operations which must be answered by management. *Decision making* is the process of choosing a specific course of action from among many possible alternatives. Determining ways and means for accomplishing the course of action decided upon is also a part of the decision-making process. Decisions which are made by management should be guided by the plans and goals of the business organization.

The businessman of 50 years ago could get by on experience and "rule-of-thumb" procedures in making his plans and decisions in a sense that is not possible today. Business operations today are complex, and technological advances make it much more difficult to keep up with competitors in products, methods, and marketing techniques. If a business is to minimize its risks today, plans and decisions cannot be based on opinions and guesswork. Effective planning and wise decision making must be based on information, and the quality of the plans and decisions can be no better than the quality of the information used. If the information used by management is inaccurate or inadequate, plans are likely to be faulty and decisions will probably be wrong. It is the function of business research to provide management with the needed accurate and adequate information.

BUSINESS RESEARCH

Business research is the systematic search for and interpretation of facts in an effort to solve specific business problems. As a result of research, businessmen are continually making decisions to produce or sell new products, change old products, change packaging designs, construct new buildings, move to new locations, reorganize the business, and use new methods of selling, advertising, and production.

Types of Research

Different kinds of research are conducted in many different fields, but the various kinds of research may be classified into two general types—pure research and applied research.

Pure Research. *Pure research* is research conducted only for the purpose of gaining knowledge. That is, the research is conducted for its own sake and is an end in itself. Experiments on the effects of color upon human emotions are examples of pure research. These experiments yield information which satisfy a scientist's curiosity. The results of pure research may, however, prove to have practical values.

Applied Research. Most research conducted by business is applied research. *Applied research* utilizes existing knowledge and searches for new knowledge in an effort to solve a problem which has a practical purpose. For example, an applied research project might have as its purpose the determination of a practical color scheme for an industrial plant. Using the data about the effects of color on human emotions, the researcher might paint a series of rooms in the plant in different colors and then determine the effects of the various colors on employee morale and productivity.

Scientific Method

Techniques and tools for doing research vary in terms of the nature of the problem for which a solution is being sought. However, all research employs basic scientific procedures which are referred to as the scientific method. The *scientific method* is a means of bringing order and system to the solution of a problem and involves following these basic steps: (1) locate and define the problem, (2) formulate hypotheses, (3) collect, classify, and analyze data, and (4) draw conclusions.

Locate and Define the Problem. One cannot, of course, go through a problem-solving process without a problem. Problems grow out of a need or a difficulty that one observes or experiences, and often this need or difficulty is experienced in attempts to solve other problems.

Having experienced a difficulty, the researcher must then define the nature of the difficulty. The exact nature of a difficulty is not always immediately understood. Often the situation demands careful observation, deliberation, and analysis prior to being able to state or define it as a problem. The essence of this process is that the researcher attempts to determine the nature of a problem before proceeding into its solution.

Formulate Hypotheses. After carefully defining a problem, the next step in the scientific method is the formulation of hypotheses. *Hypotheses* are tentative solutions to the problem which are proposed by the researcher.

Hypotheses give a sense of direction to research efforts. The proposing of tentative solutions to a problem enables the researcher to direct his efforts toward sources of data which will likely assist in solving the problem, as contrasted to a blind gathering of data in the broad area of the research study. As research progresses on a problem, it is frequently necessary to discard hypotheses and substitute other hypotheses in their places.

To illustrate the function of hypotheses, assume that Mr. Smith leaves his home in order and returns to find drawers open and articles of various sorts scattered about. A notion comes to his mind that burglary would account for the disorder. He has not seen the burglar, but this hypothesis offers a plausible explanation of the facts he has observed. At this point Mr. Smith makes a further search for facts on the basis of the burglar hypothesis. If a burglar were responsible, certain things might have happened—that is, articles of value may be missing or a window may be raised or jammed. And so, Mr. Smith tries in his search to find new facts to verify or disprove the burglar hypothesis. If he finds facts to substantiate the hypothesis, he concludes that it was a burglar. If he does not find such facts, he must then back up and attempt to formulate a new hypothesis. At this point, for example, it may occur to him that his children are mischievous and might have scattered the articles about the house.

Collect, Classify, and Analyze Data. The value of a research study depends upon the effectiveness and objectivity with which data is collected, classified, and analyzed. Two types of data may be collected —primary data and secondary data. *Primary data* is information and facts which have not been classified and analyzed by someone else.

Much primary data has not been recorded prior to the work of the researcher; rather, the data is collected by him through observation, interviews, questionnaires, or experimentation, as in the case of the researcher who painted rooms in the plant in different colors in order to measure the effects of different colors on employee morale and productivity. The major source of primary data in business research is the records of the company. To give management a basis for planning and decision making, data from the records of the accounting department, the reports of salesmen, inventory records, production reports, etc., is collected, classified, and interpreted.

Secondary data is data which has been analyzed and interpreted by someone else. For businessmen the major source of secondary data is the United States government. For example, data on gross national product, national income, industrial production, prices, etc., is published monthly by the United States Department of Commerce in the *Survey of Current Business*. Other major sources for published business information and data are discussed in the last section of this chapter.

After data has been collected, it must be classified. In the classification of data, the researcher places together data of like characteristics. For example, data with respect to chairs, tables, couches, and rugs might be placed together in a category called household furniture.

ILLUS. 24-2. The data for much business research is collected from the records and reports of the company.

When data has been classified, it must be analyzed and interpreted to discover whether it substantiates or refutes the hypotheses proposed by the researcher. If the data does not substantiate the hypotheses, the researcher must formulate new hypotheses and must analyze and interpret the data again in terms of the new hypotheses. In addition, new hypotheses may require the collection of additional data.

Draw Conclusions. The final step in the scientific method is the drawing of conclusions with respect to the solution(s) of the problem. The critical element in this step is the stating of conclusions which agree with the data which has been collected for solving the problem of the research study. Occasionally the preconceived ideas of the researcher are so strong that conclusions are made which are contrary to the facts.

Areas of Research

There are a number of areas in which business research is conducted. The most common of these are marketing research, product research, personnel research, financial research, environmental research, and economic research.

Marketing Research. *Marketing research* refers to research into all of the functions performed in the movement of goods from producer to consumer. Markets and marketing operations are constantly changing—a different group of buyers for a product may appear, the attitudes of people may change and require a new advertising approach for a product, and someone may develop a more efficient method of distribution. The businessman must have information as to what changes are taking place and are likely to take place which influence the marketing of his products.

There are several subdivisions of marketing research which usually receive the most research attention. These subdivisions are discussed below and on the next pages.

Market Research. The term market research is often confused with the broader term, marketing research. *Market research* is the study of the people who buy a company's product or who might buy a new product. Businessmen need to know who these buyers are, how many of them exist, and where they are located. A swimsuit manufacturer, for example, might do market research to find out where in the country most of his swimsuits were being purchased. This knowledge might indicate to the manufacturer that he should alter his advertising and merchandising methods.

Motivation Research. A second area of marketing research is *motivation research,* the probing into the subconscious reasons for consumer buying behavior. Motivation research, which borrows many techniques from psychology and sociology, has been of great help to business. Businessmen who know what influences people to buy one product and reject another can adapt their own product so that it will have more appeal for consumers. For example, one drug manufacturer who sold a low-priced cough syrup discovered that his product was not selling as well as a similar, higher priced product. He wondered why customers were not taking advantage of the savings which would result from buying the lower priced medicine. So the manufacturer allotted money for motivation research, and a group of consumers were interviewed for their opinions on the two products. It was learned that consumers distrusted the low-priced medicine. They felt that by paying the higher price they were getting higher quality medicine, even though this was not true. When their health was involved, they wanted the best product they could buy. The drug manufacturer raised the price of his medicine, retained the same advertising messages he had used before, and eventually gained a fair portion of the market.

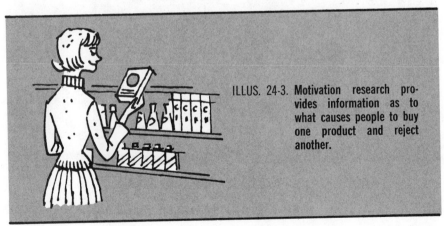

ILLUS. 24-3. Motivation research provides information as to what causes people to buy one product and reject another.

Advertising Research. Thousands of products are available to the consumer, and advertising plays an important role in selling these products. Advertising must tell a customer what is unique about the product and why he will be happier if he buys the product. To sell the product, the advertising message, layout, and medium must be as effective as possible. *Advertising research* tests the effectiveness of the advertisement and the medium which carries it.

The testing of the advertising copy and layout may be conducted before and/or after the advertisement is circulated. One of the most common methods for pretesting ads that are to be published is to show several ads to selected persons who indicate their preference. If the advertisement is to be broadcast, the selected persons listen to or watch the advertisements and state their preference.

The testing of advertisements after they appear (posttesting) is often conducted by large research agencies. The most famous agency for testing the effectiveness of published advertisements is the Starch Magazine Advertisement Readership Service. This organization sends to a sample of magazine subscribers questionnaires based upon the ads in a particular issue of a magazine. Questions such as "Did you read the advertisement on page 25?" are asked. The answers to the questions tell researchers how many people saw the advertisement, how many read part of the copy, and how many read all of the copy.

ILLUS. 24-4. A common method of determining the effectiveness of television advertising is to telephone a sample of persons and ask them what program they are watching.

Radio and television advertising may be posttested by several methods. A common one is to telephone a sample of persons and ask them which programs they are listening to or watching at the time of the call. Thus, it is learned how many people are exposed to the advertisements of the company sponsoring a program. Another method is to attach to a radio or television set a machine which automatically records which station's programs are being viewed or listened to and the times at which each station is tuned in.

Product Research. The purpose of *product research* is to improve existing products or to develop new products. The research laboratories which create new products and make improvements in old ones have as their objective the creation of products which customers will buy in preference to competitors' products. Thus, product research must be guided by the findings of marketing research as to what consumers want and will buy.

As a result of many factors, products are continuously changing— old products go out of use or are vastly improved and new products are developed. It is estimated that over 80 percent of our economy is based on products that did not exist at the beginning of this century. For a company to survive, it must continually search for ways to improve even its highly successful products; and it must be alert to the possibilities of developing new products. There are many examples of exbusinessmen who guided their businesses as did the blacksmith who based his decisions on the opinion that the automobile would never be accepted as a mode of transportation by consumers.

"Yes, sir. This is the last word in transportation. They'll never improve on it."

Veterans Administration

ILLUS. 24-5. A business must continually search for ways to improve its products.

Personnel Research. To be successful, a business needs as much information as it can get with respect to the effective utilization of human resources. This information is provided to management by *personnel research* studies in areas such as: the selection of new employees, the training of employees, the promotion of employees, the wages and benefits of employees, and the morale of workers.

Environmental Research. *Environmental research* includes not only study of employee working conditions but also study of the earth and its atmosphere. Environmental research originally dealt mainly with the physical, social, and psychological climate affecting workers. Much of the progress in employee working conditions was prompted by such research. However, environmental study has since expanded to include pollution control and is a major concern for almost all businesses.

The onset of a "throw-away" society has caused problems, as discussed in Chapter 2. Businesses are researching means of production and resource use which will diminish pollution of the environment and unwise depletion of resources. Through research, means have been found to recycle products formerly considered wastes from production or consumption.

Financial Research. The study of the financial operations of a business is called *financial research*. A constant check of a business' financial status must be maintained or the financial stability may weaken before management realizes what is happening. Financial research can be used to determine how much money will be needed in the future, where the money can be obtained, how to invest any reserve funds the company might have, and how to decrease company indebtedness.

Economic Research. In the economy the level of business activity is continually changing—business is sometimes good and sometimes not so good. The kind of *economic research* most needed by business is concerned with trends in the economy which indicate what is likely to be the general level of business activity in the future and how these trends will affect single industries or businesses. Many important business plans and decisions must be based upon some type of economic forecasting of future business conditions.

Much economic data which is extremely valuable in assessing trends and in forecasting business conditions is compiled and published by universities, state governments, and the federal government. These sources provide information such as the level of wholesale prices, the prices consumers are paying for goods and services, the average number of hours per week workers are working, the number of business failures in a given period of time, and the value of all goods and services produced in the United States in a year (gross national product). Economic researchers utilize such data in forecasting business conditions for the entire economy, in forecasting sales volume in an industry, and in forecasting the share of the industry's sales volume which a particular business will have. On the basis of these forecasts, a business can then plan its production and determine its needs for materials, supplies, labor, and equipment.

Resources for Conducting Business Research

Much needed business research is, of course, done by business itself. Most large companies have research departments or divisions which, in the main, engage in research projects related to the specific problems of the company. Since research departments are expensive to maintain, small companies must depend to a considerable degree on outside help.

ILLUS. 24-6. Even small businesses are finding it necessary to allocate funds for research.

Bureaus of business research and individual faculty members in universities conduct studies which are helpful to business. Extensive research is undertaken by various divisions of the federal government, and much of this research is available to and useful for business. Research studies which are useful to particular industries are made by *trade associations* (organizations formed by businessmen in some particular trade or industry, such as retail clothiers, plumbers, automobile dealers, and steel manufacturers). There are also many research organizations and individual consultants that may be employed by a company to conduct a particular research study.

SOURCES OF BUSINESS INFORMATION

A vast quantity of information is available on local and national business conditions and problems. Sources of information on local business conditions usually include: newspapers, Chamber of Commerce, credit bureau, retail merchant's bureau, and state departments of commerce. The sources of information on national business conditions and problems are so numerous that not all of them can be listed, but a few of the major sources are discussed below.

Chamber of Commerce of the United States

The Chamber of Commerce of the United States has many services available to members and literature that can be bought by nonmembers. A publications directory can be obtained by writing to the Chamber of Commerce of the United States in Washington, D.C. Much of the literature is of particular benefit to the small businessman. The following are examples of some of the printed pamphlets that are available: *Problem Analysis; Business and Economic Forecasting; Profits—Something for Everyone; Small Business: Its Role and Its Problems; Demand, Supply, and Prices; Why the Businessman?*

United States Department of Commerce

There are several federal agencies that provide information of value to businessmen. The principal one is the United States Department of Commerce. The literature of this department and other government agencies is available directly from the United States Government Printing Office, Washington, D. C., 20402. However, there are regional field offices of the Department of Commerce in the principal cities from which much of the literature can be obtained. The following are examples of some of the literature available to businessmen: *Distribution Cost Analysis; Market Analysis Tools; Operating Costs and Ratios—Retail Trades; Store Arrangement and Display; Survey of Current Business; Causes of Commercial Bankruptcies; Credit and Payment Terms; Aids to Retail Grocery Profits; Market Research Sources.*

United States Small Business Administration

The Small Business Administration is a federal agency created in 1953 to aid, counsel, assist, and protect the interests of small business concerns; to insure that small business concerns obtain a fair share of government contracts; to make loans to small businesses under certain conditions; to charter, license, and make loans to investment companies created to serve small businesses; and to provide funds for studies to help small business in managing, financing, and operating its enterprises.

There are 62 regional and branch offices in the principal cities. Some of the examples of the numerous printed aids available through the United States Small Business Administration are as follows: *Pricing and Profits in Small Stores; Sizing Up Small Business Locations; Buying a Small Going Concern; Methods for Improving Off-Season Sales; Basic Accounting for Small Partnerships; Stock Management in Small Stores; Improving Personal Selling in Small Business; Choosing the Legal Structure for Your Firm; How to Analyze Your Own Business; Traps to Avoid in Small Business Management.*

Public State Agencies

In many states there are services for businessmen performed by state authorities. Bulletins and other literature may often be obtained from these sources. For example, the Department of Commerce of the State of New York publishes and distributes to its citizens a series of booklets on all of the phases of starting and operating a small business.

Business Literature

Every businessman should assume that his education has just begun. He should therefore study regularly to keep himself up to date on all subjects. One of the best ways is to subscribe to at least one trade magazine. A *trade magazine* is one containing information on a particular industry or line of business. For instance, there are magazines covering coal, iron, chain stores, independent stores, dry goods, pottery, electrical appliances, and practically all other lines of industrial endeavor. Many of these are specialized according to particular products or particular types of distribution.

There are published each year hundreds of books which discuss all phases of accounting, merchandising, purchasing, stock control, advertising, promotion, and other business activities. Some of these books should go into the library of the businessman regularly.

Many city libraries make a practice of establishing special sections devoted to business and industry. Some libraries, such as the Business Branch of the Public Library of Newark, New Jersey, publish monthly and yearly bulletins showing the literature available in the field of business. In such libraries a businessman will find many books and magazines to help him keep up to date in management practices.

The sources of information in libraries are practically unlimited. In the modern public library and in some private libraries, there should be an answer to almost every problem whether it is a technical production problem, a sales problem, or a management problem. If you will take your problem to a competent librarian, that person can find for you the information you need.

REVIEW WHAT YOU HAVE LEARNED

Business Terms Checkup:

(1) planning
(2) decision making
(3) business research
(4) pure research
(5) applied research
(6) scientific method
(7) hypotheses
(8) primary data
(9) secondary data
(10) marketing research
(11) market research
(12) motivation research
(13) advertising research
(14) product research
(15) personnel research
(16) environmental research
(17) financial research
(18) economic research
(19) gross national product
(20) trade association
(21) trade magazine

Reading Checkup:

1. Name some of the changes in conditions that may affect any business.
2. How can business risks be minimized?
3. In making business plans, what are some of the things which must be taken into consideration?
4. On what must effective planning and wise decision making be based?
5. What is the function of business research?
6. Distinguish between "pure research" and "applied research."
7. What are the basic steps in the scientific method?
8. What is the difference between primary data and secondary data?
9. In business research, what is the major source of primary data?
10. What does the researcher do when he classifies data?
11. What is the most critical aspect in the process of drawing conclusions as to the solution of a problem?
12. Name the areas in which business research is most commonly done.
13. How may the effectiveness of advertising copy and layout be tested?
14. If a small business cannot afford to employ research personnel, what can it do to obtain needed research information?
15. Name several local and national sources of business and economic information.

16. Indicate some of the objectives of the Small Business Administration.
17. Name some of the industries for which there are trade magazines.

APPLY WHAT YOU HAVE LEARNED

Questions for Class Discussion:

1. Can today's businessman rely on "rule-of-thumb" procedures in making his plans and decisions?
2. Identify some of the problems faced by a business for which research information is needed in order that proper decisions can be made.
3. How does the formulation of hypotheses assist the researcher?
4. In order to solve the problem of the research study, what must the researcher do if the data do not substantiate the hypotheses?
5. Why is it important for businesses to conduct marketing research?
6. What is motivation research, and why is it important to businessmen?
7. What relationship exists between product research and marketing research?
8. The Riviera Company has a highly successful product which has captured 80 percent of the national market. Should the company spend the money to engage in research with respect to this product which has proven to be so successful in the marketplace?
9. What are some areas in which personnel research is conducted?
10. How can the results of financial research be used by businessmen?
11. What kind of economic research is needed by business?
12. Why is an accurate forecast of sales volume so important to business?

Problems and Projects:

1. You have been reminded in this chapter that one of the important aspects of business is change and that businesses must keep abreast of these changes. Make a list of as many new developments and changes as you can think of that affect business.
2. Compile a list of specific problems which could be solved through the various areas of research discussed in this chapter.
3. Make a list of all the possible sources that you can think of or discover in your community from which a businessman could obtain information on business conditions and trends.
4. Without using specific references to individual firms or persons, compile a list of problem areas in your community where environmental research could be carried on and indicate who should be responsible for each of the studies.

Case Problem 24-1:

Bill Grafton, a research consultant, was hired by Albert's Men's Shop to conduct a study of customer attitudes about the store. Grafton prepared a questionnaire which 500 of the store's customers agreed to complete. Shown below are the questions relating to employees which appeared on the questionnaire. The results of a tabulation of customer answers are shown in parentheses following each question.

a. Do owners or employees greet you as you enter the store? (80% said no.)
b. Are employees alert, courteous, and helpful? (90% said no.)
c. Do you get waited on promptly? (75% said no.)
d. Are employees neat and careful of their personal appearance? (55% said yes.)
e. Do employees know, and can they clearly explain, the merits of the goods they are selling? (85% said no.)

Required:

Using the customer-response data shown above, make conclusions and recommendations to the management of Albert's Men's Shop.

Case Problem 24-2:

A businessman operating a medium-sized men's clothing store has been using rather conservative ideas and methods for 20 years at the same location. Steady, but not large, profits have been made during all of this time. A regular customer group has been established. The building and facilities are a bit cramped and somewhat old-fashioned, although still serviceable.

The proprietor's son, just graduated from business school, is now coming into the business as a partner. The son has had part-time experience in his father's store and has had some college courses of a general business nature, such as economics. He is now enthusiastic and full of suggestions of what should be done to the business to make it the very latest in appearance, popularity, and profit-making. His suggestions are:

1. Remodel the building and install the latest modern equipment; double the present space.

2. Get rid of some of the traditional merchandise which the store has handled and put in style merchandise; add additional lines, such as sports clothing and formal clothes for men; add a young men's shop emphasizing style and snap.

3. Revamp the office, bookkeeping, and credit procedures; tighten up on small-account credit and encourage big-account buying.

4. Put on a vigorous advertising campaign locally and in the neighboring cities to draw trade.

5. To finance these changes, the young man estimates that $75,000 will be needed. Since the old business is valued at about $150,000, it is proposed to take out a mortgage on the business as security for the proposed loan.

Required:

1. Make one comment for and one against each of the five proposals.

2. What should the proprietor do about his son's suggestions?

Continuing Project:

Determine specific ways in which you can keep yourself informed as to the changing conditions of business, what steps you can take to control your business, and what types of continuing research may be necessary. Include, if possible, a specific type of research that you will conduct in anticipation of going into business.

CAREERS IN DATA PROCESSING, ACCOUNTING, RESEARCH, AND OFFICE MANAGEMENT

Careers in Information Systems. Insurance companies, manufacturing organizations, banks, wholesale and retail organizations, and the federal government use the specialized services of the systems analyst. Colleges and universities have an increasing need and use for these analysts in order to satisfy the many demands made on the data processing equipment by researchers and administrators.

The *analyst* concerns himself with planning, scheduling, and coordinating the activities which are required to develop systems for processing data and obtaining solutions to complex business, scientific, and engineering problems.

A college degree is usually necessary, as is experience. College work in mathematics, science, engineering, accounting, or business administration is desirable.

The analyst is likely to work in a large city and with large organizations. There is a growing need for junior and senior systems analysts.

The *programmer* prepares the detailed instructions for the computer. He is likely to be employed by a large organization or by the federal government. Insurance companies, banks, public utilities, transportation, retail and wholesale businesses, and manufacturing concerns use many programmers. The job is an exacting kind of analysis and requires an aptitude for logical thinking and extreme accuracy.

A college degree is desirable and courses in mathematics, physical sciences, business administration, accounting, and electronic data processing are helpful. Some persons become programmers after several years of experience in other data processing positions or after a technical schooling offered by manufacturing firms. After one year of close supervision the individual can become proficient to handle the task on his own.

There are many related jobs in data processing for operating personnel. These jobs require various amounts of education and training. While a high school diploma may be sufficient to begin the job, advancement is probably dependent upon technical or college courses in office and electronic data processing areas. Included in the operating personnel job classifications are coding clerks, keypunch operators, data typists, wiring operators, console operators, and tape librarians. Working conditions in the data processing areas are usually quite good.

Data processing equipment servicemen who know electricity and have electronic and mechanical skills find a great demand for their services. Basic to the job description is the installation, modification, and maintenance of electronic data processing equipment and systems. Many such servicemen work for computer manufacturers.

Careers In Accounting. For many years accounting has been one of the most rapidly growing professions, and it is a well-paid profession. Because of governmental requirements and scientific management in business, the need for accountants has steadily increased. Some people like to make a distinction between a bookkeeper and an accountant. A bookkeeper is generally considered to be the one who keeps the records, and the accountant is considered to be the one who prepares financial statements and interprets them. However, in many businesses one person is both a bookkeeper and an accountant.

Many kinds of jobs are available for bookkeepers and accountants in both business and government. There are specialized jobs, such as those for posting clerks and ledger clerks; and there are more important jobs, such as those for general accountants, auditors, controllers, and public accountants. A public accountant is one who does accounting work for other people instead of being employed by just one business. A certified public accountant (C. P. A.) is one who has passed a special examination in accounting, after which he has the legal authority to certify that any financial statement which he prepares is correct.

Accounting positions require absolute accuracy and honesty. To be happy in an accounting position, one must enjoy working with figures. The education of a person who expects a good future in accounting should include the study of law, budgeting, taxation, cost accounting, finance, and management. Since more and more offices are installing computers, every accountant should also learn about automated and electronic data processing.

Careers in Research. Research is one of the most rapidly expanding fields in business, and many career openings are appearing all the time. Businesses with separate research departments need qualified personnel. Research and consulting firms and laboratories also need persons trained in research procedures.

Within the various areas of research, there are openings for persons to conduct surveys, design questionnaires, and tabulate data. Research departments also need economists and statisticians who can gather and interpret data and project these data into a meaningful forecast. Eventually, a competent and experienced person can be placed in charge of directing a research study.

Research careers require college training, and an advanced degree generally is necessary. Knowledge of economics, statistics, business organization, and psychology is also a requirement.

Careers in Offices. There is great variety in the kinds of offices in which one may work and in the kinds of work performed in the office. A person might work for retail or wholesale businesses, government agencies, manufacturers, or professional people such as doctors and lawyers. Jobs available for beginning workers in the office include those of typist, stenographer, secretary, cashier, correspondent, and switchboard operator. An individual also might be given a job as operator of one of the office machines. Bookkeeping machine operator, calculator operator, duplicating machine operator, key-punch operator, and transcribing machine operator are positions one might hold. Or a person might be one of several kinds of clerks—cost clerk, filing clerk, disbursements clerk, personnel clerk, stock clerk, payroll clerk, and general clerk.

Jobs involving office functions are also available in various special departments of a business such as accounting, finance, statistics, purchasing, production, and sales; and there are supervisory jobs related to the various functions and departments.

Most employers require that their beginning office workers have specialized training in certain office procedures. Courses in bookkeeping, general business, clerical or office practice, and typewriting are some of the courses which will prepare one for an office job. Opportunities for advancement depend on the employee's ability, education, training, accuracy, honesty, behavior, and leadership.

One who begins his career as an office worker might advance to almost any management position in a business organization, such as office manager, director of purchases, credit manager, manager of finance, data processing manager, personnel director, traffic manager, and production manager. However, more and more businesses are filling management positions with college graduates who have degrees in business administration.

UNIT VII
Personnel

What are the functions of personnel management?

How may a business obtain new employees?

Why do companies need to prepare specifications for each job?

What promotion policies should be followed?

How is labor turnover computed?

BACKGROUND OF CHAPTER

People are the most important factor in business. A firm may be housed in an expensive building and may use the most modern equipment and production methods, but it wlll not be successful unless it has capable and well-satisfied employees. Thus, business now places much emphasis on the functions of personnel management.

Personnel must be carefully selected and trained. Business will suffer if managers hire persons who are not suited to a particular job or if they do not properly train employees. Policies for promoting, transferring, and discharging workers are also necessary for effective personnel management.

This chapter discusses some of the problems of obtaining employees and of training and promoting them so that a business can operate most efficiently.

CHAPTER 25

SELECTION, TRAINING, AND PROMOTION

As was discussed in Chapter 3, production of goods and services is possible when management, a factor of production, brings together the other factors of production—natural resources, labor, and capital goods. The effective utilization of labor (human resources) by management is of tremendous importance to the success of a business. If a business is to make a profit, its management must secure competent people and must give effective leadership to these people.

PERSONNEL MANAGEMENT

That aspect of management which is concerned with obtaining and effectively utilizing human resources is called *personnel management*. Not so many years ago, the functions of personnel management were thought to have been performed if all of the jobs in the business were filled. Today, however, it is commonly recognized that much more is involved if human resources are to be utilized effectively.

Functions of Personnel Management

Briefly discussed below are the functions of personnel management which are commonly performed by businesses today. The extent to which these functions are performed depends on many factors, such as the size of the business and the importance placed on personnel programs by the management.

Selecting New Employees. Hiring well-qualified employees is an important function of personnel management. For this function to be performed, it is necessary to secure applicants, to determine their qualifications, to hire those whose qualifications match the jobs to be filled, and to introduce to their new jobs those who are hired.

Training Employees. It is a function of personnel management to follow up selection procedures with effective training programs. New employees and employees transferred to new jobs must be trained, and changes which require additional training for workers are constantly occurring—changes in jobs, in machines, in processes, and in policies. Employees also need training which will prepare them for promotion.

Promoting and Transferring Employees. Another function of personnel management is to devise good policies and procedures for promoting and transferring personnel. Without such policies and procedures, personnel who have been selected and trained by a business will secure employment elsewhere.

Determining Wages and Benefits. How much compensation is received in the form of wages and other benefits is of vital concern to all workers. The determination of what is fair compensation is a function of personnel management.

Maintaining Health and Safety Programs. To be efficient, employees must be healthy; they must also be protected from accidents. Providing health and safety programs is a function of personnel management.

Negotiating with Unions. If the workers in a business are members of a union, a function of personnel management is to negotiate a labor contract with the union and to engage in collective bargaining to discuss and resolve differences arising between management and the union.

Establishing Good Human Relations. An unhappy, disgruntled worker is not an efficient worker. Assisting in the establishment of a work environment in which the morale of the workers is high and in which workers have harmonious and cooperative working relationships is an important function of personnel management.

Organizing for the Management of Personnel

In a business that has only a few employees, the proprietor or general manager performs the personnel functions. As he works side by side with his employees, he has a good understanding of them and readily appreciates their viewpoint. Likewise, the employees get to know something about the problems of their employer and, as a result, have a better attitude toward their employer and feel free to discuss their problems with him. Such conditions make for good employer-employee relationships.

Much of our modern business, however, is conducted on a large scale, and it is common to find businesses with thousands of employees.

Naturally, this bigness makes it impossible to have a close relationship between the owners and the employees. Since large businesses need employees for hundreds of different kinds of highly specialized jobs, the problems of selecting properly qualified employees, training them for their jobs, providing for their health and welfare, and stimulating them to work at their greatest efficiency are complex and important. Large businesses, therefore, require large personnel departments which are often organized into divisions representing the major functions of personnel management (see Illustration 25-1). The dotted lines in Illustration 25-1 indicate that a personnel department exists to give advice and service to other departments.

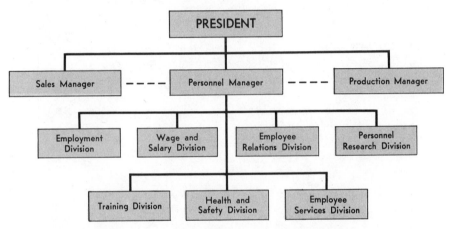

ILLUS. 25-1. Organization of a personnel department.

The three chapters in this unit and one in the next deal in detail with various aspects of personnel management. The remainder of this chapter discusses the selection, training, and promotion of personnel; Chapter 26 deals with wages, salaries, and other benefits received by personnel. Union-management relationships are discussed in Chapter 27. While the importance of establishing good human relations is important to personnel management, it is critical to the success of all managers. As a result, the topic of effective human relations in business is presented in the next unit in Chapter 29.

SELECTING PERSONNEL

A business must take the necessary time to find and hire the right people. Inadequate selection procedures can result in the hiring of unqualified workers who turn out just enough work to get by but who are not quite bad enough to be discharged. This section discusses some of the essential procedures which should be followed in selecting personnel.

Employment Requisition

As a first step in the process of securing a new employee, it is necessary to establish that a new employee is needed. In many businesses this is accomplished by issuing an *employment requisition* (a request for a worker). An example of an employment requisition is shown in Illustration 25-2.

The Sheffield Company

Employment Requisition

Number needed __1__ Date needed __7/12/--__ Date of request __5/2/--__
Job title __Receptionist__ Department __Office__
Duties __Greet visitors, operate switchboard, light typing__
Addition to force __No__ Permanent _____ Temporary _____
Replacement __For Maxine Wood__ Permanent __X__ Temporary _____
Rate of pay __$100 per week to start__ Hours of work __8:30 a.m.--5 p.m., M-F__
Education __High school graduate__
Experience __Experience as receptionist desirable but not necessary__
Charge to acct. no. __6066-B__ Signed __Evelyn Doll__ Dept. Chief
Approved __John Hendricks__ Dept. Manager

Employment Department Record	Department Manager's Acceptance
Name_____	Name_____
Address_____	Address_____
was employed transferred to fill this requisition	started work on
To begin work on_____ Rate_____	_____ at _____
Reg. No.____ Acct. No.____ Signed_____	Signed_____
Emp. Dept.	Dept. Manager

ILLUS. 25-2. Employment requisition.

Employment requisitions are sent to the personnel department. The need for an employee should be anticipated as far in advance as possible so that the personnel department will have sufficient time to find a suitable employee.

Job Specification

The employment requisition does not contain complete information about the job for which a worker is needed. The personnel department must have complete and accurate knowledge of the job to be filled before it can properly screen applicants to fill that job. One of the best ways to obtain this information is to have detailed specifications prepared for each kind of job. A *job specification* includes information as to the nature of the work done in the particular job, the necessary qualifications of the employee who is to do that work, and the opportunities that the job offers to the employee. This information is usually printed on cards, which are known as *job specification cards* (see Illustration 25-3). These cards are kept on file in the personnel department. The information on a job specification card is used in deciding how to secure qualified applicants for the job; and, after applicants are secured, the information is used in determining which of the applicants is best qualified for the demands of the job.

Cordes and Hughes, Inc.
Job Specification

Job Title Stock clerk   Department Stock room

DUTIES
Responsible for filling all orders, maintenance of stock records
as prescribed by management, appearance of stock room

EMPLOYEE QUALIFICATIONS
Education: College_____   High School___X___   Technical_____
Experience Must have some experience and knowledge of electrical trade
Physical requirements Good health
Mental requirements Accuracy, honesty, conscientiousness, systematic
habits

EMPLOYEE INFORMATION
Hours of work 8 a.m. to 4:30 p.m., Monday to Friday
Wages $95 to start; annual raise; maximum wage $120
Vacation One year, two weeks
Promotions To assistant purchasing agent

ADDITIONAL REMARKS

ILLUS. 25-3. Job specification card.

Sources for Prospective Employees

After the personnel department has received an employment requisition, it must then secure applicants for the job. Many sources of prospective employees exist, some of which will now be discussed.

Employees of the Company. Often a vacancy can be filled by transferring a present employee from some other job. Such a transfer may give an employee a chance to use his ability to a much higher degree than he did in his previous job. The policy of transfer or promotion from within the company provides a strong incentive for employees to be efficient and to train themselves for advancement. Filling a vacancy from within the firm usually creates another vacancy that must be filled from an outside source or by transfer within the company.

Friends of Present Employees. The employees of the business may recommend friends for employment.

Applications on File. A business that has earned a reputation for excellent treatment of its employees is likely to have many applications on file at all times.

Placement Bureaus. Colleges and universities; professional, technical, and trade schools; and some large high schools maintain placement bureaus to aid their graduates in obtaining positions. These bureaus can furnish lists of suitable candidates for positions. Also, the offices of many trade unions maintain lists of unemployed members and can furnish applicants for vacancies.

State Employment Service. All states have a State Employment Service which is affiliated with the United States Employment Service. Local offices throughout a state are staffed by people trained to locate and select workers in all types of occupations and to refer these workers to potential employers. The State Employment Service can be particularly helpful to small and medium-sized businesses which do not maintain complete personnel departments.

Private Employment Agencies. Another source for prospective employees is the private employment agency. Individuals looking for employment register with and provide personal data to these agencies. Payment for their services is generally made by the individuals for whom the agencies find employment. Private employment agencies usually specialize in supplying personnel of a particular kind, such as office or factory workers.

Advertising. Advertising in the daily newspaper is a common method of obtaining job applicants. This source is frequently used when workers are needed in large numbers or when they are needed immediately.

At certain times and in certain locations when the right kind of employees are difficult to obtain and when they are needed in rather large numbers, some businesses use radio and television advertising to obtain job applicants. This type of advertising is expensive and is ordinarily used only by large companies.

Procedures with Applicants

The following are procedures which are typically followed by personnel departments after applicants for a job have been obtained:

1. The applicant is interviewed to determine whether he has the general qualifications called for by the job specification card. During the interview the applicant should be given facts about

ILLUS. 25-4. An applicant should be given detailed facts about the company and the job.

the company and about the job so that he will understand what is expected of him. Detailed facts about the company and the job should also be given to the applicant so that he will not be disappointed or misled in regard to the job if he is hired. At the end of the interview, a good interviewer will have definite opinions as to the qualifications of the applicant and the level of his interest in obtaining the job.

2. If the applicant passes the preliminary interview, he may be given tests designed to show his knowledges and skills.

3. The applicant is usually given a physical examination. It is wise for a business to require an examination since it should reveal whether the applicant is physically able to do the work expected. It may also protect the business in a lawsuit if the employee later claims disability as a result of his work. The medical report becomes a part of the permanent record of the employee.

4. The references (persons who know the applicant) are investigated to see if the applicant's previous conduct has been satisfactory, and other facts are checked for accuracy. Many employers feel that references are of no value because an applicant will not give a reference unless he feels that a good recommendation can be obtained. Schools attended and former employers should be checked even though these are not given as references. Often it is possible to obtain over the telephone much more dependable answers than could be obtained in writing.

5. In many cases the applicant who has thus far proved satisfactory to the personnel department is sent to the head of the department to which he would be assigned. The department head can then interview the applicant and judge his fitness for the job.

6. When the applicant is hired, the records for the personnel department are then prepared.

Introduction to the Job

After an applicant has been hired, an introduction to his new job and to his fellow workers is an important matter. The first hours on a new job are trying ones for most people. Statistics show that a very large number of the "quitters" leave their positions during the first week and, sometimes, even on the first day. If a new employee suddenly finds himself behind a desk or a machine with scarcely a word of explanation or advice from anyone, he may well form an immediate dislike for the place, the position, and his fellow workers.

As soon as possible after he is hired, the new worker should be taken on a tour of the company which would include showing him the lunchroom, lockers for clothes, and the like. The department head should have another talk with the new employee about the business in general and his new job. The department head or the new employee's immediate supervisor should then introduce the new employee to his fellow workers, and a particularly good "mixer" in the department might be asked to take the new employee to lunch. Assuming that the company has a manual which states the policies and regulations of the business, a copy of this manual should be given to the new employee. Finally, the supervisor of the new employee should give him detailed information and directions about his job.

Follow-Up of New Employees

The personnel department should make a follow-up of each new employee to see whether the right person has been selected for the job. This practice will aid the department in the future selection of employees. By consulting the department head or supervisor, the personnel department can determine the efficiency of the new employee. By consulting the new employee, it can determine whether he is satisfied. After such a follow-up it may decide that, for the best interests of everyone, the employee should be transferred to another job or department.

TRAINING PERSONNEL

Selection methods which are effective in the employment of qualified workers should be followed up with effective training programs. The difference between the average worker in any occupation and the expert is largely a matter of training, and yet the difference in their output is enormous.

If a company has no plan for training its workers, the new employee and the employee who is transferred to a new job usually learn their jobs by a trial-and-error method. The employee works along as best he can and is corrected by his supervisor when he makes an error. The substitution of formal training programs for trial-and-error methods costs money, but it is a cost which can be easily justified in most businesses. The simplest argument in favor of a formal training program is that a company pays for a training program whether it has one or not. In a company which has no formal training program, the employees do a great deal of learning on the company's time and premises. Hence, this

ILLUS. 25-5. The difference between the average worker and
the expert is largely a matter of training.

learning, which is accompanied by costly errors, is done at company expense. It seems to follow that if money is being spent for training, the spending should be planned.

Numerous reasons exist as to why employees must be trained. Changes are constantly occurring in the business which require additional training for workers—changes in jobs, in machines, in processes, and in policies. Employees also need training which will prepare them for promotion.

Some of the different types of training programs found in business are discussed below and on the next pages.

On-the-Job Training

The most common type of training is *on-the-job training*. The employee is placed on his new job and, in effect, practices the job under close supervision until he is skillful enough to do the job with a normal amount of supervision. The intensive supervision is usually given by his supervisor who often has received training in how to teach others effectively. The major disadvantage of on-the-job training is that during the training period it slows up the production of the unit in which the job is located.

Vestibule Training

Vestibule training is conducted by company instructors in "classrooms" away from the work area. The effort in vestibule training is to simulate the regular working conditions of the job for which the trainees are being prepared. As contrasted to on-the-job training where learning and production of work are being accomplished at the same time, vestibule training concentrates the attention of the trainee on learning the job. Because the trainees can concentrate on learning the job without the pressure of actual production, vestibule training is often more effective than on-the-job training. Also, vestibule training is superior to on-the-job training in that it does not slow down production in the regular work area.

A procedures manual is a valuable aid during on-the-job and vestibule training, and it is also useful to the worker after the training has been completed. A *procedures manual* gives definite instructions for the performance of certain operations and tasks. For example, a correspondence manual describes the various styles of letter arrangement used by the business and often includes capitalization, punctuation, and grammar rules.

Apprenticeship Training

Apprenticeship training is most frequently used in skilled trades, such as printing and metal work. A worker becomes an assistant to a skilled craftsman for a period of time, usually from two to six years. During his apprenticeship, the worker learns by watching and by assisting the skilled craftsman. Often the learning which the apprentice obtains from the skilled craftsman is supplemented by formal classroom instruction.

Supervisory Training

Business has come to recognize that the supervisor occupies the key position in the business organization. Supervisors are the first line of management; that is, they are the ones who are in direct contact with the workers. To the average worker the supervisor is the company, and his attitude toward the company is largely governed by his reaction to his immediate supervisor. The increasing recognition of the need for good supervisors has led to the development of training programs which are designed to assist them in improving their performance. In the main, these programs have not concentrated on improving the technical knowledge and skill of supervisors, for most supervisors are selected for their positions because they have demonstrated excellent technical competence in their work. Rather, *supervisory training* programs usually are designed to improve the leadership and management skills of supervisors. Since most on-the-job training is conducted by supervisors, training programs are also set up to train supervisors in how to train their workers. Most often supervisory training is conducted in formal classes taught by company executives.

Executive Development

Developing executives is vital to the long-run success of a business. Training for management positions is accomplished in many different ways. Formalized courses, which are quite similar to business courses offered in undergraduate and graduate curriculums in universities, are provided by some companies. At times, management trainees are sent to universities to participate in executive development seminars, and some are sent to universities to obtain advanced degrees. Much on-the-job training is also given to management trainees. Often management trainees act as understudies for the executives whose jobs it is anticipated

ILLUS. 25-6. Subordinates should be trained so that they can step into the shoes of executives who may leave their present positions.

they will eventually hold. Some companies also rotate management trainees from job to job so that they will get a picture of the total operations of the company.

PROMOTING, TRANSFERRING, AND DISCHARGING PERSONNEL

If a business is to keep the personnel who have been selected and trained, it must have good policies and procedures for promoting and transferring personnel.

Promotions

Promotion is the advancement of an employee to a position in which he has more authority and responsibility. Usually a promotion also includes an increase in pay and results in more prestige and privileges. Promotion opportunities occur when company growth makes it necessary to create new jobs and when jobs are vacated as the result of resignation, death, or dismissal.

As much as possible, a business should follow the policy of filling vacancies in higher positions by promoting its own employees. Assuming that the company's selection program has been successful in securing well-qualified employees, these employees will be ambitious and will not stay with the company unless there are opportunities for advancement. Also, if employees feel that there are few opportunities for advancement, they will not work as hard at their jobs; and they will not be highly motivated to take advantage of the company's training programs.

Promotion policies must be carefully prepared, and it is very important that all employees understand these policies. Employees must, first of all, know the possible positions to which they might advance. To accomplish this, as will be discussed in Chapter 28, many companies provide employees with an organization chart which shows lines of authority and promotion.

Employees must also understand the factors which are considered in selecting an individual for promotion. The two basic factors which most companies consider are ability and seniority. The task of evaluating the relative abilities of employees being considered for promotion is most difficult. In the main, the decision as to which employee most deserves the promotion should be made by the immediate superior of the workers involved, for he is the one who best knows their abilities. If two or more workers have about the same abilities, the one who has been with the company the longest should receive the promotion.

Transfers

Transfer is the assignment of an employee to another job in the company which, in general, involves the same kinds of skills and responsibilities. At times transfers are made at the request of the employee, but more often they are initiated by the employee's supervisor.

Some of the reasons for transfers are: (1) employees being trained for management positions are transferred from one position to another to give them breadth of experience; (2) capable employees are transferred to jobs which give them a better chance for promotion; (3) workers are transferred to a new department which has been established because of the growth of the company; (4) older workers are transferred to easier jobs; (5) employees are transferred when it is discovered that they are not well suited to their present positions; and (6) workers are transferred when they are unable to get along well with their fellow workers.

Transfer policies and procedures must be carefully established and must be understood by employees. If the reason for a transfer is not thoroughly explained to an employee, he may without justification feel that he is being unfairly treated by the company.

"I forgot to tell you earlier, Jim, that your office is being moved down the hall."

ILLUS. 25-7. Reasons for changes must be thoroughly explained to employees.

Discharges

Discharges are unfortunate for both employer and the employee. A *discharge* involves a permanent separation of an employee from the company. In ordinary language, this means that the employee is fired. Discharge of an employee usually arises from his lack of ability, laziness, failure to get along with his supervisor, or failure to get along with other employees.

Another form of discharge is the *layoff*, which may arise because the job is eliminated due to a decline in business, adoption of more efficient procedures, or the use of automated equipment. Discharges are caused by the employee whereas layoffs are caused by changes within the company.

It is very costly to hire and train an employee. Therefore, it is very costly to discharge an employee. Proper employment methods to avoid the necessity of discharging an employee are extremely important.

Frequently the discharge of an employee is not left entirely in the hands of the department head. If the department head wishes to discharge an employee, he must consult the personnel department. Such a consultation may result in transferring the employee to some other department. In this way a low rate of labor turnover can be maintained.

LABOR TURNOVER

Labor turnover is a term used to describe the extent to which employees come and go in a business. Turnover affects the efficiency of a business because the loss of an experienced employee necessitates hiring and training a new employee.

A low turnover rate is desirable. Two of the most common formulas for computing turnover are:

$$\text{1.} \left\{ \begin{array}{c} \text{Number of employees who have} \\ \text{terminated their employment} \\ \text{with the business} \end{array} \right\} \div \left\{ \begin{array}{c} \text{Average} \\ \text{number of} \\ \text{employees} \end{array} \right\} = \left\{ \begin{array}{c} \text{Percentage} \\ \text{of labor} \\ \text{turnover} \end{array} \right\}$$

$$\text{2.} \left\{ \begin{array}{c} \text{Number of employee} \\ \text{replacements} \end{array} \right\} \div \left\{ \begin{array}{c} \text{Average} \\ \text{number of} \\ \text{employees} \end{array} \right\} = \left\{ \begin{array}{c} \text{Percentage} \\ \text{of labor} \\ \text{turnover} \end{array} \right\}$$

Let us suppose that during one year fifteen persons left the employ of a business; twelve new employees were hired to replace those who had left; and the average number of persons on the payroll was one hundred. According to the first method, the labor turnover was—

$$\frac{15}{100} = 15 \text{ percent}$$

According to the second method, it was—

$$\frac{12}{100} = 12 \text{ percent}$$

REVIEW WHAT YOU HAVE LEARNED

Business Terms Checkup:

(1) personnel management
(2) employment requisition
(3) job specification
(4) job specification cards
(5) on-the-job training
(6) vestibule training
(7) procedures manual

(8) apprenticeship training
(9) supervisory training
(10) promotion
(11) transfer
(12) discharge
(13) layoff
(14) labor turnover

Reading Checkup:

1. Name the functions of personnel management.

2. In the early days of the development of personnel management, what did businessmen regard the function of personnel management to be?

3. In a business which has only a few employees, who performs the personnel management functions?

4. How are large businesses likely to be organized for performing the functions of personnel management?

5. What is the first step in the process of securing a new employee?

6. Explain the purposes for which a job specification card is used.

7. What are some of the sources of labor supply that may be used by a personnel department?

8. What procedures are followed by a personnel department after job applicants have been obtained?

9. Why is a physical examination required by many employers?

10. Why are references given by applicants often considered of very little value?

11. Explain what might be done to introduce a new employee to the company and to his job.

12. Why should the personnel department make a follow-up of a new employee?

13. What is the most common type of training?

14. Distinguish between on-the-job training and vestibule training.

15. In what types of jobs is apprenticeship training most frequently used?

16. What information is often found in a correspondence manual?

17. When do promotion opportunities occur in business?

18. Name the factors which are most often considered when promoting an employee.

19. What are the reasons for transfers?

20. What is the basic difference between a discharge and a layoff?
21. Explain the two methods of computing labor turnover.

APPLY WHAT YOU HAVE LEARNED

Questions for Class Discussion:

1. Do you think the functions performed by personnel management are important to a business? Why or why not?
2. What is the difference between a job specification card and an employment requisition?
3. What should be accomplished in interviewing a job applicant?
4. Why do some employees leave their positions soon after they are hired?
5. Do you think all businesses should have training programs for new employees? Why or why not?
6. Is vestibule training more effective than on-the-job training?
7. What methods are used to train personnel for executive positions?
8. What kind of training is most frequently given to supervisors?
9. Why is it considered a good policy for a firm to fill vacancies in higher positions by promoting its own employees?
10. When a promotion is to be made, who should decide which of the employees will receive the promotion?
11. What advantage is there in transferring individuals from one department to another instead of discharging a person in one department when he is not needed and hiring a new person in another department?

Problems and Projects:

1. Obtain an application blank from a business and fill it out. Of the categories of information contained on the application blank, which do you think would be most helpful in assisting a company in deciding whether it should hire you?
2. Prepare a report to your class after interviewing a guidance counselor at your school who has contact with businesses who employ your school's graduates. Gather information that would help provide classmates with tips to follow when applying for a local job. Your "Do's" and "Don'ts" should cover such areas as the application blank, the interview, and the first day on the job.
3. Working with other members of your class, prepare a debate on the topic: On-The-Job Training is Superior to Vestibule Training.
4. The Gilbert Manufacturing Company has 600 employees and feels that it is necessary to have a systematic evaluation of all employees in order

to be fair to everyone and in order to discover persons who are worthy of promotion and greater responsibility. Supervisors submit periodic written reports which are evaluations of workers under them.

    (a) Indicate the advantages of showing this report to the employee.

    (b) Indicate the disadvantages of showing this report to the employee.

5. The number of employees of the Brookfield Manufacturing Company averages 250; the number of employees who have left the company in the past year is 15; the number of employee replacements is 10. Compute the percentage of labor turnover by each of the two methods illustrated in this chapter.

Case Problem 25-1:

    The Southern Textiles Company employs a large number of office workers and has worked out a plan of selecting and supervising its employees. Upon passing a preliminary interview and being hired to work for the firm, employees are subject to the following routine:

    (a) They are given a week of indoctrination, lectures, acquaintance with general company policy, departmental visits, and some routine training for a simple job.

    (b) Each beginner is assigned to a routine task with an experienced person to "learn by watching and doing."

    (c) After a period of routine work, new assignments are made to more difficult work (with more pay, too). Employee ratings submitted by supervisors determine many such placements.

    (d) For those who show aptitude, additional transfers and promotions occur every six months or year.

    (e) After several years of seasoning and training, the employees are groomed for positions as junior executives. Part of this training consists of school courses, tuition for which is paid by the company.

    (f) Junior executives may eventually reach executive status in the same organization where they started or may be transferred to branches to get their promotion.

Required:

1. What are the strong features of this plan?

2. Can you see any weaknesses?

Case Problem 25-2:

    Charles Morgan had been hired in the mail room of the Teletron Trading Corporation five weeks ago. His job was to collect mail twice daily from each office in the building, sort and process the outgoing mail, deliver outgoing mail to the local post office, and pick up incoming mail from the post office. He learned the job in one day by working with the outgoing employee, Tom Williams. Tom Williams was leaving the company because he was entering military service.

After one month, Morgan felt he was doing rather well with such little supervision. In fact, the supervisor was seldom around. A week later he received notice that he was to be discharged effective next week. Since no explanation accompanied the announcement, he went to the personnel office immediately. The personnel manager pulled a folder from the file and began reading notes that had been placed there during the past month. Morgan responded truthfully to each of the items presented:

(a) An hour late to work on the thirteenth: "My car wouldn't start, but I called to say that I would be in as soon as possible."

(b) Two offices complained that the mail had not been picked up on the second of the month: "It was my second day on the job and I couldn't remember all the stops. After the second day, I made a schedule and I haven't missed an office since."

(c) The Research Department complained that an important document had been sent regular mail that should have been sent airmail: "I didn't know the policy for deciding when and how to send items until I found and asked the supervisor. Then he gave me a pro-cedures manual to study. Tom Williams didn't tell me there was such a manual."

Several other similar complaints had been included in the personnel file, each readily explained by Morgan. According to the personnel manager, Morgan was discharged in keeping with company policy. The discharge policy is that whenever there are five or more complaints per month per employee during the first year of employment he is discharged.

Required:

1. What is your opinion of the company's discharge policy in Morgan's case?
2. Are there any personnel training problems that exist with the Teletron Trading Corporation?
3. What recommendations might be made to improve the training pro-gram?

Continuing Project:

Describe the plan that you will follow in your business for selecting employees, training employees, and promoting employees.

What are wages?

What is meant by a piece-rate plan?

What factors determine wages and salaries?

What fringe benefits may businesses offer?

Who pays social security taxes?

Who is affected by the Social Security Act?

BACKGROUND OF CHAPTER

How much compensation is received in the form of wages and other benefits is of vital concern to all workers. If an employee is unhappy about the compensation he is receiving, his morale will be low even though he is satisfied with all other aspects of working for the company.

A company may determine and pay wages and salaries in several different ways. There are also numerous fringe benefits, such as profit-sharing and group insurance plans, which a company may decide to offer its personnel. Policies and practices relating to the compensation of employees are discussed in this chapter.

CHAPTER 26

COMPENSATION AND BENEFITS

One of the most important incentives for an employee is the compensation he receives for his work. If he feels that he is being underpaid for his services or that increased effort on his part will not result in increased pay, he is likely to do the minimum amount of work necessary; but if he feels that he is being paid a just compensation or that he does have a chance to add to his salary by increased effort and efficiency, he is likely to be a better satisfied and more cooperative employee. A major problem of management is to adopt compensation plans that will bring the best results.

Since the 1930's, business and government have come to provide many benefits which supplement wages or salaries. In addition to discussing policies and practices related to the payment of wages and salaries, attention is also given in this chapter to these supplemental benefits.

WAGES AND SALARIES

Although the term wages is often used to include salaries, in this chapter *wages* is used to mean compensation paid on an hourly basis; and *salaries* is used to mean compensation of executives, supervisors, salesmen, and other employees paid on a basis other than an hourly rate.

Wage and Salary Plans

Because businesses vary so greatly in the type of work being done and in the qualifications required of their employees, many methods are used in determining employee compensation. Under some wage plans two workers doing the same kind of work are paid the same rate of pay regardless of whether one produces more than the other. There are other

ILLUS. 26-1. Workers are likely to do a minimum amount of work unless
they feel that increased effort will result in increased pay.

systems by which a good worker can earn more than a poorer worker.
The most common methods of compensation will now be discussed.

Time Wages. The payment of salaries or wages on the basis of a
year, a month, a week, a day, or an hour is probably the most common
method. Wages paid under this method are often spoken of as *time
wages*. The most common kind of time wages is the *hourly wage,* but
straight salary (a flat rate per week or month) is also frequently used.
Some of the advantages of time wages are:

1. Only a small amount of clerical work is required to determine the
   wages to be paid.
2. The employee can budget his personal expenditures better since
   he knows what pay he is to receive.
3. This method is the only satisfactory way of paying employees
   who do a variety of work, such as the employee who answers the
   telephone, serves as information clerk, and does some filing or
   record work.

The chief disadvantages of this method are:

1. It offers no immediate incentive for extra effort.
2. The conscientious worker feels that he is penalized to the advantage of a lazy fellow worker who receives the same salary.

When the time-wage method is used, the employee can be provided greater satisfaction by increases in his wage or salary rate from time to time when he merits them.

Commission. Under the *commission* plan of compensation, employees, usually salespeople, are paid a given percentage of the volume of business done by them.

The commission plan has the following advantages:

1. It provides a direct incentive to the employee to do his best.
2. It enables management to control costs. For example, the salesmen of a wholesaler are paid a commission. Thus, the selling expense represented by salesmen's salaries becomes a predetermined percentage of the selling price and varies directly with the sales volume.

Some of the disadvantages are:

1. Management cannot control employees on commission as easily as it can employees paid by other methods. For example, wholesale salesmen are likely to feel independent and, instead of working their territory intensively, may do just enough to ensure themselves a reasonable compensation.
2. Employees are likely to be interested in doing nothing except that which will directly increase their wages.
3. Salespeople working on a commission are likely to cater to customers who place large orders and to neglect those who do not.
4. The compensation is likely to vary a great deal when there are seasonal fluctuations.

Salary and Commission. Some salespeople are paid a salary plus a certain commission on their sales volume. For instance, a salesperson may be paid a salary of $100 a week plus a 2 percent commission on his sales. Such a method eliminates most of the disadvantages of the straight salary and the straight commission plans. This plan is used chiefly for salespeople and managers.

Salary and Bonus. A salary and bonus plan is similar to the salary and commission plan in that the employee is paid a regular salary. In addition to the salary, he is paid a bonus based on some quota. The quota is generally an annual or semiannual volume rather than a monthly or weekly volume. For example, a salesman may receive a salary of $175 a week; and if, at the end of six months, he has made sales of more than $15,000, he will receive a bonus of 1 percent of his total sales. Sometimes the bonus is graduated so that the last bracket of the goal offers the greatest reward. In the example just mentioned, the bonus might be 1 percent on all sales up to $15,000; 2 percent on all sales of $15,000 or more and under $18,000; 3 percent on all sales of $18,000 or more and under $20,000; 4 percent on all sales of $20,000 or more. The bonus, however, is not always a percentage; sometimes it is a definite sum of money.

The advantage of the salary and bonus plan is that it keeps the employee working harder over a longer period than he would be if he were being paid a salary plus a commission. Similarly, bonuses are granted on production bases to piece-workers in both factories and offices. Route men for dairies and laundries are often given bonuses for obtaining new customers or for getting a certain volume of sales.

Piece-Rate Plans. A common type of incentive wage in industry is the piece-rate plan. Under a *piece-rate plan* the employee is paid a fixed sum per unit of production. For example, if an employee gets 10¢ for each unit and he produces 250 units a day, he would receive $25.

ILLUS. 26-2. Although piece-rate plans are more commonly used in the factory, some office workers are paid on the basis of units of work completed.

Although piece-rate plans are much more commonly found in the factory, certain office employees may also be paid on the basis of units of work completed. For example, billing clerks may be paid according to the number of invoices they complete, and the wages of some typists and stenographers are determined by the number of lines or pages of material typed.

Piece rates for each job are usually established by means of time and motion studies. If the time and motion studies have been properly made, a piece-rate plan can have these advantages:

1. Workers are paid in proportion to their productive effort.
2. The plan of compensation encourages workers to become more skillful.
3. The plan is easily understood by employees.
4. Labor costs can be determined with a small amount of clerical effort.

Some of the disadvantages are:

1. The plan does not protect the employee against loss of earning power due to causes beyond his control, such as the breakdown of the machine.
2. The employee tends to sacrifice quality for quantity, although proper inspection can keep the quality up to the standard.
3. The rates of compensation are difficult to establish.
4. The plan is discouraging to beginners.

There are many types of piece-rate plans in use in business, and many of the variations have been made in order to avoid some of the disadvantages listed above. For example, in many plans the piece rates are used as an incentive for workers to improve their production, but the workers are guaranteed a minimum hourly wage.

In some cases individual workers and labor unions have objected to piece-rate plans. When such a plan is used as a device for speeding up production, but the piece rate is then lowered, the plan proves quite objectionable to workers. If, however, the piece-rate plan is operated fairly, it is usually advantageous to workers as well as to the employer.

Profit Sharing. *Profit sharing* takes many forms. In a very small business the owner may share profits by granting bonuses of a flat sum, such as $25 to $1,000, to his employees each year, the amount depending upon the success of the business activities of the past year. Some companies share profits by giving to their employees either a lump sum of cash or shares of stock in the company, the amount depending upon the financial success of the company and the length of service of the employee.

A brief discussion of several plans is given here:

1. The profit-sharing system of a large mail-order company is designed to encourage employee savings. The employees contribute 5 percent of their wages to a fund, and the company contributes 5½ to 7½ percent of its profits to the same fund. After contributing for ten years, the employee is entitled to make withdrawals from his account.

2. The plan of a large soap company is to have the employee purchase stock in the company. The employee has 5 percent deducted from his salary to apply on the purchase of the stock. The company contributes an additional amount. In six years the employee owns the stock; and thereafter, as long as he retains it in his possession, he receives yearly a cash profit-sharing dividend in addition to the regular dividend on the stock that he owns.

3. A manufacturer of photographic supplies makes an annual cash payment to employees, the size of which is determined by the amount of the regularly declared dividend on the company's stock and the earnings of the employee for the five preceding years.

4. A manufacturer of meat products puts into a profit-sharing retirement fund each year a sum of money that varies with the length of service of the employee and the earnings of the company in that particular year.

Factors Affecting the Amount of Wages or Salaries Paid

The amount of money which an individual receives in wages or salary is determined by numerous factors, such as: (1) the traits and abilities of the individual; (2) the relative importance of the job as compared with other jobs; (3) the seniority of the individual; (4) the supply of and demand for the particular kind of labor; (5) the prevailing wage rates in the community and in the industry; (6) the current economic conditions, including the cost of living; (7) the strength of and bargaining success of a union; and (8) certain federal and state laws (these wage and hour laws are discussed in Chapter 27). Additional attention is given below to the difficult and important task of establishing the relative importance of one job as compared to other jobs and to the influence of the cost of living upon wages.

Establishing the Relative Importance of Jobs. Great differences exist between the janitor's and the president's skill, ability, duties, responsibilities, authority, and contribution to the success of the company. There is also quite a difference in the janitor's wage as compared to the president's salary. In between these extremes are numerous other jobs which require varying degrees of skill and ability, which have quite different duties and responsibilities, and which contribute in greater or lesser measure to the company's success.

An employee is quite naturally concerned as to how much money he is earning as compared to other employees. If Joe is earning less than Bill and feels that his work is of greater value to the company than Bill's, Joe will be a very unhappy person. Thus, it is important for a business to determine the relative value of its various jobs to the company and to use this information in establishing its wage structure.

Job evaluation is the term used to refer to the process of ranking jobs in the order of their importance. Job evaluation involves the rating of jobs and should not be confused with *employee evaluation* which is the rating of workers. In job evaluation the jobs must first be analyzed to determine such things as the tasks performed, the skills needed, the responsibility required, and the nature of the working conditions. This information is then used as a basis for arranging jobs in the order of their importance.

Several different methods are used by business for ranking jobs in the order of their importance. The most commonly used method is the point system. An example of the point system is given in Illustration 26-3 on page 540. In this example the job has a value of 420 points. Thus, the rate of pay for the job would be lower than for a job with a point value of 600.

Impact of Cost of Living on Wages. A very important factor in measuring the income of a worker relates to the amount of real wages that he receives. *Real wages* represent the amount of goods and services that the money wages will buy. For example, let us assume that the monthly cost of living for Mr. Martin and his family in 1965 was $600. If the same things which made up this $600 cost in 1965 now cost $700, Mr. Martin would have to be earning $100 more per month in order to have the same standard of living as he had in 1965. From this

Skill		
1. Training	60	
2. Experience	70	
3. Versatility	40	
4. Tact and Agreeableness	20	190
Responsibility		
5. For Details	35	
6. For Quality	35	
7. For Individual Initiative	10	80
Effort		
8. Physical	25	
9. Mental	50	75
Conditions		
10. Working Environment	50	
11. Exposure to Danger	25	75
Total Points		420

ILLUS. 26-3. Point system of job evaluation.

example, it is easy to see that the amount of money that one earns is important only in relation to the cost of living. There is no real increase in wages if the cost of living rises at the same rate as wages.

FRINGE BENEFITS

Besides the regular wages and salaries that are paid employees, many workers in industry today receive supplementary benefits which are commonly called *fringe benefits*. Fringe benefits represent a sizable portion of the employer's payroll costs. It is estimated that the cost to the employer of all types of fringe benefits is over 25 percent of the regular wages and salaries paid. Some of the most common types of fringe benefits are described on the following pages.

Insurance

Many businesses have made it possible for their employees to obtain life insurance at wholesale rates through what is called *group insurance*. In some cases businesses pay part of the insurance premium. Life insurance is thus provided for workers who might not be able to pay the regular rates. Another advantage of group insurance is that no physical examination is required. Some employees would be unable to pass the physical examination required in obtaining insurance individually.

Pensions

Many businesses have pension plans. Some of the general characteristics of pension plans are:

1. The business sometimes pays the entire cost, but in many cases the employee makes a contribution.
2. Sometimes retirement is mandatory at a certain age, and at other times it is at the request of either the employer or the employee.
3. The length of service required before an employee is eligible to retire is usually from 20 to 35 years, with adjusted pensions for those who wish to retire sooner.
4. There is such great variation in the amounts of the pension payments that no attempt will be made to name them. Pension plans usually provide a minimum and a maximum monthly pension based upon the salary of the employee and his length of service.

Pay for Time Off

It is common practice to pay workers for a certain amount of vacation. Many employers pay workers for holidays even though there is no work performed. Some employers encourage all workers to vote and give them some extra time off from their work with pay to be sure that they vote. After a specified period of employment, many employees are granted a certain number of paid absences because of sickness, sickness in the family, or death in the family.

The fringe benefits discussed above are just a few of those which are provided by businesses. Among the many other supplemental benefits provided are: jury duty pay, military induction bonuses, religious holidays, rest periods, credit unions, Christmas bonuses, medical care, safety awards, and suggestion awards.

Other Programs Which Benefit and Protect Personnel

Many companies provide various services and programs which benefit and protect their employees, such as cafeterias, canteen services, hospitals, beauty shops, and recreation facilities. Three benefits of particular concern to employees and employers are discussed below: modified workweeks, health programs, and safety programs.

The Modified Workweek. In recent years firms have experimented with a variety of plans to modify the standard 40-hour, five-day workweek. The four-day week has gained popularity. By working longer hours for fewer days each week, employees are provided an extra day away from work. Forty hours of work can be completed during a 10-hour, four-day week. Another variation of the four-day week is an eight- or nine-hour day with shorter coffee and meal breaks. This variation produces a workweek of slightly less than 40 hours as does the 12-hour day for a three-day week tried by some firms.

In keeping with changing values toward work and leisure and the increased social responsibility of business, firms have introduced other modifications to the standard workweek. For example, some companies offer employees staggered work hours, allowing the work day to begin and end earlier while others may be allowed to start and finish later in the day. A four-day week may also be staggered by having some employees start on days other than Monday. This plan enables a business

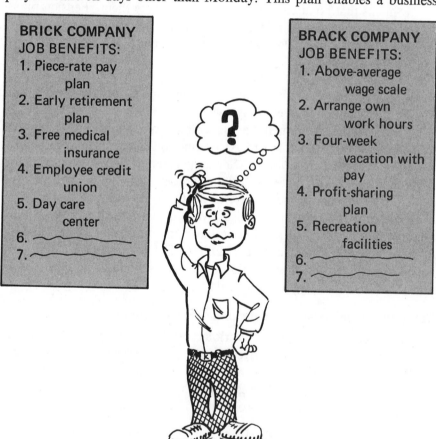

BRICK COMPANY
JOB BENEFITS:
1. Piece-rate pay
    plan
2. Early retirement
    plan
3. Free medical
    insurance
4. Employee credit
    union
5. Day care
    center
6. ⎯⎯⎯⎯⎯
7. ⎯⎯⎯⎯⎯

BRACK COMPANY
JOB BENEFITS:
1. Above-average
    wage scale
2. Arrange own
    work hours
3. Four-week
    vacation with
    pay
4. Profit-sharing
    plan
5. Recreation
    facilities
6. ⎯⎯⎯⎯⎯
7. ⎯⎯⎯⎯⎯

ILLUS. 26-4. Selecting an employer must include many job considerations.

to operate as many days a week as it likes without requiring employees to work more than forty hours per week. As a result, overtime labor costs may be reduced or eliminated.

Changes in work schedules enable employees to adjust individual life styles to the world of work. Working wives, for example, find advantages to adjusting work hours to accommodate family needs. Business benefits, too, by attracting workers who might not otherwise be available and by obtaining maximum use of expensive equipment and other resources. Absenteeism declines and worker morale and productivity increase under many of the new company-tailored plans for modifying the workweek.

The Health Program. If the employee is to do his most efficient work, he must be healthy. The person who is suffering from toothache, a stomach disorder, or other illness will not do as much work as he should and is likely to spoil materials or have accidents. Illness may also mean absence from work, which is costly to the business. The health program often has the following features:

1. A physical examination is required at the time of employment and at periodic intervals thereafter.
2. Health education is carried on by means of posters on bulletin boards, booklets, and talks. Employees are thereby taught how to prevent certain kinds of illness and how to look after their physical well-being.
3. Plant sanitation provides healthful surroundings for the employees. This often includes supervision of ventilation, heating, and lighting, as well as care of washrooms and drinking fountains.
4. A first-aid room and, in some cases, hospital service are provided. If the business does not maintain its own hospital, it may arrange with a local hospital for service to its employees.
5. Sometimes dental service is provided at a nominal cost for the benefit of employees.
6. The operation of a lunchroom, in which wholesome food is provided at reasonable prices, may be considered part of the health program.
7. Studies of fatigue are often made and are used as the basis for a more efficient planning of the employee's work. As a result of these studies, many businesses have established rest periods throughout the work day.

The Safety Program. If it were possible to compile the costs of industrial accidents during one year, the sum would be enormous. Because thousands of workers are injured and killed every year, the primary purpose of the safety program is to reduce the number of accidents.

Accidents are due to mechanical, physiological, or psychological causes. The mechanical causes are such things as unguarded machinery, defective machinery, slippery floors, and obstructed passageways. Such causes usually can be eliminated if proper care is exercised on the part of management. The physiological causes of accidents are long hours of work, inadequate lighting, tasks that are dull and monotonous, and the like. These causes cannot always be eliminated, but they can be reduced somewhat by the maintenance of proper working conditions. The psychological causes are ignorance, recklessness, carelessness, inexperience, and the like. To eliminate these causes, both workers and management must cooperate.

In large organizations specialists devote their entire time to the promotion of safety. One of the first steps in a safety program is regular inspection. Regular inspection will lead to better planning and

"Office safety training might be difficult to do. Why do you think we should make it a crash project?"

ILLUS. 26-5. Many good safety suggestions come from employees.

arrangement of equipment and to better safeguards of machinery. Inspection will also disclose bad housekeeping practices, poor handling of materials, and faulty electric wiring. Regular inspections will call attention to the need for proper maintenance of the plant and equipment.

As is implied by Illustration 26-5, page 544, one of the important sources of safety suggestions is the employees themselves. Many organizations have formed safety committees made up of employees. When employees realize that they have a part in a safety program that will protect them, they will be inclined to cooperate. Unless employees do cooperate, there cannot be a successful safety program.

There are safety regulations for businesses in many states. In addition, a federal law on health and safety exists, which will be discussed in the next section.

BENEFITS PROVIDED BY LAWS

Businesses contribute to employee benefits which are provided by the Occupational Safety and Health Act, the Social Security Act, and by workmen's compensation laws.

Occupational Safety and Health Act

When the people of America became concerned about the social and physical environment of man during recent years, they also became concerned about the environment of the work place. In a recent year, there were 14,000 job deaths and over two million disabling injuries.

Many industries have shown gradual decreases in the rate of work injuries over the years as shown in Illustration 26-6 on page 546. It can be seen that in the critical manufacturing industry the number of disabling injuries per million employee-hours worked shows a distinct increase. The rise in manufacturing injuries accompanied by man's concern about his work environment prompted Congress to act.

The Occupational Safety and Health Act was passed in 1970. The law provides for the establishment and enforcement of occupational safety and health standards. Responsibility is placed on both employers and employees. Employers must provide a work place which is free of actual or potential health and safety hazards while meeting standards prescribed by the U. S. Secretary of Labor. Employers must inform all employees of job hazards and federal standards. For their protection, of course, employees are required under the law to observe the standards.

Industrial standards developed by business and government before 1970 have been adopted under the law, and new standards have been

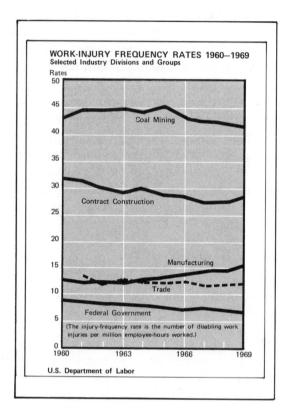

WORK-INJURY FREQUENCY RATES 1960–1969
Selected Industry Divisions and Groups

Rates

Coal Mining

Contract Construction

Manufacturing

Trade

Federal Government

(The injury-frequency rate is the number of disabling work injuries per million employee-hours worked.)

U.S. Department of Labor

ILLUS. 26-6. High job injury rates in manufacturing helped prompt the passage of the Occupational Safety and Health Act.

developed systematically as a part of the Occupational Safety and Health Act. Federal inspections and investigations are made from time to time at work places of small and large firms transacting business in more than one state. Employees, however, may request additional plant inspections and may report violations directly to the U. S. Department of Labor. Heavy penalties, including possible imprisonment, face violators of the law.

Social Security Act

The Social Security Act was passed by Congress in 1935, and it has been changed many times since then.[1] Approximately nine out of ten persons who are employed are affected by the provisions of this act.

---

[1] Congress will undoubtedly continue to amend the provisions of the Social Security Act. Literature concerning the latest provisions of the act may be obtained from any social security office.

The most important programs provided by the act (and these are programs for which employers are taxed) are: (1) old-age, survivors, and disability insurance, (2) health insurance, and (3) unemployment insurance.

Old-Age, Survivors, and Disability Insurance (OASDI). The OASDI portion of the Social Security Act provides pensions to retired workers and their families, death benefits to the survivors of workers, and benefits to disabled workers and their families. The process of figuring benefits is somewhat complicated, but the amount received is based on the amount of the contributions credited to the worker's social security account.

ILLUS. 26-7. To provide funds to pay employee social security benefits, the employer is taxed the same amount as the employee.

Workers Covered by OASDI. Most business employees are covered by the OASDI portion of the Social Security Act. Others are also covered, such as regularly employed agricultural and domestic workers, federal employees not covered by other retirement systems, state and local government employees if they so decide, and workers for nonprofit institutions on an optional basis. Many self-employed individuals and independent businessmen are likewise covered by the OASDI provisions of the Social Security Act.

Social Security Taxes. The money to pay retirement, survivors, disability, and hospital (Medicare) benefits comes from social security taxes paid by employees, employers, and self-employed. Though the tax changes from time to time, it is levied on a fixed portion of income earned each year (in 1973 the yearly tax was 5.85 percent on the first $10,800). The employer and the employee each pay this tax based on the employee's earnings during the calendar year. Self-employed persons pay a slightly higher rate of social security tax than do regular employees.

Health Insurance. The 1965 social security amendments established a broad program of health insurance for people who have reached retirement age. This program, which is commonly referred to as "Medicare," provides hospital insurance and medical insurance.

Hospital Insurance. Under the hospital insurance provisions, payments are made for hospitalization, outpatient hospital diagnostic services, posthospital care in nursing homes, and posthospital health services at home. As with the OASDI benefits, money to pay for these hospital benefits comes from social security taxes paid by employees, employers, and the self-employed.

Medical Insurance. Under the medical insurance provisions, the federal government makes payments for physicians' and surgeons' services, home health visits, and other medical and health services, such as X-rays, surgical dressings, casts, and ambulance service. The medical insurance program is a voluntary program. Those who decide to buy this insurance pay a monthly amount, and an equal amount is paid by the federal government.

Unemployment Insurance. The unemployment insurance program is, in the main, administered by the states. In order for workers in a state to participate in the program, it is necessary for the state to pass an unemployment compensation law which is in harmony with the federal law; and all states have passed such laws.

Unemployment Benefits. Unemployment insurance gives many workers some income when they are out of work. Unemployment compensation laws vary from state to state, but the worker usually receives about one half of his regular wage for a period of from three to nine months. Before unemployment benefits are received, the worker must meet certain requirements. To be eligible for benefits under most state laws, a worker:

1. Must be unemployed through no fault of his own.
2. Must register at a public employment office for a job.
3. Must be able and available for work.
4. Must be totally unemployed for the amount of time specified in the state law.

Unemployment Insurance Taxes. The money to pay unemployment benefits comes from taxes paid by the employer (in a few states employees are also taxed). Currently, a tax rate of 3.28 percent is levied on the first $4,200 of income paid to each employee (2.7 percent goes to the state fund, and .58 percent is used to pay federal administrative costs). In many states the tax rate is reduced for employers having a low labor turnover rate.

Records Required. Every employer subject to the Social Security Act must keep adequate records of earnings and taxes due. The state unemployment compensation laws also require employers to keep records similar to those required by the federal law.

Workmen's Compensation Laws

All states have workmen's compensation laws which require employers to provide insurance for a worker's death, injury, or sickness

ILLUS. 26-8. Workmen's compensation laws require employers to provide insurance for the work-connected death, injury, or sickness of a worker.

arising directly from the worker's employment. Some types of workers are exempt, such as those in agriculture, but almost all employees in business are covered by this type of protection.

In some states the law requires that payments be made directly to the state which will pay claims according to law. In other states the laws merely require that the employer must provide this kind of protection. The employer may pay the claims directly or may purchase insurance through an insurance company which will pay the claims according to law.

In the case of injury or sickness arising directly out of the work, weekly benefits are paid the worker. If the worker is killed in his employment or dies from an illness arising from his work, benefits are paid to the widow or children.

REVIEW WHAT YOU HAVE LEARNED

Business Terms Checkup:

(1) wages
(2) salaries
(3) time wages
(4) hourly wages
(5) straight salary
(6) commission
(7) piece-rate plan

(8) profit sharing
(9) job evaluation
(10) employee evaluation
(11) real wages
(12) fringe benefits
(13) group insurance

Reading Checkup:

1. Under what type of wage plan is each of the following three employees being paid? (a) $65 a week, (b) $5,500 a year, and (c) $1.90 an hour.
2. What are some advantages and disadvantages of time wages?
3. State the principal advantages and disadvantages of the commission plan of compensation.
4. What is meant by a salary and bonus plan of compensation?
5. How are piece rates for a job usually determined?
6. What are some of the advantages and disadvantages of a piece-rate plan?
7. Under a profit-sharing plan, how do employees sometimes participate in the profits?
8. What is the most commonly used method for ranking jobs in the order of their importance?
9. Name some provisions that are typically found in pension plans.

10. What are the advantages to businesses of using workweek plans that are different from the 40-hour, five-day standard?

11. Indicate some of the activities commonly provided in health programs.

12. Identify some of the causes of industrial accidents.

13. Why was the Occupational Safety and Health Act passed?

14. What are the responsibilities of the employer and employee under the Occupational Safety and Health Act?

15. What benefits are provided for those who are covered by the Social Security Act?

16. What types of workers are covered by the OASDI portion of the Social Security Act?

17. How much social security tax do employees pay in relation to the amount paid by the employer?

18. Under the health insurance program of social security, who pays for medical insurance?

19. Under most state laws, what requirements must a worker meet before he can receive unemployment compensation?

20. What kind of protection do workmen's compensation laws provide?

APPLY WHAT YOU HAVE LEARNED

Questions for Class Discussion:

1. How does the amount of skill needed in a job affect wage rates?

2. What is the advantage of a salary and bonus plan as compared to a salary plus a commission plan?

3. Give an example of how a piece-rate pay plan might be used.

4. How has business attempted to overcome some of the disadvantages of a piece-rate plan?

5. It has been claimed that straight wage rates—paying every worker the same rate—are unfair to the better workers and that some kind of piece-rate or bonus system should be used. What is your opinion?

6. Name some factors that determine basic wage and salary rates.

7. Explain the difference between job evaluation and employee evaluation in determining wage rates.

8. Explain the difference between money wages and real wages.

9. Indicate some of the fringe benefits received by workers and the importance of these fringe benefits in the total compensation received by workers.

10. If a factory keeps a record of accidents and finds that its accident rate is rapidly increasing, what are some of the personnel research problems that could be investigated?

11. Can you explain why the old-age-benefits taxes paid by a self-employed person are higher than those paid by an employed person?
12. If the unemployment tax rate is 3.28%, under what circumstances may an employer pay less than this?
13. If an employee is driving home from work and is injured in an automobile accident, will this injury be covered by workmen's compensation?

Problems and Projects:

1. Assume that there are three salesmen, Smith, Jones, and Brown, who earn base salaries of $9,000, $9,200, and $9,400 a year. They produce sales of $80,000, $92,000, and $96,000 respectively. Each is paid a 6 percent commission for all sales in excess of $40,000. Draw a table with columns for the names of the men, the sales, the base salary, the commission, and the total compensation. Complete this table with the appropriate figures.

2. The Whitehall Machine Company has 115 employees and a payroll of $600,000 a year. Assume that the employer pays a 5.85 percent social security tax and a 3.28 percent unemployment tax. The company spends $32,000 a year for life insurance on employees, $9,000 for hospital insurance, $8,300 a year for workmen's compensation, $5,700 for recreation, $13,000 as a loss on the operation of the lunchroom, and $40,000 a year for vacation time.
   (a) Compute the total cost of fringe benefits.
   (b) Compute the percentage that the total fringe benefits are of the total payroll costs.

3. Assume that for purposes of old-age benefits, Paul Baxter has had 5.85 percent deducted from $10,800 of his salary for each of 30 years before his retirement.
   (a) How much will he have paid to the federal government for social security?
   (b) How much will the employer have paid?

4. Visit your nearest social security office and obtain the following information as a basis for a report to your class on the social security system.
   (a) The current social security tax rate.
   (b) Pamphlets explaining the following employee benefits: retirement, survivors, disability, and Medicare.

Case Problem 26-1:

The Farney Company, which manufactures metal folding chairs, has twelve workers and one supervisor in one of its small assembly plants. Each employee is responsible for the total assembly of each chair so that the work of each employee is independent. A piece-rate wage plan is used.

The employees recently expressed to higher management the desire for a change in the standard 40-hour, five-day week. Higher management yesterday informed everyone that a plan for a modified workweek would be considered as long as: (1) each employee worked at least 36 hours per week; (2) weekly output for the plant did not drop; (3) the plant operated at least during the hours of 8:00 a.m. to 5:00 p.m., Monday through Friday; and (4) at least three employees be on the job at any one time except during meal hours.

The plant supervisor called a meeting of his workers to arrange a plan that would satisfy both employees and higher management. Before the meeting began, however, he knew there would be problems. A few workers were against any changes. Many had already decided personally the days and hours they preferred, and it seemed that no two preferences sounded alike. Four of the workers are women, all of whom prefer to leave work by three in the afternoon.

Required:

1. What type of modified workweek seems most likely to be effective?
2. Design a schedule for the women employees.
3. How might a modified workweek affect morale, absenteeism, and production?

Case Problem 26-2:

The Midwest Foundry Company has a pension plan under which workers can retire at age 65. A worker can retire at an earlier age on a reduced pension if he is injured. Joe Campbell, age 52, has worked for the company 25 years. He was injured six months ago while working. After several operations, the doctors have reported that he never can work again.

Required:

1. Can Joe Campbell obtain any compensation from workmen's compensation?
2. Is there any help available to Joe Campbell under federal social security?
3. Is there any other help available to Joe Campbell?

Continuing Project:

Make a list of the employees that you will need in your business. Indicate the wages and salaries that you would expect to pay each employee and the methods that you will use in making these payments. Also list any types of fringe benefits that you plan to offer your employees.

What is the history of labor unions?

How do labor unions achieve their goals?

How do management objectives conflict with union objectives?

What is collective bargaining?

Why have labor laws been passed?

How are wages and hours regulated?

BACKGROUND OF CHAPTER

Chapter 26 discussed the wages and other benefits which are received by employees. At times employees are not satisfied with their wages, their benefits, or their working conditions. In order to gain more power in negotiating with management for higher wages and other benefits, many workers have joined labor unions. As members of labor unions, workers agree to bargain as a group with the employer rather than to bargain as individuals.

This chapter explores the relationships which exist between unions and management and discusses the legislation which influences these relationships.

CHAPTER 27

LABOR RELATIONS AND LEGISLATION

As is discussed in Chapter 3, profit is the reward received by the owners of a business for producing goods and services. The management of a business directs its efforts toward increasing profits, and these efforts involve controlling costs and increasing the efficiency of the operations of the business. The efforts of management to reduce costs and improve efficiency are, at times, in conflict with the desires of workers for higher wages and other benefits. Often these differences can be resolved to the mutual satisfaction of both management and the workers, but sometimes no common ground for agreement can be found.

As business developed in the United States and elsewhere, some employers did not provide good working conditions or pay fair wages; and workers found that as individuals they had little power to negotiate with management for pay increases and better working conditions. To obtain the economic power which would enable them to gain concessions from management, many workers joined labor unions. As labor unions grew larger and more powerful, labor-management conflicts occurred which were detrimental to management, to workers, and to the general public. These conflicts led to the passage of legislation which concerns itself with the rights and responsibilities of labor unions and management.

This chapter discusses the union-management relationship and the labor laws which influence this relationship.

LABOR UNIONS AND THE UNION-MANAGEMENT RELATIONSHIP

About three out of ten workers in nonagricultural businesses are labor union members. The extent to which workers belong to unions varies by industry, by occupation, and by geographical area. Unions have been very successful in organizing workers in mining, construction, manufacturing, transportation, and public utilities. Two thirds or more of all factory production workers are organized, and certain basic industries such as steel, automobile, aircraft, meat-packing, rubber, and electrical manufacturing are almost completely organized.

Very few workers employed in agriculture, trade, banks, and insurance companies are organized. In terms of occupations, the largest unorganized groups are white-collar workers, hired agricultural workers, and domestic workers.

While union membership in white-collar and professional occupations has been relatively small, growth has occurred. In recent years the number of bargaining units among state and federal employees and teachers has increased rapidly. A continued increase in the unionization of service workers is expected.

National Unions

Although there are many single-firm unions, the strength of the labor movement resides in unions which draw their membership from workers located throughout the country. The largest and most powerful union organization in the United States is the American Federation of Labor and Congress of Industrial Organizations (AFL-CIO). Approximately 75 percent of the workers who are organized are members of national unions affiliated with the AFL-CIO.

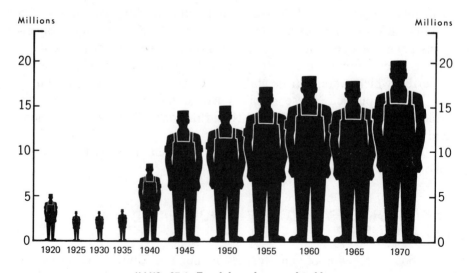

ILLUS. 27-1. Trend in union membership.

The American Federation of Labor (AFL) was formed in 1886, and originally the membership was organized according to occupations or crafts. In 1936 eight unions, some of which had belonged to the AFL, formed a separate federation which became known as the Congress of Industrial Organizations (CIO). The formation of the CIO was the result of opposition to the emphasis in the AFL on *craft unionism;* that is, the organization of workers by occupations, such as machinists, carpenters, and plumbers. Those who formed the CIO were proponents of *industrial unionism;* that is, they wanted to organize unions for skilled, semiskilled, and unskilled workers employed by the same large industry, such as the steel industry.

The difficulties between the AFL and CIO did not prevent the growth of unionism; and with the passage of time, both the AFL and CIO became mixtures of craft and industrial unions. Many efforts to merge the two federations were made over the years, and finally in 1955 the AFL and CIO merged to form the AFL-CIO.

A number of strong national unions are not affiliated with the AFL-CIO. Two of the largest independent unions are the Teamsters and the United Automobile Workers.

Union Objectives and Tactics

Labor unions have numerous objectives. The most important objectives are:

1. Higher wages and shorter hours.
2. The *closed shop* in which the employer agrees to hire only persons who are union members, and all new employees must join the union.
3. The *union shop* in which the employer may hire nonunion workers, but they must eventually join the union.
4. An arrangement by which employees who are members of the union must continue to be members or be discharged from their jobs.
5. An arrangement whereby the employer agrees to hire only union members and to give preference to union members when workers are laid off.
6. Recognition of unions as the bargaining agent of employees.
7. Requiring the employer to withhold union dues from the pay of the workers and to pay the dues directly to the union.
8. Agreements with employers whereby rights and privileges of an employee are determined by his length of service.

ILLUS. 27-2. To receive higher wages is an important objective of labor.

In order to enforce their demands or to gain their objectives, labor unions have followed certain practices in dealing with employers:

1. A *strike*—a refusal of employees to work until their demands have been fulfilled.
2. A *walkout*—another term for a strike.
3. A *sitdown strike*—a strike in which workers do not leave their places of work but simply refuse to work.
4. A *slowdown strike*—a strike in which the workers continue to work but at a reduced speed.
5. *Picketing*—placing one or more persons at the entrance to the place of business with the purpose of inducing others not to enter. It is a common practice during a strike to picket the employer.
6. A *boycott*—a practice of union members of refusing to purchase products from a company whose employees are on strike.

Management Objectives and Tactics

The important management objectives which have conflicted with union objectives are:

1. *Profit.* Management's responsibility is to make a profit for the owners of the business. To fulfill its responsibility in the competitive world of business, management must attempt to reduce costs and improve worker efficiency.

2. *Retain managerial authority.* For an organization to function effectively, management must have the authority to require workers to perform assigned tasks. Management vigorously dislikes any infringement by unions in the realm of its authority, as, for example, having to consult a union before transferring, disciplining, or discharging a worker.

3. *Nonunion shop or open shop.* In general, management prefers a nonunion shop; that is, it prefers not to have its workers represented by a union. If workers are organized, management prefers an open shop. In an *open shop* management may hire union members, or it may hire workers who are not members of the union.

In its conflicts with unions, management has used the following techniques in efforts to combat the power of organized labor:

1. *Employers' associations.* Employers' associations, such as the National Association of Manufacturers, perform many functions

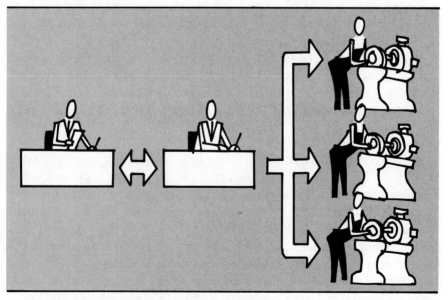

ILLUS. 27-3. To retain managerial authority is an important objective of management.

for their members—research, *lobbying* (influencing legislators regarding proposed laws), promoting the industry, etc. In the area of union-management conflict, the major effort of employers' associations has been in promoting management's viewpoint with the public and with governments at the local, state, and federal levels.

2. *Injunction.* An *injunction* is a court order directing a person(s) to refrain from doing a certain act(s). Courts issue injunctions in order to give protection against irreparable damage. Prior to World War I, injunctions were commonly issued by courts to prevent almost all kinds of strike activity. Today, however, injunctions are usually only issued to prevent damage to company property and to restrict certain picketing activities.

3. *Lockout.* A *lockout* is a work stoppage instituted by management. Management "locks the gates" and refuses to let workers enter the premises until they withdraw their demands.

4. *Hiring new employees.* In an effort to force regular employees who are out on strike to return to their jobs because of fear that they might lose them, management has sometimes hired new employees to operate the business.

5. *Blacklist.* A *blacklist* is a list of names of union "troublemakers" which is circulated among employers to prevent their hiring the persons listed. Although it was once a common practice, "blacklisting" is now illegal.

6. *"Yellow-dog" contract.* The *"yellow-dog" contract* was another management device, now illegal, which required the new worker to sign a statement that he was not a member of a union, would not join a union, and could be discharged if he did join a union.

Collective Bargaining

The basic characteristic of a labor union is that its members agree to bargain as a group with the employer for higher pay and other benefits rather than to bargain with the employer as individuals, a process which is known as *collective bargaining*. The procedure of collective bargaining involves representatives from management and labor meeting together to discuss and to resolve their differences. If management and labor are able to resolve their differences, which is often the case, they state their agreement in a contract which is called the *labor contract*. Labor contracts are usually quite lengthy and cover such things as: wages, hours, fringe benefits, seniority, disciplinary procedures, grievance procedures, and the length of time the contract will remain in force. Both management and labor are bound by the terms of the labor contract.

The negotiations between representatives of management and labor do not always result in agreement being reached on all issues. If the negotiations reach a point where neither party is willing to compromise further, they may attempt to resolve their differences by means of mediation or arbitration.

Mediation. At times, management and labor attempt to resolve their differences by securing the help of a *mediator,* a disinterested third party. The mediator, or mediators, listens to the arguments of both sides and suggests ways in which labor and management might compromise in arriving at a solution to the existing problem. Labor and management are not obligated to accept the mediator's suggestions.

Often community leaders or university professors serve as mediators; and since the establishment of the Federal Mediation and Conciliation Service in 1947, its staff has often been used to help settle disputes.

Arbitration. Management and labor also attempt to resolve their differences by means of *arbitration.* When this means of settling disputes is used, management and labor agree in advance that they will

ILLUS. 27-4. Labor and management are bound by the decision made by an arbitration board.

be bound by the decision of the arbitrator. Thus, as contrasted to the mediator, the arbitrator has the power to make a decision which will settle the dispute. Although arbitration may be entrusted to an individual, usually an arbitration board is used. Generally, the arbitration board consists of three persons—one chosen by labor, one chosen by management, and a third person agreeable to both management and labor.

LABOR LEGISLATION

Conflicts between labor and management led to the passage of federal legislation. The three important laws which currently define the rights and responsibilities of unions and management are: the Wagner Act, the Taft-Hartley Act, and the Landrum-Griffin Act. In addition to these laws, this section also discusses labor legislation which regulates wages and hours and discriminatory practices.

Wagner Act

In 1935 Congress passed the National Labor Relations Act, which is commonly known as the Wagner Act. This act is our basic labor law. The Wagner Act guaranteed the right of workers to organize unions and the right of these unions to bargain collectively with employers. The act also created the National Labor Relations Board to administer the provisions of the act. The National Labor Relations Board was given the power to hold secret elections in which employees could decide which union, if any, they wanted as their representative for bargaining purposes. The Board was also given the authority to prevent employers from engaging in the following activities which were designated as "unfair labor practices":

1. Interference in any way with the right of employees to organize unions and bargain collectively.
2. Domination or interference with the formation of or administration of a labor union.
3. Financial contribution to or other support of a union.
4. Discrimination of any kind against employees which would tend to encourage or discourage membership in any labor union.
5. Discharge of or any discrimination against an employee who has given testimony under the act.
6. Refusal to bargain collectively with the union chosen by the majority of the employees as its representative.

Taft-Hartley Act

Employers felt and, after a time, other groups came to feel that the Wagner Act favored unions; and in 1947 Congress passed the Labor Management Relations Act (Taft-Hartley Act). The effort in the Taft-Hartley Act was to restore a balance of power between management and labor. Except as it is amended by the Taft-Hartley Act, the provisions of the Wagner Act remain in force.

The basic "unfair labor practices" which were designated by the Wagner Act were not changed by the Taft-Hartley Act, but it added the following "unfair union practices":

1. Restraint or coercion of employees who are exercising their rights as defined in the act—e.g., threats by unions that employees will lose their jobs unless they support the union's activities.
2. Causing an employer to discriminate against an employee because of his union activities—e.g., causing an employer to discharge an employee because he has circulated a petition urging a change in the union's method of selecting shop stewards.
3. Refusal to bargain collectively with an employer.
4. Engaging in a *secondary boycott* (a boycott of a person or a firm not engaged in a dispute) or engaging in *jurisdictional strikes* (stopping work because of a dispute between different unions).
5. Charging excessive initiation fees to keep new members out of a union.
6. Requiring employers to pay for work employees have not done (a practice that is called *featherbedding*).

Other important provisions of the Taft-Hartley Act are:

1. Unions may be sued for breach of contract.
2. The closed shop is outlawed.
3. If in the judgment of the President of the United States a controversy or strike exists which imperils the national health or safety, he may obtain a court injunction forbidding the action for a period of 80 days. During the "cooling off" period, further efforts to settle the dispute are to be made.
4. The act allows states to adopt more restrictive legislation against union-membership requirements than is provided by the act itself, and many state legislatures have passed so-called "right to work" laws which provide that an individual does not have to join a union in order to obtain and hold a job.

Landrum-Griffin Act

In 1959, as a result of investigations of union activities which revealed corrupt and irresponsible practices, Congress passed the Labor-Management Reporting and Disclosure Act (Landrum-Griffin Act). In the main, the law deals with internal union affairs by providing new safeguards for rank-and-file members and by placing additional restrictions on the activities of unions and their officers.

The first part of the act is a "bill of rights" for rank-and-file members which is designed to insure their rights to participate in union affairs, to be informed of union agreements, and to have fair hearings in disciplinary actions. Other parts of the act provide for reporting procedures which have as their purpose the prevention of and detection of illegal or unfair practices. Unions must file a detailed report of their internal affairs with the Secretary of Labor, and any changes which occur must be reported annually. Unions must also file an annual financial report with the Secretary of Labor which includes information as to salaries paid to officers and to employees who receive more than $10,000 a year from the union. The act requires employers to report

ILLUS. 27-5. The rights of rank-and-file union members to participate in and to be informed of union affairs are protected by the Landrum-Griffin Act.

annually any payments made or received which relate in any way to the rights of the employees to organize and to bargain collectively.

Wage and Hour Laws

Several laws dealing with wages and hours have been passed which affect labor and management.

The Fair Labor Standards Act (FLSA), which was enacted by the federal government in 1938 and has since been amended several times, is often referred to as the Wage and Hour Law. In general, the provisions of this act cover workers employed in industries engaged in interstate commerce or in the manufacture of goods shipped in interstate commerce. The act also covers employees of certain retail and service establishments whose sales volumes exceed a prescribed amount. The FLSA exempts from its provisions many different types of workers, such as executives, administrators, and professional employees; but some of the exemptions apply to only one provision of the act. The determination as to whether a particular employee is exempt from one or more provisions of the act is somewhat complicated. Thus, it is advisable for an employer to comply with the provisions of the FLSA until he is certain that some or all of his employees are exempt from some or all of the law's provisions.

The major provisions of the FLSA deal with overtime payments and minimum wage rates. For most employees covered by the act, the employer must pay a minimum hourly wage for the first 40 hours of work during a week, and he must pay 1½ times the regular hourly rate for all work in excess of 40 hours.

Under another federal law, the Walsh-Healey Public Contracts Act, there are special regulations for work done on federal government contracts. For example, the rate of pay for over 40 hours weekly or eight hours in any day must be at the rate of 1½ times the regular hourly rate.

In addition to the federal laws just discussed, many states have laws which set minimum wages for regular and overtime work and which ensure that men and women will receive equal pay if they are performing the same work. Many other state laws exist which relate to wages. For example, most states require regular payment of wages due an employee. As a rule payday is seven to ten days after the work period ends. The Department of Labor in the state should be contacted if a business has any doubts as to whether or not it is complying with all of the state laws.

Discriminatory Laws

The movement toward increased social responsibility within the American economic system applies to employers and to employees. While businesses have become increasingly responsive to society's needs (see Chapter 2), unions, too, have become very concerned about the social welfare of workers. State and federal laws dealing with various forms of discrimination have been enacted to promote fair treatment of all workers. Legislation has focused, in particular, on discriminatory employment practices involving sex, race, and age.

The Equal Pay Act, passed in 1963, is a federal law which affects the wages received by some employees. Under this law employers are not permitted to pay different amounts of wages to male and female employees doing work on jobs requiring equal skill, effort, and responsibility and which are performed under similar working conditions. This law applies to employers who are subject to the provisions of the Fair Labor Standards Act.

The Civil Rights Act, passed in 1964, contains a section called "Equal Employment Opportunity." This law prohibits employers from discriminating against applicants or employees because of sex, race, color, religion, or national origin.

In addition, state and federal laws have been passed which outlaw other forms of discrimination. The Discrimination in Employment Act,

ILLUS. 27-6. The federal Equal Pay Act and laws in some states require that men and women must receive equal pay if they are performing the same work.

which became effective in 1968, makes it illegal for employers, unions, and employment agencies to discharge or refuse to hire or otherwise discriminate against persons aged 40 to 65. Employers and employees in all states should be familiar with their rights and duties regarding the fair social treatment of workers.

REVIEW WHAT YOU HAVE LEARNED

Business Terms Checkup:

(1) craft unionism
(2) industrial unionism
(3) closed shop
(4) union shop
(5) strike
(6) walkout
(7) sitdown strike
(8) slowdown strike
(9) picketing
(10) boycott
(11) open shop
(12) lobbying

(13) injunction
(14) lockout
(15) blacklist
(16) "yellow-dog" contract
(17) collective bargaining
(18) labor contract
(19) mediator
(20) arbitration
(21) secondary boycott
(22) jurisdictional strikes
(23) featherbedding

Reading Checkup:

1. Approximately how many of the workers in the labor force are union members?
2. Name the basic industries in which almost all of the production workers are members of unions.
3. What occupations have the fewest union members?
4. What is the largest and most powerful union organization in the United States?
5. What is the difference between craft unionism and industrial unionism?
6. Why was the Congress of Industrial Organizations (CIO) formed?
7. Name two of the larger unions which are not affiliated with the AFL-CIO.
8. What is a labor contract, and what are some of the things usually covered in a labor contract?
9. What are the main means of settling labor-management disputes?
10. What is the difference between mediation and arbitration?
11. What are the three most important laws which currently define the rights and responsibilities of unions and management?
12. Is it legal for an employer to discharge a worker because he belongs to a union?

13. Can a union legally boycott an employer who is not involved in a labor dispute?
14. Must an employer bargain collectively with his employees?
15. What is an injunction, and how may an employer use it to prevent a union from interfering with the operation of his business?
16. How do the provisions of the Fair Labor Standards Act affect the amount of wages paid employees?
17. How do the provisions of the Equal Pay Act affect the amount of wages paid employees?
18. Name three laws that are designed to reduce discriminatory practices.

APPLY WHAT YOU HAVE LEARNED

Questions for Class Discussion:

1. What are the objectives of labor unions?
2. What management objectives are sometimes in conflict with the objectives of unions?
3. What is the basic characteristic of a labor union?
4. What tactics have unions used in trying to force management to accept their demands?
5. What tactics has management used to combat the power of organized labor?
6. Explain what you feel may be some of the advantages or disadvantages of using mediation in labor-management disputes.
7. Why was it necessary to pass labor laws?
8. What is the basic purpose of the Wagner Act? The Taft-Hartley Act? The Landrum-Griffin Act?
9. Management is prevented by law from engaging in certain "unfair labor practices." What are some of these practices?
10. Labor is prevented by law from engaging in certain "unfair union practices." What are some of these practices?
11. What types of job discrimination have been made illegal?

Problems and Projects:

1. Joe Speck, an employee of the Battelle Manufacturing Company, a company doing a national business, was a member of a union which had a dispute with the Battelle Manufacturing Company. He was fired by the company for giving testimony against the company. Can he be fired legally?
2. The employees of the Blue Ridge Baking Company do not belong to a union. A union, in attempting to get the employees to join, set up a picketing line, attempted to induce customers to boycott the company, and tried to prevent workers from entering the plant. Is this legal?

3. Make a list of companies in your community which have employees who are members of unions. For each company indicate the union or unions to which their workers belong.

4. Interview a local businessman and a local labor leader with respect to their views concerning organized labor. Report the results of your interviews, and add a statement which identifies your point of view about the value of labor unions.

5. Paul Watson is a driver for the Overland Trucking Company, which operates across state lines. Last week Watson worked ten hours a day for six days and received for this work his straight-time pay of $4 an hour. Does his work and his payment of wages conform to the requirements of the Fair Labor Standards Act? Explain your answer.

Case Problem 27-1:

Helen Thomson and Maria Garcia are employed by the Dickens Company. Helen Thomson has been an extremely efficient, friendly, and cooperative worker. To increase the number of women in higher level jobs, management has offered her a supervisory position; but she is upset about management's point of view toward pay. The salary offered her is only two-thirds that for comparable positions held by men in the company. She has been told that all the supervisors are men, most of whom have large families and who need the higher salary. Further, management claims that the workers might not produce as much under a woman supervisor, so they prefer to pay her less.

Maria Garcia, on the other hand, has been employed by the firm for 35 years. She had been asked to consider early retirement but refused. The reason management requested an early retirement was to get a young person to learn a new but complicated method for performing her duties. Maria is willing to learn the new method but management feels that due to age she will not learn as well as a younger person will. In addition, they add, "all that training will be lost when you retire in only a few years." Because of her refusal to retire early, Maria feels that management has made the job uncomfortable. "I have been given odd working hours from week to week and my duties have been increased; they are trying to drive me away from working here."

Required:

1. What do both situations have in common?
2. Is the Dickens Company violating any laws? If so, which ones?
3. What action might be taken by Helen Thomson and Maria Garcia to correct the situation?
4. Do you agree with management's reasons for offering Helen Thomson less salary and for asking Maria Garcia to retire early?

Case Problem 27-2:

The River Sand and Gravel Company has 100 employees. The employees did not belong to a labor union, but union agents succeeded in convincing some of the employees that they should join the union. The union finally claimed that more than half the employees belonged to the union and that therefore the union would represent the employees in dealing with the company. The company protested. A secret election was held and a total of 56 employees voted for the union. The union officials then insisted that the company negotiate a labor contract for all employees.

Required:

   1. The company insisted that it would deal only with employees and would not deal with labor union officials. Does the company have a legal basis for its arguments?
   2. Does the company have to discharge the 44 employees who did not join the union?
   3. Do the 44 employees have to join the union?

Continuing Project:

Assume that your employees belong to a union. Prepare a labor contract which you believe is fair to you and to your employees.

CAREERS IN PERSONNEL MANAGEMENT AND LABOR RELATIONS

Many opportunities for personnel jobs exist in private business and in government. The knowledge that you have gained in this unit may help you decide whether you are interested in or suited for a career in personnel management.

There are three levels of employees within the personnel department of a business. Heading the department is the personnel director. Below him are the specialists in various areas of personnel management, such as wage administration and employee training. These specialists may have titles of testing director, wage and salary administrator, or employee services director. Below the specialists are the staff assistants and clerical employees.

Many persons start their careers in personnel work as staff assistants or clerical employees. The beginner may be assigned to such jobs as keeping personnel records, maintaining bulletin boards, and distributing the employee newspaper. As he gains knowledge about the company's operations and the functions of the personnel department, he may give tests to job applicants, interview applicants, or prepare material for employee training manuals. Eventually he may become responsible for such important tasks as establishing wage and salary policies and fringe benefits policies.

It is possible to enter personnel work without a college education, but more and more businesses are requiring college training of their personnel management employees. With a high school education an individual might begin working in another department within the company and be transferred to the personnel department after he learns about the company's operations and shows an aptitude for dealing with employees. Some companies also have training programs for new personnel workers.

Anyone planning to enter the field of personnel management should have a knowledge of the principles of human relations, business organization and administration, sociology, psychology, public speaking, English, labor economics, political science, and statistics.

In this unit you learned about the importance of the union-management relationship. Careers in labor relations may be found within the personnel department of a business or within a separate department, often called the industrial relations department. A separate department for labor relations is most likely to be found in a large company.

A business firm is not the only place in which one may pursue a career in labor relations. Labor unions hire lawyers, economists, and statisticians who perform for the union much the same jobs as are performed by labor relations employees in private business. There are also positions in labor relations, particularly in the areas of arbitration and mediation, in various government agencies.

Even though there is a demand for experts in labor relations, it is a difficult field for a beginner to enter. Most companies want to hire persons who have a college degree and several years experience in various aspects of employee relations and business administration.

A new employee in a company's labor relations department might receive his training by first helping to conduct studies of union demands concerning such things as seniority practices, overtime pay, and rehiring policies. As the employee becomes more experienced, he may be assigned to help handle grievance cases. The top position in the department is that of labor relations director, whose responsibility is to negotiate labor contracts, handle collective bargaining cases, and help other top executives set labor relations policies for the company.

To become successful in labor relations, a person must study labor legislation, labor economics, business administration and organization, and personnel management.

UNIT VIII
Management Functions

What is management?

What kinds of work do managers perform?

Is a supervisor a manager?

What devices do managers employ for planning purposes?

Why do businesses use organization charts?

What characterizes a good organization?

BACKGROUND OF CHAPTER

Successful businesses are characterized by good management. The work performed and the skills needed by managers are of concern to those who employ management personnel, especially business owners and personnel directors. While good management has many dimensions, basic functions have been identified around which the role of managers can be studied.

In this chapter you will get an overview of management and learn how managers effectively plan and organize. The importance of setting goals and employing planning tools will be presented. In addition, you will learn about the value of organization charts and the elements of good organization.

CHAPTER 28

PLANNING AND ORGANIZING FUNCTIONS

A distinct characteristic of successful businesses is sound management. As you will recall from Chapter 3, management is one of the four factors of production. The other three are labor, capital goods, and natural resources or land.

Profitable long-run businesses do not happen by accident. Forming, organizing, and operating a business requires varied knowledges and skills. A knowledge of the role managers play is essential in appreciating the responsibilities involved in running a firm and in deciding whether one wishes to be considered for a managerial job.

NATURE OF MANAGEMENT

What is management? What do managers do? Who is classified as a manager? In the next few paragraphs, you will find answers to these basic questions.

Meaning and Functions of Management

Defining management is not easy because management involves many elements. Generally *management* is the process of achieving the goals of an organization by utilizing people and other resources. Other resources include such things as money, equipment, buildings, and materials. Management is a process, not a single act or event, which occurs over time. Defined as a process, management involves complex man-to-man and man-to-machine types of relationships. Upon completion of your study of business principles, you may wish to review the full meaning of management.

To aid in defining management, studies have been done which have attempted to specify what managers do. No matter what kind or size of business, the studies reveal that managers do essentially the same general types of work. Whether the president of a large manufacturing company or the supervisor in a small retail business, a manager performs these four functions: (1) planning, (2) organizing, (3) leading, and (4) controlling.

Planning means deciding what has to be done and determining how objectives are to be met. Organizing involves getting set up to be able to do the necessary work that has been planned. A manager leads when he guides the employees and controls when he checks to see that the work has been done as planned. In addition to performing the four managerial functions, managers are also often involved in doing routine nonmanagerial types of work.

Managerial and Nonmanagerial Employees

A *manager* is one who works with others and spends the majority of his time performing tasks that are categorized as planning, organizing, leading, and controlling. A manager may be an owner of a business or an employee.

An employee who performs as many as three of the four functions of management would not normally be labeled a manager. Nonmanagerial employees may plan, organize, and control their own work to a limited extent on a regular basis but do not usually lead or direct other employees. A newly employed typist, for example, spends some time planning the typing of a report, organizing the materials and equipment, and controlling by proofreading and correcting errors. The majority of time, however, is spent in actual typewriting—a nonmanagerial task.

An employee who is engaged in all four management functions is a manager. There are various levels of managerial responsibility just as there are various levels of nonmanagerial responsibility. As used in this text, a *supervisor* is the first level manager; he performs all four managerial functions on a limited basis. An *executive* is a manager above the supervisory level with broad responsibilities. In large businesses, of course, there may be several managerial levels between supervisors and top executives.

Another way of distinguishing low from high level managers is the time spent on each function. High level managers spend much more time planning and organizing than do low level managers. A low level manager, such as a supervisor, spends the bulk of time leading employees and controlling their performance. To be labeled a manager at any level, all four managerial functions must be performed, as shown in Illustration 28-1.

ILLUS. 28-1. A manager performs all four functions of management.

THE PLANNING FUNCTION

Of the four functions of management, the first and most important is planning. *Planning* means to look ahead, to set goals, and to consider ways of attaining goals. Unless planning occurs, the organizing, leading, and controlling functions serve little purpose. Planning, therefore, is the foundation of good management; and central to effective planning is the establishment of realistic goals.

Setting Goals

Whether a firm is new or old, or large or small, it must set goals or objectives. Goals that are clearly established and properly communicated to employees stand the best chance of being reached. Well-defined objectives provide a solid basis for managers to organize, lead, and control their departments or companies successfully.

Precise Goals. Goals must be specific and meaningful. The goal "to make a profit" is vague; "to increase sales by $5,000 in the next six months" is specific. Managers cannot set such goals haphazardly. In setting profit goals, for example, consideration must be given to such factors as (1) general economic conditions of the country and local area, (2) past sales records, (3) demand for products or services, (4) role of competitors, (5) financial resources of the firm, and, for some businesses, (6) the season of the year. Many large firms employ specialists to help prepare detailed goals.

Clear and Coordinated Goals. Goals should be clear and coordinated. For a small enterprise goals may be clearly established in the mind of the owner and easily stated orally to the few employees. Once a firm begins to employ two or more managers, goals require more attention. Although each department within a business has separate goals, all goals must be coordinated. Assume, for example, that the sales manager of a firm wishes to increase sales and that the advertising manager wishes to reduce advertising costs during a certain year. To boost sales, the firm will normally have to increase advertising. It is evident that the sales manager and the advertising manager have good intentions but conflicting goals. Managers must work together so that goals become consistent and coordinated.

Long- and Short-Term Goals. Successful businesses develop long- and short-term goals. *Long-term goals* cover a period beyond one year and *short-term goals* are for one year or less. Long-term goals are stated in general terms because they point the general direction and provide a basis for establishing short-term goals. Once long-term goals are defined, goals for the upcoming year can be planned in detail. Each manager then considers what must be done next week, next month, and next quarter to reach the one-year goals and the long-term goals. The planning process moves from long-term general goals to short-term specific goals. Good planning helps management detect and solve problems before they arise as shown in Illustration 28-2 on page 577.

Planning Devices

Successful firms use devices that have proven to be helpful during the planning process.

Budgets. The most popular planning device is the budget. As you learned in Chapter 22, financial budgets assist managers in arriving at goals and in determining how to reach those goals. Financial budgets,

ILLUS. 28-2. Planning enables management to achieve goals efficiently.

such as sales and advertising budgets, are especially valuable in planning to achieve short-term goals.

Schedules. While budgets help in financial planning, schedules are of value in planning for the most effective use of time. A *schedule,* for most business purposes, is a time plan for reaching objectives. Schedules specify the task to be completed by a department or individual and the approximate time required to complete the task. A supervisor may adopt a schedule to plan the work to be done by each employee for the day or week, such as shown in Illustration 28-3. Schedules might be used by a production manager to plan the completion and shipment of orders.

WORK SCHEDULE FOR JULY 23			
Special Order Department			
Employee	Order 532	Order 533	Order 534
Shenker, M.	X		
Duffy, P.	X		
Gaston, S.		X	
Robinson, J.		X	
Kingston, C.			X

ILLUS. 28-3. Schedules are used by managers as planning devices.

Standards. Another planning device used by managers is that of setting standards. A *standard* is a yardstick or measure by which something is judged. Sixteen ounces is the yardstick used to judge whether an item weighs a pound. In business, standards are set to determine when the quality of work, for instance, reaches that which is desired. Because standards are used to control as well as to plan, types of standards are presented in Chapter 29. Not only is setting standards a part of a manager's job, but so is knowing when to revise outdated standards.

Policies. As part of planning, managers frequently establish policies. *Policies* are guidelines used in making decisions regarding specific problem situations. A policy is often a general rule to be followed by the entire business or by specific departments. A broad policy might state that "all employees must have at least a high school education." An applicant with only three years of high school would be rejected under this policy. Policies help to reduce misunderstandings and encourage consistent solutions to similar problems.

Procedures. A *procedure* is an orderly list of steps to be followed for performing certain work. For routine tasks, procedures improve business efficiency and are of special help to employees. The procedure shown in flow-chart form in Illustration 28-4 on page 579 would be of great help to a new employee in the catalog order department for the Johnson Company. Experienced employees can help managers design new procedures and improve old ones.

THE ORGANIZING FUNCTION

Planning is an extremely important function of management but a plan that is not executed lacks meaning. Before a plan can be executed, however, a business must be organized. *Organizing* means to structure or arrange relationships between people, the work to be done, and the facilities so that goals are achieved. When a manager organizes, he takes steps that will enable his business, division, or department to reach its objectives. To better understand the organization function, one should become familiar with the organization chart.

Role of Organization Charts

A common device used in organizing is the organization chart which can be seen in Illustration 28-5 on page 580. Others may be found elsewhere in the chapter. An *organization chart* is a visual device which

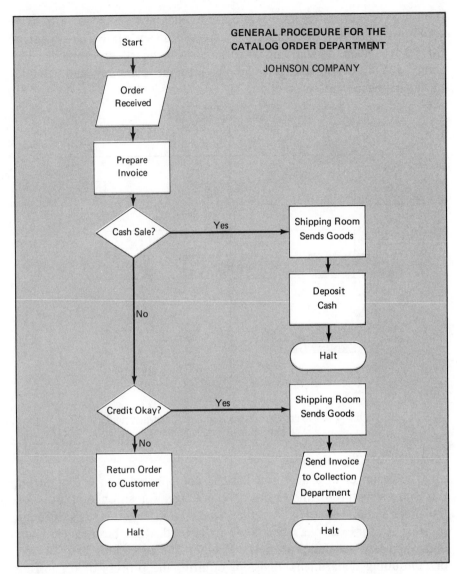

ILLUS. 28-4. Procedures may be placed in flow-chart form.

shows the structure of an organization and the relationships among workers and divisions of work. The important role of the organization chart is to: (1) indicate each employee's area of responsibility and to whom each reports; (2) coordinate the divisions of work and to make those divisions clear; (3) show work to be done; and (4) indicate lines of promotion.

Large organizations usually present to each new employee a booklet which explains the organization of the business and shows an organization chart. By understanding an organization chart, an employee has some idea of where and how he fits into the company and what is ahead in the way of promotion.

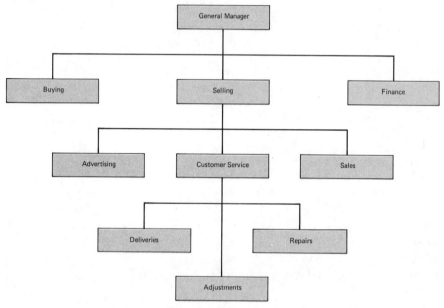

ILLUS. 28-5. Possible divisions of work activities to be performed in a retailing firm.

Elements of Organization

The manager of a new firm has the complicated task of organizing the entire structure of the business. A manager for an ongoing firm, on the other hand, cannot ignore the organization function; organization must occur, for example, when goals are revised, when business expands, and when key personnel are lost. Whether one is a manager of a new or continuing department, division, or firm, the process of organizing involves three elements: the division of work, the facilities, and the workers.

Division of Work. In establishing an organizational structure, the total work to be done must be divided into units, such as departments. The first consideration is the grouping of activities into broad natural divisions, such as buying and selling. For firms with few employees, this may be all that is needed to divide the work into manageable units. For larger firms the major divisions need to be further divided into smaller units before departments of reasonable size can be formed. Separating the work of the firm into logical units and grouping related units into divisions facilitates (1) forming departments composed of related tasks, (2) arranging the flow of work within and among departments, and (3) assigning responsibilities to employees.

Major divisions of work vary with the type of firm. Use of three divisions, however, is rather common. A retail store might be divided into buying, selling, and finance. A manufacturing firm's divisions might include production, marketing, and finance. Most firms have a finance division (also known by other titles such as administration) which includes accounting, data processing, and other office-type work.

As a business grows, the number of major divisions must be increased or new units must be added to existing divisions. When a retail outlet expands, the basic divisions of buying and selling may be subdivided. Selling might be subdivided into advertising, personal selling, and customer service. Buying, on the other hand, might include purchasing, shipping, and storing. The organization chart in Illustration 28-5 on page 580 shows possible divisions of work for a retail store. Determining how to divide work into meaningful units is based on (1) the type of work to be done in each business and (2) the amount of work to be done.

Facilities. While divisions of work are being established, the physical aspects of organizing must also be considered. These aspects include providing proper equipment and materials for performing tasks and arranging the layout of the facilities so that all work flows smoothly.

The layout of the work must be such that it will minimize wasted motions, backtracking, and uneven flow. An office clerk, for example, who files frequently not only needs appropriate file cabinets but the cabinets should be located close to his desk in order to save steps.

Physical working conditions also have an effect on the morale of workers. Job satisfaction is influenced by such things as lighting, temperature control, ventilation, color of walls, cleanliness of the building, quality of tools and equipment, and such added conveniences as parking facilities and lunchrooms.

Workers. Dividing the work into manageable units and providing adequate facilities must be done with the workers in mind. In fact, organizing involves establishing a harmonious relationship between the work to be performed, the facilities needed, and the employees, so that productivity will be at its best. In part, organization is a successful marriage between man, his materials, and his work.

Characteristics of Good Organization

When a business is operated by one man, there is no need for an organization—all of the work is performed by one person. The need for organization arises when two or more persons join their efforts in working toward a common end. When two or more persons engage in any kind of cooperative activity, be they members of a football team or construction workers building a house, they can accomplish better results if the overall task is divided so that each member has certain specific duties to perform. Thus, as soon as one employee is hired by a business, the problem of organization begins because responsibility must be assigned and the needed authority must be delegated. Attention is now given to basic characteristics of good organization that apply to the management of workers.

Responsibilities are Assigned and Authority is Delegated. *Responsibility* is the obligation to do an assigned task. In a good organization the assigned tasks are clearly defined so that each individual in the organization knows exactly the tasks for which he is responsible.

Authority is the right to make decisions with respect to work assignments and to require subordinates to perform assigned tasks in accordance with the decisions made. Authority is delegated from the top of the organization down through the lower levels. One of the greatest mistakes in business is to assign responsibilities to employees without giving them sufficient authority to carry out those responsibilities. Each employee and each supervisor should know specifically: (1) what his job is supposed to accomplish, (2) what his duties are, (3) what authority he has, (4) who his boss is, (5) who reports to him, and (6) what is considered satisfactory performance of his duties.

Unless employees know specifically their responsibilities, duties, and authority, they are not likely to do their best work. Furthermore, there is likely to be a state of confusion existing most of the time; for instance, the person handling credits and the person handling sales may get into disputes through misunderstandings. There are all sorts of handicaps that may arise if there is no definite organization for a business.

An organization chart showing personnel and departments definitely places responsibility and shows authority. When responsibility and authority are understood, overlapping duties can be eliminated easily. By pointing out authority, such a chart can also be instrumental in eliminating friction between individuals and between departments.

The organization charts shown in Illustrations 28-6, 28-7, and 28-8 illustrate how a business may grow from a one-man enterprise into a partnership with specialized duties and then expand as additional employees assume certain responsibilities.

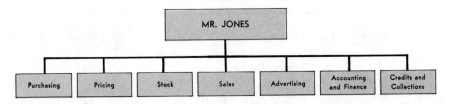

ILLUS. 28-6. Work performed by the owner of a one-man business.

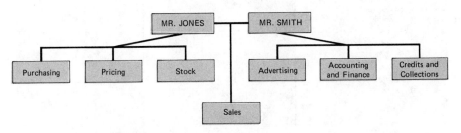

ILLUS. 28-7. Divisions of work in a partnership.

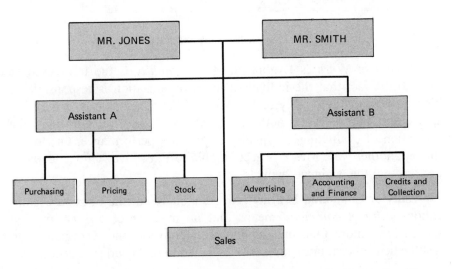

ILLUS. 28-8. Divisions of work and delegated authority in an expanded partnership.

Illustration 28-9 shows in more detail how the authority is delegated and the tasks are performed in a small retail store operated by the owner and two employees.

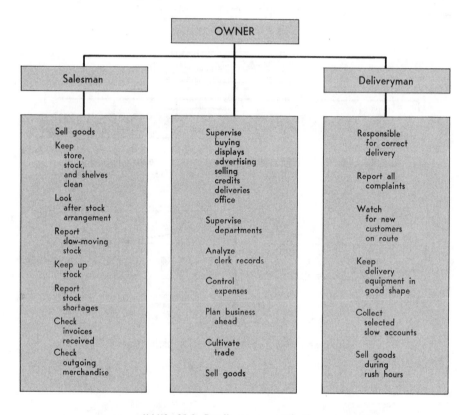

ILLUS. 28-9. Retail store organization.

Quality of Work Is Evaluated. *Accountability* is the term used to refer to the fact that the individual in an organization is responsible to his superior for the quality of his work. When Executive X assigns responsibility and delegates authority to Mr. Y, Executive X assumes the obligation of evaluating the quality of Mr. Y's performance. Or, to say this in another way, Mr. Y is accountable to Executive X for effectively performing the assigned work.

Unity of Command Is Practiced. As a characteristic of good organization, *unity of command* means that no member of an organization should have more than one supervisor. Confusion and disorganization result when subordinates have work assigned to them and are accountable to more than one supervisor. For example, an individual who is assigned work by two supervisors may not know which assignment to perform first, or he may receive conflicting instructions with respect to the same work assignment.

ILLUS. 28-10. When a worker has more than one supervisor, confusion and disorganization result.

A Reasonable Span of Control Is Maintained. *Span of control* refers to the number of employees who are directly supervised by one person. The executive who supervises too many individuals will be overworked and unable to perform his functions effectively. On the other hand, waste of valuable executive time results if an executive has too few persons to supervise. In general, the span of control can be larger at the lower levels than at the upper levels of an organization. For example, the manager of a unit in a department store might supervise 15 or more workers while the president might find it difficult to supervise the work of three or four vice-presidents.

Types of Organization Structures

The two principal types of internal organization structures that are used in business are (1) the line and (2) the line-and-staff organization.

Line Organization. A *line organization* means that all authority and responsibility may be traced in a direct line from the president down to the lowest administrative unit in the organization. A line organization is shown in Illustration 28-11 (sales is the only area for which the complete organization is shown). The lines which join the personnel indicate the lines of authority. The lines show, for example, that the president has authority over the sales manager, that the sales manager has authority over the assistant sales manager, that the assistant sales manager has authority over the branch managers, and that the branch managers have authority over the salesmen.

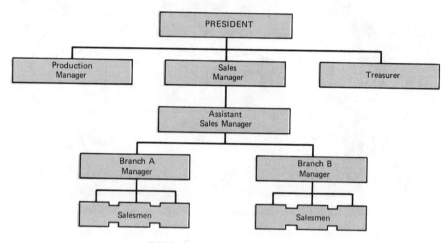

ILLUS. 28-11. Line organization.

In a line organization the president has direct control over all units of the business, but responsibilities are passed along from one person to another down to the lowest level of the organization. Under this form of organization, each person is responsible to only one superior executive, who in turn is responsible to someone else. Very little red tape is involved because the line of action is direct. This type of organization can be very efficient if the manager is capable, for new ideas can be put into effect immediately.

Line-and-Staff Organization. Most large businesses use the *line-and-staff organization*. As a business grows larger and larger, the work increases in amount and in complexity. The result is that line personnel have more and more difficulty in maintaining specialized competence in all of the areas for which they are responsible. To solve this problem and still retain the advantages of direct and definite lines of authority, staff specialists are added to the line organization to give advice and assistance to line personnel. Staff personnel have no authority over line personnel—

that is, staff personnel cannot require anyone in the line organization to perform any task. Thus, line personnel are still responsible to only one supervisor.

The line-and-staff organization in Illustration 28-12 is like the line organization in Illustration 28-11 except for the addition of two staff specialists—the advertising specialist and the marketing research specialist. The fact that their responsibility is to give specialized advice and assistance to the sales organization of the business is indicated in the organization chart by the broken lines.

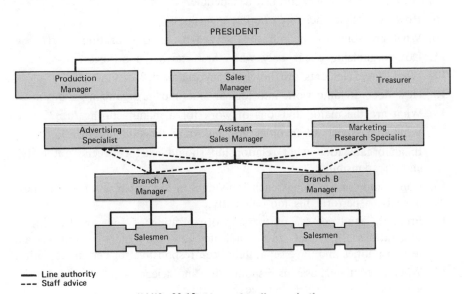

ILLUS. 28-12. Line-and-staff organization.

REVIEW WHAT YOU HAVE LEARNED

Business Terms Checkup:

(1) management
(2) manager
(3) supervisor
(4) executive
(5) planning
(6) long-term goals
(7) short-term goals
(8) schedule
(9) standard
(10) policy

(11) procedure
(12) organizing
(13) organization chart
(14) responsibility
(15) authority
(16) accountability
(17) unity of command
(18) span of control
(19) line organization
(20) line-and-staff organization

Reading Checkup:

1. Why is it difficult to define management?
2. What four functions do managers perform?
3. What managerial function do nonmanagerial employees rarely perform?
4. What is the most important management function?
5. List five factors that might influence the setting of profit goals?
6. Should short-term goals be determined before long-term goals?
7. Name five planning devices that managers find useful.
8. How might a supervisor use a schedule?
9. How do policies help in running a business?
10. What are some of the purposes served by an organization chart?
11. Does organizing occur only when first starting a business?
12. What three elements are involved in organizing?
13. How does dividing work into logical units aid in organizing a business?
14. What are the major divisions of work for a manufacturing firm?
15. What two aspects of facilities are important to good organization?
16. In an organization what relationship should exist between "authority" and "responsibility"?
17. Name some of the things each individual in the organization must know if he is to perform his job efficiently.
18. From the study of the partnership organization of Jones and Smith in Illustrations 28-7 and 28-8, indicate how they have shared certain responsibilities and have separately been responsible for certain activities.
19. When Executive X assigns responsibility and delegates authority to Mr. Y, what obligation does Executive X assume?
20. What is meant by "unity of command"?
21. To what does "span of control" refer in an organization?
22. What type of organization is used by most large businesses?
23. How does a line-and-staff organization differ from a line organization?
24. Refer to Illustration 28-12 and explain what authority the advertising and marketing research specialists have over other employees.

APPLY WHAT YOU HAVE LEARNED

Questions for Class Discussion:

1. How is a supervisor's job different from a top executive's job?
2. What is meant by the statement from the chapter that says after a firm begins to employ two or more managers goals require more attention?

3. Explain how your schedule of classes is related to a business schedule.

4. Explain how the procedure in Illustration 28-4, page 579, can help a new employee whose job is to handle cash sales.

5. What are some of the dangers of the failure of a businessman to assign duties and responsibilities to others?

6. Why is it important for each individual in the organization to have only one supervisor?

7. Explain why it is important for an executive to have an appropriate number of subordinates under his supervision.

8. Why do businesses use a line-and-staff organization?

9. If the sales manager of a nationwide organization and the branch manager of a district office both have jurisdiction over salesmen working out of this district office, what can be done to avoid misunderstandings among the salesmen?

10. Some organizations have a policy that is stated somewhat as follows: "Decisions should be made at the lowest possible level consistent with responsibility and the nature of the action to be taken." What do you think of this policy?

11. A manager of a local store stated that he does not practice all of the management advice offered in this chapter yet claims to be very successful. How would you respond?

Problems and Projects:

1. Obtain a statement of goals from a local business or from a student organization in your school. Write an explanation of how the goals help those who plan the operation of the organization.

2. You and a friend plan to open a laundromat with twelve washing and four drying machines. Write several policies that will help you to plan the running of the business.

3. Draw an organization chart for an automobile dealer and service station based upon the following facts:

   (a) The owner of the business is J. M. Gray.

   (b) The business consists of a service station, a new- and used-car sales department, a repair department, and a parts department.

   (c) Gray's son, John, acts as his assistant but also manages the parts department and supervises to a certain extent all the other functions.

   (d) B. L. O'Hara and three assistants have charge of the repair department.

   (e) O. P. Thompson has charge of the new- and used-car sales department, but a young man by the name of Larry Williams spends most of his time with the used cars.

(f) Gray's nephew, Jim Blake, takes care of the service station with the assistance of two young boys.

4. Three men operate a hardware store as partners. They have divided the work and the responsibilities as follows: (a) Woodrey, buying; (b) Foster, office; and (c) Dunn, sales. Using a simple organization chart, expand these titles so as to show in greater detail the work and the responsibilities of each man.

5. Invite an administrator in your school to visit your class. As he describes each major activity that he performs, decide with your classmates to which management function—if any—each activity belongs.

Case Problem 28-1:

Bill Jordan started a business twenty years ago as a one-man business. It grew slowly for a while because Jordan did all the work. As the business expanded, he hired more people. The business now employs one hundred persons. He is the president and manages the business personally. He has an open-door policy and all employees are permitted and expected to come to him for answers to their problems. He has given responsibility to his sales manager, his production manager, and a purchasing agent, but he makes all the decisions or approves the decisions before they are made. He feels that an organization chart is not needed because everybody knows how the organization operates, and they understand that he is the boss.

Required:

1. Explain what you think would be the efficiency of an organization of this type.
2. How do you think the department heads and the employees would feel about this kind of organization and management?
3. Do you have any suggestions for the improvement of this business?

Case Problem 28-2:

Three partners, Barton, Benson, and Evans, operate a garage in which they sell automobiles, operate a service station, and operate a repair shop. All three partners do the buying and selling. They all quote allowances on trade-ins of old cars. They all give instructions to the men in the repair shop. They alternate in keeping the bookkeeping records. The banking is done by any one of the partners.

Required:

1. Criticize the buying procedure.
2. Criticize the procedure of quoting allowances on old cars.

3. Criticize the supervision, including instructions given to the repair shop.
4. Criticize the method of keeping books and doing the banking.
5. Draw up an organization chart with an explanation of how you think the business should be operated.
6. Write two policies for the repair shop.

Case Problem 28-3:

The Toyline Company makes and sells a line of children's toys. In six months, retail stores will begin buying the firm's products on a large scale in preparation for the Christmas shopping season. The marketing manager is confident that sales will be higher this year than last. Thus, he has just hired and is training several new salesmen for the upcoming rush period. Increased advertising has also been planned.

The production manager, on the other hand, has been running into difficulties getting raw materials from the firm's only supplier. Production has been cut by 20 percent during the last two months, and the inventory of finished goods is less than planned. The production manager, not having received word to the contrary, had planned to keep the finished goods inventory at last year's level. There is no indication as to when the raw material problem will be solved. In addition, the local union has been discussing a possible strike.

Required:

1. Discuss the problems that exist in the Toyline Company.
2. How can the problems be solved?

Continuing Project:

Assume that in your business firm you will have at least one employee. Prepare a list of policies to be followed and draw an organization chart showing the duties and the responsibilities of all persons.

What are essential qualities of sound leadership?

How does a manager achieve good human relations?

How are standards used in controlling?

What can be gained from comparing planned goals with actual achievement?

Why are control devices sometimes unsuccessful?

BACKGROUND OF CHAPTER

In Chapter 28 you learned about the planning and organizing functions of management. The leading and controlling functions are presented in this chapter.

Employees need effective leadership if the work that has been planned and organized is to be completed. The leadership style of executives has a great deal to do with how productive workers might be. Ineffective leadership often results in poor human relations and low productivity. Good managers must possess desirable leadership qualities.

Leadership plays a key role in controlling business operations. In addition to motivating workers, managers must exercise certain controls if goals are to be achieved.

CHAPTER 29

LEADING AND CONTROLLING FUNCTIONS

Employees are either managers or nonmanagers. Often nonmanagerial employees hope to become managers. Therefore, employees should be aware of the functions of management so that (1) differences between the work of managerial and nonmanagerial employees are understood, (2) authority and responsibility are known, and (3) relationships among management functions are seen.

The work of managers is classified into four general functions. Two of the functions—planning and organizing—were presented in Chapter 28. The third function, leading, and the fourth, controlling, are presented in this chapter.

THE LEADING FUNCTION

At any organizational level, a manager must know where he is going (planning) and how to get there (organizing). *Leading,* the third function of management, is the ability of a manager to direct employees in such a way that the goals are achieved. Thus, building morale and motivating employees to work effectively are essential ingredients of sound leadership. In fact, effective leaders understand human relationships and take them into consideration when directing employees.

Human Relations and Morale

Since humans are complicated beings, definitions of good human relations can be quite complicated. Simply stated, though, *good human relations* exist when a group of people get along well together as contrasted to a group in which there are arguments, misunderstandings, hostility, and suspicion. Management has come to recognize that good human relations are essential in business organizations.

In order to make a profit, the management of a business must strive to accomplish the goals of the organization in the most efficient manner possible. For a long time as business and industry were developing, management in its efforts to increase productivity placed great emphasis on technological improvements in machines and methods and tended to overlook the aspirations, drives, motivations, and satisfactions of the human beings who made up the organization. Then management came to realize that friction and conflict between individuals and between groups resulted in low output, poor-quality work, high labor turnover, high absenteeism, unnecessary grievances, and other conditions which decreased productivity and profits. Or, to say this in another way, management recognized that greater productivity is achieved by people who are enthusiastic about their jobs and who have a spirit of cooperation in working with others in accomplishing the company's goals. Thus, a prime objective of management today is the maintenance of and improvement of good relations among employees and between employees and management.

ILLUS. 29-1. Friction and conflict decrease productivity and profits.

Employee Morale. In making efforts to achieve good human relations, management is attempting to preserve and foster what is commonly called good morale. *Morale* is a state of mind which reflects an individual's attitudes toward his job, his fellow workers, and his employer. Depending on the attitudes of the individual, his morale may be high, low, or at any number of levels in between.

The level of the morale of the personnel in any organization is the result of numerous complex factors. In general, though, high morale may be said to exist in a business when its employees:

1. Receive satisfaction from their jobs.
2. Take pride in their work and in the company.
3. Respect and cooperate with the people with whom they work and for whom they work.
4. Have a feeling of belonging to the work group of which they are a part.
5. Approve of the pay scales and promotional opportunities.
6. Are loyal to the company and abide by its rules, regulations, and policies.

Low morale is, of course, the opposite of high morale and may be said to exist when the attitudes and feelings of employees are opposite to those listed above.

Measuring Employee Morale. Too often, when faced with decreasing profits, management considers last of all the possibility that employee morale may not be at a desirable level. Although morale is an intangible which is difficult to measure, there are several means which can assist management in evaluating the organization's morale.

Examine Records of Productivity. If production and/or sales are dropping, it may be caused by unhappy employees who are not doing their best work.

Study Labor Turnover Figures. Labor turnover, as discussed in Chapter 25, is the change caused by the loss of an experienced employee and the hiring of a new employee. High labor turnover is rather good evidence that the morale of the organization is not what it should be.

Obtain Absenteeism and Tardiness Reports. Staying away from or reporting late for a job is a way of escaping a job the employee does not like. An upward trend in absenteeism and tardiness may be nothing more than a flu epidemic, but it may also be evidence of discontented workers.

Study Grievances Which Are Filed. Expressed grievances reveal specific problems which are making employees dissatisfied. Insight as to the morale of the organization can be obtained from a study of the quantity of and nature of these grievances.

Conduct Morale or Attitude Surveys. In order to try to determine the satisfactions and dissatisfactions of employees, morale or attitude surveys may be conducted. Although information for these surveys is sometimes secured by interviewing employees, true opinions are more likely to be expressed if the employee is asked to fill out a questionnaire which he does not sign. Questionnaires may contain such questions as: "Do you feel that this plant is a safe one in which to work?"; "Do you think your wage is a fair one?"; "Do you think your foreman is well qualified for his job?"

Achieving Good Human Relations

Management has given much attention to methods which would be effective in maintaining and improving the morale of business organizations. Some of the more important of these methods relate to executive leadership, supervisory leadership, communications, and employee participation.

Executive Leadership. The possession of leadership abilities by the company's executives is the most important single ingredient in achieving good human relations. An important aspect of this is that having confidence in the leadership abilities of the executives is an essential part of job satisfaction for employees. Employees want to feel that their leaders know their jobs and that they are making sound decisions in directing the company.

To be effective leaders, executives must possess a certain amount of technical knowledge and skill, such as in accounting or sales management. The task of executives today, though, is increasingly becoming that of giving leadership to individuals and to groups. Thus, today's executives must possess human relations skills. As a matter of fact, in many important positions, the executive's ability to work with people is more important than his technical knowledge and skill.

The human relations skills that executives possess are particularly important to an organization, for their skills set the example which will be followed by subordinates throughout the organization. Illustration 29-2 contains a list of some of the things executives should and should not do in their relationships with personnel.

Supervisory Leadership. Supervisors are the first line of management; that is, they are the ones who have the most contacts with workers who

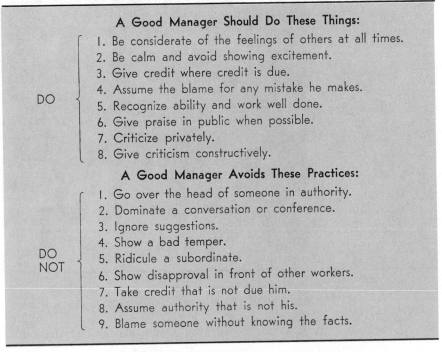

A Good Manager Should Do These Things:

DO

1. Be considerate of the feelings of others at all times.
2. Be calm and avoid showing excitement.
3. Give credit where credit is due.
4. Assume the blame for any mistake he makes.
5. Recognize ability and work well done.
6. Give praise in public when possible.
7. Criticize privately.
8. Give criticism constructively.

A Good Manager Avoids These Practices:

DO
NOT

1. Go over the head of someone in authority.
2. Dominate a conversation or conference.
3. Ignore suggestions.
4. Show a bad temper.
5. Ridicule a subordinate.
6. Show disapproval in front of other workers.
7. Take credit that is not due him.
8. Assume authority that is not his.
9. Blame someone without knowing the facts.

ILLUS. 29-2. Some managerial do's and don'ts.

are not part of management. As with executives, supervisors must possess human relations skills in giving leadership to individuals and groups. Since the attitude of a worker toward the company is largely governed by his reactions to his immediate supervisor, it is particularly important for supervisors to possess good human relations skills. An inefficient and inequitable supervisor often gives his workers a distorted picture of the company's policies and attitudes. The fact that about one third of all labor turnover can be attributed to poor supervision underscores the importance of good supervision in reducing employee dissatisfaction.

The major activities of a supervisor are connected with scheduling and assigning work, reviewing work, and instructing employees. Good human relations are established among workers when their supervisor:

1. Has prestige in the organization.
2. Has good morale and, thus, sets a good example for his workers.
3. Is friendly.
4. Is fair in his treatment of employees.
5. Is interested in the welfare of the workers.
6. Obtains a fair share of privileges and income for his workers.

ILLUS. 29-3. The attitude of a worker toward the company is greatly influenced by his attitude toward his immediate supervisor.

7. Selects and develops a working group whose members like each other.
8. Secures the participation of workers in devising work methods and in setting work goals.
9. Gives clear instructions as to the job to be done.
10. Leads his workers to a record of outstanding performance.
11. Keeps his workers informed as to what is going on in the company.

Communications. The level of employee morale depends in great measure upon the effectiveness of communications between employees and management. Ill will and lack of interest in the business result from poor communications. For example, if poor communications exist when an employee is hired, he will not know what the specific duties of his job are. Thus, he cannot perform his job properly and will probably be criticized by his supervisor.

If communications between employees and management are not good, management will not know what is displeasing employees, and no attempt can be made to correct a situation which is causing low morale. Also, employees who are kept in the dark about the business cannot be expected to feel that they are a part of the business. Thus, they cannot feel loyal to the business or completely satisfied with their jobs.

"I know you can't see much back there, but,
believe me, without you the whole act would collapse."

ILLUS. 29-4. Employees who are kept in the dark about the business are
likely to be dissatisfied with their jobs.

Employees want to know almost everything about what is going on in the company for which they work. Specifically, they want to know such things as:

1. What are the conditions of employment, rates of pay, hours of work, vacations, and sick pay?
2. What is the history of the company, and what are its policies?
3. How is the business doing in relation to other companies?
4. Who sells our products, and what are the best-liked features of our products?
5. Are new products being developed?
6. How does our productivity compare with previous years?

If a company does not provide answers to questions such as those listed above, employees will get some kind of answers via the "grapevine"; and some of the answers they get will be based on rumors and misinformation.

Communications Between Management and Employees. Many different means can be used for effecting the needed communications between employees and management. Much information is relayed to the employees through their supervisors. Employee manuals which contain information about the company's history, policies, organization, rules and regulations, benefits, activities for employees, and the like, are very useful means for transmitting information to employees. Bulletin boards can be used to post announcements. Financial reports may be sent to the employee's home for an explanation of the earnings for a year or some shorter period.

Human nature being what it is, it is not possible to have such good human relations that workers will have no complaints. Actually, the fact that no complaints are being received from workers can be a danger signal that all is not as it should be in the organization. Workers should be encouraged to express their dissatisfactions, for a "bottled-up" dissatisfaction can result in a delayed explosion which is out of proportion to the problem.

Employees with complaints often communicate their dissatisfactions to their supervisor who, if he cannot resolve the difficulty, will communicate the problem to a higher level of management. Management should, however, provide a definite procedure by which employees can voice their grievances.

Communications Among Managers. In addition to communications between employees and management, much exchange of information

ILLUS. 29-5. **Workers should be encouraged to express their dissatisfactions.**

must, of course, take place among the members of management. All levels of management must receive and send information which will enable each manager to discharge his responsibilities effectively. Such information is often contained in reports and memorandums. For example, the production manager must have sales, purchasing, and finance reports so that he can schedule production. Much of the needed exchange of information among managers is also accomplished in committee meetings, in conferences, and by telephone.

Employee Participation. Another method which managers can use to maintain and improve morale is to give employees opportunities to participate in making suggestions and in reaching decisions with respect to problems with which they are concerned. For example, the problem as to how overtime work will be assigned is one which can easily lead to worker dissatisfaction. If management unilaterally makes the decision as to how overtime work will be assigned, there is much more chance for worker dissatisfaction than if workers are given the opportunity to participate in reaching the decision.

Participation in making decisions about problems which concern him gives each employee a needed feeling of importance and makes him feel that he is really a part of the business organization. Each employee who has participated in reaching a decision that a particular procedure will be used is also motivated to assist in making the procedure a success. As discussed in Chapter 2, some managers have also attempted to make work more stimulating by providing variety in highly specialized jobs (job enlargement) and by allowing employees to make job decisions that might otherwise be made by superiors (job enrichment) in the work situation.

Since an experienced employee knows more about his particular job than anyone else, a business should have some system for securing his participation in making suggestions for improving that job. The opportunity to make suggestions is good for the morale of a worker, and, of course, his morale is further raised if his suggestion is adopted by management.

Many companies have located throughout the building suggestion boxes into which employees can drop their suggestions. A committee collects the suggestions periodically and discusses them. For ideas which are adopted, some sort of recognition—usually a sum of money— is given to the person who contributed the suggestion. If a suggestion cannot be used, it is desirable to explain to the contributor why it could not be used.

THE CONTROLLING FUNCTION

The last function of management—controlling—is closely related to the planning, organizing, and leading functions. Planning is concerned primarily with setting goals, and organizing is concerned with making arrangements to meet the goals. Leading involves guiding employees so that goals will be reached. The *controlling* function involves judging the success of meeting the goals and then taking corrective action, if necessary, when goals are not being achieved. Through control procedures it is also possible to discover why goals are not being reached and to decide upon possible corrective steps. Illustration 29-6 shows how the four functions of management (planning, organizing, leading, and controlling) are connected.

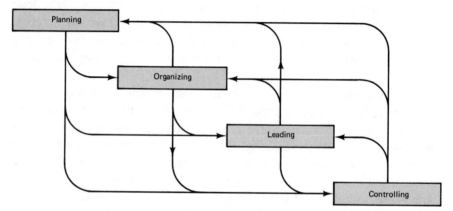

ILLUS. 29-6. Each function of management is directly related to every other function.

The important role of the controlling function relative to planning, organizing, and leading may be seen best by example. The manager of a small grocery store, The Modern Market, decided that within a six-month period sales could be increased by 10 percent (the planned goal). The amount of display space was expanded slightly, a new employee was hired, and the advertising budget was increased (the organizing function). All employees were informed of the goal and, to stimulate sales efforts, individuals and departments that contributed most to increasing sales volume would be awarded cash prizes (the leading function). At the end of the first month, the manager was anxious to discover whether the goal (10 percent increase in sales) had been reached. The accountant provided sales figures which showed an increase of 9 percent (the controlling function).

Although the goal was nearly reached the first month, the manager was not fully satisfied. The accountant provided controlling information with the sales volume broken down by departments. After carefully examining sales, the manager found that all but one department had actually increased sales by 10 percent or more. However, sales in the meat department had increased by only 6 percent, thereby reducing the total average sales to 9 percent. This information provided a clue as to why sales did not increase overall by 10 percent. To increase sales by 10 percent during the second month of his campaign, The Modern Market manager can give more attention to increasing sales in the meat department.

In the above example, the manager was able to: (1) judge the success of his plan, (2) detect why the goal was not fully reached, and (3) take immediate steps to reach the six-month goal. Controlling enables managers to achieve both short-term and long-term goals. Various types of controls are available to managers but the success of controlling efforts rests with the human factor.

Types of Controls

The types of controls that managers exercise vary with the size of the firm and the nature of the firm. There are as many as four distinct types of controls; namely, (1) quantity controls, (2) quality controls, (3) time controls, and (4) cost controls.

Quantity Controls. Quantity controls are used frequently in business. Production managers specify the minimum number of units to be produced per hour, day, or month by individual workers or groups of workers. Sales managers establish the number of prospects that salesmen must contact daily or weekly. And the office supervisor may set an acceptable day's work for the typist by the number of letters typed or indicate to a keypunch operator the number of cards expected to be processed.

Standards, which were discussed in Chapter 28, are determined by managers in the planning stage. The standards become the means for judging success and for applying controls. For example, by setting fair standards, slow and incompetent employees can be identified as well as fast, competent ones. Employees can be evaluated easily on the basis of quantity standards.

Quality Controls. Quantity controls alone are often not enough to judge an employee, a product, or a service. A fast worker, for example, can be very inaccurate; a slow worker can be extremely accurate. As shown in Illustration 29-7, the quality of the work performed is as important a measure of success as the quantity produced.

Standards for quality may also be established as a part of the planning function. Perfection—no defects—may be the only acceptable standard for much of the work in business. A light bulb that does not work will not sell or a letter with errors is not mailable. While perfection is a desirable standard, it may not always be practical to hire hundreds of people to examine each finished product. Sampling a few bulbs every hour, however, may be enough of a spot check to catch faulty batches of bulbs.

Quality standards cannot be lowered. Numerous defective products reaching consumers will decrease sales eventually. When customer confidence is lost, the reputation of the business suffers. Management invites bankruptcy when quality controls are not given adequate attention.

ILLUS. 29-7. Quality controls are as important as quantity and time controls.

Time Controls. Quantity and quality controls are tied in with time controls. That which is done in business can be measured by time. Time standards, however, are more important for some businesses, or for certain departments, than for others. A building contractor, a baker, and a newspaper editor normally have strict timetables to meet. For such firms, delays may cause an immediate financial loss.

There are various time control devices that managers use. Schedules, which are used for planning, also serve as time control aids. For example, a schedule may indicate a planned series of events and show, too, when events actually occur. The production goal for the week, for instance, may be planned and posted on Monday. On Friday the actual units produced are displayed. The difference between "planned" and "actual" figures, if any, aids in evaluating the production department and provides helpful information for planning future production goals.

Schedules, like other planning devices, are also controlling devices. The close relationship between planning and controlling is shown in Illustration 29-8.

ILLUS. 29-8. Effective controlling is closely related to good planning.

Cost Controls. In the final analysis, the success or failure of a firm is measured in money—profit or loss. While trying to increase profits, managers are constantly aware of two specific objectives: (1) to increase sales and (2) to decrease costs. Not all managers or employees are directly connected with work that will increase sales. However, most employees and managers do influence costs. Wasting material or taking more time than necessary to perform a task adds to the cost of doing business. Increased costs, without a proportionate increase in sales, will decrease profit. Businesses must be cost conscious at all times.

Generally more attention is given to cost controls in business than to any other type of control. The control devices used, as a result, are numerous. One of the main purposes of the accounting department is to provide cost information in detail. This is why the head of an accounting department is often called a controller. Most managers, however, act as cost controllers in some way.

The most commonly used controlling device is the budget. Budgets, like schedules and standards, are also planning devices. When a budget is prepared it is a planning device; after that it is a controlling device. Actual cost figures are collected and compared with estimated or planned figures. Such comparisons permit judgments about the success of planning efforts and provide clues for making changes that will help assure that goals are reached.

Controls and Employee Support

Control devices usually involve people. While most workers are not enthusiastic about controls, they generally accept the need for necessary controls. Certain control measures are self-explanatory such as the need to punch time clocks. Other controls may seem less obvious or even of doubtful value; therefore, less than full support will be given them. Two rules should be kept in mind when dealing with controls: (1) control devices should be created with care, and (2) control measures should be explained adequately in order to win employee support.

REVIEW WHAT YOU HAVE LEARNED

Business Terms Checkup:

(1) leading   (3) morale
(2) good human relations   (4) controlling

Reading Checkup:

1. Why should employees be aware of the functions of management?
2. What are the four functions of management?
3. What are some of the characteristics which employees have when there is good morale in the business organization?
4. In conducting a morale or attitude survey, how should the opinions of workers be obtained?

5. What is the most important single ingredient in achieving good human relations?

6. List at least six things a manager should do to achieve good human relations when dealing with employees.

7. What practices should a manager avoid in his dealings with employees?

8. What individual in the company has the greatest impact on a worker's attitude toward his job?

9. Name some of the characteristics of a good supervisor.

10. What are some of the things employees want to know with respect to their jobs and the business organization?

11. Identify some of the means by which management may communicate with employees.

12. To what level of management do employees usually express their dissatisfactions?

13. What three results may be gained from effective controlling?

14. What are the major types of controls?

15. Why are quality controls important?

16. Why are cost controls important?

17. List two planning devices that are also used as controlling devices?

18. When does a budget become a cost control device?

19. What two rules should managers follow when dealing with control devices?

APPLY WHAT YOU HAVE LEARNED

Questions for Class Discussion:

1. How is the leading function of management related to the planning function?

2. What are some of the ways in which management can attempt to determine the level of the morale of the organization?

3. Explain why you feel that a good manager will not criticize or show disapproval of a worker in the presence of other workers.

4. Why must a good manager or supervisor know his people well enough to determine how much praise may be given to an employee?

5. Explain how a good manager will use constructive criticism to get better results.

6. What do you think of a manager who places a supervisor in charge of a group of workers and then frequently goes directly to the individual workers and gives them instructions or criticizes them?

7. How important are good communications to the morale of an organization?

8. Should workers be encouraged to express their dissatisfactions about their jobs?

9. Should employees participate in making decisions about problems which concern them?

10. Should management solicit from employees suggestions as to how their jobs can be improved?

11. What types of controls could be used for a delivery man whose job is to take packages from a store to customers' homes?

12. Why should a manager compare his planned budget figures with the actual figures?

13. What types of control devices are of questionable value?

Problems and Projects:

1. List some questions you would include in a morale survey.

2. In this chapter it is emphasized that wages alone do not create job satisfaction or job happiness. Write a report on the subject, "Factors in Job Happiness that May Be More Important than Wages."

3. By working with several class members, debate the following topic from the employee's point of view: Quantity standards are more important to most supervisors than quality standards.

4. Interview a manager. Then give an oral report to the class based on the answers you get to such questions as these:

    (a) What is the official title of the person?

    (b) How many employees work under the manager?

    (c) What percent of a typical working day is spent planning, organizing, leading, and controlling?

    (d) What are the most common types of problems that arise in working with employees?

Case Problem 29-1:

The Industrial Chemical Company normally employs 500 men and women. The production manager also serves as employment manager and personnel manager of the plant. The company has high and low periods of production. During the low periods, the least productive workers are laid off and some are discharged. Many do not return when they are needed so new employees are hired. The turnover averages about 15 percent. Working conditions are fair. Wages are fair in relation to those of similar industries. The production manager considers his plan to be the least expensive method of operating.

Required:

1. What do you think would be the morale conditions among employees in this plant?
2. What do you think would be the efficiency in this plant?
3. What are some of the things that could be done to avoid such a high labor turnover?

Case Problem 29-2:

The Battery Shop specializes in selling five major types of automotive batteries. About the same quantity of each type is sold yearly. The manager, who is concerned about maintaining the quality of his products, keeps monthly records of the number of each type of defective battery that is returned within the guarantee period. When the number of complaints received about any one battery is excessive, the battery is dropped from the inventory and replaced by a new and, hopefully, better one from a different manufacturer. Here is the manager's report for a recent period:

TYPE AND NUMBER OF DEFECTIVE BATTERIES

Battery	Monthly Average for Prior Year	Jan.	Current Year Feb.	Mar.
A	18	18	16	17
B	10	5	4	7
C	7	6	12	15
D	3	5	2	4
E	12	16	21	22
Total	50	50	55	65

Required:

1. For the three-month period, which two batteries have the best quality record?
2. Which two batteries seem to be declining in quality?
3. If the manager decides to drop one of the batteries (to be replaced by a new one), which one should it be?
4. How does the manager control business operations by use of the above record?

Continuing Project:

Describe what you will do to maintain good human relations within your business and what controls you will employ to assure that your product or service will meet with customer satisfaction.

CAREERS IN MANAGEMENT

The demand for managers in nearly all business areas far exceeds the supply of qualified candidates. An individual with an interest in becoming a manager and who has the necessary education and leadership skills will have little difficulty finding employment in business or government. Estimates are that over 250,000 new managers are needed each year in the United States. By looking at the classified advertisements in leading newspapers, one will discover proof of the shortage and, thus, the need for managers.

Managers are needed at different levels in every business field. Manufacturing, finance, insurance, retailing, construction, transportation, and service are only a few of the general fields requiring men and women with leadership ability. In large companies, one may have to choose whether he wishes to manage in such areas as production, marketing, personnel, or finance. In small firms, managers must be able to manage in more than one area. The higher one moves up the management ladder, the more areas he will manage.

Most new managers do not start, however, at the top. While the way to the top of the ladder differs somewhat from industry to industry, most new managers in medium to large firms are placed in training programs while assigned to a specialized department. In other cases, trainees may be made special assistants or assistant managers to line or staff executives. After a reasonable period of time, such as from two months to two years, a successful management trainee is moved to other departments to gain experience and to better understand different aspects of the firm. As one gathers added experience at the lower managerial levels and as he is found to be an effective leader, opportunities exist for moving to middle and top management positions.

In addition to holding a management position, a new trainee is usually expected to attend seminars (special training sessions). Experienced managers of the company may lead the seminars and discuss selected management problems. Also, speakers from outside the firm may give lectures on management principles and effective practices. Even in small firms, new managers will have an opportunity to discuss management problems with experienced executives on an informal basis.

While experience is the true test of an effective manager, education has become a major requirement for entrance into most management training programs. For supervisory positions, a high school education is the minimum expected. Many supervisory positions, however, now require some college training. Specialized programs in community colleges (junior colleges) are highly desirable for entering management at the initial level.

For middle- and top-level management positions, a four-year college degree is expected. While most managers today have attended college, there are still examples of men and women who made it to the top with a high school education or less.

Training in general business administration is highly desirable though some firms may require training in specialized fields, such as marketing, production, or finance. Courses of value to potential managers include business organization and management, accounting, business law, data processing, economics, and mathematics. Gaining business experience in school work-study programs, summer employment, and part-time jobs, is desirable.

Other than education, managers must possess skills in human relations, decision making, written and oral communications, and planning. While in school, one may reveal his managerial interest and ability by active membership in organizations, participation in school events, and election to offices in various organizations.

UNIT IX
Government and Business

How does government control monopolies?

What is meant by fair trade laws?

How can trademarks be protected?

What is the Environmental Protection Agency?

What is the Bureau of Standards?

What financing information must businesses provide consumers?

BACKGROUND OF CHAPTER

One of the principles upon which our economic system is founded is the right of an individual to own and operate his own business. There is no law which prevents anyone from starting a legitimate enterprise such as a store, lumberyard, or manufacturing plant. However, there may be laws to keep a person from starting a business exactly where he wants and to keep him from running the business just as he pleases.

For the good of our society, national, state, and local governments regulate certain business operations. This chapter will discuss some of the limitations which government has placed on business to protect businesses and consumers.

CHAPTER 30

GOVERNMENT REGULATIONS

Many federal and state laws passed in recent years have tended to regulate the freedom of business enterprises in their relations with labor, society, and competitors. Governmental regulations cover licensing, wages, hours of work, working conditions, competition, prices, products, and numerous other aspects of business. Within the limits of these laws and as long as they do not infringe upon the rights of others, businessmen can exercise their freedom.

Most businessmen feel that business must be regulated to some extent for its own protection as well as for the protection of the public. Of course, every businessman probably has his own definition of regulation and the extent to which business should be regulated. In part, the extent of governmental regulation is determined by federal and state constitutions, laws, regulatory commissions, and court decisions.

Business operations and transactions that are completely or essentially confined to a state are called *intrastate commerce*. Each state has the right to control those business activities that are carried on within the state.

Under the Federal Constitution the federal government is given the right to regulate *interstate commerce*, or commerce among the states; and no state is permitted to impose duties on imports or exports. Every year the federal government passes new laws regulating commerce among the states. Every year the various states pass new laws regulating business within those states.

REGULATIONS TO MAINTAIN COMPETITION

As defined in Chapter 3, competition is the rivalry among sellers for the customer's dollar. In an effort to win customers from other sellers, a business improves its products, develops new products, and

ILLUS. 30-1. The federal government regulates businesses which are engaged in interstate commerce.

searches for more efficient operating methods to keep prices low. Competition thus helps the consumer get quality products at fair prices. It also benefits society by tending to make businesses use this country's productive resources efficiently.

Competition, however, does not always operate smoothly by itself. To provide for fair competition, government often must pass certain regulating laws.

Control of Monopolies

While competition is highly desirable, there are situations where competition may not be preferred. As you learned in Chapter 3, a monopoly exists when competition is lacking for a product or service or when producers can control the supply and price. A single producer, for instance, can keep prices unreasonably high by deliberately limiting supply. The original producer of a completely new product, for example, has a temporary monopoly. However, the monopoly is eliminated by competitors who are attracted by profit possibilities.

Monopolies are not necessarily undesirable; sometimes they represent very efficient forms of production. It is rather the question of control or use that determines whether or not monopolies are socially desirable.

The Sherman Antitrust Act and various other federal laws, as well as many state laws, attempt to prevent or to control monopolies. Whenever there is a monopoly such as that which exists in the telephone and telegraph industry, the federal government reserves the right to regulate that industry.

Business Monopolies. Monopolies operated by business firms exist in a number of service industries such as in transportation and communications. The federal government grants monopolies to airline companies. This policy is based on the assumption that the public would not be benefited, but would probably be harmed, if new airline companies were established in competition with those already in existence; for such competition might make it impossible for any of the airlines to make a profit.

The federal government, through the Civil Aeronautics Board, governs rates for the transportation of products and people between specified points. Nevertheless, the airlines compete with one another on the basis of services and conveniences. Take, for example, the airlines that operate between New Orleans and Philadelphia. Each company may have a feature which makes its airline route more attractive than its competitors. One airline might have more comfortable seats and better food service. One may fly nonstop and use more modern planes.

ILLUS. 30-2. The federal government regulates various types of business monopolies.

It may be seen, therefore, that airlines have a partial monopoly in that no new airline can be established without permission of the Civil Aeronautics Board. The existing airlines, however, do compete with one another.

The federal government also regulates railroads, truck lines, bus lines, power companies, telegraph companies, telephone companies, and television and radio stations if they operate in interstate business. Most of these companies are also subject to state regulations.

Government Monopolies. The United States Postal Service, an independent establishment of the federal government, is one form of governmental monopoly. No private enterprise is allowed to compete with the governmental postal service except in the parcel post branch. No company, for example, can establish a service to handle first-class letters, although express companies and other transportation agencies are permitted to handle shipments comparable to parcel post.

In some places the federal government operates large power companies as monopolies. The federal government also has a monopoly over the buying and production of materials used in the development of atomic energy.

Promotion of Fair Competition

In an attempt to minimize the number of monopolies and thus encourage competition, federal and state governments have passed protective laws and have created agencies to enforce the laws.

Federal Trade Commission. The Federal Trade Commission is the outgrowth of a demand made by competing manufacturers for protection from unfair methods of competition. This commission is therefore charged with the administration of most of the federal laws having to do with fair competition. To minimize the number of cases of unfair business practice it must handle, the commission has provided operating guidelines for various industries.

Codes of Fair Practice. The Federal Trade Commission has authority to organize conferences within industries for the purpose of establishing rules of fair trade practice. More than 150 industries are now operating under sets of rules established in this manner. The conference is usually called at the request of the industry, but it may be called by the Federal Trade Commission. Consumers are included in the conference. After rules have been set up and approved by the Federal Trade Commission, they, in a sense, become a form of law of

1. To promote free and fair competition by preventing price fixing, unfair methods of competition, and unfair or deceptive trade practices.
2. To prevent sellers from discriminating in price arrangements among buyers.
3. To protect the public and other businesses by preventing false or deceptive advertising.
4. To enforce the truthful labeling of wool and fur products.
5. To protect consumers from wearing apparel or fabrics that are dangerously flammable.
6. To protect buyers from the misrepresentation of the real value of automobiles.

ILLUS. 30-3. Principal functions of the Federal Trade Commission.

that industry pertaining to fair competition. The rules are of two types: (a) those that become the basis of legal action and that the Federal Trade Commission will enforce and (b) those that members of the industry agree to follow but that remain optional. It will be seen that those in the first group really become laws. Those in the second group are not really laws, but they are very influential in the industry.

Public Initiated Action. A complaint may be registered with the Federal Trade Commission by an individual, a business concern, or an association. A letter of complaint stating the facts in the case may be submitted. Some of the causes for complaint are adulteration, mislabeling, misleading selling schemes, false advertising, selling refinished goods as new, selling imitations of products, and otherwise misrepresenting an article to the extent that the competitor will be damaged or the public misled.

The procedure in filing a complaint before the Federal Trade Commission is outlined in the following example: Dealer A discovers that Dealer B is selling a product that he is misbranding and misrepresenting. Dealer B is able to undersell Dealer A and therefore causes Dealer A a loss of business. Because Dealer B sells his product in interstate commerce, he is subject to the jurisdiction of the Federal Trade Commission. Dealer A writes a complete letter of complaint to the Commission. The latter asks for such additional information as it needs; or if the complaint is serious enough, it sends an investigator to gather additional facts. The case will then be called for a hearing. If the Federal Trade Commission decides, however, that there is insufficient evidence to bring an action or if the matter is settled without necessity for an action, the

1. Any act that restrains trade.
2. Any monopolies except those specifically authorized by law, such as public utilities.
3. Price fixing, such as agreements among competitors.
4. Agreements among competitors to divide territory, earnings, or profits.
5. Gaining control over the supply of any commodity in order to create an artificial scarcity.
6. False or misleading advertising.
7. Imitation of trademark or trade name.
8. Discrimination through prices or special deals.
9. Price-cutting on branded merchandise on which minimum prices have been established by the producer or distributor.
10. Pretending to sell at a discount when actually there is no reduction in price.
11. Offering so-called "free" merchandise with a purchase when actually the price of the article sold has been raised to compensate for the "free" merchandise.
12. Misrepresentation as to the quality, the composition, or the place of origin of a product.
13. Selling secondhand or reclaimed merchandise as new merchandise.

ILLUS. 30-4. Types of practices prohibited by the Federal Trade Commission.

case may be dismissed. If it is called for a hearing, both dealers will be called to testify. If a decision is rendered against Dealer B, the commission will issue an order requiring Dealer B to cease carrying on the unfair trade practice specified in the complaint.

Government Initiated Action. Investigations of unfair business practices may be initiated by the business community, by individuals, and directly by the Federal Trade Commission. Regardless of who initiates the investigation, when the Federal Trade Commission has a complaint against a business, it ordinarily will make the complaint known. If there is a violation of the law, the business is often instructed informally to *cease and desist,* or in other words, to quit that practice which is prohibited by the law. If the business refuses or ignores the instruction, then a formal order to cease and desist is issued. Of course, a business has the right to defend itself before the Federal Trade Commission and can carry the case to a court if necessary.

Robinson-Patman Act. The original act under which the Federal Trade Commission was formed is called the Federal Trade Commission

Act. It has been amended many times. Another important law is the Robinson-Patman Act, which attempts to prevent discrimination in selling. It is largely the outgrowth of abuses that arose out of selling to certain preferred customers at much lower prices than to other customers.

To be guilty of a violation of the Robinson-Patman Act, there must be discrimination as to price or service and an injury to the trade (the buyer or a competitor). Under the Robinson-Patman Act the buyer and the seller are equally guilty if the seller discriminates in price, service, or any other way and the buyer accepts the discrimination. For instance, assume that Merchants A and B are competitors and that a manufacturer sells to Merchant A at one price but gives a special discount to Merchant B. The manufacturer and Merchant B are both guilty of violating the Robinson-Patman Act.

The Robinson-Patman Act permits the giving of special concessions if merchandise is bought in large quantities, but there must be no special concessions between buyers who obtain the same quantity under similar conditions.

Control of Advertising. The Federal Trade Commission Act was amended to provide for federal jurisdiction over false advertising in interstate commerce. Under this amendment, which became effective in 1938, it is unlawful for an advertiser to disseminate (circulate) false advertising to induce the purchase of foods, drugs, devices, or cosmetics, or to participate in any other unfair methods of competition. This amendment is devised to protect honest businessmen.

The following specific acts are prohibited:

1. In general, all unfair methods of competition in commerce, as well as unfair or deceptive acts or practices, are declared unlawful.
2. It is unlawful to disseminate false advertising in order to induce purchases of foods, drugs, devices, or cosmetics. Publishers, radio and television broadcasters, advertising agencies, and other advertising media are relieved from liability under the Federal Trade Commission Act unless they refuse to furnish the commission with the name and the address of the manufacturer, packer, distributor, seller, or advertising agency that has caused the dissemination of such advertisements.
3. *False advertising* is unlawful and is defined as being "misleading in a material respect," including the failure to reveal facts as to consequences possible from using the advertised commodities.

There are numerous state laws that attempt to prevent dishonest advertising. Federal and state efforts to control advertising have been only partially successful. The slowness of the legal process through our courts and regulatory bodies is one major cause of continued unfair advertising by dishonest and unethical business operators.

Fair Trade Laws. Another important amendment to the Federal Trade Commission Act is sometimes called the Fair Trade Enabling Act (also known as the Miller-Tydings Act of 1937). Under this act states are permitted to pass laws allowing producers and distributors to fix the price of branded or labeled merchandise. The state laws are commonly called fair trade laws. Commodities sold in this manner are often referred to as *fair traded.*

Fair trade laws permit manufacturers of nationally branded products to make resale price agreements with wholesalers and retailers. In such agreements minimum retail selling prices are set, which allow retailers to make a fair profit. Retailers may charge more, but not less, than the fair trade price. Under the McGuire Act of 1952, after one fair trade agreement has been signed by a producer and a distributor and other distributors have been so informed, the agreement then applies to all distributors in the state. This provision is called the *nonsigners clause.* Manufacturers of competing goods or services cannot make agreements among themselves to fix prices or to divide markets.

In general, the fair trade laws permit price cuts below the contract minimum (a) when a dealer's stock of a particular commodity is being closed out with the purpose of discontinuing that commodity; (b) when damaged, secondhand, or deteriorated goods are being disposed of and the fact is clearly made known to the public; and (c) when the goods are being disposed of by a court order.

Since the federal law and the various state laws were passed, there has been confusion concerning the status of fair trade agreements. At one time most of the states had adopted such laws; now less than half have enforceable fair trade regulations.

Points of view toward fair trade laws vary among businessmen and consumers. Large stores object because they are prevented from setting the lowest possible prices, but this enables the small business to compete successfully pricewise. Manufacturers prefer fair trade laws because more stores, large and small, can handle the merchandise; also, product reputation is protected when stores are not allowed to offer goods as loss leaders. Consumers prefer low prices for goods so are generally against legalized price fixing for branded goods.

Estimates are that less than 10 percent of nationally branded goods are fair traded. Fair trade agreements today apply mainly to selected types of products, such as electrical appliances, phonograph records, sporting goods, drugs, cosmetics, liquors, and tobacco.

Fair trade agreements have declined in popularity for several reasons. First, since many state courts have not strongly supported fair trade agreements, producers and distributors have not pushed hard to enforce or to enter into agreements. Second, agreements may be legally evaded rather easily, such as when a dealer sells appliances involving trade-ins. By offering a high value on the product traded in, the net price to the buyer is lowered.

Despite the possibilities of evading fair trade agreements on branded and labeled goods, businessmen must be aware of the existence and nature of the laws in their respective states.

REGULATIONS AFFECTING PROPERTY RIGHTS

Society, by means of its government, places certain limitations on property rights; and, under certain circumstances, it grants special property rights.

Limitations on Property Rights

Taxation, which is discussed in detail in Chapter 31, is one of the first actions of society in governing the use of private property by individuals and organizations. The government also has the right to take property in time of an emergency, such as a war, or for the public good, as in the widening of a street or the building of a new highway. This right is referred to as the right of *eminent domain*. When property is taken in this manner, the government must prove that the taking of the property is for the general welfare of society and must pay the owner a fair price for the property.

The government also limits the rights of individuals and organizations in the use of property. Federal, state, and local laws prohibit the use of private property in maintaining a public nuisance or in promoting an unlawful enterprise. For instance, governments are permitted to seize and to sell automobiles that have been used in illegally transporting and selling liquor.

Special Property Rights

Society, through its government agencies, grants certain exclusive privileges as a reward for special services that are rendered to it. These privileges are a special form of private property. Among the most important of these privileges are franchises, patents, copyrights, and trademarks.

Public Franchise. A *public franchise* is a contract that permits a person or organization to use public property for private profit. No individual member of society, however, has any special right to use public property except through some special grant by society. Cities frequently give private companies and individuals the right to use the streets for operating streetcars or buses, or for erecting electric power lines or telephone lines.

Patent. A *patent* is an agreement between the federal government and an inventor which grants to the inventor the exclusive right for 17 years to make, use, and sell his invention under a legal form of monopoly. Through the laws of the government, the patent holder can seek protection in case some other person infringes upon his right by duplicating the invention without permission. This protection is a reward for the inventor's services in making his invention available for the general use of society. He is permitted to profit by this protection; and other members of society are prohibited from duplicating the article or the process covered by the patent.

Copyright. A *copyright* is similar to a patent in that it is an official federal grant of the exclusive right for 28 years (renewable for 28 more) to reproduce, publish, and sell literary or artistic work. An example of a copyright can be seen at the back of the title page in the front of this book.

Trademark. A *trademark* is a distinguishing name, symbol, or special mark placed on a good or service that is legally reserved for the exclusive use of the owner. Many articles are sold under trademarks and trade names. Many of these products are highly advertised and well known. Obviously, if more than one person or company is permitted to use the same trademark or trade name, buyers may become confused; and the original owner of the trademark or trade name may suffer considerable damage.

Sometimes a trademark is used locally, but the company may grow and eventually operate nationally. The company may then discover that another firm in some other part of the country is using the same trademark or trade name. In order to protect the owner of the trademark or trade name, provisions are made for its registration under federal laws administered by the U. S. Patent Office in the Department of Commerce. Thus, by registering its trademark or trade name, a business has some protection in case another company wishes to use the same name or tries to register it. Registration provides a legal basis of preventing another from using the same trademark or trade name.

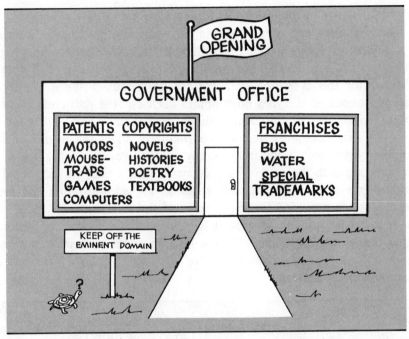

ILLUS. 30-5. Special property rights are granted by federal, state, and local governments.

REGULATIONS PROTECTING THE GENERAL WELFARE

Certain laws which affect the operations of businesses have as their basic purpose the protection of the public's general welfare. Among these laws are those relating to building and zoning, business licensing, environmental controls, and financing.

Building and Zoning Regulations

It might be assumed that a business could construct a building of any kind any place it wishes. However, there are many state, county, and city regulations in regard to the type and construction of a building for a certain purpose or the type of business that can use an existing building. Many of these regulations deal with safety factors.

Zoning relates to the location in which a certain type of building may be constructed. For example, a business building usually cannot be constructed in a residential zone. There are also various classes of business and industrial zones. A dirty and noisy industry cannot build a plant near a good residential section.

Licensing of Businesses

City, county, and state government agencies have used licensing as a device for limiting and controlling those who plan to enter particular types of businesses. For instance, one may be required to obtain a license for the operation of a certain hazardous business. In some cities businesses of all types must obtain licenses. It is particularly common to license restaurants, beauty shops, barber shops, and other forms of service establishments that may particularly affect the health of the community. In most states and in many cities there are special licensing laws that regulate the sale of such items as liquor and tobacco. Under a licensing system inspectors are required for administering the law, and revenue is provided for the support of the government. Under the system a license may be revoked if the business is not operated according to the standards specified in the law. In order to start a business that must be operated under a license, one must file an application in accordance with the law.

ILLUS. 30-6. Local and state governments use licensing to limit and control those who plan to enter certain types of businesses.

It is well to study not only the individual state laws but also the local city ordinances. Many types of licenses are required, and one may be subject to a fine if he fails to apply properly and get a license. It is possible that both a state license and a city license will be needed.

If a corporation or business organized in one state attempts to operate in another state, a license is usually required. Such businesses are required to register, to obtain a license, and to pay a fee. Sometimes there is an annual tax involved.

Licensing practice usually involves registration, the paying of a fee, sometimes inspection, sometimes regulations, and sometimes an annual tax.

1. Restaurants and food-handling businesses
2. Barber shops and beauty shops
3. Cleaning and laundering establishments
4. House-to-house peddlers and solicitors
5. General stores
6. Liquor stores
7. Finance and lending institutions
8. Dealers and local distributors
9. Transportation businesses
10. Businesses operating in a foreign state
11. Hotels and motels
12. Insurance companies

ILLUS. 30-7. Common types of businesses requiring a license.

Environmental Regulations

People have become increasingly concerned about the natural environment. As a result, environmental protection laws have been passed by federal and state governments in recent years. These laws often directly affect the way businesses operate. Agencies have been created to recommend laws and to enforce existing laws.

In 1970 the Council on Environmental Quality was created within the executive office of the President of the United States to recommend national environmental policy. The Environmental Protection Agency was created in the same year to administer and enforce various anti-pollution laws. The Environmental Protection Agency may set industrial standards to assure that the laws are being implemented. Some of the federal environmental laws deal with water and air pollution and the conservation of natural resources.

In 1965 the Federal Water Quality Act was passed, which requires states to establish water pollution standards and procedures for enforcing the standards. All states have complied and many have passed rather rigorous laws in an attempt to control water pollution by the business community.

Strict air pollution laws have also been passed. The Air Quality Act of 1967 created a National Center for Air Pollution Control which has the power to establish air standards to be met by each state. Under emergency conditions, federal authorities may shut down factories, halt motor traffic, or curtail air pollution from any source.

The federal government exercises control over the consumption of certain natural resources, such as oil. States also exercise control over the consumption of oil and coal. The purpose of these controls is to prevent the waste of these natural resources which are important to everyone.

Financial Regulations

To protect citizens from dishonest practices in financial dealings and to protect the country from economic disturbances, the federal and state governments have passed laws which regulate financial transactions.

Legislation covering security transactions are especially significant. *Securities,* in most cases, are stocks and bonds. The general purposes of legislation are:

1. To require the public disclosure of information indicating the true worth of securities offered for sale to the public.
2. To penalize those who offer securities for sale through fraud and misrepresentation.
3. To place definite duties upon persons who sell securities.

Detailed information and procedures are available to businesses wishing to offer securities for sale. The Securities and Exchange Commission administers all federal laws affecting securities; an appropriate office should be contacted for state regulations and procedures.

Federal and state laws control banking transactions as well. Through the Federal Reserve System, which was discussed in Chapter 17, the federal government is able to exercise strong controls over interest rates and other credit activities. States regulate the legal and contract interest rates and other technical aspects of banking. Each state also controls the operation of insurance companies.

REGULATIONS PROTECTING CONSUMERS

Regulations protecting consumers have been in existence for years. Much of the legislation in recent years has been prompted by active consumer organizations at the local and state levels. The interest in consumer welfare has gained momentum to the point where special consumer agencies and divisions have been established in many state governments. As a result, some of the states have passed effective consumer legislation. Successful state laws may prompt the passage of comparable national laws.

Consumer legislation frequently aids business firms although businessmen sometimes resist such laws before passage. Whether for or against consumer legislation, firms must be aware of the various laws in effect and of those being proposed. Many of the laws pertain to product safety and to the consumer's right to information.

Product Safety

Products that may cause injury or death have been of special concern to consumers. Foods and drugs, in particular, have received the greatest legislative action. Because nonfood products may also be harmful, laws have been passed in this area as well.

Regulation of Foods and Drugs. The Federal Food, Drug, and Cosmetic Act, administered by the Department of Health, Education, and Welfare, regulates all foods and drugs that are sold across state lines. The law specifically prohibits the following acts:

1. The introduction or the delivery for introduction into interstate commerce of any food, drug, device, or cosmetic that is *adulterated* (diluted or not pure) or *misbranded* (not marked properly as to label or description).
2. The adulteration or the misbranding of any food, drug, device, or cosmetic in interstate commerce.
3. The receipt in interstate commerce of any food, drug, device, or cosmetic that is adulterated or misbranded, and the delivery or the offered delivery thereof.
4. The giving of a guarantee that is false.
5. The alteration, mutilation, destruction, obliteration, or removal of the whole or any part of the labeling of, or the doing of any other act with respect to, a food, drug, device, or cosmetic, if such act is done while the article is held for sale after shipment in interstate commerce and results in the article being misbranded.

Under this act poisonous cosmetics may be barred from interstate traffic; but certain cosmetics, which contain coloring that may cause irritation, may be sold if they are marked with the proper warnings.

Any food that is injurious to health is barred from interstate commerce. Unsafe amounts of harmful ingredients may not be added to any food product. The law makes it mandatory that harmful sprays on fruits and vegetables be thoroughly washed off before shipments of the products may cross state lines. Any type of food that may be *contaminated* (spoiled or injured) during the process of manufacture or packing may be subjected to regulation and licensing by the Food and Drug Administration in order to assure wholesomeness of the product.

Regulation of Nonfood Products. Legislative activity dealing with the safety of nonfood products has increased at the federal and state levels. Some of the legislation deals with labeling and handling substances which are dangerous to life and health. The Hazardous Substance Labeling Act of 1960, for example, requires cautionary labeling of a wide range of household products. For the purpose of reducing deaths and injuries, auto and highway safety bills were passed in 1966. A health-warning message must appear on cigarette packets. Other safety laws have been proposed or passed at the federal and state levels.

Consumer Information

One of the rights of consumers is the right to information about products and services. Information that is needed to make intelligent purchasing decisions is available in different forms.

Knowledgeable salesmen may provide prospective buyers with detailed data about products. Information is also obtainable from product literature and from published sources, such as government reports and magazines. The *Consumer Bulletin* and the *Consumer Reports* periodicals, published by independent consumer organizations, rate the quality of consumer goods which have been laboratory tested. Buying information is available through course offerings at educational institutions and through businessmen who speak to consumer groups.

Standards. In an effort to reduce confusion when purchasing products, federal and state governments have created standards for weights, container sizes, grades of products, and the like. These standards benefit businessmen as well as consumers. The major federal agencies which are responsible for setting and administering standards are the National Bureau of Standards, the Department of Agriculture, and the Food and Drug Administration.

The principal functions of the Bureau of Standards are those that pertain to (a) the making of tests, (b) the establishment of standards, and (c) the control of weights and measures. This bureau has established standards for many products. If a manufacturer wishes to produce

ILLUS. 30-8. Laws require sellers to give consumers helpful buying information.

a product according to these standards, the bureau will furnish him with the necessary information.

The United States Department of Agriculture administers many laws that affect the businessman and consumer. Some of the primary functions of the department have been to standardize the names, grades, and measurements of food products. Meat, butter, and egg inspection is conducted under the jurisdiction of this department. Probably the most important functions that affect the businessmen are those pertaining to grading and inspection programs that assure the quality and wholesomeness of food.

The law permits the Food and Drug Administration to set minimum *standards of identity* for foods after conducting public hearings. That is, for each commonly named food, such as jelly, it can write a definition with minimum standards. Only foods meeting these standards may be marketed under that name. Foods that do not meet the standards but that are clean and wholesome may be marketed but must be labeled *substandard*. Even these must meet all standards of sanitation and nutrition.

Truth in Packaging. Despite the efforts of governments to establish fair product standards, until recently the packaging of commodities was mostly unregulated. Competition in packaging and labeling is as keen as price competition. In the process of designing and labeling merchandise in an appealing manner, consumers are sometimes misled.

Nonstandard weights and measures are often employed. "King size," for example, might be smaller or larger than "giant size" or "large economy size." With a highly competitive consumer product, producers find that rather than raise the price, it is more advantageous to reduce the quantity and to redesign the package so that the contents appear unchanged.

The frustrating experiences of consumers led to the Fair Packaging and Labeling Act of 1966, which is more popularly called the Truth in Packaging Law. Under this law, expressions such as "giant quart" are forbidden. Also, manufacturers must provide specific information about a product's contents, including a clear statement of the net quantity in each package. While the government may not establish standard package sizes, the law allows government officials to urge industry to develop standardized packages. The general purpose of the law is to simplify comparison shopping.

Truth in Lending. The Consumer Credit Protection Act of 1968, Title 1 of which is commonly known as the Truth in Lending Act, was passed to inform consumers of the cost of borrowing and the cost of purchasing on credit. The actual cost of loans made by lenders must be placed in writing at the time funds are borrowed and the cost must be expressed (1) in total dollars and cents and (2) as a percentage of the amount borrowed. The percentage must be expressed as a simple annual rate on the unpaid balance. Similar provisions apply to credit purchases.

Prior to the passage of the law, credit terms were confusing to most consumers. Interest rates on installment purchases, for example, might not have been revealed or the rates might have been expressed in misleading ways. Service charges added to interest rates only made the cost of financing that much more difficult to calculate.

With the Truth in Lending Act, the actual cost of credit must be revealed to buyers. A portion of a typical department store's monthly credit statement is shown in Illustration 30-9. The finance charge of

$5.27 is shown separately and the interest rate of 1½ percent a month on the unpaid balance is equal to an annual rate of 18 percent. Many states have passed laws establishing maximum annual percentage rates that may be charged.

DALTON'S DEPARTMENT STORE						
This statement covers transactions for the 30-day period ending on billing date shown below.						
Billing Date	Previous Balance	Purchases	FINANCE CHARGE	Payments	Credits	New Balance
May 8	351.50	.00	5.27	.00	.00	356.77

To avoid additional *finance charge* pay the *new balance* before the above date next month.

FINANCE CHARGE, if any, is computed on Previous Balance by applying Periodic Rate of 1½%, corresponding ANNUAL PERCENTAGE RATE 18%. Minimum FINANCE CHARGE is 50¢ on previous balances.

ILLUS. 30-9. Retailers are required to reveal finance charges and annual percentage rates on credit sales to customers.

REVIEW WHAT YOU HAVE LEARNED

Business Terms Checkup:

(1) intrastate commerce
(2) interstate commerce
(3) cease and desist order
(4) false advertising
(5) fair traded
(6) nonsigners clause
(7) eminent domain
(8) public franchise
(9) patent

(10) copyright
(11) trademark
(12) zoning
(13) securities
(14) adulterated
(15) misbranded
(16) contaminated
(17) standards of identity
(18) substandard

Reading Checkup:

1. What are the differences between interstate and intrastate commerce?
2. Give some examples of business monopolies.
3. Name some government monopolies.
4. What agency of the government is primarily charged with the administration of fair trade laws?

5. Name at least three different kinds of practices that are prohibited under the laws administered by the Federal Trade Commission.

6. Who may make a complaint to the Federal Trade Commission in regard to an unfair practice?

7. If a business is accused of violating a law administered by the Federal Trade Commission, what is the first step taken by the Commission when the violation is determined to exist?

8. What is the essential purpose of the Robinson-Patman Act?

9. Describe the advertising practices that are prohibited by federal laws and regulations.

10. What is the Fair Trade Enabling Act?

11. Does the Fair Trade Enabling Act, and laws permitted under it, allow competing manufacturers to agree on and to fix prices among themselves?

12. On what types of goods are fair trade agreements most likely to be found?

13. Why does the federal government grant patents and copyrights?

14. How can a business prevent another from using an original trade name or trademark?

15. Name the two types of regulations on construction of buildings.

16. Give at least three common types of businesses that are required to obtain a license before they can operate.

17. Which federal agencies recommend and enforce environmental laws?

18. What are the general purposes of legislation affecting securities?

19. Where do federal consumer protection laws often originate?

20. Give at least one example of a practice that is prohibited by the Federal Food, Drug, and Cosmetic Act.

21. List various sources of product information available to consumers.

22. What agencies are primarily concerned with standards?

23. In what ways do the functions of the United States Department of Agriculture affect businessmen?

24. What conditions prompted the passage of the Truth in Packaging and Truth in Lending laws?

APPLY WHAT YOU HAVE LEARNED

Questions for Class Discussion:

1. Why is it desirable to keep the number of monopolies at a minimum?

2. Is a code of fair practice established by the Federal Trade Commission as effective as a law passed by Congress?

3. Explain whether you think that it is legal under the Robinson-Patman Act for a firm to sell goods to an independent retailer for $2 a dozen in 10-dozen lots and to sell the same item to a large chain store for $1 a dozen in lots of 10,000 cases.

4. A large store advertises a popular item at half price but has only 12 available. Is this false or deceptive advertising?

5. If you publish a magazine in which false advertising appears, are you subject to any liability under the regulations of the Federal Trade Commission?

6. You are a retail druggist selling a brand of toothpaste which has a fair trade price established on it under the federal law and the laws of your state. You have bought and paid for the merchandise and decide to sell it below cost in order to attract customers. In other words, you plan to use it as a "loss leader." May you do this?

7. Give your argument as to why you think prices under fair trade laws are fair or unfair.

8. Explain why zoning regulations are necessary.

9. Explain some of the problems of a corporation that is incorporated in Illinois and does business in all of the other 49 states.

10. How might the National Air Quality Act affect manufacturing firms?

11. How do terms such as "king size" and "giant size" confuse consumers?

Problems and Projects:

1. Three manufacturers that sell nationally discuss prices of a product that they all manufacture but which has become unprofitable to each. They feel that it is foolish to sell at a loss. They all agree to raise prices, but they do not agree on how much each will charge. Do you consider this action legal? Explain.

2. The Excello Food Products Company: (a) Sells to all customers a product in lots of 1-5 cases at $3.00 a case; in lots of 6-10 cases at $2.80 a case; and in lots of 11-15 cases at $2.60 a case. Is this fair and legal? (b) It has a chance to sell to a large chain store and contemplates selling in lots of 1,000 cases at $2.10 a case. Is this legal?

3. Two large corporations operating in several states are highly competitive and have eliminated most of the small competitors. The two firms reach an agreement that one corporation will be permitted to operate in certain large cities and the second corporation in another group of cities without competition from each other. What do you think of this action as a basic business principle and of its legality?

4. Make a list of the various types of regulations, licenses, and restrictions on businesses in your community (ignore federal regulations).

5. Examine some labels of food products and report the kind of information that you discover on these labels pertaining to contents, standards, grades, or inspection.

6. Assume that you are about to buy a new product such as an automobile, a television, or a record player. Determine which product is best for your needs by comparing competing national brands and prices. Check the *Consumer Bulletin* and *Consumer Reports* for information. Write a report defending your brand choice.

Case Problem 30-1:

The Confectionary Company was organized as a corporation to manufacture and sell candy in an area covering three states. The basic ingredients in the candy includes sugar, syrup, nuts, coloring, molasses, milk, vanilla, butter, and a preservative. The plant is located in a large city.

Required:

1. What are some of the local or state governmental regulations to which this company will be subjected?
2. To what federal regulations will this company be subjected?

Case Problem 30-2:

Gerald Moore ran a bakery in Newark, New Jersey. His business was wholly intrastate. His competitor, Mead's Fine Bread Company, which was one of several corporations held under interlocking ownership and management, engaged in an interstate business. Mead cut the price of bread in half in Newark but made no price cut in any other place in New Jersey or any other state. As the result of this price cutting, Moore was driven out of business. He then sued Mead for damages for violation of the Robinson-Patman Act. Mead claimed that the price cutting was purely intrastate and therefore did not constitute a violation of the federal statutes.

Required:

1. How should the court decide?
2. Why?

Case Problem 30-3:

The Smith Company is a discount store in a state with a typical fair trade law. Three lines of watches are handled. Line A includes inexpensive watches which are produced and sold locally under a private label. Line B is medium-priced and is a national brand; while the store has not signed a fair trade agreement, the producer announced it had signed such an agreement with a competing jewelry store in a nearby community in the state.

Line C includes high-quality watches and the store has signed a fair trade agreement with the manufacturer.

Required:

1. May Line A or Line B be sold at less than the producer's recommended selling price? Explain.
2. Under what conditions may Line C be sold at less than the recommended selling price?

Continuing Project:

Based upon the type of business you have selected, investigate the federal, state, and local regulations, including licenses, that apply to your business. Find out what zoning regulations are involved, and indicate whether your business can operate in the location that you have selected.

What are the methods of levying taxes?

What taxes might a business be required to pay?

What special taxes do corporations pay?

Why are license fees charged?

What are assessments?

What are the purposes of levying tariffs?

BACKGROUND OF CHAPTER

Taxes are one of the greatest operating expenses of a business. Many taxes are hidden —they are included in the purchase price of raw materials or merchandise, the rent, the electricity bill. Taxes also are paid directly on wages, property of all kinds, and, finally, on profits. Many businesses also pay for licenses.

Every business must take taxes into consideration because it will fail if it cannot pay its taxes. This chapter explains some of the theories of taxation and discusses most of the taxes which are important to a businessman.

CHAPTER 31

TAXATION OF BUSINESS

All citizens pay taxes directly or indirectly, but much of the tax revenue required to support federal, state, and local governments is collected from business. Businesses pay through sales, gross receipts, and property taxes. Also, sole proprietorship and partnership businesses pay as individuals so that a large amount of business tax is included in the individual income tax. Taxes collected by the federal government account for two thirds of all taxes collected, while the various state and local government taxes account for the other one third.

TAX OBJECTIVES AND POLICIES

Because taxes are such an important part of the cost of operating a business, the businessman must, of course, have a thorough knowledge of the various kinds of business taxes. He should also have an understanding of the basic tax objectives and policies being followed by federal, state, and local governments.

Objectives in Assessing Taxes

Taxes are used by government to accomplish two goals—to raise revenue and to regulate. A tax may be levied for either or both of these purposes. For example, liquor and tobacco are highly taxed for regulation as well as for revenue purposes. The belief is that the levying of high taxes on liquor and tobacco products will discourage their use.

Taxes on interstate commerce offer another good example of taxes levied for both revenue and regulation. The Constitution of the United States provides that the federal government shall regulate commerce between the states; but over a long period of time, the states have found a means of regulating commerce through a system of taxation. Many of these state laws have been tried in the federal courts and have been

ILLUS. 31-1. Taxes take a large percentage of the income of many businesses.

declared constitutional in spite of the fact that they tend to regulate commerce between the states. Some of the state tax laws that tend to regulate interstate commerce are given in Illustration 31-2.

Fairness in Taxation

It is difficult for government to find methods of levying taxes fairly and in sufficient amount to meet government expenses. The question of fairness has always caused much debate. One problem is the determination of who will, in fact, pay a tax which is levied by government. For example, a manufacturer may have to pay taxes on the goods he manufactures; but since the tax is part of the cost of producing the product, this cost is eventually passed on to the customer.

With respect to fairness in taxation, three basically different policies are followed by government—proportional taxation, progressive taxation, and regressive taxation.

1. Taxes on margarine to protect producers of butter.
2. Taxes on out-of-state motor trucks.
3. Use taxes on goods bought outside the state and brought into the state.
4. Discriminatory taxes against certain products produced outside the state.
5. Taxes on foreign corporations for doing business within the state.

ILLUS. 31-2. State tax laws which tend to regulate interstate commerce.

Proportional Taxation. If the rate of tax remains the same regardless of the base on which the tax is imposed, the type of tax policy is called *proportional taxation.* For example, the tax rate on real estate per thousand dollars of valuation is always the same regardless of the amount of real estate owned by the taxpayer. However, the principle of proportional taxation is not followed in many other forms of taxation.

Progressive Taxation. Another theory of taxation is that taxes should be based upon the ability to pay. This principle of taxation is called *progressive taxation.* The principle of progressive taxation is usually followed in income taxation. For example, a person with a low income is taxed at a lower rate than a person with a large income.

Regressive Taxation. The third type of tax policy is *regressive taxation* in which the actual rate of taxation becomes lower as the tax base increases. While general sales taxes are often thought to be proportional, they are actually regressive because those with lower incomes pay a larger proportion of their incomes in taxes. Suppose, for example, that two people live in a state with a 5 percent general sales tax. The first person has an annual income of $5,000, all of which must be spent to live. The tax on the $5,000 would be $250 ($5,000 $\times$ 5%). The second individual has an annual income of $10,000 but is able to save $1,500. This individual would pay sales taxes of $425 ($8,500 $\times$ 5%) which would be 4.25% of his total income. Even though the second person pays more dollars in sales taxes ($425 to $250), the rate of tax based on income is lower (4.25% compared with 5%). Therefore, the general sales tax is regressive.

KINDS OF TAXES

Taxation has become so complicated that the average businessman spends a great deal of time in filling out tax forms, in computing taxes, and in making various reports. In many businesses the various taxes take a great percentage of the income. Illustration 31-3 on page 640 gives examples of the types of taxes that a business operating in only one state might be required to pay.

A corporation doing business in several states will be subjected to numerous additional taxes, some of which may overlap. If a business is organized in one state, it probably will have to obtain a special license to do business in another state and will be subjected to the various taxes enforced in both states.

Federal income tax	Property tax—intangible property
State income tax	Sales tax
Local income tax	Federal excise tax
Payroll taxes	Franchise tax
Federal social security tax	Gasoline tax
State unemployment tax	Corporation taxes
State workmen's insurance tax	Severance tax
Property tax—real estate	Licenses
Property tax—personal	Motortruck licenses and taxes
Property tax—merchandise	Assessments

ILLUS. 31-3. Most common business taxes.

Federal Income Tax

A *federal income tax* is imposed upon individuals and certain business establishments. Illustration 31-4 shows the sources of taxes by the federal government and the expenditures for a recent year. Almost two thirds of the taxes come from individual and corporate income taxes. Employers are required to withhold income taxes from the pay of employees and give this money to the government. Different report forms are provided for the individual, the sole proprietorship business, the partnership, and the corporation. Accurate bookkeeping records are required in order that the true income can be reported and the tax computed accurately. The income tax return gives instructions and provides a detailed form for reporting the various information that is required. Illustration 31-5 on page 642 implies the many types of records a business must maintain to file its federal income tax forms.

Under the federal income tax regulations a business pays the tax based upon its profits. In other words, it is permitted to deduct all its operating expenses, including state and local taxes, before arriving at a profit on which the tax is imposed. Owners of corporations are taxed twice: the profits of the corporation are taxed and then when the owners receive the earnings through dividends, the owners must pay personal income taxes on these profits from the business.

Partnerships and sole proprietorships are not taxed in the same manner as corporations. In fact, there is no federal income tax on the partnership or sole proprietorship but only upon the earnings which each owner receives from the business. In this way a partner or a sole proprietor escapes the double taxation that is imposed upon owners of a corporation.

Income from Federal Taxation	
Individual and Corporation Income Taxes	63%
Social Insurance Taxes and Contributions	23%
Excise Taxes	9%
Customs, Estate, and Gift Taxes	3%
Miscellaneous Receipts	2%
Expenditures of Tax Funds	
National Defense	41%
Health and Income Security	28%
Interest	9%
Commerce and Transportation	5%
Education	4%
Veterans	4%
Agriculture	3%
Space Programs	2%
International Affairs	2%
Other	2%

Source: U. S. Bureau of the Census, *Statistical Abstract of the United States: 1971*

ILLUS. 31-4. Revenue and expenditures of federal government.

Certain small corporations have the privilege of reporting their income and being treated for federal income tax purposes as if they were partnerships. In order to do this, it is necessary for all stockholders to agree that the corporation will be treated as a partnership. By this device a small corporation can escape the double taxation imposed on other corporations and stockholders.

State and Local Income Tax

In many states and cities there is an income tax that is similar in many respects to the federal income tax. However, the state income tax rates are always lower than the federal income tax rates. The state income tax is imposed upon individuals and businesses in essentially the same manner as the federal income tax.

In some states and cities there is a *gross income tax* on all income, which operates in a manner very similar to the payroll tax which is a tax on all wages. In other words, the gross income tax is levied as a percentage of the total income of each individual and business.

Social Security Taxes

Almost all businesses are subject to federal social security taxes that provide for old-age pensions, medical care, and other benefits.

SCHEDULE C (Form 1040) Department of the Treasury Internal Revenue Service	**Profit (or Loss) From Business or Profession** (Sole Proprietorship) ▶ Partnerships, joint ventures, etc., must file on Form 1065. ▶ Attach to Form 1040.	19--

Name as shown on Form 1040 — Grant J. and Helen Wells, 918 Marsh Street, Muncie, Indiana | Social security number 303 24 1150

A Principal business activity ......Retail Store............; product ......Furniture.............
  (See separate instructions)   (For example: retail—hardware; wholesale—tobacco; services—legal; manufacturing—furniture; etc.)

B Business name ......Silverline Store......   C Employer Identification Number 27-0118224

D Business address ......139 McKinley Avenue, Muncie, Indiana......   47306
E Indicate method of accounting: (1) ☐ cash; (2) ☒ accrual; (3) ☐ other.   (ZIP code)

F Was there any substantial change in the manner of determining quantities, costs, or valuations between the opening and closing inventories?
  ☐ YES ☒ NO. If "Yes," attach explanation.

G Were you required to file Forms 1096 and 1099 or 1087 for the calendar year 19-- ? (See "Item G" in separate instructions for Schedule C.)
  ☐ YES ☒ NO. If "Yes," where were they filed? ......

1 Gross receipts or gross sales $..136,354.18.. Less: Returns and allowances $......1,341.11......			$ 135,013	07
2 Inventory at beginning of year (if different from last year's closing inventory attach explanation)	31,216	09		
3 Merchandise purchased $..78,901.88.. less cost of any items withdrawn from business for personal use $......none	78,901	88		
4 Cost of labor (do not include salary paid to yourself)				
5 Material and supplies				
6 Other costs (explain in Schedule C–1)				
7 Total of lines 2 through 6	110,117	97		
8 Inventory at end of this year	28,321	90		
9 Cost of goods sold and/or operations (subtract line 8 from line 7)			81,796	07
10 Gross profit (subtract line 9 from line 1)			53,217	00
OTHER BUSINESS DEDUCTIONS				
11 Depreciation (explain in Schedule C–2)	811	67		
12 Taxes on business and business property (explain in Schedule C–1)	1,153	39		
13 Rent on business property	7,200	00		
14 Repairs (explain in Schedule C–1)	125	00		
15 Salaries and wages not included on line 4 (exclude any paid to yourself) . . .	22,642	76		
16 Insurance	250	36		
17 Legal and professional fees	300	00		
18 Commissions				
19 Amortization (attach statement)				
20 Retirement plans, etc. (other than contributions made on your behalf—see separate instructions)				
21 Interest on business indebtedness	119	78		
22 Bad debts arising from sales or services	531	41		
23 Depletion				
24 Other business expenses (explain in Schedule C–1)	6,123	57		
25 Total of lines 11 through 24			39,257	94
26 Net profit (or loss) (subtract line 25 from line 10). Enter here and on line 35, Form 1040. **ALSO** enter on Schedule SE, Part I, line 1			13,959	06

SCHEDULE C–1. EXPLANATION OF LINES 6, 12, 14, AND 24   **C**

Line No.	Explanation	Amount	Line No.	Explanation	Amount
12	Personal Prop Tax	$ 133.39	24	Misc. Expense	$ 418.50
12	FICA Taxes	600.00			
12	Unemp Comp Taxes	420.00			
14	Repair Store Equip	125.00			
24	Advertising	3,854.26			
24	Tel & Tel Expense	258.15			
24	Heating & Lighting	908.20			
24	Sta & Supplies	187.18			
24	Truck Expense	497.28			

ILLUS. 31-5. Federal income tax profit (or loss) statement.

Employees must also make contributions. Almost all employers are also subject to federal and state taxes for unemployment insurance, a Social Security Act program which pays benefits to unemployed persons for a specified length of time.

Property Tax

In every state there is some form of *property tax* on tangible property, and in some states there are two or more property taxes. For instance, there may be a real property tax, a personal property tax, and an intangible property tax. A *real property tax* is a tax levied on land and buildings. A *personal property tax* is a tax on such items as furniture, machinery, merchandise, and equipment. In many states there is a special property tax on merchandise. An *intangible property tax* is a tax on assets such as money in the bank, notes, stocks, bonds, and other securities. The businessman should familiarize himself with all the tax laws of his state to be sure that he gets the proper forms at the right time and reports his taxes accurately. If he is delinquent (late) in paying his taxes or attempts to avoid the payment of them, he will be subject to a penalty.

A tax on property—whether it is real, personal, or intangible—is stated in terms of mills or in terms of dollars per thousand of assessed valuation. It is most frequently quoted in terms of mills. A tax of 28 mills is $28 a thousand or, on a percentage basis, 2.8 percent. At this rate the tax on $2,000 would be $56.

Sales Tax

The *sales tax* (a tax usually collected on each retail sale) is a very common means of raising revenue. There is now a sales tax in almost

ILLUS. 31-6. In order to provide the proper forms and pay the correct amounts, a businessman must be familiar with all tax laws.

every state. Although there is no uniformity in the administration of these taxes, in nearly every case the retailer is responsible for the collection of the tax and in turn must pay this tax to the state government. It is therefore important for the businessman to be familiar with the sales tax law of his state so that he can be sure to collect the tax properly and to keep records that will enable him to report the tax correctly.

In most states that have sales taxes, the taxes are imposed on most items that are sold at retail. However, in states that do not have general sales taxes, there are often special sales taxes on such items as gasoline, cigarettes, liquor, and other selected items.

Excise Tax

The *excise tax* is usually a federal tax. An excise tax is imposed upon the manufacturer, wholesaler, or retailer as a percentage of the value of certain items sold. This is also a sales tax because it is included as part of the selling price.

Business or Service Taxes

Business or *service taxes* can rightfully be called *privilege taxes.* They are sometimes also referred to as *benefit taxes.* Those who pay them derive a privilege or direct benefit from federal, state, or local governments. Franchise and gasoline taxes are in this classification.

Franchise Tax. A *franchise tax* is charged to public utilities and certain other companies that are granted concessions or privileges. An example is a charge of so much a mile for each bus using the city streets.

Gasoline Tax. The *gasoline tax* is sometimes classed as a benefit tax, for it is usually levied to pay for the construction and maintenance of roads. It is in the form of a sales tax.

Other Service Taxes. Other good examples of service taxes are those imposed on corporations, particularly on life insurance companies. Since a corporation is an artificial being created by the state, it is subject to the regulations of the state and must pay for the privilege of its existence. Life insurance companies usually pay on the basis of their gross income or their net income.

Business or service taxes are direct taxes for those on whom they are imposed, although they frequently result in indirect taxes on the consumers. In some states certain taxes have been imposed on public utilities without the possibility of the taxes being passed on to the consumers. For instance, a state may impose a 2 percent tax on the sale of electricity and gas. The public utility may be prevented from passing this charge on to the consumer since the rates for the gas or electricity have already been established and cannot be raised.

Corporation Taxes

Besides many other taxes imposed upon a corporation, a corporation has to pay a special *corporation* or *organization tax* at the time the state permits the corporation to organize. The corporation is also taxed on its capital stock each year. This tax is called a *corporation franchise tax.*

If a corporation organized in one state wishes to do business in another state, it is called a foreign corporation and usually must pay for a permit to do business in the other state. This permit is sometimes called an *entrance tax*. Some states impose a franchise tax, which in the case of a foreign corporation is sometimes called a *corporation privilege tax.*

Severance Tax

A *severance tax* is levied as a charge against the consumption of natural resources. For example, certain states charge a percentage on the oil that is pumped, the ore that is mined, and the timber that is cut. These taxes are levied on the assumption that the state is granting the privilege of deriving a profit from the consumption of natural resources.

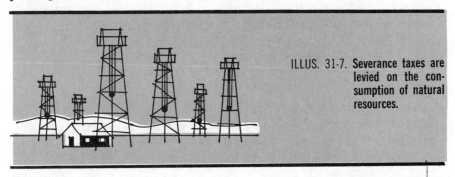

ILLUS. 31-7. Severance taxes are levied on the consumption of natural resources.

License Fees

The purpose of a *license* is to give government control over the entrance of persons into certain types of businesses or the sale of certain types of products. In such licensed businesses no one is permitted to operate without a license. Some licenses merely cover the cost of operating the license system and whatever inspection, enforcement, or regulation is necessary. In many cases, however, government has seen fit to increase license fees in order to produce additional revenue with which to operate other governmental functions. Licenses, therefore, serve both as a means of control and as a means of producing revenue.

Motortruck Licenses and Taxes

Motortrucks used for transporting goods are subject to a license tax. Often each truck must be licensed in all states in which it travels. States also impose taxes on one or more of the following bases: capacity of the truck (or trailer), the number of wheels, the actual load carried, or the distance traveled.

Assessments

Ordinarily, assessments are not classified as taxes. In a very practical sense, however, assessments are taxes since they are imposed upon property owners with the idea that the value of their property will be increased as a result of the improvements for which the assessments are made. Thus, in theory, an *assessment* is a charge by local government for some direct benefit or improvement to property. For example, when sidewalks, highways, or sewers are built, the adjoining property owners are often assessed these costs. There may be some serious arguments and lawsuits as a result of the assessments because it is often argued that the property owner receives no benefit, or at least not in proportion to the amount of the assessment. For example, a city may decide to widen and improve a street in front of a business for the purpose of expediting the flow of "through" traffic. The improved street might actually be a disadvantage to the business, however, if traffic moves through faster and people do not stop to buy.

Tariffs

Tariffs are taxes levied upon imports for (a) protection, (b) revenue, or (c) both protection and revenue. When they are collected, they are often called *customs*. The common practice of levying tariffs on imported foreign products is the result of the desire of domestic producers to have the national market to themselves. But tariffs are sometimes used to protect industries that are vital to our national defense, infant industries, and certain other industries that might be destroyed by the competition of foreign goods. While the tariff on imports gives the domestic producer some short-term protection from the competition of foreign producers, it also tends to cause other countries to retaliate by placing tariffs on their imports of our products. In the long run our tariffs cause other countries to put tariffs on our goods so that we have difficulty exporting.

Very early in the history of the United States, certain manufacturers, notably in the textile field, sought governmental protection by the encouragement of high tariffs. They argued that infant industries should be protected and encouraged and that in case of war certain industries were necessary; they also defended the idea that high tariffs brought about high standards of living.

One argument for high tariffs is to shut out competition from other countries where low wages are paid. It is often asserted that manufacturers in the United States cannot compete with products produced with low wages in other countries; however, wages are not the only answer to this problem. Efficiency and productivity are the factors that make it possible for American manufacturers to compete. Of course, it is true that if a foreign country has the same productivity and efficiency as the United States but with lower labor costs, that country can produce goods more cheaply than American manufacturers.

There is a basic economic principle that if there were no tariffs anywhere in the world, each country would produce the things that it could produce best and would import from other countries goods that could be produced better in other countries. In this way everybody in the world would secure the advantage of the most efficient production, and everybody would have the most goods for the least money. However, because of the competitive nature of countries in world trade, it is doubtful that countries will limit their production. Tariffs are probably a permanent condition.

REVIEW WHAT YOU HAVE LEARNED

Business Terms Checkup:

(1) proportional taxation
(2) progressive taxation
(3) regressive taxation
(4) federal income tax
(5) gross income tax
(6) property tax
(7) real property tax
(8) personal property tax
(9) intangible property tax
(10) sales tax
(11) excise tax
(12) business or service tax
(13) privilege tax
(14) benefit tax
(15) franchise tax
(16) gasoline tax
(17) corporation or organization tax
(18) corporation franchise tax
(19) entrance tax
(20) corporation privilege tax
(21) severance tax
(22) license
(23) assessment
(24) tariffs
(25) customs

Reading Checkup:

1. What is the main source of federal taxes?
2. One type of tax policy is called proportional taxation. Explain why it has this name.
3. It is claimed that the owners of a corporation pay a tax twice on the income of the corporation while the owners of a partnership pay only once. Explain what is meant.
4. How are the gross income tax, state income tax, and payroll taxes similar?
5. What are the three types of property on which there is commonly a tax?
6. Name some types of special sales taxes when there is no general sales tax.
7. Give some examples of businesses operating under a franchise tax.
8. Besides some of the normal taxes paid by a proprietorship or a partnership, what are some of the special taxes that are paid by a corporation?
9. What are the purposes of a license?
10. Why is an assessment not considered to be a tax?
11. What are the purposes for which tariffs are levied on imports?

APPLY WHAT YOU HAVE LEARNED

Questions for Class Discussion:

1. Give your arguments as to which you feel is the fairest kind of tax—a proportional tax, a progressive tax, or a regressive tax.
2. Is the gasoline tax a benefit tax in your state?
3. Do you consider a gross income tax (on all income without deductions) fair? Explain.
4. Many people feel the sales tax is one of the fairest taxes. Why?
5. For what reason do you consider a franchise tax to be fair?
6. Many businessmen contend that they are tax collectors for government but receive no compensation for this service. In the following examples, who provides the free tax collection for the government: (a) personal income tax (withholding), (b) sales tax, (c) social security (old-age and survivors insurance), (d) admission tax, and (e) excise tax on airline tickets.
7. If we had state tariffs on most products, how would these tariffs affect manufacturing and marketing in the United States?

Problems and Projects:

1. On real estate assessed or valued at $17,560, compute the tax if the tax rate is 29.40 mills.

2. The Fairmont Manufacturing Company is located in a state where there is a tax on machinery, equipment, and inventory of goods available for sale. The depreciated value of the machinery and equipment at taxing time is $56,000. For tax purposes the company may list the machinery and equipment at 50 percent of this value.

Goods manufactured and available for sale (inventory) at cost for each month during the year were as follows:

January	$32,000	July	$48,000
February	44,000	August	40,000
March	52,000	September	32,000
April	60,000	October	28,000
May	60,000	November	32,000
June	56,000	December	36,000

For tax purposes the company must compute the average monthly value of goods available and list this for tax purposes at 50 percent of the average monthly value. The tax rate is $32.36 a thousand.

(a) Compute the value of the machinery and equipment that will be reported for tax listing.

(b) Compute the value of the manufactured goods that will be reported for tax listing.

(c) Compute the total tax that must be paid.

3. If the real estate tax rate is 34 mills per dollar of valuation:

(a) What is the tax per thousand dollars of valuation?

(b) What is the tax on real estate valued at $25,000?

(c) Using your local tax rate, compute the real estate tax on the valuation of $25,000.

4. The National Manufacturing Corporation is a closely owned corporation with only eight stockholders. Its earnings for the past year and the computation of federal income taxes are as follows:

$146,000 subject to normal tax of 22 percent	$ 32,120
25,000 exemption from surtax for all corporations	
$121,000 subject to 26 percent surtax	31,460
Total federal income taxes	$ 63,580
Net income	$146,000
Total federal income taxes	63,580
Profit after taxes	$ 82,420

H. M. Bradford is one of the eight stockholders. He owns 10 percent of the stock and has been receiving an average of $5,000 of dividends. These dividends plus his other income of $11,000 caused him to pay last year a personal federal income tax of $3,780.

Bradford and the other stockholders have considered taking advantage of the federal income tax law which permits a corporation with ten or fewer stockholders to report its income and for individual stockholders to pay taxes as if the business were a partnership. All the net income of the corporation is considered as income to the stockholders regardless of whether the earnings are paid out in dividends to the stockholders.

In the example above, if the stockholders take advantage of this provision, Bradford would have had to report income from the corporation amounting to $14,600 (10% of $146,000) which, plus his $11,000 of other income, would have made a total of $25,600, on which he would have had to pay a federal income tax of $7,500.

Would you recommend that this company consider taking advantage of this provision in the federal income tax law?

5. A store building valued at $45,000 for tax purposes is rented for $600 a month. The real estate tax rate is 96 mills; the repairs and insurance average $750 a year; the depreciation is figured at 4 percent of the value; and there is a gross income tax of 3 percent. Compute the net income from this property for the owner.

6. Alex Shore earns a salary of $700 a month. For old age, survivors, disability, and health insurance benefits his wages up to $10,800 a year are taxed at 5.85 percent; the employer is taxed on the same wages at 5.85 percent; the employer is also taxed 3.28 percent on wages of $4,200 for unemployment insurance.

(a) What is the total tax paid by the employee each year?

(b) What is the tax paid by the employer?

(c) If Alex Shore were self-employed, he could still be covered for old age, survivors, disability, and health insurance benefits; but his income up to $10,800 would be taxed at a rate of 8.0 percent (nothing for unemployment). What would his tax be?

Case Problem 31-1:

The National Tobacco Company manufactures cigarettes and does business in every state. It has branch offices and warehouses in 15 different states from which cigarettes are shipped to wholesalers and retailers. It also has salesmen traveling in all states.

Required:

1. Make a list of the types of taxes that you think this corporation must pay.

2. Which of these taxes do you think enter into the cost of the product and are eventually paid for by the individual who buys and uses the cigarettes?

Case Problem 31-2:

The Sunrise Publishing Company owns real estate assessed at $115,000 on which there is a tax of $24 a thousand. It owns equipment amounting to $80,000 on which there is a property tax of $3 a thousand. It pays a state workmen's compensation tax of 1 percent on salaries amounting to $52,000. The old-age benefits tax, called FICA tax, amounts to a total of 5.85 percent on wages amounting to $84,000. License fees of various kinds amount to $380 a year.

Required:

1. List and compute each of the taxes and show the total.
2. If the sales of this firm amount to $278,000 for the year, figure the percentage of the income from sales that is spent for taxes.

Continuing Project:

Make a study of all the types of taxes for which your business will be liable and estimate the cost of each tax.

CAREERS IN GOVERNMENT AND TAXATION

Taxation has not only imposed a tremendous financial burden directly on business, but it has also imposed a tremendous work burden of record keeping on business. All businessmen are tax collectors for local, state, and federal governments. A businessman must keep numerous records and file numerous reports. Some of these reports require days or even weeks to prepare.

Even in a small business the businessman will spend a considerable amount of his time handling tax matters and the records and reports that are necessary. In big businesses large staffs of employees are kept busy handling problems and work related to taxation.

Tax problems are so numerous and so complicated that specialists are needed to handle the work. There are many opportunities in business for persons to specialize in this field. The education and experience that are needed are in accounting, law, and taxation.

In government at all levels there are many tax experts who are accountants. They must supervise the collection of taxes and audit the books of taxpayers. The United States Internal Revenue Service has many offices and a large staff devoted to auditing records and collecting taxes. States, counties, and cities also have large staffs for these purposes.

Many other opportunities exist in government service on all levels for persons who have a sincere desire to serve the public. Jobs include those of inspecting food products, enforcing laws and regulations, approving loans, and rendering services to business.

There are opportunities for persons with all types of education and especially for those with a business education. In governmental accounting jobs one needs a good knowledge of accounting, law, and taxation. In other fields of governmental service, one may need education in special fields such as insurance, finance, chemistry, health, or agriculture. Most government jobs require that the applicant pass a civil service test.

INDEX